T0397182

REPRESENTATIONS AND RIGHTS OF THE ENVIRONMENT

Attending to the 'Cry of the Earth' requires a critical appraisal of how we conceive our relationship with the environment, and a clear vision of how to apprehend it in law and governance.

Addressing questions of participation, responsibility and justice, this collective endeavour includes marginalised and critical voices, featuring contributions by leading practitioners and thinkers in Indigenous law, traditional knowledge, wild law, the rights of nature, theology, public policy and environmental humanities. Such voices invite us to broaden our horizon of meaning and action, modes of knowing and being in the world, and envision the path ahead with a new legal consciousness; they must play a decisive role in comprehending and responding to current global challenges.

A valuable reference for students, researchers and practitioners, this book is one of a series of publications associated with the Earth System Governance Project. For more publications, see www.cambridge.org/earth-system-governance.

SANDY LAMALLE is an international consultant and associate researcher at Loyola Sustainability Research Centre, Concordia University. She is a member of the International Law Association Committee on the Implementation of the Rights of Indigenous Peoples, and has worked as a legal adviser for international organisations. She co-founded the innovation research network on environmental governance *Notre Golfe*.

PETER STOETT is Dean and Professor at the Faculty of Social Science and Humanities at Ontario Tech University. He is also Co-Chair of the Intergovernmental Science-Policy Platform for Biodiversity and Ecosystem Services (IPBES) Global Assessment of Invasive Alien Species and Their Control; and was a coordinating lead author for the United Nations *Sixth Global Environmental Outlook*.

The **Earth System Governance Project** was established in 2009 as a core project of the International Human Dimensions Programme on Global Environmental Change. Since then, the Project has evolved into the largest social science research network in the area of sustainability and governance. The Earth System Governance Project explores political solutions and novel, more effective governance mechanisms to cope with the current transitions in the socio-ecological systems of our planet. The normative context of this research is sustainable development; earth system governance is not only a question of institutional effectiveness, but also of political legitimacy and social justice.

The **Earth System Governance series** with Cambridge University Press publishes the main research findings and synthesis volumes from the Project's first ten years of operation.

Series Editor

Frank Biermann, Utrecht University, the Netherlands

Titles in print in this series

Biermann and Lövbrand (eds.), *Anthropocene Encounters: New Directions in Green Political Thinking*

van der Heijden, Bulkeley and Certomà (eds.), *Urban Climate Politics: Agency and Empowerment*

Linnér and Wibeck, *Sustainability Transformations: Agents and Drivers across Societies*

Betsill, Benney and Gerlak (eds.), *Agency in Earth System Governance*

Biermann and Kim (eds.), *Architectures of Earth System Governance: Institutional Complexity and Structural Transformation*

Baber and Bartlett (eds.), *Democratic Norms of Earth System Governance*

Djalante, Siebenhüner (eds.), *Adaptiveness: Changing Earth System Governance*

Behrman and Kent (eds.), *Climate Refugees*

REPRESENTATIONS AND RIGHTS OF THE ENVIRONMENT

Edited by

SANDY LAMALLE

AND

PETER STOETT

CAMBRIDGE
UNIVERSITY PRESS

CAMBRIDGE
UNIVERSITY PRESS

Shaftesbury Road, Cambridge CB2 8EA, United Kingdom

One Liberty Plaza, 20th Floor, New York, NY 10006, USA

477 Williamstown Road, Port Melbourne, VIC 3207, Australia

314–321, 3rd Floor, Plot 3, Splendor Forum, Jasola District Centre, New Delhi – 110025, India

103 Penang Road, #05–06/07, Visioncrest Commercial, Singapore 238467

Cambridge University Press is part of Cambridge University Press & Assessment,
a department of the University of Cambridge.

We share the University's mission to contribute to society through the pursuit of
education, learning and research at the highest international levels of excellence.

www.cambridge.org
Information on this title: www.cambridge.org/9781108488297

DOI: 10.1017/9781108769327

© Cambridge University Press & Assessment 2023

First published 2023

Printed in the United Kingdom by TJ Books Limited, Padstow Cornwall

Bookcover: Photopgraph of Mind Eye, Sculpture by Artist Olga Ziemska, Respir'Art Sculpture
Park, Dolomite Mountains of Italy, 2015.

A catalogue record for this publication is available from the British Library.

Library of Congress Cataloging-in-Publication Data
Names: Lamalle, Sandy, editor. | Stoett, Peter John, editor
Title: Representations and rights of the environment / edited by Peter Stoett, University of Ontario;
Sandy Lamalle, Concordia University.
Description: Cambridge, United Kingdom ; New York, NY : Cambridge University Press, 2023. |
Includes bibliographical references and index.
Identifiers: LCCN 2022000040 (print) | LCCN 2022000041 (ebook) | ISBN 9781108488297 (hardback) |
ISBN 9781108708401 (paperback) | ISBN 9781108769327 (epub)
Subjects: Law and Environmental Humanities.
Classification: LCC K3585 .R465 2022 (print) | LCC K3585 (ebook) | DDC 344.04/6–dc23/eng/20220202
LC record available at https://lccn.loc.gov/2022000040
LC ebook record available at https://lccn.loc.gov/2022000041

ISBN 978–1-108–48829–7 Hardback
ISBN 978–1-108–70840–1 Paperback

In memory of those who opened the path before us,
And for our generation and the next.

'The Great Peace begins as a seed in our hearts.
The dream stirs us all to consider our action onto future generations.
The 'how' is revealed in our hoping.'

Ven. Dyani Ywahoo (Cherokee Elder)

With

Poets and Healers

We are invoking

You

Goddess of Memory

and the transmission of Knowledge

Daughter of Earth Gaia and Heaven Ouranos

Symphony of celestial bodies and divinities

Inventor of the Words and Language

Mother of the nine Muses

O Mnemosyne

– Help us recollect

what was left on the side of Time

Join the pieces of knowledge of our being human

Remember the diversity of realms and languages

Ways of knowing and being in the world

Reconcile meaning and being

With all our relationships

Make forms and paths

For common living

understanding

and healing

Contents

Part II　Recollection 145

Part III　Perspectives 231

Illustrations

Artworks

Figures

Tables

Contributors

Marten Berkman is a Visual Artist living with his family and practising his art in the boreal forest upstream from Whitehorse, Yukon in Canada's subarctic. With an artistic practice inspired by the land and our relationship with it, Marten creates digital media of our inner and outer geographies. From a background in drawing, painting, printmaking and photography, his media have evolved to include film-making, stereoscopy and interactive stereo 3D video installation. His works have appeared locally, nationally and internationally in print, theatres, galleries, festivals (Planet in Focus, Interactive Futures, Electric Fields, ISEA), and been commissioned for events ranging from the 2010 Winter Olympics to TAIS Frame Anomalies, to Gwaandak Theatre's *Map of the Land, Map of the Stars*. He has recently completed *Remote Sensibility VIII: The Ecology of Perception*, a multichannel stereo 3D video installation in collaboration with elders, astronauts and artists.

Greta Bird has long been an Activist, Scholar and Advocate in the area of justice and Australia's First Nations peoples. Her education on the injustice of colonisation and the *terra nullius* fiction began in stories shared in bush camps, prisons and court houses during ethnographic research. Books such as *The Civilising Mission: Race and the Construction of Crime* and *The Process of Law* in Australia contributed to bringing issues such as the 'invasion' of Australia, genocidal white practices and the wrongful denial of First Nations sovereignty to a broad readership. She currently teaches at the University of South Australia, prior to which she worked for many years as Associate Professor in the School of Law and Justice at Southern Cross University.

Jo Bird is a Researcher associated with the University of South Australia. Jo is interested in the intersections between human rights, environmental law and bioethics in both Australia and internationally. She has an undergraduate background in arts and law, which included studies in environmental law. Jo obtained an Australian postgraduate award to complete a Ph.D. in law at the University of Melbourne. Jo was awarded the Vallejo Ganter scholarship to conduct research in Malaysia and has also travelled to Mexico, working with *No Mas Muertes*, a human rights NGO. Jo currently works with Professor Irene Watson on an Australian Research Council grant on Indigenous Knowledges and Law.

Vincent Blok is Associate Professor in Philosophy of Responsible Innovation at the Philosophy Group, Wageningen University (the Netherlands). In 2005, he received his Ph.D. degree in philosophy at Leiden University with a specialisation in philosophy of technology. Blok's research group is specialised in business ethics, philosophy of technology and responsible innovation. Together with six Ph.D. candidates and four postdocs, he is involved in several (European) research projects. His books include *Ernst Jünger's Philosophy of Technology: Heidegger and the Poetics of the Anthropocene* (Routledge, 2017) and *Heidegger's Concept of Philosophical Method* (Routledge, 2020). Blok has published over hundred journal articles in, e.g. *Environmental Values*, *Business Ethics Quarterly*, *Synthese* and *Philosophy & Technology*, and in multidisciplinary journals like *Journal of Cleaner Production*, *Public Understanding of Science* and *Journal of Responsible Innovation*.

See www.vincentblok.nl for more information on his current research.

Valérie Cabanes is a Legal Expert in International Law, specialising in Human Rights and Humanitarian Law. She is the Honorary President of *Notre Affaire à Tous*, a member of the Executive Committee of the Global Alliance for the Rights of Nature and one of the experts of the UN Harmony with Nature initiative network. After two decades in NGO fieldwork, in 2013 she launched a European citizens' initiative on the crime of ecocide then co-founded in 2015 the *NGO Notre Affaire à Tous* on the initiative of the 'Case of the century' (Climate case against the French government supported by two million citizens). In 2015, she contributed to the drafting of the project of a Universal Declaration of Humankind Rights and to a proposal for amendments to the Statute of the International Criminal Court on the crime of ecocide. She notably wrote Un nouveau droit pour la Terre. *Pour en finir avec l'écocide* (Seuil, 2016) translated: *Rights for Planet Earth* (Natraj, 2018); *Homo Natura en harmonie avec le vivant* (Buchet/Chastel, 2017); *Des droits pour la Nature* (Utopia, 2016); *Crime climatique, stop!* (Seuil, 2015); *Les procès climatiques* (Pédone, 2018); *Collapsus* (Albin Michel, 2020).

John Crowley is Chief of the Section for Research, Policy and Foresight in the UNESCO Division of Social Transformations and Intercultural Dialogue. Since joining the UNESCO Sector for Social and Human Science in 2003 he has also been a programme specialist in social science (2003–05) and head of the communication, information and publications unit (2005–07), chief of section for ethics of science and technology (2008–11) and team leader for global environmental change (2011–14). Before joining UNESCO, he worked as an economist in the oil industry (1988–95) and as a research fellow at the French National Political Science Foundation (1995–2002). From 2002 to 2015, he was editor of the UNESCO-published *International Social Science Journal*. He contributed to the *UNESCO World Report on Social Sciences* (2013) on the implications of environmental transformations.

Kevin Ka'nahsohon Deer is a Mohawk Faithkeeper and Teacher, Kahnawake, Quebec, and the Vice-President of the Indigenous technical Institute in Tyendineaga, Ontario. He has taught at the *Karonhianonhnha* Mohawk Immersion School (since 1989). In the older traditional teachings in the Longhouse, he helps to perform the ceremonies, songs, speeches and dances of the Mohawk people. He is also a resource person on Iroquoian world view, philosophy treaties, land claims, and native-European historical perspectives. He has been deeply involved in the Mohawk language and spiritual revitalisation of his nation for the past thirty-six years. During the 1990 Oka Crisis, he was involved in peace negotiations to try to resolve the dispute between the Iroquois Confederacy and the federal and provincial government representatives. He received his bachelor's in education at McGill University in June 1996. He was involved with the First Nations Chiefs of Police Association as an Elder (2003–06), and has been a community representative on the police commission (Peacekeeper Services Board) for the past ten years. He is passionate about Indigenous spiritual knowledge of Turtle Island that must be shared and understood by all the newcomers to the New World.

Jean-Pierre Delville is Bishop of Luke (Liège), Belgium. He holds a bachelor's in theology from the Gregorian University of Rome and a degree in biblical sciences from the Pontifical Biblical Institute. He has a doctorate in biblical philology (Catholic University of Louvain-la-Neuve). He became a priest in 1980 and was first vicar, then professor in the Liège Seminar and at the Catholic University of Louvain-la-Neuve. He was director of the *Revue d'histoire ecclésiastique/Louvain Journal of Church History*. His publications focus on the history of exegesis in the sixteenth century, the history of Liège in the Middle Ages to the present time. In 2010, he was elected president at the Research Institute on Religions, Spirituality,

Cultures, Societies. He became Bishop of Luke in 2013, and wrote a guiding document called 'Kairos' (favourable occasion), in which he promotes the involvement of Christians in society, and particularly for society's more disadvantaged people. He undertook a systematic pastoral visit of the deaneries of the diocese, putting an emphasis, in particular, on the evangelical message and community involvement.

Yaëll Emerich is an Associate Professor at the Faculty of Law at McGill University, where she teaches mainly property law and secured transactions. She has been director of the Paul-André Crépeau Centre for Private and Comparative Law (2016–18) after being interim director (2013). Doctor in private law from Quebec and French universities, she holds a postdoctorate from McGill, a master's in private law from Paris II, a DEA in philosophy of law from Paris II and a DEA in private law from Lyon 3, where she has been a research fellow. Professor Emerich teaches and publishes primarily in the areas of property and secured transactions from a comparative perspective. She was a MacCormick Fellow at the University of Edinburgh and a visiting professor at the Université de Lyon 3 and at the Royal University of Phnom Penh. She headed a research grant from the *Fonds de Recherche Société et Culture Québec* addressing the law of sureties from a transsystemic perspective and is currently heading a research grant from the Social Sciences and Humanities Research Council on transsystemic property law. Her ongoing areas of research include property, possession, trusts and theories of property.

Matthias Fritsch is Professor of Philosophy at Concordia University, Montreal. His research interests are social, political and moral philosophy (in particular, democratic theory and justice between generations) as well as nineteenth- and twentieth-century European philosophy (especially German critical theory, phenomenology and deconstruction). He is the author of *The Promise of Memory: History and Politics in Marx, Benjamin, and Derrida* (State University of New York Press, 2005); *Taking Turns with the Earth: Phenomenology, Deconstruction, and Intergenerational Justice* (Stanford University Press, 2018). He co-edited *Reason and Emancipation* (Humanity Books, 2007) and *Eco-Deconstruction: Derrida and Environmental Philosophy* (Fordham University Press, 2018). He has also published a range of articles in scholarly journals, and translated authors such as Heidegger, Gadamer and Habermas into English. He has been a Humboldt Fellow in Frankfurt and a Visiting Research Professor in Kyoto, and is a Senior Research Fellow at Western Sydney University. While continuing to write on environmental and intergenerational ethics, he is working on a monograph on phenomenology and the sources of normative critical theory.

Sandy Lamalle is an International Consultant and Associate Researcher at the Loyola Sustainability Research Centre, Concordia University, Montreal. She is the co-convener of the ESGRREW. She worked as a legal consultant in London, and as a legal adviser in international organisations in Brussels and Geneva, including the European Union and United Nations. She holds a Ph.D. in international law (Geneva) and in European Union law (Strasbourg), and led research projects in Europe, Asia, Australia and America, notably on international cooperation, legal language and communication. She has been a participant in intercultural dialogue processes, such as the China–Europe Forum and the Canadian Commission on Truth and Reconciliation. She has written legal reports, notably on the participation and responsibility of non-state-actors and the implementation of the rights of Indigenous peoples. She has published on reconciliation, legal personality, legal pluralism, translation, conceptual evolution, legal linguistics and semiotics. She was an editor for the *International Journal for the Semiotics of Law*, and has co-edited the first interdisciplinary and intersectoral book mobilising knowledge on the environmental governance of the Saint-Lawrence River (2018).

Caroline Laske holds graduate and postgraduate degrees in law from the University of Cambridge, in linguistics and translation studies from the University of Birmingham, and a Ph.D. in legal history from the University of Ghent. Her research activities as a university researcher (University of Durham, Free University of Brussels, University of Ghent) and her work as a legal expert and specialist consultant for EU and international agencies, have taken her across a number of fields. Today her research interests lie at the intersection of law, history and linguistics, and she has applied linguistics methodologies to study legal concepts, comparative law and legal translation. She also works on the legal capacity that medieval women enjoyed or lacked and on the relations between Anglo-Norman England and medieval Flanders. She is currently a postdoctoral research fellow at the Ghent Legal History Institute and has been appointed Heinz Heinen Fellow at the Bonn Centre for Dependency and Slavery Studies and within the Cluster of Excellence 'Beyond Slavery and Freedom. Asymmetric Dependencies in Pre-modern Societies'.

Deborah McGregor (Anishinaabe) is an Associate Professor at the Osgoode Hall Law School and Faculty of Environmental Studies at York University. She currently holds a Canada Research Chair in Indigenous Environmental Justice. Her research focuses on Indigenous knowledge systems, water and environmental governance, environmental justice, forest policy and management, and Indigenous food sovereignty. Her research has been published in a variety of national and international journals and she has delivered numerous public and academic presentations relating to Indigenous knowledge systems, governance and sustainability. She is co-editor (with Alan Corbiere, Mary Ann Corbiere and Crystal Migwans) of the Anishinaabewin conference proceedings series. She recently co-edited with Rochelle Johnson and Jean Paul Restoule *Indigenous Research: Theories, Practices, and Relationships* (2018).

Michelle Maloney holds a BA (political science and history) and laws (hons.) from the Australian National University, and a Ph.D. in law from Griffith University. She is Co-Founder and National Convenor of the Australian Earth Laws Alliance (AELA), Adjunct Senior Fellow, Law Futures Centre, Griffith University; and Director of Future Dreaming Australia – an organisation created by Indigenous and non-Indigenous leaders to promote cross-cultural sharing of governance and ecological knowledge in Australia. Michelle is on the Executive Committee of the Global Alliance for the Rights of Nature and the Steering Group for the Ecological Law and Governance Association. Michelle has thirty years' experience designing and managing climate change, sustainability and environmental justice projects in Australia, the UK, Indonesia and the USA, and this includes ten years working with Indigenous colleagues in Central Queensland on a range of community development, sustainability and cultural heritage projects. Michelle met and fell in love with Earth jurisprudence and Wild Law in 2009 and since 2011 has been working to promote the understanding and practical implementation of Earth-centred governance – with a focus on law, economics, ethics, education and the arts – through her work with AELA.

James Meadowcroft is Professor at the Department of Political Science and the School of Public Policy and Administration at Carlton University, and has recently completed a fourteen-year term as a Tier 1 Canada Research Chair in Governance for Sustainable Development. He has written widely on environmental politics and policy, democratic participation and deliberative democracy, national sustainable development strategies, and socio-technical transitions. His recent work focuses on energy and the transition to a low carbon society and includes publications on conceptual innovation in environmental policy, multilevel environmental governance, smart grids, the politics of socio-technical transitions and negative carbon emissions. He is a member of the Scientific Steering Committee of Earth System Governance Project (ESG). He was the initiator of the ESG Taskforce on Conceptual Foundations. He is also Research Director, alongside David Layzell and Normand Mousseau, of the Transition Accelerator, which engages diverse societal stakeholders to co-create visions of a socially desirable net-zero future and build out transition pathways.

Dorine van Norren is a Diplomat, Scientist and Artist. She holds a master's in international and Dutch law (1995) and a Ph.D. in law and development studies (2017), Tilburg University and University of Amsterdam), entitled 'Development as Service: A Happiness, Ubuntu and *Buen Vivir* interdisciplinary view of the Sustainable Development Goals', for which she did research in Bhutan, Ecuador and South Africa. She studied law in Amsterdam and South Africa (Cape Town) and French for a year in Lyon, France. She worked as a diplomat in Sri Lanka (Colombo) and Turkey (Ankara) and held several positions at the ministry of foreign affairs (Southern Africa, North America, European Integration desks). She was attached to the Advisory Council of International Affairs, as an executive secretary for the Commission on Development. She is currently seconded to the Ministry of Education, Culture and Science, as a coordinator for UNESCO. She has published several scientific articles on development cooperation. She has written several blogs and opinion articles for *OneWorld, The Broker, Atlantisch Perspectief, NRC, Trouw, De Helling, Down to Earth magazine, Economische Statistische Berichten, Diplomat Magazine.* She regularly gives national and international lectures on the themes of her Ph.D. In 2019–20, her first exhibition entitled *The Wheel of Values* was shown in the Africa Study Centre in Leiden University, Alliance Française Rotterdam and the Rathenau Institute in The Hague.

Arnaud Paturet is a Lawyer in Private Law, a classical Historian and Researcher at the CNRS (UMR 7074 Centre for Theory and legal analysis) who also teaches at the École normale supérieure in Paris and in various other institutions (Centre national de la fonction publique territoriale, École nationale supérieure de Police, Institut du travail social de la région Auvergne, Université Clermont-Auvergne section Lettres-Histoire). His research is focused on legal history and Roman law as the projection of modern images and cognitive representations. He has researched and written on concepts and legal categories, the legal concept *res*, religion, slavery, bodies and disability, death and funeral rituals, with a strong societal connotation beyond legal categories. He uses a methodology combining historical sociology, anthropology and legal science.

T8aminik Rankin is an Algonquin Hereditary Chief and Medicine Man. He was born in the forests of northern Abitibi and named in Algonquin *Kapiteotak* ('He who is heard crying or singing from afar'), in a family that had managed so far to preserve the nomadic lifestyle of his ancestors. He was guided on his spiritual path notably by his father and William Commanda. He later became Grand Chief of the Algonquin Nation. Since being recognised as an elder by his peers in 2006, he has devoted himself to the role of teacher and spiritual leader. He is a survivor of the painful era of Indian Residential Schools and gives a vibrant testimony about forgiveness and reconciliation in the book *We Were Called Savages*. In 2013, T8aminik and Marie-Josée co-founded the NGO Kina8at, dedicated to reconciliation and the transmission of traditional knowledge and Native American culture. T8aminik is a Member of the Order of Canada, Knight of the National Order of Quebec, and a recipient of the Diamond Jubilee of Queen Elizabeth II. He is Honorary President of the Circle of Peace of Montreal, Member of Religions for Peace World Council and of the *Ethics in Action Committee* in Notre Dame University, Indiana.

Nicole Rogers is an Associate Professor in the School of Law and Justice, Southern Cross University and a founding member of the School. She researches and publishes in the areas of performance studies theory and the law, wild law/Earth jurisprudence and interdisciplinary climate studies encompassing climate litigation, climate activism and climate fiction. From 2014 to 2017, Nicole instigated and, together with Michelle, co-led the Wild Law Judgment Project. She is co-editor of *Law as If Earth Really Mattered: The Wild Law Judgment Project* (Routledge, 2017). Her 2019 Routledge monograph Law, *Fiction and Activism in a Time of Climate Change* was shortlisted for the 2020 Hart–SLSA book prize.

Mahisha Sritharan is a Research Assistant at York University. Her research focuses on environmental justice, climate change and Indigenous knowledge. Mahisha holds a master's in environmental studies from York University and a BA in environmental geography and health studies from the University of Toronto. Through her research work experiences, she has been able to apply an interdisciplinary approach to understanding social determinants of health and their relationship to environmental justice.

Peter Stoett is Dean of Social Science and Humanities at the University of Ontario Institute of Technology in Canada. He is the co-convener of the ESGRREW. He was the founder and Director of the Loyola Sustainability Research Centre, and Chair of the Department of Political Science at Concordia University in Montreal. His main areas of expertise include international relations and law, global environmental politics, and human rights. He has conducted research in Europe, eastern, southern and western Africa, central America and Asia. He has published over ten books and fifty articles/chapters on various aspects of global environmental justice and human rights and works frequently with the United Nations on related issues. He is a Senior Fellow with the Earth System Governance Project, and an Expert Member of the Commission on Education and Communication of the International Union for the Conservation of Nature.

He is also an Expert Member of the Commission on Education and Communication of the International Union for the Conservation of Nature.

Marie-Josée Tardif is recognised as an Algonquin Elder and Writer. For more than fifteen years she was a journalist on the main radio and TV channels in Quebec and Canada (Radio-Canada, RDI, LCN), and in the UK. She trained with David Ciussi, the French specialist in conscious communication, and devotes most of her time to groups or individuals in their learning of a more constructive and humane communication, based on principles of self-awareness and mindfulness. She received two Sacred Pipes from the elders of the Algonquin Nation (2007 and 2015), and recognised as a 'kokom', an elder and teacher of the Algonquin philosophy and traditional medicine. Marie-Josée is the author of best-seller *On nous appelait les Sauvages* (2012; translated in 2019, *We Were Called Savages*). She also wrote *La Leçon de Sitar ou l'Art de vibrer de toutes ses cordes*. Member of the Religions for Peace Women of Faith Network Council, Ethics in Action Committee, created by the Vatican, the United Nations, Religions for Peace and Notre Dame University, to develop an interreligious moral consensus on the major challenges of integral sustainable development. She is the co-founder with T8aminik Rankin of the Indigenous association *Kina8at*.

Preface

The authors of this remarkable collection offer critical perspectives on some of the most challenging issues of our time, interrogating understandings of rights, representations and environment. They offer a rich discussion that spans cultures, knowledge systems and academic disciplines to explore the intersections of community, representation, nature and law. They champion a more caring vision that affirms life, respect and reverence for nature, solidarity with the poor and marginalised, and reconciliation with Indigenous peoples.

Over millennia human societies have forged complex and evolving relationships with their natural surroundings, continuously transforming themselves and the world around them. But today the human presence – our technology, agriculture and industry, our sheer numbers together with those of our domesticated animals – dominates the terrestrial biosphere, increasingly threatening the survival of non-human species and ecosystems. At this critical juncture, where it has become urgent to shift the human development trajectory onto more sustainable lines, it is important to reflect on ideas, beliefs, representations and legal systems, to understand the quandary we confront, consider voices and perspectives which have been silenced, and to explore alternative futures.

The volume is organised into three parts which engage with *challenges* in the current political and legal landscape explore *recollections* of the past and of fields and modes of knowledge, and survey *perspectives* for what might be. The discussion is ambitious, bridging cultures, disciplines and imaginaries and challenging the reader to engage with ideas that they may find novel, difficult or even disconcerting. But such reflection on past and future, which highlights plural ways of being and knowing, is essential to rethink our relationships with one another, and with the non-human natural world. For as we try to develop more just and caring relationships, it is vital to reconsider our activities and habits, goals and beliefs, loyalties and ethics. In that optic, the authors emphasise that how we envision the environment determines how we define environmental problems and their solutions. And the book proceeds to offer a pragmatic reflection on the shortcomings of modern legal frameworks, on current alternative practices in different countries (notably of the global south), and on possible new pathways in law and governance.

This book has its origins in the Working Group on Representations and Rights of/for the Environment set up though the Taskforce on Conceptual Foundations of Earth System Governance. It illustrates the diversity of scholarship embraced by the Earth System Governance network. And it attests to the enthusiasm of Sandy Lamalle and Peter Stoett who have gathered such distinguished contributors to deal with complex topics that include decolonising the Anthropocene, advancing legal communication and understanding with Indigenous legal traditions and systems, defining environmental justice and democracy, identifying and appraising systems that recognise the rights of nature, and defining effective local and international legal frameworks.

James Meadowcroft
School of Public Policy
Carleton University

Acknowledgements

This edited volume is the fruit of a growing and maturing process. Born out of a convergence of questioning, the Workgroup on the Representations and Rights of the Environment (ESGRREW) was co-founded by Sandy Lamalle and Peter Stoett in 2015–16 as part of the Taskforce on Conceptual Foundations of Earth System Governance. In 2017, ESGRREW launched an intercultural and interdisciplinary Dialogue & Research Process in partnership with Future Earth, under the patronage of UNESCO and the Canadian Commission for UNESCO. Since then, the process has been nurtured by various events organised in Canada and Europe: it has assumed a life of its own, and we are hopeful it will continue to flourish and contribute to transforming global thinking.

We would like to express our deep appreciation and gratitude to all the authors, participants, partners and sponsors of the ESGRREW for the inspiring cooperation, meetings and discussions we have had in recent years, and thanks to whom this book now sees the light of day:

- Faculty of Social Science and Humanities, Ontario Tech University, Canada, for financial support in order to prepare this book (2019), and for hosting the ESGRREW symposium 'Addressing Climate Change: Technology, Law and Ethics' (25 January 2018);
- Centre for Legal Theory and Empirical Jurisprudence at KU Leuven (Belgium) for support in the preparatory steps of this book (2019);
- Loyola Sustainability Research Centre, and the Loyola College for Diversity and Sustainability at Concordia University, Montreal, for general support of the ESGRREW, and their financial and logistical support in the organisation of the ESGRREW launch event (12–13 April 2017);
- Canadian Law & Society Association for sponsorship and financial support of the ESGRREW launch event (2017);

- Montreal Hub of Future Earth for general support of the ESGRREW Intercultural and Interdisciplinary Dialogue & Research Process, and for financial support of the ESGRREW launch events (2017);
- UNESCO and Canadian Commission for the UNESCO for patronage (2017);
- Canadian Commission of the UNESCO for support in the organisation and hosting of the ESGRREW Session 'Traditional Indigenous Knowledge, Earth Law and Environmental Justice', at the 57th CCUNESCO AGA in Montreal (26 May 2017);
- World Humanities Conference and the University of Luke (Liège, Belgium) for support and hosting of the ESGRREW Symposium 'Opening New Paths in the Representations and Rights of the Environment: The Role of Humanities' (10 August 2017);
- Canada Council for the Arts for financial support for the art exhibition of Marten Berkman at the World Humanities Conference in Belgium (2017);
- Délégation Générale du Québec in Brussels for financial support of the ESGRREW Symposium at the World Humanities Conference in Belgium (2017).

We would like to thank in particular the following.

James Meadowcroft for entrusting us with the mandate of convening a research group and programme in the ESG Taskforce on Conceptual Foundations, and for his support and participation in ESGRREW events.

For their support of ESGRREW: Anne-Hélène Prieur-Richard, Christina Cook, Jean-Patrick Toussaint, Paul Shrivastava, Raymond Paquin, John Crowley, Luiz Oosterbeek, Jean Winand, Sébastien Goupil, Angèle Cyr, Lyndsay Campbell, Alain Lebeaupin (†), Juan Pablo Cerrillos Hernandez, Anna Dederichs, Michel Audet.

For their participation in ESGRREW events and contribution to the discussions: Kathleen Mahoney, Daniel Hoornsveg, Tamara Thermitus, Marie-Josée Tardif, T8aminik Rankin, Kevin Ka'nahsohon Deer, Juliette Scott, Josiane Pouliot, Deborah McGregor, Mahisha Sritharan, Marten Berkman, Arnaud Paturet, John Crowley, Jean-Pierre Delville, Caroline Laske, Michèle Perrin-Taillat, Nicole Rogers, Michelle Maloney, Greta Bird, Jo Bird, Yaëll Emerich, Dorine van Norren, Colin Robertson, Valérie Cabanes, Matthias Fritsch, Brendan Mackey, Sarah Burch.

For their support and kind help in organising ESGRREW events: Rebecca Titler, Adan Suazo, Joanne Downs, Maura Matesic, Thomas McMorrow, Heather Marcille, Fabienne de Smet, Alison Psathas, Alexandra Salmon-Bobek, Xavier Le Guyader, Eleanor Haine-Bennett, Marike Bontenbal, Steve Whitaker, Derek Cooke, Stéphane Grétry, Marie d'Acremont, Go Okui.

We are very grateful to the authors of this book for their inspirational work, their spirit of openness to other cultures, fields of knowledge, ways of being and thinking, and for their patience with the editorial process.

Finally, we would like to address our special thanks to:

Olga Ziemska and Marten Berkman for their mesmerising artworks firing imagination, and for the beautiful photos illustrating this book, notably the photo of *Mind Eye* on the cover.

Emma Kiddle, Frank Biermann and Ruben Zondervan for their support in this book project.

Sarah Lambert and the team at CUP for their patient help in bringing it to fruition.

Cristina for her support, inspiration and love.

Oliver for his faith, support and partaking in this exploration.

Without you all, this fascinating, hopeful journey would not have been possible.

 Earth System Governance   Taskforce on Conceptual Foundations

Organisation · Commission
des Nations Unies · canadienne
pour l'éducation, · pour l'UNESCO
la science et la culture ·

United Nations · Canadian
Educational, Scientific and · Commission
Cultural Organization · for UNESCO

 futurearth

 WORLD HUMANITIES CONFERENCE
Challenges and Responsibilities for a Planet in Transition

Canadian   Association
Law and Society Canadienne
Association   Droit et Société

 Québec
Délégation générale
Bruxelles

 OntarioTech UNIVERSITY

 UNIVERSITÉ Concordia UNIVERSITY

FACULTY OF
ARTS AND SCIENCE

Loyola Sustainability Research Centre

Loyola College for
Diversity and Sustainability

1

An Introduction

Towards the Multifold Vision

SANDY LAMALLE AND PETER STOETT

Observing the sun rising in the awakening light of dawn, the heart rejoices in beauty. Our vision and attitude towards the world form our perception, so tells the Poet of multifold vision and imagination (Blake 1821). He describes different worlds shaped by different states of mind. In the state of single vision (Ulro), of logic, measurements and data capture, the sun is a 'guinea-form, an average star, in an average galaxy'. In the twofold vision (Generation), which 'understands biological cycles, productive seasons, farming, and, in the modern world, has fostered great advances in manufacturing', the sun is a 'celestial nuclear furnace which forged the building blocks of life, such as carbon'. In the threefold vision (Beulah), where 'there is an awareness and desire for felt relationships', 'ethics, morality and justice', the glorious Sun is sharing heaven with the resplendent Moon, and is 'praised for its warmth and light'. In the fourfold vision (Eternity), relational knowledge is combined with 'multivalent perception and creative powers of imagination', 'space is fractal and time fluid', the Sun like 'the cosmos is alive and pluriform'. We can 'perceive the interior vitality of the world as well as its interconnecting exteriors', and 'make sense of the best of the other states: the discernment of Ulro, the expansiveness of Generation and the feeling of Beulah … The geniuses of science and the arts work hand-in-hand, illuminating each other', and 'imagination's ingenuity isn't only spectacular and fun, but generative and lasting' (Vernon 2020). These different worlds spring from different modes of vision. And each vision can open on to a wider world by a shift of conscience. Artist Olga Ziemska embodied such multifold imagination of the Poet in her sculpture featured on the cover of this book, entitled *Mind Eye*.[1]

---

[1] Located 2,000 metres high in the Respir'Art Sculpture Park, Dolomite Mountains of Italy, 2015.

1.1 The Change in Vision

The Messengers came knocking at the Western door of the House of Mica. They had come before – but this time the door opened.[2] On 22 November 1993, at the United Nations headquarters in New York, they delivered their message: 'Cry of the Earth – The Legacy of the First Nations'. Seven delegations from the Four Directions, with knowledge keepers and spiritual leaders, gathered for a historic conference.[3] For the first time, they shared with the world ancestral knowledge, transmitted orally, regarding the ecological, spiritual and ethical crises confronting humanity (McFadden 2005: 80, 110). They called for an awakening of people, for action and unity:

It is time to mend the Sacred Hoop of life on our Earth Mother.

(Arvol Looking Horse)

We must join hands with the rest of creation, and speak of common sense, responsibility, brotherhood and peace ... we are the generation with the responsibility and option to choose the path with a future for our children.

(Chief Oren Lyons)

We must live in harmony with the natural world and recognize that excessive exploitation can only lead to our own destruction. We cannot trade the welfare of our future generations for profit now. We must stand together, the four sacred colours of man, as the one family that we are ... We (human beings) are a spiritual energy that is thousands of time stronger than nuclear energy. Our energy is the combined will of all the people with the spirit of the natural world, to be of one body, one heart, and one mind for peace.

(Chief Leon Shenandoah)

In the wake of the message delivered at the conference, as 'a gesture of hope and deed of unity', people gathered for a 3,700-mile walk which started on 23 June 1995, from the ancestral territory of the Wampanoag Nation (The People of the Morning Light) along the Atlantic Ocean by Cape Cod, Massachusetts, to the shore of the Pacific Ocean at Santa Barbara, California, ending on 2 February 1996 (McFadden 2001: 101). Elder William Commanda sponsored this walk joining the two oceans in the perspective of 'unit[ing] people of all races and religions for healing the Earth now and the Future generations' (The Sunbow Walk for the Earth, Respect and Harmony with all Creation).

The door opened for the Messengers at a time when a change in vision was expressed around the world, 'a phase-change in human understanding of the

---

[2] Three times since 1923, when Deskaheh (1873–1925), the Mohawk representative for the Haudenosaunee (Six Nations Iroquois Confederacy), went to Geneva to speak at the League of Nations, the ancestor of the United Nations.

[3] It included seven delegations representing the Hopi, Maya, Huichol, Lakota, Mi-kmaq, Haudenausenee (Iroquois Confederacy) and Mamiwinini (Algonquin) Nations of North America.

environment' (Primavesi 1998: 75). Since the 1960s, the damages to nature and the earth had been raised notably by scientists (Carlson 1962) and theologians (Moltmann 1980; Berry 1988). And in the 1992 Rio Declaration issued by the United Nations Conference on Environment and Development, 'nature' and 'the earth' are presented as 'threatened natural environment' (Meadowcroft 2017: 57–60). Since then, the environment understood as 'physical environment', 'the natural world, as a whole or in a particular geographical area, especially affected by human activity', manifests 'an implicit problematization of human interactions with our surroundings' (Meadowcroft 2017: 54–55). With the gradual change in vision came to light not only 'the destruction of nature and eco-systems', but also 'the devaluation of living creatures', 'the wholesale exploitation of the Earth' with 'the related oppression of multitudes of human beings' (Grear 2013: 971), and 'a spiritual crisis of the human race' (Regenstein 1991: 153; Vaughan-Lee and Berry 2013). The crisis has been caused 'by how we imagine the world to be – the ideas we have about what constitutes those things we call 'nature', what makes humans human, and how we understand relationship between peoples and the places within which they live' (Bohannon 2014: 3). Such a realisation raised 'very deep questions about the underlying worldviews of thought paradigms within which we are operating', and made 'critical reflexion crucial' (Rawles 1998: 134–36, 43; Spretnak 2011: 6; Sofoulis 2018: 821–22).

Indeed, the change in vision was already blurring the landscape over a century ago. Reflection on the history of what we understand as the modern scientific operating paradigm shows its roots, evolution and interweaving with society, social representations and philosophy across centuries (Morrow 2011). At the beginning of the twentieth century, exploration at both the subatomic and extra-galactic levels described 'rips in the fabric of reality' as science then conceived the world to be (Trinh 2019; Espagnat 1994). Such rips – animated by revolutionary thinking in science, technology and eventually ethics – put into question concepts and values of a worldview focused on substance, structure and mechanistic behaviour, dividing reality into categories, opposing subject to object; an epistemology which assumed scientific descriptions to be objective, independent of the human observer and the process of knowledge (Capra 2010: 325, 331). The rip started tearing apart the fabric of many fields of knowledge, decomposing the modern paradigm and beginning to unveil a new scenery in science (Stengers 2010), physics and biology (Capra 2010; Espagnat 1994); social sciences and geography (Harvey 1989; Giddens 1990; Morin 2001; Latour 2004; Johnston et al. 1996: 466); the philosophy of science (Whitehead 1929; Canguilhem 1967; Andler et al. 2002); philosophy (Cadava et al. 1991; Dews 2007; Plumwood 2002); the philosophy of language (Peirce [1878] 1958; Wittgenstein [1953] 1969; Jackson 1988), representations in arts and science (Friggs and Hunter 2010);

theology (Sittler 2004); anthropology (Clifford 2003; Alliot 1983; Ingold 2011; Ratto 2016) and law (Unger 1976; MacCormick 1978; Carty 1990; Rouland 1991; Bankowski and Scott 2000; Kennedy 2006; Koskenniemi 2006; Delmas-Marty 2008).

The manifestations in the different fields are the fragmentation, objectification, cracking of the object and disintegration of the subject, until collective representations and conceptual frameworks of intelligibility no longer provide a coherent, meaningful and effective story (Capra 2010: 325; Ingold 2011; Korten 2015: 1; Cyrulnik and Morin 2018: 11, 16, 21; Carty 2007: 198–99, 231). 'The deepest crises experienced by any society are those moments of change when the story becomes inadequate for meeting the survival demands of a present situation' (Berry 1988: 123). Such change has led to reconsidering the contours of the fields as well as knowledge itself. Understood by epistemologists as a 'propositional attitude', a mental or social representation works as a framework for thought and action (Gélinas and Bouchard 2013). Representations as truth claims 'are at once scientific, philosophical and religious' (Kull, in Favareau et al. 2017: 20), and are constitutive of narratives used in different fields of knowledge (Nash 1994). As Heisenberg highlighted the crucial role of the observer on reality in quantum physics, and participative theory emerged in sociology and anthropology, the understanding of the process of knowledge became an integral part of one's understanding of reality. In that sense, if our apprehension of the world is mediated by our own approach and representations, then the current predicament denotes a crisis of perception (Capra 2010: 331, 325).

Observing the sun rising – experiencing colours, sounds and myriads of sensations. According to neuroscientists, the 'vast majority of these sensations are ignored by our conscious mind, while those that we recognize and name become perceptions' (Lipari 2014). Linking lived experience with mental representations, perception is both an interpretative and creative activity, which combines sensory perception with notions of time and space, experience and intuition (Merleau-Ponty 1996; Watzlawick 1978), and which participates in making reality intelligible (Bouveresse and Rosat 2003). It also implies that 'we feel our histories as well as think of them' (Dian Million, in Lucchesi 2019), as representations and emotions are entangled in structured narratives in one's community or culture (Cyrulnik and Morin 2018: 55). Perception can thus be approached as 'a process of distilling sensations into linguistic and culturally distinct patterns – that describes, names, and gives meaning to those sensations' (Lipari 2014). 'So what perceptions get named, as well as how they get named, is ultimately a social and political matter', which dimensions of language are 'not limited to what we name' (Lipari 2014). Representations are therefore active components of shared social and material realities, shaped by language and culture, and by different ways of experiencing the world.

Accompanying the change in vision in different fields of knowledge, the Messengers came to remind us that our experience of the world as humans, as our capacity for communion (Vernon 2019), encompasses all the dimensions of our being and relationships. 'At the forefront of contemporary science, the universe is no longer seen as a machine composed of elementary building blocks. We have discovered that the material world ultimately is a network of inseparable patterns of relationships; that the planet as a whole is a living, self-regulating system' (Capra 2010: 8). The new physics is an integral part of the new worldview that is now emerging, or re-emerging, in many contested conceptual spaces (Capra 2010: 8, 327), and shedding light on 'the inherent relatedness of all in life' (Spretnak 2011: 199). 'We are profoundly relational beings who have been living – with some difficulty – in anti-relational (mechanistic) systems of thought and ways of doing things' (Spretnak 2011: 6). The biological sciences are now more likely to observe life in terms of 'information and communication systems nested in larger communicative systems . . . including natural and cultural environments' (Wheeler 2016). The change of our perception of reality with quantum physics and biology led many 'to reconsider our approach to science and lead our way back to the ancient spiritualities' (Capra 2010: 331, 6), rejoining substance with process, and reconnecting all the dimensions, from the heart to the stars. This is a 'recovery of relational knowledge' (Donati 2004; Einstein and Infeld 1993; Ricœur 1983; Kalka 1985; Whitehead 1938: 12–13), reminiscent of such knowledge in the Vedas and Taoism; as well as in the European tradition, with Heraclitus dynamic balance, according to which with material reality, there is also flow and movement (Fagot-Largeault 2006–07).

Conceiving all relations as vibrating waves on the cosmic ocean, like Pythagoras' music of the spheres[4] (Martineau 2010) – this is the ancient sense of *Cosmos* in the Greek world where heaven and earth, gods and humans are linked in a community (Pythagoras, in Plato's Gorgias, 507e–508a). *Rita* in Hinduism, *Dharma* in Buddhism, *Tao*, *Ch'eng* and *Jen* in the Chinese world: 'These are the ancient perceptions of the ordering, or the balancing, principles of the universe, the principles governing the interaction of all those basic forces constituting the earth process' (Berry 1988: 19). They remind us that from 'time immemorial, to recognize and act according to these principles was the ultimate form of human wisdom' (Spretnak 2011: 59). Human knowledge grew in that light. Up to the seventeenth century, 'the goal of science was wisdom, understanding of the natural order and living in harmony with it' (Capra 2010:

---

[4] According to which the planets and stars move to musical ratios, therefore producing a symphony.

335). This recollection in the perspective of current challenges inspired the United Nations General Assembly Resolution 66/288 of 27 July 2012, entitled *The Future We Want*, which recognised that 'planet Earth and its ecosystems are our home', and that 'in order to achieve a just balance among the economic, social and environmental needs of present and future generations, it is necessary to promote harmony with nature', a more holistic approach to reality. This approach leads us to rebalance our notion of responsibility from a focus on the individual to a focus on the relational process involved (McNamee and Gergen 1999): rediscovering traditional knowledge, such as the *Ubuntu* principle of connectedness and mutual construction in South Africa, the Anishinabe *8itokotati8in* principle meaning our interdependency and solidarity in North America, or *Ngarlimbah*, the Walmajarri concept of unity and reciprocity between people, spirit and environmental realms in Australia.

These principles invite us to rethink of our existence as 'interbeing': 'We interare, they interare, everyone interis' (Thich Nhat Hahn). Re-envisaging science and society in that light, 'we see the world more fully' – it can produce 'a new species of knowledge, a new way of being in the world' (Kimmerer 2020: 46, 47). New approaches and theories have emerged in various fields of knowledge and practice in that perspective about 'representational activity creating reality', such as ontological levelling and non-representational methods like practice theory and performance studies (Sofoulis 2018: 821). This relational shift is a 'fundamental change of worldview that is occurring in science and society – a change that is nothing less than the unfolding of a new vision of reality – and the social implications of cultural transformation' (Capra 2010: 6). Because the 'stories we choose to shape our behaviours have adaptive consequences' (Kimmerer 2020: 30), 'this is a moment of unprecedented opportunity to create a future consistent with our nature and possibility as living beings born of a Living Earth born of a Living Universe … Communications technologies now give us the capacity as a species to choose our common story with conscious intention' (Korten 2015:1).

1.2 Opening on to the 'Fourth World'

> We come full circle in this place – The Stranger and the Ancient Race.
> *(Elder Jane Crane)*[5]

The Messengers to the House of Mica recalled our interrelatedness and exhorted us to unite, while the obstacles they encountered to deliver their message exposed the dividing barriers still standing before the fourth world – imperialism, oppression,

---

[5] Elder Jane Crane (2014) in Heppner (2020).

discrimination and ignorance. These barriers made this world 'the most distant from the political and economic core': the 'populations were decimated by direct violence, structural violence, and disease, and survivors were forcibly relocated into territorial enclaves representing a fraction of the land and resource base they had originally occupied' (Wilmer, in Beier 2009: 187, 193). The peoples of this world are 'among the poorest of the poor, and thus the most threatened segment of the world's population in terms of social, economic and environmental vulnerability' (International Labour Organization 2017). Barriers of historical negative representations, prejudices and reductive scientific categories kept out of reach millenary languages, cultures and wisdom (Clarkson et al. 1992: 9; Battiste 2000: 5; Jansen and Pérez Jiménez 2017: 28; Menski 2005: 396; Castillo and Strecker 2017: 28). Such barriers prevented access to information outside of the dominant meaning system, and precluded understandings of other modes of knowledge and living, legal traditions and systems, and integral forms of spirituality (Clarkson et al. 1992: 9–10; Napoleon 2007: 1–2; McCaslin 2005: 3–4; Menski 2005: 394; Beier 2009: 197; Berry 1988: 184; Sousa Santos 2014: 238). That world displaying its ontological specificity (Stewart-Harawira, in Beier 2009: 216) belongs to the 370 million Indigenous peoples spread out in more than 90 countries around the world, with about 4,500 distinct cultures and as many different languages and dialects (Castillo and Strecker 2017: 25). They 'are stewards of about 80 percent of the world's remaining biological diversity and account for 90 percent of its cultural diversity' (Dowie 2017: xiii). If they are characterised by 'a special condition, namely that of collectively facing specific forms of social injustice that are the consequence of colonialism' (Pulitano 2012: 29), and clear common issues across the globe (Bellier and Legros 2001), they hold a vision which is 'key to the future survival of humanity' (IISD 1992: 7).

Removing barriers, restoring sight. The Sustainable Development Goals of 2015–30 recognise that all our needs are intertwined with each other's and with our environment, and that 'delivering social justice and protecting the environment are closely linked' (Future Earth Report 2020: 10; IISD 1992: 7; Boff 1997: 319–27). This demands addressing poverty and inequality, as well as marginalisation and discrimination (Stoett 2012; Fox and Stoett 2016: 567–68). While this was recognised regarding the 'third world' in peace and development approaches, the United Nations Declaration on the Rights of Indigenous Peoples (UNDRIP 2007) recognised and defined these issues regarding the 'fourth world', stating principles, standards and guidelines to that end (Pulitano 2012: 29). Many countries and regions have started removing barriers (ILA Kyoto Report 2020). Indigenous peoples' collective rights to their traditional lands, cultural heritage, self-determination and autonomy, as well as to the reparation and redress for the wrongs they have suffered, are now recognised as rules of customary international law (ILA Sofia Report 2012). The participation and leadership of Indigenous peoples is presently considered necessary for the 'transformative and cross-sectorial systemic change required to deal with the climate crisis' (IPCC 2018, 2019; Díaz et al. 2019). It is notably based on the consideration that 'respect for Indigenous knowledge, cultures and traditional practices contributes to sustainable and equitable development' (UNDRIP, para. 11) (Roué and Nakashima 2002). It includes their 'distinctive spiritual relationship' to their lands, territories and resources, with their right to 'uphold their responsibilities to future generations in this regard' (UNDRIP, art. 25). The Declaration on Cultural Diversity recognises the 'contribution of traditional knowledge, particularly with regard to environmental protection and management of natural resources, fostering synergies between modern science and local knowledge' (UNESCO 2001, Action Plan, para. 14). The importance of Indigenous knowledge, innovation and practice to the conservation and sustainable use of biological diversity is notably asserted in the UN Convention on Biological Diversity (CBD) (CBD 1992, art. 8). The World Conference on Science (Budapest, 1999) urged governments to promote understanding of Indigenous knowledge systems, to generate the necessary intellectual space and create a conceptual framework open to it (Battiste 2002: 6). Global assessment programmes, such as the Intergovernmental Science-Policy Platform on Biodiversity and Ecosystem Services (IPBES) have been developing 'constructive ways of creating synergies across knowledge systems'. Such 'complementarities ... have advanced the understanding, and in many cases improved management of ecosystems, critical natural resources and biodiversity' (Tengö et al. 2014: 582–83, 588).

As with the ancient parable of the Elephant in India, 'situated knowledges support epistemological pluralism and recognize that every body of knowledge illuminates some aspects of the world'. According to such a 'situated knowledge ecology', 'a diversity of knowledge types is valued' (Sofoulis 2018: 821; Haraway 1988). By acknowledging 'the uniqueness of each knowledge system, we can go well beyond a mere pluralist approach to knowledge. Dialogue can become a tool for social cohabitation, as well as for discovering and enhancing knowledge' (Mazzocchi 2006: 465). In that respect, the policy of engagement of the United Nations Development Programme (UNDP) with Indigenous peoples specified that not only 'their land and resource management, sciences and knowledge' were 'a resource for the whole world', but also 'their ways of life, cultures, governance, political and justice systems, and healing practices' (UNDP 2001). Intelligence of reality, as *inter-ligere* (linking between), requires a community of practice in which the different perceptions of the members interact in order to reach a structured vision, a common sense. It involves the 'co-creation' and 'co-nurturing' of a common research, practice and living (Lévesque et al. 2009; McGregor 2018).

Such a co-creation at the society level is the purpose of reconciliation processes, and concerns not only knowledges or knowledge systems, but the recognition of the specificity of Indigenous peoples, laws and systems, and the experience of constituting with them a common space of meaning (Lamalle 2020b: 168). There is thus a further and decisive step in opening on to the fourth world. Reconciliation notably signifies 'reaching out to the other to build understanding and relationships' (Carmichael 2010). Reconciliation as 'ontological encounter and real intercultural dialogue' goes beyond the content of specific knowledge, cognitive approaches and practices. It demands the recognition, understanding and interaction with Indigenous law and legal traditions (Beier 2009; Napoleon and Friedland 2016; Castillo and Strecker 2017: 351). Notions of law and justice in Indigenous legal traditions are very different from their understanding in modern legal systems (McCaslin 2005: 3–4), notably in their form and process (Menski 2006: 394). The recent revitalisation of Indigenous law and languages in various countries contributed to highlight their structural and conceptual differences: 'within Indigenous justice systems, there is more emphasis on duties, obligation and responsibilities', and the most distinct aspect of such a worldview is 'the intimate linkage between the natural world, spirituality, and collective relations' (Dorough 2009: 274), which implies the connection to the heart and to the earth (Castillo and Strecker 2017: 75). This encompasses all aspects of Indigenous ways of life – such as ontology with all as integral components of 'one system' is shared by many Indigenous cultures around the world, including not only 'ritual, economic, residential and kinship rules and conventions, but also what we would call natural laws and technological rules' (Austin-Broos and Merlan 2017: 11). The recognition of Indigenous law therefore challenges both the current definitions of 'law' and 'environment' in modern legal systems. In that regard, the experience of reconciliation in Canada has unlocked and pushed the doors for 'ontological encounter and intercultural dialogue' since the Royal Commission on Aboriginal Peoples (1991–96), dismantled the scaffolds of discrimination and cleared the windows of perception with the important work of the Truth and Reconciliation Commission (TRC) (2008–15). As an ethical space of encounter and dialogue, the TRC launched the process of co-creation of new representations and practices with Indigenous law and approach to justice (Lamalle 2015: 22–23). We have been removing barriers. We have discovered another world. We are now beginning to unfold a new vision of law and society.

1.3 A New Legal Consciousness

Describing the Coronavirus as an 'SOS signal' for humankind, leaders at the World Health Organization (WHO), CBD and World Wildlife Fund (WWF) explain that pandemics, such as the one experienced since the beginning of 2020, are the result of humanity's destruction of the environment and 'a warning to us to mend our broken relationship with nature'.[6] As witnesses to the Cry of the Earth, the harm done to human well-being and the natural world is now tangible for everyone (UN HRC Report 2019: 13). A 'change in societal values and perceptions' is called for, meaning 'that previously accepted practices are now deemed problematic' (Meadowcroft 2017: 63–65). The current situation is 'not only a crisis of the physical environment but also a crisis of the system of representation and of the institutional structures through which contemporary society understands and responds to environmental change' (Bergthaller et al. 2012: 262).

While the fabric of a fragmented world (Cyrulnik and Morin 2018: 11, 16, 89) is progressively falling to pieces, solutions remain embedded in the conceptual, methodological and institutional weft of that fabric. Political options are limited in an objectified world which is approached by an 'environmental governance based in markets, exchange and offsets' (Godden 2012: 264; Korten 2015: 25) and restricted by a narrative about 'management of natural resources', 'carbon trading', 'distribution of environmental costs and benefits', and 'negotiation of environmental limits'. Such structures and approaches raised 'serious concern about legitimacy and accountability, prompting patterns of responses to those concerns in many areas of global governance' (Godden 2012: 264–65; Grear 2013: 969–70). How we envision the environment affects how we envision the environmental problems and their solutions (Bohannon 2014: 4–6). Considering that 'discourses are embedded in language', 'an environmental discourse is a 'social construct' reflecting how people interpret, give meaning to and represent the environment' (Dryzek 1997: 7).

Law is a vital component of environmental governance, since it 'acts as a key locus for the generation and affirmation of discursive knowledge about the environment. In turn, though, this knowledge frames the assessment of the efficacy of various types of legal responses' (Godden 2018: 267–71). As the place of intersection of various fields of knowledge and practice, the legal field displays the same fragmenting and objectifying pattern that has proven inadequate to address current challenges (Grant et al. 2013: 957, 963; Grear 2013: 971; ILC 2006). With the change in vision transforming different fields of knowledge, 'a new imagination is required' (Thomas-Pellicer et al. 2016: 2): 'we need a Copernician

---

[6] The lead of the UN Convention on Biological Diversity, Elizabeth Maruma Mrema, the World Health Organization Director for Environment and Health, Maria Neira, and the Head of the WWF International, Marco Lambertini, 'Pandemics result from destruction of nature', say UN and WHO, Damian Carrington, environment editor 17 June 2020. According to scientists on emerging infectious diseases, diseases like SARS or Ebola, as wells the spread of older diseases such as malaria, are linked to the deforestation and destruction of ecosystems, to the manipulation and traffic of fauna and flora and to climate change.

shift in law and governance' (Regenstein 1991: 168; Biermann et al. 2012; Kotzé and Kim 2018: 3–4). Conceptual narratives have an impact on law and policymaking (Meadowcroft and Fiorino 2017), and paradigm shifts go through a transition phase during which the understanding of old concepts are modified and new concepts emerge (Miller 1996: 258). If the term 'environment' has become a concept in policymaking and law during the last century (Meadowcroft 2017: 62), it expresses the awareness of a problematic relationship of humankind with its world at different scales – with its vision of reality.

The polysemic term 'nature' has also been used as a more general notion in policymaking, gathering different conceptions which evolved throughout time, as well as understandings in different languages (Milton 1998: 88). It designates notably the notion of what is or what appears to be a general property of being, the process of growth, the result of that process, the whole of what is apart from humankind, a living being, and several representations of nature, some of which are constitutive of the seven of the International Union for the Conservation of Nature (IUCN) categories (6 + 1b) (Ducarme and Couvet 2020). With the awareness of such a diversity, 'there may be a need to engage these different conceptions and representations in a kind of dialogue' (Ducarme and Couvet 2020). As environmental problems occur across borders at the local and global levels, 'decisions are made based on shared understandings of the problems or solutions, or motivated by dominant perceptions or interpretations of the law and the environment' (Jessup and Rubenstein 2018: 4). For this reason, the importance of defining problems and goals in a collaborative manner, with the largest participation, was stressed in the Millennium Ecosystem Assessment and in different national and international fora (UN Millennium Declaration 2000; Millennium Ecosystem Assessment 2004; UN World Summit 2005). It means addressing the questions of representation and participation of marginalised peoples, notably from the fourth world (Sousa Santos and Rodriguez-Garavito 2005: 22), but also nurturing an effective and open dialogue valuing different perspectives, modes of knowledge and approaches (Sousa Santos 2014: 238). 'It is the active co-participation of situated speakers in creating contexts of relevancy, constraint and possibility for each other's immediately subsequent actions which provides the emergent structure upon which social understanding and (later) language ultimately rests' (Favareau 2017: 13). In the policy–legal arena, 'a shared way of apprehending the world ... enables those who subscribe to it to interpret bits of information and put them together in coherent stories of accounts' (Dryzek 1997: 8).

At the international level, as stories and representations are inscribed in languages, the challenge is communicating between different cultures, languages, legal systems and traditions in the speciality language of law and policy (Lamalle

2020a: 91; Gounelle 2005; Carty 1991: 67; Gessner 1994). Comparative law proposes several classifications of legal systems on the basis of various criteria, such as language, structure of legal thought or cultural traditions (Sousa Santos 2004: 302f.). For instance, among classifications considering legal thought or language, various systems are suggested such as the French, Germanic, Scandinavian, English, Russian, Chinese, Islamic and Hindu systems. Such classifications leave other legal traditions unexplored, such as the ones in the fourth world comprising Indigenous laws and traditions in Africa, the Americas and Australia (Glenn 2004: 61). Yet there is a conceptual language in international law, which operates with certain representations. The critique drew special attention to that conceptual language (Carty 2007), which was formed in European jurisprudence since the seventeenth century (Koskenniemi 2001: 9; Nijman 2004), and which is rooted in the *jus commune* inherited from Roman law (Mattila 2012: 220, 224, 246). Not only was such conceptual language spread out by colonisation, notably in English, French, Dutch and Spanish (Mattila 2012: 331, 386, 432), but it was also used to shape international institutions (Koskenniemi 2001). The limits and impacts of such a conceptual and methodological frame on the apprehension of the international reality were denounced, notably with regard to the environment (Pahuja 2011; Sousa Santos 2014: 124, 237; Ramlogan 2002). 'If legal theory is to engage seriously with globalisation and its consequences a critical re-examination of its agenda, its heritage of ideas, and its conceptual tools is called for' (Menski 2005:16, 46), so that the international language can effectively become an 'instrument of the legal dynamic' (Gounelle 2005: 114).

In the same way that the discourse can be framed in terms of a narrative structure with certain representations and concepts (Dews 2007: 292, 296; Nash 1994; Rouland 1991: 182), or in terms of a certain mode of knowledge and approach (Sofoulis 2018: 821), there are also linguistic and jurilinguistic frames according to legal traditions and systems (Mattila 2006; Legrand 1996: 60; Gémar 1995). Such frames constitute a certain perspective which determines the understanding and apprehension of the world (Wittgenstein 1953 [1969]: 214; Geertz 1973; Spivak 2012). The perspectives and frames which condition a way of apprehending the world are especially determinant in international legal language. The use of a lingua franca, a vehicular language in debates and negotiations in international fora and organisations, comes with a certain perspective inherent to the language and legal tradition, such as the use of English[7] and the perspective of the common law tradition (Mattila 2012: 446). It comes as well with the challenge of legal translation in other languages, cultures and legal systems (Wagner et al. 2014; Scott 2017; Gotti and Williams 2010;

---

[7] About 85 per cent of international organisations use English as a formal language of negotiation (Mattila 2012).

Mattila 2006; Steiner 1998). Being unaware of such a jurilinguistic perspective can become a limitation and prevent other perspectives, concepts and approaches from being expressed, understood or taken into account (Mattila 2012: 454). For instance, as linguistic structures in a specific language have an influence on thinking in that language, 'grammar is [not] just the way we chart relationships in language', 'it also reflects our relationships with each other': 'Saying 'it' makes a living land into 'natural resource' (Kimmerer 2020: 57–58). The revitalisation of Indigenous languages such as *Anishinaabemowin* and *Kanyen'kéha* (Anishinabe and Mohawk) led to the rediscovery of a 'grammar of animacy' relating all forms – from humans, animals, trees and rocks to rivers – and highlighting other ways of apprehending and living in the world (Kimmerer 2020: 58; Milton 1998: 89). Linguists have also remarked that 'the West's Indo-European languages favour nominalization, an emphasis on the naming of things (nouns) rather than on process-oriented ways to express aspects of subtle, dynamic relationships' present in other languages favouring verbs or relations (Spretnak 2011: 55). In addition to that linguistic level, as a legal language describes a specific world, which uses its own concepts, narratives and methods, its translation into another language and legal system can be perplexing and illustrate the limits of such an exercise (Lamalle 2014; Howard 2018). For instance, in the study of concepts in different cultures, 'looking for concepts of nature is not simply a matter of looking for words which can be translated as nature'. Concepts may not 'carry a label', be 'terminologically covert and expressed through actions rather than words' (Milton 1998: 90).

Considering these different frames, the emergence of a global legal science calls for a 'consciousness of diversity', and a 'pluralistic vision of legal theory' (Menski 2005: 7), which includes co-constitutive approaches (Chual and Engel 2019). It implies taking into account critical approaches and opening the debate to other fields of knowledge (Broekman and Cata Backer 2013: 127; Goodrich 1986: 21). Such 'a space of conceptual negotiation can be seen as a new ontology that emerges in the context of cosmopolitical connections' (Arregii in Bold 2019: 183–84). Shedding another light on the current predicament, this opening of the international language of law and policy participates in the paradigmatic change towards a 'new common sense' (Sousa Santos 2004: 60, 121) – a change which can light up a new legal consciousness and give form to the multifold vision.

1.4 Joining Forces: Nurturing a Common Space

'We are not defending nature. We are nature.' This slogan, exhibited as an advertisement on the front of a bus stop in Paris in 2015, was part of a semiotic campaign on the meaning of our world-defining concepts during the negotiations at the UN Climate conference COP21.[8] In the last decades, contexts of negotiation at the international level were confronted to include and recognise other definitions, understanding and experiences of 'the environment', notably with alternative conferences such as the International Forum on Globalisation (IFG) (Korten 2015: 13)[9] and the International Indigenous Peoples Forum on Climate change (IIPFCC)[10] (Morgan 2011) – drawing attention to different actors and perspectives. These alternative fora became a systematic practice in parallel with intergovernmental conferences, gathering critical and marginalised voices. Such an evolution made clear there was a discrepancy in representations and a need for an effective space of encounter and dialogue. This focus on the meaning-making contexts also made salient the shift in approach in terms of process which is accompanying the change in vision (Capra 2010: 330), fostering new epistemological frameworks in law and policymaking (Bartel, in Philippopoulos-Mihalopoulos and Brooks 2017: 164; Slaughter and Ratner 1999: 294; Raustiala 2000: 403; Biermann 2014: 15). The scope is adjusted, with normative considerations, on: what characterises the process, who participates in the process and what is its outcome. The development of collaborative governance, practice theory, co-production and action research (Nicolini 2012; Innes and Booher 2010; Bartels and Wittmayer 2014) gave way to the relational policy analysis of a world of becoming, in which knowledge as encounter 'aims at shared understanding and joint transformation' (Wagenaar 2011). As we co-create meaning-making contexts, we can therefore open an inclusive and ethical space (Ermine 2007), where different perspectives can join forces to shape a common understanding of our world in law and policy.

In this light, the Working Group on Representations and Rights of the Environment (ESGRREW) was created in 2015–16 in order to gather different voices and open an effective intercultural dialogue with a wider approach in law and governance (Murtagh, in Bold 2019: 116; Eberhard 2008; Le Roy 2004; Biermann 2014: 43), encompassing different fields of knowledge, legal systems and traditions (Beier 2009: 5; Eberhard and Vernicos 2006; Menski 2006). The ESGRREW was inaugurated in the framework of a global research alliance, the Earth System Governance Project (ESG), which seeks to widen the scope and approach of governance, and 'to break down disciplinary boundaries', with a focus on advancing 'a more holistic understanding of planetary earth', based on the

---

[8] The 21st Conference of the Parties to the 1992 United Nations Framework Convention on Climate Change.
[9] Notably, the Seattle World Trade Organization Protest in 1999 raised awareness on the role and impact of corporate actors (Korten 2015).
[10] It includes statements such as: the Lyon Declaration of the First International Forum of Indigenous Peoples and Local Communities on Climate Change (2000); Hague Declaration of the Second International Forum on Indigenous Peoples and Local Communities on Climate Change (2000); Anchorage Declaration of the Indigenous Peoples' Global Summit on Climate change (2009).

principles of inclusiveness, differentiation and solidarity (Biermann 2014: 15–24, 27, 43). With a renewed understanding of the process of law and policymaking in relation to biological, social and ecological processes, the ESG approach differs 'from concepts of government, and from the notion of management', advancing the perspective of 'a global stewardship of the planet based on cooperation, coordination, and consensus building among actors at all levels' (Biermann 2014: 20). The ESGRREW came out of the ESG Taskforce on Conceptual Foundations, reflecting a critical concern with 'how ideas are inter-linked with real social forces and interests' (Meadowcroft, Gupta and Stevenson 2014). It explores 'key ideas and concepts that are coming to frame international discussion of the challenge of governance', with a view to 'understanding, refining and critically interrogating' the 'thought categories we use to make sense of the world' and which 'provide the foundation for contemporary theory and practice in the environmental domain' (Meadowcroft, Gupta and Stevenson 2014). The ESGRREW examines conceptual frameworks which apprehend reality in law and legal systems, and their synchronic and diachronic evolution. The 'conceptual reimagining is part of the process of political and policy change, and the character of that reimagining influences how debates and actions play out … what they tell us about the past and what they portend for the future' (Meadowcroft and Fiorino 2017: 356). In that regard, the focus of ESGRREW is on the articulation of different representations and systems of representation of the environment and their formulation in law and governance – in legal language, institutional organisation and social practice.

This book is the expression of a collective endeavour: the critical reflexion conducted in the framework of the ESGRREW Process of Dialogue & Research. This international process was launched on 12–13 April 2017 in Montreal, in partnership with Future Earth[11] and under the patronage of UNESCO and the Canadian Commission of UNESCO. This process intends to contribute to the dynamics of 'new ethical thinking' as identified by the World Commission on the Ethics of Scientific Knowledge and Technology (COMEST report 2015) in bridging and reducing knowledge divides, ensuring public participation, asserting at all relevant levels the value of local, Indigenous and traditional knowledge, and strengthening ethical and institutional frameworks. For its Process of Dialogue & Research, the ESGRREW endorsed the principles and values of the Diversity and Inter-cultural Dialogue established by the 2001 UNESCO Declaration, 2005 Convention on the Diversity of Cultural Expression, 2012 UN Resolution 67/104, UNESCO Action Plan 194 EX/10 and 2016 Roadmap for 2013–22. It also adopted 'Reconciliation as principle', as defined in the Final Reports of the Canadian Truth

---

[11] Future Earth mobilises scientists to respond to global environmental change and supports transformation towards global sustainability, strengthening partnerships with policymakers and other stakeholders.

and Reconciliation Commission (2015) in all dimensions of society, in particular in law and governance, and based on the respect of the UN Declaration on the Rights of Indigenous Peoples (UNDRIP). Reconciliation is understood as the 'healing of relationships', notably creating 'a more equitable and inclusive society by closing the gaps in social, health, and economic outcomes that exist' with Indigenous peoples.

As such, reconciliation requires removing 'barriers to understanding' such as racism, systemic discrimination and prejudices. It means approaching the other without objectification in constituted forms or in a fixed alterity (Milton 1998: 98). Such barriers exist in science. Their removal recently allowed the realisation that millenary Medicine wheels – structures of stones made by Indigenous peoples[12] – were complex systems of representation and astronomical observatories (Trinh 2019: 81–85). Contrary to the eroding scientific paradigm of a fragmented reality, such traditional systems of representation are integrated forms of knowledge connecting botanical, social, political, spiritual and astronomical knowledges (Trinh 2019: 428–29). Enlightening the principles of interdependence and responsibility, Indigenous Medicine wheels are dynamic conceptual frameworks for all aspects of life and knowledge: they can represent various aspects of reality at different scales (Thumbadoo 2005: 23). As the work of the Canadian Truth and Reconciliation Commission established, effective dialogue necessitates removing barriers to understanding, such as negative representations and stereotypes, not only between fields of knowledge, languages, legal traditions and institutions, but also between peoples, social groups and individuals (TRC Report 2015). They concern notably reductive representations in the media 'narrowly framing questions about environmental activism', instead of promoting the duty to consult and effective participation in decision-making (Mahoney 2017). The ESGRREW Process of Dialogue & Research has cultivated an inclusive space of interaction encouraging intercultural and interdisciplinary dialogue – with critical, conceptual and pragmatic objectives. As formulated in traditional knowledge, it signifies 'integrating the messages and strengths of all directions into the circle of life' (Thumbadoo 2005: 105). In that optic, the research unfolds the scope of law and governance with various fields of knowledge and practice, inside and outside academia.

Humanities, and environmental humanities in particular, play an important role in that respect, contributing to 'a new configuration of knowledge' (Nye et al. 2013). Such a role involves 'acknowledging the differences and diffractions in worldviews, histories, subjectivities, relations and practices that various

---

[12] Such medicine wheels structures in stones can be found in Big Horn, Wyoming, in South Dakota, Montana, Saskatchewan, Alberta, and in the valleys of Ohio and Mississippi. Such structures were denied as forms of knowledge, but are now recognised by scientists (Trinh 2019: 85).

communities (both human and non-human) engage in, with respect to their environment' (Neimanis et al. 2015: 71). The research in that direction generated a new integral dimension of humanities with specific fields of inquiry overlapping with social and natural sciences (Neimanis et al. 2015: 71; Wheeler, in Favareau et al. 2017: 27–28). They can be approached as 'sociocultural imaginations' (Neimanis et al. 2015: 81), or 'sense-making fields wherein humans cultivate and negotiate relations with the world, both emotionally and rationally, while also creating identities for themselves' (Appadurai 1996: 5). Their understanding has an important influence on 'the conceptual development of environmental or ecological imaginaries' and on how we deal with the crisis of perception (Neimanis et al. 2015: 81). In that light, the Outcome Document of the World Humanities Conference 'A New Humanities Agenda for the 21st Century' (UNESCO-CIPSH 2017) affirms 'the essential role of the humanities in fostering epistemological decolonisation', in 'rethinking the meaning of humanism in the face of ongoing crises', and in 'promoting pluralism with due regard for Indigenous and traditional knowledge'.

Reminiscing the old humanist tradition of 'non separated knowledge' both the *trivium* and *quadrivium*[13] were taught 'to climb back up to Unity' in a community where all were equal (Critchlow, in Martineau 2010: 3–5). At the end of the Middle Ages, the *studia humanitatis* designated the study of what 'characterises human beings': grammar, rhetoric, history, moral philosophy and poetry. Today, environmental humanities can help us reconnect knowledges and reconcile different dimensions and relationships of our being human – in relation to oneself, other humans, living beings, the earth and elements, to past, present and future. Rallying with Hermes, we can trace back the old tradition of studying the signification of languages and discourses, through theology, legal interpretation and philological approaches to language. Such a tradition sheds light on the continuity between these approaches in human and social sciences, in making sense of the world and elaborating common knowledge, including in the lived experience and its spiritual expressions – reconstituting an intersubjective symbolic reality, and as a reminder that there are discursive and non-discursive symbolic forms. Bringing to light the ontological question, such approaches recall the living experience of humans in meaning-making communities like religions and spiritualities in a large sense (Meslin 1988: 27; Bohannon 2014: 2; Gira 2001: 33). As such, theology has been a source of conceptualisations for law and society, notably with canon law, scholastic discussions and elaboration of legal and political theory (Gaudemet 2005: 298–300; Kantorowicz 1989; Burns 1988). The

---

[13] The *trivium* (grammar, logic and rhetoric) and the *quadrivium* (arithmetic, geometry, music and astronomy) of Pythagoras were structured on the cardinal objectives of truth, beauty and goodness.

role of humanities in the legal field was constitutive of its expansion and evolution, in particular in the movement of vertical translation of concepts between theology, philosophy and philology (Lamalle 2014). Such a role was decisive in the process of elaboration of a legal science and legal language with the medieval glossators and post-glossators who inquired into pragmatic elements of Roman law (Mausen 2003: 1394), in its systematisation with Budé and Leibniz during the Renaissance, as it is determinant now with the contemporary critique and reassessment of legal conceptual frameworks, scope and language, notably with the evolution of international law and institutions, globalisation, decolonisation, new technologies and the ecological crisis (Pahuja 2011; Bankowski and Scott 2000; Fleerackers and Broekman 2020; Benyekhlef et al. 2015; Daniel et al. 2015; Philippopoulos-Mihalopoulos and Brooks 2017). Humanities call attention to the ontological, epistemological, cultural and theoretical components of legal and political discourses, frameworks and institutions. As such, they are 'necessary extensions of humans' cognitive bearing as a species', in order 'to understand the limits of human agency and its continuity with the agency' of other beings and processes of the planet (Cobley, in Favareau et al. 2017: 14). They also contribute to 'a global and detotalizing perspective on life and interpersonal relations' (Petrilli 2014: 330).

The legal field is therefore at the junction of an important process of transformation of collective representations, as well as institutional, social and individual practices. There is notably a broadening of participation to different actors, and an increasing concern for responsibility, such as the responsibility of states (Crawford ILC 2001), international organisations (Gaja ILC 2005), companies (Global Pact) and non-state actors (Gal-Or et al. 2015). Most recent developments include the work on 'a legally binding instrument to regulate, in international human rights law, the activities of transnational corporations' (OEIGWG 2019). At the same time, as in other fields of knowledge, the subject–object dichotomy, fragmented and disembodied rationality, and core narrative concepts are put into question (Grear 2013: 971; Philippopoulos-Mihalopoulos 2017: 11, 14). It concerns notably the 'objectification of the natural world', and deficiency of the current conceptual framework to apprehend reality in the legal language, and allow effective participation and regulation in environmental law and governance (Ramlogan 2002; Philippopoulos-Mihalopoulos and Brooks 2017: xvi, 6–9). In that regard, it seems that 'neither human rights law nor environmental regulation and governance regimes have to date delivered the paradigm shift required' (Bosselmann 2011; Grear 2013: 969). To that end, there are calls to bring issues of environmental justice (Holder and McGillivray 2017) and green criminology (Stoett and Omrow 2021) to the centre of legal research, highlight the continuum between nature and culture (Nikolić 2017; Austin-Broos and Merlan 2017), and develop 'new, inclusive and interdisciplinary methodologies for reassessing the human–environment interface'. The responsibility of legal scholarship is, in that light, to re-envisage legal theory with new narratives, concepts and approaches, to develop 'practical strategies to guide policymaking' and a 'more holistic and socially embedded environmental education' (Philippo-poulos Mihalopoulos and Brooks 2017: xvi; Bergthaller 2012: 263). Guided by these different considerations and objectives in its Process of Dialogue & Research, the ESGRREW organised international working sessions, conferences, symposia and an immersive art exhibition, with participants from various cultures and fields of knowledge, encompassing art, history, philosophy, political science, international relations, sociology, law, traditional knowledge, theology, geography, economics, environmental sciences, engineering, anthropology, linguistics and semiotics. The flow of such an abounding experience cannot be condensed into a book. It instilled hope, hindsight and perspective into the reflection presented in this volume – an opening deliberation of relational intelligibility (McNamee and Gergen 1999).

1.5 Relational Intelligibility

The perspectives gathered in this volume take various shapes of account and narrative modes, including stories of individual and collective experience, manifested in essays, transcribed oral discussions with Indigenous Elders, and scientific argumentations and reasonings. These differences participate in our comprehension, in a relational intelligibility – 'to cleanse the doors of perception and regain serious contact with different dimensions being' such that 'human beings can cooperate with the imagination and awaken as new acuity arises' (Vernon 2020). Therefore, it is not just our sight which is mobilised in creating a context conducive to the joint goal of reaching a common sense, but the different dimensions of human experience. We expose here our deliberations: a first look at the present landscape with a view to identifying the challenges, a second look throughout time and dimensions to recollect what was left on the trail, and a third look on the horizon of possibilities.

1.5.1 Challenges

How we approach knowledge and 'make sense of the planetary system and the Anthropocene' is decisive in our common endeavour. Head of Research at UNESCO, John Crowley expounds on the responsibility of environmental humanities in the current context of institutional frameworks and international debates in his chapter. He sheds light on the twofold task of the environmental humanities: 'understanding of the human dimension of ecosystemic processes, which means the ways in which patterns of human beliefs (all the way from elaborate cosmologies to common sense embedded within practical culture) influence environmental outcomes mediated through human behaviour', and to 'shape the systems of meaning around action to respond to environmental challenges'. One important insight in that respect is that 'systems that involve human beings are systems of structures of action that are, at the same time, processes of distribution of meaning'. He observes that there is a recent scientific realisation of a unitary planetary system which implies 'the interconnections between physical, biological and social sciences', while Gaia was already narrated in ancient traditions. 'The humanities help to bridge the spheres of understanding and action through the medium of language broadly understood'. This puts the 'scientistic' paradigm under another light: 'the "safe operating space" cannot be adequately understood in purely scientific and technological terms', nor thought as standing 'outside politics' (see Chapter 2). Rather, it involves different participants, fields and types of knowledge. Ethics and dialogue thus 'require a new kind of politics, incorporating new modes of representation – something that goes beyond the authoritative allocation of resources or problem-solving'. It notably means 'rooting politics in conscious-ness' and reshaping 'political communities as expanded discursive and narrative space(s)' (Chapter 2).

An important challenge in that respect is 'Decolonising the Anthropocene Conceived as a Universalising Project': 'the extension and enactment of colonial logic which systematically erases difference'. Canada Research Chair in Indigenous Environmental Justice Deborah McGregor and researcher Mahisha Sritharan draw attention to 'the violence at its core (among peoples, with other living beings and Mother Earth), and call[s] for the consideration of Indigenous philosophies and processes of Indigenous self-governance as a necessary political corrective', taking into account 'Indigenous knowledge systems and legal traditions' in climate change research. In that perspective, the UNDRIP 'should form an integral part of any climate change policy or public discourse on the matter', be it internationally or nationally. In any case, 'climate change policies and programmes should recognise and address ongoing colonialism that continues to alienate Indigenous peoples', and 'engage with Indigenous legal and intellectual traditions to derive environmental and climate change policy and approaches'. In the Anishinabek tradition, 'knowledge-seeking or acquisition must consider the ancestors and future generations'. It involves 'the conception of humanity's relationships with 'other orders of beings' and 'laws, protocols and practices over time to ensure that relationships remain in balance including rocks, trees and water, and that life would continue'. 'It challenges the human-focused nature of current legal systems and promotes laws that protect nature in its own right'; challenging 'the dominant neoliberal paradigm that regards nature as property and a resource'. 'Indigenous peoples have their own climate change stories, and embedded within them are solutions' (Chapter 3).

Opening the channels of perception, artist Marten Berkman explores 'our relationship with the land'. Our experience of the world mediated by the artist is 'a door opened in ourselves to our presence in the land'. He questions the way we perceive the world 'from the vantage point of our manufactured spaces': 'what is our contemporary conduit for sensitive relationship with the earth?' He observes that 'urban and industrial culture functionally separates the land from our consciousness'. If the way we see the world informs the way we treat the world, 'perception is the key to a maturing relationship with it'. As a photographer and film-maker, he awakens our sensibility to a sense of presence in the land – to 'the ecology of our perception'. 'This implies the necessity to expand our focus from quantitative deduction of the problem and solutions, to ensuring we have the inner connections and relationships necessary for qualitative response to environmental stress.' Is there 'a contemporary visual palette which will ignite our consciousness to immaterial experiences, even ancestral memories?'. Approaching 'technology as ecology', he uses a 'technological means to capture the very presence of the land three-dimensionally', for 'stereoscopic vision', and dissolves the separation between subject and object, by allowing the viewer to participate in landscapes as reflected shadows on the land. He reminds us that 'Beauty and wonder are essential experiences in human–more-than-human relationships', and 'different art forms [can] speak eloquently for the ineffable'. He calls out to 'imagine the creative force unleashed when our industrious nature is in concert with all of nature, when systems analysis encompasses the largest system, when decisions are based on head, hands and heart'. If how we see the world is often defined by the world we have created and the technology we use, then 'art can be part of that essential bridge' (see Chapter 4).

Engaging with Indigenous legal traditions raises the challenges of widening the scope of legal communication and reconciling law with the different dimensions of being. In her chapter, volume co-editor Sandy Lamalle invites us to 'contemplate the legal field beyond the barriers and borders of modern constituted forms'. In order to address the fragmentation and hiatus in the legal narrative, she contemplates the evolution of legal practice at the national and international levels, and the implications of taking into account the different relationships highlighted in Indigenous law, 'catalysing both the ontological questioning and its response', notably raised by critiques on legal categories and core concepts. Focusing attention on the insights of linguistics, literature, translation and pragmatic semiotics as applied to law, she emphasises that approaching different legal traditions requires 'a change of perspective and attitude on the legal forms and modes of expression'. In the case of Indigenous legal traditions, such a change in perspective 'extends the realm of legal communication to different modes of presence to the world'. In that sense, reconnecting legal traditions contributes to reminiscing and reconstituting the legal experience in its integrity. As a response to the 'challenge of a common legal sense', she contends that the semiotic approach enables to visualise the legal landscape on a wider horizon of legal communication. 'It allows us to study the narrative semiotics of different legal traditions, such as the dances, storytelling, artefacts like Wampum belts and protocols for ceremonies in Indigenous law.' Such approaches bring to light 'the existence of different forms of legal conscience'. Beyond the operation of translation, therefore, what is at stake in the evolution of the legal language and practice is the constitution of 'a common semiotic space' (see Chapter 5).

1.5.2 Recollection

Reminiscing the different relationships and dimensions of being, Traditional Indigenous Knowledge describes 'spiritual consciousness as the highest form of politics'.[14] In the spirit of reconciliation, Knowledge Keepers from the Anishinabe and Mohawk traditions share their insights in Chapter 6. According to Kokom Marie-Josée Tardif, 'our relationship with Mother Earth is a sacred relationship with a being'. 'The status of women in society and the way they are treated are directly related to the way the relationship with the 'environment' is defined.' 'The unbalance we experience today worldwide is linked to the "climate change within ourselves"', and 'we need to reconcile ourselves with the feminine qualities of our being on a spiritual level'. 'The mind has to be reconciled with the heart and body, and the two poles masculine and feminine have to be in balance.' Hereditary Chief T8aminik Rankin, survivor of the residential schools, talks about 'healing our relationships and walking on the path of reconciliation with ourselves, with other beings and with Mother Earth'. 'We need to open our heart and see through it the life within us and around us, not just through the intellect.' This transformation also concerns 'the healing process from colonisation and oppression of Indigenous peoples, and all the oppressed'. Faithkeeper Kevin Ka'nahsohon Deer calls attention to 'the change in consciousness to see, to hear and to speak differently'. Expressing 'gratitude through sacred ceremonies, songs, dances, rituals, and speeches' is an essential part of living and law. 'In the Haudenosaunee tradition, we offer greetings and thanks, our gratitude', including all, 'from the Earth our Mother to the Stars'. He underlines that 'the law of the land is not human-made,

---

[14] Action of remembering or recollecting. Originating from medieval Latin *recollectio* and the verb *recolligere*, it denotes the action of 'gathering things together again'.

but a greater natural law, the Great Law of Peace', according to which 'in every decision we make, we must consider the impact on the seventh generation'. Kokom Marie-Josée Tardif evokes an important step in the recognition of Indigenous peoples' spirituality. 'At the 2019 Conference of Religions for Peace, we adopted a Final Declaration with a commitment to take care of the earth'. It notably states: 'Leaders and partners in the fight against environmental degradation, our Indigenous brothers and sisters remind us we are 'guardians and caretakers of earth'; 'Our different experiences of the sacred make clear that we are, at root, relational', and that 'our well-being is intrinsically shared' (see Chapter 6).

Recalling the Franciscan tradition in the Church,[15] which values affect and gratitude as a mode of knowledge, solidarity with the poor and with the whole of creation, Pope Francis[16] raises concern 'On care for our common home' in his Encyclical *Laudato Si*. His Excellency Monseigneur Jean-Pierre Delville, Bishop of Liège, resituates the encyclical in its historical and theological signification, in the framework of 'the social encyclicals of the popes', 'for the dialogue with the different cultures' and 'the progress of the whole humanity in the direction of justice and solidarity'. 'Pope Francis has accentuated this orientation' notably with a focus on 'the dialogue for peace and reconciliation'. Intended as a contribution to the COP 21, *Laudato si* questions the modern 'epistemological paradigm' and 'promotes solidarity with the poor as well as stewardship of the Earth, putting an emphasis on the spiritual, moral and social dimensions of the current environmental crisis'. Fostering an 'integral ecology', 'inseparable from the notion of the common good, a central and unifying principle of social ethics', the Pope states that 'the establishment of a legal framework which can set clear boundaries and ensure the protection of ecosystems has become indispensable'. He asserts 'the necessity of a global ecology', 'concerted political action' and 'international solidarity', considering the 'ecological debt' that exists, 'between the global north and south'. In that regard, Mgr Jean-Pierre Delville presents *The Amazon* (Rome 2019)[17] and *Querida Amazonia* (2020),[18] which give concrete application to *Laudato si*, and affirm 'the right of the original peoples to the land and its boundaries, and to self-determination and prior consent'. The Pope notes that 'the way in which Indigenous peoples relate to and protect their territories is an indispensable measure for our conversion to an integral

---

[15] The Franciscan tradition spans eight centuries, 'evoking a change in one's consciousness or awareness of others, and in one's relationship to others, not only to humans but to all of creation' (Delio 2003).

[16] His Holiness Pope Francis, Head of the Catholic Church and Sovereign of the Vatican City State, is the first Jesuit pope, the first from the Americas, the first from the Southern Hemisphere and from outside Europe since the eighth century. He chose his name in honour of Saint Francis of Assisi and *Laudato si* is the beginning of his *Canticle of the Creatures*, praising all creatures, especially Brother Sun.

[17] The Final Document of the Special Assembly of the Synod of Bishops for the Pan-Amazon Region.

[18] The Apostolic Exhortation of Pope Francis.

ecology'. With the recognition of Mother Earth, he asserts that 'the voice of women should therefore be heard, they should be consulted and participate in decision-making', and 'their leadership must be more fully assumed in the heart of the Church' (see Chapter 7).

Reminding us that the 'conceptual language' of modern legal systems and international law finds its roots in Roman law, legal history specialist Arnaud Paturet examines thoroughly the *jurisprudentia* and its evolution. He investigates the history of the 'current division in the legal landscape into persons, things and actions' (*persona, res, acta*) originating from Gaius and legal rhetoric. If today, such a division is merely reduced to a subject–object dichotomy, with the legal subject as the centre of categorisations and 'only raw material for building the legal order', objectifying the rest of the legal world, it was not so in Roman law. 'There was no clear separation between *res* and *persona*, subject and object.' 'The modern notion of 'thing' emerged from the theorisation of the subjective rights of a legal person, to have a full power on the 'thing' (*potestas*). Shedding light on the original meaning and use of *res*, Arnaud Paturet reflects on the Roman legal framework, which was 'human-centred' in civil law, as in modern legal systems: concerning the regulation of 'property, trade, patrimonial transmission, family organisation or, to a certain extent, order and security'. There were nevertheless *mores* (traditions, customs) and 'a Roman religion, on which depend[ed] the prosperity of the city, to promote good relationships between men and gods through rituals', noting that 'many deities represented natural elements'. Roman law formulated various concepts in that regard, such as *res communes omnium*, a 'regime of the air, the water of the sea and its shores'. Today, the difficulties with the legal categorisation is 'the apprehension of all natural elements and animals'. 'In a mature legal system', 'legal science is supposed to develop the conceptual tools necessary to apprehend reality'. It means addressing to that end the modern 'ontological duality of legal taxonomy', notably as applied to property (see Chapter 8).

Highlighting 'the continuous interaction between the way legal thought creates meaning in language and language creates realities in law', legal language expert Caroline Laske inquires into the semantic history of the legal language with regard to the definition of our relationship with the environment. 'Law is a specialised language.' Such language 'is at the heart of the normative nature of law and of its prescriptive and performative functions'. Using 'electronic corpus linguistics methodologies', she analyses 'how conceptual meanings have shifted throughout time' constituting 'the language of social and political thought'. She remarks that 'in an international or supranational context, legal concepts and terms can be used differently in different languages and studying the semantic content can provide deep-level understanding of such differences'. She describes her inquiries into the

British National Corpus (BNC), American English Corpora and ECOLEX (an information service on environmental law operated jointly by the Food and Agriculture Organization (FAO), the International Union for the Conservation of Nature (IUCN) and the United Nations Environment Programme (UNEP)). She notably observes that 'Environmental laws and regulations in the sense of protecting and preserving the environment rather than merely upholding landowners' rights against adverse interference with their land by others, is a relatively new phenomenon'. It was during the late 1990s that 'the concept of environment took on and consolidated the specific meaning relating to the effect of human activity'. Environmental law language and terminology expanded rapidly, with urgency, and 'from a whole panoply of underpinning philosophical, scientific, legal and socio-economic conceptual thinking'. Neglecting to address such underpinnings, 'skipping the stages of debate over fundamentals and incremental growth and acceptance', 'debates went directly to the important, but narrower, question about the merits of the suite of policy instruments available to achieve the … protection objectives'. Raising concern over content and legitimacy, such underpinnings need to be addressed 'for a maturing of environmental law' (see Chapter 9).

1.5.3 Perspectives

Venturing into new paths, Valérie Cabanes, legal activist at Earth Law Alliance, takes us on a journey to different initiatives toward the establishment of an effective legal framework for the protection of nature. In particular, the movement for the Rights of Nature intends to 'rethink the law beyond humanity alone', and to 'recognise the inalienable rights of living systems and species and their specific rights'. Such rights 'must be distinguished from individual liberties' which 'are accompanied by duties and linked to the capacity of free will'. They must be 'recognised in national constitutions and courts of law as intangible rights'. Such an approach emerged from the observation that current environmental laws are ineffective, notably as 'nature is considered to be property in almost every country's legal system', which 'gives its owner the right to damage or destroy it'. Examining legal practice, she looks into cases that deliberate the recognition of specific rights of rivers, animals and mountains. She also delves into the intergovernmental negotiations which were initiated at the United Nations on the principle of Harmony with Nature since 2009. In the optic of an 'Earth-centred worldview', with a 'respect and reverence for the Earth and its natural cycles', she also reports initiatives to recognise 'Nature as a subject of law'. As such, 'Nature can be represented and defended in court by any individual, community, people or nation and has an inalienable right to restoration'. She advocates a further initiative, regarding responsibility enforcement, with the movement for the recognition of 'ecocide as an international crime', a new legal category characterised as a 'severe damage to any part or system of the global commons, or to Earth's ecological system'. (See Chapter 10)

Addressing the issue of property with respect to current environmental challenges, law professor Yaël Emerich envisions how property law could be rethought in common law and civil law systems. In such systems, for instance, 'legislation regarding air or water pollution primarily aims to protect human health and economic growth'. In reaction to such 'anthropocentrism', 'environmental ethics, such as biocentrism and ecocentrism, have been adopted by some jurists, mainly from the common law tradition'. 'Biocentrism holds that every living entity on Earth has intrinsic value' and 'Ecocentrism' recognises 'that Nature as a whole has intrinsic value'. A paradigm shift is necessary to transform 'Property law concepts, particularly ownership', 'to account for human beings and their relationship with Nature'. 'Exploring the theory that Nature should be granted personhood and subjective rights', Yaël Emerich proposes another approach 'in which Nature would be the subject of legally protected interests'. She notes that 'the possibility of recognising a new subject of law, distinct from physical and legal persons, has already been proposed in Quebec civil law in relation to trusts'. Re-examining the subject–object dichotomy, she reconceptualises 'ownership and its narrative', in a perspective which is 'relational, socially limited, and functional': 'a reconciliation of the private and collective property regimes'. She also demonstrates 'how property law, and more specifically concepts ... such as common patrimony and patrimony by appropriation, can be used to better protect nature as part of a commitment to sustainable development'. Taking into account 'our membership within an Earth community that is broader than the human community', 'there are a variety of ways to adapt property law to environmental challenges' – 'different concepts and values may be necessary, including the categorisation of certain resources as non- appropriable through the notion of common things and a more dynamic management of resources using a trust patrimony by appropriation' (see Chapter 11).

Taking on both challenges of *inventio* and performative action, legal activists Nicole Rogers, Greta Bird, Jo Bird and Michelle Maloney (National Convenor at the Australian Earth Laws Alliance), stand up to reimagine and re-enact the common law. 'Performance and performative writing can play a key role in opening up an extralegal space for new representations of non-human species and Earth itself.' The first initiative they launched is the Wild Law Judgment Project, 'a collaborative, cross-institutional endeavour' to rewrite judgments in the perspective of Wild Law. Envisaging Wild Law as a place of resistance to prioritise 'the well-being of all lifeforms on Earth over short-term economic benefits', they question whether 'legal scholars, as both insiders and outsiders, [can] *perform* law differently to achieve wild Earth-centred outcomes'. In their reflection, they take heed of the perspective of Aboriginal law, highlighting that 'First Nations peoples define and perform law quite differently', 'in song and ceremony, in living to care for Mother Earth', action embedded in the definition that 'law is what cares for country'. In that sense, '[T]he strengthening of an Earth jurisprudence and the chance to protect the planet may follow from recognition of First Nations laws'. The second initiative is 'the Rights of Nature tribunals [which] constitute an unconventional performative forum for recognition of non-mainstream representations of Earth and its communities'. They are 'comprised of lawyers and ethical leaders from Indigenous and non-Indigenous communities around the world', 'focusing on wild law, including Rights of Nature and ecocide'. They have 'raised awareness of the need for a reform of international law, to provide people, who have fallen victim to the practices of multinational corporations, with unfettered access to justice'. Contributing to a paradigm shift, 'they can empower lawyers, citizens and activists with new concepts, a new vocabulary, and a transformative vision for our legal and governance systems'. (See Chapter 12.)

From the perspective of environmental justice and democracy, philosopher Matthias Fritsch applies a pragmatic and innovative approach to the question of the representations and rights of future people with respect to the environment. He draws attention to the realisation that 'globalising capitalism inherently favours the present, at the expense of past and future generations', contrary to long-term policies required for climate change and environmental sustainability. He contends that '[D]emocracies must be able to sustain their sovereignty over time, but they must also understand sovereign power as globally and intergenerationally shared'. 'Taking turns among rulers and the ruled is a normative idea inherent to the concept of democracy.' He observes that '[P]resentism is often related to the short-term thinking said to be brought on by democracy's relation to free market competition', and 'to the dependence of national governments on global markets and the economic movement of capital'. 'Thus, taking democratic turns with generations above all calls for stemming the economic interference in an ecological embedding of democratic institutions.' Matthias Fritsch moves on to identify and list 'new proposals regarding how to reform existing democratic institutions' throughout the world. Placing 'democracy in historical time', 'taking turns should be thought of, less as a form of government, and more as a dimension of political experience and institutionalisation'. As such, '[c]onversations and dialogue in general ... calls for the institutionalisation of granting all a turn at being heard'. And, in any case, 'future generations are already what we might call 'spectrally' present in the here and now'. Such 'co-presence of past and future generations is often defended by various Indigenous views, for instance, the well-known Great

Law of Peace (Gayanashagowa) of the Iroquois (Haudenosaunee) Confederacy and its reference to the principle of seven generations'. 'Part of the solution to democracy's short-termism, then, lies not just in addressing intergenerational fairness, but intra-generational equality' (see Chapter 13).

Considering the impact of market economy and actors, and fostering a responsible approach for our economic activities, philosopher Vincent Blok addresses the normative and social dimensions of a circular, bio-based economy (CBE). Such an economy is defined as 'an industrial system that is restorative or regenerative by intention and design. It replaces the 'end-of-life' concept with restoration, shifts towards the use of renewable energy, eliminates the use of toxic chemicals, which impair reuse, and aims for the elimination of waste through the superior design of materials, products, systems, and, within this, business models.' In that perspective, 'the transition to the CBE is a complex process of co-evolution of economic, technological and institutional developments at multiple levels and at a long-time scale'. However, 'current practices in the CBE are framed by the market logic', focusing 'on profits, efficiency and operational effectivity', while with 'a social logic', 'actors [would] focus on the public good and benefits for society'. He affirms therefore that we need to take into account the normative and social dimensions to the transition to the CBE. 'In first instance, we have to acknowledge that sustainable development, which is the main aim of the CBE, is a normative concept.' In that sense, 'the transition to the CBE requires fundamental reflection on the role of economic actors in the social and ecological environment with significant consequences for their business practices'. Realising 'that the economy is a subsystem of the larger biosphere of planet Earth', 'the human economy must fit well with the processes and relationships of the Earth's economy'. In that respect, 'the biosphere of planet Earth must operate as a normative standard' for our shared well-being. To that end, the concept of 'responsible innovation' can help to articulate the normative and social dimensions of the transition towards a new economy. (See Chapter 14.)

In the final chapter of this volume, exploring the implementation of Indigenous law concepts and principles in policymaking, Dutch diplomat and researcher Dorine van Norren appraises the best practices and limits to the articulation between ancient and modern legal traditions. In contrast with the normative objectification of the environment, which is 'no longer treated as living or as a sacred force', '[g]uardianship of nature is revered in many Indigenous traditions as a self-evident fact'. She looks into 'three traditions of the Global South: from Asian Buddhism in Gross National Happiness (GNH), to African *Ubuntu* (collective) thought and Latin American *Buen Vivir* (Good Living) derived from Native American traditions'. She presents her field research and reflections on such approaches and principles, and looks specifically at how they shape law and policies in South Africa, Bhutan and Ecuador, as 'all three countries actively promote their alternative Indigenous view on international relations and development'. *Buen Vivir* and *Ubuntu* are Indigenous concepts of social justice and interdependence with nature. Core principles of the 'notion of Gross National Happiness' are 'respect for nature, compassion, and balance "between spiritual and material aspects of life"; moderation and interdependence of all things'. She explains that if the application of the *Ubuntu* principle is through legal interpretation and jurisprudence in South Africa, GNH policy in Bhutan consists in 'sustainable and equitable socio-economic development' and '(strong) biodiversity conservation'. Ecuador and Bolivia adopted rights to nature in constitutional and legislative measures, in order to promote the Indigenous view of life in their modern legal system and language resulting from colonisation. It is rather 'an attitude (a mental, practical and interrelational approach) that is promoted'. It means the 'Rights of nature are closely intertwined with collective rights and with the principle of free prior informed consent (FPIC)' – that is with the implementation of the UNDRIP. (See Chapter 15) If such conceptualisations are intermediary steps towards a new consciousness, they can inspire us to embrace the guardianship of nature.

In this experience of relational intelligibility, as makers of meaning, shapes and relations, we have realised with the Poet, that a new vision of ecology is 'not one of managed exploitation (Ulro), nor managed consumption (Generation), or even managed cooperation (Beulah), but instead one aimed at radically extending awareness of the ecologies of which we are a part' (Vernon 2020). It is our hope that this volume will help readers forge this new critical and light-bearing awareness, and inspire them to encourage others along that path.

References

Alliot, M. (1983). Anthropologie et juristique: Sur les conditions de l'élaboration d'une science du droit. *Bulletin de liaison du Laboratoire d'anthropologie juridique de Paris* 6: 83–117.

Andler, D., A. Fagot-Largeault and B. Saint-Sernin (2002). *Philosophie des sciences*. Paris: Gallimard Folio.

Appadurai, Arjun (1996). *Modernity at Large: The Cultural Dimensions of Globalization*. Minneapolis: University of Minnesota Press.

Austin-Broos, D. and F. Merlan (eds.) (2017). *People and Change in Indigenous Australia*. Honolulu: Hawaii University Press.

Bachelard, G. (1938). *La formation de l'esprit scientifique*. Paris: Vrin.

Bankowski, Z. and A. Scott (2000). *The European Union and Its Order: The Legal Theory of European Integration*. Oxford: Blackwell.

Bartels, K. P. R. and J. M. Wittmayer (2014). Symposium introduction: Usable knowledge in practice. What action research has to offer to critical policy studies. *Critical Policy Studies* 8(4): 397–406.

Battiste, M. (2000). *Reclaiming Indigenous Voice and Vision*. Vancouver: University of British Columbia Press.

Battiste, M. (2002). 'Indigenous knowledge and pedagogy in First nations education: A literature review with recommendations', for the national Working Group on education and the Minister of Indian Affairs, Indian and Northern Affairs Canada (INAC). Ottawa.

Baudrez, M. and T. di Manno (eds.) (2005). *Liber Amicorum Jean-Claude Escarras, La communicabilité entre les systèmes juridiques*. Brussels: Bruylant.

Bellier, I. and D. Legros (eds.) (2001). Mondialisation et stratégies politiques autochtone. *Recherches amérindiennes au Québec* 31(3): 3–12.

Benyekhlef, K., E. Amar and V. Callipel (2015). ICT-driven strategies for reforming access to justice mechanisms in developing countries. *World Bank Legal Review* 6: 325–43.

Bergthaller, H., R. Emmet, A. Johns-Putra et al. (2014). Mapping common ground: Ecocriticism, environmental history and the environmental humanities. *Environmental Humanities* 5(1): 261–76.

Berry, T. (1988). *The Dream of the Earth*. San Francisco: Sierra Club Books [repr. Berkeley, CA: Counterpoint, 2015].

Biermann, F. (2007). Earth system governance as a crosscutting theme of global change research. *Global Environmental Change* 17(3–4): 326–37.

Biermann, F. (2012). Planetary boundaries and earth system governance: Exploring the links. *Ecological Economics* 81: 4–9.

Biermann, F. (2014). *Earth System Governance: World Politics in the Anthropocene*. Cambridge, MA: MIT Press.

Boff, L. (1997). *Cry of the Earth, Cry of the Poor*. Maryknoll, NY: Orbis.

Boisson de Chazournes, L. and V. Gowlland-Debbas (2001). *The International Legal System in Quest of Equity and Universality. Liber amicorum Georges Abi-Saab*. The Hague: Martinus Nijhoff.

Bold, R. (ed.) (2019). *Indigenous Perceptions of the End of the World: Creating a Cosmopolitics of Change*. New York: Palgrave Macmillan.

Bosselmann, K. (2011). A vulnerable environment: Contextualising law with sustainability. *Journal of Human Rights and the Environment* 2(1): 45–63.

Bouveresse, J. and J.-J. Rosat (eds.) (2003). *Philosophie de la perception: Phénoménologie, grammaire et sciences cognitives*. Paris: Odile Jacob.

Boyd, D. R. (2019). *Report of the Special Rapporteur on the Issue of Human Rights Obligations Relating to the Enjoyment of a Safe, Clean, Healthy and Sustainable Environment*, 40th session of the Human Rights Council. A/HRC/40/55.

Broekman, J. M. and L. Cata Backer (2013). *Lawyers Making Meaning*. Dordrecht: Springer.

Burns, J. H. (ed.) (1988). *The Cambridge History of Medieval Political Thought c. 350–c. 1450*. Cambridge: Cambridge University Press.

Cadava, E., P. Connor and J.-L. Nancy (eds.) (1991). *Who Comes after the Subject?* New York: Routledge.

Canguilhem, G. (1967). Mort de l'homme ou épuisement du Cogito. *Critique* 24(242): 599–618.

Canoe, L. and Tom Porter (2001). Sounding a basic call to consciousness. In S. McFadden (ed.), *Profiles in Wisdom: Native Elders Speak about the Earth*. New York: Authors Choice Press, 19–34.

Capra, F. (2010). *The Tao of Physics: An Exploration of the Parallels between Modern Physics and Eastern Mysticism*. Boulder, CO: Shambala Publication.

Carlson, R. (1962). *Silent Spring* [40th anniv. ed. 2002]. New York: Mariner.

Carmagnat, F. (1994). L'invention des sciences modernes (Isabelle Stengers). *Réseaux* 12 (65): 129–31.

Carmichael, L. (2010). Reconciliation: some stumbling blocks, assumptions, dilemmas'. Consultation Report for Effective & Sustainable Reconciliation Conference St George's house, Windsor, 21 May 2010.

Carty, A. (ed.) (1990). *Post-Modern Law, Enlightenment, Revolution and the Death of Man*. Edinburgh: Edinburgh University Press.

Carty, A. (1991). Critical international law: Recent trends in the theory of international law. *European Journal of International Law* 2(1): 66–97.

Carty, A. (2007). *Philosophy of International Law*. Edinburgh: Edinburgh University Press.

Castillo, M. M. and A. Strecker (eds.) (2017). *Heritage and Rights of Indigenous Peoples*. Leiden: Leiden University Press.

Castree, N., M. Hulme and J. D. Proctor (eds.) (2018). *Companion to Environmental Studies*. New York: Routledge.

Chual, L. J. and David M. Engel (2019). Legal consciousness reconsidered. *Annual Review of Law and Social Science* 15: 335–53.

Clarkson, L., Vern Morrissette and Gabriel Régallet (1992). *Our Responsibility to the Seventh Generation, Indigenous Peoples and Sustainable Development*. Winnipeg: International Institute for Sustainable Development.

Clifford, J. (2003). *On the Edges of Anthropology*. Chicago: Prickly Paradigm Press.

Cobley, P. (2017). What the humanities are for: A semiotic perspective. In Kristian Bankov and Paul Cobley (eds.), *Semiotics and Its Masters*. Berlin: De Gruyter Mouton, vol. 1, 3–24.

Code, L. (2006). *Ecological Thinking: The Politics of Epistemic Location*. Oxford: Oxford University Press.

COMEST (2015). *Report on Ethical Perspective on Science, Technology and Society: A Contribution to the Post-2015 Agenda*. Paris: World Commission on the Ethics of Scientific Knowledge and Technology.

Cooper, D. E. and J. A. Palmer (eds.) (1998). *Spirit of the Environment: Religion, Value and Environmental Concern*. London: Routledge.

Cyrulnik, B. and E. Morin (2018). *Dialogue sur notre nature humaine: L'unité dans la diversité*. Marabout: Éditions de l'Aube.

Daniel, C.-É., G. A. Legault and L. Bernier (2015). La régulation des nanotechnologies, le débat national français et le dialogue social: Nanomonde, grandes attentes normatives? *Lex Electronica* 20(1): 93–125.

Delio, I. (2003). A Franciscan View of Creation: Learning to Live in a Sacramental World, Synthesis provided by: Marie Puleo, A Franciscan View of Creation: Learning to Live in a Sacramental World. The Franciscan Heritage Series, Vol. 2.

Delmas-Marty, M. (2008). Les forces imaginantes du droit. *Cours au Collège de France*, 6.

Dews, P. (2007). *Logics of Disintegration, Poststructuralist Thought, and the Claims of Critical Theory*. London: Verso.

Díaz, S., J. Settele, E. Brondízio, H. T. Ngo, M. Guèze, J. Agard et al. (2019). Summary for policymakers of the global assessment report on biodiversity and ecosystem services of the Intergovernmental Science-Policy Platform on Biodiversity and Ecosystem Services, http://ipbes.net/sites/default/files/downloads/spm_unedited_advance_for_posting_htn.pdf

Donati, P. (2004). La relation comme objet spécifique de la sociologie. *Revue du MAUSS* 2(24).

Dorough, D. S. (2009). The significance of the Declaration on the Rights of Indigenous Peoples and its future implementation. In C. Charters and R. Stavenhagen (eds.), *Making the Declaration Work: The United Nations Declaration on the Rights of Indigenous Peoples*. Copenhagen: IWGIA, 264–78.

Dowie, M. (2017). *The Haida Gwaii Lesson: A Strategic Playbook for Indigenous Sovereignty*. San Francisco: Inkshares.

Dryzek, J. (1997). *The Politics of the Earth: Environmental Discourses*. Oxford: Oxford University Press.

Ducarme, F. and D. Couvet (2020). What does 'nature' mean? *Palgrave Communications* 6: 14.

Eberhard, C. (ed.) (2008). *Traduire nos responsabilités planétaires: Recomposer nos paysages juridiques*. Brussels: Bruylant.

Eberhard, C. and G. Vernicos (eds.) (2006). *La quête anthropologique du droit*. Paris: Karthala.

Einstein, A. and L. Infeld (1993). *L'évolution des idées en physiques, des premiers concepts au théories de la relativité et des quantas*. Paris: Flammarion.

Ermine, W. (2007). Ethical space of engagement. *Indigenous Law Journal* 6(1): 193.

Espagnat, B. (1994). *Le réel voilé: analyse des concepts quantiques*. Paris: Fayard.

Fagot-Largeault, A. (2006). *Cours sur l'ontologie du devenir, Collège de France*, Chaire de philosophie des sciences, Série de cours années 2006–07, 2007–08, 2008–09. Available on the website of the Collège de France.

Favareau, D., K. Kull et al. (2017). How can the study of the humanities inform the study of biosemiotics? *Biosemiotics* 10: 9–31.

Fleerackers, F. and Broekman, J. (2020). *Legal Thoughts Convert: Rethinking Legal Thinking*. Dordrecht: Springer.

Fox, O. and P. Stoett (2016). Citizen participation in the UN Sustainable Development Goals consultation process: Toward global democratic governance. *Global Governance* 22: 555–74.

Frigg, Roman and Matthew Hunter (eds.) (2010). Beyond mimesis and convention: Representation in art and science. *Boston Studies in the Philosophy and History of Science* 262: 26.

Future Earth Report (2020). *Our Future on Earth, Science Insights into Our Planet and Society*.

Gal-Or, N., C. Ryngaert and M. Noortmann (eds.) (2015). *Responsibilities of the Non-State Actor in Armed Conflict and the Market Place. Theoretical Considerations and Empirical Findings*. Leiden: Brill.

Gaudemet, J. (2005). *Corpus iuris civilis: Dictionnaire de la culture juridique*. Paris: Presses universitaires de France, 1394–98.

Geertz, C. (1973). *Interpretation of Cultures*. New York: Basic Books

Gélinas, C. and Y. Bouchard (2013). An epistemological framework for indigenous knowledge. Université de Sherbrooke, 45th Algonquian Conference, 18 October.

Gémar, J. C. (1995). *Traduire ou l'art d'interpréter. Langue, droit et société. Eléments de jurilinguistique*. Tome 2: Application. Sainte-Foy: Presses de l'Université du Québec.

Gessner, V. (1994). Global legal interaction and legal cultures. *Ratio Juris* 7(2): 132–45.

Ghiselin, M. T. (1997). *Metaphysics and the Origins of Species*. New York: State University of New York Press.

Giddens, A. (1990). *The Consequences of Modernity*. Cambridge: Polity.

Gira, D. (2001). *Au-delà de la tolerance: La rencontre des religions*. Paris: Bayard.

Glenn, P. (2004). *Legal Traditions of the World*. 2nd ed. Oxford: Oxford University Press.

Godden, L. (2018). Climate change: Limits discourses at the interface of international law and environmental law. In B. Jessup and K. Rubenstein (eds.), *Environmental Discourses in Public and Environmental Law*. Cambridge: Cambridge: University Press, 263–85.

Goodrich, P. (1986). *Reading the Law: A Critical Introduction to Legal Method and Techniques*. Oxford: Blackwell.

Gotti, M. and C. Williams (eds.) (2010). *Legal Discourse across Languages and Cultures*. Berne: Peter Lang.

Gounelle, M. (2005). Communicabilité en droit international public. In M. Baudrez and T. di Manno (eds.), *Liber Amicorum Jean-Claude Escarras. La communicabilité entre les systèmes juridiques*. Brussels: Bruylant, 107.

Grant, E., L. J. Kotzé and K. Morrow (2013). Human rights and the environment: In search of a new relationship. Synergies and common themes. *Oñati Socio-Legal Series* 3(5): 953–65.

Grear, A. (2013). Towards a new horizon: In search of a renewing socio-juridical imaginary. *Oñati Socio-Legal Series* 3(5): 966–90.

Hall, S. (1997). *Representations: Cultural Representations and Signifying Practices*. London: Sage/Open University.

Haraway, D. (1998). Situated knowledges: The science question in feminism and the privilege of partial perspective. *Feminist Studies* 14(3): 575–99.

Haraway, D. (2008). *When Species Meet*. Minneapolis: Minnesota University Press.

Harvey, D. (1989). *The Condition of Postmodernity: An Inquiry into the Origins of Cultural Change*. Oxford: Blackwell.

Harvey, D. (1996). *Justice, Nature and the Geography of Difference*. Oxford: Blackwell.

Hayes, Z. (2002). The cosmos, a symbol of the divine. In D. M. Nothwehr (ed.), *Franciscan Theology of the Environment: An Introductory Reader*. Quincy, IL: Rochester OSF Franciscan Press, 249–67.

Heppner, D. H. (2020). The stranger and the ancient race: Collective responsibility in educational research. *Journal of Indigenous Research* 8: art. 10.

Holder, J. and D. McGillivray (2017). Bringing environmental justice to the centre of environmental law research: Developing a collective case study methodology. In A. Philippopoulos-Mihalopoulos and V. Brooks (eds.), *Research Methods in Environmental Law: A Handbook*. Cheltenham, UK: Edward Elgar.

Holm, P., J. Adamson, H. Huang, L. Kirdan, S. Kitch, I. McCaldman et al. (2015). Humanities for the environment: A manifesto for research and action. *Humanities* 4(4): 977–92.

Howard, R., L. A. Ciudad and R. de Pedro Ricoy (2018). Translating rights: The Peruvian Languages Act in Quechua and Aymara. *Amerindia* 40: 219–45.

ILA (2012). *Report of the Committee on the Implementation of the Rights of Indigenous Peoples, Sofia Conference, International Law Association, August 2012*.

ILA (2016). *Final Report of the Committee on Non-State Actors, Johannesburg Conference, International Law Association, August 2016*.

ILA (2020). *Resolution and Final Report of the Committee on the Implementation of the Rights of Indigenous Peoples*, adopted at the ILA Conference in Kyoto, International Law Association, December 2020.

ILC (2006). *Report on the Fragmentation of International Law. International Law Commission*, UN Doc. A/CN.4/l.682.

Ingold, T. (2011). *Redrawing Anthropology: Materials, Movements, Lines*. Aldershot, UK: Ashgate.

Innes, J. E. and D. E. Booher (2010). *Planning with Complexity: An Introduction to Collaborative Rationality for Public Policy*. London: Routledge.

International Labour Organization (2017). *Indigenous People and Climate Change, Gender, Equality and Diversity Branch*. Geneva: International Labour Organization.

IPBES (2019). *Global Assessment Report of the Intergovernmental Science-Policy Platform on Biodiversity and Ecosystem Services*. Bonn: IPBES Secretariat.

IPCC (2018). *Global Warming of 1.5 °C, an IPCC Special Report on the Impacts of Global Warming of 1.5°C Above Pre-industrial Levels and Related Global Greenhouse Gas Emission Pathways, in the Context of Strengthening the Global Response to the Threat of Climate Change, Sustainable Development, and Efforts to Eradicate Poverty*. Geneva: Intergovernmental Panel on Climate Change.

IPCC (2019). Summary for policymakers. In *Climate Change and Land: An IPCC Special Report on Climate Change, Desertification, Land Degradation, Sustainable Land Management, Food Security, and Greenhouse Gas Fluxes in Terrestrial Ecosystems*.

Jackson, B. S. (1988). *Law, Fact, and Narrative Coherence*. Merseyside, UK: Deborah Charles.

Johnston, J., D. Gregory and D. M. Smith (eds.) (1996). *Dictionary of Human Geography*. 3rd ed. Oxford: Blackwell.

Kalka, R. (1985). La structure de la métaphysique de la relation chez Thomas d'Aquin. *Journal philosophique du Centre de recherche philosophique Saint Thomas d'Aquin* (5): 218–39.

Kantorowicz, E. (1989). *Les deux corps du Roi, essai sur la théologie politique au Moyen Âge*. Paris: Gallimard.

Kennedy, D. (2004). The disenchantment of the logically formal legal rationality. *Hastings Law Journal* 55(5): 1031–76.

Kennedy, D. (2006). The last treatise: Project and person. *German Law Journal* 7(12): 982–92.

Kimmerer, R. W. (2020 [Milkweed Editions 2013]). *Braiding Sweetgrass: Indigenous Wisdom, Scientific Knowledge and the Teachings of Plants*. Harmondsworth, UK: Penguin.

Korten, D. C. (2015). *Change the Story, Change the Future: A Living Economy for a Living Earth*. Report to the Club of Rome, Living Economies Forum. Oakland, CA: Berrett-Koehler.

Koskenniemi, M. (2001). *The Gentle Civilizer of Nations: The Rise and Fall of International Law 1870–1960*. Cambridge: Cambridge University Press.

Koskenniemi, M. (2005). International law in Europe: Between tradition and renewal. *European Journal of International Law* 16(1): 113–24.

Koskenniemi, M. (2006). Fragmentation of International Law: Difficulties arising from the diversification and expansion of international law. Report of the Study Group of the International Law Commission, International Law Commission, A/CN.4/L.682.

Kotze, L. (2018). Reflections on the future of environmental scholarship and methodology in the Anthropocene. In O. Pedersen (ed.), *Perspectives on Environmental Law Scholarship*. Cambridge: Cambridge University Press, 140–61.

Kotze, L. J. and R. E. Kim (2019). *Earth System Law: The Juridical Dimensions of Earth System Governance*. New York: Elsevier.

Lamalle, S. (2014). Multilevel translation analysis of a key legal concept: persona juris and legal pluralism. In Le Cheng, K. K. Sin and A. Wagner (eds.), *Ashgate Handbook on Legal Translation*. Abingdon, UK: Routledge, 299–312.

Lamalle, S. (2015). Reconciliation in Canada: A healing force for social and institutional change. *Indigenous Law Bulletin* 8(16): 20–23.

Lamalle, S. (2020a). De l'entendement juridique et des perspectives jurilinguistiques, actes du colloque le droit au prisme des langues. *Revue de droit international et de droit comparé* 1.

Lamalle, S. (2020b). L'horizon de la sémiotique juridique. In Y. Emerich, A. S. Hulin and S. Lamalle (eds.), *Coder–Décoder: Linguistique et concepts juridiques*. Montreal: Éditions Yvon Blais.

Latour, B. (2004). *Politics of Nature*. Cambridge, MA: Harvard University Press.

Le Roy, E. (2004). Pour une anthropologie de la juridicité. *Cahiers d'Anthropologie du Droit* 241–47.

Legrand, P. (1996). Comparer. *Revue internationale de droit comparé* 48(2): 279–318.

Lévesque, C., É. Cloutier and D. Salée (eds.) (2011). Co-construction des connaissances en contexte autochtone, Actes de colloque, Réseau de recherche et de connaissances relatives aux peuples autochtones (DIALOG) et Institut national de la recherche scientifique (INRS). *Cahier DIALOG* 2013–03.

Lipari, L. (2014). *Listening, Thinking, Being: Toward an Ethics of Attunement*. University Park: Pennsylvania State University Press.

Lucchesi, A. H. (2019). Spirit-based research: A tactic for surviving trauma in decolonizing research. *Journal of Indigenous Research* 7(1): art. 4.

MacCormick, N. (1978). *Legal Reasoning and Legal Theory*. Oxford: Oxford University Press.

Mahoney, K. (2017). Reconciliation, Indigenous knowledge and earth law: Getting rid of the stereotypes. Paper presented at launch of the ESGRREW Process of Dialogue & Research, 13 April, Concordia University, Montreal.

Martineau, J. (ed.) (2010). *Quadrivium: Number, Geometry, Music, Heaven*. Glastonbury, UK: Wooden Books.

Mattila, H. (2006). *Comparative Legal Linguistics, Language of Law, Latin and Modern Lingua Francas*. Christopher Goddard (trans.). Aldershot, UK: Ashgate.

Mattila, H. E. S. (2012). *Jurilinguistique comparée: Langages du droit, latin et langues modernes*. Jean-Claude Gémar (trans.). Montreal: Yvon Blais.

Mausen, Y. (2003). Scolastique juridique. In D. Alland and S. Rials (eds.), *Dictionnaire de la culture juridique*. Paris: Presses universitaires de France, 1394–98.

Mazzocchi, F. (2006). Western science and traditional knowledge. *EMBO Reports* 7(5): 463.

McFadden, S. (ed.) (2001). *Profiles in Wisdom: Native Elders Speak about the Earth*. New York: Athours Choice Press.

McFadden, S. (2005). *Rainbow Warriors*. New York: Harlem Writers Guild Press.

McGregor, D. (2018). From 'decolonized' to reconciliation research in Canada: Drawing from Indigenous research paradigms. *ACME: An International Journal for Critical Geographies* 17(3): 810–31.

McNamee, S. and K. J. Gergen (eds.) (1999). *Relational Responsibility Resources for Sustainable Dialogue*. Thousand Oaks, CA: SAGE.

Meadowcroft, J. (2017). The birth of the environment and the evolution of environmental governance. In J. Meadowcroft and D. J. Fiorino (eds.), *Conceptual Innovation in Environmental Policy*. Cambridge, MA: MIT Press, 53–73.

Meadowcroft, J., Gupta and Stevenson (2014). Work Plan, Taskforce on Conceptual Foundations, Earth System Governance Project, 15 December, www.earthsystemgovernance.net/conceptual-foundations

Menski, W. (2005). *Comparative Law in a Global Context: The Legal Systems of Asia and Africa*. Cambridge: Cambridge University Press.

Menski, W. (2006). *Comparative Law in a Global Context: The Legal Systems of Asia and Africa*. 2nd ed. Cambridge: Cambridge University Press.

Merleau-Ponty, M. (1996). *Le primat de la perception et ses conséquences philosophiques.* Lagrasse: Éditions Verdier.

Meslin, M. (1988). *L'expérience humaine du divin, Coll. cogitatio fidei*, 150. Paris: Éditions du Cerf.

Meyer, M. (1999). *Pour une histoire de l'ontologie.* Paris: Presses universitaires de France.

Millennium Declaration (2000). UNGA, 55th session (8 September 2005), A/RES/55/2.

Millennium Ecosystem Assessment. (2004). Proceedings of the International Conference. Bridging Scales and Epistemologies: Linking Local Knowledge and Global Science in Multi-Scale Assessments. Alexandria, Egypt, www.millenniumassessment.org/en/Bridging.Proceedings.html

Miller, A. (1996). *Intuitions de Génie: Images et créativité dans les sciences et les arts.* Paris: Flammarion.

Milton, K. (1998). Nature and the environment on Indigenous and traditional cultures. In D. E. Cooper and J. A. Palmer (eds.), *Spirit of the Environment.* London: Routledge, 81–94.

Moltmann, J. (1980). Reconciliation with Nature. Methodist Conference in London, distributed by North American Conference on Religion and Ecology (NACRE). Washington, DC.

Moltmann, J. (1990). Human Rights and Rights of Nature (NACRE). International Conference on Caring for Creation, Washington, DC, 15–17 May.

Morgan, R. (2011). *Transforming Law and Institutions, Indigenous Peoples: The United Nations and Human Rights.* Aldershot, UK: Ashgate.

Morrow, K. (2011). Ontological vulnerability: A viable alternative lens through which to view human/environmental relations. *Journal of Human Rights and the Environment* 2(1): 1–4.

Napoleon, V. and H. Friedland (2016). The inside job: Engaging with Indigenous legal traditions through stories. *McGill Law Journal/Revue de droit de McGill* 61(4): 725–54.

Nash, C. (ed.). (1994). *Narrative in Culture: The Uses of Storytelling in the Sciences, Philosophy and Literature.* London: Routledge.

Neimanis, A., C. Åsberg and J. Hedrén (2015). Four problems, four directions for environmental humanities: Toward critical posthumanities for the Anthropocene. *Ethics and the Environment* 20(1): 67–97.

Ness, B. and R. Zondervan. (2017). The Taskforce on Conceptual Foundations of Earth System Governance: Sustainability science. *Challenges in Sustainability* 5(1): 1.

Nicolini, D. (2012). *Practice Theory, Work and Organization: An Introduction.* Oxford: Oxford University Press.

Nijman, J. E. (2004). *The Concept of International Personality: An Inquiry into the History and Theory of International Law.* The Hague: TMC Asser Press.

Nikolić, M. (2017). All that is air melts into city: Minoritarian apparatuses for a more-than-human. In A. Philippopoulos-Mihalopoulos and V. Brooks (eds.), *Research Methods in Environmental Law: A Handbook.* Cheltenham, UK: Edward Elgar.

Nye, D. et al. (2013). Background document on emergence of the environmental humanities. MISTRA, www.mistra.org/en/mistra/application-calls/completed-application-calls/environmental-humanities.html

Pahuja, S. (2011), *Decolonising International Law: Development, Economic Growth and the Politics of Universality.* Cambridge: Cambridge University Press.

Peirce. C. S. ([1878] 1958). How to make our ideas clear [1878]. In *Values in a Universe of Chance: Selected Writings, 1839–1914.* Garden City, NY: Doubleday.

Petrilli, S. (2014). *Sign Studies and Semioethics: Communication, Translation and Values.* Berlin: de Gruyter Mouton.

Philippopoulos-Mihalopoulos, A. and V. Brooks (eds.) (2017). *Research Methods in Environmental Law: A Handbook*. Cheltenham, UK: Edward Elgar.

Plumwood, V. (1993). *Feminism and the Mastery of Nature*. London: Routledge.

Plumwood, V. (2002). *Environmental Culture: The Ecological Crisis of Reason*. London: Routledge.

Primavesi, A. (1998). The recovery of wisdom. In D. E. Cooper and J. A. Palmer (eds.), *Spirit of the Environment: Religion, Value and Environmental Concern*. London: Routledge, 69–80.

Pulitano, E. (ed.) (2012). *Indigenous Rights in the Age of the UN Declaration*. Cambridge: Cambridge University Press.

Ramlogan, R. (2002). The environmental and international law rethinking the traditional approach. *Vermont Journal of Environmental Law* 3.

Ratto, M. (2016). Making at the end of nature. *Interactions* 23(5): 26–35, interactions.acm .org

Raustiala, K. (2000). Sovereignty and multilateralism. *Chicago Journal of International Law* 1(2): 401–419.

Rawles, K. (1998). Philosophy and the environmental movement. In D. E. Cooper and J. A. Palmer (eds.), *Spirit of the Environment*. London: Routledge, 125–38.

Regenstein, L. G. (1991). *Replenish the Earth*. London: SCM Press.

Richmond, L., B. R. Middleton et al. (2013). Indigenous studies speaks to environmental management. *Environmental Management* 52(5): 1041–45.

Ricœur, P. (1983). *Temps et récit*. Paris: Seuil.

Roué, M. and D. Nakashima (2002). Indigenous knowledge, peoples and sustainable practice. In P. Timmerman (ed.), *Social and Economic Dimensions of Global Environmental Change*. Vol. 5 of T. Munn (ed.), *Encyclopedia of Global Environmental Change*. Chichester, UK: Wiley, 314–24.

Rouland, N. (1991). *Aux confins du droit. Anthropologie juridique de la modernité*, Paris: Odile Jacob.

Santos-Granero, F. and G. Mentore (eds.) (2006). Special issue in honor of Joanna Overing: In the world and about the world: Amerindian modes of knowledge. *Tipití: Journal of the Society for the Anthropology of Lowland South America* 4(1): 57–80.

Scott, J. (2017). Legal translation: A multidimensional endeavour. *Comparative Legilinguistics* 32: 37–66.

Short, W. J. (2004). A Franciscan language for the 21st century. *AFCU Journal: A Franciscan Perspective on Higher Education* 1: 1–9.

Silbey, S. (2008). *Legal Consciousness in New Oxford Companion to Law*. Oxford: Oxford University Press.

Sittler, J. (2004). *The Care of the Earth*. Minneapolis, MN: Fortress Press.

Slaughter, M. and S. Ratner (1999). Appraising the methods of international law: A prospectus for readers, symposium on method in international law. *American Journal of International Law* 93(2): 291–302.

Sofoulis, Z. (2018). Representation and reality. In N. Castree, M. Hulme and J. D. Proctor (eds.), *Companion to Environmental Studies*. Abingdon, UK: Routledge, 819.

Sousa Santos, B. de (2002). *Toward a New Legal Common Sense*. 2nd ed. Cambridge: Cambridge University Press.

Sousa Santos, B. de (2004). *Vers un nouveau sens commun juridique: Droit, science et politique dans la transition paradigmatique*. N. Gonzales Lajoie (trans.). Paris: LGDJ.

Sousa Santos, B. de (2014). *Epistemologies of the South: Justice against Epistemicide*. Boulder, CO: Paradigm.

Sousa Santos, B. de and C. A. Rodiguez-Garavito. (2005). *Law and Globalization from Below*. Cambridge: Cambridge University Press.

Spivak, G. C. (2012). The politics of translation. In L. Venuti (ed.), *The Translation Studies Reader*. New York: Routledge, 312–30.

Spretnak, C. (2011). *Relational Reality, New Discoveries of Interrelatedness that Are Transforming the Modern World*. Topsham, ME: Green Horizon Books.

Steiner, G. (1998). *After Babel, Aspects of Language and Translation*. Oxford: Oxford University Press.

Stengers, I. (2010). *Cosmopolitics I*. R. Bononno (trans.). Minneapolis: University of Minnesota Press.

Stoett, P. J. (2012). *Global Ecopolitics: Crisis, Governance and Justice*. Toronto: University of Toronto Press.

Stoett, P. J. and D. A. Omrow (2021). *Spheres of Transnational Ecoviolence: Environmental Crime, Human Security, and Justice*. New York: Palgrave Macmillan.

Tanasescu, M. (2015). *Environment, Political Representation, and the Challenge of Rights: Speaking for Nature*. New York: Palgrave Macmillan.

Tengö, M. et al. (2014). Connecting diverse knowledge systems for enhanced ecosystem governance: The multiple evidence base approach. *Ambio* 43: 579–91.

Thomas-Pellicer, R., V. de Lucia and S. Sullivan (eds.) (2016). *Contributions to Law, Philosophy and Ecology: Exploring Re-embodiments*. New York: Routledge.

Thumbadoo, R. V. (2005). *Learning from a Kindergarten Dropout: A Reflection on Elder William Commanda*. Ontario: Circle of All Nations.

Trinh, X. T. (2019). *Le vertige du cosmos*. Paris: Flammarion.

Truth and Reconciliation Commission of Canada (TRC) (2015a). Report, *Honouring the Truth, Reconciling for the Future*.

Truth and Reconciliation Commission of Canada (TRC) (2015b). Report, *Principles of Truth and Reconciliation*.

UNESCO (2000). Science for the twenty-first century: A new commitment. Official document of the World Conference on Science, Budapest, 7 July 1999.

UNESCO and CIPSH (2017). *A New Humanities Agenda for the 21st Century*. Outcome document of the World Humanities Conference, 6–11 August, Liège, https://arts-and-society.org/w-h-c-outcome-document/

UNGA Resolution (2011). *Harmony with Nature*. A/RES/65/164.

UNGA Resolution (2012). *The Future We Want*. A/RES/66/288.

UNGA Resolution (2015). *Transforming Our World: The 2030 Agenda for Sustainable Development*. A/RES/70/1.

Unger, R. (1976). *Law in Modern Society: Towards a Criticism of Social Theory*. New York: Free Press.

UN HRC (2019). *Report of the Special Rapporteur, Issue of Human Rights Obligations Relating to the Enjoyment of a Safe, Clean, Healthy and Sustainable Environment*. United Nations General Assembly, A /HRC/40/55.

UN Secretary-General (2010). Report. A/65/314.

UN Secretary-General (2019). Human rights obligations relating to the enjoyment of a safe, clean, healthy and sustainable environment. A/74/161.

Vaughan-Lee, L. and W. Berry (eds.) (2013). *Spiritual Ecology: The Cry of the Earth*. Point Reyes, CA: Golden Sufi Center.

Vernon, M. (2019). Divine transports. *Aeon* (Nov.), https://aeon.co/essays/how-trance-states-forged-human-society-through-transcendence

Vernon, M. (2020). The four-fold imagination. *Aeon* (4 Sept.), https://aeon.co/essays/what-we-can-learn-from-william-blakes-visionary-imagination

Wagenaar, H. (2011). *Meaning in Action: Interpretation and Dialogue in Policy Analysis*. Armonk, NY: M.E. Sharpe.

Wagner, A., K. K. Sin and Le Cheng (eds.) (2014). *Ashgate Handbook on Legal Translation*. Abingdon, UK: Routledge.

Watzlawick, P. (1978). *La réalité de la réalité*. Paris: Éditions du Seuil.

Wheeler, W. (2016). *Expecting the Earth: Life, Culture, Biosemiotics*. London: Lawrence & Wishart.

Whitehead, A. N. (1929). *Process and Reality: An Essay in Cosmology*. Cambridge: Cambridge University Press.

Whitehead, A. N. (1938). *Modes of Thoughts*. New York: Free Press.

Wittgenstein, L. ([1953] 1969). *Philosophical Investigations*. G. E. M. Anscombe (trans.). Oxford: Blackwell.

World Summit (2005). Final Document, 24 October 2005, UNGA, 60th session A/RES/60/1.

Part I

CHALLENGES

2

Environmental Humanities

Politics, Dialogue, Ethics

JOHN CROWLEY

Introduction

This chapter has two purposes. First, it offers a vision of environmental humanities as an interdisciplinary endeavour that involves the core disciplines of the humanities as well as their connections with other disciplines and ways of working within the academy and beyond. And, second, it draws some conclusions from that vision for the kinds of issues of politics, dialogue and ethics that arise from the real-world problems which demand the attention of the environmental humanities. In other words, I will operationalise some of the key messages that the environmental humanities might have to propose in light of the situation in which we find ourselves. This is a matter first of *characterising* that situation. Environmental humanities can help us make sense of the challenges that arise – albeit not in isolation. The point of the exercise is not to oppose a realm of humanities or humanistic thinking about environmental challenges to a scientific mode of thinking, but, on the contrary, to seek appropriate forms of integration between them. And, second, I should like to consider how humanities thinking can bear on *action* issues that arise from the situation as thus characterised. What kind of action? How can it be justified? Through which practical mechanisms can it be pursued?

2.1 Defining the Humanities

In recent years, there has been a boom of interest in environmental humanities, giving rise inter alia to a journal that carries the title and to various research networks that have defined themselves precisely by those words. UNESCO itself has contributed to and benefited from this boom in particular by putting environmental humanities at the heart of the overall humanities dynamic promoted by the World Humanities Conference held in Liège in 2017, and by its follow-up activities. The boom is a consequence of two overlapping movements, which intersect at a time of intense self-questioning about the humanities, both in the academy and beyond.

On the one hand, the natural sciences have produced an image of the current predicament of the planetary system that challenges the humanities to consider its meaning. If there is an age called the Anthropocene, then the humanities, by the very definition of the self-study of humankind, need to take it seriously. It is a secondary matter whether this takes the form of exploring and refining the concept as originally developed by geologists or, as in the case of Bruno Latour (2015), questioning the coherence of the conceptual language. What counts is that such debates cannot fail to engage the humanities. On the other hand, symmetrically, the humanities are driven to interrogate their foundational idea of the 'human'. Pressures and counter-pressures relating to the homogenising and normalising way in which the 'human' has historically been conceived – whether as a set of blind spots or as a deliberate hegemonic project – go back several decades. More recently, concerns about race, class and gender have intersected with a series of new questions about three kinds of boundaries of the human: with respect to animals, with respect to emerging technological entities and with respect to the planetary system. In this sense, the idea of the Anthropocene – whether endorsed or rejected – is the site of a dual internal and external pressure on the humanities, which both explains and justifies the boom.

So far, I have avoided defining the humanities. A working definition is therefore in order, not so much to prescribe any principle of division of the intellectual realm, but rather to point to certain historically and institutionally defined domains and to their implications.

The historical division between the social sciences and humanities is in many respects arbitrary, but it is embedded in the real structures of academic life. It corresponds, roughly speaking, to a distinction between two clusters of disciplines: one, the centre of gravity of which is probably best defined by economics, political science and sociology; and another, the centre of gravity of which is probably best defined by philosophy, languages and literature, as well as the disciplines related to the arts and, in most but not all academic systems, history. This distinction should not be overstated: concepts and methods have circulated between the two clusters since they started to emerge in something like the contemporary form at the end of the nineteenth century, and individuals often straddle the division by training or taste. Nonetheless, there is a routine, everyday logic to it.

History is an interesting case in this regard because it sits precisely at the dividing line between the social sciences and the humanities and has developed differently in different intellectual and institutional traditions. In France in particular, there has been a strong tendency to attach history to the social sciences as a consequence of the influence and legacy, not just intellectually but institutionally, of the *Annales* school of Marc Bloch and Lucien Febvre, and later Fernand Braudel. The *Annales* school not only defined history as a social science, one of the *'sciences de l'Homme'*, but also created a series of institutions designed to promote that idea, including the central, foundational presence of history in the École des hautes études en sciences sociales and the very close relationship established between history, sociology and anthropology.[1] By contrast, in the British tradition, even though many historians might subscribe to the *Annales* methods of historical analysis, history is, generally speaking, anchored rather in the humanities. Thus, historical research is funded in the UK less by the Economic and Social Research Council than by the Arts and Humanities Research Council. The division is purely institutional, but it has consequences. In particular, different funding mechanisms entrench different intellectual traditions and promote different career paths. UNESCO's own institutional structures follow the UK model. However arbitrary the package of disciplines may be judged in intellectual terms, philosophy, history, the arts, and languages and literature, are what UNESCO works with as 'the humanities', institutionalised in the International Council of Philosophy and Human Sciences, established at UNESCO's initiative in 1951 alongside its sister organisation, the International Social Science Council, to give substance at the global level to the mechanisms of international scientific cooperation.

Within this division, 'environmental humanities' may be defined for present purposes as philosophy, history, the arts, languages and literature applied to environmental questions. While very diverse, these questions cluster, in humanities terms, around understanding of the ways in which environmental systems operate – understanding, for instance, of the human dimension of ecosystemic processes, which means the ways in which patterns of human beliefs (all the way from elaborate cosmologies to common sense embedded within practical culture) influence environmental outcomes mediated through human behaviour.

---

[1] An anecdotal indication of this difference was given by discussion on what name to use in French for the World Humanities Conference given that UNESCO is committed to planning and publicising such events bilingually. For many French speakers involved in the discussion, the term *'humanités'* appeared artificial, whereas *'sciences humaines'* would have seemed more natural and more 'French'. On the other hand, others worried that establishing in the very name of the event the contrast between 'humanities' in English and *'sciences humaines'* in French might detract from the institutional purpose of uniting stakeholders behind a shared action plan. After extensive consultation, including with UNESCO's specialist translation service, and with stakeholders in the various French-speaking institutions, it was decided, as a pragmatic compromise rather than a substantive theoretical choice, to use *'humanités'* in French to render 'humanities' in English.

2.2 Interpreting Systems

That these ideas are fashionable should not detract from their importance. Not that they are original: on the contrary, they synthesise a fairly extensive body of existing work. Nonetheless, the humanities have an essential contribution to make to the scientific understanding of socio-ecosystems in a broad sense, up to and including the planetary system as a whole. Of course, systems can be understood in objectivistic scientific manner, from the outside, in terms of the laws by which they operate, and much of scientific value can thus be produced. These are the methods of the natural sciences, but equally of many of the social sciences, which consider systems and try to define them in terms of their internal laws of operation and interactions with other systems. The difference between the natural and social sciences in this respect is that socio-ecosystems include human agency as a constitutive component. Because human agency is a matter of beliefs and values as well as behaviour and formal institutions, understanding how beliefs and values operate, where they come from, the internal tensions within them, and the ways in which beliefs mediate systems of action is crucial to systemic understanding. One cannot, even in principle, analyse how socio-ecosystems work without reference to what people *think* about how they work.

In epistemological terms, there are well-known examples within science, including the purely physical sciences, of the ability to describe systems without reference to detailed description of the entities that compose them. For instance, in order to analyse the temperature of a system, it is not necessary to consider the properties of each individual molecule within the system. Well-developed techniques of statistical mechanics, dating back 150 years, allow direct macroscopic description of the system as a whole. It is not impossible in principle to imagine techniques to describe systems that include human behaviour without reference to the human behaviour itself, in the same way that is not impossible in principle to develop macroeconomic models that make no reference to their microeconomic foundations. On the other hand, success in these areas has so far proved elusive. Experience thus suggests that, at least for practical purposes, the capacity to provide real insights on such a basis is rather limited.[2]

It follows that, if we want to know how socio-ecosystems work, we have to be sensitive to the role of human behaviour and its value-driven, belief-oriented underpinnings. At the same time, in addition to understanding how things work, we have the parallel task of trying to understand and indeed shape the systems of meaning around action to respond to environmental challenges. This does not

---

[2] This point should not be overstated, however, and one should be wary of declaring future intellectual developments to be 'impossible'. Interesting results have been obtained by applying techniques from physics to the analysis of collective behaviour, e.g. of crowds or of online communities (initially devised to address animal behaviour such as bird flock murmuration).

mean that the environmental humanities, as such, are necessarily some kind of political programme to achieve specific outcomes – although in practice they may be, and the people engaged in humanities research into environmental issues may have a political agenda. Rather, it is the very nature of the humanities to study the ways in which human thought is expressed through the full range of cultural productions – music, dance, literature, art, philosophy, material culture – and, at the same time, to produce expressions of that culture which are part of the objects of study.

In other words, systems function, and in addition they acquire meaning. It is the core business of the humanities to remind us, first, that the ways in which systems function are not insensitive to what they mean. Systems that involve human beings are systems of structures of action that are, at the same time, processes of distribution of meaning. Second, the humanities stress that the process of studying these things itself produces meanings which are part of what needs to be studied. Systems may be changed by the analysis conducted on them. Not, of course, by the mere fact of thinking about them in different terms. The thinking, however local, is a constituent of the system and contributes to its overall state, but the system has a relational character that cannot be exhaustively reduced to local variables. Systemic properties are emergent generally speaking – and certainly are when the systems under consideration include human feedback loops. Nonetheless, the ability to reshape the language within which a system gives an account of itself has effects on the system itself that grow in magnitude as the language is disseminated.

2.3 Representing the Anthropocene

An important issue in this regard is representation in the context of the Anthropocene. Representation is an interestingly ambiguous word, which refers simultaneously to multiple semantic fields that are connected, including by the history of the word itself, but at the same time points towards very different conceptual configurations. To represent something is to make it present (in some meaningful sense) even though it is absent (in some other, equally meaningful sense).

The constitutive ambiguities of 'representation' are familiar and have been the subject of an extensive literature in political theory. Something is represented when something else stands in its place, but there are many tricky questions about what makes such an operation possible, legitimate or effective, and for which purposes, and what its consequences might be for the entities involved and for the system of which they are part. The issues are complex enough in the case of concrete entities that have the empirical capacity to speak for themselves but choose, or are required, to stand aside while their representative speaks or acts in their name. Things get considerably more tangled when considering abstract entities that must be constituted through representation to acquire personhood or concrete entities that, for whatever reason, cannot literally speak for themselves.

At the same time, the legal and political issues of representation are intimately tied up with the equally venerable and familiar question of artistic representation, which induces a certain relation between an entity – again, concrete or abstract – and its image in a very broad sense. One immediate feature of this relation, which sheds light on the underlying complexities of legal/political representation, is that representation involves not just two entities – the second standing for the first – but four. The artist creates the terms on which one thing may stand for another – possibly in radically new and unexpected ways – but succeeds only to the extent that an audience of some description buys into and gives credence to the representation. Hence the view that representation is a form of magic, something dishonest and potentially dangerous, a view that runs in various forms from Plato to Bourdieu.

The question of the Anthropocene raises in stark and fascinating form these very familiar general questions about representation. Politically, the hypothesis that human activity is the primary force shaping the planetary system raises the question how non-human interests can be reflected within political deliberation and perhaps, more profoundly, what the very nature and composition of an Anthropocenic political community might be. Ethically, these questions point to the intimate connection between representation and responsibility. Imaginatively, the Anthropocene invites reflection on what it might mean for humanity to think of itself as the reflexive component of a self-conscious planetary system, and what it might mean for any particular human to think and act as a member of such a largely unrepresented humanity. And artistically, it is a challenge to find forms of representation, whether visual or not, or perhaps artistic forms that renounce the ambition to 'represent', that can give an account or an image of the Anthropocenic planetary system and thus – as in previous generations for the crown, the state, the nation, the people or the proletariat – provide an imaginative basis for its political constitution.

The creative dynamic of representation is even more clearly visible in the legal field. Endowing some entity with legal personhood changes its character – to the point of literally creating it. When referring to individual human beings, the transformation may seem subtle, though the significance of, say, a child acquiring on maturity the legal right to speak and act in its own name is hardly trivial, any more than the symmetrical process of a previously autonomous person losing legal capacity. The implications are more obvious, and more dramatic, when something is brought into existence by the very fact of being legally represented, as in the case of a corporation or a state, or sees its standing fundamentally changed by operation of law, as when natural entities such as mountains or rivers are constituted as legal persons. Furthermore, this dynamic of creation is not a one-off. Rather, it is an aspect of the ongoing process by which a representative speaks for the thing represented and, by giving a certain expression to its identity and interests, constitutes it.

The legal and artistic meanings of representation come together in the political domain. One of the most famous images in political philosophy is the frontispiece of the second printing of Hobbes' *Leviathan* (1651), which shows a composite sovereign constituted of the multiple bodies of the subjects and achieving unity through a single head and two hands that hold the staff of authority and the sword of power. This image crystallised a certain understanding of the nature of power, authority and sovereignty that had enormous consequences, not just in the immediate European context of the mid-seventeenth century but considerably beyond, for domestic politics as well as for the understanding of the nature of law in the international domain. However, the unique fame of this visual representation of political representation should not blind us to the fact that it is typical. There are many other kinds of images, in the broad sense, that have similarly transformed systems by transforming how they are understood.

The effect of such images for the body politic is analogous to the epiphanic moments often described in autobiographical accounts, where the protagonist finds him or herself profoundly changed simply by a sound, a smell, an image, a performance, a landscape. It constitutes a transformation that, by changing self-perception, changes identity, whether for individuals or for systems. This is not a normative judgement. It simply points to the fact that systems are mediated, inter alia, by the account they give of themselves. Hence the intimate connection with the humanities, part of the core business of which is to engage with understanding the various aspects of *meaning*. The domains of systemic analysis and interpretation are thus not ontologically separate, but rather constitute distinct but complementary modes of analysis that coexist in intimate dialogue. Every human system can thus, without contradiction, be analysed in terms of certain structural principles or understood as a space of human action, and the discursive space of interpretive conflict is an important aspect of how systems manage contradictions between what they are in fact and the formal principles on which they operate.

In other words, the humanities help to bridge the spheres of *understanding* and *action* through the medium of language broadly understood. One of our challenges in the face of the environmental situation of the planet is to bridge the gap between our ability to give an account of the system and our ability to act within it to achieve supposedly desirable goals.

2.4 Making Sense of the Planetary System

The 'account' of the planetary system is, of course, first and foremost a scientific one. Indeed, the idea of a 'planetary system' – of the interconnections between physical, biological and social sciences – is an outcome of improved knowledge, over the past forty years, of the interdependencies that make it meaningful to speak of a planetary system, in the singular. The intuition that such a system exists is far from new, notably in ancient traditions and texts such as the Vedas or Taoism. Its symbolic representation is at least as old as the famous 'Earthrise' photograph, taken from Apollo 8 in orbit around the Moon.[3] An understanding of the actual mechanics and dynamics of the planetary system, beyond its mere existence, is more recent, however, and intimately connected with the development of new satellite observation capacities and new capacities for numerical simulation, both closely connected to the emergence in the late 1980s of human-induced climate change as a scientific and political challenge.

The importance of science in representing the Anthropocene is hard to overstate. It is from science, much more than from philosophy, that the *idea* emerged of the planetary system as ultimately unitary, indifferent to familiar distinctions between the physical, the biological and the social. It is through science, in a very real sense, that the planetary system speaks – to us at least. We have no intuitive grasp of, or even everyday capacity to observe, except at a very local level, tectonic movements, deep ocean currents, atmospheric temperature profiles or the large-scale dynamics of rain forests and the species that inhabit them. Our scientific and technological observations, on the other hand, are ever more highly developed and our ability to make sense of the dynamics is constantly increasing, albeit imperfect. We have growing evidence of our collective impact, however unplanned and in many respects inadvertent, underpinning the increasingly insistent idea that we might deliberately manage the planetary system as a whole, as local environmental systems have already been managed – often inadequately – for decades.

At one level, this emphasis on science is both necessary and desirable. It is an important issue in ethics to consider knowledge and its implications, including both knowledge of past causal chains and foreknowledge – often imperfect and at best probabilistic. In many codes, both moral and legal, responsibility will be treated differently according to the degree of knowledge an agent had, or could reasonably be expected to have, of the consequences of action or inaction. In environmental ethics, this finds expression in the idea that specific responsibilities fall on those who have knowledge of systemic risks, in addition to the

---

[3] The relations between the various forms of intuition of planetary interdependency, their symbolic representations and the practical processes of space management that derive from them, are the subject of Peter Sloterdijk's *Spheres* (2011–16, 3 vols.).

responsibilities inherent in causal contribution to their occurrence or attendant on capacity to act without self-harm. The rather tangled area of climate ethics draws its complexity – and distinctive interest – from the way in which all three of these grounds of responsibility interact, each bringing different agents into play in different ways.[4]

However, emphasising science can also be a problem. To illustrate, let me refer to a major event from March 2012: the 'Planet Under Pressure' conference, which took place in London and was the point of origin of Future Earth. The outcome declaration of the conference, elaborated as a kind of foundational charter for the future organisation and at the same as a high-level political statement, expresses a strikingly scientific understanding of what was at stake in designating the planet as 'under pressure'.[5] To summarise at the risk of simplification, the declaration states that we know through the natural sciences that the planet is indeed under pressure, in the sense that the ability of the planetary system to endure in something like its current state cannot be assumed. The challenge, on the basis of scientific knowledge, is thus to find ways within the system of acting to alleviate the pressure and create – in a characteristic phrase of the time – a 'safe operating space' for humanity.

As a metaphor, the idea of a 'space' follows quite naturally from the notion of 'planetary boundaries', which was the framing of the foundational research from which the conference itself stemmed (Rockström et al. 2009).[6] The boundaries here are the limits beyond which certain characteristic cycles defining the balance of the planetary system can no longer operate sustainably. There are for instance, levels of inorganic input to the nitrogen cycle beyond which no natural processes can be expected to ensure absorption and recycling, leading to an open-ended build-up of compounds – mostly various kinds of nitrates – that have significant and well-known negative impacts, through water contamination notably. The nitrogen cycle, though not the best known in public debate, was the one with respect to which the boundary had already been breached by 2010. Better known is the greenhouse gas cycle, with reference to carbon dioxide because of its long atmospheric persistence. As is now widely known – though still not infrequently denied – there is a natural cycle, involving vegetation in particular, that sets limits to the amount of carbon dioxide that can be recycled. Beyond those limits, excess

---

[4] UNESCO's World Commission on the Ethics of Scientific Knowledge and Technology (COMEST) has devoted several reports to these issues ('The Ethical Implications of Global Climate Change', 2010; 'Background for a framework of ethical principles and responsibilities for climate change adaptation', 2013; 'Ethical Principles for Climate Change: Adaptation and Mitigation', 2015), which are all available at www.unesco.org. Building inter alia on the reports, UNESCO's General Conference adopted in 2017 its Declaration of Ethical Principles in Relation to Climate Change.

[5] www.igbp.nct/download/18.6b007aff13cb59eff6411bbc/1376383161076/SotP_declaration-A5-for_web.pdf

[6] For a subsequent review of the origins and development of the notion, see also Steffen et al. (2015).

carbon dioxide emitted by non-cyclical human activities will build up primarily in the atmosphere where increasing concentrations are expected to drive global temperature increases and regional climate transformations, with a range of negative consequences. A part of the excess will also be absorbed by the oceans, leading to acidification, which is detrimental to many marine animals, plants and processes.

In other words, once the planetary system breaches those boundaries, it finds itself in a state – or more precisely an unstable dynamic – in which it can no longer be taken for granted that it is the same planetary system. Rather, the environment relevant to human civilisation will be in flux, in transition between systems, with no guarantee that whatever new cyclical state emerges will still accommodate humans, at least at the level of civilisation and planetary dominion by which we have, for some centuries, defined ourselves. The idea of the Anthropocene as self-undermining is a familiar one in the literature. It finds one striking expression, for instance, in James Lovelock's idea that 'Gaia', as a self-regulating planetary system, is effectively protecting itself against human impact through a process of rapid warming that will lead to a 'warm world' – by which Lovelock means a global average temperature increase of 6 °C – in which human populations will be reduced to preindustrial levels (Lovelock 2009). In response to such scenarios, activist movements have arisen calling for depopulation as a deliberate individual and collective strategy. For present purposes, however, a different aspect of the issue is in many ways more important. If the planetary system ceased to be the same system, then we would lose the scientific knowledge about it that defines one important aspect of the Anthropocene, viz. its reflexivity. The Anthropocene thus lies within the planetary boundaries; outside lies a wild, unknown, dangerous future that humans – insofar as they survive at all – would need to navigate without the maps and navigational tools they have patiently developed over centuries.

This is why the space within the planetary boundaries is defined as a 'safe' one. The choice of word is interesting, and in some ways odd for a species that has long defined itself, both existentially and culturally, as surviving in the face in danger. Heroes, in all the stories I am aware of, are those that venture outside safe spaces in order to confront the wild unknown and return with something of value to their group – or, if they fail to return, to be remembered as those who at least tried. Those who declared that humanity's space needs to be 'safe' were obviously not thinking along those lines; they were not deliberately proposing that human survival demands timidity within the confines of our collective shelter. But nor were they sensitive to the cultural baggage that the language of safety carries with it. One reason for taking for granted, in the context of this international science conference, the positive value of the word 'safe' was, no doubt, the second part of the Anthropocene exit scenario sketched in the previous paragraph. The safety within the boundaries is existential, but, as noted above, it is also epistemic; it reflects the role of science in establishing the boundaries in the first place, and thus its necessary role in managing what goes on within them. Outside the boundaries, we would no longer know what we are doing. We would lose foreknowledge of the consequences of our choices. We would again – as before the science of the integrated planetary system emerged – be feeling our way, constantly exposed to the risk of inadvertent impacts that might well be catastrophic and detected too late.

This is why the space was defined as a safe *operating* space, which brings in the dimension of *governance*: defining how the Anthropocene planetary system, of which humans and their societies are an integral, self-conscious component, should be governed, in light of accumulated scientific knowledge, to stay within the planetary boundaries of safety. This a complex question, and there are clearly quite different ways of envisaging it. What is interesting about the 'Planet Under Pressure' declaration is how it picks a specific angle, which is explicitly that the natural sciences have the answer to the technical question how the planetary system should be steered – which path it should follow – but need help from the social and human sciences in defining how to get and stay on that path. In other words, as it was common to say at the time, governing the Anthropocene is doing 'as science demands'.[7] This is what I called earlier a 'scientistic' paradigm – the view that the planetary boundaries stand outside politics and determine conditions of political possibility.

2.5 Navigating the Anthropocene

The idea of navigating the Anthropocene by restricting or even rolling back human encroachment on natural systems is understandable and may even have some practical efficacy in specific areas – plastic pollution being perhaps the best example. But it nonetheless has severe limitations, both conceptual and practical, that make it hard to envision as a comprehensive template.

First, the whole point of the Anthropocene hypothesis, and of the political language developed around it, is to stress that it goes considerably beyond human impact on the planet. It is, rather, about moving from the planet conceived as something apart from the humans that live on it to the notion of a planetary system that includes, through its systemic dynamics, all its human and non-human

---

[7] This characteristic slogan underwent something of an eclipse in subsequent years, partly because of the conceptual limitations discussed here, and partly because it came to appear politically ineffective. It is striking, however, that it has resurfaced more recently as the leitmotif of the youth climate action movement of which Greta Thunberg is the best-known spokesperson.

components. One can, of course, seek to roll back human encroachment, perhaps to the point of voluntary extinction, as some have argued. But unless humans literally disappear entirely, or unless we renounce all scientific understanding and all technological capacity, such footprint reductions are still a management technique, deliberately designed and implemented to fulfil a chosen objective, and thus requiring ongoing monitoring and accountability in order to be meaningful. In other words, to put it very simply, one cannot have both Anthropocenic responsibility and traditional ideas of 'nature' as separate from humanity and technology.

Second, there is no way of thinking about these issues that can dispense with the essential point that human flourishing is, by definition, an essential component of Anthropocenic viability. Sacrificing humans, or human civilisation, or more modestly human standards of living, to save the planet does not somehow give birth to a planet immune from human impact. It simply produces an alternative management framework in which human needs have been relatively downgraded within an overall Anthropocenic utilitarian calculus. And if humans have intrinsic value in the same sense and to the same extent as tigers, free-flowing rivers and wetlands, a strong burden of proof falls on anyone using consequentialist arguments to justify sacrifices of human well-being.[8] It is necessary to show that the proposed measures can be reasonably expected to produce the desired benefits for the relevant non-human entities, which means a high, serious level of scientific understanding of planetary interdependencies. Human knowledge, which is one dimension of human flourishing, is thus indispensable if the planet is to be protected against the worst human excesses. This is not a paradox: it is simply one statement of the Anthropocenic political problem. Of course, many approaches to improving the survivability of the Anthropocene do not depend on sacrificing human flourishing but rather on critically interrogating it, in particular, by stressing its intangible rather than its material components. Once resource consumption comes to be seen not as a proxy for human flourishing but as a possibly dispensable tool for achieving it, some problems look easier. The point, however, is that even in the worst-case scenario, the question of human flourishing cannot drop out of the Anthropocene calculus.

What this means is that, without questioning in any way the science of planetary boundaries, the 'safe operating space' cannot be adequately understood in purely scientific and technological terms, as if its inside and outside could be neatly

---

[8] Many strands of thought, both within environmental thinking and in opposition to it, would adamantly reject that idea that humans have no distinctive intrinsic value for the purposes of these discussions. However, in the terms of the present paragraph, this would only increase the burden of consequentialist proof, possibly to the point where it cannot be met. My point is that the problem only disappears or becomes trivial if humans do not have *at least* as much intrinsic value as non-human entities – a position that would not be about managing or even navigating the Anthropocene but rather exiting from it entirely.

segregated. Not only can Anthropocene survival governance not be cordoned off in this way (which suggests that the very phrase 'safe operating space' is probably quite misleading), it probably cannot be reduced to a technical calculus at all. The Anthropocene is inherently a space of meaning, devoid of definite boundaries, in which the tasks are to make sense of, as much as to act with reference to, the science of planetary interdependency. One important dimension of the sense that needs to be made is ethical: interpreting the responsibilities that arise from knowledge – about the system as such, about past causal dynamics within, about its possible future paths. Another dimension is political: imagining the institutions and procedures that can represent the Anthropocene and its denizens, taking full account of the ambiguities of representation as referred to above. Failure to connect the spheres of understanding and of action will simply undermine both.

2.6 Scoping the Anthropocenic Political Community

Which brings me back to politics. Given the above sketch of the scientific and conceptual issues, how do the environmental humanities bear on what politics could or should look like in the Anthropocene? My outline suggestion is that the distinctive features of the humanities, as modes of intellectual inquiry, correspond well to the nature of the political challenges we face collectively, as humanity: to make sense of, to develop mechanisms for, to operate within a political community of a radically new kind. What is new is that this political community needs to extend beyond familiar parameters in a number of ways – not just the parameters of the Western tradition of political philosophy or political theory but also those of, for instance, the Islamic or Confucian traditions. How far this claim can be generalised, I am not sure. But, at the very least, the point is not limited to the tradition that runs, say, from Plato to Weber by way of Hobbes.

The familiar parameters concern how to organise the affairs of people who share a concrete social space defined by history, geography and something like 'organic solidarity' in the Durkheimian sense: participation in a system of division of labour that functions both structurally to organise social relations in a certain way and, and at the level of ideas, to define the appropriate distribution of functions within that social group. More concretely, states are recognised in international law on the basis of territory, population and government, which poses the question of political community along three dimensions: what makes a territory more than just a space on a map; what makes a population more than just a mass of persons who happen to occupy that territory at a particular time; and what makes administration of that space and those persons more than simply management?

Organising the political affairs of a community, as thus interpreted, is complicated enough within the parameters of limited territories and reasonably well-defined populations. In the Anthropocene, in addition to the many familiar problems of political theory, new dimensions of organic solidarity become relevant, including both the composition of the population and the time horizon that emerges from scientific understanding of planetary interdependency. In other words, we need to take account, inter alia, of the necessary and troubling presence within our political horizon of future generations, which challenge understandings of time itself. Because we know how we could affect future generations, our knowledge carries with it a responsibility to consider the consequences not just of our present choices, but even of configurations over which we may not have any direct control.

To use a pop culture reference, consider the series *Early Edition*, which aired in the United States on CBS from 1996 to 2000, and both dramatises and simplifies in a neat way the ethics of foreknowledge. The series, set in Chicago, follows the adventures of a man who mysteriously receives each *Chicago Sun Times* newspaper the day before it is actually published, and who uses this knowledge to prevent terrible events. One has to assume, of course, both the credibility of the source and the protagonist's capacity to act on foreknowledge to change the future, but both assumptions are relevant also for the Anthropocene and not in themselves deeply problematic: the credibility is that of science and the capacity to act stems from the fact that science produces scenarios which, by definition, have not happened yet, and at the same time provides evidence for the kinds of actions that might influence which scenario comes to be actualised.

The question is: what follows from receiving the 'early' edition of tomorrow's paper – which nicely encapsulates the idea of foreknowledge in general? In the case of the series, the protagonist comes to feel, as presumably others would in the same circumstances, a responsibility to ensure that the next day's horrible headline never happens. Of course, this is a TV drama, so the headline is usually something both immediately horrible and fairly straightforward in terms of preventive action, such as the death of two young children in a fire, with twenty-four hours to stop the fire starting or get the victims out in time. If the next day's headline was – say – 'World's Hungry Still Top One Billion', it's far less clear what the protagonist could do with his twenty-four hours of foreknowledge.

This is just a TV series, but the serious point stands. Knowledge carries with it responsibility in terms not of some speculative new ethics, but of the kinds of ethical frameworks that we are already intimately familiar with, and indeed are embedded in many of our legal systems. Thus, assigning responsibility in civil law has a lot to do with the presence or absence of foreknowledge. If one could not have foreseen the consequences of an act or omission, meaning in most legal systems that no reasonable person could have foreseen them, one is in principle legally blameless. How one feels morally about dramatic consequences is, of course, a different and less determinate matter. Correlatively, civil liability for consequences arises (prima facie) when they were foreseeable, whether or not they were actually foreseen. Failure to foresee things that should have been foreseen is, in this context, a form of negligence. These basic ideas do not really depend on the details of civil law, which may vary considerably between jurisdictions: it is rather the basic intuition with which most people would be at least broadly familiar. If you know something, specific responsibilities may follow; and when you're ignorant about something, you may have a responsibility to find out.

So, there is a sense in which climate science is giving us an 'early edition' of Earth's futures. But it's a much more complex sense than in the TV series and, less obviously, something more elusive than our familiar moral and legal intuitions about the connection between liability and foreknowledge. Instead of having unambiguous forewarning of something that *will* happen if we fail to act and is preventable by reasonably well-identified steps, we have clouded forewarning of things that *might* happen with significant uncertainty as to how they might be prevented.

The nature of the Anthropocene is to offer a conceptual framework to make sense of a planetary system that is in important respects human-driven, but through much more distended and diffuse causal chains than are embedded in established moral and legal paradigms. It follows that much more distant contemporaries than we are used to thinking about come to be encompassed within our moral horizon – or, perhaps more precisely, that the location of that horizon is much less determinate than it used to be. In the foundational concepts of sociology, organic solidarity operates in tandem with nation-building as an analytical and normative framing that defines the units within which the question of political community arises. In late modernity, in the context of what is generically called globalisation, organic solidarity and nation-building part company, thus weakening the analytical basis for the normative principles on which modernity was based – including, in legal terms, the United Nations Charter.[9]

This point should of course not be overstated. The nation state is the regulatory principle of modernity, anchored in the sociological paradigm, but it has always coexisted with older alternatives, born within pre-modern empires, that emphasise the moral duty to consider the good of humanity as a whole. Stoicism offers one important ancient template, some features of which are taken over into distinctively modern paradigms such as Kantianism and utilitarianism. Indeed, the idea that moral and even political universalism might emerge from reflexive, enlightened nationalism still has relevance, as elegantly summarised in Jaurès'

---

[9] This point is central to the sociology of Anthony Giddens (e.g. *The Consequences of Modernity*; *Modernity and Self-Identity: Self and Society in the Late Modern Age*) but has also been widely picked up in other bodies of work.

dictum, from his 1910 essay *L'armée nouvelle*, that 'un peu d'internationalisme éloigne de la patrie; beaucoup d'internationalisme y ramène'. What is new, perhaps, is that a feature – indefinite spatial and temporal extension of horizons of moral concern – that was previously optional, and embedded in specific philosophical frameworks, now comes to look like a functional and normative requirement. Furthermore, it is not exhausted by the responsibility to consider the geographically and temporally distant consequences of our actions. If there is anything true in the idea that the planetary system is an integrated system of which humans are the conscious part, which is what the Anthropocene ultimately means philosophically, then the Anthropocenic political community, at least in principle, includes a wide variety of concrete and abstract non-human entities with which we cannot avoid engaging.

The question is how we engage with them and what kinds of responsibilities, if any, arise therefrom – which also raises the question of the language in which we can engage with non-human entities. And the centrality of language in this regard brings us back to the heart of the matter: the role of the humanities in making sense of the Anthropocene.

Does that mean that we should put on hold practical action to address issues such as climate change until we have a new comprehensive understanding of the integrated planetary system? No. We need to advance, hard as it may seem, on two coordinated fronts: achieving what can be achieved with the systems as they are, and at the same time ambitiously and comprehensively rethinking the systems. And the connection between these tasks is conceptual, but also practical. Any attempt to act within an inadequate system necessarily pushes against its boundaries and limitations, thereby revealing them and creating breaches through which new thinking and new action potentials can circulate. Systemic change never comes gradually; it is inherently catastrophic in the strict mathematical sense of the word. But the gradual build-up of counter-pressures and hypothetical alternatives creates the conditions in which, at least in principle, sudden phase change can occur without being, in the ordinary, non-technical sense of the word, a catastrophe.

One of those counter-pressures, which also bears the germ of an alternative, is, precisely, interrogation of the notion of an Anthropocenic political community.

Such a political community, like any other, is necessarily an ethical community in the sense that it arranges its collective affairs in light of a certain framework of assignment of responsibility and of judgement about the relative desirability of outcomes, on the basis not of unanimity or even consensus but of a discussion space, the linguistic structure of which precisely defines the political community. Which is to say that a political community is, among other things, a community of people who have common terms on which to disagree about things – a context of argument within which they can talk to one another without necessarily agreeing, but which includes the possibility of agreement. Such a discussion space certainly does not mandate the ethics required for an Anthropocenic community. At most, it makes possible the necessary rethinking of responsibility beyond inherited consequentialist frameworks, which are poor tools to assign to anyone, in particular, responsibility for any outcome of systemic significance, or the various kinds of virtue ethics or deontologism, which need to assume a clear definition of the moral identity of the members of the political community, so that duties can be assigned to them corresponding to their ethical status. Yet in a heterogeneous community that needs to be constructed anew in the light of new circumstances, it is unlikely that one could rely on any stable background pattern of deontological assignment to say to an entity of hypothetical type X127 'these are your duties'. Whether such assignment might be produced by positive law is of course a different matter, to be assessed at a more practical level.

In addition to inviting us to revisit and reimagine principles of responsibility, the constitutive ethics of the political community entail principles of inclusion. Whose interests deserve consideration, whose voice counts? As Bruno Latour (2004) puts it, how many of us are there? In the case of a concrete political community of people occupying a specific territory, this may be easy enough in practice, leaving only the question how such a community arranges its business. By contrast, in the kind of political community that would need to emerge to deal with the issues of the Anthropocene, there is no a priori definition of the group within which the questions arise. Deciding who constitutes the community goes hand in hand with trying to work out how the community should organise itself, which raises questions about who should be 'in' or 'out', who counts as an entity for the purposes of the analysis and, of course, how heterogeneous entities can be brought within a common framework. This includes, obviously, entities that do not have the commonly established aptitudes and qualities that allow them to speak for themselves, and therefore exist politically through modes of representation which, while neither mysterious nor necessarily new, raise certain questions about their basis and application.

2.7 Dialogue in the Anthropocene

The connection between politics and ethics thus gives rise to the question of *dialogue*. Specifically, an Anthropocenic political community probably requires new modes of dialogue and of analysis of the political, connected to new modes of representation. Traditionally, the question of dialogue has arisen either on the basis of a prior, shared linguistic and cultural background, or in the context of conquest or absorption. Strictly speaking, neither configuration corresponds to the situation under discussion, which is a context of heterogeneity, stemming from a new understanding of things that were always already present, but are henceforth seen in a different light. So, in the absence of ontological commonality – if the political community is not composed of the same kinds of beings – and of the presumption of shared language, how can we talk to one another? What can 'dialogue' look like with the climate, the ocean or the Siberian tiger? Some modalities of exchange with such entities are familiar and deeply unequal. Effectively, we submit them to 'questioning' in precisely the sense used by the Spanish Inquisition, using science to *extract* information from them, sometimes in ways that are literally inquisitorial questionings, i.e. torture, sometimes in less invasive ways. We also use the technologies derived from science to control entities and, again, *extract* economic benefit from them, e.g. by cultivation, breeding, hunting, mining. What is clear, however, is that such extractive procedures are not in any true sense dialogical: the entities under questioning get no chance to ask any questions back, still less to be part of defining what counts as a question. The only way they can respond is, effectively, by participating or refusing to participate in the exchange. Metaphorically, one could indeed say that when a species goes extinct it is, at a certain level, telling us that it no longer wants to talk to us because there are no shared language and no shared discursive space within which to exchange.

In other words, what lies at the heart of the nexus of politics, dialogue and ethics is the disconnection between the knowledge we have and our apparent incapacity to exercise the correlative responsibility. The powerful mechanisms of dialogue that science offers being one-sided, how, by contrast, could the conditions be created – by leveraging rather than neglecting the power of scientific questioning – for other entities to talk back to us in ways that aren't simply evasive or self-destructive? And while the examples above were of concrete non-human entities, the point applies equally to abstract non-human entities (the atmosphere, the biosphere, etc.) and to humans themselves, as illustrated by the historically impoverished forms of dialogue within which Indigenous peoples were often enclosed. Clearly, just talking is already a form of dialogue, but a rather weak one, which is indifferent to the status of the entities engaging in it and to their different modes of engagement. After all, I don't think we would want to say that the torturer engages in 'dialogue' with the victim of torture – certainly not in any sense that is normatively meaningful. By contrast, the kind of dialogue that underpins a political community requires, not necessarily a precondition of equality, but at least a balance between entities that recognise one another as each occupying a legitimate space in their community (thus acknowledging it, at least implicitly, as their shared community) and engaging in dialogue oriented towards maintenance and perhaps even enrichment of the community.

The reflection on ethics required by the politics of the Anthropocene, which will be talkative insofar as it adds indefinitely many voices, will also involve meta-ethical consideration of the nature and limits of ethics. Similarly, dialogical processes within the Anthropocenic political community necessarily entail a process of discussion about the nature, limits and possible transformations of dialogue, which fits very naturally with what the humanities have to bring in terms of traditions of scholarship and specific intellectual tools.

2.8 Doing Politics in the Anthropocene

Ethics and dialogue in the Anthropocenic political community thus require a new kind of politics, incorporating new modes of representation – something that goes beyond the authoritative allocation of resources or problem-solving but, at the same time, cannot rely on a clearly established alternative framing. There are several interesting contributions to the question of what a politics of radical heterogeneity would look like – the work of Laclau and Mouffe (2001), for instance – but often, within the post-Marxist tradition, concerned only with relations among humans, incorporating environmental issues at best as external constraints. In fact, the Anthropocene calls for a radical meta-political approach, which puts the very nature of the political at the heart of politics. Usually, on the other hand, in order to make everyday politics work, we bracket the question of what politics is. Indeed, the dysfunctions of contemporary political systems are often due to the way in which the question of the political keeps invading the space of ordinary politics, destabilising established political forces and institutions, the constitutional balance between executive, legislative and judicial power, and the established cultural representations of the nature of political authority. A meta-politically driven crisis can answer its own questions only by a process of re-establishment, for which the necessary conditions may or may not be met.

There are thus three processes to be considered for these purposes: studying, imagining and making things happen. They are intertwined – neither identical, nor separable. Merely studying things by mobilising the environmental humanities will not automatically put those disciplines to work to encourage new kinds of imaginings – still less produce desirable outcomes, such as a sustainable, harmonious universe within which collective survival, flourishing and happiness are ensured. On the other hand, without the imaginings, it is hard to see how the structural tendencies towards possibly terminal crisis could be headed off. And this in turn gives rise to certain profound political difficulties.

Alternatives set within observable structural trends are no more than options within a predefined set of possibilities. However radical they may appear, they are still, by assumption, within the system. On the other hand, aspirational possibilities that cannot be connected analytically to observable structures and dynamics cannot be worked towards – they can only be hoped for. This does not mean that radical forms of imagination are inconceivable. Observably, they exist. Nor does it mean that they have no effects. On the contrary, the world is changed when changes in the language through which it is seen become embedded in social common sense. What it does mean, on the other hand, is that they cannot be formulated as a political programme. This is not a new problem either theoretically or practically. It lies, for instance, at the heart of Jacques Derrida's reflections in the 1990s on Marxism and messianism (Derrida 1993), and more generally underpins the philosophical idea of an 'event', as theorised, in addition to Derrida, by Deleuze, Badiou and others. An event – uncontrollable, unpredictable, unknowable – is the point at which systems suddenly change from one state to another. It can be imagined and aspired to, but it can neither be planned for nor predicted.

There are two obvious differences between the Anthropocene and earlier contexts defined by the fault line, the unbridgeable gap, between radical imagination and structural constraint. The first is that the Anthropocene is, at least in its origins, entirely defined by scientific knowledge of its patterns of interdependence, suggesting that it inherently leaves less space for imaginative reconstruction. The second is that, unlike in familiar political configurations, the issues cannot be limited to arrangements among humans within non-human settings. The non-human components of the Anthropocene are henceforth active, dynamic and equipped with at least some capacity to express themselves.

However, these differences, which superficially make the traditional problem of political transformation impossible to resolve because they create radical heterogeneity between the imagined event (paradigmatically, climate breakdown) and the analysed system, in fact establish genuinely new action potentials. Reconciling radical imagination with reformist action is a perennial problem that has plagued all political movements with transformative ambitions. Yet, in the Anthropocene some intriguing directions emerge for radically imaginative reformism. Nor are these possibilities solely theoretical. Real-world dynamics that exemplify at least some of these possibilities are also observable. And, strikingly, the political possibilities are anchored in the kinds of considerations on ethics and dialogue that have been sketched above.

The first direction is the Anthropocene as lived experience. There is no contradiction in the idea of a scientific paradigm being accessible through non-scientific channels once one recognises that the idea of interdependence is distributed and disseminated. It is accessible at any point of the system through a multitude of forms and connections. The point is not, obviously, that any farmer observing the soil, or insects, or the migration dates of birds can thereby approximate a global circulation model of the Earth's climate. But, as one would expect from the perspective of the humanities, the intuition and lived experience of connectedness can run deeper, if less precisely, than the ability to simulate systems. Rooting politics in consciousness is not new: the principle is central, in several different variants, in the Marxist tradition. But the Anthropocene has the potential to sharpen the politics of consciousness, and to connect it to an expanded ethics of diffuse responsibility, by giving an account of experience that is informed by and illuminates the abstract system – thereby making it concrete – and at the same time offering transformative options even at the individual level. By this I do not mean that system-level change can be achieved by individual action, especially if the individuals involved are few. But their transformation is real, as they go off-grid, or become vegan, or put their energy into roof-top gardening, or even simply look at things differently, and by transforming themselves they offer a language of transformation that in turn modifies the language of the system as a whole. Which is, no doubt, why debates around these issues become tense and, on social media, often vitriolic: individual transformations in their multiple forms, and parallel refusals to transform oneself or to be transformed, are not simply individual choices that can coexist – they are clashing expressions of systemic dynamics, in other words political processes mediated, sometimes deliberately, sometimes unwittingly, through individual action.

The second, overlapping direction is the Anthropocene as expanded discursive and narrative space. The lived experience referred to above is one that, however solitary, cannot be solipsistic. It is, in the older language of romanticism, a form of communion with nature, except that it makes apparent, through its very structure as experience, that nature is not something external, nor is it a passive medium, but rather an active interlocutor that answers in ways that are not only, and not primarily, sublime or ineffable, but rather chime, very practically, with modes of self-understanding. This can easily be caricatured as the tree-hugging tendency of the transformative movement, but the point – underwritten by the science of the Anthropocene – is that there is nothing mystical or irrational in listening to plants, animals, rivers or mountains. The only condition is to accept imperfection and ambiguity – but is it that different among humans? – and the impossibility of speaking back in anything like the same terms. Philosophically, this corresponds to the corollary of one of Wittgenstein's most famous dicta: 'if a lion could talk, we could not understand him' (Wittgenstein 1958: 223). Which entails that the ability to understand – albeit limited, and mediated through a language, whether scientific or poetic, that the interlocutor does not share – shows that, to that extent, the interlocutor is speaking. And therefore, if 'the limits of my language mean the limits of my world', the imaginative and scientific extension of my language extends, by that very token, my world (Wittgenstein 1922: §5.6). And, again, this ethically significant transformative process does not depend on collective action, though it may be enhanced by it.

These connections between politics, dialogue and ethics mediated by the internal logic of the environmental humanities, do not determine 'what is to be done' in the Anthropocene. On the contrary, the idea that a unique and well-defined political programme follows from the internal logic of the Anthropocene is precisely the kind of 'scientism' that I sought to dismiss above. Politics is about disagreement, and even the tools and methods of ethics and dialogue can only offer ways of managing the disagreements, not a technique for eliminating them. What does emerge from the discussion, on the other hand, is that there are things to be done: it is not just a matter of waiting for catastrophe to strike or for its absence to spare us. Furthermore, the possibilities are not limited to a macro-scale paralysed by insurmountable coordination problems. Small-scale and even individual transformation is meaningful even if it does not scale up – and what cannot be scaled up can, perhaps, be disseminated. And what is most truly transformative is the work of the imagination to reshape political communities. By default, or by habit, it is often taken for granted that the reshaping can only be geographical, based on the correct observation – discussed above – that the Anthropocene expands horizons of ethical concern. But while the Anthropocene may indeed give rise to distinctive forms of cosmopolitanism, this is not a requirement of politics or ethics in the Anthropocene, nor, perhaps, is it even the most natural implication. Local expansions of ethical horizons, to our co-dependent non-humans and to their imaginative meaning for us, are equally important in principle, and perhaps more likely to be of practical relevance in the short term. Following Voltaire's Candide, 'il faut cultiver notre jardin', not as quietistic withdrawal, important as that may be, but, especially now that our 'garden' is in some sense planetary, and inextricably tangled up with ourselves, with full awareness of the political and ethical implications.

References

Derrida, J. (1993). *Spectres de Marx. L'État de la dette, le travail du deuil et la nouvelle internationale*. Paris: Galilée. [*Specters of Marx: The State of the Debt, the Work of Mourning, and the New International*. P. Kamuf (trans.). London: Routledge, 1994.]

Giddens, A. (1990). *The Consequences of Modernity*. Cambridge, UK: Polity.

Giddens. A. (1991). *Modernity and Self-Identity: Self and Society in the Late Modern Age*. Cambridge, UK: Polity.

Laclau, E. and C. Mouffe (2001). *Hegemony and Socialist Strategy: Towards a Radical Democratic Politics*. 2nd ed. London: Verso.

Latour, B. (2004). *Politiques de la nature, Comment faire entrer les sciences en démocratie*. Paris: La Découverte. [*Politics of Nature: How to Bring the Sciences into Democracy*. C. Porter (trans.). Cambridge, MA: Harvard University Press, 2004.]

Latour, B. (2015). *Face à Gaïa. Huit conférences sur le nouveau régime climatique*. Paris: La Découverte. [*Facing Gaia: Eight Lectures on the New Climatic Regime*. C. Porter (trans.). Cambridge, UK: Polity, 2017.]

Lovelock, J. (2009). *The Vanishing Face of Gaia: A Final Warning*. New York: Basic Books.

Rockström, J. et al. (2009). Planetary boundaries: Exploring the safe operating space for humanity. *Ecology and Society*, 14(2): art. 32.

Sloterdijk, P. (2011, 2014, 2016). *Spheres* (3 vols.). Los Angeles, CA: Semiotext(e).

Steffen, W. et al. (2015). Planetary boundaries: Guiding human development on a changing planet. *Science*, 347(6223).

UNESCO COMEST Report (2013). *Background for a Framework of Ethical Principles and Responsibilities for Climate Change Adaptation*. Paris.

UNESCO COMEST Report (2015). *Ethical Principles for Climate Change: Adaptation and Mitigation* Paris.

UNESCO's General Conference (2017). Declaration of Ethical Principles in Relation to Climate Change.

UNESCO's World Commission on the Ethics of Scientific Knowledge and Technology (COMEST) Report (2010). *The Ethical Implications of Global Climate Change*. Paris.

Wittgenstein, L. (1922). *Tractatus Logico-Philosophicus*. London: Routledge & Kegan Paul.

Wittgenstein, L. (1958). *Philosophical Investigations*. 2nd ed. Oxford: Blackwell.

3

Decolonising the Dialogue on Climate Change

Indigenous Knowledges, Legal Orders and Ethics

DEBORAH MCGREGOR AND MAHISHA SRITHARAN

Introduction

Climate change will have enormous impact on the livelihoods of indigenous peoples. Already, many rural communities are being forced to adapt their way of life due to the changing environment.

Their livelihood systems are often vulnerable to environmental degradation and climate change, especially as many inhabit economically and politically marginal areas in fragile ecosystems in the countries likely to be worst affected by climate change. While indigenous peoples are among the least responsible for the problem, they are among those most vulnerable to it.

(IASG 2008: 19; 21)

The Anthropocene inadvertently and unintentionally signals what we are arguing here: that *the Anthropocene as the extension and enactment of colonial logic systematically erases difference*, by way of genocide and forced integration and through projects of climate change that imply the radical transformation of the biosphere.

(Davis and Todd 2017: 769, italics in original)

Indigenous peoples in Canada score far worse on virtually all indicators of well-being than the general public, a situation which has been directly attributed to historical and ongoing processes of colonisation (Ananya 2014; Delormier et al. 2017; Greenwood et al. 2015). It is generally well recognised that Indigenous peoples are the most impacted and vulnerable population affected by climate change internationally and in Canada (Ford et al. 2010). It is also recognised that Indigenous peoples have contributed far less to the climate change crisis than most other groups (Whyte 2017). Climate change has exacerbated existing inequalities in profound ways, particularly along gender dimensions (Native Women's Association of Canada 2007; Vinyeta et al. 2015; Williams et al. 2018). Historical and ongoing processes of colonisation have resulted in the widespread loss of connection and access to the lands that supported traditional Indigenous environmental governance systems and that enabled adaptation to major environmental change, including climatic (Kermoal and Altamirano-Jiménez 2016; Whyte 2017). Indigenous peoples have already had to undergo immense adaption as a result of colonialism and have shown remarkable resilience in the face of dramatic environmental and climate changes.

Indigenous knowledges over the millennia have enabled resilience and adaptation to significant and devastating environmental change for Indigenous peoples. Indigenous knowledges continue to transform to support Indigenous peoples in the face of climate change (Pearce et al. 2015; Whyte 2017). Indigenous peoples in Canada have identified Indigenous knowledge systems (IKS) as central to supporting and enabling adaptive capacity, resilience and sustainability in the face of climate change (Cameron et al. 2019; McGregor 2017b). As such, the government of Canada is focusing more attention on incorporating traditional knowledge into climate change research and programmes, particularly community-based monitoring. Less attention has been directed towards how IKS can contribute to well-being and self-determined futures in climate change research. Furthermore, climate change policies and programmes have not been informed by the recognition of Aboriginal and treaty rights, including those outlined in the United Nations Declaration on the Rights of Indigenous Peoples (UNDRIP).

In terms of Indigenous knowledge research and Indigenous peoples, Cameron (2012), Todd (2015) and Whyte (2017) point out that climate change research focused on Indigenous knowledge and Western science has thus far failed to apply an analysis of historical and ongoing colonialism to understanding how climate change is impacting Indigenous communities. Such impacts are much more clearly recognised by Indigenous peoples themselves, however. In the 2002 Kimberley Declaration, for example, Indigenous contributors stated that, 'Since 1992, the ecosystems of the earth have been compounded in change. We are in crisis. We are in an accelerating spiral of climate change that will not abide by unsustainable greed' (Kimberley Declaration 2002). The Kari-Oca 2 Declaration (2012) agreed, noting that: 'The exploitation and plunder of the world's ecosystems and biodiversity, as well as the violations of inherent rights of Indigenous peoples that depend on them, have intensified.'

This chapter draws on a paper prepared for the Earth System Governance Representations and Rights of the Environment Workgroup (ESGRREW) symposium 'Addressing Climate Change: Technology, Law and Ethics' (2017) and builds upon the knowledge, experiences and perspectives shared at that event. This contribution also aims to introduce distinct considerations that must be accounted for in climate change discussions relating to Indigenous peoples. It was originally delivered in the context of a community of scholars interested and engaged in discussions relating to legal, political and technological solutions to address climate change.

My contribution was informed by my involvement in the Chiefs of Ontario (COO) and Ontario First Nation Young Peoples' Council (OFNYPC) collaboration for an Elders and Youth Gathering on climate change 'Reconnecting with Mother Earth' held in 2017 (herein referred to as the Gathering). The Gathering brought together First Nations young people, Elders and practitioners to learn from each other and share knowledge about how climate change affects the lived experiences of First Nations peoples in Ontario. It had a specific focus on IKS and how they can assist communities in dealing with climate change. The main goal of the gathering was for youth and Elders to learn from each other about climate change and develop a path forward for how to address challenges that climate change is posing to the lives and livelihoods of First Nations peoples.

This contribution will focus on the necessity of realising that understanding the relationship between Indigenous peoples and climate change in Canada requires a distinct decolonising lens to envisioning a self-determined climate change future. Further, I will analyse the tension that emerges when considerations of IKS/ traditional knowledges come into play in discussions of climate change adaptation, mitigation and resilience.

3.1 Context: Colonisation and the Anthropocene

Heather Davis and Zoe Todd, in their analysis of the role of colonisation in fully appreciating the Anthropocene, offer an invaluable diagnosis of the underlying structures, assumptions and values that underlie the contemporary planetary crisis. In their work 'On the Importance of a Date or Decolonizing the Anthropocene', they write:

Our contention here is that the Anthropocene, if explicitly linked to the beginnings of colonization, would at least assert it as a critical project that understands that the ecocidal logics that now govern our world are not inevitable or 'human nature', but are the result of a series of decisions that have their origins and reverberations in colonization. From this place, we can begin the project of decolonizing the Anthropocene. However, without recognizing that from the beginning, the Anthropocene is a universalizing project, it serves to re-invisibilize the power of Eurocentric narratives, again replacing them as the neutral and global perspective. By linking the Anthropocene with colonization, it draws attention to the violence at its core, and calls for the consideration of Indigenous philosophies and processes of Indigenous self-governance as a necessary political corrective, alongside the self-determination of other communities and societies violently impacted by the white supremacist, colonial, and capitalist logics instantiated in the origins of the Anthropocene.

(Davis and Todd 2017: 753)

Following David and Todd's analysis, Kyle Whyte asserts that:

Colonially induced environmental changes altered the ecological conditions that supported Indigenous peoples' cultures, health, economies, and political self-determination. While Indigenous peoples, as any society, have long histories of adapting to change, colonialism caused changes at such a rapid pace that many Indigenous peoples became vulnerable to harms, from health problems related to new diets to erosion of their cultures to the destruction of Indigenous diplomacy, to which they were not as susceptible prior to colonization. Indigenous peoples often understand their vulnerability to climate change as an intensification of colonially-induced environmental changes.

(Whyte 2017: 154)

Whyte lays out a set of assumptions that are critically important in understanding Indigenous self-determined climate change futures. These are:

1. Anthropogenic (human-caused) climate change is an intensification of environmental change imposed on Indigenous peoples by colonialism.
2. Renewing Indigenous knowledges, such as traditional ecological knowledge, can bring together Indigenous communities to strengthen their own self-determined planning for climate change.
3. Indigenous peoples often imagine climate change futures from their perspectives: (a) as societies with deep collective histories of having to be well-organised to adapt to environmental change and (b) as societies who must reckon with the disruptions of historic and ongoing practices of colonialism, capitalism, and industrialisation.

(Whyte 2017: 153–54)

The view offered by Kyle Whyte challenges the dominant discourse that posits Indigenous peoples solely as a vulnerable population in global and regional discussions of climate change. Whyte acknowledges that while indeed Indigenous peoples are vulnerable, they also possess experiences, derived in part from living through historical and ongoing colonialism, that have equipped them with knowledge and experience of how to survive catastrophic environmental change. In other words, Indigenous peoples have adapted and survived to this point, and have utilised their own IKS to do so.

Indigenous rights, IKS and environmental sustainability are interwoven concepts. They have been expressed by Indigenous peoples in international fora through various environmental declarations over the past three decades. Indigenous peoples have called for the recognition of IKS for decades, culminating in the acknowledgement of IKS in the United Nations Declaration on the Rights of Indigenous Peoples (UNDRIP). For example, UNDRIP, article 31 states that:

Indigenous peoples have the right to maintain, control, protect and develop their cultural heritage, traditional knowledge and traditional cultural expressions, as well as the manifestations of their sciences, technologies and cultures, including human and genetic resources, seeds, medicines, knowledge of the properties of fauna and flora, oral traditions, literatures, designs, sports and traditional games and visual and performing arts. They also have the right to maintain, control, protect and develop their intellectual property over such cultural heritage, traditional knowledge, and traditional cultural expressions.

(UNGA 2007)

Despite improvements made internationally, nationally and locally in recognising IKS as valuable in addressing challenges, IKS continue to be marginalised in relation to Western-based knowledge, particularly with regard to climate change (Samuel 2019).

Recognition of IKS has not necessarily resulted in their robust application on the ground, and Indigenous peoples continue to see their territories exploited, their rights ignored and planetary destruction ongoing. Indigenous peoples, among others, have observed that 'Imperialist globalisation exploits all that sustains life and damages the Earth. We need to fundamentally reorient production and consumption based on human needs rather than for the boundless accumulation of profit for a few' (Kari-Oca 2 Declaration 2012). IKS in their various forms challenge the dominant political and economic world order and call for fundamental change in order to achieve sustainability for all beings on Mother Earth (McGregor 2016).

There are examples where IKS have been recognised, valued and promoted, including by international organisations such as UNESCO and the United Nations Environment Programme (UNEP) (see also Nakashima et al. 2012). Despite numerous such examples of the recognition of IKS, there has thus far been limited overall impact. According to the most recent report of the Intergovernmental Panel on Climate Change (IPCC), the planet's health continues to deteriorate (IPCC 2018). The United Nations Intergovernmental Science-Policy Platform on Biodiversity and Ecosystem Services (IPBES) released its global assessment report in May 2019 and the findings are equally troubling. The IPBES report indicates that on the current trajectory, we can expect massive species extinction, with one million species potentially disappearing within a few years (IPBES 2019). Both reports call for transformative change to address the current global challenges we all face.

Thus, despite the inroads in recognising IKS in environmental governance, Indigenous assessments of the world climate and environmental crisis have found global solutions lacking (McGregor 2016). Compared to the thousands of years during which Indigenous peoples have generated IKS in order to maintain sustainable relationships with Creation, the field of IKS in the international arena is very recent. To date, research in this area has focused on how IKS can be incorporated into non-Indigenous-derived climate change. A significant concern with this approach is that:

It is born out of a fundamentally contradictory system in which climate knowledge is predominantly created by, and composed of, the voices of scientists from within those industrialized or western countries whose model of human interaction with ecological systems has so far proven to be unpromising and destructive.

(Samuel 2019: 51)

In other words, climate knowledge of Indigenous peoples and others has been marginalised in these broader processes. Indigenous peoples have not been able to contribute their own climate change knowledge, yet they do indeed have their own climate change stories, and embedded within them are solutions (McGregor and McGregor 2019).

Given this context, it is simply not rational for Indigenous peoples to rely on global, national and regional economic and political frameworks for climate justice and a sustainable future. Various international Indigenous environmental declarations over the decades have articulated similar sentiments and challenges and have offered calls to action to reorient the dominant world order's unsustainable paradigm to one that calls for living well with the Earth (McGregor 2016).

3.2 Climate Change Policy and Colonialism

As noted above, scholars have argued that dramatic and devastating environmental change is not new to Indigenous peoples, but can be understood as a continuation of the challenges many had to overcome as a result of colonialism (Reo and Parker 2013; Reo et al. 2017; Whyte 2017). Adaptation to climate and other environmental change is something that Indigenous communities have had to do in the past in order to survive to the present (Kimmerer 2013; Reo and Parker 2013). Whyte states that 'colonially-driven environmental change destroyed ecosystems on which Indigenous peoples relied, boxed Indigenous peoples into small reservations that were fractions of their original territories, or simply displaced Indigenous peoples from their homelands to new ecosystems' (2017: 155).

Indigenous peoples have thus already had to undergo immense adaption as a result of the impacts of colonialism, including alienation, dispossession and relocation from their traditional territories. The reserve system offers an example of such dispossession. A product of colonialism, the reserve system further disenfranchises Indigenous communities that are being impacted by climate change (Whyte 2017). In many places around the world, people are having to face the reality of seeing their homes and homelands disappear as a result of rising sea levels (Khedun and Singh 2014). Colonial institutions such as the reserve system frequently inhibit or prevent Indigenous peoples from adapting to such dramatic changes as they are prohibited from leaving the limited parcels of land to which they have been confined by the ruling government. The reserve system specifically limits the mobility of Indigenous peoples, a strategy they had employed to deal with environmental change historically.

Environmental change brought on by invasive species is another issue that is likely to worsen with climate change; as Reo et al. (2017) state, since the arrival of Europeans, Indigenous peoples have had to contend with and overcome many threats of invasive species. Reo et al. explain also that Indigenous people often attempt to work with non-Indigenous groups to address invasive species concerns. However, they are often ignored or engaged by others too late to have an impact on mitigation and adaptation. Indigenous nations are all too often 'consulted' *after* the problem has become out of control. Moving forward, 'Indigenous nations need to be directly involved in developing any environmental change policies that aim to generate, or happen to constrain, future options for their societies' (Reo et al. 2017: 214).

The UNDRIP offers a helpful framework for facilitating Indigenous communities' recovery from colonialist activities that limit their capacity to adapt to undesirable change. UNDRIP should form an integral part of any climate change policy or public discourse on the matter, particularly as it relates to Indigenous and human rights, yet currently it does not. This observation is true of climate change policy that is put forward both internationally (Paris Climate Agreement) and nationally (Pan-Canadian Framework on Clean Growth and Climate Change).

These policies fail to consider the rights and interests of Indigenous peoples as well as historical and ongoing processes of colonisation. It is widely recognised, internationally and in Canada, that Indigenous peoples are more vulnerable to the impacts of climate change than other peoples due to distinct connections to the natural world (Centre for Indigenous Environmental Resources (CIER) 2006). Indigenous peoples 'are among the poorest of the poor, and thus the most threatened segment of the world's population in terms of social, economic and environmental vulnerability' (International Labour Organization 2017). In Canada, the situation is similar, as Indigenous peoples are confronted with disparities and disadvantages in every conceivable indicator of well-being (Anaya 2014). Climate change will exacerbate these challenges as Indigenous peoples continue to seek justice in their relationships with dominant, broader society.

It is for this reason that I suggest that current climate policy in the Canadian context does not address in any substantial way the concerns and interests of Indigenous peoples. As long as governments in Canada (federally and provincially) continue to undermine Indigenous peoples in terms of sovereignty, authority, jurisdiction and application of Indigenous laws in relation to the land, current climate change policy will continue to fail Indigenous peoples. Colonial and later Canadian policies, laws and practices have been intended to deny Indigenous peoples sovereignty over their lands, and the climate change agenda has not sought to resolve this issue. Canada continues to rely on the exploitation of Indigenous lands and resources in order to advance its own national interests. Climate change policies and programmes at the very least should address the following three points:

1. Recognise and address ongoing colonialism that continues to alienate Indigenous peoples from their lands/waters and creates the conditions for climate change vulnerability.
2. Recognise and respect the aims of the UNDRIP in climate change efforts at every level.
3. Engage with Indigenous legal and intellectual traditions to derive environmental and climate change policy and approaches.

If environmental and/or climate policy does not address the fact that the interests and concerns of Indigenous peoples are rooted in a colonial history and self-determined climate futures must be supported, they risk further entrenching an ongoing colonial legacy that alienates Indigenous peoples from their lands and livelihood.

3.3 IKS: The Ongoing Tension

For thousands of years, Indigenous peoples generated and passed on knowledge resulting in sustainable relationships with all of Creation. Indigenous peoples have thus been seeking knowledge to support their existence as peoples and nations for millennia. IKS have enabled resilience and adaptation to significant and devastating environmental change throughout (Whyte 2017). Indigenous nations framed their IKS through their own ontological and epistemological foundations and methods (Kermoal and Altamirano-Jimenez 2016). In this sense, IKS speaks to our (as Indigenous peoples) responsibility to knowledge; it is not enough to 'obtain', 'harvest', 'acquire' or 'tap into' such knowledge. We are bound to respect the knowledge and all its sources, comprised of all our relations, both human and non-human.

IKS thus moves explicitly beyond the strictly human dimension. In the Anishinabek tradition,[1] for example, knowledge-seeking or acquisition must consider the ancestors and future generations. This ontology also includes the spirit

---

[1] The Indigenous term *Anishinabe* has various transcriptions in English: Anishinaabe, Anishinabek, Anicinape.

world, such that protocols must be respected for how we acknowledge and show respect to the spirits that can help us in our daily lives (Dumont 2006). Indigenous activist Winona LaDuke describes IKS (LaDuke uses 'TEK', or traditional ecological knowledge) as 'the culturally and spiritually based way in which Indigenous peoples relate to their ecosystems' (LaDuke 1994, 127). The major difference between Indigenous and non-Indigenous conceptions of TEK is that Indigenous peoples see TEK as much more than a 'body of knowledge'; rather, it is a 'way of living', it is about how one relates to Mother Earth (Kimmerer 2012). From an Indigenous perspective, IKS are more of a 'verb' than a noun; they are something that we do, rather than simply subject matter to study and document (McGregor 2005). IKS obligate us to act on knowledge and assume responsibility for what we know (McGregor 2017b).

Indigenous knowledges continue to transform to support Indigenous peoples in the face of climate change (Pearce et al. 2015; Whyte 2017). Indigenous peoples in Canada have identified IKS as central to supporting and enabling adaptive capacity, resilience and sustainability in the face of such change (Cameron et al. 2019; McGregor 2017b). In recent decades, climate change research involving Indigenous peoples and traditional knowledge has shown that the generation, innovation and transmission of traditional knowledge itself is threatened by climate change. Indigenous knowledge is taught, and relationships with the land are sustained, through social engagement within and among families, communities and other societies (Kermoal and Altamirano-Jiménez 2016; Tobias and Richmond 2014). The knowledge that has traditionally been passed on in support of identity, language and purpose has been disrupted at an intergenerational level (Lemke and Delormier 2017). This scenario results in a significant tension that Indigenous communities must grapple with: the intergenerational transmission and application of traditional knowledges, in the form of land-based ways of life, languages and food security systems, for example, are threatened by climate change; yet, at the same time, these same practices enable adaptation and resilience to this unique threat (McGregor 2019).

Furthermore, Cameron (2012) observes how research involving Indigenous peoples that has focused on incorporating Indigenous knowledge into Western frameworks has often failed to include colonialism in its analysis of how climate change is impacting Indigenous communities. Cameron states that, 'climate change itself, as a number of Indigenous leaders and scholars have made clear, is thoroughly tied to colonial practices, both historically and in the present, insofar as greenhouse gas production over the last two centuries hinged on the dispossession of Indigenous lands and resources' (2012: 104). When the experiences of Indigenous communities in Canada are tied to the historical impact of colonialism and its continued reverberations, it is a huge oversight to fail to incorporate the lasting impact of colonialism as it plays into the issue of climate change.

3.4 Indigenous Legal Traditions and the Well-Being of the Earth

The influence of IKS is becoming more evident in the emerging field of Indigenous law. Indigenous legal traditions have particular relevance in transforming the current unsustainable paradigm that dominates the environmental and climate change landscape. Many scholars point to the fact that the recognition of Indigenous legal traditions is key to achieving justice for both humans and non-humans. Indigenous laws flow from different sources (from the land, the Creator, the spiritual realm) and are embedded in Place, although laws can be negotiated across nations and large geographic spaces, as seen in nation-to-nation treaties. Indigenous laws convey particular types of relationships with, and responsibilities to, each other as peoples, the natural world or environment, the ancestors, the spirit world and future generations (Borrows 2010; Johnston 2006). For example, Anishinabe legal scholar John Borrows affirms that, 'Anishinaabek law provides guidance about how to theorize, practice, and order our associations with the Earth, and does so in a way that produces answers that are very different from those found in other sources' (2010: 269). In this sense, by grounding conceptions of Indigenous justice (and injustice) in Anishinabek law, possibilities open up for creativity and innovation in understanding and enacting our appropriate relations with all beings in Creation.

One defining characteristic of IKS and laws involves the conception of humanity's relationships with 'other orders of beings' (King 2013), or what Melissa Nelson (2013) calls the 'more-than-human world'. Indigenous systems draw on a set of Indigenous metaphysical, ontological and epistemological assumptions about the place of humanity in the world which describe how people should relate to all of Creation (Borrows 2010; Craft 2017). As well, many Anishinabek characterise the Earth itself as a living entity with feelings, thoughts and agency (Craft 2018). According to Craft (2014), responsibilities lie at the heart of Anishinabek legal structure. Anishinabek legal obligations and responsibilities consider relationships among all our relations, including the spirit world, the ancestors, those yet to come and other powerful beings that inhabit the peopled cosmos. These legal considerations are supported by IKS, which emphasise not just the practice of acquiring knowledge and perhaps utilising it, but also acquiring the knowledge needed to ensure harmonious and just relationships. The Anishinabek developed laws, protocols and practices over time to ensure that relationships with other orders of beings remained in balance, and that life would continue. In this sense, as knowledge can come directly from the 'natural world', all beings/entities/peoples have responsibilities to carry out to ensure the continuance of Creation to support life. Fundamentally, *Indigenous laws are meant to allow for good relations* and ultimately for each living being to live well (Craft 2014). John Borrows adds that 'Duties and obligations are central to relationships under Anishinabek law' (Borrows 2010: 59). He also states that natural law is one source of Indigenous legal orders and that natural law flows directly from experiences; including living and observing the natural world/Creation; understanding how the Earth maintains its functions; and lessons on how to read laws from the land/water/ nature.

As I have stated, Indigenous laws are not limited to relationships among persons. Anishinabe/Metis scholar Aimee Craft writes that 'Legal relationships between beings are structured on the basis of spirit. Spirit and life exist beyond the indicators of breathing entities and far beyond the human realm. For example, rocks, trees and water are all beings with whom Anishinabe are in legal relationships' (2018: 57).

The application of Indigenous legal orders to seeking justice provides an excellent example. The United Nations World Water Development Reports (2014–19) all reveal serious challenges ahead, globally, regionally and locally, in relation to climate change impacts on water security. By 2030, the world is projected to face a 40 per cent global water deficit under the business-as-usual (BAU) scenario (Water for a Sustainable Future 2015) and it is expected that climate change will exacerbate these conditions.

The application of Indigenous legal orders and knowledge systems in addressing the water crisis lies in how we understand and relate to water as a living entity. More specifically, in the Anishinabek tradition, an ontologically important aspect of Indigenous knowledge and legal systems is that the lands and the waters themselves are recognised as relatives and teachers, and they are a significant source of knowledge (Kimmerer 2013). We learn from them about how to be in the world, and they also form a critical source of law (Borrows 2010; Craft 2014). 'Responsibilities do not begin and end with the human relationships' (Craft 2018: 57). In other systems of law, water is treated as a subject, a commodity, resource or object, often to be owned, bought, sold, extracted and used (McGregor 2015; Wilson et al. 2019; Chiblow 2019).

For the Anishinabek, our sources of knowledge are thousands of years old, even millions or more when you consider some relatives. Over time, we developed our own epistemologies for understanding and relating to these relatives and teachers. Such worldviews, in which everything is alive and must be related to as such (Dumont 2006), offer distinctly alternative understandings and practices to influence currently dominant conceptions of law, knowledge and justice.

Water is understood to be a living entity, with agency and power to affect change (McGregor 2015; Chiblow 2019). '*Anishinabe – nibi inaakonigwin* (water law) tells us that water is life – *nibi onje biimassdiiziiwin*. We are born of water. Not only does it give and take life, it is also a living being in and of itself that relies on a larger web of relationships to be well and to bring wellness to other beings' (Craft 2018: 56). There are tremendous implications to be realised if Indigenous conceptions of water are taken seriously. Yet major societal transformation is required in water governance at every scale and scope for water security to be achieved for people and for water and all the life that water supports. Anishinabe scholar Deb Danard writes that the first incorrect assumption people make is that they think they can govern water. In fact, the way that people are 'governing' water (or think they are) has resulted in a global 'water crisis' as the world water reports reveal in every iteration. She argues that water governance must occur from the perspective of water or be led by water. She writes beautifully of this idea, saying:

The concept of a governance structure by the water for the water may sound impossible. However, it is within this impossibility that there is possibility. Water will continue to demonstrate its creative and destructive form, doing the work that the water was instructed to follow at the beginning of Creation, nourish life. As human beings connecting to the water inside and outside of us, we begin to understand that governance from perspective of water. In the spirit of decolonizing thought, when we connect to water we understand the desire of water to fulfil its teaching to nourish life and our desire as human beings to continue to exist from the blessing of waters generous gift. As with any gift, we are indebted to the water and should attempt to 'repay' that debt with love and gratitude. Continued attempts to rigidly and systemically control the power of water demonstrates the limitations of man-made governance as being a centric belief of man in domination over natural laws.

(Danard 2013: 119)

Water (*nibi*) must be related to in fundamentally different ways than is currently practised.[2] There exist in western legal tradition concepts such as the rights of Mother Earth, nature and legal personhood which may bear some similarities to Indigenous ontologies relating to water. Similar ideas have been taken up internationally in various fora. Most notably, the Universal Declaration of the Rights of Mother Earth reflects concepts embedded in Indigenous cosmovisions that acknowledge the Earth itself possesses being, or agency, and rights. Indigenous laws based on traditional knowledge and ways of being recognise the rights of Mother Earth through a covenant of duties, obligations and responsibilities

---

[2] Notably according to the principles of *Zaagidowin* (love/taking care of), harmony and healing.

(Borrows 2010; Craft 2018). Indigenous cultures have held these traditions since time immemorial.

Conceptual frameworks that uphold the rights of Mother Earth are gaining ground and have been enacted through constitutional and legal mechanisms in Ecuador and Bolivia. The rights of Mother earth expressed in Bolivia and Ecuador are based on Indigenous concepts of 'living well' (Chuji et al. 2019; Gudynas 2011, see also Chapter 15 in this volume). This Indigenous paradigm directly challenges the dominant neoliberal paradigm that regards nature as property and a resource. Ecuador has adopted in its Constitution specific mention of the rights of Mother Earth. Bolivia adopted the Law of Rights of Mother Earth (2010), which outlines principles that seek harmony with Mother Earth and obligations and duties of the state and people to protect and uphold the rights of Mother Earth. The law established an Office of Mother Earth to ensure compliance with the law. In New Zealand, the Whanganui River iwi and the Crown entered into an agreement to recognise the Whanganui River as a living and legal entity (Salmond 2014).

The Rio+ 20 Future We Want Declaration (2012) has also recently recognised the concept of Mother Earth (article 39). The recognition of the rights of the Mother Earth in a UN Sustainable Development Declaration (albeit limited) reflects the persistence of Indigenous peoples' influence, despite continued exclusion from the development of such documents. Indigenous peoples have been effective in opening up the dialogue of an expanded view of sustainability by sharing their understanding of Mother Earth and humanity's obligations to her.

Indigenous peoples' continued assertions of the importance of recognising the rights of Mother Earth to live are no longer simply philosophical reflections. They are becoming a reality in state legal systems. Emerging conceptual frameworks such as Earth Jurisprudence, Earth Justice and Wild Law are gaining currency and slowly becoming the topic of much dialogue and debate. Earth Jurisprudence in particular (Schillmoller and Pelizzon 2013) is a legal philosophy that emphasises the interconnections and interdependence of humanity and the natural world. It challenges the human-focused nature of current legal systems and promotes laws that protect nature in its own right (nature not as property). (See Chapters 10–12 in this volume.)

Some scholars have pointed out that extending conventional notions of environmental justice and sustainable futures to a narrative that is inclusive of non-human entities through a 'rights of nature' discourse demonstrates innovation that will lead to a more sustainable path forward (O'Donnel and Talbot-Jones 2018). Although such ideas have many critics and sceptics, they are gaining currency. Although the innovations in rights of nature discourse and earth jurisprudence are inspired or born out of, at least in part, Indigenous cosmologies, they rely on state recognition for their development. Indigenous laws and knowledges do not. They are embedded in the land, in the spirit world, and in all beings and entities themselves. Craft cautions that while the recognition of the rights of water, or personhood of water, is an important step toward much needed change, it has its limitations. She writes that:

> While pragmatically useful to contest state control over water. Western legal mechanisms can fall short of the legal relationships that currently exist between Indigenous peoples and water. The danger is that by using non-Indigenous legal mechanisms for the affirmation and framing of sacred relationships in non-Indigenous languages, we may lose the spirit of the relationships itself. Many have argued that corporations can have rights and are legal persons, so can other non-human entities. However, distinctions should be drawn between corporations (as non-living beings) and water (as living being with whom we are in relationship). Anishinabe *inaakonigewin* (law) sees water as living, spirited being.
>
> *(Craft 2019:103)*

While we are not 'there' yet, the rights of nature approach does hold potential. Indigenous scholars agree that there is room in state systems to include Indigenous legal concepts (Borrows 2010, 2019; Craft 2018).

3.5 Insights from the Elders and Youth Gathering on Climate Change

> Our laws, culture, and language are what keep us strong, and we have to ensure these are passed on and practiced by current and future generations. The stronger we are, the more able we will be to deal with climate change.
>
> We have a responsibility to teach young people so our knowledge can be passed on to future generations. That will be what keeps us strong.
>
> We need to start teaching our kids about what our ancestors know and what their reason was for living on traplines in certain seasons and by lakes etc … Most kids don't understand so we need to get those teachings to the next generation. We have knowledgeable Elders but there's a gap because kids don't know the language so we need to teach our children the language.
>
> *(McGregor, 2017a)*

Elders and youth at the gathering offered further guidance for what a self-determined climate change future might look like. Strengthening and supporting IKS should form a core aspect of climate change mitigation and adaptation strategies. Elders and youth emphasised the importance of reconnecting with our own identity, culture, traditions, history and treaty relationships as a critical adaptation strategy. Youth and Elders alike felt that through being grounded in identity, through reconnection with land, through youth cultural camps and land-based activities, youth leadership will be strengthened. It was felt that strong identity and culture contributes to individual and collective abilities to handle crises, including current and future challenges such as climate change. There was a significant willingness from the Elders to reconnect with the youth through initiatives like youth–Elder mentorship programmes.

Youth and Elders agree that learning ancestral, traditional knowledge (TK) is critical to long-term survival. IKS have ensured our collective survival and will continue to do so. Elders and youth both agree that learning our own legal traditions/systems/laws, ceremonies and knowledge is of high priority. The main way offered to learn about IKS is through land-based activities and learning ancestral languages, as these languages contain knowledge and understanding of the world that are critical to survival.

It was felt that learning about and from the land will assist First Nations in addressing climate change impacts. The current education system does not foster this type of education. Learning from Elders is a priority because First Nations want to continue to hunt, fish and gather medicines (practise the way of life that sustained them for thousands of years). The key to First Nations survival is not to replace traditional activities on the land, but to revitalise the ability to exercise traditional roles and responsibilities to the Earth, to exercise treaty rights, enact sovereignty and self-determination. Historical and ongoing colonialism continues to impact communities and their well-being. Many communities experience crisis after crisis and continued disruption of their connection to the Mother Earth through resource development/extraction. Historical and ongoing colonialism continues to impact communities and their well-being. Elders and youth indicated that Indigenous peoples have to focus on life, on our Indigenous legal systems and our own laws, protocols, traditions, knowledge and spirituality because the other laws and governance regimes are failing. Indigenous peoples have to rely on their strengths.

Asserting and enacting First Nations sovereignty and self-determination are especially relevant in climate change discussions. Several areas were identified as key elements in allowing Indigenous peoples to take care of themselves, others and Mother Earth. These are: culture–language–life; ceremonies–spirituality–mind; governance; water–land–life; community–social–education; economy; health–wellness. Elders and youth emphasised full support for health and wellness leadership programming related to reclaiming traditional roles and responsibilities. It was felt that such programming would be critical to climate change adaptation in First Nations communities. The need for further discussion and education was apparent as many participants continue to experience first-hand the impacts of climate change, made all the worse by historical and present environmental challenges (e.g. due to the legacy of damaging forestry and mining practices, including degraded water).

In many respects, the Elders and youth at the gathering were calling for a decolonising of current legal and policy regimes that continue to undermine Indigenous self-determination and thus capacity to adapt to climate change. Elders and youth pointed out that there is no single solution to climate change and that creativity and innovation are required on an ongoing basis.

Perhaps the most critical recommendations made at the Gathering centred around re-establishing the connection between youth and Elders. Intergenerational learning was regarded as vital for climate change adaptation. Youth and Elders agreed that learning ancestral traditional knowledge (TK) is critical to our long-term survival. IKS served our ancestors and communities in the past and will continue to do so. Opportunities to learn and enact responsibilities form an important aspect of adaptation and building on strengths. Enacting responsibilities involves continued and sustained advocacy to protect Mother Earth.

Gathering participants expressed concerns regarding unsustainable development in their territories. Industrial contamination (e.g. from forestry, mining, hydroelectric development) continues to degrade the landscape and has had tremendous negative impacts on First Nations people. Participants also pointed out the impact of such activities on the plants, wildlife, fish and Mother Earth in general. These activities continue and unless they are dealt with, First Nations will continue to face environmental injustices. Participants pointed out that climate change makes all past and present environmental challenges worse.

Governments (federal and provincial) continue to let environmental destruction and degradation occur, with future government-supported threats looming, such as the siting of high-level nuclear waste on First Nation lands. Governments expect First Nations to continue to bear the burden of negative impacts. As Elders and political leadership pointed out, environmental destruction is directly related to the economic, social and cultural challenges First Nation communities continue to experience.

Therefore, to adequately address climate change, First Nations must continue to advocate to protect the lands and waters (Mother Earth) and assert treaty rights. It is not an option; it is a responsibility. Advocacy also includes advancing First Nation education (including public schools where most children/youth attend school) that includes teaching of First Nation history, treaties, culture, traditions and knowledge. Elders and youth also mentioned that advocacy occurs in research and program development. There is an enormous lack of research and programmes that are First Nation-specific. Mainstream or government-sponsored plans, strategies and programs intended to address climate change generally do not serve First Nations.

3.7 Self-Determined Climate Change Futures

When industry comes in they abide by provincial and federal laws while First Nations people go by old ways and there is anger over government/industry telling people to follow regulations.

When we talk to Elders, they tell us that change is happening with the land and how much has changed with the land including loss. We are told what we can do to bring it back.

(McGregor, 2017a)

The rationale for an exploration of a distinct Indigenous climate change future stems from the view that adaptation in any meaningful way must originate from Indigenous peoples themselves. In Canada, at least, solutions conceived by others (usually the state, but not exclusively so) aimed at addressing the so-called Indian problem have had devastating consequences. In 1996, following five years of study, the Royal Commission on Aboriginal Peoples concluded that 'the main policy direction, pursued for more than 150 years, first by colonial then by Canadian governments, has been wrong' (RCAP 1996). Two decades later, the 2015 Truth and Reconciliation Commission (TRC) drew similar conclusions, highlighting the colonialism and racism that continue to plague Indigenous aspirations on every conceivable front (Anaya 2014). From an Indigenous point of view, climate change 'solutions' that perpetuate ongoing colonial processes constitute a grave injustice. Renewing Indigenous knowledges can bring together Indigenous communities to strengthen their own self-determined planning for climate change.

Elders and youth alike agree that IKS can assist Indigenous communities in strengthening their capacity to formulate self-determined solutions. When elements of IKS are extracted from Indigenous communities to serve a climate change agenda not of their own choosing or making, this constitutes another form of colonialism. Self-determined solutions must emerge from Indigenous communities directly, and as such are a distinct and necessary alternative to the supposed 'decolonising' of existing climate change policies and programmes being undertaken by certain governments, academic institutions, and others ('colonisers'). Suggestions from the Gathering around effectively decolonising climate change discussions include the need to:

- Engage Indigenous peoples as nations (at all scales and levels). Indigenous peoples should not be an 'afterthought' or an 'add-on'. They are not 'interest groups' or 'stakeholders'.
- Respect and recognise IKS (or TEK) holistically, not just as data to include in other models, paradigms or research. Support Indigenous-led climate change research. Adopt a knowledge-sharing paradigm and reject the predominant 'data

extraction' model that characterises much climate change research that attempts to incorporate IKS.

- Recognise that climate change is not compartmentalised; it impacts every aspect of the lives of Indigenous peoples. Climate change solutions that focus on one aspect only, e.g. food security, while not addressing water security, community well-being are short-sighted and will have limited utility in Indigenous communities.
- Recognise that Indigenous communities have been resilient and have coped with, adapted to and survived through devastating losses due to environmental change.
- Recognise that both environmental resilience and impacts are gendered and thus adaptation strategies must account for gender.
- Support the recovery of traditional systems of governance, land-based activities and Indigenous conceptions of well-being.

These suggestions are not exhaustive, but they require dramatically different climate change solutions than are currently proposed by governments at every level. Recommendations from Indigenous peoples call for an end to colonisation and the devastating harm it causes Indigenous peoples. Insights from the Elders and youth point to an urgent need for a radically different set of political, governing and legal orders to address climate change. The status quo is failing miserably, as each new IPCC report reveals. As peoples who have suffered incredible losses due to historical and ongoing colonialism in all its various forms, including massive environmental change, Indigenous peoples continue to seek a future that sustains all life on earth. Perhaps it is time to really listen.

References

Anaya, J. (2014). *The Situation of Indigenous Peoples in Canada*. Report of the Special Rapporteur on the Rights of Indigenous Peoples.

Borrows, J. (2010). *Canada's Indigenous Constitution*. Toronto: University of Toronto Press.

Borrows, J. (2019). *Law's Indigenous Ethics*. Toronto: University of Toronto Press.

Cameron, E. S. (2012). Securing Indigenous politics: A critique of the vulnerability and adaptation approach to the human dimensions of climate change in the Canadian Arctic. *Global Environmental Change* 22: 103–14, https://doi.org/10.1016/j .gloenvcha.2011.11.004

Cameron, L., D. Courchene, S. Ijaz and I. Mauro (2019). The Turtle Lodge: Sustainable self-determination in practice. *AlterNative: An International Journal of Indigenous Peoples* 15: 13–21, https://doi.org/10.1177/1177180119828075

Center for Indigenous Environmental Resources (CIER) (2006). *How Climate Change Uniquely Impacts the Social, Physical, and Cultural Aspects of First Nations*. Prepared for the Assembly of the First Nations. Winnipeg: Center for Indigenous Environmental Resources.

Chiblow, S. (2019). Anishinabek Women's Nibi Giikendaaswin (Water Knowledge). *Water* 11(2): 209.

Chuji, M., G. Rengifo and E. Gudynas (2019). Buen Vivir. In A. Kothari, A. Salleh, A. Escobar, F. Demaria and A. Acosta (eds.), *Pluriverse: A Post-Development Dictionary*. New Delhi: Tulika Books, 111–14.

Craft, A. (2014). *Anishinaabe Nibi Inaakonigewin Report: Reflecting the Water Laws Research Gathering*. Retrieved from University of Manitoba Human Rights Research (CHRR) and the Public Interest Law Centre (PILC), http//static1 .squarespace.com

Craft, A. (2018). Navigating our ongoing sacred legal relationship with Nibi (water). In *UNDRIP Implementation More Reflections on the Braiding of International, Domestic and Indigenous Laws*. Waterloo: Centre for International Governance Innovation, 53–61.

Craft, A. (2017). Giving and receiving life from Anishinaabe nibi inaakonigewin (our water law) research. In J. Thorpe, S. Rutherford and A. Sandberg (eds.), *Methodological Challenges in Nature: Culture and Environmental History Research*. New York: Routledge, 105–19.

Craft, A. (2017). "Navigating Our Ongoing Sacred Legal Relaionship with Nibi (Water)." In J. Borrows, L. Chartrand, O. Fitzgerald, R. Schwartz eds. Braiding legal Orders: Implementing the UNDRIP (Waterloo: CIGI), 101–110.

Danard, D. W. (2013). Be the water. *Canadian Woman Studies* 30(2): 115–20.

Davis, H. and Todd, Z. (2017). On the Importance of a date or decolonizing the Anthropocene. *ACME: An International Journal of Critical Geographies* 16(4): 761–80.

Delormier, T., K. Horn-Miller, A. M. McComber and K. Marquis (2017). Reclaiming food security in the Mohawk community of Kahnawake through Haudenosaunee responsibilities. *Maternal and Child Nutrition* 13(S3): 1–14. https://doi.org/10.1111/mcn.12556

Dumont, J. (2006). *Indigenous Intelligence*. Sudbury, ON: University of Sudbury.

Ford, J. D., L. Berrang-Ford, M. King and C. Furgal (2010). Vulnerability of Aboriginal health systems in Canada to climate change. *Global Environmental Change* 20: 668–80, https://doi.org/10.1016/j.gloenvcha.2010.05.003

Greenwood, M., S. de Leeuw, N. M. Lindsay and C. Reading (eds.) (2015). *Determinants of Indigenous Peoples' Health*. Toronto: Canadian Scholars' Press.

Gudynas, E. (2011). Buen Vivir: Today's tomorrow. *Development* 54(4): 441–47, https://doi.org/10.1057/dev.2011.86

Inter-Agency Support Group on Indigenous People's Issues (IASG) (2008). *Collated Paper on Indigenous Peoples and Climate Change, United Nation Permanent Forum on Indigenous Issues*. New York: United Nations Economic and Social Council.

International Labour Organization (2017). *Indigenous People and Climate Change, Gender, Equality and Diversity Branch*. Geneva: International Labour Organization.

IPBES (2019). Summary for policymakers of the global assessment report on biodiversity and ecosystem services of the Intergovernmental Science-Policy Platform on Biodiversity and Ecosystem Services. Bonn: IPBES Secretariat.

IPCC (2018). Summary for policymakers. In V. Masson-Delmotte, P. Zhai, H.-O. Pörtner, et al. (eds.). *Special Report: Global Warming of 1.5 °C*. Geneva: World Meteorological Organization, www.ipcc.ch/sr15/chapter/spm/

Johnston, D. (2006). *Respecting and Protecting the Sacred* [Research Paper, prepared for the Ipperwash Inquiry], www.attorneygeneral.jus.gov.on.ca

Kari-Oca 2 Declaration (2012). Presented at the Indigenous Peoples' Global Conference on RIO + 20 and Mother Earth, Rio de Janeiro, Brazil.

Kermoal, N. and I. Altamirano-Jiménez (eds.) (2016). *Living on the Land: Indigenous Women's Understanding of Place*. Edmonton, AB: AU Press.

Khedun, C. and V. Singh (2014). Climate change, water, and health: A review of regional challenges. *Water Quality, Exposure, and Health* 6: 7–17, https://doi.org/10.1007/s12403-013-0107-1

Kimberley Declaration (2002). International Indigenous Peoples' Summit, Kimberley, South Africa.

Kimmerer, R. W. (2012). Searching for synergy: Integrating traditional and scientific ecological knowledge in environmental science education. *Journal of Environmental Studies and Sciences* 2(4): 317–23.

Kimmerer, R. W. (2013). *Braiding Sweetgrass: Indigenous Wisdom, Scientific Knowledge and the Teachings of Plants.* Harmondsworth, UK: Penguin.

King, C. (2013). *Balancing Two Worlds: Jean-Baptiste Assiginak and the Odawa Nation 1768–1866.* Saskatoon, SK: Cecil King.

LaDuke, W. (1994). Traditional ecological knowledge and environmental futures. *Colorado Journal of International Environmental Law and Policy* 5: 127.

Lemke, S. and T. Delormier (2017). Indigenous peoples' food systems, nutrition, and gender: Conceptual and methodological considerations. *Maternal and Child Nutrition* 13(s3): 1–12. https:// doi.org/10.1111/mcn.12499

McGregor, D. (2015). Indigenous women, water justice and Zaagidowin (love, women and water. *Canadian Woman Studies/Les Cahiers de La Femme* 30(2/3): 71–78.

McGregor, D. (2016). Living well with the earth: Indigenous rights and the environment. In D. Short and C. Lennox (eds.), *Handbook of Indigenous Rights.* New York: Routledge, 167–80.

McGregor, D. (2017a). *Taking Care of Each Other: Taking Care of Mother Earth.* Summary and Highlight Report, 'Reconnecting with Mother Earth' Elders and Youth Gathering on Climate Change November 4th–5th, 2017. Chiefs of Ontario.

McGregor, D. (2017b). Anishinabe knowledge and water: Honouring our responsibilities. In S. Hutchings and A. Morrison (eds.), *Indigenous Knowledges: Proceedings of the Water Sustainability and Wildfire Mitigation Symposia.* Adelaide: University of South Australia, 93–121.

McGregor, D. (2019). Reconciliation, colonialism and climate change. In C. Tuohy, S. Borwien, P. Loewen and A. Potter (eds.), *Policy Transformation in Canada: Is the Past Prologue?* Toronto: University of Toronto Press, 139–47.

McGregor, D. and H. McGregor (2019). All our relations: Climate change storytellers. In C. Sandilands (ed.), *Rising Tides: Reflections for Climate Changing Times.* Halfmoon Bay, BC: Caitlin Press, 125–29.

Nakashima, D., K. G. McLean, H. Thulstrup, A. R. Castillo and J. Rubis, United Nations University Staff and United Nations Educational (2012). *Weathering Uncertainty: Traditional Knowledge for Climate Change Assessment and Adaptation.* Tokyo: United Nations University.

Native Women's Association of Canada (2007). *Aboriginal Women and Climate Change.*

Nelson, M. (2013). The hydromythology of the Anishinaabeg: Will Mishipizhu survive climate change, or is he creating it? In J. Doerfler, N. J. Sinclair and H. K. Stark (eds.), *Centering Anishinaabeg Studies: Understanding the World through Stories.* East Lansing: Michigan State University, 213–33.

O'Donnell, E. and J. Talbot-Jones (2018). Creating legal rights for rivers: Lessons from Australia, New Zealand, and India. *Ecology and Society* 23(1): 7. https://doi.org/10.5751/ES-09854-230107

Pearce, T., J. Ford, A. Cunsolo Willox and B. Smit (2015). Inuit traditional ecological knowledge (TEK), subsistence hunting and adaptation to climate change in the Canadian Arctic. *Arctic* 68(2): 233–45.

Reo, N. and A. Parker (2013). Re-thinking colonialism to prepare for the impacts of rapid environmental change. *Climate Change* 120(3): 671–82, https://doi.org/10.1007/s10584-013-0783-7

Reo, N. J., K. Whyte, D. Ranco, J. Brandt, E. Blackmer and B. Elliott (2017). Invasive species, Indigenous stewards, and vulnerability discourse. *American Indian Quarterly* 41(3): 201–23.

Royal Commission on Aboriginal Peoples (RCAP) (1996). *People to People, Nation to Nation: Highlights from the Report of the Royal Commission on Aboriginal Peoples.* Ottawa, ON: Ministry of Supply and Services.

Salmond, A. (2014). Tears of Rangi: Water power, and people in New Zealand. *HAU: Journal of Ethnographic Theory* 4(3): 285–309.

Samuel, S. (2019). Witsaja iki, or the good life in Ecuadorian Amazonia: Knowledge co-production for climate resilience. In International Labour Organization & School of Geography and the Environment (ed.), *Indigenous Peoples and Climate Change Emerging Research on Traditional Knowledge and Livelihoods.* Geneva: International Labour Organization.

Schillmoller, A. and A. Pelizzon (2013). Mapping the terrain of earth jurisprudence landscape, thresholds and horizons. *Environmental and Earth Law Journal* 3(1): art. 1.

Tobias, J. K. and C. A. M. Richmond (2014). That land means everything to us as Anishinaabe . . .: Environmental dispossession and resilience on the North Shore of Lake Superior. *Health Place* 29: 26–33.

Todd, Z. (2015). Indigenizing the Anthropocene. In H. Davis and E. Turpin (eds.), *Art in the Anthropocene: Encounters among Aesthetics, Politics, Environments and Epistemologies.* London: Open Humanities Press, 241–54.

United Nations General Assembly (UNGA) (2007). United Nations Declaration on the Rights of Indigenous Peoples.

Vinyeta, K., K. Powys Whyte and K. Lynn (2015). *Climate Change through an Intersectional Lens: Gendered Vulnerability and Resilience in Indigenous Communities in the United States.* Portland, OR: US Department of Agriculture, Forest Service, Pacific Northwest Research Station.

Whyte, K. (2017). Indigenous climate change studies: Indigenizing futures, decolonizing the Anthropocene. *English Language Notes* 55: 153–62.

Williams, L., A. Fletcher, C. Hanson, J. Neapole and M. Pollack (2018). *Women and Climate Change Impacts and Action in Canada: Feminist, Indigenous, and Intersectional Perspectives.* Canadian Research Institute for the Advancement of Women and the Alliance for Intergenerational Resilience.

Wilson, N. J., L. M. Harris, A. Joseph-Rear, J. Beaumont and T. Satterfield (2019). Water is medicine: Reimagining water security through Tr'ondëk Hwëch'in relationships to treated and traditional water sources in Yukon, Canada. *Water* 11(3): 624, https://doi.org/10.3390/w11030624

4

Our Relationship with the Land

An Ecology of Perception

MARTEN BERKMAN

Introduction

How do we perceive the rest of nature meaningfully from the vantage point of our manufactured spaces? This is the question which has inspired my art practice for many years, and stems from early and formative experiences with the web of life. Whether it is the life teeming in a freshwater spring, nesting in forests, blooming in oceans or surviving tenaciously on the remote reaches of the planet, we impact this life that so many of us probably never see first-hand. Our impact is from the manifestation of our nature, which is creative, industrious and prolific. Unfortunately, our impact threatens the stability and viability of the only biosphere we can call home. How can human nature be connected to, instead of orphaned from, the rest of nature? No matter how much data we acquire about the crises we create for ecosystems, there remains tremendous inertia to apply the principal remedy: changing our behaviour. This implies the necessity to expand our focus from quantitative deduction of the problem and solutions, to ensuring we have the inner connections and relationships necessary for qualitative response to environmental stress. Evolution on a cultural level will not happen unless affected on the level that drives our deepest 'decision-making': our hearts. What is our contemporary conduit for a sensitive relationship with the earth? If the way we see the world informs the way we treat the world, is perception the key to a maturing relationship with it? This question inspires my artistic practice, which I call 'Remote sensibility: the ecology of perception'.

4.1 Origins and Meaning of Remote Sensibility

Remote sensing is the process of detecting and monitoring the physical characteristics of an area by measuring its reflected and emitted radiation at a distance from the targeted area. Special cameras collect

> remotely sensed images of the Earth, which help researchers 'sense' things about the Earth.
>
> *(definition courtesy of the US Geological Survey)[1]*

My connections with the rest of the natural world have been innate since childhood, and have pervaded my work throughout my life. Yet I experience an irony every day, the seeming dichotomy in our culture between the human and the more-than-human. On the one hand, we can be passionate about wilderness, and on the other, passionate about our industriousness in turning that nature into commodities we need. Both perspectives are real, and often mutually exclusive.

Or are they? Is not our industriousness our own very nature? Is our lifeway essentially dissimilar from any other species finding or creating its niche on the planet? Where then does the duality and conflict take place? When does human nature become dissonant with the rest of nature?

We care for what has meaning for us, and the meaning of landscapes may be as diverse as the people on the planet. Visual art, photography and film have been wonderful vehicles for me to reflect on the meanings I discover, and to share these meanings with those who have shared experiences of wonder and humility with the Earth.

But I appreciate there are many who do not have this shared experience of 'nature', and for whom the photograph of a place might not have more meaning than the intellectually *associated* meaning of symbol or character (e.g. when used in a shampoo advertisement or superhero film), or the *aesthetic* experienced in the interaction of light and dark, composition and form (i.e. the experience of visual pleasure, without context of its evolutionary origins). Is this dearth of direct experience responsible for our lack of appreciation for the larger systems we are a part of, or of the impact of our behaviour on them?

In first world global urban industrial culture, experiences of undomesticated habitats may be no more immediate than through an aeroplane window or the background scenery of an advertisement for a car. Even those of us living in or close to wild areas may have a livelihood dependent on the unravelling of ecological systems with our industrial capacity. Quantitative data collected for land use planning and resource extraction may be as technologically mediated, precluding qualitative knowledge which would only be arrived at with our head, heart and feet on the ground. In each of these instances, our perspectives of and relationships with place are shaped by the technology we create, surround ourselves with and use. In other words, the tools and living spaces it has been our nature to create, may perceptually separate us from the nature we are indelibly a part of.

---

[1] See definition at www.usgs.gov

Culture reflects values celebrated in our lifeway. How can we on the one hand enjoy pretty pictures of wilderness, yet perpetuate an industrial practice which diminishes and distances us from the subject of what we consider 'aesthetic'? For a culture physically removed from large and vibrant ecological systems, can art provide the vehicle for discovering meaning in the remote environments we are intimately connected to but never experience first-hand? As an artist, what visual language and tools can I use to effectively open a door to discovering meaning in the landscape for a largely Western, technological culture which is separated from it? In a technological society, are technological interfaces our windows of perception into the material and immaterial qualities of the world? Like the fire ignited in our soul by music or poetry, is there a contemporary visual palette which will ignite our consciousness to immaterial experiences, even ancestral memories, before we have ever got our feet dirty in a wetland or touched the sky from a mountain top? What is the means to our remote sensibility?

These questions have been a constant throughout my life, leading to my artistic practice. To provide insight into its origins, meaning, experimentation and implications, I will share the journey that took me there.

Artwork 4.1 Remote Sensibility V (tundra pond, Peel watershed, Yukon; Ottawa, capital of Canada), stereo 3D video installation 2009.
How do we dissolve the perceptive and emotive distance between remote geography and the manufactured spaces which impact it?

4.2 From Domesticated to Unconditioned

My own cultural roots originate in the Netherlands, one of the most domesticated and densely populated countries on the earth. This is literally a manufactured landscape, a condition shared by over half of humanity. It was from this backdrop that both my parents were inspired to move to Canada after the Second World War, where they met and started a family. When I was 4, they bought land in the countryside which was to be my playground, where I had formative years of play and discovery close to life and the land. Whether through the material sustenance of fish, raspberries, fiddleheads and groundhog, or the sensual stimulation of swimming, fireflies, aurora and autumn, these years are characterised by unmediated engagement in the rest of nature. I vividly remember one afternoon as we picked raspberries at the intersection of grassland and forest, along the walls built of stones left by glaciers. Here I crawled and gazed under the canopy of delicate leaves to discover a veritable universe: small lichens, mushrooms, mouse dens, and insects; an overwhelming richness and diversity of colours, patterns, forms and scale. And each element was a manifestation of and vessel for life.

This experience of wonder was echoed in a freshwater spring, where plants, insects and animals of extraordinary diversity formed a constellation of life from the micro to the macro in a cubic metre of water. Even when life was stilled in the depths of winter, beauty was elicited by the elements, as exquisite snow crystals tumbled and gathered in the wind, forming sinuous drifts that engaged like sculpture. It was a sense of wonder which I would always carry with me. And it is this experience of wonder which I would like to acknowledge and revisit – how it informs for us, and illuminates, different ways of knowing.

As a child, I felt challenged by the perfection of nature contrasting with the seeming imperfection of our human behaviour. If I knocked a stone over in the woods, I felt my conscience could live with it if another animal could have done it as well. However, human endeavour, such as building a road through those same woods, seemed at the expense of the natural order, and was difficult to accept, to reconcile. The transition from rural to urban seemed disjointed: our creations, manifestations of short-term ideas, seemed incredibly clumsy and awkward in the bigger picture. Classmates in the suburbs laughed at the demise of an animal impacted by a vehicle, when I grieved. While I wandered wetlands on a Saturday morning, friends were watching cartoons while eating chocolate-covered sugarbombs – and I was very envious! How was I to reconcile these human and more-than-human worlds? How was I to reconcile human nature with the rest of nature?

I sought answers by studying visual arts and geography, and found insight, inspiration and challenges in both. In geography, I noted how in studies of

Artwork 4.2 Untitled (barn window), Lithograph, 38×56 cm, 1987

ecosystems and humans, overwhelming arguments for changing our behaviour were quantitative: the measurements of ecological impacts due to our behaviour, and the practical changes necessary to mitigate them. Yet this knowledge was old. The numbers may have grown, but cause and effect were not new, nor was our ongoing challenge in mitigation. I felt that for our behaviour to evolve, change had to happen on several different levels.

Though led to the arts by my heart, I was at times stunned by the assault of art that needed to shock, or had an almost clinical separation from subject for the sake of irony. I observed an artist creating a work with a foetus skeleton inside a deep fryer, and observed my own recoil at life creating a representation of its self-consuming immolation. Yet I also realised that this was perhaps a metaphor for many contradictions in our nature, and an essential manifestation of the inner world of this artist. It has struck me how art, that unpredictable emanation of what our creativity demands of us, is an essential inner barometer. It fathoms depths of consciousness and unconsciousness beyond our finite intellect. Whether from shock or wonder, it is an inner barometer I trust. It is interesting how the 'readings' of this inner barometer were essential wind to fill my sails, and perhaps speaks to what ultimately reaches, touches, drives us all.

At the same time as undertaking my undergraduate studies, I was making a concerted effort to discover the earth, and perhaps myself along the way. I had a yearning for remote places, far from the domestication and conditioning of my species' impact. I returned from Ungava Bay to paint whale bones that seemed to course with the energy of life that had run through them. A walk across the Arctic Circle inspired lithographs of stark granite, fresh from the epic effects of tectonic and glacial forces. I was also discovering the camera as a wonderful sketchbook, a very portable instrument I could take with me on my excursions.

Walks in remote places had sometimes been limited by how much food and fuel one could carry, so I searched for places to travel by kayak, and was delighted how rivers in Patagonia could take one deep into otherwise relatively inaccessible

Artwork 4.3 Ungava Whale, acrylic on canvas, 137×165 cm, 1986

Artwork 4.4 Untitled (snow, granite, Baffin Island, Nunavut), lithograph, 61×85 cm, 1986

sections of desert. In a quiet journey into the Patagonian badlands, I revelled in the silence and light. But in this desert, other dimensions were revealed. Where sediments had eroded, dinosaur bones and ancient forests protruded from hillsides. Literally seventy million years of life lay before me like an open book. After several days camping in one location, I noticed strange shards of stone quite different from the surrounding rock. It turned out that camp was in the middle of a Palaeolithic toolmaking site, littered with shards of obsidian. This was confirmed by a broken arrow tip, likely damaged in a hunt and discarded. It was a humbling and awe-inspiring moment to be camping in the same location as distant cousins, who were using the technologies of our ancient shared relatives. I discovered later in Puerto Natales that these were the Aónikenk, more commonly known as the Tehuelche, and found a photograph in the museum of these people. Apparently, they had been forced from the land they lived and hunted on, and were eventually wiped out in many areas from the cumulative effects of European colonisation. For me, it was an intimate, sobering and humbling encounter.

Continuing the strategy of exploring the desert by following water courses led to a hike along a river fed by the snow melt from Bolivia, which carved a beautiful valley near San Pedro de Atacama in Chile. High on the valley rim were more stone tools. Judging by the aeolian erosion, some were very old. In this same desert is Chuquicamata, the largest open pit copper mine in the world. In this beehive of industrious activity, I recognised that this was an extension of the very chippings in stone I had encountered in Patagonian and Atacama deserts, practised by ancestors for thousands upon thousands of years. This industrious nature seems to be an indelible part of human nature. Yet through the escalation and scale of this industriousness, humans have come into conflict with the rest of the living world.

I was honoured to receive an invitation to do a master's in geography, and my interest would have been ecology and adaptation. However, my intuition compelled me to explore other remote and extreme environments on the planet, and contemplate these journeys artistically. I joined climbing expeditions in the Himalayas, and organised several long walks in solitude and with a friend in the High Arctic. It was on Ellesmere Island that I had another epiphany. For here, life was pushed to such extremes that it could not be taken for granted. Once again I stared back through time, as carboniferous layers of rock released wood still organic after ten million years. It was then that I came across a circle of stones, likely of Dorset or Thule origin, likely a thousand years old.

It was joyous to imagine a family living, children playing, in this location on the edge of possibility. Around me, musk oxen grazed on the whispers of vegetation supported by the breath of water released in the short moment of summer. How the hares, arctic fox and other mammals survive such a veritable vacuum of energy filled me with awe. It struck me then just how precious, and precarious, this biosphere is. Like the limits of the biosphere which we quickly reach when we climb just a few kilometres vertically, a matter of a few degrees latitude towards the poles puts life on the threshold of possibility. In the vast silence, gazing

Artwork 4.5 Stone Circle (Thule tent ring, Ellesmere Island, Nunavut), silver print from 120 mm film, 23×30 cm, 1990

through time, touching the edge of where life was possible, my heart brimmed with delight.

> the air is full,
> and empty.
> ridges embrace the sky.
> in a chasm
> of silence
> a raven's wings
> pass by.

(Marten Berkman, 1990)

How could life, and the places which support it, ever be taken for granted?

A portfolio of photographs from these high Arctic walks was published as the book *Chasms of Silence*. Canadian poet and novelist Anne Michaels wrote the foreword, where she ruminated on the threshold of negation reflected in these elemental images:

when the human animal, dying at high speed, seems to hold a version of infinity ...

The power in this journey for me was the departure from the familiar, the habituated mind set free in an environment that I was not conditioned for.

Artwork 4.6 The Wind Brings Us Our Dreams (candle ice, Lake Hazen, Ellesmere Island, Nunavut) silver print from 120 mm film, 23×30 cm, 1990

The yearning created by this journey was to share the depth of experience, the profound invigoration of perspective, born from extreme geographies. However, I questioned if this would translate for a person without the shared, direct experiences of stones, bones and wind.

As a photographer, what was going through my head and heart was how to capture the very sense of presence in this profound place, so full in its elementality, emptiness and silence. This begged representation of dimensionality, possibly through holography, but practical means escaped me. This intuition was to be realised many years later in concert with Anne's prose when evolving technology would expand the visual palette.

4.3 Together Today for Our Children Tomorrow

I found my home in the north. When I discovered the Yukon, I also found the space, the silence and the elementality which were my muses. Here in a world between the extremes of the high arctic and the lakes and woods of the south, I built a cabin and settled in the boreal forest. I was soon enjoying the very welcoming community of 35,000 people in a territory larger than Germany. I did not hesitate joining friends exploring mountains, lakes and rivers, humbled by a land where thousands of caribou could migrate by our camp in a single day, where sun never set in summer, where aurora danced in the energy vacuum of winter.

The humility I found seemed in stark contrast to many cultural expressions about the wild, which seemed more about egos dominating the wilderness than our connections with it. The digital revolution enabled small video cameras to reach the hands of independent producers and artists like me. Thus I was inspired to create my film *Cascade de Lumière*, in which I documented a journey in the arctic down the Firth River to the Beaufort Sea, but focused on the inner journey this river took us on. Needing to express more than what we could literally see, I experimented with choreography[2] in seeking a better language for the depiction of our inner journey. I discovered how different art forms could speak eloquently for the ineffable.

I was asked if I would like to contribute photography to raising public awareness about a pristine watershed in the heart of the Yukon territory, the Peel watershed, and I jumped at the opportunity. This large watershed holds many overlapping values: traditional territory to four First Nations (Na-Cho Nyäk Dun, Tetlit Gwich'in, Vuntut Gwich'in, Tr'ondëk Hwëch'in); ecological integrity; subsistence; beauty; tourism; and oil, gas and mineral values. At that time, the Peel watershed was about to be the subject of a land use planning process, a requisite of the Umbrella Final Agreement between the territorial and federal governments and Yukon First Nations. The land use plan was an incredible process, where all stakeholders were given opportunity to have a voice. In a territory where non-Indigenous culture was historically motivated by resource extraction, from furs to the Klondike Gold Rush, to modern mines for gold, lead and zinc, Indigenous voices now have a legal framework within which to be effectively heard, expressing values born of eons living intimately and interdependently on the land.

The path to the Umbrella Final Agreement had been started many years earlier. In 1973, Chief Elijah Smith and representatives of the Yukon Native Brotherhood met with then Prime Minister Pierre Trudeau in Ottawa. They presented him a document which championed principles born of a relationship with the land that was countless generations old, expressed aptly in its title 'Together Today for Our Children Tomorrow'. It would be the guiding document in negotiating land claims and self-governing agreements between the Yukon First Nations and the federal and territorial governments. In keeping with the inclusive thinking which characterises Indigenous communities, it championed the requisite to hear all voices in land use planning processes.

---

[2] Choreography is the movements used by dancers, especially in performing ballet or the art of planning such movements (*Cambridge Online Dictionary* (08.11.2019)).

Artwork 4.7 Snake River Stones, 35 mm colour transparency, 2003

I witnessed first-hand the public consultation sessions for the Peel watershed where voices, both Indigenous and non-Indigenous, young and old, from many walks of life, had a safe venue to stand and be heard for the values that were their reality. This was in stark contrast to only a few years previously when proposed federal regulations on placer mining operations to protect stream water quality were met by threats and intimidation, including towards members of the public and NGOs who expressed their support. In the Peel planning process, it was extraordinary to hear the passion of people standing up for the values they identified in the land. Unfortunately, the government of the time rejected the plan arrived at through this planning process, and came up with their own plan which protected far less of the land than the First Nations wanted and the Commission recommended. It did favour the desires of one stakeholder group, the resource sector. I respect the validity of this mineral industry: it is a reflection of a significant part of our nature. Mineral extraction is as natural to us as our first chippings in stone, and almost all the technology we depend on is made from mineral products, the fruit of curiosity, problem-solving, passion and creativity. However, cultural, ecological, spiritual and sustainable economic interests were given second ranking to the resource industry values. Is this a balanced reflection of our nature?

Four First Nations and two conservation societies then partnered to challenge the government's plan. Through appeals and counter-appeals, the dispute went all the way to the Supreme Court of Canada.[3] In the end, respect was championed, and the original land use plan arrived at through consultation has now been accepted. It had got this far through incredible passion and commitment by many people, across many walks of life and cultures, who spoke for justice and fairness,

---

[3] *First Nation of Nacho Nyak Dun* v. *Yukon*, 2017 SCC 58.

because they had a safe place to do so. Thanks to the legacy and vision of the Yukon First Nations manifesto from 1973, that 'safe place' exists as a legal condition of land use planning. The document expressed Indigenous values that I believe non-Indigenous cultures need to learn from: the recognition that deep, resilient solutions come from inclusive, circular processes. This is a wake-up call to the fact that we all originally come from the land, and are orphaned as long as we live in the delusion that we are separate from it. That quantitative values are balanced with qualitative values, ensures resilient solutions by acknowledging all aspects of our nature.

On the Snake River, Tetlit Gwich'in elder Elizabeth Hansen told me how in her language, there is no word for wilderness. For her culture, there is no separation from the living land to which identity and being are inextricably tied. This contrasts starkly with my urban and industrial culture, where romantic notions of nature can contrast with and seem to contradict our own industrious nature. How do we transcend this duality we create?

4.4 Three Rivers: Wild Waters, Sacred Places

In 2003, when the future of the Peel watershed was still uncertain, the Three Rivers Project was launched by Juri Peepre, founder and executive director of the Yukon chapter of the Canadian Parks and Wilderness Society, in partnership with Yukon Arts Centre and curator Scott Marsden. I was one of many creators invited to join these teams made up of artists, writers, photographers, film-makers and conservationists from across Canada and the USA. Every team was accompanied by representatives from the First Nations communities whose traditional lands include the Peel watershed. We travelled down three of the watershed's rivers (the Wind, Snake, Bonnet Plume), with the goal of learning about the land from first-hand experience, and the rich stories shared by the First Nations elders. Stories and inspirations about this land would ultimately be shared with the Canadian public through visual art, writing, photography and film. It was an outstanding cultural investment: in an age of remote sensing, it allowed for remote sensibility.

Remote sensibility is the term I use to describe the qualitative sensitivity necessary for a culture that is far from the landscapes and ecosystems it impacts. I consider remote sensibility to be the acknowledgement of the emotive, subjective experience of the land, through first-person experience of remote geographies. Sending out teams of artists was the perfect way to accomplish this, as it honours the many ways of knowing and viewing the world, through the head, the hands and the heart. The fruits of these artistic journeys were an exhibition and film entitled *Three Rivers: Wild Waters, Sacred Places* (2004) and a book called *Three Rivers:*

Artwork 4.8 Duo Lakes, Snake River, Peel Watershed, Yukon, 35 mm colour transparency, 2003

Yukon's Great Boreal Wilderness (2005). The group exhibition toured across Canada, and provided an intimate, diverse, intuitive reflection of the land.

I wondered, was my work principally viewed by those who were already sensitised to the land? When attending the World Wilderness Congress in Anchorage, Alaska, in 2005, I had an inspiring experience. In the founding congregation of the League of Conservation Photographers, eminent conservation biologist Dr George Schaller acknowledged and applauded how conservation photography had advanced by leaps and bounds in the last thirty years. But he also challenged his audience with a sobering reality: we were still headed towards ecological collapse. This made me ask myself, how effective was my kind of work in addressing our ecological crisis and the evolution of our behaviour? Who was this work actually reaching? This reverberated with my questions of why the industriousness and creativity which are part of our nature, were also responsible for the very orphaning of ourselves from the rest of life on the planet, a duality at the core of our being. For a culture functionally and perceptually so far from remote intact ecosystems, what meaning is actually carried in an image of 'nature', when there is no shared experience of the subject? This inspired a deconstruction of my photographic process, a challenge to vigorously investigate image and the meaning it conveys, and our own relations with the subjects in the process.

4.5 Ancestral Memories

Acknowledging the fact that we all come from and are dependent on the land, but are not necessarily conscious of this relationship, I created a body of work which asked what role the medium played in our actual perceptions of it. This was a deconstruction of my photographic process, to challenge my own assumptions and vocabulary in the medium.

- I wondered what meaning does an image of a mountain carry, for those who have no shared experience of the subject? Is there an ancestral memory that it kindles, from when we all gazed out on the land?
- What meaning does a black-and-white image hold? Or is its meaning in fact informed by seeing the world in tones of grey, an echo of the uncondi-tioned, undomesticated mind we had as infants, before our colour vision developed?
- What meaning does a photograph of an animal carry, if we have not shared in a direct experience of the subject? Especially when our first encounters with 'nature may be plastic toys of extinct and endangered species?
- A recent political debate over compromising the birthing grounds of caribou belies our insulation from the needs of other mammals, while we care passion-ately for the families we know. Would our compassion expand, if we knew how to 'know' or directly experience these species in the tundra? How can imaging of the land facilitate such knowing?
- What does a portrait in fact reveal about ourselves, when devoid of the essential relationships which begin under our skin and extend through the earth, rivers, atmosphere?

This also led to an expansion of what 'nature' really implied. Where did the separation of human and nature take place, as we gaze at matter transformed by life and time (a weathered stone, a fossil, a Neolithic obsidian blade) or did it?

4.5.1 Stillness as a Catalyst for Presence

It was during this process that I discovered what I had been intuiting years previously on Ellesmere Island: a technological means to capture the very presence of the land three-dimensionally. Stereoscopic vision is a faculty which is essential to countless species. It is an incredible faculty of the brain to combine two optical stimuli to perceive and navigate three-dimensional space. I have found the faculty to be intimately entwined with my emotional self, belying the connection between self and place. In a world of predominantly two-dimensional media, stereoscopy opens a door to presence.

Artwork 4.9 Pillar of Light (British Mountains, Ivvavik National Park, Yukon) digital photographs, 2005

With digital tools now available, I was able to capture stereoscopic video of remote geographies, and create installations which dissolved the perceived separation between natural and manufactured spaces. Stereoscopic imaging actually pre-dates photography, and has been used with photography for over a century and a half. With contemporary technologies, high-resolution imagery can be captured stereoscopically, and projected life-size. I explore it as a means to juxtapose realities which are otherwise perceptually disparate but functionally inseparable. In *Remote Sensibility V*, a stereo 3D large-format video projection depicts the heart of an urban centre, juxtaposed with vegetation blowing in the wind on a rocky ridge (see Artwork 4.10). The urban centre is Ottawa, political capital of Canada, where legislation is passed that affects remote geographies. The windswept ridge is in the Canadian Arctic, the destiny of which is

Artwork 4.10 Remote Sensibility V, stereo 3D video projection, 20 min loop, 2.1×3.8 m, 2009

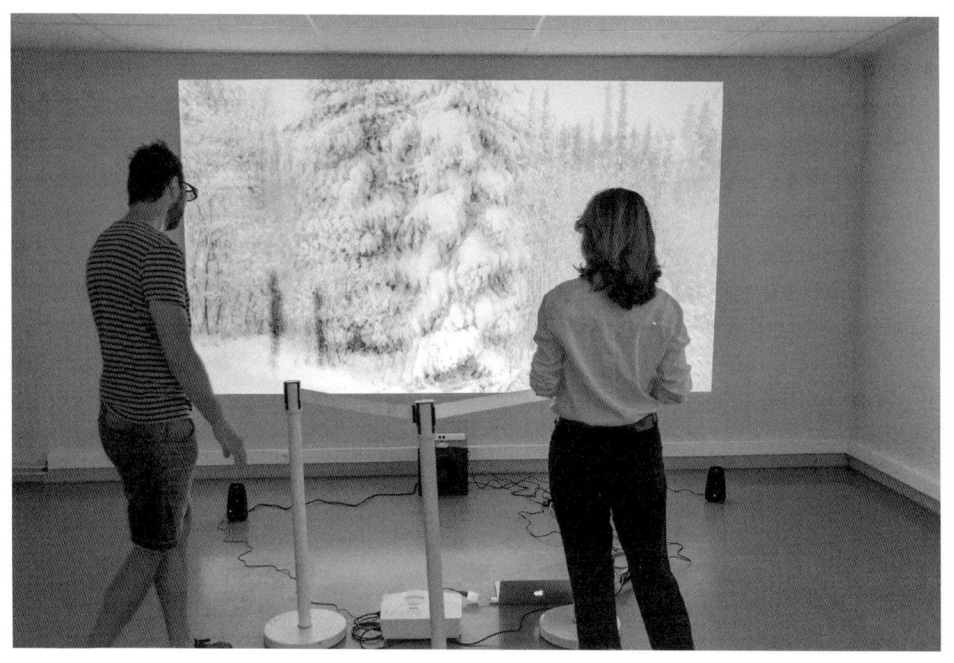

Artwork 4.11 Hart to Heart: reflections/réflexions, interactive stereo 3D video installation (World Humanities Conference, Liège) 2017

Artwork 4.12 Murs intérieurs/Inner Walls, anaglyph stereo 3D print on vinyl, stereo photo collage, 1.2×2.1 m, 2014

profoundly impacted by the legislation passed in a distant parliament. It is intriguing to behold viewers return to sit several minutes with a topographical feature which does not change except for the waving of vegetation in the wind. As an 11-year-old boy commented in the gallery, 'thank you for taking me to a place I could never get to'. Perhaps the illusion of dimensionality is the catalyst to a sense of presence in the land that our species has known for the majority of its existence.

In the curated group show 'Untrue North', I experimented with large-format stereo 3D anaglyph prints to recreate forms in contexts that are normally outside our consciousness. For example, one installation in the gallery is the life-size amount of ore (1,000 kg) required to create 1 gram of gold using the cyanide heap leach process. It provokes the question: would our ecological footprint be the same if we lived intimately with the consequences of its extraction? I also explored this form of imaging to virtually perforate the floors of interior and exterior manufactured spaces. Such perforations provide visible metaphors for our relationship with landscapes that we are connected to, but do not see first-hand. Below the floor, a pregnant woman on the boreal forest floor reflects the fecundity that exists outside our manufactured spaces. Through the wall of an urban building, we perceive the boreal forest, and the poetry it inspires. These installations serve not only as metaphor, but as vehicles to surprise and delight, where our conditioned experience of imaging is challenged by scale and perceived form.

Artwork 4.13 Chasms of Silence, still from stereo 3D video installation, 2014

And here I want to share again what I had first dreamed of when taking my long walks in the Arctic: to be able to bring a sense of immediacy and direct presence to the viewer. Revisiting Baffin Island in the Eastern Arctic, I captured stereo 3D video, and composed a video installation. Adapting Anne Michaels' prose, her words were woven into the landscape as text between boulders left by glaciers; words and stones like apostrophes in time. The orchestration of virtual form, sound and text became a multifaceted visual poem. Mediated by the artist, is a door opened in ourselves to our presence in the land – perhaps kindling an ancestral memory?

4.5.2 Dissolving Separation of Subject and Object to Become Subject and Subject: Technology as Ecology

However, an aspect that still challenges me is the passive experience of viewing these geographies, whether through photography or video installation. I wanted to blur the separation between subject and object, if not physically, then perceptually, and metaphorically, as a means to offer a more personal encounter with landscapes that are thousands of kilometres distant. The tool for helping to dissolve this separation from subject matter is creating interactivity.

With my friend Baptiste Bohelay who is an artist and expert in coding, we melded digital stereo imaging and software programming to create interactive stereo 3D video installation. It was a playful means to let the viewer participate in landscapes they may never see first-hand. Sensors pick up viewers in the gallery space, and we are portrayed as reflected shadows of ourselves, made up of particles, which move with us between trees, behind stones, in these

Artwork 4.14 Projection intérieure projection (Marten Berkman and Baptiste Bohelay) still from interactive video installation, 2014

geographies which are otherwise far away. Presenting landscape in this interactive medium offers a two-way portal to a connecting experience.

Unlike traditional Indigenous knowledge, born of intimate contact with the land over generations of time, urban and industrial culture functionally separates the land from our consciousness. This form of installation is a participatory metaphor, offering technology as part of our ecology, which it must be, if we are to become perceptively and functionally 'of the land'. It is the self-realisation necessary if our nature is to be in harmony with instead of at odds with the rest of nature. Imagine if inherent in our architecture, was the representation of ecosystems and footprints that are indelibly a part of our lifeway. Imagine if our systems design finally expanded to be conscious of systems reality, which is our earth system, that we are a member of. Imagine if all the incredible human ingenuity, industriousness and creativity, which is our inherent nature, manifest in all we see manufactured around us was enlightened simply through experience and perception, to consider the rest of the world in our systems design. How resilient our designs would be, when conscious of the extraordinary living designs of nature. We are nature in ourselves ... cognitively affirmed by biology, archaeology, palaeontology ... it is the delusion we suffer if we think ourselves separate from it. To dissolve the delusion, is to make us conscious again of what Indigenous elders remind us of. And then we are agents, not impediments to the beauty and strength and creativity of this living world, this wondrous anomaly in this solar system that we can never take for granted. It all hinges on our perception. The way we see the world is the way we treat the world, and how we see needs to catch up with the paradigm it has been our nature to create. And that is the ecology of our perception.

4.5.3 Beauty and Wonder: Essential Experiences in Human–More-than-Human Relationships

Here I wish to return to an experience I shared earlier; the sense of wonder. I propose we look carefully at the experiences of wonder and beauty. What happens in these states? I offer that in these moments, our sense of self dissolves. For a moment there is neither I nor that, there simply is. We live a moment in the most exquisite experience of reality, one where we perceive reality, and that is the reality of totality, of connection. For a moment, duality has evaporated, the delusion of separation has been lifted, the conditioning of mind has been dissolved. I wrote already of this as the dissolving between subject and object. But this is in fact the dissolving between subject and subject. Interconnectedness also means two-way, multifold interaction and responsibility.

How frustrated so many Indigenous peoples must be, and have been, in encountering the colonial perception of cognitive separation from, and delineation of, the world. We are like adolescents when we assume what we know is the truth, that what we understand is the extent of reality, and when we project this assumption onto the world. Science has been a fantastic tool of and for our mental faculty. Unlike the realities we imagined in our minds and projected onto the world, which inevitably lead to conflict when encountering other projected realities, science assumes we know nothing until we can create a hypothesis and test it. However, we have suffered when we have assumed our quantitative knowledge to be sufficient, when we have let this tool be the defining instrument of our reality. We are as prone to projecting realities arrived at through our science, as we have been in projecting realities arrived at through our imagination. Science has been used to qualify our actions, when this instrument is driven by hubris instead of humility. We are not dispassionate, impartial creatures, and science can be compromised as a result.

In fact, if we are to pay careful attention to the scientific discipline, we must acknowledge that we cannot make the assumption that the mind is the only qualified means of knowing. What other means of knowing do we exercise daily, and meaningfully throughout our lives? Are many of the challenges we face due to making decisions based on quantification alone? And if we venture into the realms of other means of knowing in the more-than-human world, what are the qualifiers that nurture successful outcomes?

4.6 Listening to Our Elders, Our Astronauts, Our Artists

I am drawn to where experience looms large, and this is found in traditional knowledge, in science and in art. A current project inspired by a journey on the Hart River in the Yukon's Peel watershed, aspires to reflect multiple means of knowing in finding common ground in our values and aspirations as humans. When Jimmy Johnny, Elder of the Na-Cho Nyäk Dun First Nation, speaks of the value in the water and the land, he does so with the lens of time, generations upon generations spent in intimate relationship with the earth. When Canadian astronaut Julie Payette speaks about her perspective on the uniqueness and fragility of the earth's atmosphere, the only thing making life on this planet possible, she is speaking from the perspective born of science and engineering at the pinnacle of resource extraction and manipulation: from space in orbit around the earth. And when artists speak wordlessly about beauty and wonder in the air, land, water, light and life, we are sharing the perspective transcending our cognition, but trusting instead in the barometer of the heart, articulated through the disciplines of our respective artistic vocabularies.

Like the complexity of ecosystems, of seemingly infinite relationships in eternal flux, our cultures and lifeways are in constant interaction and evolution. Of the seemingly infinite barriers we are currently facing, it is incredible to behold that common to all our endeavours and aspirations is the thread of life that we are gifted to be a part of. So many means of knowing, some of which are shared in this current project, appear to point in the same direction, that all life is connected, not separate, and no mental construct will ever succeed in separating us from reality. Imagine the creative force unleashed when our industrious nature is in concert with all of nature, when systems analysis encompasses the largest system, when decisions are based on head, hands and heart.

It has been our nature to arrive at the urban and industrial point we now have. This realisation of our aspirations, our dreams, our industriousness, our creativity, has produced undisputed rewards. However, the paradigm we create in the Anthropocene is our peril, and the peril for all life, if our consciousness is not in tandem with our impact. At the moment we are collectively realising the hubris of adolescent behaviour, when our situation begs humility and respect. Remote sensibility is just one means for art to be the vehicle for our awareness, nurturing our awareness of a reality we impact but may never know first-hand. Without first-hand knowledge, are we forever thwarted from the type of knowing from generations of intimate connection to the land, or from kilometres out in space? What are the conduits of feeling that inform our hearts, and that set our inner compass? Artists are specialists in fathoming the depths of our many means of knowing and sharing this journey through multiple media. Are these the catalysts to transforming our behaviour?

Can we experience wonder in the rest of nature from the vantage point of our manufactured spaces? The fact we are part of nature ourselves, implies the answer is absolutely yes. How we live in the world is defined by how we see the world, and how we see the world is often defined by the world we have created, the technology we use. If our technologies are the necessary interface between the heart of our urban spaces and the remote geographies we impact but do not see first-hand, then art can be part of that essential bridge. Like traditional knowledge and science, art practices strike me as essential in the maturing relationship we have with the rest of life as an industrious species. And the bridges art creates may be the triggers to seek out the land first-hand, to reacquaint with what was the reality of our ancestors.

And so, I found it necessary, and exciting, to move beyond the classic landscape photograph. Multidisciplinary art may reflect how our approaches to our challenges need to be multidisciplinary, reflecting multiple ways of knowing, including fundamentally, the deep wisdom of the heart. The technologies that have been our nature to create also shape our human world and can orphan us from the more-than-human world. This begs technology to then become a vehicle, not an impediment, to our ancient relationship with the rest of nature. With this palette, the artist as mediator becomes essential for our perception to keep abreast of our relationship with the land from the vantage point of our manufactured spaces.

I aspire in my own practice – whether digital collage reflecting layers of meaning, stereoscopic projection dissolving the distance to remote geographies, interactive installation blurring the duality between ourselves and the land we behold – that these mediums are our remote sensibility. When open to the intuitive, the circular, the qualitative, the emotive, creativity with our technology becomes a part of our ecology: the ecology of our perception.

Acknowledgements

My deep gratitude to:

My late parents John and Anneke Berkman, who sowed the seeds of a lifelong connection to the land, and my late uncle and visual artist Henk Berkman who sowed the seeds of art;

Peoples of the Yukon First Nations, on whose traditional territories I live, explore and am inspired;

Jimmy Johnny, Elizabeth Hansen, Joanne Snowshoe, Robert Alexie Sr., Julie Payette, David Suzuki, Kim Hudson, the late Neil Colin, Juri Peepre, John Lammers, John Witham, who generously shared their time, their stories, and their wisdom;

Jill Pangman for the endless generous support to so many who have travelled so deep in the land thanks to her knowledge, skill and passion;

Sue Staniforth, Jill Pangman and Ron Cruikshank and Joe Jack for editorial review;

Sandy Lamalle and Peter Stoett for doing the critical academic work in fostering multidisciplinary and cross-cultural understanding of the land and our relationship with it.

My wife Jennifer, and daughters Sya and Willow, without whose patience, love and support, my creative work would not be possible.

References

Selected Artworks, Films, Exhibitions

Cascade de Lumière, experimental docudrama, 23', 2008. Official selection, Rendezvous du Cinema Quebecoise 2008; Vancouver international, Mountain Film Fest; Moondance; Wild and Scenic Environmental Film Fest, broadcast on PBS; Winner, second place, MITY award, Dawson City International Short Film Festival.

Chasms of Silence, Berkman, Folio Gallery/ Waterous, 1999, ISBN 0–9680175–4-1: limited edition portfolio of high arctic black-and-white landscape photography, with a foreword by poet and novelist Anne Michaels (finalist, Banff Mountain Book Awards, 2000).

The Ecology of Perception (2017) presentation, and solo exhibit of S3D interactive video and anaglyph works (*Hart to Heart*; *Remote Sensibility V*, *projection intérieur projection*, *Abimes de Silence*, *Murs Intérieurs*, *Le Chevalet*) curated by Sandy Lamalle, 2017 UNESCO World Humanities Conference (Challenges and Responsibilities for a Planet in Transition), Liége, Belgium.

Hart to Heart (2015) interactive S3D video installation (20'): Available Light Film Festival, Yukon Arts Centre; curated by Andy Connors, ISEA (International Symposium of Electronic Arts) Vancouver, BC; 'In It' VR showcase – Confluence Gallery, Emily Carr University, Vancouver, BC; curated by Maria Lantin; 'Mountain Art' – Walter Phillips Gallery, Banff Centre, AB. Curated by Jen Mizuik.

Remote Sensibility VIII: The Ecology of Perception (2019) multichannel, parallelogram and interactive S3D video installations, Yukon Arts Centre Gallery, curated by Mary Bradshaw.

Three Rivers, documentary, Canadian Parks and Wilderness Society, 20', 2004.

See my website www.martenberkman.com

Further Reading

Alexander, C. (1977). *A Pattern Language: Towns, Buildings, Construction*. Oxford: Oxford University Press.

Council of Yukon First Nations: Nations, History. See the website http://cyfn.ca

Hudson, K., 2 ways of knowing: The power of linear and circular thinking. See the website https://2wkblog.com/

Peepre, J. (2005). *Three Rivers: The Yukon's Great Boreal Wilderness*, Harbour Publishing.

Robertson, P. (2004). *Three Rivers/Wild Waters, Sacred Places*, Exhibition catalogue, Yukon Arts Centre, Whitehorse, Yukon.

Yukon Land Use Planning Council. www.planyukon.ca

5

A Common Space of Legal Communication

SANDY LAMALLE

Introduction

The Messengers had come to the House of Mica to voice the 'Cry of the Earth'.[1] For the last two decades of climate change negotiations, Indigenous peoples have tried to explain their message in alternative fora, with a critical movement to the modern approach of the environment. Like Indigenous languages, law and legal traditions, their message seemed to be in an unknown idiom. The authors of this book, and other participants in the ESGRREW Process of Dialogue and Research, highlighted the challenges of an effective dialogue with Indigenous peoples on such issues, and in particular with regard to Indigenous legal traditions, their recognition and understanding. Indigenous peoples around the world are especially affected by climate change, and they 'can make important contributions to solutions, through traditional knowledge, legal systems and cultures that have proven effective at conserving land, water, biodiversity and ecosystems, including forests' (UNGA 2019: 14). The United Nations Programme of Action for the Second International Decade of the World's Indigenous Peoples promoted 'access to justice', 'full and effective participation', 'non-discrimination and the inclusion of Indigenous peoples in the design, implementation and evaluation of international, regional and national processes regarding laws, policies, resources, programmes and projects' (2005–15, UNGA Resolution 60/142). If now several countries have recognised the rights of Indigenous peoples in their constitutional systems (UNGA 2014: 2–5), the 2014 Report of the UN Secretary General recommended to 'recognise and strengthen Indigenous people' 'own forms of governance', and 'take into account their distinct identity' (UNGA 2014: 17). In that optic, the upcoming International Decade for Indigenous Languages (UNESCO 2020 – Los Pinos Declaration) will

---

[1] Conference 'Cry of the Earth – The Legacy of the First Nations', 22 November 1993, at the United Nations headquarters in New York. It included seven delegations, representing the Hopi, Maya, Huichol, Lakota, Mikmaq, Haudenausenee (Iroquoian) and Mamiwinini (Algonquin) Nations of North America.

contribute to saving and revitalising languages (Harrison 2020), and 'provid(ing) intergenerational transfer of intangible cultural heritage and knowledge to assist us in facing future global challenges'. Such languages are a testimony to the multifarious changing and entwining relationships of all living things over millennia and time immemorial. They tell of the human story of survival, adaptation and transformation – of what makes us all related in the past, present and future. They were celebrated worldwide during the United Nations International Year of Indigenous Languages in 2019 (UN Proclamation 71/178), with the objectives of 'increasing understanding, reconciliation and international cooperation'. In this perspective, and with regard to the objectives set out in the United Nations Declaration on the Rights of Indigenous Peoples (UNDRIP) and the 2030 Agenda on Sustainable Development, we also need to reacquaint ourselves with Indigenous legal traditions.

Different legal systems and traditions[2] around the world are recognised in addition to common law and civil law systems. Due to historical factors of subjugation and based on 'comparative approaches to law on Western grounds' (Clarkson et al. 1992: 9), Indigenous laws and traditions were not considered as 'law' or 'legal systems' (Menski 2005: 394; Napoleon 2007: 1–2). Most Indigenous legal orders, also called 'chthonic systems' enter into that category, such as Native African, Australian and American laws and customs (Menski 2005: 396). Their full recognition challenges the modern understanding of law founded on state institutions (Morgan 2011: 126; Anaya 2004), as well as its legal mode of knowledge, expression and communication (Gunn 2018; Lamalle 2014b). Although many countries have recognised Indigenous legal traditions, such as those of South Africa and Pacific Island states (LCC 2006: 26), prejudices, discrimination and reductive categories have been preventing full recognition on an equal footing (Beier 2009: 197; Sousa Santos 2014: 127; Castillo and Strecker 2017: 28–29). International legal frameworks should be open 'to integrate the diversity of the global society and involve Indigenous Peoples' ontologies as well' (May 2017: 351). To that end, UNDRIP asserts 'the right to the dignity and diversity of their cultures, traditions, histories and aspirations', and 'States shall take effective measures . . . to combat prejudice and eliminate discrimination and to promote tolerance, understanding and good relations' (art. 15). They should also 'ensure that Indigenous peoples can understand and be understood in political, legal and administrative proceedings' (art. 13.2). It means we need to take in to account not only another worldview, but also another way of approaching and understanding law and governance. Such 'ontological encounters' call into

---

[2] A legal tradition can be understood as 'a set of deeply rooted, historically conditioned attitudes about the nature of law, about the role of law in the society and the polity, about the proper organization and operation of a legal system and about the way law is or should be made, applied, studied, perfected and taught' (Law Commission of Canada 2006: 4).

question the bias and limits in approaching the other through certain structures and organised forms (roles and functions), through categories (as reified forms, concepts, procedures and modes of government), or through a certain definition and apprehension of the legal subject (Dorough, in Morgan 2011: 126; Lamalle 2014a). In that regard, they bring into perspective how we approach other legal traditions and systems, and how we translate our understanding of reality into legal language and practice. With the revitalisation of Indigenous languages, cultures and laws, 'effective ontological encounters' are therefore both a condition for reconciliation, and a time to reappraise legal communication. Such a dialogue between legal traditions invites us to widen our legal horizon and redefine accordingly the definition of the landscape in law and governance.

   This chapter mobilises, in that perspective, diverse disciplines as applied to law, including philosophy, literature, sociology, anthropology, linguistics and semiotics. In particular, it highlights how semiotics can open the scope of research to different forms of legal conscience, and contemplate the specificity of a legal narrative, language or tradition. This reflection takes into account the critique of the modern legal rationality and subject, pragmatics and the critique of language and translation. The research focus is on the relationship between Indigenous law, common law, and civil law traditions and systems, with notably a case study of the Reconciliation process in Canada. In such an intercultural process, the operation of translating legal concepts and rationales is tested to its limits (McCaslin and Wanda 2005: 3–4), and 'shared frameworks' are called for in order to engage with Indigenous legal traditions (Napoleon and Friedland 2016). In response, this chapter reflects on legal translation and the way we apprehend different forms of legal conscience, with a view to opening a space of legal understanding and communication. It notably sheds light on how, on one side, the critique of current modern legal systems in the common law and civil law traditions raised concerns over fundamental issues in relation to how we conceive and practise law; and how, on the other side, Indigenous law and traditions, which were not recognised as such and ignored, offer a wider scope for comprehension, as well as responses to the crisis of modern legal systems. In this light, the first section explores the definitions of the legal landscape; the second ponders the approach of the legal subject; the third brings into focus the challenges of legal communication and reconciliation.

5.1 Defining the Legal Landscape

The legal field is at the junction of all aspects of life in society. If the legal categories of law determine the reality of the legal world (Carty 1991: 77), cultures and languages play a crucial role in defining the legal landscape. In modern law, as in other scientific discourses, legal narratives are based on representations (Rouland 1991). Representations and conceptual frameworks provide a structure of thought (Ost 2005; Grize 1982), and constitute the matrix of social practices, generating their institutionalisation (Jodelet 2006). The alternative fora to international negotiations, on climate change notably, have brought to the fore (Korten 2015: 13; Morgan 2011), the existence of different representations of the world and 'environment', ways of knowing and forms of knowledge, as well as different legal traditions (Sousa Santos 2014: 237). Acknowledging that diversity in the legal field, in particular at the international level, calls for a critical re-examination of the legal landscape, considering legal rationality, conceptual framework and language (Menski 2005: 16, 46; Gounelle 2005: 114). In that perspective, we will bring into focus the critique of law (Section 5.1.1), how we approach Indigenous law (Section 5.1.2), and the challenges of legal translation (Section 5.1.3).

5.1.1 The Critique of Law

Usually designated as 'Western' legal traditions, common law and civil law traditions are quite different in their rationale, institutions and processes, and were constituted in the framework of different cultures, languages and countries. Nevertheless, they share common conceptual roots in the *jus commune* inherited from Roman law, as well as historical and linguistic interweaving (Mattila 2012: 220, 224, 246). It has been developed in European jurisprudence since the seventeenth century, notably regarding the Westphalian treaties, and used to shape international law and institutions (Koskenniemi 2001: 9; 2005: 115; Carty 2007; Nijman 2004). Such conceptual language was spread out by colonisation notably in English, French, Dutch and Spanish, with the subjugation of other legal traditions and systems (Mattila 2012: 331, 386, 432). The limits and impacts of that conceptual and methodological frame on the apprehension of international reality were emphasised, notably with regard to social justice and the environment (Pahuja 2011; Wilmer 2009: 191; Sousa Santos 2014: 124, 237; Ramlogan 2002). The critique underlined the lack of 'equity between different ways of knowing and different forms of knowledge' (Sousa Santos 2014: 237), and the necessity of 'positioning actual lived experience at the centre of consideration' in lieu of current 'disembodied rationality' (Philippopoulos-Mihalopoulos and Brooks 2017: 6, 14). The legal categories and representations are contested on various grounds. Critical environmental law exposes the objectification of the 'natural world', the focus on human agency, and 'challenge(s) the human/non-human divide on which most of legal regulation is based' (Philippopoulos-Mihalopoulos and Brooks 2017: 8). The critique put an emphasis on the inability of legal categories to apprehend reality through the subject–object dichotomy, atomisation of subjects into individuals and states, the empty universalism of abstract designations unable to grasp the specificity and diversity of agents (Pelizzon and O'Shannessy 2016: 212), and the fragmentation of law into different, conflicting branches and regimes (Pedersen 2018; Philippopoulos-Mihalopoulos and Brooks 2017: 6–10; ILC 2006). According to philosophers and legal theorists: 'The possibility of a new imagination [would] hinge(s) then on the desarticulation of a set of key conceptual referents through which Western modernity apprehends and constructs the world' (Thomas-Pellicer et al. 2016: 2).

The critique of the legal landscape, notably described in international negotiations, thus concerns the legal narrative structure which is based on certain representations and concepts (Dews 2007: 292, 296; Nash 1994; Rouland 1991), a certain mode of knowledge and approach (Sofoulis 2018: 821), as well as linguistic and jurilinguistic frames (Mattila 2006; Kimmerer 2020). All such frames constitute a certain perspective which determines the understanding and apprehension of the world (Wittgenstein [1953] 1969: 214; Geertz 1973; Spivak 2012). They are deemed problematic on the pragmatic level of formulating and implementing law, in particular environmental law, and addressing the different dimensions of the ecological crisis (Kotzé 2018; Bergthaller et al. 2012: 262). Such critique converges with the critiques of modern legal rationality, in particular in legal anthropology and sociology, which foster a wider legal scope to approach other legal traditions, with new epistemological frameworks for analysis (Murtagh 2019: 116; Eberhard 2008; Le Roy 2004), and a broader approach to law and governance encompassing different fields and modes of knowledge (Beier 2009: 5; Eberhard and Vernicos 2006; Menski 2005). This implies reappraising subjugated legal systems and traditions. While classifications of legal systems in comparative law may be based on various criteria, such as language, structure of legal thought or cultural traditions (Sousa Santos 2004: 302f.), such classifications usually leave unexplored the ones in the fourth world, comprising Indigenous laws and traditions in Africa, America and Australia (Glenn 2004: 61).

5.1.2 *Approaching Indigenous Law*

With the re-emergence of Indigenous cultures and the development of processes of reconciliation, Indigenous laws and traditions are being revitalised, and legal communication between legal traditions is being rekindled. If historical 'ways of encountering' other legal traditions were modelled on state experience (Wilmer 2009: 191), prejudices and reductive categories (Castillo and Strecker 2017: 28–29), reconciliation involves the reappraisal of the relationships, taking into account Indigenous perspectives and 'understanding of human associational patterns', law and governance (Morgan 2011: 144; Wilmer 2009: 198; Napoleon 2007; Borrows 2002). In this regard, the term 'legal system' may be used to refer to 'a state-centred legal system where law is managed by legal professionals in legal institutions that are separate from other social and political organizations', and the term 'legal order' can be used, in contrast, 'to describe law that is embedded throughout social, political, economic, and spiritual institutions' (Napoleon 2007). Indigenous legal traditions situate knowledges in their social, environmental, economic and symbolic contexts – their relationships with the lands therefore having the 'highest possible meaning' (Deloria 1992: 62; Castillo and Strecker 2017: 344). Such 'intimate linkage between the natural world, spirituality, and collective relations' (Dorough 2009: 274) makes intelligible that in 'Indigenous justice systems, there is more emphasis on duties, obligation and responsibilities within these collectivities' (Dorough 2009: 274). 'Indigenous laws typically are non-prescriptive, non-adversarial and non-punitive. They generally promote values such as respect, restoration and consensus and are closely connected to the land, the Creator and the community' (Law Commission of Canada 2006: 3). Sets of 'moral principles, ethics, and values that are given expression in regulatory codes ... govern relationships with the environment and with one another' (Stewart-Harawira 2009: 216).

While fragmentation, atomisation and objectification are causes of serious concern in modern legal systems and societies, Indigenous legal traditions and orders, which have perpetuated for millennia, are 'based upon the inter-relatedness of all living things – this includes our ancestry whether past, present or future as well as our natural environment, plants, animals, trees, mountains, water, birds, rocks etc. As all life is interrelated, we are encouraged to strive for peace, balance and harmony' (Victor 2007: 22–23). This ontology with all as integral components of 'one system' is shared by many Indigenous cultures around the world – it encompasses not only 'ritual, economic, residential and kinship rules and conventions, but also what we would call natural laws and technological rules' (Austin-Broos and Merlan 2017: 11). Unlike 'notions of justice as deterrence and punishment, the old indigenous tradition of justice as healing aims at achieving balance and harmony in families and communities' (McCaslin 2005: 3–4). And converging with the critique of legal categories and disembodied rationality in modern legal systems, Indigenous 'understandings of justice as healing originate from the lived experience of people' (McCaslin 2005: 3–4, 17). Thanks to much resilience and strength, the revitalisation of Indigenous legal traditions in Canada since the 1990s made salient their specificity and approach to law (Victor 2007): making explicit their values and principles in constitutions and contemporary legislation; restoring practices and institutions such as potlatches and Elders Councils; reintroducing holistic methods of justice, such as healing circles and peacemaker initiatives (TRC Report 2015; LCC 2006: 25). Notably with regard to their effective and positive results, different programmes and projects throughout the country have created hybrid and independent structures in communities, based on Indigenous laws, as alternative or as principal modes of law and justice (Jaccoud 2014). The implementation of the recommendations of the Truth and Reconciliation Commission (TRC) since 2015, also based on Indigenous laws and traditions, has put in practice another understanding of law and justice, addressing different dimensions of living in society. Recognising Indigenous legal traditions, beyond making them commensurate with another tradition or legal system (Povinelli 2002), therefore entails the 'development of Indigenous knowledges and methodologies as part of a transformative political process' (Cunneen 2014: 53).

Such developments further highlighted the structural and conceptual differences between legal traditions, but also put into perspective the responses brought by Indigenous legal traditions to the ailments of modern law and society.

5.1.3 Challenges of Legal Translation

Dialogue and communication between legal traditions come with the challenge of legal translation between legal languages (Wagner et al. 2014; Scott 2017; Gotti and Williams 2010; Mattila 2006; Steiner 1998). The use of a lingua franca, or vehicular language, in debates and negotiations tends to involve a certain perspective inherent to the language and legal tradition concerned (Mattila 2012: 446). Being unaware of such a jurilinguistic perspective can become a limitation and prevent other perspectives, concepts and approaches from being expressed, understood or taken into account (Mattila 2012: 454). For a long time, Indigenous languages were forbidden in many countries,[3] but there is now a re-emergence of languages and cultures. Their protection and revitalisation is not only a way to preserve the world's cultural diversity, it also contributes to peace building and development (UNESCO Conventions 2003 and 2005; Castillo and Strecker 2017; UNDP 2001: para. 11). Most Indigenous languages of the world developed as spoken languages without a writing system, as they are living oral traditions (Report of the International Expert Group Meeting on Indigenous Languages 2008). Another specificity emphasised by linguists is that the structure of Indigenous languages is quite distinct from other languages (Howard et al. 2018). In contrast with the objectification in modern legal and scientific languages, the 'language of animacy' in Algonquian and Iroquoian languages, favour verbs, relating entities together in a same dynamic (humans, animals, trees, plants, rocks,

---

[3] Languages are disappearing notably due to historical and contemporary oppression of Indigenous peoples (Pulitano 2012: 29).

elements) and designating life forces and relationships (Kimmerer 2020: 57–58). Regarding the current ecological predicament, Potawatomi botanist Kimmerer asserts that in the modern world 'the language of animacy teeters on extinction, not just for Native peoples, but for everyone', and that 'maybe a grammar of animacy could lead us to whole ways of living in the world' (Kimmerer 2020: 58).

The revitalisation and translation of Indigenous languages in several countries stressed the challenges, obstacles and limits of legal translation. There are notably determining factors in the choice of translation strategies and methodologies. Such factors can create an unbalance or asymmetry between the source and target languages, caused by the different modes of communication used in the languages (e.g. oral or text), cultural or ideological bias, legal or political status of a language (Spivak 2012). For instance, in the translation of the Peruvian Languages Act in Quechua and Aymara, linguists noted that the 'codification of traditional justice' tends 'to be primarily oral and the principles of customary law that hold within the communities are not generally consigned to writing' (Howard et al. 2018: 221). In Mexico, 'Tzeltal translators embedded the content of the United Nations Declaration of Human Rights in a genre (Mantalil) recognizable to Tzeltal speakers, as it has a perlocutionary effect insofar as it guides listeners on how to live their lives; it expresses the idea of 'law' in Tzeltal' (Pitarch 2008 in Howard et al. 2018: 225). Such a perlocutionary act – understood as an utterance which has consequential effects on the feelings, thoughts or actions of both audience and speaker – is a modality of legal communication with another mode of perception, usually called direct perception. Indigenous translators considered what the legal text meant in their own law and used their own mode of legal communication and narration: a specific form of speech. In order to re-establish the balance between the source and target languages, legal translation needs to take into account the cognitive structures and legal semiotics of the Indigenous languages, with their specific modes of narration and modalities of legal communication (Lamalle 2020a: 96). The translation of the Constitution of Columbia in seven Amerindian languages raised other challenges: 'Translation problems arising from the divergent conceptual systems within which the diverse tongues are embedded may be harder to overcome, particularly when it is a matter of legal language' (Howard et al. 2018: 220). This means that the operation of legal translation requires considering not only the modalities of communication, structural differences and possible unbalances in translation approaches, but also the conceptual systems specific to a certain legal language. Legal translation can be envisaged, in that optic, as 'a space of possibilities, an autonomous realm of "cross-cultural events"', a space 'which enables other positions to emerge' (Wagner et al. 2014), opening the scope of legal communication and modalities of dialogue.

If the critique of modern legal rationality showed the concerns and limits of the definition of the legal landscape, the difference of perspective with Indigenous legal traditions is ontological and calls for other modalities of relationship, dialogue and translation (Poirier 2008). The rehabilitation of such traditions and the relationships with their legal orders require, in practice, to acknowledge that ontological dimension (Beier 2009; Carty 2007).

5.2 Approaching the Legal Subject

Ontology has been excluded from modern law since the eighteenth century due to 'the normative evolution of law and its disentanglement from religious, metaphysical and ontological questions', disconnecting law from its own perspective (Carty 1990: 6). If different factors have enkindled the questioning on being, notably scientific and technological developments or globalisation, the current ecological crisis has put the ontological question at the centre of deliberations. In the legal field, such reflexivity was fostered by the evolution of society and law, by the experience of fragmentation, incoherency and lack of effective legal instruments, by critical reflection on such experience, and by the development of legal theory and practice with the insights of other fields of knowledge. The dialogue with other legal traditions can further shed light on current issues, their causes and possible remedies. As modern law focuses on the regulation of human beings and social institutions, and sets aside the 'environment' as a separate concern or object in current legal narratives and frameworks, critical and pragmatic reflections have raised the question of its apprehension in law – impelling further reflection on the legal subject, therefore reopening the ontological question in the legal field (Pelizzon and O'Shannessy 2016: 218). We now focus on such ontological reflexivity in law (Section 5.2.1); see how Indigenous law and traditions constitute a response to the ontological questioning (Section 5.2.2), and consider the evolution of legal narrative and categories (Section 5.2.3).

5.2.1 Ontological Reflexivity in Law

In the context of a crisis of representation in various fields of knowledge (Briggs and Hunter 2010; Bergthaller et al. 2012; Miller 1996), the critique in linguistics and philosophy on the modern subject particularly contributed to the ontological questioning in law and society (Canguilhem 1967; Cadava et al. 1991; Carty 2007: 198; Sousa Santos 2004; Goodrich 1987; Kennedy 1987, 2006). Like the disintegration of the representation of the modern subject in philosophy (Boyle 1991: 469), arts and sciences (Chakravartty 2010), such process in international law was brought to light after the development of international organisations and the *ratione materiae* and *personae* extensions of the scope of international law (Carty 2007: 198–99, 231; Bederman 1996; Barbéris 1983; Lamalle 2014a). This process was already transforming representations in civil law and common law systems (Amselek and Grzegorczyk 1989; Commaille and Jobert 1998; Goodrich 1987; Kennedy 1997), and concerns both the conception of the modern subject, as ontological stance, and its legal designation by the concept of legal personality.

The understanding and use of the modern notion of subject (*subjectus*) in Western legal systems resulted from an evolution and secularisation of debates, in relation to the notion of person through different fields of knowledge: notably from the theological works of Dun Scotus and William of Occam in the Middle Ages (meaning as submitted to natural law with an autonomy); the political works of Hobbes and Pufendorf (meaning as submitted to a sovereign authority); and to the works of the Enlightenment philosophers (meaning a free and rational person). The subject, drawing from such reflections and definitions, was equated to the individual (a human being), defined as person. The notion of person, which served as representation for the concept of legal personality, is understood as a philosophical, political and legal subject (Lamalle 2014b). Contrary to its genealogy, use and understanding in the Justinian institutions in Roman law, the person as subject is approached as the centre of legal reasoning and logic in modern law (Villey 1968: 663), understood as having power (*potestas*) over objectified things (*res*) (see Chapter 8 in this volume). Such conception of the legal subject led to the subject–object dichotomy, and the distinction between persons and things became 'a keystone of the semantic architecture of Western law' (Pelizzon and O'Shannessy 2016: 213). In that context, the law is a quality of the person, and *persona juris*, the legal designation of the person is then defined as the quality of the legal subject (Grzegorczyk 1989: 23). Such equations associate exclusively the legal designation *persona juris* to human beings (and by analogy, through the process of personification, to institutions as fictive persons or *persona ficta*), as the owner of rights and obligations (Villey 1968: 664). The construction of *persona juris* as designating the legal subject was thus characterised by the modern representation of a person as an independent, autonomous, rational, free and capable being. Such representation led to dominating and fragmenting approaches to the world, and to obstacles in apprehending realities in law and legal reasoning as separate personified units (such as institutions, biological cells, foetuses, virtual realities, cities, animals, forests, rivers). It has been criticised since its formulation in the eighteenth century, notably in relation to the notions of will, independence, autonomy, interest and patrimony (Delmas-Marty 2008; Dubreuil 2005; Viala 2001: 681; Pelizzon and O'Shannessy 2016: 218), as well as the absence of content of legal personality as a legal designation (Boyle 1991: 489).

Contemporary legal theory still struggles with the consequences of personification, in particular in common law systems, despite its becoming obsolescent as a mode of representation with the development of legal technique. 'The reflections of Jellinek in German political theory, Michoud in French legal theory and Ferrara in Italian legal theory all managed to get beyond personification in civil law systems and acknowledged the concept of *persona juris* as a legal tool' (Lamalle 2014b: 304–05). However, the concept approaching reality in terms of roles acts as an empty category (Subramanian and Chung 2005: 81, 83), as a 'ready-made character of the subject' (Boyle 1991: 489). However, 'the human subject cannot be reduced to the logic of identity and the social roles through which it is articulated. Humanity transcends and at once subtends the logic of roles and identities' (Petrilli 2021). And the construction of the legal subject as 'a *persona* masking the concrete particularities of the individual humans hinged indeed on the transformation of the complex modalities of human interaction into a rarefied legal mode that presupposed the erasure of the embodied, experiential' person (Thomas-Pellicer et al. 2016: 5, 6). The 'concrete materiality of person goes out', as well as the life-animating experience and *affectus*, including intentions, principles, sentiments and emotions. This is what makes the singularity and specificity of each entity, as *haecceitas* according to Scotus, and quiddity for each community: 'that is everything in its unique being' (Delio 2003; see also Chapters 6 and 7 in the present volume).

The crisis of legal categories, and in particular the concept of *persona juris*, in national and international law (Carty 2005) is a symptom but also a window of opportunity to address gaps in legal apprehension and ontological considerations in the context of global law (Lamalle 2014a). It is an opportunity, not only to extend the legal landscape to other entities and realms, but also to formulate distinctions between different types of entities according to their own specific legal attributions (such as animals, rivers, forests, ecosystems) – differentiating legal attributions rather than facts (Le Moigne 2000: 416). These are objectives of the movement for the Rights of Nature (see Chapters 10–12 and 15 in this volume), apprehending in law the more-than-human realm (Boyd 2017). Extending 'legal personhood to elements of eco-systems and to the earth system itself' (Burdon 2013) is one of the envisaged means for meeting the main challenge accompanying the attribution of rights to nature: addressing the specificity of entities ('rivers have rivers rights') in relation to the adaptation of the concept of legal personality or thing, and in the way we approach legal taxonomy and reasoning.

The difficult apprehension of the subject in international law set in motion a process of questioning on the law, its instruments and representations (Cosnard 2005: 3), notably with regard to the diversification of actors and their influence in the development of international law (Gaja 2003; Ruggie 2011). And it challenged the effectivity and relevance of the concept of legal personality in practice (Johns 2010; Nijman 2004; Sellers 2005; Ruiz-Fabri 2005), despite its evolution and development as a legal designation in jurisprudence, in particular regarding international organisations (Lamalle 2014a). It is important to note that the concept of *persona juris* has not been translated in Indigenous law and traditions due to historical factors of subjugation (Lamalle 2014b). In the current context of change and reappraisal, the question takes another form: how could it allow the expression of such laws and traditions? The critique of the conception of the subject as independent and rational was also debated in international law as a discourse conditioned by history and culture (Koskenniemi 2005: 115) and influenced by social and cultural assumptions about the nature of human beings (Naffine 2003). One of the critiques formulated from an Aboriginal Australian perspective of law, is that law is perceived 'not simply as a force that externally influences individual behavior but rather is an intrinsic part of the individual as well as nature' (Watson, in Pelizzon and O'Shannessy 2016: 215). Another critique, in relation to the approach of the subject, concerns the notion of rights, notably as a metaphor translated into other languages and legal systems. For instance, such a notion translated into Chinese has a quite different meaning (Mannoni 2020). Another critique of rights concerns how we approach our relationship with the land: 'In Western thinking, private land is understood to be a "bundle of rights", whereas in gift economy property is a "bundle of responsibilities"' (Kimmerer 2020: 28). The Indigenous peoples' understanding of property rights as 'collective entitlements subordinated to the imperative of environmental and cultural preservation' also challenges current conceptions. It would mean expanding the legal canon beyond individual rights, new notions of rights that go beyond the idea of individual autonomy, and incorporate a 'solidaristic understanding of entitlements grounded on alternative forms of knowledge' (Sousa Santos and Rodriguez-Garavito 2005: 14, 15). In that direction, in the *Lhaka Honhat* case in 2020, the Inter-American Court of Human Rights interpreted the right to property to include communal rights of Indigenous peoples and not just abstract title.[4] Indigenous peoples have called for the 'multicultural reconstruction of human rights, as to counter the liberal and individualist bias', including social and collective rights, rights for the Earth and natural entities (Sousa Santos and Rodriguez-Garavito 2005: 21), while there has been an ongoing critique of the separation between human and environmental rights (Sousa Santos 2005; Thomas-Pellicer et al. 2016: 3; Grant et al. 2013). The possibility of a new approach to the legal landscape would depend therefore, not only on a change of concepts, but on effective ontological

---

[4] Inter-American Court of Human Rights, *Caso Comunidades Indígenas Miembros de la Asociación Lhaka Honhat (Nuestra Tierra)* v. *Argentina* (6 Feb. 2020).

encounters and dialogue to 'frame and articulate this profound interconnection of rights through the particular political and spiritual philosophies of the Indigenous Nations' (Stewart-Harawira 2009: 222; on reappraising of the notion of rights, see Chapter 15 in the present volume).

5.2.2 *Reconnecting and Re-embodying the Legal Subject*

Considering the modern disembodied rationality, disintegrated subject and fragmented legal field, Indigenous relational landscapes appear as a much-needed response to solve current crises (Bold 2019: 91) by opening at different scales the encompassing eagle view: reconnecting and re-embodying. Indigenous law and traditions recognise and address the relationships with particular human and non-human entities that inhabit that order, such as plants, trees, animals, rocks, natural elements, spirits, gods, kin, ancestors, future generations – not necessarily with nature as a designated whole (Milton 1998: 89). In that light, Indigenous narratives are centred on relations (Borrows 2010). Concepts and practices of 'relational personhood' are present in different Indigenous legal traditions, such as the concept of *Jukurrpa* among the Warlpiri in Australia (Vaarzon-Morel 2017; Costa 2009). Indigenous law enlightens, in a wider ontological understanding, the recognised need to 're-embed the subject in hubs or nexi of relations' and to recognise and address the more-than-human realm in the critique of modern law (Carty 2007; Thomas-Pellicer et al. 2016: 16). It means approaching a living interconnected world, 'expanding and re-imagining relations with spiritual agencies' (Bold 2019: 3). In Indigenous law and language, this approach takes the shape of oral legal narratives specifying the mode of relationships with different entities, such as water for instance, recognising their specificity and advising behaviour accordingly (Craft 2014: 19, 39; King 2007: 454). This relational worldview highlights responsibility, solidarity and ethics of care, as a 'strong focus on people and entities coming together to help and support one another' (Hart 2010: 13). Such an approach is echoed in contemporary scientific reassessments of the human person as a 'network-self': 'beyond psychological and biological approach (containers), beyond consciousness and self-awareness, memory approach: but complexity and multidimensionality of persons' (Wallace 2019). It recognises the 'social embeddedness, relatedness and intersectionality of selves'. But it goes beyond 'social identities … as membership in communities (local, professional, ethnic, religious, political), or in virtue of social categories (such as race, gender, class, political affiliation) or interpersonal relations (such as being a spouse, sibling, parent, friend, neighbour)'. The relations themselves matter and are 'social but also physical, genetic, psychological, emotional and biological' (Wallace 2019). As a part of the ontological change in science (Fagot-

Largeault 2006; Spretnak 2011: 199), the key is a shift in focus from units to relations. In that sense, legal apprehension would address relations, as it is already the case in various legal traditions (Lamalle 2014b), and as Indigenous creation stories invite us to do (Erdoes and Ortiz 2013). Some methodologies in international law highlighted that turn to a certain extent, notably that of the 'legal process' and 'new legal process', which tried to approach the processes of legal creation and interpretation, redirect the attention to legal practice and institutional relations (Slaughter and Ratner 1999: 294). A further step would be to include the relationships with more-than-human entities, resituating humans and (legal) meaning-making in that wider interwoven legal pattern and semiosis (Peirce [1878] 1958; Favareau et al. 2017: 11–12).

In that light, meaning is embedded in practice and human beings are in a 'web of significance' (Geertz 1973: 5). In approaching that web, we are reminded that the 'meaning–constitutive aspect of language cannot be examined in separation from its knowledge–constitutive aspect' (Dews 2007: 292). If language plays a role with mental representations in 'mediating between minds', the notion of direct perception, as highlighted in phenomenology with the example of Indigenous modes of knowledge, comes as an 'alternative to representational approaches' with body mediations (Rival in Castree et al. 2018: 278). Indeed, such cognitive approaches take other forms of expression, such as walk, chant, dance, ceremonies, beyond words, through action, in time and movement (Descola 2006–07). Indigenous law and traditions are structured around the experiencing being and include the various dimensions of being. 'The Indigenous world view, which reconnects mind, body and spirit, brings a holistic vision to a society that is accustomed to approaching life in a fragmented, compartmentalized fashion' (Clarkson et al. 1992: 75), in the direction fostered by the critique of modern law, 'from universality towards lived knowledge' (Nikolić 2017). This approach notably 'deals with the multiple ways in which bodily processes and sensory life interrelate in the production of particular ways of knowing': for instance, for the Piaroa 'social consciousness and moral reasoning can be crafted into knowledge forms by sensory processes engaged with achieving an aesthetics of action' (Overing, in Santos-Granero and Mentore 2006). With a living language expressing knowledge forms (through speech, gestures, artwork, rhythm and music), these cognitive structures gave rise to 'poetics of knowledge', which need to be considered in 'poetics of translation'. In a relational perspective, if the former is the art of creating relations of awareness and conscience, then the latter is the art of creating relations of transformation and understanding. In both instances, it is about giving shape to relations of meaning. In this perspective, Indigenous law and traditional ways are reminiscing modes and parts of ourselves we had forgotten as human beings in a modern legal landscape. They recall the existence of poetics of knowledge. According to Indigenous ways, 'we understand a thing only when we understand it with all four aspects of our being: mind, body, emotion and spirit', while 'science privileges only one, possibly two, of those ways of knowing' (Kimmerer 2020: 47). In such a context, and understanding of legal relationships, making an agreement involves therefore all dimensions of being, with embodied and felt knowledge. Reconnection with the heart, in that sense, contributes to realising our 'relationships and responsibility to Creation' – it includes an ethics of care, and sentiments like respect and gratitude, as in the Haudenosaunee 'thanking address' (King 2007: 454–56). This brings to light the integrity of the human being in Indigenous law, reminding us that law, in a much larger sense, is not human-made only, and concerns the more-than-human realm, including natural elements (see Chapter 6 in this volume).

In this light, responding to the call of Indigenous legal traditions is a process of critical significance: re-envisaging being human in all its dimensions and relations in the legal field – re-embodying law and knowledge (Stewart-Harawira 2009: 211; Thomas-Pellicer et al. 2016), and reinhabiting the world with 'the multiple, overlapping spheres of community, authority, and interdependency that actually exist in human experience' (Dorough in Morgan 2011: 126). Remedying 'modernity's ontological and epistemological trajectory of disembodiments' (Thomas-Pellicer et al. 2016: 2), such an ontological shift would contribute to responding to the critique of modern law and to the crisis of modern representations. It would also provide a specific framework for decolonising legal narratives (see Chapter 3 in this volume) and allow the expression of other legal traditions, envisaging it both as a response to the current ecological predicament and restoration of legal integrity.

5.2.3 *The Evolution of Legal Designations and Narrative*

This ontological shift means approaching a living and interconnected experience of reality. Oral narration displays therefore the same characteristics, as narratives are dynamic forms of relational patterns of thought, and orality is inscribed in the experience of a present moment. For instance, in the Anishinabe legal tradition, where 'the law of water (*Anishinaabe nibi inaakonigewin*) is structured by a set of relations between founding principles' and the responsibility of guardians of water, such legal relations are explained in specific oral narratives about water, contextualising people in concrete situations (Craft 2014: 19, 39). We note that such narratives are also told in 'languages of animacy' (Kimmerer 2020: 57), that is Indigenous languages in which not only humans but also other beings are considered animated entities. For instance, in Anishinabe, the term *peciko* designates an animated entity and includes notably animals, trees, plants, rocks and rivers (Esipan 2020). It is usually translated as 'person' or 'living being', but such a translation tends to convey the representations attached to that term in English, and leads to personification in case it is applied to other realities, as is the case with institutions (juridical persons). This is not so in the Anishinabe language: *peciko mitik* (a tree entity) does not have the same ontic characteristics as a *peciko asini* (rock entity) and is addressed differently in its relationships with *anishinabek* (human entities). Indigenous poetics of knowledge and legal attributions are different and consider a body of ontic knowledge, that is, 'knowledge pertaining to the distinctive nature of particular types of entity' (Mulhall 1996: 4). Another determining point regarding Indigenous narratives is they have a wider understanding of the verbs used in relation to human entities, as their legal scope comprehends a diversity of entities and relations, their application to other entities do not use an anthropomorphic and restrictive analogy. This example is particularly enlightening:

> In the old times, our elders say, the trees talked to each other. But Scientists decided long ago that plants were deaf and mute, locked in isolation without communication. The conclusion was drawn that plants cannot communicate because they lack the mechanisms that animals use to speak. There is now compelling evidence that our elders were right – the trees are talking to one another. They communicate via pheromones, hormone like compounds that are wafted on the breeze, laden with meaning.
>
> *(Kimmerer 2020: 20)*

Such an example questions our understanding of communication and sheds light on the necessary awareness of our own perspective, on the existence and possibility of a depersonified language and a communication beyond words and representations. 'There is a serious problem with using (human) language as the model for analyzing other species' communication in hindsight. It leads us to treat every other form of communication as exceptions to a rule' (Deacon 1997: 52). We need to distinguish between 'aspects of semiosis that are unique to human semiosis, and those that are common across one or more species' (Favareau 2017: 13).

These two considerations – about the use of the term 'person' and the reduction of legal language to human meaning-making (anthroposemiosis) – are decisive in the attempts to transform law and legal intelligibility to face up to current social and ecological challenges. In the legal cases recognising rights or personality to other entities such as rivers, in different countries (see Chapter 10 in this volume), the approach of personification shows its limits, as the representation of the legal subject. And it is important to draw attention to the overlapping of semantic use and the necessity to differentiate between two understandings. First, the use of the term 'person' to designate 'animated entities' in Indigenous legal traditions does not attribute human qualities to other entities but recognises their ontic specificity.

And the use of the term 'person' in modern legal language in English, which refers to a personified conception of the legal subject, with human qualities and attributions, leads to the analogy of 'fictive persons' as applied to institutions.

In arguing the shift from object to subject, advocates for rivers sometimes draw on the powerful yet arguably superficial analogy of corporate personhood, a legal state of affairs where an abstraction metamorphises into a robust subject capable of suing and being sued. As the Colorado case study shows, however, the analogy of the corporation is not always helpful. Perhaps, more fundamentally, the analogy is inapt. After all, the corporation is both a human construct and a fictionalised human person. By contrast, rivers are natural features that exist independently of human construction and imagination (Clark et al. 2019: 830).

We need to differentiate the legal designation in Indigenous legal traditions. For instance, in Ecuador, the Vilcabamba River was not approached as a person, but as a 'divine' part of nature (Clark et al. 2019), reminding us of the *res divini juris* in Roman law, as belonging to another realm and law beyond the human, with specific ontic faculties (see Chapter 8 in this volume). This recognition is found within the Ecuadorian state liabilities towards the achievement of the *good living* or *sumak kawsay* (see Chapter 15 in this volume). In India, a similar reasoning was applied on the basis of the divine nature of the Ganges and Yamuna rivers, and moral duty to protect them as Hindu divinities, as sacred entities. In that case, one of the terms envisaged for the legal designation of the rivers was 'juristic entities' (Clark et al. 2019: 832), avoiding personification and placing them in another category of entities, different from human entities. Beyond the subject–object dichotomy, the Yarra River/Birrarung in Australia was described as a 'living and integrated natural entity' deprived of legal personhood (Clark et al. 2019: 833). In that case, legal personhood is associated with human qualities and set aside in order to emphasise the specificity of the river as a different entity. In doing so, the legal designation is denied its function because of its mode of representation, identified with the modern understanding of a human being as legal subject. In that reflection, it seems either we remove the mode of representation of the legal designation, or we change the conception of the 'person' as legal subject. An element in favour of the latter option is the evolution of the meaning of the notion of 'person' throughout time and its use in different fields of knowledge, recalling the initial characteristics of the concept of *persona* in Roman law: 'that which perpetuates in time and that which stands before – the designation' (Lamalle 2014b: 303–04). In the twentieth century, as a reaction to the conception of an independent subject, the use of the term 'person' in common language was differentiated from the term 'individual' as a way of underlining its relational quality (Dubreuil 2005). In that sense, the change in use of the term would come from a renewed approach of the person in the common space and language, and from the understanding of legal personality as a designation with content, in a colourful and vibrating legal landscape, beyond the black-and-white subject–object dichotomy. The former option involves renaming legal designations altogether. Either way, the recognition and legal designation of water, and other entities, in the legal landscape – as bringing them to existence in the legal world – is an advancement in the apprehension of diverse realities in the legal language and reasoning, and a much-awaited reform of the modern legal frame of intelligibility.

Furthermore, the ontological shift entails addressing relations. Such insight is present in the recognition of 'the interrelationship between the right to water and the right to a healthy environment' (Clark et al. 2019: 835), but clouded by the current structure of thought in law. The realisation of the interdependent relation between humans and water, and its different dimensions was acknowledged in the case of the Ganga and Yamuna rivers, pointing to their 'spiritual and physical sustenance', and their support to the life, health and well-being of the entire community (Clark et al. 2019: 835). Addressing relationships between entities, in their specificity and different dimensions, in terms of responsibility and ethics of care, may be another important step in the reform of legal institutions and narrative. In that regard, taking into consideration Indigenous poetics of knowledge and narratives, with their specific semantic content (see Chapter 9 in this volume), reasoning and repertoire of interpretation (Potter and Wetherell 1987) can also be a source of inspiration and creativity in the legal field. Opening that space of dialogue between legal traditions will help adapt the current legal language and practice to such relational legal ontology and consciousness (Chual and Engel 2019).

5.3 Legal Understanding and Co-Meaning-Making

As presented in Chapter 1 in this volume, effective dialogue requires removing 'barriers to understanding': discrimination, historical negative representations, reductive categories and ignorance of other modes of knowledge (Clarkson et al. 1992: 9; Battiste 2000: 5; Jansen and Pérez Jiménez 2017: 28). Entering that dialogue with Indigenous legal traditions and orders (Sousa Santos and Rodriguez-Garavito 2005: 2; Mazzocchi 2006: 463), we need to 'follow the traces of oral traditions and local practices' (Menski 2005: 396). It implies a change of perspective (Wittgenstein [1953] 1969: 214) and attitude (*Einstellungsänderung* in Broekman 2016) from the understanding and practice of law in Western legal systems, and a reappraisal of the legal scope, methods and instruments. In that space of legal dialogue and 'conceptual negotiation' (Arregii 2019: 183–84), the encounter 'aims at shared understanding and joint transformation' (Wagenaar 2011), towards a 'new common sense' (Sousa Santos 2004: 60, 121). To meet that challenge we need to recognise other forms of legal expression and communication. To that end, legal semiotics can shed light on other forms of legal conscience and communication (Section 5.3.1) and help open a space of legal understanding (Section 5.3.2), for reconciliation and legal co-meaning-making (Section 5.3.3)

5.3.1 Approaching Other Forms of Legal Conscience

Considering other legal traditions means approaching reality and the legal landscape differently. We need to acknowledge the specificity of 'Indigenous cosmopolitics', and the fact that it is another form of knowledge which requires a participative epistemology (Poirier 2008). Considering the development of pragmatics and the philosophy of language in the study of law, the exercise of legal interpretation can be extended to new practices. In legal language, as in other scientific languages, giving meaning and making sense is a question of narration (Broekman 2016: vi). The legal discourse and practice approached as a narrative based on representations can be studied with the techniques of semiotics (Jackson 1988; Nash 1994). Considering that legal meaning is enclosed in forms, such as representations and concepts of law, we can only perceive it through those forms (Dews 2007: 292). We can thus apprehend a variety of legal significations with the study of the 'narrative semiotics' in different legal traditions (Kalinowski 1988: 92). Regarding the ontological dimension of legal practice and discourse, legal semiotics opens the analysis to the form of law and 'the content of the legal conscience' (Jackson 1988: 65): the narrative forms and modalities taken in that tradition, highlighting the elements which are characteristic to its social representations and practices. In that light, studying the narrative semiotics of a legal conscience specific to a legal tradition can help to identify both form and content of legal communication in that tradition. This approach allows us to take into account Indigenous ontologies, their cognitive structures and the 'frame of perception and understanding of a legal community' (Legrand in Pedro Ricoy et al. 2018: 163). Such a frame of perception conditions the modalities of legal expression and communication. The study of the narrative semiotics therefore allows us to consider other modalities of legal narration, beyond a certain understanding of law, legality and language (Le Roy 2004; Alliot 2003; Rival in Castree et al. 2018; Kohn 2013). We can then adjust our focus on legal communication itself. As we noted, in Indigenous legal traditions, conceptual frameworks take another form in oral narratives such as creation stories, and the range of legal communication goes beyond the dimension of language spoken or written, with songs, dances, ceremonies and artefacts.

If we approach language as a system of symbolic communication and perception of meaning – through the experience of different dimensions of being – as an alternative to representational approaches, ritual communication appears as a practice where 'the opposition between symbolic and material dimensions of life disappear' (Harries-Jones 2004). Such a unique feature has a performative character in Indigenous legal communication, the meaning being in the ritual itself. Indigenous ceremonies and certain oral declarations, such as Mantalil in Tzeltal, present that feature, and their legal meaning needs to be apprehended *in acta*. In studying the narrative semiotics of such legal traditions, we can identify various distinctive elements, like the modalities of communication (e.g. text, oral declaration, protocol of meeting, ceremonies, artefact, song, dance), what is to be communicated (e.g. will, intention, agreement), and the significations used to that end founding the narrative (e.g. concepts, narrative modes). We can focus attention on distinctive features of Indigenous legal communication, and open a wider horizon of legal understanding, starting a process of comprehension in which we can interact with others, and expand our own knowledge horizon. As legal language evolves, and there are instituting functions of law, it can be envisaged as 'an instrument of action, an operative tool' (Husson 1986: 982). Conceptual elaboration has therefore a key role in creating new modalities of communication. However, decentring human language and detaching it from its exclusive articulation to representation allow us to give account of other modes of signifying, make a distinction between representation and language, and rehabilitate the experience of meaning through different dimensions of being (Kohn 2013; Rival in Castree et al. 2018). In this light, the legal language extends beyond the frames of modern law and representations, with a broader range of modes of legal communication.

5.3.2 Legal Understanding and Modalities of Legal Communication

On a wider horizon where we can contemplate the legal landscape beyond the walls and borders of the constituted forms of Western modern law (Ogden and Richards 1989: 4), we can now recognise and distinguish the specific modes of Indigenous legal communication. From this viewpoint, the limits to communication and to the translation of such practices and significations, underlined in different contexts, can be reconsidered (Sousa Santos 2004: 302; Salée and Lévesque 2016). As in Indigenous traditions, legal expression does not usually take the shape of a written text, its use as a privileged form of legal communication in modern law hindered legal communication with Indigenous peoples (Gunn 2018). On a wider horizon of legal communication, we can take into consideration forms of expression other than words, and mobilise both the insights of jurists and linguists, but also that of legal sociologists and anthropologists (Lamalle 2020a). The translation of the specific narrativity of Indigenous legal traditions can embrace Indigenous methodologies which are holistic, relational and rooted in

Indigenous ontology (Craft 2014). That context includes 'legal and political rituals' (Birkland 2011: 90) with other modes of perception, such as the performance of Haka, which is a chanted dance of the Aboriginal peoples of the South Pacific, recognised as a form of legal communication. Opening the field of communication to legal consciences other than Western legal traditions, we can consider oral legal traditions, ceremonies, as well as artefacts such as Wampum belts made of shells, which are considered sacred objects (Moses 2018).

> One of the first Wampum belts to mark a treaty between Indigenous Peoples and European traders ... is call(ed) the Two-Row Wampum. Here is its description: Two rows of blue, each symbolizing a different nation. Separated and surrounded by three rows of white; one for peace, another for friendship and the last for forever. The Two-Row Wampum was an agreement made between the Haudenosaunee and the Dutch upon European arrival in North America. The Wampum ensured that Europeans and First Nations, while living side by side on the same land, would refrain from interfering in each other's nations.
>
> *(Sadongei 2004: 17–19)*

Wampum belts are used to mark legal agreements between peoples and are of 'particular significance with regards to treaties and covenants made between Indigenous peoples and European colonial powers'. It includes 'the Hiawatha Belt (the belt of the Haudenosaunee, the Covenant Chain Wampum of 1764, and the Two-Row Wampum Belt (*Kaswentha*)' (Parmenter 2013). The study of colonial-era documentary records, corroborating Haudenosaunee (Iroquoian) oral tradition regarding the Two-Row Wampum belt, shows recitations of the tradition in documentary sources from 1656 to 1755. Integrating Indigenous oral tradition, notably through documentary record, could contribute to the 'reconciliation of historical knowledge' (Parmenter 2013). Modes and forms of legal communication also comprise diplomatic protocols (Beier 2009). For instance, the 'Covenant Chain represents the long tradition of diplomatic relations in North America, and is often invoked when discussing contemporary affairs between the state and Indigenous peoples' (Parmenter 2013).[5] Among the Indigenous modalities of legal communication for the negotiation and agreement of treaties, there is the pipe-smoking ceremony, signifying 'to the Creator the intention of the parties to keep the terms of the agreement in a strong binding manner' (Gunn 2018). Such Indigenous diplomatic protocols were followed by both parties in negotiating and concluding many treaties with Western representatives.

Due to the lack of translation of treaties in Indigenous languages, and consideration for other Indigenous modalities of legal communication (such as Wampum belts and oral recitations), different issues were raised concerning their

---

[5] The Covenant Chain is the name given to the complex system of alliances between the Haudenosaunee and Anglo-American colonies in the early seventeenth century (Parmenter 2013).

interpretation, as it is currently based on the written text in English (Gunn 2018: 11). In such contexts, the 'textual approach' of interpretation of the treaty is limiting. In current international practice, if the International Law Commission considers interpretation as a 'holistic exercise', including different approaches to interpretation such as 'textual, contextual, teleological, historical, intentions of the parties' (Aspremont and Gardiner 2020: 34–36), it concerns written documents most of them written in English, and further material usually refers to other documents such as dictionaries, publications of doctrine or other international and regional treaties. Articles 31 to 33 of the Vienna Convention on the Interpretation of Treaties 'reflect rules of customary international law' on interpretation in the jurisprudence of the International Court of Justice (Merkouris and Peat 2020: 3). In that context, article 32 allows for 'material' outside the treaty to be considered for interpretation; and article 33 concerns multilingual treaties, with the general principle that no one language is superior to another (Gunn 2018: 14). Such provisions in positive law can help balance translation and interpretation to a certain extent, as the notion of 'material' could be understood *lato sensu* and include other forms of communication, such as storytelling or artefacts. Nevertheless, such material would still be considered as being outside the treaty.

The Inter-American Commission Court of Human Rights is considered to have 'provided a multicultural scope to many rights of the American Convention on Human Rights to incorporate 'Indigenous' culture in all its dimensions', such as freedom of expression (article 13) which includes the right of Indigenous peoples to speak in their own language because it 'ensures the expression, distribution and transmission of culture'. Litigation shows that 'traditional habits and customs' are taken seriously by the Court, and agreed with the fact that 'Indigenous peoples' view of the universe' contributes to the evaluation of protected rights (Burgorgue-Larsen 2020: 17–18). In such a framework therefore it should be possible to envisage the recognition and consideration of other modalities of legal communication on an equal level.

If there is more sensitivity to other legal traditions in legal practice, there is still an epistemic gap concerning the recognition and inclusion of Indigenous legal traditions and law, in particular the modalities of Indigenous legal communication in Indigenous languages as well as ceremonies, storytelling or artefacts. Towards such recognition, 'the African Commission on Human and Peoples' Rights (ACmHR) demands that the African Charter should be interpreted in 'a culturally sensitive way', taking into full account the different legal traditions of Africa's diversity' (Merkouris and Peat 2020: 26). In that perspective, perhaps the interpretive approach of the 'integration technique' and the 'combinaison normative' techniques, usually referring to other international or regional instruments, might help in including Indigenous law, legal concepts and modalities of legal communication.

As we observed, Indigenous languages are embedded in specific cognitive structures and modes of knowledge, requiring consequent translation of both content and mode of communication. In that perspective, the specific Indigenous languages, forms of speech, protocols and modalities of legal communication involved in concluding a treaty would need to be recognised as such, and taken into consideration for its interpretation. For instance, oral stories and artworks, like Wampum belts, are designed to express the meaning and scope of the treaties. In the Indigenous perspective, treaties are considered as 'living agreements rather than as mere documents', as a 'living relationship beyond the particular promises' and 'expressed in terms of kinship' (Gunn 2018). Such modalities and understanding are inherent to the treaty concluded, and is therefore not only another key of interpretation, but also another mode of perception of its meaning, as embodied and felt knowledge forms. Disregarding such modalities of legal communication is not only truncating legal discourse, but also depriving legal interpretation of a larger legal conscience and understanding. Translating the content of the legal message into words only and in a textual approach, without having regard to the modalities of communication, is to miss whole dimensions of the message. Concerning the operation of translation, there are different ways of transmitting both information and modality of communication (like oral recordings), and such considerations could be discussed and specified in agreements. By opening the field of legal communication to wider legal consciences, we can address different conceptual frameworks, dimensions of being and modalities of expression – broadening the realm of legal understanding.

5.3.3 Co-creating a Common Semiotic Space in Law and Society

Reflecting on such considerations in our legal thinking and practice, we can work towards the constitution of the shared framework which is called for in Indigenous legal traditions. As narrative semiotics helped us in approaching other forms of legal conscience and expression, semiotics, as a wide-angle instrument, allow us to look at relations of meaning beyond categorial and conceptual structures (Lamalle 2020b). Indeed, the notion of semiotic space can be described as a place structured by relations of meaning in the framework of certain constituted forms, significations and representations. Such forms can be identified in terms and concepts, but also beyond words, on the different dimensions where relations of meaning and significations are structured. It can be a place like a building, such as a court, with the protocol of a trial and the content of a legal discourse; or a longhouse, with a certain protocol for a ceremony, and the content of a story. On another level, a legal system can also be considered as a semiotic space. The semiotic space emerging from the interaction between two or more legal systems and traditions is a place of negotiation of meaning and significations (Lamalle 2020b). As a space in between different 'thought worlds', it is an 'ethical space' of recognition and respect, where 'appropriate, ethical and human principles' guide the interaction (Ermine 2007). Such a space of cross-cultural exchanges implies the recognition of the different languages and modalities of legal communication: facilitating the co-creation of a 'common semiotic space', towards 'a new common sense, liberating' (Sousa Santos 2004: 60, 121). The capacity to conceive new significations (in words, protocols of meeting and ceremonies, institutions, artefacts) with mutual legal understanding is also part of the operation of legal translation, as a third space of transformation and communication (Wagner et al. 2014). It means going a step further to entering another semiotic space: it is co-creating a common semiotic space with new relations of meaning.

The example of the TRC in Canada illustrates the creation of a new semiotic space in law and society with Indigenous peoples and their legal traditions. It is a space in which the definitions of the relationships with Indigenous peoples are reconsidered, and in which Indigenous approaches, principles, medicine and law can find expression and application. In such a space, the negative representation and discrimination are publicly contested, and new social representations are collectively formulated (Lamalle 2015). The conclusions of the TRC, on the basis of such new social representations, launched a process restructuring the relations of meaning into new forms and significations in law and society, with new concepts, institutions and processes. This 'process of reconciliation' is renewing the relationships with Indigenous peoples and law 'on a basis of inclusion, mutual understanding, and respect' (TRC Report 2015: 27), and towards a renewed 'vision of justice' (Cunneen and Rowe 2014). In its conclusions, the TRC also considered 'justice' from an Indigenous law perspective, as 'healing relationships' (McCaslin 2005). And 'the reclamation of Indigenous heritage, culture, knowledge, and jurisprudence is an integral part of the healing process' (McCaslin and Youngblood Henderson 2005: 17). The TRC fostered Indigenous traditional approaches to justice and health (with witnesses, sharing circles, traditional medicine, community support) in partnership with Health Canada, in order 'to address the relationship between the spiritual, emotional and physical in a holistic manner' (TRC 2015: 29–31). In the context of Canada, it means also healing intergenerational trauma of colonisation, forced assimilation and residential schools. Such 'traumatic events are part of larger historical formations that have profound effects for both individuals and communities', and are also 'built into ongoing social relations, roles, practices and institutions' (Kirmayer et al. 2000: 16). As discrimination, loss of language and culture, and disconnection from the land have led to socio-economic inequalities and health disparities, 'reconciliation must create a more equitable and inclusive society' (McNally and Martin 2017).

The TRC designed a roadmap for change in that direction with ninety-four Calls to action. 'This roadmap builds on substantive Indigenous leadership, resilience, and creativity' (McGibbon 2019) and includes a list of '10 Principles of Reconciliation' the first being the 'adoption of the United Nations Declaration on the Rights of Indigenous Peoples (UNDRIP) as a framework for reconciliation'. Such a process aims to create a 'space of liberation and transformation', to foster a change of social representations and narratives, fill the gap of inequalities and rebalance relationships in various sectors. In that new semiotic space, many First Nations concluded new agreements with the federal government to renew relationships, and a diversity of actors across Canada endorsed the TRC's Calls to action and the UNDRIP: federal, provincial and Indigenous governments, as well as churches, businesses, associations, municipalities, schools and universities. And following the recommendations of the TRC, law societies, bar associations and law schools in Canada have initiated reforms to that end, notably training law students, lawyers and judges about Indigenous law.[6] The semiotic space opened by the TRC is intended to expand to the whole of Canadian society, and implies the negotiation of legal meaning and significations with the semiotic and linguistic spaces of the legal systems of common law, civil law and Indigenous law. The TRC understands reconciliation as 'a mutual process to be engaged in by Indigenous and non-Indigenous peoples alike, and with the potential to contribute to a change in the narrative and conceptions of political morality that can henceforth inform the political culture' (Stanton 2017: 38). This is a new space of legal communication and transformation towards the creation of a new legal narrative and practice. In such a space, the recognition of Indigenous languages[7] and law involves taking into account Indigenous poetics of knowledge, conceptual frameworks and modalities of legal communication. It requires also poetics of translation which are in accordance with the narrative semiotics specific to Indigenous legal traditions. If 'co-creating' and nurturing such a common semiotic space of legal communication is a major challenge, it is also a historical chance to reconcile with Indigenous legal traditions, modes of knowledge and ontologies (Lévesque et al. 2009; McGregor 2018).

---

[6] For instance: Canadian Bar Association, Responding to the Truth and Reconciliation Commission's Calls to Action, March 2016.
[7] Notably with the Indigenous Languages Act – An Act Respecting Indigenous Languages. Bill C-91 introduced in 2019, received royal assent 21 June 2019.

Conclusion

The revitalisation and promotion of Indigenous languages made salient the existence of obliterated idioms and ways of being in the world. Reacquainting with Indigenous legal traditions, we realise a broader comprehension of legal language and communication.

In affirming the operative and performative characters of language, semiotics opens a new horizon of meaning, and allow us to approach legal consciences and languages in the diversity of their forms, significations and modalities of expression.

We have now the possibility to remove the barriers to legal understanding, for co-meaning-making in a wider scope of legal intelligibility with different legal traditions. This is a further step for the reconciliation with Indigenous peoples. This is also an opportunity to respond to the critique of law and to the ecological crisis – restoring legal integrity, by acknowledging the different relations and dimensions of being human in law with the more-than-human realm. Such an ontological actualisation, in accordance with other legal traditions, translates a relational approach of the legal landscape.

In order to enact the paradigm shift, which is called for, our challenge consists not only in bringing to light a common space of legal communication, but also in co-creating altogether a new legal framework.

Acknowledgements

This is a reflection with long roots in time and space. I am grateful to all those who encouraged and nurtured its growth on different continents. During the preparation of this chapter, I conducted a research visit in legal theory to the KU Leuven Law Faculty in Belgium. I am very appreciative and thankful to professors Jan Broekman and Frank Fleerackers for their kind welcome and the inspiring discussions we had on legal philosophy, language and semiotics. *In de geest van taal. Met al mijn dankbaarheid.*

References

Alliot, M. (2003). Anthropologie et juristique: Sur les conditions de l'élaboration d'une science du droit. In C. Kuyu (ed.), *Le droit et le service public au miroir de l'anthropologie*. Paris: Karthala, 283–305.

Amselek, P. and C. Grzegorczyk (eds.) (1989). *Controverses autour de l'ontologie du droit*. Paris: Presses universitaires de France.

Anaya, J. (2004). *Indigenous Peoples in International Law*. 2nd ed. Oxford: Oxford University Press.

Arregui, A. G. (2019). This mess is a 'World'! Environmental diplomats in the mud of anthropology. In R. Bold (ed.), *Indigenous Perceptions of the End of the World: Creating a Cosmopolitics of Change*. New York: Palgrave Macmillan, 183–202.

Aspremont, J. and R. Gardiner (2020). Methodological observations on interpretation in international law, ILA Study Group on the Content and Evolution of the Rules of Interpretation. Kyoto Conference.

Austin-Broos, D. and F. Merlan (eds.) (2017). *People and Change in Indigenous Australia*. Honolulu: Hawaii University Press.

Barbéris, J. A. (1983). Nouvelles questions concernant la personnalité juridique internationale. In *Collected Courses of the Hague Academy of International Law* (179). Leiden: Brill, 145–304.

Battiste, M. (2000). *Reclaiming Indigenous Voice and Vision*. Vancouver: UBC Press.

Bederman, D. J. (1996). The souls of international organizations: Legal personality and the lighthouse at Cape Spartel. *Virginia Journal of International Law* 36(2): 275–377.

Beier, J. (2009). *Indigenous Diplomacies*. New York: Palgrave Macmillan.

Bergthaller, H., R. Emmet, A. Johns-Putra et al. (2012). Mapping common ground: Ecocriticism, environmental history, and the environmental humanities. *Environmental Humanities* 5: 261–76.

Birkland, B. (2011). *An Introduction to the Policy Process: Theories, Concepts and Models*. London: Routledge.

Bold, R. (ed.) (2019). *Indigenous Perceptions of the End of the World: Creating a Cosmopolitics of Change*. New York: Palgrave Macmillan.

Borrows, J. (2002). *Recovering Canada: The Resurgence of Indigenous Law*. Toronto: University of Toronto Press.

Borrows, J. (2010). *Canada's Indigenous Constitution*. Toronto: University of Toronto Press.

Boyd, D. R. (2017). *The Rights of Nature: A Legal Revolution that Could Save the World*. Toronto: ECW Press.

Boyle, J. (1991). Is subjectivity possible? The postmodern subject in legal theory. *University of Colorado Law Review* 62: 489–524.

Broekman, J. (2016). *Meaning, Narrativity and the Real: The Semiotics of Law in Legal Education IV*. Dordrecht: Springer.

Burdon, P. (2013). The earth community and ecological jurisprudence. *Oñati Socio-Legal Series* 3(5): 815–37.

Burgorgue-Larsen, L. (2020). *Final Report on the Inter-American Commission of Human Rights (iacom.hr) & the Inter-American Court of Human Rights (IACtHR)*. ILA Study Group on the Content and Evolution of the Rules of Interpretation, 29 November–13 December, Kyoto.

Cadava, E., P. Connor and J.-L. Nancy (eds.) (1991). *Who Comes after the Subject?* London: Routledge.

Canguilhem, G. (1967). Mort de l'homme ou épuisement du cogito? *Critique* 1: 599–618.

Carty, A. (ed.) (1990). *Post-Modern Law, Enlightenment, Revolution and the Death of Man*. Edinburgh: Edinburgh University Press.

Carty, A. (1991). Critical international law: Recent trends in the theory of international law. *European Journal of International Law* 2(1): 66–97.

Carty, A. (2005). International legal personality and the end of the subject: Natural law and phenomenological responses to new approaches to international law. *Melbourne Journal of International Law* 6: 534–52.

Carty, A. (2007). *Philosophy of International Law*. Edinburgh: Edinburgh University Press.

Castillo, M. M. and A. Strecker (2017). *Heritage and Rights of Indigenous Peoples*. Leiden: Leiden University Press.

Castree, N., M. Hulme and J. D. Proctor (eds.) (2018). *Companion to Environmental studies*. New York: Routledge.

Chakravartty, A. (2010). Truth and representation in science: Two inspirations from art. In R. Frigg and M. Hunter (eds.), *Beyond Mimesis and Convention: Representation in Art and Science*. Dordrecht: Springer, 33–50.

Chual, L. J. and David M. Engel (2019). Legal consciousness reconsidered. *Annual Review of Law and Social Science* 15: 335–53.

Cosnard, M. 2005. Rapport introductif. In *Le sujet en droit international*. Paris: Pedone, 3–35.

Costa, R. da (2009). Indigenous diplomacies before the nation-state. In J. Beier (ed.), *Indigenous Diplomacies*. New York: Palgrave Macmillan, 61–77.

Clark, C., N. Emmanouil, J. Page and A. Pelizzon (2019). Can you hear the rivers sing? Legal personhood, ontology, and the nitty-gritty of governance. *Ecology Law Quarterly* 45(4): 787.

Clarkson, L., V. Morrissette and G. Régallet (1992). *Our Responsibility to the Seventh Generation: Indigenous Peoples and Sustainable Development*. Winnipeg: International Institute for Sustainable Development (IISD).

Commaille, J. and B. Jobert (1998). *Les métamorphoses de la régulation juridique*. Paris: LGDJ.

Craft, A. (2014). *Anishinaabe Nibi Inaakonigewin Report*. Reflecting the Water Laws Research Gathering conducted with Anishinaabe Elders, 20–23 June 2013 at Roseau River, Manitoba. University of Manitoba's Centre for Human Rights Research (CHRR) and the Public Interest Law Centre (PILC).

Cunneen, C. and S. Rowe (2014). Changing narratives: Colonised peoples, criminology and social work. *International Journal for Crime, Justice and Social Democracy* 3 (1): 49–67.

Delio (2003). *A Franciscan View of Creation: Learning to Live in a Sacramental World*, Synthesis provided by: Marie Puleo, The Franciscan Heritage Series, Volume 2.

Delmas-Marty, M. (2008). *Les forces imaginantes du droit*. Cours au Collège de France, Cours no. 6.

Deloria, V. Jr. (1992). *God Is Red: A Native View of Religion*. Golden, CO: Fulcrum Publishing.

Descola, P. (2006–07). 'Modalités de la figuration', Anthropologie de la nature. Cours au Collège de France, 'Ontologie des images'.

Dews, P. (2007). *Logics of Disintegration, Poststructuralist Thought, and the Claims of Critical Theory*. London: Verso.

Dorough, D. (2009). The significance of the Declaration on the Rights of Indigenous Peoples and its future implementation. In C. Charters and R. Stavenhagen (eds.), *Making the Declaration Work*. Copenhagen: IWGIA, 264–78.

Dubreuil, E. H. (2005). *The Personalism of Denis de Rougemont: Spirituality and Politics in 1930s Europe*. Cambridge: Cambridge University Press.

Eberhard, C. (ed.) (2008). *Traduire nos responsabilités planétaires: Recomposer nos paysages juridiques*. Brussels: Bruylant.

Eberhard, C. and G. Vernicos (eds.) (2006). *La quête anthropologique du droit*. Paris: Karthala.

Erdoes, R. and A. Ortiz. (2013). *American Indian Myths and Legends*. New York: Doubleday.

Ermine, W. (2007). Ethical space of engagement. *Indigenous Law Journal* 6(1): 193–203.

Esipan (2018). *Guide linguistique Anicinape*. Quebec: Kina8at.

Fagot-Largeault, A. (2006–08). *Ontologie du devenir*. Paris: Cours au Collège de France.

Favareau, D. et al. (2017). How can the study of the humanities inform the study of biosemiotics? *Biosemiotics* 10: 9–31.

Frigg, R. and M. Hunter (eds.) (2010). *Beyond Mimesis and Convention: Representation in Art and Science*. Dordrecht: Springer.

Gaja, G. (2003). *First Report on the Responsibility of International Organisations*. 26 March, ACN.4/532

Geertz, C. (1973). *Interpretation of Cultures*. New York: Basic Books.

Glenn, H. Patrick (2003). La tradition juridique nationale. *Revue internationale de droit comparé* 2: 276–78.

Goodrich, P. (1987). *Legal Discourse: Studies in Linguistics, Rhetoric and Legal Analysis*. New York: Macmillan.

Gotti, M. and C. Williams (eds.) (2010). *Legal Discourse across Languages and Cultures*. Berne: Peter Lang.

Gounelle, M. (2005). Communicabilité en droit international public. In M. Baudrez and T. di Manno (eds.), *Liber Amicorum Jean-Claude Escarras. La communicabilité entre les systèmes juridiques*. Brussels: Bruylant.

Grant, E., L. J. Kotzé and K. Morrow (2013). Human rights and the environment: In search of a new relationship. Synergies and common themes. *Oñati Socio-Legal Series* 3(5): 953–65.

Grize, J.-B. (1982), *De la logique à l'argumentation*. Geneva: Droz.

Grzegorczyk, C. (1989). Le sujet de droit: Trois hypostases. *Archives de Philosophie du Droit* 34: 9–32.

Gunn, B. L. (2018). Exploring the International Character of Treaties 1–11 and the Legal Consequences, in *Canada in International Law at 150 and Beyond*, Paper No. 5, January, Centre for International Governance Innovation.

Harries-Jones, P. (ed.) (2004). Semiotics, evolution, energy, and development: In honor of the work and life of Gregory Bateson. *Seed* 4(1): 1–2.

Harrison, K. D. (2010). *The Last Speakers: The Quest to Save the World's Most Endangered Languages*. Washington, DC: National Geographic.

Hart, M. A. (2010). Indigenous worldviews, knowledge, and research: The development of an Indigenous research paradigm. *Journal of Indigenous Voices in Social Work* 1(1): 1–16.

Hewitt, J. G. (2016). Indigenous restorative justice: Approaches, meaning and possibility. *University of New Brunswick Law Journal* 67: 313–35.

Howard, R., L. Andrade Ciudad and R. de Pedro Ricoy (2018). Translating rights: The Peruvian Languages Act in Quechua and Aymara. *Amerindia* 40: 219–45.

Husson, C. A. D. (1986). Expanding the legal vocabulary: The challenge posed by the deconstruction and defense of law. *Yale Law Journal* 95: 969–91.

ILC (2006). *Report on the Fragmentation of International Law*. International Law Commission. UN Doc. A/CN.4/l.682.

Jaccoud, M. (2014). Peuples autochtones et pratiques d'accommodements en matière de justice pénale au Canada et au Québec. *Archives de politique criminelle* 1(36): 227–39.

Jackson, B. S. (1988). *Law, Fact, and Narrative Coherence*. Merseyside, UK: Deborah Charles.

Jansen, M. and G. A. Pérez Jiménez (2017). The Indigenous condition: An introductory note. In M. M. Castillo and A. Strecker (eds.), *Heritage and Rights of Indigenous Peoples*. Leiden: Leiden University Press, 25–39.

Jodelet, D. (2006). La Place de l'expérience vécue dans les processus de formation des représentations sociales. In V. Haas (ed.), *Les savoirs du quotidien: Transmissions, appropriations, représentations*. Rennes: Presses universitaires de Rennes, 235–55.

Johns, F. (ed.) (2010). *International Legal Personality*. New York: Routledge.

Kalinowski, G. (1988). Sémiotique. *Droit et Société* 8: 91–98.

Kennedy, David (1987). *International Legal Structures*. Baden-Baden: Nomos.

Kennedy, D. (2006). The last treatise: Project and person. *German Law Journal* 7(12): 982–92.

Kennedy, Duncan (1997). *A Critique of Adjudication* (fin de siècle). Cambridge, MA: Harvard University Press.

Kennedy, Duncan (2004). The disenchantment of the logically formal legal rationality. *Hastings Law Journal* 55: 1031–76.

Kimmerer, R. W. (2020). *Braiding Sweetgrass: Indigenous Wisdom, Scientific Knowledge and the Teachings of Plants*. Harmondsworth, UK: Penguin.

King, J. T. (2007). The value of water and the meaning of water law for the Native Americans known as the Haudenosaunee. *Cornell Journal of Public Law and Policy* 3(16): 449.

Kirmayer, L. J., M. E. Macdonald and G. M. Brass (2000). *The Mental Health of Indigenous Peoples*. Montreal: McGill University.

Kohn, E. (2013). *How Forests Think: Toward an Anthropology Beyond the Human*. Berkeley: University of California Press.

Korten, D. C. (2015). *Change the Story, Change the Future: A Living Economy for a Living Earth*. Oakland, CA: Berrett-Koehler.

Koskenniemi, M. (2001). *The Gentle Civilizer of Nations: The Rise and Fall of International Law 1870–1960*. Cambridge: Cambridge University Press.

Koskenniemi, M. (2005). International law in Europe: Between tradition and renewal. *European Journal of International Law* 16: 113–24.

Kotze, L. J. (2018). Reflections on the future of environmental scholarship and methodology in the Anthropocene. In O. Pedersen (ed.), *Perspectives on Environmental Law Scholarship*. Cambridge: Cambridge University Press, 140–61.

Kotze, L. J. and R. E. Kim (2019). *Earth System Law: The Juridical Dimensions of Earth System Governance*. New York: Elsevier.

Lamalle, S. (2014a). L'évolution conceptuelle dans le langage juridique international ou la traduction d'une nouvelle littéralité. *Revue Semiotica* 201: 145–65.

Lamalle, S. (2014b). Multilevel translation analysis of a key legal concept: *Persona juris* and legal pluralism. In Le Cheng, K. K. Sin and A. Wagner (eds.), *Ashgate Handbook on Legal Translation*. Abingdon, UK: Routledge.

Lamalle, S. (2015). Reconciliation in Canada: A healing force for social and institutional change. *Indigenous Law Bulletin* 8(16): 20–23.

Lamalle, S. (2020a). De l'Entendement juridique et des perspectives jurilinguistiques, Actes du Colloque Le droit au prisme des langues. *Revue de droit international et de droit compare* 1: 69–100.

Lamalle, S. (2020b). L'horizon de la sémiotique juridique. In Y. Emerich, A. S. Hulin and S. Lamalle (eds.), *Coder–Décoder: Linguistique et concepts juridiques*. Montreal: Éditions Yvon Blais.

Law Commission of Canada (2006). *Justice within: Indigenous legal traditions*. www.lcc.gc.ca

Le Moigne, J. L. (2000) Sur quelques topiques de la complexité … des situations que peut connaître le juriste dans ses pratiques. *Droit et Société* 46: 407–27.

Le Roy, E. (2004). Pour une anthropologie de la juridicité. *Cahiers d'Anthropologie du Droit*: 241–47.

Lévesque, C., É. Cloutier and D. Salée (eds.) (2011). Co-construction des connaissances en contexte autochtone, Actes de colloque, Réseau de recherche et de connaissances relatives aux peuples autochtones (DIALOG) et Institut national de la recherche scientifique (INRS). *Cahier DIALOG* 2013–03.

Lévesque, C., É. Cloutier, D. Salée, S. Dugré and J. Cunningham (2009). Aboriginal people in Québec cities: Scientific perspectives and societal challenges. *Cahier ODENA* 2009–02.

McCaslin, D. W. (ed.) (2005). *Justice as Healing: Indigenous Ways, Writings on Community Peacemaking and Restorative Justice, Native Law Centre, University of Saskatchewan*. St Paul, MN: Living Justice Press.

McGibbon, E. (2019). Truth and reconciliation: Healthcare organizational leadership. *Healthcare Management Forum* 32(1): 20–24.

McGregor, D. (2018). From 'decolonized' to reconciliation research in Canada: Drawing from Indigenous research paradigms. *ACME: An International Journal for Critical Geographies* 17(3): 810–31.

McNally, M. and D. Martin (2017). First Nations, Inuit and Métis health: Considerations for Canadian health leaders in the wake of the Truth and Reconciliation Commission of Canada Report. *Healthcare Management Forum* 30(2): 117–22.

Mannoni, M. (2020). Rights metaphors across hybrid legal languages, such as Euro English and legal Chinese. *International Journal for the Semiotics of Law* 34: 1375–99.

Mattila, H. (2006). *Comparative Legal Linguistics, Language of Law, Latin and Modern Lingua Francas*. Christopher Goddard (trans.). Aldershot, UK: Ashgate.

Mattila, H. E. S. (2012). *Jurilinguistique comparée: Langages du droit, latin et langues modernes*. Jean-Claude Gémar (trans.). Montreal: Éditions Yvon Blais.

May, M. (2017). Desacralizing landscapes: Maya heritage in the global picture. In M. M. Castillo and A. Strecker (eds.), *Heritage and Rights of Indigenous Peoples*. Leiden: Leiden University Press, 333–55.

Mazzocchi, F. (2006). Western science and traditional knowledge. *EMBO Reports* 7(5): 463.

Menski, W. (2005). *Comparative Law in a Global Context: The Legal Systems of Asia and Africa*. Cambridge: Cambridge University Press.

Merkouris, P. and D. Peat (2020). *Final Report*. ILA Study group on the content and evolution of the rules of interpretation, 29 November–13 December, Kyoto.

Miller, A. (1996). *Intuitions de Génie: Images et créativité dans les sciences et les arts*. Paris: Flammarion.

Milton, K. (1998). Nature and the environment on Indigenous and traditional cultures. In D. E. Cooper and J. A. Palmer (eds.), *Spirit of the Environment*. London: Routledge.

Morgan, R. (ed.) (2011). *Transforming Law and Institutions, Indigenous Peoples, the United Nations and Human Rights, Non-State Actors in International Law*. Aldershot, UK: Ashgate.

Moses, J. (2018). *Traditional Care of Sensitive Canadian Indigenous Materials, Delaware Band, Six Nations of the Grand River*. Government of Canada: Canadian Conservation Institute.

Mulhall S. (1996). *Heidegger and Being and Time*. London: Routledge.

Murtagh, C. (2019). Shifting strategies: The myth of Wanamei and the Amazon. Indigenous REDD+ Programme in Madre de Dios, Peru. In R. Bold (ed.), *Indigenous Perceptions of the End of the World: Creating a Cosmopolitics of Change*. New York: Palgrave Macmillan, 115–39.

Naffine, N. (2003). Who are law's persons? From Cheshire Cats to responsible subjects. *Modern Law Review* 66: 346, 351.

Napoleon, V. (2007). Thinking about Indigenous legal orders. Research paper, National Centre for First Nations Governance, Canada.

Napoleon, V. and H. Friedland (2016). The inside job: Engaging with Indigenous legal traditions through stories. *McGill Law Journal/Revue de droit de McGill* 61(4): 725–54.

Nash, C. (ed.) (1994). *Narrative in Culture: The Uses of Storytelling in the Sciences, Philosophy and Literature*. London: Routledge.

Nijman, J. E. (2004). *The Concept of International Personality: An Inquiry into the History and Theory of International Law*. The Hague: TMC Asser Press.

Nikolić, M. (2017). All that is air melts into city: Minoritarian apparatuses for a more-than-human. In A. Philippopoulos-Mihalopoulos and V. Brooks (eds.), *Research Methods in Environmental Law: A Handbook*. Cheltenham, UK: Edward Elgar, 482–508.

Ogden, C. K. and I. A. Richards (1989). *The Meaning of Meaning: Practical Criticism*. New York: Mariner.

Ost, F. (2008). La septième cite: La traduction. In C. Eberhard (ed.), *Traduire nos responsabilités planétaires: Recomposer nos paysages juridiques* Brussels: Bruylant, 87–100.

Pahuja, S. (2011). *Decolonising International Law: Development, Economic Growth and the Politics of Universality*. Cambridge: Cambridge University Press.

Parmenter, J. (2013). The meaning of Kaswentha and the two Row Wampum Belt in Haudenosaunee (Iroquois) history: Can Indigenous oral tradition be reconciled with the documentary record? *Journal of Early American History* 3: 86–87.

Pedro Ricoy, R. de, R. Howard and L. Andrade Ciudad (2018). Translators' perspectives: The construction of the Peruvian Indigenous Languages Act in Indigenous languages. *Meta, Journal des traducteurs/Translators' Journal* 63(1): 1–276.

Peirce, C. S. ([1878] 1958). How to make our ideas clear. In *Values in a Universe of Chance, Selected Writings, 1839–1914*. Garden City, NY: Doubleday.

Pelizzon, A. and G. O'Shannessy (2016). Autonomous legal persons and interconnected ecosystems: An 'ecological' self towards the age of re-embodiment'. In R. Thomas-Pellicer, V. de Lucia and S. Sullivan (eds.), *Contributions to Law, Philosophy and Ecology: Exploring Re-embodiments*. New York: Routledge, 224–38.

Petrilli, S. (2021). The law challenged and the critique of identity with Emmanuel Levinas. *International Journal for the Semiotics of Law* 35: 31–69.

Philippopoulos-Mihalopoulos, A. and V. Brooks (eds.) (2017). *Research Methods in Environmental Law: A Handbook*. Cheltenham, UK: Edward Elgar.

Pitarch, P. (2008). The labyrinth of translation. In P. Pitarch, S. Speed and X. Leyva-Solano (eds.), *Human Rights in the Maya Region*. Durham, NC: Duke University Press, 91–121.

Poirier, S. (2008). Reflections on Indigenous cosmopolitics: Poetics. *Anthropologica* 50(1), L'expérience et la problématique de la (dé)colonisation: Autour de l'œuvre d'Éric Schwimmer/(De)colonization as experience and field of enquiry: The work of Eric Schwimmer (2008), 75–85, *Canadian Anthropology Society*.

Potter, J. and M. Wetherell (1987). *Discourse and Social Psychology: Beyond Attitudes and Behaviour*. London: SAGE.

Povinelli, E. A. (2002). *The Cunning of Recognition: Indigenous Alterities and the Making of Australian Multiculturalism*. Durham, NC: Duke University Press.

Pulitano, E. (2012). *Indigenous Rights in the Age of the UN Declaration*. Cambridge: Cambridge University Press.

Ramlogan, R. (2002). The environmental and international law: Rethinking the traditional approach. *Vermont Journal of Environmental Law* 3: 1–15.

Report of the International Expert Group Meeting on Indigenous Languages (2008). UN Document: E/C.19/2008/3, http://documents.un.org

Rouland, N. (1991). *Aux confins du droit: Anthropologie juridique de la modernité*. Paris: Odile Jacob.

Ruggie, J. (2011). *Report of the Special Representative of the Secretary-General on the Issue of Human Rights and Transnational Corporations and Other Business Enterprises, Guiding Principles on Business and Human Rights: Implementing the United Nations 'Protect, Respect and Remedy' Framework*, A/HRC/17/31.

Ruiz Fabri, H. (2005). Les catégories de sujets du droit international. In *Le sujet en droit international*. Paris: Pedone, 55–71.

Sadongei, A. (2004). What about sacred objects? In S. Ogden (ed.), *Caring for American Indian Objects: A Practical and Cultural Guide*. St Paul, MN: Minnesota Historical Society Press, 17–19.

Salée, D. and C. Lévesque (2016). The politics of Indigenous peoples–settler relations in Quebec: Economic development and the limits of intercultural dialogue and reconciliation. *American Indian Culture and Research Journal* 40(2): 31–50.

Santos-Granero, F. and G. Mentore (eds.) (2006). Special issue in honor of Joanna Overing: In the world and about the world: Amerindian modes of knowledge. *Tipití: Journal of the Society for the Anthropology of Lowland South America* 4(1): 57–80.

Scott, J. (2017). Legal translation: A multidimensional endeavour. *Comparative Legilinguistics* 36: 37–66.

Sellers, M. N. S. (2005). International legal personality. *American Journal of International Law* 11: 67–78.

Slaughter, M. and S. Ratner (1999). Appraising the methods of international law: A prospectus for readers, symposium on method in international law. *American Journal of International Law* 93(2): 291–302.

Sofoulis, Z. (2018). Representation and reality. In N. Castree, M. Hulme and J. D. Proctor (eds.), *Companion to Environmental Studies*. Abingdon, UK: Routledge, 819.

Sousa Santos, B. de (2004). *Vers un nouveau sens commun juridique: Droit, science et politique dans la transition paradigmatique*. N. Gonzales Lajoie (trans.). Paris: LGDJ.

Sousa Santos, B. de (2014). *Epistemologies of the South: Justice against Epistemicide*. Boulder, CO: Paradigm.

Sousa Santos, B. de and C. Rodriguez-Garavito (2005). *Law and Globalisation from Below: Towards a Cosmopolitan Legality*. New York: Cambridge University Press.

Spivak, G. C. (2012). The politics of translation. In Lawrence Venuti (ed.), *The Translation Studies Reader*. New York: Routledge, 312–30.

Spretnak. C. (2011). *Relational Reality, New Discoveries of Interrelatedness that Are Transforming the Modern World*. Topsham, ME: Green Horizon Books.

Stanton, K. (2017). Reconciling reconciliation: Differing conceptions of the Supreme Court of Canada and the Canadian Truth and Reconciliation Commission. *Journal of Law and Social Policy* 26: 21–42.

Steiner, G. (1998). *After Babel, Aspects of Language and Translation*. Oxford: Oxford University Press.

Stewart-Harawira, M. (2009). Responding to a deeply bifurcated world: Indigenous diplomacies in the twenty-first century. In J. Beier (ed.), *Indigenous Diplomacies*. New York: Palgrave Macmillan, 207–24.

Subramanian, N. and S. Chung (2005). Measuring the evolvability of legal personality. *Ius Gentium* 11: 79–133.

Thomas-Pellicer, R., V. de Lucia and S. Sullivan (eds.) (2016). *Contributions to Law, Philosophy and Ecology: Exploring Re-embodiments*. New York: Routledge.

Truth and Reconciliation Commission of Canada (2015). *Summary of the Final Report. Report Honouring the Truth, Reconciling for the Future.* http://nctr.ca/reports.php

UNESCO (2003). Convention for the Safeguarding of the Intangible Cultural Heritage and UNESCO.

UNESCO (2005). Convention on the Protection and Promotion of the Diversity of Cultural Expressions.

UNESCO (2020). Outcome Document. Los Pinos [Chapoltepek]: Making a Decade of Action for Indigenous Languages, High-level closing event of the International Year, 27–28 February, Mexico City, Mexico.

United Nations Development Programme (2001). *Policy of Engagement with Indigenous People.*

United Nations General Assembly (2014). Report of the Secretary-general, *Achievement of the Goal and Objectives of the Second International Decade of the World's Indigenous Peoples*, 6 August, A/69/271.

United Nations General Assembly (2015). *Transforming Our World: The 2030 Agenda for Sustainable Development*, 25 September, A/RES/70/1.

United Nations General Assembly (2019). Report of Special Rapporteur, Human rights obligations relating to the enjoyment of a safe, clean, healthy and sustainable environment, 15 July, A/74/161.

Vaarzon-Morel, P. (2017). Reconfiguring relational personhood among Lander Warlpiri. In D. Austin-Broos and F. Merlan (eds.), *People and Change in Indigenous Australia*. Honolulu: Hawaii University Press.

Viala, A. (2001). La définition de l'état de droit: L'histoire d'un défi à la science juridique. *Revue Européenne de Droit Public* 13(1): 673–691.

Victor, W. (2007). Indigenous Justice: Clearing space and place for Indigenous epistemologies. Research paper for the National Centre for First Nations Governance.

Villey, M. (1968). *La formation de la pensée juridique moderne*. Paris: Presses universitaires de France.

Wagenaar, H. (2011). *Meaning in Action: Interpretation and Dialogue in Policy Analysis*. Armonk, NY: M.E. Sharpe.

Wagner, A., S. King-Kui and Le Cheng (2014). Legal translatability process as the 'third space': Insights into theory and practice. In Le Cheng, K. K. Sin and A. Wagner (eds.), *Ashgate Handbook on Legal Translation*. Abingdon, UK: Routledge.

Wallace, K. (2019). The network self: Relation, process, and personal identity, *Aeon*.

Wilmer, F. (2009). Where you stand depends on where you sit? In J. Beier (ed.), *Indigenous Diplomacies*. New York: Palgrave Macmillan, 185ff.

Wittgenstein, L. (1969). *Philosophical Investigations*, G. E. M. Anscombe (trans.) [1953], 3rd ed. Oxford: Blackwell.

Part II
RECOLLECTION

6

Traditional Indigenous Knowledge and the Relationship to Mother Earth

WORDS FROM GRANDMOTHER MARIE-JOSÉE TARDIF, GRANDFATHERS T8AMINIK RANKIN AND KEVIN KA'NAHSOHON DEER

Introduction

These difficult times we live in were foreseen by spiritual visionaries across the world. My ancestors warned us about this time and the choice we would have to make, in the Seven Fires Prophecy, which was inscribed in sacred Wampum shell in the late 1400s. The Prophecy holds a vision for the future where we honour our relationship and responsibility to Mother Earth and all creation; celebrate our individual gifts and diversity, and still; recognize and respect our place within a Circle of all Nations.

It is of crucial importance that the people of the world: respond immediately to the plight of the many oppressed by exploitation, social injustice and racism; animate the human capacity for forgiveness, compassion, love and reconciliation, and; create a global synergy to insure the improvement of the lives of all. This path will lead us to love, sharing, respect, responsibility, compassion, healing, reconciliation, equality and justice. We shall then light the Eighth fire together and become A Circle of All Nations – a Culture of Peace.

(William Commanda, A Circle of All Nations – A Culture of Peace*)*

Our relationship with Earth is decisive in the reflection on the representations and rights of the environment. The way we approach her determines our relationship with her and with other beings, now and in time – with ancestors and future generations – as well as who we are as humans.

In the spirit of peace and reconciliation, this chapter gathers the testimonies of North American Indigenous knowledge keepers from Anishinabe[1] and Mohawk

---

[1] The word Algonquin refers to a language family, gathering various Indigenous languages such as Anishinabe, Innu and Atikamekw. The Algonquin people refer to themselves as Anishinabe (ani-shi-nabey) in their language. It means 'human being'.

peoples.[2] They are leading figures in Canada and abroad, well known for their devoted and relentless social and spiritual engagement: Anishinabe Elder Oteimin Kokom Marie-Josée Tardif; Hereditary Algonquin Chief and medicine man T8aminik Kapiteotak Rankin; and Mohawk Elder faithkeeper and teacher Kevin Ka'nahsohon Deer.

They each talk about guiding principles in their respective traditions about human beings and all our relationships, and through their individual experience, shed light on specific steps we are to take at this time of crisis and in the future.

Marie-Josée Tardif, a leader in Anishinabe cultural and spiritual revitalisation talks about restoring the balance with the feminine and our being human (Section 6.1); T8aminik Rankin, a survivor of the notorious residential school system and a leader on reconciliation talks about healing our relationships and walking on the path of reconciliation with ourselves, with other beings and with Mother Earth (Section 6.2); Kevin Deer, a leader in Iroquoian language and spiritual revitalisation, talks about the change in consciousness to see, to hear and to speak differently, and the future generations (Section 6.3).

6.1 A Vision of Hope for the Future: Restoring Balance with the Feminine – Words by Grandmother Marie-Josée Tardif

The vision for the future we are formulating at this time is decisive for us human beings, for all the beings and for Mother Earth.

In 2019, the Conference of Religions for Peace was an important event for the Indigenous peoples, as on a rare occasion, we were invited to take the floor as one of the religions of the world. With Grandfather T8aminik Rankin, we participated in the conference in Germany, which gathered 900 participants from 125 countries. After five years of participation, thanks to the secretary general of the organisation, we were given a much bigger role as new members of the board of the administrative council of the organisation Religions for Peace. This is an important step in the recognition of other spiritualities of the world, different from the more institutionalised religions of the Bible and from other spiritualities recognised as religions, such as Buddhism or Hinduism. It is also an important evolution in the recognition of Indigenous peoples and their rights, in particular in relation to the protection of Mother Earth. In Canada, there was a Commission on the Murdered and Missing Indigenous Women in order to address this major problem in society. If we take the example of policies against the environment and Indigenous Peoples such as the ones in Brazil at the moment, we also realise that the status of women

---

[2] If Anishinabe tradition belongs to the Algonquin linguistic family, the Mohawk tradition belongs to the Haudenosaunee (People of the Longhouse and Iroquoian linguistic family). These two traditions, one patrilineal and nomadic, the other matrilineal and semi-sedentary, present complementary visions.

in society and the way they are treated are directly related to the way the relationship with the 'environment' is defined. When we instrumentalise women, we do so with the Earth and vice versa. And the cultures which value and respect the feminine, also respect the Earth.

Such a consideration is decisive when we have to deal with the oppression of women, as is the case in many countries. At some point, during the conference, I spoke in front of religious representatives, some of them from radicalised movements and countries, of the place of women and what needs to change. Women, and the way to relate to the feminine, has to do with the unbalance we experience today worldwide. It is what I call the 'climate change within ourselves'. We can only change ourselves individually and need to reconcile ourselves with the feminine qualities of our being on a spiritual level: interiority, intuition, emotions, symbolism, prayer, meditation, silence, gestation, the part trusting the cycle of life. The modern world is dominated by the masculine qualities found within each one of us, which are also important, such as exteriority, action, science, rationality, logic, spoken and written words, but to the detriment of the feminine dimension.[3] It is expressed through a certain mode of knowledge, which is science, and through a certain aspect of our being, the mind and its rationality, as it is in the spirit of conquering expressed in colonisation. We need to restore the balance between these two poles. The Anishinabe tradition praises Mother Earth and the feminine qualities, along with the masculine qualities.

We have met so many young people who are anxious and afraid, who think they have to always be perfectly happy. They are ignorant of the natural cycles, with gestation, with rest, with grief. They do not accept sadness and other emotions in their lives and cannot grow. Instead, they are too often convinced they must take medications and drugs not to live the change and transformation they need, and that life generously offers to us.

There is now an awakening, and we need to keep and nurture hope. The mistake would be to try to 'help' the Earth by science only, and technological tools as a control over materiality. The solution requires us to change our way of seeing and living: to see with the 'eyes of the heart'. The mind has to be reconciled with the heart and body, and the two masculine and feminine poles have to be in balance.

During a colloquium on the environment, in Chantilly, France, there was a presentation on the necessity to calculate, assess, quantify and put a price on the resources of the Earth. The idea is that there is a threshold we cannot overcome – with such a logic of division we cannot relate with our whole being to the Earth,

---

[3] This reflection is present in different spiritual traditions; see for instance the work of Annick de Souzenelle on the religions of the Bible, and the translation and exegesis on this subject.

nor to all her beings. Grandfather William Commanda,[4] who was a major spiritual leader in the Anishinabe tradition, used to ask: 'How can you sell your mother?' How can we divide our mother up on an Excel spreadsheet? Grandfather's message and lifelong commitment was linked to concern and responsibility for the plight of Mother Earth, and the need to alert the world's peoples to the urgent necessity to rebalance our priorities, needs and values. In his teachings, our salvation is interconnected with the salvation of Mother Earth, and vice versa.

I find it interesting how the culture and spiritual tradition of Indigenous peoples around the world have been portrayed as infantile and naive since the time of colonisation, when Indigenous people have tried to share their knowledge and understanding of the balances existing between human beings and other beings, and with Mother Earth. These are sacred relationships, and we need to realise we have to consider our relationship with the Earth as a sacred relationship with a being. It implies not just our mind or body, it implies our heart as well as our whole being.

In the 2019 Religions for Peace conference, we adopted a Final Declaration, in which there is a commitment as 'us, members of religions for Peace' to take care of the environment:[5]

We gather in hope, convinced that the sacred calls all humanity into shared responsibility for our common good, care for one another, the earth, and its entire web of life.

We commit to urgent action against the climate crisis. We will mobilise religious communities to protect the earth – including the promotion of 'green congregations'. Leaders and partners in the fight against environmental degradation, our Indigenous brothers and sisters remind us, 'when Mother Earth suffers, human beings suffer; when human beings suffer, Mother Earth suffers'. We, guardians and caretakers of earth, endorse the Faiths for Forests Declaration. We commit to raise awareness about tropical deforestation and to educate our religious communities about the dire spiritual and sustainability crisis. We will take action to live ecologically balanced and sustainable lifestyles and advocate for government policies to protect rainforests, defend the rights of Indigenous peoples, and fulfil their pledges to the Paris Agreement on climate change.

The Declaration also mentions the idea of 'shared well-being' as a common understanding of sacred interconnectedness between all the beings and with Mother Earth:

---

[4] Algonquin Chief William Commanda Ojigkwanong (1913–2011) opened a path of reconciliation among Indigenous Peoples and with Mother Earth. He was an Elder from Kitigan Zibi Anishinabe in Maniwaki, Quebec; the great-grandson of Pakinawatik and keeper of three sacred wampum shell belts of historic and spiritual importance: the 1400s Seven Fires Prophecy Belt about 'choice', the 1700 Welcoming Belt about 'sharing' and the 1793 Jay Treaty Border Crossing Treaty Belt, about 'borderlessness'. His ancestors inscribed their legends, prophecies and agreements in these artworks over many centuries. Carrier of the Seven Fires Prophecy, William was the spiritual guide to the 1995 Sunbow Five Walk, which carried the prayers of Indigenous peoples across the North American continent, to raise awareness of the abuses to Mother Earth. William was a chief of Kitigan Zibi reserve and recipient of awards, such as the Wolf Project and Harmony, for his efforts to foster harmony between all the peoples, through the creation of a Circle of all Nations.

[5] Declaration of the 10th World Assembly of Religions for Peace, 23 August 2019, Lindau, Germany.

Our heart's inner-most experiences of the sacred and our outer-most social lives cry out to be connected in a state of positive peace that Religions for Peace calls, 'Shared Well-Being'. Our different experiences of the sacred make clear that we are, at root, relational: radically related to the sacred and to all that is caused or embraced by the sacred. As fundamentally relational, our well-being is intrinsically shared. Helping the other, we are helped; injuring the other, we wound ourselves.

Shared Well-Being also calls for a robust notion of the 'common good' that can serve all of us in our efforts to virtuously unfold our rights-protected human dignity. The supreme good for us is the sacred, even as we understand it differently. The common good includes the earth with its air, water, soil, and web of life. The common good also includes just institutions that help each to develop her or his human dignity. These call all of us to a shared and grateful responsibility. Each person is to draw from the common good; each is to help build it up. Advancing Shared Well-Being is concrete. We commit to advancing Shared Well-Being by preventing and transforming violent conflicts, promoting just and harmonious societies, nurturing sustainable and integral human development, and protecting the earth.

And of particular importance to our commitment in Canada and in the world, the Declaration states also that 'we adopt *The Peace Charter for Forgiveness and Reconciliation*, convinced that transforming violent conflicts requires the healing of historical wounds and painful memories, forgiveness, and reconciliation. We commit to integrating efforts for healing into all our conflict resolution work.'

In the Anishinabe tradition, understood as a way of living and seeing the world, there is no division, all aspects of life are present and have a place. There is no duality or conflict between matter and spirit, body and soul, humans and nature. If in Africa, we talk about the Ubuntu principle (see Chapter 15 in this volume), in the Anishinabe tradition we talk about *8itokotati8in* (pronounced: wi-to-ko-ta-ti-win) meaning our interdependency and solidarity.

In my own spiritual development, as I come from a Quebequer family and grew up in a modern environment, then learned and lived in the traditional way of the Anishinabe and was recognised as an Elder and knowledge keeper, I had to reconcile the different views of these two cultures. I think we all have to deal with the relationship between masculine and feminine poles of ourselves as these two cultures seem to embody. The masculine side wants to have control, and the feminine side teaches us how to accept the natural cycles, things beyond power relations and transformation of ourselves. Have you noticed how in most of the recognised religions, we salute the Sky and the Father? We then forget the Earth, the Mother of all. Both need to be praised, both masculine and feminine poles.

If we continue to approach Earth as an object and reduce our relationship to her as an instrument to other ends, it is a grave mistake. Such a mistake means our refusal to change and keep the unbalanced and dysfunctional domination of the masculine side. This is the most part of the problem and also solution of the environmental crisis, as the societal one. If we accept to rebalance masculine and feminine sides, we will go in another direction: value the feminine dimension of being. Then modes of knowledge other than science will have their place in this world, and respectful relationships between human beings and with the Earth can replace colonisation, domination and coercion. In that sense, the Earth also has rights, as do all beings on the planet. Even though this approach is still masculine and in the modern framework of designating crimes against the planet, it might be a first step towards rebalancing the two poles. For the Anishinabe, who see the Earth as their Mother, there is no need for rights when we counterbalance freedom with a deep sense of responsibility.

I would like to give an example here of our modern disconnection with natural cycles and Mother Earth. With *Kina8at* (kee-na-wat), the association we created to share the Anishinabe tradition, we are working with the Canadian Spatial Agency on a project, and we realise concretely how science and the scientific approach may prevent us from realising who we are as human beings. For the scientists we meet, it is often difficult to know or accept what it means to be human beings, with their right to experience emotions, to trust their intuition or simply 'be', when they are trained to dedicate most of their time to think, do or have. Those going to space are going further and further from Mother Earth. And in the meantime, most express a fear of nature, as unknown and uncontrolled forces – that fear is the fear of being oneself. This is why we enjoy so much working with them: they are used to exploring outer space, so we help them explore their inner space. Walking on the sacred path is an important realisation for many of them to accept and reconcile with Mother Earth and with their feminine side.

Today fear pervades all generations. If we think of the Second World War, most testimonies relate that people did not lose hope. Nowadays, anxiety, cynicism, lack of empowerment are contagious. It is like we are living through a third world war; we need mobilisation on a world scale, we need to stand shoulder to shoulder, and come together to care for the Earth and each other in order to take the road to Peace. This is our challenge. Many people have to speak to each other, change the current vision together of who we are as humans and what we are doing. It starts with our relationship with ourselves as individuals, then with the balance of the two masculine and feminine poles, then with the Earth and all the other beings. We have no right to lose Hope for us, for our ancestors and for the future generations.

6.2 Healing Relationship: The Path of Reconciliation – Words by Grandfather T8aminik Rankin

I am Anishinabe, a human being, and as such I have never abandoned Mother Earth, nor forgotten the teachings of the forest, nor the beauty of each season and its fruits. My people, the Mami8inini, were nomads, travelling on birch-bark canoes, on the waters of the Harricana River in North-West Quebec.

Today, the world is much different from when I was born, more than seventy years ago. The first changes came when I was still living with my parents. The government forbade us to live in the forest and we could no longer eat the animals, nor the berries or drink water, as they had all been contaminated by the wood and mining industries. In the 1960s, my people were poisoned by mercury which contaminated fish, and many people died as a consequence. But thanks to modern medicine, most of us were healed and saved. It means that we cannot live as we used to, aware now of how industry pollutes and destroys. We kept on praying so that people would realise what they were destroying: the rivers, the forest, the animals, the people.

Today, there is an awakening about what we are doing to ourselves and Mother Earth, in particular regarding the economy and its impact on future generations. We recently participated in a peaceful campaign to raise awareness of the issue of gas and oil extraction and its consequences on Mother Earth, such as the pollution of water, soil and all the animals that has happened in many places already. The people suffer too from all this directly in their body, their mind and their heart. Mother Earth cries every morning – we want to show calmly and peacefully that such projects will do harm. The message is a positive one, as we invite reconciliation with Mother Earth. In order to do that, we need to start with ourselves. We need to open our heart and see through it the life within us and around us, not just through the intellect.

To that end, with *Kina8at*, the organisation we created with *Oteimin Kokum* (Grandmother Marie-Josée); and with the new Dominique Rankin Foundation, we take people (entrepreneurs, doctors, engineers, etc.) from different walks of life into the forest and onto the river in canoes, in order to reconnect them to their heart, the elements, the animals and Mother Earth. The canoe is made of birch bark, as are the baskets to transport food – on the canoe, we ride silently, cradled by the water, between earth and sky. It teaches us balance and reminds us of our place as human beings.

The land is that of our ancestors, the river was a road for nomadic peoples. Today, with highways and cars, travelling means pollution and contamination of soil and water.

Throughout the hardships in my life, I gradually learned not to live through emotions of anger, fear or anxiety. Once the heart is opened, we see differently. I travelled to many places in Canada and to foreign countries, and it was a sad spectacle to see all those children who did not even know what a fish was and needed to reconnect with Mother earth. In order to teach, one has to change the approach, one has to cleanse oneself from within, give oneself love and hope, so that one can give that to others.

During the Religions for Peace World Conference in August 2019 in Bavaria, Germany, about 900 persons gathered to talk and share views on the current destruction of the Earth. We emphasised the fact that when Mother Earth suffers, we all suffer. The question of the status of women and their suffering is linked to Mother Earth. What we call the medicine of women, among the Anishinabe, has to do with the protection of water and of the Earth, as well as sound and singing.

6.2.1 Healing People and Mother Earth

For six years, I have participated in the Truth and Reconciliation Commission in Canada to help our people heal the trauma of the residential schools. The Commission was established to collect the testimonies of the survivors of residential schools (more than 5,000 children died), and many were broken physically and psychologically. From the late nineteenth century until the 1990s in Canada, 150,000 children of our peoples were taken away from their parents and locked up in schools managed by churches. They were to be civilised. Instead, they were deprived of their language, culture, pride and self-esteem. They were severely abused. I have survived and healed, after years of struggling with anger and alcohol, thanks to my parents, my spiritual guides and my community – despite discrimination and economic difficulties. This is why I wanted to help others heal during the Commission. People need to understand who they are again, to accept what happened. In Anishinabe, we do not have a word for *forgiving* or *pardon*. Rather, we talk about acceptance, which is quite a different concept. If I had waited for forgiveness from the priests and nuns who raped me, so that I would feel better, I would still be waiting. This has never happened to this day. By insisting on the notion of acceptance, the elders taught me to 'own' my story. They walked next to me on my healing journey, helping me regain by myself my inner power and freedom.

Thanks to traditional medicine and healing circles, when came the time of the Truth and Reconciliation Commission, we were able to help in the process of witnessing the trauma endured by our people,[6] giving the teachings of our ancestors on Mother Earth, the elements, the pride in who we are, truth which is in ourselves, love, fortitude, respect and acceptance of what happened in our own history. I suffer when I see the Earth suffering, and many people who are

---

[6] In Canada, the Commission on Truth and Reconciliation (2008–15) worked with Health Canada and traditional medicine men and women to help survivors of the residential schools in the process of giving testimony of their experience. Traditional Indigenous knowledge keepers and healers helped with unlocking traumatic memories from the mind, heart and body of survivors, and starting healing.

disconnected from the Earth. If we want to heal ourselves, our relationships and people, we need to realise and acknowledge our relationship with Mother Earth.

Reconciliation means 'becoming one again'; it is a path towards unity within persons, communities, institutions and societies.

To give an example, during the conference in Germany, we were talking about what was sacred during a big ceremony outside. When I was given the microphone, I asked everyone: 'Do you really want to walk on the sacred Earth? Then take off your shoes, feel the Earth under your feet and go.' It was quite something to watch all these religious people, businesspeople, politicians and scientists barefoot in the park where we were gathered! It was such a simple thing to do, but, for many people, it was a realisation. Aggression leads to destruction; reconciliation with Mother Earth and with oneself leads to life and health. Such is the journey we have with people coming to our land and on the river – it is a spiritual journey. No tourism, no cameras. It is not about doing but being. Finding one's balance in the canoe in relationship with oneself and the natural elements.

In the Anishinabe tradition, we have the Prophecy of the Seven Fires. The spiritual guide who succeeded my father, on my road as a hereditary chief and medicine man, was William Commanda. He passed away a few years ago, he was 97. Grandfather William was the protector of the Wampum belt describing the Prophecy.[7] By that Wampum belt, we know that a long time ago, our ancestors had foreseen the arrival of the white people on the continent. They had announced that the arrival of the white people would generate great suffering and pain among the peoples, but they also announced that there would be reconciliation in the end. Each fire corresponds to a time in the future. At that time of great challenges, it is said that the Earth is not burnt everywhere and there is still hope.

I believe the new generations will be able to establish reconciliation between the peoples and with Mother Earth. But we need to have people who lead by example. We have to show by example, we have to build that road. The more that people start healing, the more robust is the road to reconciliation with Mother Earth.

6.3 A New Consciousness: To See, to Hear, to Speak Differently – Words by Grandfather Ka'nahsohon Kevin Deer

We the people of the Longhouse belief have a custom that before we do anything that involves gathering the people, we do what we call in our Mohawk language *Ohen:ton Karihwatehkhwen* which translates as 'the matters that we put before everything else'. It follows a specific pattern which I will describe briefly.

---

[7] The term 'wampum' refers to beads made from purple and white mollusc shells on threads of elm bark. Wampum belts are artworks conveying legal, political, historical and spiritual significance.

We always start by addressing all the people that are assembled. We offer greetings and thanks that we are still alive, that we are in peace, that our basic needs are still being met and that we are happy. Then we acknowledge all of the waters and rivers, we acknowledge the medicine plants and roots for good health, we acknowledge all of the grass, we acknowledge the insects, we have the knowledge of the flowers and the plants, we acknowledge the strawberries who are the leaders of the fruits, we acknowledge our life supporters: the three sisters (the corn, beans, squash), we acknowledge the free animals, we acknowledge all the trees and the forests, we acknowledge all of the birds and their leader the bald eagle, we acknowledge the mighty winds and the smaller winds, we acknowledge our grandfather the Thunder Beings, we acknowledge our Elder Brother the Sun, we acknowledge our Grandmother the Moon, we acknowledge the stars and the star stories, we acknowledge our ancestors and the Enlightened Messengers, and we finally acknowledge the Great Spirit – The Creator (*Shonkwaia'tison* – the one who made our body) for all the sources of life that sustains our daily lives.

As Indigenous People of Turtle Island (North America) we have our own Creation Stories which describe in detail who we are, where we come from, why are we here and where we go after our physical death. The common denominator that we all understand is that the Earth is our Mother and that we were all given original instructions when the first *Onkwehon:we* (original true beings) were made and given the freedom to enjoy this sacred garden. All that was asked of us in return was to give thanks. We express our gratitude through sacred ceremonies, songs, dances, rituals and speeches which all consist of giving thanks for all the gifts that we receive every day in the sacred cycle and web of life. We still do these ceremonies today so that our lives may continue as we look forward to the unborn faces to come out of the Mother Earth and that they may inherit a happy, safe, clean, beautiful, healthy, peaceful and loving home.

As a faithkeeper at the Mohawk Trail Longhouse in Kahnawake, I have been entrusted to maintain and perform these sacred responsibilities. I also have been a Mohawk Immersion School Teacher for the past thirty years and in the last two years offered Mohawk language classes for natives living in the city of Montreal. I am deeply involved with maintaining our Mohawk language along with the spiritual revitalisation of many *Kahnawakehro:non* based on Iroquoian worldview and philosophy. I am also very intrigued in early native and non-native relationships, the Doctrine of Discovery, historical treaty perspectives, so-called native land claims, the Royal Proclamation of 1763, the British North America Act, Indian Act, Constitution Act of Canada 1982, First Nation Treaty Rights and Native Political Sovereignty.

Today we human beings are facing an existential crisis. Due to capitalism, along with a flawed economic and monetary model, we are now witnessing the wanton destruction of the natural world and of the necessities that sustains human life. If these necessities are depleted, then millions of human beings will die because we cannot live and survive without clean air, freshwater and food. So whatever harm we cause to the earth, we also cause to ourselves. We need to understand that there are many economic false prophets who offer us the lie of a good life as long as they can make a profit. The economic engine that drives North America is based on fossil fuels and resource extraction.

We the Iroquois (Haudenosaunee) have a story that talks about our relationship to our Grandfather Thunder Beings who send their lightning bolts down to prevent giant horned serpents from rising out of the earth. The story recounts that if these horned serpents ever came out of the earth, they would destroy and kill the people. These horned serpents today are representative of the fossil fuels and all its by-products. If we continue to extract and bring this negative energy up and out into the world, then humans will feel the wrath of Mother Earth's fury even more so in the form of more flooding, more hurricanes, more tornadoes, more earthquakes, more droughts, more rain and hail, more forest fires, more diseases, more smog, more pollution, etc. The future of human life is at the precipice. We either change direction or maintain the status quo. If we maintain the idea of 'business as usual' then we are heading into the abyss of more worldwide suffering and pain. This is where the life of all humans in the future is headed if we do not rethink our consciousness with our Mother Earth regarding how we see her, how we hear her, how we speak about her and what we do to her.

The Mother Earth's body is sacred and precious. We are supposed to be living in harmony and communion with her, not asserting dominance or dominion over her. With the introduction of money came the flawed concept of wealth which divided people into socio-economic classes and groups causing wars between those who have money and the power and the labourers and slaves. Today the kings of the New World are the multinational corporations who have reduced us to nothing but mere economic slaves. We had a great prophet known as the 'Peacemaker-*Rononhsion-niton*' who established the Five Nations Iroquois Confederacy which is based on the principles of peace, equity and balanced reasoning. He eliminated war by eliminating territorial boundaries and used the concept of 'One Dish with One Spoon' meaning that the land in all its resources would be equally shared among the Five Nations. This idea was supposed to spread to the four directions; north, east, west, south (NEWS) because the good news had arrived that love and peace replace hatred and revenge. Unfortunately, this plan was not able to be fulfilled because individuals began to hack and cut at the white roots of peace, so the great tree never grew to reach its pinnacle for the whole world to see. But now with modern technology this message can get out quicker than before as a means bringing a new hope for some of the people in the world.

When the peacemaker completed the league he specifically cautioned the Chiefs and the leadership to never argue or fight among themselves because he said if this ever happened the people would lose faith and they would take matters into their own hands. If that happened, then men would begin to fight again. He stated that if we ever began fighting among ourselves, we would be reduced to disgrace; if that ever happened, then we would evoke this ceremony to call upon his return and an intervention would begin. On Sunday, 6 May 1990, we did this ceremony in Tyendineaga, Ontario calling for his return. The spiritual intervention did begin but it is a transcendence to a higher plane of spiritual consciousness. Also, our ancestors of Turtle Island who all have entered into the ancestral realm began to reveal their knowledge and power to us, their grandchildren of today, who are still connected to them in the ancient traditional ceremonial ways. The prophecies of the Indigenous Peoples of Turtle Island are all coming true. All the environmental degradation, pollution, killings, war, disease that we are witnessing today was all foretold. One of the stories of the Longhouse talks about a little boy who would lead the people back into the forest to a mountaintop. Once there he would take the hair of our women and braid it into a string and unite our women as one because our power and strength lies within our women. Today our women are rising up and getting stronger again in fulfilling their roles and responsibilities. In the symbolic house where one door is the eastern seaboard, the other door is the western seaboard, and the roof of that house is the sky, most men in this house are out of balance with themselves and as a result lots of women along with the Mother Earth are suffering. But we are now in a time when great changes are upon us; women will take a leading role in the healing, nurturing and wellness that needs to occur.

I will conclude by saying this: since the prophecy of the White Buffalo Calf Woman was fulfilled in the spring of 1994, with the birth of the first white buffalo calf, numerous animals, fish and birds have been appearing as white albinos. The sacred animals covered in white are messengers reminding us through their outward appearance that we human beings need to get back to a whiter, purer, cleaner and deeper spiritual way of being. So, it is up to each and every one of us to make the necessary actions in our daily lives to be the eyes, the ears and the voice of our loving Mother, Earth!

6.4 Epilogue

In the Prophecy of the White Buffalo Calf Woman, shared by different Indigenous peoples in North America, it is said that the Spirit of the white Buffalo will help unify all the peoples of humanity to return to spirituality and heal the damage caused by pollution. The prophecy underlines the responsibility of all people to address these issues – as one heart, one mind and one spirit. The healing concerns each and every one of us, within ourselves and with all our relationships (past, present and future), including with all the different beings (like animals, plants and trees), the elements and Mother Earth – for harmony, balance and equality, in order to create a global culture of peace.

In the Haudenosaunee's *Basic Call to Consciousness*,[8] spiritual consciousness is the highest form of politics. It is recalled that we must live in harmony with the natural world, and that the law of the land is not human-made, but a greater natural law, the Great Law of Peace. According to that Great Law, in every decision we make, we must consider the impact on the seventh generation. This principle is based on an ancient philosophy considering that the decisions we make today should result in a sustainable world, generations into the future. This principle must guide the decisions being made about community, water, subsistence, but also about relationships; we have to be aware of the implications of our actions, and every decision should result in good relationships, generations into the future. Each generation has a responsibility to ensure the survival of the seventh generation.

Acknowledgements

Respecting the traditional way of communicating knowledge, this chapter was prepared on the basis of oral discussions, with Marie-Josée Tardif, T8aminik Rankin, and Ka'nasohon Kevin Deer in 2019 and 2020, and transcribed by Sandy Lamalle, who is grateful to the Elders for their teachings and permission to share them in this chapter. *Mik8ec. Niá:wen.*

References

Akwesasne Notes (ed.) (1978). *Basic Call to Consciousness*. Summertown, TN: Book Publishing Company.

Declaration of the 10th World Assembly of Religions for Peace, 23 August 2019, Lindau, Germany.

Rankin, D. and M.-J. Tardif (2020). *We Were Called Savages*. B. Vrignon (trans.). Winnipeg: Vidacom [orig. Fr. pub.: D. Rankin and M.-J. Tardif, *On nous appelait les sauvages: Souvenirs et espoirs d'un chef héréditaire Algonquin*. Montreal: Éditions Le jour, 2011].

Souzenelle, A. de. (2000). *Le féminin de l'être: Pour en finir avec la côte d'Adam*. Paris: Albin Michel.

Truth and Reconciliation Commission of Canada (2015). *Honouring the Truth, Reconciling for the Future*. Toronto: James Lorimer.

Vasantha Thumbadoo. (2005). *Learning from a Kindergarten Dropout: William Commanda – Ojikwanong, Cultural Sharings and Reflections*. Kanata: Circle of All Nations.

[8] Akwesasne Notes (1978).

7

The Encyclical Letter *Laudato si'* of Pope Francis

Roots and Actuality

JEAN-PIERRE DELVILLE

Introduction

Pope Francis raised the alarm about ecology in his encyclical letter *Laudato si'* – *On Care for Our Common Home*, of 24 May 2015. This letter sounds much like the famous Fifth Symphony of Ludwig van Beethoven, where the percussive notes of the opening pattern (the famous 'pom-pom-pom-pom'!) are followed by an elaborated musical development. In *Laudato si'* also, the Pope launches a solemn warning, which is followed by a complex argumentative discourse. The encyclical is a symphony in which the Pope gathers all aspects of the ecological crisis, and leads to the concept of 'integral ecology' (Chapter 4), in which the different sides of ecology are bound with human life, and in particular with the plight of the poor. The recipients of the Encyclical *Laudato si'* (LS) are a very broad public: 'The Encyclical is destined to every man of good will and is not reserved to Christians' (LS 62). This chapter will further explore the LS and discuss its implications for the rights and representation of nature. It will be completed by the analysis of the Final Document *The Amazon* (TA) of the Special Assembly of the Synod of Bishops for the Pan-Amazon Region, held in Rome in October 2019, and by the presentation of the principal elements of the post-synodal apostolic exhortation of Pope Francis, *Querida Amazonia* (QA) of 2 February 2020. Such documents propose a concrete application of the Encyclical *Laudato si'* in the world of today.

Historical Context

The encyclical must be presented in its historical context and the framework of the social encyclicals of the popes. In 1885, Leo XIII published *Immortale Dei. De civitatum constitutione christiana*, about the connection between society and Christianity. But it was not enough: the Pope realised that the misery of the poor was structural in society, and he asked for a structural answer. So, he wrote the encyclical *Rerum novarum. De opificum conditione* (1891) about the dramatic condition of the workers. In answer to the growth of the communist movement promoted by Karl Marx, he promoted the notion of natural and distributive justice and recommended founding Christian syndicates, or trade unions, Christian cooperatives, Christian funds of mutual help. In 1901, he wrote *Graves de communi re*, about the notion of Christian democracy. In 1931, Pope Pius XI wrote *Quadragesimo anno* as a response to the economic crisis of 1929, and he insisted on the notion of social justice. Contemporary of that movement, the two world wars pushed the Church to act in favour of peace.

With those experiences, Pope John XXIII published *Mater et magistra* (1961) on the relationship between Church and society. He opened the Second Vatican Council (1962–65), specifically with the intention of focusing the role of the Church on promoting justice and dialogue between different cultures. To that end, he wrote the encyclical *Pacem in Terris* (1963) in order to promote peace in the world in the time of the Cold War. The Council wrote a synthesis of the social learning of the Church in his Constitution *Gaudium et Spes* (1965), which stresses the dialogue between Christians and society, for justice, peace and family life. It recommended founding in every diocese a commission *Justitia et pax* in order to stimulate the application of the Pastoral Constitution *Gaudium et spes*. After the Council, the orientation was taken to promote the bond between spirituality and social engagement. Pope Paul VI wrote the encyclical *Populorum progressio* (1967) on the topic of social progress for all of humanity towards justice and solidarity. In 1971, he published *Octogesima adveniens. Apostolic Letter to cardinal Roy*, concerning justice, development, emigration, the situation of women and social responsibility. John Paul II developed this action for the promotion of justice in the world and the suppression of communist dictatorships. In 1981, he wrote *Laborem exercens* on the meaning of work and the role of the worker. On the right of ownership, the Pope writes (14):

Christian tradition has never upheld this right as absolute and untouchable. On the contrary, it has always understood this right within the broader context of the right common to all to use the goods of the whole of creation: the right to private property is subordinated to the right to common use, to the fact that goods are meant for everyone.

In 1987, in the Encyclical *Sollicitudo rei socialis*, John Paul II insisted on the concept of development. In *Centesimus annus* (1991), a hundred years after *Rerum novarum*, John Paul II criticises neoliberalism and the conception of capital for their lack of consideration for humankind and the earth. In 2005, Benedict XVI published *Deus caritas est: On Christian love*, in which he develops the link between justice and love. In 2009, he wrote *Caritas in veritate: On human integral development in charity and truth*, in which he insisted on ecology, finance and political engagement. Pope Francis has accentuated this orientation in his apostolic exhortation *Evangelii Gaudium* (2013), in which he shed light on key elements of the Gospel with regard to the social integration of the poor in society and the dialogue for peace and reconciliation. In this context he wrote, in 2015, the encyclical *Laudato si'* (LS), in which he expresses his vision of the future of the earth and humanity. He intended the encyclical as a contribution from Catholics to the COP 21 in Paris (the twenty-first Conference of the Parties to the 1992 United Nations Framework Convention on Climate Change). He benefited from the reflections of many episcopal conferences in the world, and insisted on an ecology based on the integrity of humankind and nature.

Plan of the Encyclical

The plan of the encyclical can be understood in light of the 'see–judge–act' method, which can be defined as: (1) observing the situation; (2) evaluating the problem and its cause; (3) proposing solutions.

Chapter 1 ('What is happening to our common home') is concerned with the first phase of the method 'to see'. It is an analysis of the ecological situation of the world.

The second phase of the method 'to judge', with the evaluation of the problem and its cause, covers three chapters: Chapter 2 ('The Gospel of creation'), which presents the Judeo-Christian tradition on ecology; Chapter 3 ('The human roots of the ecological crisis'), which identifies the causes of the ecological problem, and advances the abuse of technology; and Chapter 4 ('An integral ecology'), which presents the thesis of the Pope: the necessity of a global ecology, which encompasses all aspects of human life, because 'everything is interconnected', as he regularly says.

The third phase of the method 'act', proposing solutions, animates the reflection in Chapter 5 ('Lines of approach and action'), and insists on political action at the global level, and in Chapter 6 ('Education and ecological spirituality') which proposes personal guidelines and a spirituality motivating this commitment.

Sources of Inspiration

The Pope's sources of inspiration include the reflections of his predecessors, especially Benedict XVI, and his own personal thoughts. Pope Francis is inspired by many declarations of the local episcopal conferences, including from Japan, Canada, Brazil, Argentina, the Dominican Republic, Mexico, Paraguay, Bolivia, New Zealand, Asia, Latin America. He highlights the work of local churches and shows that the issues raised in the encyclical had been addressed for years by communities and grass-roots organisations of the Church. He refers also to the Ecumenical Patriarch Bartholomew, chief of the Orthodox Church, who is a great specialist of the question. He also uses the declarations of the international meetings on this topic (such as Rio, 1992). He also bases his reflections on the work of an author he studied for his doctorate thesis, Romano Guardini (1885–1968), in particular his book *The End of Modern Times*. He is inspired by the figure of Saint Francis of Assisi, whose name he took as Pope and whose commitment he values for the solidarity with nature. Therefore, he took as a title for the encyclical the beginning of the Canticle of the Creatures of Saint Francis: *Laudato si'*.

Laudato si, mi Signore, cum tucte le Tue creature, spetialmente messor lo frate Sole, lo qual è iorno, et allumini noi per lui.

Be praised, my Lord, through all your creatures, especially through my lord Brother Sun, who brings the day; and you give light through him.

(St Francis of Assisi, Canticle of the Sun)

Issues Outlined

The great intuition through the document is that the ecological crisis must be measured by its repercussions for human life and, in particular, for the life of the poor. The poor are the first victims of the current situation: they suffer from lack of water, mismanagement of garbage, climate change, poor economic situations, the destruction of natural resources and food insecurity notably resulting from monocultures (Chapter 1).

7.1 To See (Chapter 1)

Chapter I ('What is happening to our common home') follows the logic of observing and examines the situation of the ecology on earth. The analysis addresses the four elements in nature: air, water, earth and fire, the overall impact on humans.

7.1.1 Air

On this, the Pope writes: 'The climate is a common good, belonging to all and meant for all. At the global level, it is a complex system linked to many of the essential conditions for human life. A very solid scientific consensus indicates that we are presently witnessing a disturbing warming of the climatic system' (LS 23). Thus the Pope refutes climate scepticism and warns of the gravity of the situation.

7.1.2 Water

Next he draws our attention to the water: 'Fresh drinking water is an issue of primary importance, since it is indispensable for human life and for supporting terrestrial and aquatic ecosystems' (LS 28). The Pope continues his analysis speaking about the situation in Africa and about the quality of water available to the poor. 'Our world has a grave social debt towards the poor who lack access to drinking water, because they are denied the right to a life consistent with their inalienable dignity' (LS 30).

7.1.3 Earth

The Pope emphasises that the situation of the earth is linked to the economy: 'The earth's resources are also being plundered because of short-sighted approaches to the economy, commerce and production. The loss of forests and woodlands entails the loss of species which may constitute extremely important resources in the future, not only for food but also for curing disease and other uses' (LS 32). A consequence is the loss of biodiversity, 'the disappearance of thousands of plant and animal species which we will never know' (LS 33).

7.1.4 Fire

Referring to the tropical forests, the Pope writes: 'The ecosystems of tropical forests possess an enormously complex biodiversity which is almost impossible to appreciate fully; yet when these forests are burned down or levelled for purposes of cultivation, within the space of a few years, countless species are lost and the areas frequently become arid wastelands' (LS 38).

7.1.5 Human Beings

The Pope sets out the consequences of the degradation of the environment for human life. He complains about the decline in the quality of human life (LS 43). He underlines inequality on the planet: 'The human environment and the natural environment deteriorate together; we cannot adequately combat environmental degradation unless we attend to causes related to human and social degradation'. In fact, the deterioration of the environment and of society affects the most vulnerable people on the planet: 'Both everyday experience and scientific research show that the gravest effects of all attacks on the environment are suffered by the poorest (Bolivian Bishops' Conference 2012: 17)' (LS 48). So, we have 'to hear both the cry of the earth and the cry of the poor' (LS 49). He adds: 'A true 'ecological debt' exists, particularly between the global north and south, connected to commercial imbalances with effects on the environment, and the disproportionate use of natural resources by certain countries over long periods of time' (LS 51).

7.1.6 The Weakness of Reactions

The Pope concludes his first chapter with a call to international solidarity: 'The establishment of a legal framework which can set clear boundaries and ensure the protection of ecosystems has become indispensable; otherwise, the new power structures based on the techno-economic paradigm may overwhelm not only our politics but also freedom and justice' (LS 53). He remarks that, until now, our reactions have been weak: 'It is remarkable how weak international political responses have been. The failure of global summits on the environment make it plain that our politics are subject to technology and finance' (LS 54). But it remains possible to do something: 'In some countries, there are positive examples of environmental improvement: rivers, polluted for decades, have been cleaned up; native woodlands have been restored; landscapes have been beautified thanks to environmental renewal projects; beautiful buildings have been erected; advances have been made in the production of non-polluting energy and in the improvement of public transportation' (LS 58).

7.2 To Judge

7.2.1 Through the Christian Approach (Chapter 2)

As the whole encyclical 'is not reserved to Christians', it includes nevertheless 'a chapter dealing with the convictions of believers'. The reason is that: 'science and religion, with their distinctive approaches to understanding reality, can enter into an intense dialogue fruitful for both' (LS 62). To judge and evaluate the situation, the Christian faith can bring many resources. Therefore, Chapter 2 is entitled 'The Gospel of the creation'. The Pope offers a new reading of the Bible, especially of the accounts of the Creation and of the action of Jesus.

7.2.1.1 Creation of the World and Dignity of the Human Person

The accounts of the Creation in the Bible are not descriptive accounts of the reality; their literary genre is that of the myth, which allows understanding through a narrative: 'The creation accounts in the book of Genesis contain, in their own symbolic and narrative language, profound teachings about human existence and its historical reality' (LS 66). Therefore, the conclusion of the first account of the creation (Gen 1:1–31) is important and underlined by the Pope: 'After the creation of man and woman, "God saw everything that he had made, and behold it was very good" (Gen 1:31). The Bible teaches that every man and woman is created out of love and made in God's image and likeness (cf. Gen 1:26). This shows us the immense dignity of each person' (LS 65).

7.2.1.2 Risk of Sin and Violence

Such a dignity includes liberty, and liberty includes the ability to do evil. Therefore, the second account of creation (Gen 2:4–3:24) presents the breakdown of the relationship between God, man and earth: 'They suggest that human life is grounded in three fundamental and closely intertwined relationships: with God, with our neighbour and with the earth itself. According to the Bible, these three vital relationships have been broken, both outwardly and within us. This rupture is sin' (LS 66). The sin leads to violence and murder: 'In the story of Cain and Abel, we see how envy led Cain to commit the ultimate injustice against his brother, which in turn ruptured the relationship between Cain and God, and between Cain and the earth, from which he was banished' (LS 70).

The sin can be overcome, through Christ, who gives us his grace, and in communion with the saints. Saint Francis of Assisi received such grace in a full way: 'It is significant that the harmony which Saint Francis of Assisi experienced with all creatures was seen as a healing of that rupture. Saint Bonaventure held that, through universal reconciliation with every creature, Saint Francis in some way returned to the state of original innocence' (LS 66). Such an attitude is valuable for every human being: 'This responsibility for God's earth means that human beings, endowed with intelligence, must respect the laws of nature and the delicate equilibria existing between the creatures of this world' (LS 68).

7.2.1.3 Creation as Nature in Relation

The notion of creation must not be understood as the description of a physical process, but in the sense of a relationship between God and man, including a distinction between God and man. So, creation means more than 'nature':

In the Judeo-Christian tradition, the word 'creation' has a broader meaning than 'nature', for it has to do with God's loving plan in which every creature has its own value and significance. Nature is usually seen as a system which can be studied, understood and controlled, whereas creation can only be understood as a gift from the outstretched hand of the Father of all, and as a reality illuminated by the love which calls us together into universal communion.

(LS 76)

At the same time, Judeo-Christian thought demythologised nature. While continuing to admire its grandeur and immensity, it no longer saw nature as divine. In doing so, it emphasises all the more our human responsibility for nature [. . .] If we acknowledge the value and the fragility of nature and, at the same time, our God-given abilities, we can finally leave behind the modern myth of unlimited material progress. A fragile world, entrusted by God to human care, challenges us to devise intelligent ways of directing, developing and limiting our power.

(LS 78)

For this notion of creation, Pope Francis again gives the example of Saint Francis of Assisi and his Canticle of the Creatures, from which he took the title of his encyclical (LS 87): 'When we can see God reflected in all that exists, our hearts are moved to praise the Lord for all his creatures and to worship him in union with them. This sentiment finds magnificent expression in the hymn of Saint Francis of Assisi:

> Praised be you (Laudato si), my Lord, with all your creatures,
> especially Sir Brother Sun,
> who is the day and through whom you give us light.
> And he is beautiful and radiant with great splendour;
> and bears a likeness of you, Most High.
> Praised be you, my Lord, through Sister Moon and the stars,
> in heaven you formed them clear and precious and beautiful'
> *(St Francis of Assisi, Canticle of the Creatures, 113–14)*

7.2.1.4 The Call to a Universal Communion

If we all are part of the creation, we all are called to a universal communion. Ecology calls for human fraternity: 'The created things of this world are not free of ownership: "For they are yours, O Lord, who love the living" (Wis 11:26). This is the basis of our conviction that, as part of the universe, called into being by one Father, all of us are linked by unseen bonds and together form a kind of universal family, a sublime communion which fills us with a sacred, affectionate and humble respect' (LS 89). The Pope shows how this point of view is still far from the situation in reality:

We fail to see that some are mired in desperate and degrading poverty, with no way out, while others have not the faintest idea of what to do with their possessions, vainly showing off their supposed superiority and leaving behind them so much waste which, if it were the case everywhere, would destroy the planet. In practice, we continue to tolerate that some consider themselves more human than others, as if they had been born with greater rights.

(LS 90)

7.2.1.5 Universal Destination of Goods Creation

Another consequence of the ownership and of the universal communion is 'the principle of the subordination of private property to the universal destination of goods, and thus the right of everyone to their use'. It is 'a golden rule of social conduct and "the first principle of the whole ethical and social order" (John Paul II 1981: 626)' (LS 93), following the words of S. John Paul II. This principle was explained in 1979: 'The Church does indeed defend the legitimate right to private property, but she also teaches no less clearly that there is always a social mortgage on all private property, in order that goods may serve the general purpose that God gave them' (John Paul II 1979: 209). He added: 'God gave the earth to the whole human race for the sustenance of all its members, without excluding or favouring anyone' (John Paul II 1991: 831). This principle was put concretely by the bishops of Paraguay: 'Every campesino has a natural right to possess a reasonable allotment of land where he can establish his home, work for subsistence of his family and a secure life. This right must be guaranteed so that its exercise is not illusory but real (Paraguayan Bishops' Conference 1983: 2, 4, d)' (LS 94). Pope Francis adds: 'The natural environment is a collective good, the patrimony of all humanity and the responsibility of everyone. If we make something our own, it is only to administer it for the good of all. If we do not, we burden our consciences with the weight of having denied the existence of others' (LS 95).

7.2.1.6 *Jesus and the Tenderness of His Gaze*

In the New Testament, Jesus gives a new impulse to the vision of nature in relation with God:

Jesus took up the biblical faith in God the Creator, emphasising a fundamental truth: God is Father (cf. Mt 11:25) ... With moving tenderness he would remind them that each one of them is important in God's eyes: 'Are not five sparrows sold for two pennies? And not one of them is forgotten before God' (Lk 12:6). 'Look at the birds of the air: they neither sow nor reap nor gather into barns, and yet your heavenly Father feeds them' (Mt 6:26).

(LS 96)

So, the respect for the birds becomes a starting point for respect of the men. 'Jesus lived in full harmony with creation, and others were amazed: "What sort of man is this, that even the winds and the sea obey him?" (Mt 8:27)' (LS 98).

7.2.1.7 *Jesus and His Cosmic Issue*

The humanity of Christ opens the way to his divinity. That conviction shows the role of Christ in the whole cosmos. That is explained by the apostle Paul, in his letter to the Colossians, and by the evangelist John in his Gospel:

In the Christian understanding of the world, the destiny of all creation is bound up with the mystery of Christ, present from the beginning: 'All things have been created though him and for him' (Col 1:16). The prologue of the Gospel of John (1:1–18) reveals Christ's creative work as the Divine Word (Logos); first, it shows the divinity of the Word of God:

'In the beginning was the Word, and the Word was with God, and the Word was God' (Jn 1:1); and afterwards, it shows the humanity of the Word of God: 'The Word became flesh and made his dwelling among us'

(Jn 1:14).

Thus, the Pope can write: 'From the beginning of the world, but particularly through the incarnation, the mystery of Christ is at work in a hidden manner in the natural world as a whole, without thereby impinging on its autonomy' (LS 99). So, we can look at the future with an intense hope: 'This leads us to direct our gaze to the end of time, when the Son will deliver all things to the Father, so that "God may be everything to every one" (1 Cor 15:28)' (LS 100).

7.2.2 Through an Anthropological Approach (Chapter 3)

Chapter 3 ('The human roots of the ecological crisis') offers an anthropological approach in order to understand the roots of the ecological crisis, in particular the abuse of technology and in the excesses of anthropocentrism.

7.2.2.1 Abuse of Technology

We can observe that 'humanity has entered a new era in which our technical prowess has brought us to a crossroads' (LS 101). But technology does not always signify progress:

There is a tendency to believe that every increase in power means 'an increase of progress itself', an advance in 'security, usefulness, welfare and vigour; an assimilation of new values into the stream of culture' (Guardini 1965: 87; trans. in English Guardini 1998: 82), as if reality, goodness and truth automatically flow from technological and economic power as such.

(LS 105)

Technology also means power: 'Yet it must also be recognised that nuclear energy, biotechnology, information technology, knowledge of our DNA, and many other abilities which we have acquired, have given us tremendous power' (LS 104). Against such a power, 'we cannot claim to have a sound ethics, a culture and spirituality genuinely capable of setting limits and teaching clear-minded self-restraint' (LS 105).

7.2.2.2 Anthropocentrism

But 'the basic problem goes even deeper: it is the way that humanity has taken up technology and its development according to an undifferentiated and one-dimensional paradigm. This paradigm exalts the concept of a subject who, using logical and rational procedures, progressively approaches and gains control over an external object' (LS 106). There is a globalisation of the technocratic paradigm: 'It can be said that many problems of today's world stem from the tendency, at times unconscious, to make the method and aims of science and technology an epistemological paradigm which shapes the lives of individuals and the workings of society' (LS 107). 'The technocratic paradigm also tends to dominate economic and political life. The economy accepts every advance in technology with a view to profit, without concern for its potentially negative impact on human beings. Finance overwhelms the real economy' (LS 109). Ecology cannot be reduced to technological problems:

> Ecological culture cannot be reduced to a series of urgent and partial responses to the immediate problems of pollution, environmental decay and the depletion of natural resources. There needs to be a distinctive way of looking at things, a way of thinking, policies, an educational programme, a lifestyle and a spirituality which together generate resistance to the assault of the technocratic paradigm.
>
> *(LS 111)*

Modern anthropocentrism has paradoxically ended up prizing technical thought over reality, since

> 'the technological mind sees nature as an insensate order, as a cold body of facts, as a mere given, as an object of utility, as raw material to be hammered into useful shape; it views the cosmos similarly as a mere space into which objects can be thrown with complete indifference' (Guardini 1965: 63; trans. in English Guardini 1998: 55).
>
> *(LS 115)*

Often, what was handed on was a Promethean vision of mastery over the world, which gave the impression that the protection of nature was something that only the faint-hearted cared about. (LS 116)

Hence, we should not be surprised to find, in conjunction with the omnipresent technocratic paradigm and the cult of unlimited human power, the rise of a relativism which sees everything as irrelevant unless it serves one's own immediate interests. There is a logic in all this, whereby different attitudes can feed on one another, leading to environmental degradation and social decay. (LS 122)

Any approach to an integral ecology, which by definition does not exclude human beings, needs to take account of the value of labour. (LS 124)

7.2.2.3 Biological Technologies

A peculiar case is the role of the biological technologies: 'It is difficult to make a general judgement about genetic modification (GM), whether vegetable or animal, medical or agricultural, since these vary greatly among themselves and call for specific considerations. The risks involved are not always due to the techniques used, but rather to their improper or excessive application' (LS 133). The use of biological technologies for GM cereals is problematic:

Although no conclusive proof exists that GM cereals may be harmful to human beings, and in some regions their use has brought about economic growth which has helped to resolve problems, there remain a number of significant difficulties which should not be underestimated. In many places, following the introduction of these crops, productive land is concentrated in the hands of a few owners due to 'the progressive disappearance of small producers, who, as a consequence of the loss of the exploited lands, are obliged to withdraw from direct production' (Episcopal Commission in Argentina 2005: 19).

(LS 134)

7.2.3 To Judge through an Integral Ecology (Chapter 4)

Pope Francis introduces in Chapter 4 his personal suggestion of an 'integral ecology'. He insists on the fact that everything is interconnected and that ecology must also consider the human being: 'Since everything is closely interrelated, and today's problems call for a vision capable of taking into account every aspect of the global crisis, I suggest that we now consider some elements of an integral ecology, one which clearly respects its human and social dimensions' (LS 137). The notion of 'integral' has been important for the Catholic Church since the beginning of the twentieth century, and suggests a complete point of view of a situation. It refers to Jacques Maritain (1882–1973) who developed in his studies the notion of 'integral humanism'.

7.2.3.1 Social, Economic, Cultural and Human Ecology

There is a social and economic ecology:

If everything is related, then the health of a society's institution has consequences for the environment and the quality of human life. 'Every violation of solidarity and civic friendship harms the environment' (Benedict XVI 2009: 687). In this sense, social ecology is necessarily institutional, and gradually extends to the whole of society, from the primary social group, the family, to the wider local, national and international communities.

(LS 142)

There is a cultural ecology:

Together with the patrimony of nature, there is also an historic, artistic and cultural patrimony which is likewise under threat. This patrimony is a part of the shared identity of each place and a foundation upon which to build a habitable city ... Culture is more than what we have inherited from the past; it is also, and above all, a living, dynamic and participatory present reality, which cannot be excluded as we rethink the relationship between human beings and the environment.

(LS 143)

There is an ecology of daily life: 'Authentic development includes efforts to bring about an integral improvement in the quality of human life, and this entails considering the setting in which people live their lives' (LS 147). This also extends to the building of houses and transport: 'Lack of housing is a grave problem in many parts of the world, both in rural areas and in large cities, since state budgets usually cover only a small portion of the demand' (LS 152).

That leads to human ecology: 'Human ecology also implies another profound reality: the relationship between human life and the moral law, which is inscribed in our nature and is necessary for the creation of a more dignified environment' (LS 155).

7.2.3.1 The Common Good

All this supposes the notion of common good: 'An integral ecology is inseparable from the notion of the common good, a central and unifying principle of social ethics. The common good is "the sum of those conditions of social life which allow social groups and their individual members relatively thorough and ready access to their own fulfilment" (Second Vatican Ecumenical Council, Pastoral Constitution of the Church)' (LS 156). The concept of common good has its origin in Aristotle (384–322 BC), and was expressed again by Thomas of Aquinas (1224–74): it is at the origin of the democratic movement in medieval Europe (Delville 2018). It was later used by a neo-Thomist such as Antoine Pottier (1849–1923) to justify social justice (Delville 2019). And the notion of common good can also be found in different cultural traditions (see Chapter 15 by Van Norren in this volume).

Common good concerns future generations: 'The notion of the common good also extends to future generations. The global economic crises have made painfully obvious the detrimental effects of disregarding our common destiny, which cannot exclude those who come after us' (LS 159).

7.3 To Act

Pope Francis offers in Chapters 5 and 6 different paths of action at the institutional and personal levels. He insists first on the necessity of global action.

7.3.1 At the Political Level (Chapter 5)

In Chapter 5 ('Lines of approach and action'), he addresses the topic of international and local political action. The situations of injustice and the uncontrolled exploitation of natural resources require political intervention: 'Interdependence obliges us to think of one world with a common plan' (LS 164).

7.3.1.1 The Role of International Organisations

Pope Francis mentions the 1992 Earth Summit in Rio de Janeiro, which proclaimed that 'human beings are at the centre of concerns for sustainable development' (Rio Declaration: Principle 1) (LS 167). International regulation is necessary for lowering pollutant gas emissions and for the governance of the oceans:

Enforceable international agreements are urgently needed, since local authorities are not always capable of effective intervention. Relations between states must be respectful of each other's sovereignty but, must also lay down mutually agreed means of averting regional disasters which would eventually affect everyone. Global regulatory norms are needed to impose obligations and prevent unacceptable actions, for example, when powerful companies or countries dump contaminated waste or offshore polluting industries in other countries.

(LS 173)

Referring to John XXIII and Benedict XVI, Pope Francis asks the reinforcement of international institutions:

Given this situation, it is essential to devise stronger and more efficiently organised international institutions, with functionaries who are appointed fairly by agreement among national governments, and empowered to impose sanctions. As Benedict XVI has affirmed in continuity with the social teaching of the Church: 'To manage the global economy; to revive economies hit by the crisis; to avoid any deterioration of the present crisis and the greater imbalances that would result; to bring about integral and timely disarmament, food security and peace; to guarantee the protection of the environment and to regulate migration: for all this, there is urgent need of a true world political authority, as my predecessor Blessed John XXIII indicated some years ago' (Benedict XVI 2009: 67).

(LS 175)

7.3.1.2 The Role of Nation States

Pope Francis also looks to the authority of the national governments:

Given the real potential for a misuse of human abilities, individual states can no longer ignore their responsibility for planning, coordination, oversight and enforcement within their respective borders . . . But political and institutional frameworks do not exist simply to avoid bad practice, but also to promote best practice, to stimulate creativity in seeking new solutions and to encourage individual or group initiatives.

(LS 177)

Such a policy needs time:

Here, continuity is essential, because policies related to climate change and environmental protection cannot be altered with every change of government. Results take time and demand immediate outlays which may not produce tangible effects within any one government's term. That is why, in the absence of pressure from the public and from civic institutions, political authorities will always be reluctant to intervene, all the more when urgent needs must be met.

(LS 181)

On 'short-termism', see Chapter 13 by Matthias Fritsch in this volume. Such a policy also calls for transparency in decision-making:

An assessment of the environmental impact of business ventures and projects demands transparent political processes involving a free exchange of views. On the other hand, the forms of corruption which conceal the actual environmental impact of a given project, in exchange for favours, usually produce specious agreements which fail to inform adequately and to allow for full debate.

(LS 182)

7.3.1.3 Relation between Politics and the Economy

Politics and the economy must be in dialogue for human fulfilment:

Politics must not be subject to the economy, nor should the economy be subject to the dictates of an efficiency-driven paradigm of technocracy. Today, in view of the common good, there is urgent need for politics and economics to enter into a frank dialogue in the service of life, especially human life. Saving banks at any cost, making the public pay the price, foregoing a firm commitment to reviewing and reforming the entire system, only reaffirms the absolute power of a financial system, a power which has no future and will only give rise to new crises after a slow, costly and only apparent recovery ... The financial bubble also tends to be a productive bubble. The problem of the real economy is not confronted with vigour, yet it is the real economy which makes diversification and improvement in production possible, helps companies to function well, and enables small and medium businesses to develop and create employment.

(LS 189)

7.3.2 To Act at the Personal Level (Chapter 6)

Pope Francis asks for 'Ecological education and spirituality' (Chapter 6) in matters of ecology. This brings us towards a new lifestyle: 'Many things have to change course, but it is we human beings above all who need to change. We lack an awareness of our common origin, of our mutual belonging, and of a future to be shared with everyone' (LS 202). 'When people become self-centred and self-enclosed, their greed increases. The emptier a person's heart is, the more he or she needs things to buy, own and consume' (LS 204). 'A change in lifestyle could bring healthy pressure to bear on those who wield political, economic and social power' (LS 206).

7.3.2.1 Education and Ecology

Pope Francis calls for education in the perspective of a covenant between humanity and the environment:

Environmental education has broadened its goals. Whereas in the beginning it was mainly centred on scientific information, consciousness-raising and the prevention of environmental risks, it tends now to include a critique of the 'myths' of a modernity grounded in a utilitarian mindset (individualism, unlimited progress, competition, consumerism, the unregulated market). It seeks also to restore the various levels of ecological equilibrium, establishing harmony within ourselves, with others, with nature and other living creatures, and with God.

(LS 210)

Such an education is very useful: 'We must not think that these efforts are not going to change the world. They benefit society, often unbeknown to us, for they call forth a goodness which, albeit unseen, inevitably tends to spread' (LS 212). Pope Francis, who is a professional educator, adds:

Ecological education can take place in a variety of settings: at school, in families, in the media, in catechesis and elsewhere ... In the family we receive an integral education, which enables us to grow harmoniously in personal maturity. In the family we learn to ask without demanding, to say 'thank you' as an expression of genuine gratitude for what we have been given, to control our aggressiveness and greed, and to ask forgiveness when we have caused harm. These simple gestures of heartfelt courtesy help to create a culture of shared life and respect for our surroundings.

(LS 213)

7.3.2.2 Ecological Conversion

All Christians are called on to live an ecological conversion: 'So what they all need is an "ecological conversion", whereby the effects of their encounter with Jesus Christ become evident in their relationship with the world around them' (LS 217). 'In calling to mind the figure of Saint Francis of Assisi, we come to realise that a healthy relationship with creation is one dimension of overall personal conversion, which entails the recognition of our errors, sins, faults and failures, and leads to heartfelt repentance and desire to change' (LS 218). But ecological conversion is also communitarian:

Isolated individuals can lose their ability and freedom to escape the utilitarian mindset, and end up prey to an unethical consumerism bereft of social or ecological awareness. Social problems must be addressed by community networks and not simply by the sum of individual good deeds ... The ecological conversion needed to bring about lasting change is also a community conversion.

(LS 219)

So, the Pope concludes:

I ask all Christians to recognise and to live fully this dimension of their conversion. May the power and the light of the grace we have received also be evident in our relationship to other creatures and to the world around us. In this way, we will help nurture that sublime fraternity with all creation which Saint Francis of Assisi so radiantly embodied.

(LS 221)

7.3.2.3 Joy and Peace

Sobriety as an ecological way of life brings joy and peace:

Such sobriety, when lived freely and consciously, is liberating. It is not a lesser life or one lived with less intensity. On the contrary, it is a way of living life to the full. In reality, those who enjoy more and live better each moment are those who have given up dipping here and there, always on the look-out for what they do not have.

(LS 223)

It concerns all of human life: 'We have to dare to speak of the integrity of human life, of the need to promote and unify all the great values' (LS 224). 'Inner peace is closely related to care for ecology and for the common good because, lived out authentically, it is reflected in a balanced lifestyle together with a capacity for wonder which takes us to a deeper understanding of life' (LS 225).

7.3.2.4 Civic and Political Love

The Pope underlines also the social dimension of love: 'We must regain the conviction that we need one another, that we have a shared responsibility for others and the world, and that being good and decent are worth it' (LS 229). Furthermore:

Love, overflowing with small gestures of mutual care, is also civic and political, and it makes itself felt in every action that seeks to build a better world. Love for society and commitment to the common good are outstanding expressions of a charity which affects not only relationships between individuals but also 'macro-relationships, social, economic and political ones' (Benedict XVI 2009: 642). That is why the Church set before the world the ideal of a 'civilisation of love' (Paul VI 1976: 709).

(LS 231)

7.3.2.5 Sacramental Signs and the Celebration of the Day of Rest

Concretely, the spirituality of ecology can be experienced in the Sacraments:

The Sacraments are a privileged way in which nature is taken up by God to become a means of mediating supernatural life. Through our worship of God, we are invited to embrace the world on a different plane. Water, oil, fire and colours are taken up in all their symbolic power and incorporated in our act of praise. The hand that blesses is an instrument of God's love and a reflection of the closeness of Jesus Christ, who came to accompany us on the journey of life. Water poured over the body of a child in Baptism is a sign of new life.

(LS 235)

'It is in the Eucharist that all that has been created finds its greatest exaltation. Grace, which tends to manifest itself tangibly, found unsurpassable expression when God himself became man and gave himself as food for his creatures' (LS 236).

Another concrete sign of the ecological spirituality is Sunday, as a day of rest: 'Sunday, like the Jewish Sabbath, is meant to be a day which heals our relationships with God, with ourselves, with others and with the world ... And so the day of rest, centred on the Eucharist, sheds its light on the whole week, and motivates us to greater concern for nature and the poor' (LS 237).

7.3.2.6 The Trinity and the Relationship between Creatures

Finally, the Pope evokes the role of the Trinity in the reflection about ecology: 'The world was created by the three Persons acting as a single divine principle, but each one of them performed this common work in accordance with his own personal property. Consequently, "when we contemplate with wonder the universe in all its grandeur and beauty, we must praise the whole Trinity" (John Paul II 2000: 112)' (LS 238).

Pope Francis concludes with a reflection on Maria and on the eternal life: 'At the end, we will find ourselves face to face with the infinite beauty of God (cf. 1 Cor 13:12), and be able to read with admiration and happiness the mystery of the universe, which with us will share in unending plenitude' (LS 243).

He offers the readers a prayer for our Earth (LS 246):

> All-powerful God, you are present in the whole universe
> and in the smallest of your creatures.
> You embrace with your tenderness all that exists.
> Pour out upon us the power of your love,
> that we may protect life and beauty.
> Fill us with peace, that we may live
> as brothers and sisters, harming no one.
> O God of the poor,
> help us to rescue the abandoned and forgotten of this earth,
> so precious in your eyes.
> Bring healing to our lives,
> that we may protect the world and not prey on it,
> that we may sow beauty, not pollution and destruction.

After an analysis of the situation and an evaluation of the ecological needs, the Pope adds paths of action and ways of contemplation. He stresses the fact that everybody is able to do something and to discover the joy in a new relation of contemplation with his brothers and sisters, with the cosmos and with God. So, the dramatic symphony I evoked at the beginning becomes a 'pastoral symphony' which gives readers peace and hope for their action in favour of ecology.

7.4 The Synod of the Amazon

A special assembly of the Synod of Bishops for the Pan-Amazon region was held in Rome (6–27 October 2019), and concluded with the adoption of a Final Document, dated 26 October, entitled *The Amazon: New Paths for the Church and for an Integral Ecology* (TA). Pope Francis took the initiative to convene such an assembly to address the ecological challenges and social problems of the region, as well as the organisational issues of the local church. The final document sets out important guidelines for the implementation of the *Laudato si'* Encyclical in the field. On 2 February 2020, Pope Francis published his post-synodal apostolic exhortation *Querida Amazonia* (*Dear Amazon*) (QA), an intense and personal document, in order to provide the Church with the official guidelines that he intends to draw from the work of the Synod of Bishops on Amazonia. First, he presented officially the final document of the Synod, which should be 'read in its entirety' (QA 3), thus giving this text a special value. The apostolic exhortation presents the dream of Pope Francis for the Amazon (QA 7). Let us take up his ecological dream: 'I dream of an Amazon that jealously preserves the irresistible natural beauty that decorates it, the overflowing life that fills its rivers and forests'. Knowing that everything is connected, Pope Francis adds a social dream: 'I dream of an Amazon region that fights for the rights of the poor, the original peoples and the least of our brothers and sisters, where their voices can be heard and their dignity advanced.' He gives also his vision of a cultural dream: 'I dream of an Amazon region that can preserve its distinctive cultural riches, where the beauty of our humanity shines forth in so many varied ways.' He concludes with an ecclesial dream: 'I dream of Christian communities capable of generous commitment, incarnated in the Amazon region, and giving the Church new faces with Amazonian features.'

7.4.1 The Findings

In terms of findings, the Synod document underlines the importance of the Amazon for the climatic balance and the danger that the Amazon runs with the forest fires that ravage it:

The scientific community warns of the risks of deforestation, which to date comprises almost 17% of the whole Amazon Forest. This threatens the survival of the entire ecosystem, endangering biodiversity and changing the cycle of water that is vital for the survival of the tropical forest. In addition, the Amazon plays a critical role as a buffer against climate change and provides invaluable and fundamental life support systems related to air, water, soil, forests and biomass. At the same time, experts remind us that by using advanced science and technologies for an innovative bio-economy of standing forests and flowing rivers, it is possible to help save the rainforest, protect the ecosystems of the Amazon and its indigenous and traditional peoples and, at the same time, provide sustainable economic activities.

(TA 11)

Pope Francis specifies: 'In a cultural reality like the Amazon region, where there is such a close relationship between human beings and nature, daily existence is always cosmic' (QA 41). 'Water is queen; the rivers and streams are like veins, and water determines every form of life' (QA 43). The Synod document stresses, as does the Encyclical, that everything is connected:

In the jungle, not only is the vegetation intertwined between one species and another, but the peoples also interrelate among themselves in a network of alliances that enriches all. The jungle thrives from interrelations and interdependencies, and this happens in all areas of life. Thanks to this, the Amazon's fragile equilibrium has endured for centuries.

(TA 43)

The Pope refers to a mosaic of more than 110 peoples in voluntary isolation (*Pueblos Indígenas en Aislamiento Voluntario* (PIAV)) that make up the Amazon. He values the diversity of their languages, skills and cultures (QA 29). The Synod document also highlights the problems of land ownership and the conflicts that arise in this regard:

The greed for land is at the root of the conflicts that lead to ethnocide, as well as the criminalisation of social movements and the murder of their leaders. The demarcation and protection of land are obligations of national States and their respective governments. However, significant portions of the Indigenous territories lack protection; and those already demarcated are being invaded by extractive interests such as mining and forestry, large infrastructure projects, illicit crops, and large estates that promote monoculture and extensive cattle ranching.

(TA 45)

The Pope specifies:

The businesses, national or international, which harm the Amazon and fail to respect the right of the original peoples to the land and its boundaries, and to self-determination and prior consent, should be called for what they are: *injustice and crime*. When certain businesses out for quick profit appropriate lands and end up privatising even potable water, or when local authorities give free access to the timber companies, mining or oil projects, and other businesses that raze the forests and pollute the environment, economic relationships are unduly altered and become an instrument of death.

(QA 14)

7.4.2 Evaluation

In terms of judging the situation, the Final Document of the Synod updates the concept of integral ecology:

Catholic Social Teaching, which for a long time has dealt with the ecological issue, is today enriched with a more comprehensive view of the relationship between the Amazon peoples and their territories, always in dialogue with their ancestral knowledge and wisdom. For example, recognising the way in which indigenous peoples relate to and protect their territories is an indispensable measure for our conversion to an integral ecology.

(TA 79)

The Pope writes: 'The equilibrium of our planet also depends on the health of the Amazon region' (QA 48). 'From the original peoples, we can learn to *contemplate* the Amazon region and not simply analyse it, and thus appreciate this precious mystery that transcends us' (QA 55). The Final Document of the Synod makes an original and unexpected proposal; it suggests defining an ecological sin:

We propose to define ecological sin as an action or omission against God, against one's neighbour, the community and the environment. It is sin against future generations, and it is committed in acts and habits of pollution and destruction of the harmony of the environment. These are transgressions against the principles of interdependence, and they destroy networks of solidarity among creatures (*Catechism of the Catholic Church*, 340–44) and violate the virtue of justice.

(TA 82)

7.4.3 Action

Turning to the proposals for action, the Synod proposes the creation of ministries in the Catholic Church responsible for ecological action and support for displaced persons: 'We want to create ministries for the care of our common home in the Amazon, whose function is to take care of the territory and its waters together with the indigenous communities, and a ministry of welcome for those who are displaced from their territories towards the cities' (TA 79). Specifically, the document adds:

We also propose to create special ministries for the care of our common home and the promotion of integral ecology at the parish level and in each Church jurisdiction. Their functions include, among others, the care of the territory and of the waters, as well as the promotion of the Encyclical *Laudato si'*, taking up the pastoral, educational and advocacy program in its Chapters 5 and 6 at all levels and structures of the Church.

(TA 82)

The Synod is also struck by the role of women in Amazonian culture and calls for the development of the place of women in society and in the Church:

The ancestral wisdom of the Aboriginal peoples affirms that Mother earth has a feminine face. The work of women in both the Indigenous and western worlds is multifaceted: they instruct children and transmit faith and the Gospel, they inspire and support human development. The voice of women should therefore be heard, they should be consulted and participate in decision-making and, in this way, contribute with their sensitivity to Church synodality. We value the role of women, recognising their fundamental role in the formation and continuity of cultures, in spirituality, in communities and families. Their leadership must be more fully assumed in the heart of the Church, recognised and promoted by strengthening their participation in the pastoral councils of parishes and dioceses, and also in positions of governance.

(TA 101)

The Synod also envisages adapting the liturgy to the Amazonian culture: 'We should give an authentically catholic response to the request of the Amazonian communities to adapt the liturgy by valuing the original worldview, traditions, symbols and rites that include transcendent, community and ecological dimensions' (TA 116). Pope Francis adds: 'it is good to combine ancestral wisdom with contemporary technical knowledge' (QA 51). Integral ecology 'has an educational dimension' (QA 58).

With regard to political commitment, the Synod insists on the necessary coordination of efforts at the international level:

The Church participates in international solidarity that must recognise and support the central role of the Amazon biome for the equilibrium of the planet's climate. The Church encourages the international community to provide new economic resources for its protection and for the promotion of a model of just and solidary development, with the protagonism and direct participation of local communities and native peoples in all phases from planning to implementation, thereby also strengthening the tools already developed by the United Nations Framework Convention on Climate Change, Rio de Janeiro, 1992.

(TA 68)

Pope Francis adds that, faced with such difficulties, 'the answer is not to be found, in 'internationalizing' the Amazon region, but rather in a greater sense of responsibility on the part of national governments' (QA 50).

Turning to achievements, Pope Francis announced, on 3 November 2019, that he would create a separate department for Amazonia within the Dicastery for the Service of Integral Human Development, in accordance with a request expressed in the Final Document of the Synod.

Conclusion

In conclusion, we can see how important Pope Francis' Encyclical *Laudato si'* is for theoretical reflection as well as for implementation in the field. It is based on the statements of many local episcopates and is inspired by studies on the subject by many scientists. It introduces the notion of integral ecology, underlining how everything is linked and how poor people are the first to suffer from the situation of climate change and social crisis. It calls for commitment at the personal and structural levels.

The convocation of the Synod for the Amazon is a tangible sign of the validity of Pope Francis' analysis. This Synod, confirmed by Pope Francis in his apostolic exhortation *Querida Amazonia*, gives concrete expression on the ground to the evolution of the ecological environment. It brings to light the injustices and the suffering that result for individuals. It proposes a new commitment for the local church and for the universal Church. For this, the Synod adopts the 'see–judge–act' logic of Pope Francis. In the 'seeing', the Synod underlines the urgency of the situation of ecological imbalance and the problems linked to the occupation of land. In the 'judging', the Synod shows the relevance of the concept of integral ecology for the Amazon and invites us to recognise an 'ecological sin', which is the result of all the shortcomings observed in this area. This notion resonates with the legal concept of 'ecocide' as presented in Chapter 10 by Valérie Cabanes in this volume.

In 'acting', the Synod proposes the establishment of church ministries to monitor ecology and promote responsible attitudes in this area. It emphasises the role of women in this regard. It suggests the development of a liturgy tuned to Amazonian cultures. At the social and political level, the Synod insists on the coordination of efforts to be promoted among all international organisations. Admittedly, the implementation of such a programme requires considerable human, technical and political resources. But it is important to map out the path of humanity's future in connection with God, its Creator, beyond even material contingencies, based on hope, nourished by faith in Christ.

References

Benedict XVI (2009). Encyclical Letter *Caritas in Veritate* (29 June), 67. In *Acta Apostolicae Sedis,* 101.

Bolivian Bishops' Conference (2012). Pastoral Letter on the Environment and Human Development in Bolivia. *El universo, don de Dios para la vida* (23 March), 17.

Congregation for the Doctrine of the faith and Dicastery for Promoting Integral Human Development (2018). *Oeconomicae et pecuniariae quaestiones. Considerations for an Ethical Discernment Regarding Some Aspects of the Present Economic–Financial System,* 6 January, Rome.

Delville, J.-P. (2015). Introduction. In *Pape François, Loué sois-tu! Laudato si'. Namur. Fidélité,* 11–14.

Delville, J.-P. (2018). Godefroid de Fontaines (1250–1309), théoricien des idées démocratiques à l'Université de Paris et inspirateur de la Paix de Fexhe. In

Christophe Masson and Bruno Demoulin (eds.), *La Paix de Fexhe (1316) et les révoltes dans la Principauté de Liège et dans les Pays-Bas méridionaux*. Brussels: Archives générales du Royaume, Studies in Belgian History, 5, 27–34.

Delville, J.-P. (2020a). Antoine Pottier and the neo-Thomist roots of social justice. In Wim Decock and Peter Heyrman (eds.), *Neo-Thomism in Action: Law and Society reshaped by Neo-Scholastic Philosophy, 1880–1960*. Louvain: Louvain University Press, 279–89.

Delville, J.-P. (2020b). Introduction. In *Pape François, Chère Amazonie. Querida Amazonia*. Namur. Fidélité, 3–7.

Episcopal Commission for Pastoral Concerns in Argentina (2005). *Una tierra para todos*.

Francis of Assisi (1999). Canticle of the Creatures. In Regis J. Armstrong et al. (eds.), *Francis of Assisi: Early Documents – The Saint*. New York: New City State, vol. I, 113–14.

Francis of Assisi (2003). Canticle of the Sun. In K. Esser (ed.), *François d'Assise, Écrits*. Paris: Éditions du Cerf, 342–45.

Francis (Pope) (2015). *Encyclical letter Laudato si'. French edition: Pape François, Loué sois-tu ! Laudato si'*. Introduction: Mgr Jean-Pierre Delville. Namur. Fidélité.

Francis (Pope) (2020). *Post-synodal Exhortation Querida Amazonia. French edition: Pape François, Chère Amazonie, Querida Amazonia*. Introduction: Mgr Jean-Pierre Delville. Namur. Fidélité.

Guardini, R. (1965). *Das Ende der Neuzeit*. 9th ed. Würzburg [Eng. ed.: *The End of the Modern World*, Wilmington, NC: ISI Books].

John Paul II (1979). Address to Indigenous and rural people, Cuilapán, Mexico (29 January). *Acta Apostolicae Sedis* 71: 209.

John Paul II (1981). Encyclical Letter *Laborem exercens* (14 September). *Acta Apostolicae Sedis* 73: 626.

John Paul II (1991). Encyclical Letter *Centesimus Annus* (1 May 1991). *Acta Apostolicae Sedis* 83: 831.

John Paul II (2000). *Catechesis* (2 August 2000). 4. In *Insegnamenti* 23/2 (2000), 112.

Paraguayan Bishops' Conference (1983). *Pastoral Letter El campesino paraguayo y la tierra* (12 June 1983), 2, 4.

Paul VI (1976). Message for the 1977 World Day of Peace. *Acta Apostolicae Sedis* 68: 709.

Rio Declaration on Environment and Development (14 June 1992), Principle 1.

Second Vatican Ecumenical Council (1965). *Pastoral Constitution on the Church in the Modern World Gaudium et spes*. Rome, 7 December 1965.

Synod of Bishops (2019). Special assembly of the Synod for the Pan-Amazon Region. Rome. 26 October. Final document. *The Amazon: New Paths for the Church and for an Integral Ecology*. www.vatican.va/roman_curia/synod/documents/rc_synod_doc_20191026_sinodo-amazzonia_en.html.

8

Persons, Things and Nature in Roman Law

Reflections on Legal History

ARNAUD PATURET

Introduction

The question of our relationship with nature cannot overlook the legal dimension, as law is a powerful lever for harmonising relationships between people, and regulates the relationship between people and their environment. However, contemporary legal systems do not always have the essential tools to address or manage this relationship, because current legal categories relegate nature to an object which humankind can use and exploit, and over which it has control, whereas, in fact, it remains the very condition of human existence. The will of the legislator is not necessarily to blame because its work potentially remains blocked by legal taxonomies – mainly the watertight dichotomy between subjects and objects, persons and things – which constrain the reasoning and ability to legislate. This systemic gap in the law could be filled by reflecting on other ways of thinking, taking for example the legal concept of 'thing', which is applied to natural entities and the idea of nature. In order to reflect on such a categorisation, we need to look at how, throughout legal history, legal operators have dealt with this issue. This context highlights all that the human sciences, and in particular the history of law and institutions, can contribute to the conception of representations and rights of the environment. The law of ancient Rome remains an essential reference due to its high degree of elaboration and influence on contemporary law. The division of legal designations established in Roman law is at the root of contemporary legal categorisation between actions, persons and things (*actiones, personae, res*). This explains why Roman law is considered as a matrix of European legal systems or, at least, as a key of interpretation to understand their evolution, to the point that some authors speak of 'benchmarks' (Rampelberg 2005). It might be wrong to believe that Romans were the only inventors of Western law, but as the Justinian *Digest* and sharp casuistic testimonies substantiate, they have undoubtedly developed a full conceptual framework and the magnificent figure of the jurist as an inventor and architect.

The current terminology of European legislation, including that of civil and common law systems, shows a continuity in legal history since our Roman precursors. Yet, if we focus on the very substance of certain fundamental lexical elements which structure the legal world, this perpetuation has to be analysed rather as an important conceptual metamorphosis. Indeed, there are areas of contemporary law where very few Roman ideas remain, even when the terms used are similar. To prove it, I will study a fundamental concept of law, which usually designates the object of a legal relationship, namely the 'thing', an entity that all legal systems have integrated under various terms. The Latin word for it is *res*, thing in English, *Sache* in German, *chose* in French, *cosa* in Italian. This concept designates as a legal subject an entity different from a human being, in a thought movement of anthropocentrism where the human being stands at the centre of the legal system and its intellectual justification.

In contemporary French law, when it comes to defining the 'thing', the informed jurist commonly replies as follows: the term 'thing' means 'a movable or immovable object characterised by its own material existence and likely to be the object of rights' (Cabrillac 2002: 66; in the same sense Cornu 1987: 173). From this fundamental definition derives a taxonomy relative to the vocation or to the retained quality of the thing: common, expendable, corporeal or incorporeal, frugiferous, gender, out of trade, without master, etc. What must be remembered from this classification, which excludes all substantialism, is that it essentially considers material goods that exist independently of the subject, and do not belong exclusively to the legal world (as opposed to rights). In the first place, this means that the 'thing' is not created by law – which comes only to describe it – but that its initial existence in the known world precedes its monopolisation by the legislator. In the second place, to consider the 'thing' as a pure object of desire or will, according to the common understanding, amounts to classifying it as a simple means in the face of the emitting will – which would be an end. In short, this framework creates a structural opposition between subject and object, to which I will return, and which structures our thinking as well as our reasoning (Paturet 2017: 70).

Indeed, the contemporary legal definition of the 'thing' (Cornu 1987: 173) joins a set of equivalences in the usual language, insofar as it is fashioned in an almost intuitive way, without any scientific filter. If we read the French Littré dictionary (Littré 1968: 921–23), which refers to various meanings for the term 'thing', we find this opposition between subject and object. The 'thing' is the 'indeterminate designation of all that is inanimate … In terms of grammar, a thing is said as opposed to a person. The pronoun that always refers to things (it) never refers to people ... What is actually, in reality as opposed to what is a word, a name '. In comparison, it is quite the same in English dictionaries: the word 'thing' means '1. entity, idea, action, etc., that exist or may be thought about or perceived; 2. inanimate material object (e.g. take that thing away)' (Thompson 1993: 948). There are, of course, other meanings of the term, but the one that structures our perception by designating any concrete object in relation to animate beings is particularly solid. It has also caused reversals between the word and what it really means according to the sensibility of the observer. A human being who loses his autonomy would deviate from the human norm characterised by free will and become a 'poor thing' (Laporte 1986: 575), considered as being deprived of his humanity, even if he remains a human being biologically, whereas the words which designate him could dehumanise his person. It is the same considering relationships of domination when one is in dependence, under the total domination of the other, the second would have made the first 'his thing', according to the commonly accepted idea. In the hollow of these metaphors, of those impossible analogies used in language to finally express a disgrace de facto, it is a whole mental universe that encompasses the law and all the rest, by forming an implacable schema that structures our thinking around a meta value: the human on one side and the entities deemed inanimate on the other.

8.1 The Evolution of Legal Doctrine

It is not uncommon for societal paradigms to be based on a strong historical–ideological grounding. By following the outline of many textbooks of historical introduction to law or law history, written by prominent French Romanists (Giffard 1938: 3 or Girard 1929), we are invited to locate the genesis of this modern legal concept of 'thing' in Roman law – in particular in the separation made in the didactic book conceived by the jurist Gaius in the second century AD.[1] This famous volume, whose structure built the landscape of the legal phenomenon, influenced many modern codifications. It presents a fundamental division of the law in the following way: 'all the rights we use are relative to persons, things, or actions. But let's first look at the persons' (Gaius, Inst. 1.8).[2] Following this orientation, the manual was composed of four books. The first dealt with persons, the second was dedicated to things, the third was on obligations and the fourth focused on legal actions (*actiones*). The volume's structure, taken separately from the content of the work, suggested that Roman law thematically separated persons and things into two distinct and tightly closed categories. However, a careful

---

[1] Probably because it remains the most accessible and educational source.
[2] Omne autem ius quo utimur uel ad personas pertinet, uel ad res, uel ad actiones. Sed prius videamus de personis.

reading of the text does not lead to the same assessment as it reveals that the *homo* (man) – thus the bodily support of the person – integrates the category of corporeal things in the same way as a ground clothes or gold (Gaius, Inst. 2.13), precisely in the second book devoted to 'things'.

Before going into the heart of the matter, I would like to present a preliminary clarification. In order to understand the evolution of the notion of 'thing', we must overcome an automatism, which is based on our contemporary vision that assumes a clear differentiation between subject and object. This configuration, by extension, leads to certain forms of unavailability, like that of the human body (Hermitte 1988), which is a limit to the disposition of oneself – based on the dignity of the human person. Such limit exists in that framework because the human being could not be a 'thing', as it is identified to the person, which may be the subject of a contract or agreement.

It is important to remain cautious regarding these modern legal constructions as they may tend to bias our reading of ancient law systems by insidiously formatting our minds. When one goes through Paul-Frédéric Girard's famous textbook (1929: 260–76), the principle is posited frankly, if not demonstrated: 'Things are everything that exists in nature. But the law does not study them in themselves, not more than persons. It studies people as subjects of rights. It studies things as objects of rights. In this way, things are divided following many views' (1929: 260). The examination frame of Roman law seems to be clear, and revolves around the salience of the subject–object couple.

In reading the analysis of the famous German Romanist Max Kaser (1971: 36) concerning the *res*, a study that remains very rigorous from the scientific point of view, and seems at first sight much less incisive than that of Girard, it has to be seen, as Yann Thomas pointed out (1981: 414), that it bears some prejudice. Kaser holds that the word 'thing' can have three different meanings in Roman law. First, the term refers to corporeal elements that have their own existence. Second, it means in a broader sense everything that can be the subject of a private law or a civil trial (object of law), including the son of a family and a woman under marital power. Third, it is a category of property. What may be surprising here is that the *res* is not considered in the juxtaposition of its meanings, but rather in the supposed chain of moments in which it is situated in relation to the subject: the thing in itself external to the subject; the thing for the subject or thing-object and finally the thing incorporated in the subject (Thomas 1981: 414). The interpretation here is from the angle of a subjectivist premise, in the perspective of the concept of will. This leads to a biased interpretation of the notion of *res* in Roman law, a caricature of roman categories, since we start from the presupposition of the separation between subject and object. It should be observed furthermore that Kaser's analysis is caught between this modern prejudice of reasoning in relation to the all-powerful human subject, and the constraints posed by an objective reading of Roman sources, which imply the possibility of a coexistence of the notion of person and thing concerning the slave, even though the author's methodological approach opens the way to the sealing of these categories.

8.2 Roman Law, Nature and Subject

Before going back to the Roman notion of *res*, it is necessary to introduce the main principles of the legal system shaped by the jurists of the Roman Empire, in terms of theoretical conception, but also and especially from the point of view of the relationship maintained with their environment. Such a context is commonly approached in modern law as what is called 'inanimate things'.

The reading of Justinian's *Digest* shows that Roman law was organised in concentric circles consisting of natural law or *ius naturale* (first circle), the law of people or *ius gentium* (second circle) and civil law or *ius civile* (third circle). Natural law was characterised above all by universality (that is to say, its socio-territorial non-demarcation) and freedom. These characteristics have led certain authors (Carbonnier 1992: 417) to indicate that *ius naturale* was another name to designate justice. This explains why Roman jurisconsults considered slavery to be contrary to natural law. Natural law is defined, according to Ulpian in D.1.1.1.3, as a universal law governing all animate beings: not only human beings but also all creatures and animals of the sea, earth and sky.[3] All beings obey this common norm, which is organised mainly around the union of the male and the female, to perpetuate the different species.[4] One might think that this notion of *ius naturale*, known by the Romans, and conceived as transcendent to humankind – encompassing humankind and the total context in which human life is inscribed – could have served as a basis for other sub-areas of law, since it applies to the animals of the earth, the sea and the birds, according to Ulpien. First, it could have served as a basis for the *ius gentium* or law of the people, which constitutes a universal law applicable to all people according to Ulpian in D.1.1.1.4.[5] Conforming to Hermogenian in D.1.1.5, this legal section introduces wars and distinguishes peoples, while regulating all the acts of existence. The famous jurist explains in D.1.1.1.4 that he took into account the *naturalis ratio*, but that it is a properly human law.[6] Therefore, it remains difficult to identify the *ius gentium*, as the natural part of natural norm reserved for man, or, on the contrary, as a way to

---

[3] Ius naturale est, quod natura omnia animalia docuit: nam ius istud non humani generis proprium, sed omnium animalium, quae in terra, quae in mari nascuntur, avium quoque commune est.

[4] Hinc descended maris atque femina coniunctio, quam our matrimonium appellamus, hinc liberorum procreatio, hinc educatio: videmus etenim cetera quoque animalia, feras etiam istius iuris peritia censeri.

[5] Ius gentium est que gentes humanae utuntur.

[6] Hoc solis hominibus inter se commune sit.

dispense with the natural law in a socialising movement controlling the apprehension of the natural. An initial part of the answer to this could be found in the definition of the third normative circle, in this case the *ius civile*. This subsystem is analysed as a particularised, specified and perfected version of the *ius gentium*, instituted within the restricted framework of the city and the *civitas*. It consists of rules that left a certain degree of latitude to the legal operators, since the civil law should not deviate totally from the principles of natural law (*ius naturale*) and the law of the people (*ius gentium*) but did not have either to conform completely to them according to Ulpian in D.1.1.6.[7]

At this stage, we can see that Roman law theory attempts to prevail over nature (and the law deriving from its organisation) through the human norm; although the natural norm can still play a role, according to the Roman jurists themselves. It is clear that there are many references to nature in their argumentation (Thomas 1998: 201–04), but not necessarily in the sense that we may think. The understanding that would fit in the wake of Aristotelian realism is that nature provides universally valid rules which are binding on the legislator – because it does not appear in the foundation of the theoretical constructions of the institutionalisation of law. On this point, the views of the Roman jurists were different from those promoted by the Stoic or Ciceronian tradition, in which nature received an eminent place. Thus Cicero repeatedly affirmed in *De legibus* (1.6, 11; 13) that law comes from nature,[8] but such point of view was not defended by classical Roman jurists. In their reasoning, *natura* was never an indispensable concept in order to justify or verify a proposition, nor an ultimate safeguard from the point of view of the legal rationale (*ratio iuris*) but was considered aberrant in the absolute. Their approach was different. The aim was to address the question of rationalising rules for the social process. Thus, in this perspective, law could not find its source in *natura* and the latter does not form the foundation of any standards because the roman jurisconsults chose to emancipate themselves from it.

The source of the meta values governing the law (*ius*) would rather be found in the *mores* (tradition, customs), therefore, as an understanding of social relations. In short, this is a non-natural moral criterion related to a pre-legal human organisation. The *mos* is an institution of the *patres*, a memory of the past, which concerned initially the religious ceremonies (Festus 146, 3), the *memoria* governing an organisation which is the object of a social consensus (Varro in Servius, Ad. Aen. 7.601) on ideas of good people (Quintilien, Inst. Orato., ch. 6 *in fine* about the *consuetudo*). Cicero indicates that *res romana* continues thanks to

---

[7] Ius civile est, quod neque in totum a naturali vel gentium recedit nec per omnia ei served: itaque cum aliquid addimus vel detrahimus iuri communi, ius proprium, id is civil efficimus.

[8] In fine: quo facilius ius in natura esse positum intellegi possit.

these *mores* (Cicero, *De re publica*, V, 1 *Moribus antiquis res romana virisque* . . .). So we are dealing with a human parameter that is contextual and subjective, because the *mos* is an aspect of culture. Let us recall that none of the definitions given by the ancient lexicographers establish a link between the two concepts. On the contrary, *mos* is an anthropocentric – and even civic – process from which nature is absent and in which the subject of law is placed in the centre.

However, nature or *natura* is not totally marginalised by Roman jurists, since they could use it to eventually extend the scope of legal rules. Adoption is one of the representative examples of this use, and it illustrates that human will could prevail over the natural order, even though there are some limits.[9] Adoption was regulated by the important field of family law, a branch of the law which was dear to the Romans.

There are many examples showing how nature is apprehended as a tool at the service of the law, without constituting its basis or feeding it. Rather, the understanding of the law seems to be human-centred, a configuration which appears in modern legal systems. In fact, natural law was abandoned early by Roman jurists, because the category itself was quickly exhausted regarding their purpose. Indeed, the essence of Roman law is civil law, which deals with the *civitas*, i.e. the citizens and especially their place of habitual residence, and the city as civilisational territory. It was where legal rules regulated property, trade, transmission of property, family organisation or, to a certain extent, order and security. The perimeter of the *civitas* delineated a human and Roman community.

Nevertheless, jurists were aware of the existence of a specific category of *res* produced by nature – independently of any human action – within specific domains of qualification. Some domains were common to all under natural law, according to Marcian (D.1.8.2) or even public use under the law of people (Marcien D.1.8.2 and 4,[10] Florentin D.1.8.3). This was notably the regime of the air, the water of the sea and its shores (Marcian in D.1.8.2.1): although these 'things' were not of particular interest for legal operators, it must be agreed that the notion of *res communes omnium* (the things common to all) plays a fundamental role in the human–*res* relationship (Mannino 2014: 40). Such qualification was used as a model for the things with co-ownership by the citizens: roads, theatres, baths and others. On the other hand, nature also produced goods for private ownership according to Paul in D.41.2.1.1. This is the case with wild animals which, as soon as they were captured, belonged to the one who controlled them in the context of a so-called natural possession, as Neratius recalls in D.41.1.14 pr.

---

[9] See IJ.1.11.4 and the comments by Javolenus (D.1.7.16) and Justinian IJ.1.11.14.
[10] Quaedam naturali iure communia sunt omnium, quaedam universitatis.

because these elements were initially produced by *natura* and could not become the commonly held property of the Romans.

We must stop here to examine the law in order to draw up a first assessment. The civil law process used by legal actors recognises the existence of things produced by nature, and almost always ensures domination by humankind over nature as part of an anthropocentric process. This is a legal construction in which the civil law is posited as a tool of human institutionalisation of all identifiable tangible and intangible elements, whether those created directly by human beings or those defined as natural. According to this approach, the individual asserts himself as the owner of a collective property, or at least of a collective use of the external nature, as if the latter were always objects of the law, since it is always called 'res'. Thus, one can detect the origins of the ideological framework of modern law systems in Roman legal taxonomies. This idea of the omnipotence of human beings would not be so absolute, if one went beyond raw qualifications to consider other parameters.

There is much to be said about the analysis of the relationships maintained by the Romans with the natural elements which surrounded them, and on which they relied to ensure their existence and sustenance. They were first and foremost relationships of a religious character. The Roman religion is certainly a human and cultural creation, hence of civic essence, and does not fit into the scheme of a so-called naturalistic religion. However, it should be noted that some deities represent the power of external nature. But the aim of Roman religion, on which depends the prosperity of the city, was precisely to promote good relationships between men and gods through rituals. We would say here that nature (deified) is considered as a partner to contribute to the prosperity of the city. Many religious acts associate entities external to human beings, whether these are divinised or whether they take more trivially part in the religious act within the framework of the sacrifice, for example various animals. Many deities represented sometimes frightening natural elements: Jupiter *Fulgurator* (the god of lightning) or Tonans (the god of thunder) to quote the best known; Neptune, the god of the seas and oceans; Tellus, the goddess personifying the earth in formation; Mars *Sylvanus*, the tutelary god of the forests to whom are given offerings for the health of the oxen. Everywhere in the countryside, altars were raised to the country deities. The law applied to religion and its modalities, for instance in the qualification of places as sacred or religious by jurists, in order to indicate their unavailability to the human trade. Religion constituted a space of dialogue between the territories controlled by man, and those that were not, such as the residence of the gods. Sacred groves, caves and deep ponds inspired fear, and mortals simply identified and delineated these places. We thus see here that the form of almost absolute control of nature operated by law is not evidenced in relation to the exercise of religious practices, in which there is more a form of partnership or even existence of fear. This is reflected in religious procedures tinged with prudence narrated by Cato, when it comes to entering a *lucus* (sacred wood) and opening a clearing or cultivating the land.

To insist on the role of nature, it suffices to recall that the ancient Roman economy was originally based on an agrarian and pastoral model. The Romans were initially farmers and shepherds. Their sector of activity was very dependent on nature and impacted by its hazards. They imagined nature as a partner in their existence. This aspect predominates, for example, in agronomic books such as those of Cato the Elder or Columella. This approach was also reinforced by the knowledge in biology or physics at that time. It caused a mixture of feelings of humility, complicity and fear in relation to the various components of *natura*. Thus, it is particularly striking to discover this very specific relationship with nature in the writings of Latin agronomists. There is, of course, a whole method for operating an agricultural domain, but also this complicity with nature, which is often the subject of deification and whose benevolence must be conciliated. Ceres, the goddess of growth (regarding the harvest), Liber the god of germination, and Pales the god of herds, were among the most important deities of the peasant world. To this should be added Robigus who preserved the wheat from rust, Flora who ensured the flowering of the plantations, Consus who protected the grain. Each part of a cultivated plant was placed under the protection of a tutelary deity.

Among various examples to understand and illustrate the relationship of the Romans with nature we will take that of the river. The power of the river is indisputable, especially in the case of large floods that reveal the force of water and nature that humans are doomed to endure. Despite technical progress and precautions to curb this type of phenomenon, it must be noted that man was mostly helpless in front of such natural hazards. These showed the power of nature. The moving water of the rivers struck the imagination and sensibility of Latin writers like Lucretius (De nat.rr.1.277–97), a very famous poet born around 98 BC. He gracefully tells us how much aquatic power can carry away whole woods, make the strongest bridges wobble, and destroy dikes and rocks. The author evokes with great panache the corporeity of certain natural elements that we feel much more than we see; they are considered as bodies – *corpora*.

More prosaically, the Roman lawyer focused on facts and approached elements such as rivers as incorporeal things, as if such categorisation expressed the elements on which man could not have control. Poetry does not bother with technical constraint because corporeality accommodates itself to the impalpable, and the artist can consider that there are things that live and flourish independently of him. The poet can see beyond cultural and legal categories, connect to more universal and deeper understandings, and can open paths for a renewed vision of our relationship with nature. The lawyer is also in his own way a poet who recomposes the world with the tools of law, but the legal constructions do not always give him the necessary latitude.

In addition to poets, nature's fluvial power did not leave the Roman jurists unmoved. Fluvial power was the subject of detailed descriptions in Gromatici's writings, the famous *agrimensores* specialists in surveying; and everyone knows the importance that the Romans attributed to territorial demarcation and rites of foundation. Among them, a certain Siculus Flaccus, active under Diocletian and whose work owed much to his predecessor Hygin, presented a singular approach. For the surveyor, the river was an exception (*modus fluminis is exceptus*), beyond the control of man, that is, left to the river itself considered as a living entity (De Cond. Agr. 235–38). More than a body, the stream was considered as an autonomous entity. The writer almost conferred personality on the river. The latter has a natural strength, a physical faculty to overtake the shores with violence, but one that will eventually return to its course after causing damage (see approaches in Chapter 3; and contemporary cases of legal personality conferred on rivers, in Chapters 10 and 11 in this volume).

This turn of thought is not trivial and sheds light on Roman conceptions of the perception of entities considered to be external to human beings. Admittedly, Romans intended to dominate what surrounded them and exercise their influence on their environment. However, within this ideological framework, humans were not the only ones being part of a conceptual category presenting an autonomy. Things on which man could not have control, such as rivers or natural elements, were also considered autonomous. Given these facts, one can realise why Roman law did not distinguish between subjects and objects in the modern sense. It must be remembered that this legal system constitutes in the studied space of the Roman city, a cultural vector, in the sense that the great values presiding over social organisation were found within the law (*ius*). The dividing subject–object line is not that clear in the ancient spirit of Roman law. Despite some measure of legal domestication of nature and its components, legal procedures echoed the idea that voluntary autonomy was not the exclusive privilege of man.

To illustrate this view, I will now take the case of the animal, starting with the sacrificial rite. This case is very representative because it is about the essential act of the Roman religion, itself considered as a very structured practice of the public and private social domains. Roman society was organised around a civic theocracy in which citizenship was accompanied by necessary religious acts. The modalities of Roman sacrifice were complex but relatively well known. Such ceremonials were executed meticulously (Scheid 2005: 72–84), and the custom was to sacrifice specific victims in terms of animal, breed, age, sex or colour according to the god honoured by the ritual. The offerings included, depending on the circumstances, horses, cows, pigs, dogs, roosters. In all sacrificial settings, public or private, it was fundamental to observe the attitude of the animal victim at the moment of the fatal blow. The sacrificed beast was supposed to show his consent by lowering his head (Scheid 2005: 74–76). Any manifestation of fear or panic by a victim, as well as any other disorder was prohibited, because it represented a very bad omen for the sacrificer, and therefore for the beneficiary community of the act. Regardless of the detail of these sacrificial modalities, what is striking is what – in modern terms – we would call the 'will of the animal', an ontological perspective which resulted from a form of personification. On a general level, it must be admitted, despite naturalist appearances, that Roman religion was anthropocentric in its practice, as it was carried out within the institutional frameworks of the city or family, or even other human group, but the detail of the ritual shows that there was a close collaboration with the animal because both the animal and man contributed to the perfection of the rite.

Far from being anecdotal, this idea of animal autonomy has penetrated the legal field. In Roman law, by derivation, a kind of will was granted to the animal through the concept of 'noxious abandonment', which attested to the link maintained between the fault and the direct author of the fault. The owner of the animal that had committed an offence could abandon the beast to the victim to avoid prosecution.

This system corresponds to the principle of *noxales actiones* as defined by Gaius (lib. 2 ed. pro D.9.4.1, see also Girard 1929: 720–26; De Visscher 1947) which concerned private crimes. These legal remedies were an extension of an evolution that had seen private vengeance turned into a legal act when the victim had accepted the reparation of the damage (De Visscher 1947: 19). Such remedies could be offered to make amends for a harmful act caused by a thing or an individual under the authority of the *paterfamilias* (head of the household). These disputes were frequent as evidenced in Gaius D. 9. 4 de *noxalibus actionibus*.

In these cases, the *pater* had to answer for the actions of the entities qualified by the law as pertaining to his *potestas*, because he was responsible for those who were under his power. If the *dominus* was condemned to pay a sum in compensation for damage resulting from the action of a third entity under its power, he kept the possibility, until the possible implementation of the *actio judicati*, to be released from his responsibility by delivering the culprit to the victim, operating in this way a noxal abandonment. This hypothesis concerned, in particular, the *servus* (slave) or the family son and, by extension, any individual *alieni iuris* who could not act directly in law, unlike the *sui iuris*.

In other words, Roman law recognised the autonomy of the subject without linking it de facto to legal personality. Another legal remedy, quite similar and also noxal, existed in cases where quadrupeds caused damage. This is the *actio de pauperie*, an ancient recourse from the law of the Twelve Tables according to Ulpien (D.9.1.1) and presumably applicable to all quadrupeds and not only to those part of *res mancipi* (Pessi 1997: 285–300). This last category grouped things of a certain value in the Roman imaginary, which were subject to the process of cession of the *mancipatio*. By the *actio de pauperie*, the *dominus* of the animal kept the possibility of giving the quadruped to the plaintiff to free himself from his obligation to pay the estimated value of the damage. This legal action applied whenever the animal had caused damage due to bestial behaviour that escaped the control of the master, and that the latter had not caused directly. For example, if a horse a little too fiery hurt another horse or if a dangerous horse harmed someone. On the other hand, if a person loaded a beast of burden too heavily and the animal reversed the loading onto another person, thus causing harm, it was logically the beast's driver who was pursued by means of *actio legis aquiliae*.

What must be remembered from the *responsa* collected in D.9.1 *Si quadrupes pauperiem fecisse dicatur* is that the *actio de pauperie* came *into* play whenever the unpredictable instinct of the animal guided his act, in a chain reaction that escaped human control. However, a horse excited by pain does not fit in this context, because it is perfectly well known that a suffering beast can behave or react violently, and that it is in line with a cause-and-effect relationship known by man. The legal remedy applied fundamentally to the unpredictability of nature, beyond human control despite his efforts. Certainly Ulpian reminds us that an animal is only capable of *damnum sine injuria*, i.e. it cannot have the intention to harm. This is because the animal is considered to be devoid of reason in the human sense (D.9.1.1.3). Nevertheless, the 'noxal abandonment' of the animal, which functioned in the same way as that of the slave or the son of a family, attributed a form of guilt to the beast, and consequently a beginning of personification, even though the animals were classified in the category of things.

However, we remain within the framework of an anthropocentric law because the jurists indicated that the damage caused by a domestic animal was *contra naturam*. This means that it was against the peaceful nature of the animal destined to serve man as if the latter was taking possession of the thing, but also the very nature of the domesticated animal, which was literally included in the *domus* (house), therefore in the civilised, human and private perimeter of the family circle. Thus, nature had a double meaning for jurists. On the other hand, the damage caused by wild animals was a case of *force majeure*, because they were characterised by their natural ferocity. A bear which escapes from someone (his master) and then harms another person could not be attached to any master because his savagery meant it was beyond human control and therefore any *dominium*: the principle of the *actio de pauperie* was not applicable (D.9.1.10).

These last remarks establish an important gap between the approach of the jurists and the overall mental approach of the Romans. If Roman society undoubtedly allowed the emergence of a legal conscience of nature, it nevertheless was not translated as such in the law. And that remains the whole problem of the contemporary world. Most of us have realised that man depends on nature, and nature should be treated accordingly. On the other hand, the shape of the legal system is unable to make this partnership effective and include nature, considered in all its manifestations, as a real actor, even a subject of law.

8.3 Things and Persons in Roman Law: A Porous Taxonomy

Considering these different examples of the understanding and use of *res* in Roman law, it appears that Roman law, taken in its systemic dimension, did not contain a clear division between subject and object, between person and thing, between the exclusive autonomy of an all-powerful subject and the total passivity of what is considered as an object.

Therefore, attempting to analyse the notion of Roman *res* from the point of view of the subject of rights (Thomas 1981: 414–15) would be a false track, as it seems to be confirmed by a lexical approach. Starting with our oldest sources, namely the law of the Twelve Tables, dating from around 450 BC, the word *res*, the 'thing' was associated with *lis* (litigation) or *causa* (court proceedings). This is attested by a note from the grammarian Festus (Lindsay 1965: 103):[11] *Litis cecidisse* literally means 'to be stripped of its cause'. The term applied to the person who had lost his case (*lis*) in that he did not succeed (*causa*) in the case (*res*) before the court. The original central meaning of *res* was 'the case' which is examined through a contradictory debate. The *res* was then the subject of a debate, a thing legally analysed as a component of the legal system and not in its relation to the subject, nor was it a legal designation of a perceptible material entity in nature. From a conceptual point of view, this understanding is very different from the concept of a corporeal thing external to the subject, prior to the law and qualifying what it designates.

It is the initial meaning of *res* which was applied to different situations. First of all, it was applied to the pecuniary interest of the plaintiff. When a judge was invited to determine the pecuniary aspects of the dispute, the loser was condemned to a *res aestimata*, a recurring expression emanating from the Roman jurists representing a *pecunia* (sum of money). Thus, in the law of the Twelve Tables 5.3 (Girard-Senn 1977: 57 and also in Ulpian, *Regulae*, 11.14), the term *res* was juxtaposed to *pecunia* in order to designate the property which the father of a family could dispose of at will. As always in Roman law, the concept is understood

---

[11] Litis cecidisse dicitur, who eius rei, of qua agebat, causam amisit.

as designating an abstract idea – purely juridical and without any materiality – in the sense as it remains in the case law; it is not a physical qualification. The Romans knew the modern notion of 'things' through the subcategory of *res corporales*, but the addition of the epithet reveals an obvious artifice of the jurists; it was permissible to enunciate *corpus* (body) and not *res* (thing) just as it was this bodily characteristic that exhausted the meaning of such category.

Moreover, it must be pointed out that Roman law never intended to strictly separate things and persons (Paturet 2010: 6–8). The *familia* (family) was a major legal actor of Roman society and the second fundamental circle of power after the state (not in the modern sense but taken as the organ of an organisation). The *familia* was at the same time (1) a subject, by the things and the rights that were held by the representative of the *potestas* (capacity to act): the all-powerful *paterfamilias* (head of the household), and (2) an object in that it was the tangible entity to which such rights were precisely applied.

It must be admitted that the *familia* consisted of a composite which was diffuse at first sight: persons and property (house), relatives under power, slaves, land, equipment, etc. This conception was not the result of a legal approach devoid of community ideology but rather resulted from a strong societal characteristic, as it appears in Cato's *De agricultura*. A chapter of this book (Goujard 1975, Caton, Agr. 141) describes the modalities of a *suovetaurilian* sacrifice, in favour of the god Mars, in the framework of a rite of protection (*lustratio*) for the purpose of agricultural exploitation. The way in which the text is arranged shows that extended protection was expected from the divinity. The *domus* (house) included the family relations by blood, but also all those under the domination of the *dominus*, as well as all real estate and movable property in a remarkable unit circumscribed by the limits of the domain and including what contributed to its prosperity. Things and persons were amalgamated through the power relationship of the *paterfamilias*.

There is another fundamental example which attests the finesse of Roman legal constructions. In contemporary analyses, the category of slave in Roman law is understood as an object resulting from an objectification process. The reasoning is actually much more subtle. We must understand that the *servus* (slave) was considered differently by the Roman jurists according to the circle of law in which it fitted (Paturet 2010: 9–18). According to natural law (*ius naturale*), all men were equal (Mommsen and Krüger 1973, *Digest* 1. 1. 1. 3 and D. 50. 7. 32) and therefore slavery could not not exist. The law of the people (*ius gentium*) recognised war and conquest, and by consequence, the fruits of the latter as well as the domination by one man over another (Mommsen and Krüger 1973, *Digest*, 1. 5. 4. 1). Civil law (*ius civile*) eventually developed the partial and necessary adjustment of the *servus* to place it in the sphere of appropriation, even though his humanity was never questioned. In that regard, there was no contradiction in Roman law, even though such an approach would seem inconceivable in contemporary law. It was precisely the human qualities of the slave which assured his 'value' and caused an extraordinary price variation ranging from a few sesterces for any individual, through very high prices for a medical doctor, to millions for a magnificent eunuch. It is important to notice that the *servus* was ranked – when it came to qualifying it as a good – in the category of *res mancipi*. The latter persons (as opposed to *res nec mancipi*) were subject to the process of cession, called *mancipatio* due to the material value attached to them in an agrarian or pastoral economy. This process shows a specific consideration of the *servus* in the marketplace (Paturet 2010: 4–5).

The closest Latin word to our modern concept of the thing-object could be, much more than '*res*', the word *bona* meaning 'goods'. In French law, this designates any material thing available for appropriation, but also the wealth or assets of these physical entities in relation to their holder. '*Bona*' synthesises perfectly the construction of law around the relation of a subject to an object. It was rarely used by the jurisconsults of Rome, because such an externality of *ius* regarding the object was foreign to them. Therefore, classical jurists used the concept of *dominium* more readily, which implied a link with the status of the person by qualifying the individual (master, owner) rather than *proprietas* (property), which was related to the thing in order to express a property relation. To affirm 'I own' as a social position is not comparable to the sequence 'this thing is my property'.

This turn of thought is the result of an acute conception of property – even if the Roman jurists did not really have a systematic definition – constructed from the point of view of the owner status and not transferred to the appropriated element. Quiritary, peregrine or provincial property (among others, Halpérin 2010: 16) were all modes of appropriation based on the quality of the subject (the owner), and not on the nature of the object in question. This was before the changes brought by the Byzantine Emperor Justinian (Krüger 1970, Code of Justinian 7.25.1).

However, the logic of imputation to the subject could slip in some cases on the side of things. In this sense, the Romans also foresaw ways of assigning and qualifying things attributed to divinities (Gaius 2: 1–9, Gaius 1965: 38) which, we could say, are 'passive' subjects, although the Romans never ventured to qualify them legally. These *res divini iuris* were always considered from the angle of unavailability to men and not from the *dominium* side of divinity. This is explained by the idea that the Romans strictly separated the world of men from that of the gods and did not apply concepts used to characterise human power to them by analogy. The only solution offered was to designate the thing devoted to the deities according to their legal qualification made by men: *res sacrae* for that dedicated to the great gods, and *res religiosae* for those abandoned to the *Mânes* (these things were actually the tombs that contained dead bodies).

In view of all these considerations and while there is still much debate on these issues, it appears that Roman law could not serve as a clear matrix for the modern conception of things as tangible goods, since the approach of *res* was much more complex and fundamentally different.

8.4 The Thing in French Law: An Avatar of the Invention of Subjective Right

In French law, the modern concept of 'thing' is based on another approach, and on the theorisation of a subjective right that came later than Roman law in legal history. This eventually evolved towards a structuring asymmetry – active (person–subject) and passive (thing–object) – of legal isomorphism.

This subjectivisation of law is analysed as a 'prerogative granted by law and allowing a person to use one thing or to require another person to perform a service' (Cabrillac 2002: 150). It is the idea of a right that is not justified by the natural order of things, and therefore may not be invoked by the judge beyond any request of the parties – as a non-objective right – validated by the competent will, which can give it up because it is a prerogative of all individuals (Cornu 1987: 374).

It is difficult to identify the precise moment of this doctrinal elaboration, no doubt it resulted from an evolution in legal thinking. Roman law did contain the very first germs of property, as evidenced by a passage from the *Institutes* of Justinian (Krüger 1972, IJ.2.4.4). The text in question analyses it as *plenam habere in rem potestas* (i.e. to have a full power on the 'thing'). We detect here the idea that the *potestas*, which nowadays we would see as the necessary attribute of a subject, finds its roots in the *res*, which could constitute a very distant genesis of the right attributable to the subject. On this basis, all the doctrinal elaboration remained to be accomplished. This one proceeded in a gradual way.

The role of Guillaume d'Occam (around 1285 to 1349) concerning the theorisation of the notion of subjective right was highlighted by Michel Villey (1964: 97–127), whose analysis was the subject of a controversy – but we cannot enter into the detail of this debate here (see Meyer 2006: 292; Piron 2008 to name a few). On the margins of these quarrels, it must be admitted that Occam's thought led to the intellectual shaping of a legal revolution. The author operated a distinction between the *ius fori* or law in courts, and the *ius poli* derived from the divine will which was superior to the former. The divine law was analysed as the expression of the divine will which conceded prerogatives to the individual. Occam also established a connection between *ius* (law) and *potestas* (capacity to act): all rights are powers attributed by a positive law. Here we have a rupture with the Roman conceptions of law – *jus est ars boni and aequi*; law is the art of the good and fair (Mommsen and Krüger 1973, D.1.1.1). According to Occam, the law determines precisely the portion of power that the individual holds, and of which he cannot be deprived without cause or fault on his part, and that can be argued in court. This power found particular emphasis on things because of the natural concession of divine origin, for the benefit of the higher rational beings that are men. Because of their quality, men are perfectly free to enjoy this use or not.

In essence, it should be said that this idea was further transformed with the (very) positivist philosophy of Thomas Hobbes (1588–1679), who wrote that the right as independent power relating to the 'thing' was part of the logic of natural law. This right was then associated to the notion of freedom, which is a specific element of human nature that distinguishes man from all animate or inanimate nature. It consisted of the possibility for the individual to use his power as he saw fit. The right of nature was therefore an automatic validation from the point of view of the person (Hobbes 1921, Leviathan, ch. XIV, Anthony: 211–36). The right that has become power, or even unlimited freedom, implied an absolute domination over 'things'. These all-powerful subjective rights were then constructed as opposed to the objects on which they bore. From this came a paradigmatic view of the *res* in antithesis with the subject of power. This principle subsequently appears in Kant's *Groundwork of the Metaphysics of Morals* (1724–1804). Kant writes that only man can be considered as an end in himself while 'things' are means (Kant 1979, § 55 and p. 98, A. Philonenko).

This dichotomy is found in Hegel's (1770–1821) *Elements of the Philosophy of Law*. He defined the thing as that which is 'immediately different from the free spirit … the outside in general. One thing, something not free, without personality and without right' (Hegel 1940: 88). 'Everything … receives as a substantial goal (which it does not have in itself), as destination and as soul, my will. It is the right of appropriation of man over everything' (Hegel 1940: 92). The relationship of power has turned into a meta-model that cannot be crossed between people (the self) and things (the exteriority of nature) into two asymmetrical categories that can no longer be interwoven. At the end of this process enshrined in modern codifications, there is almost nothing left of the original Roman *res*, except the notion of corpus.

8.5 Some Contemporary Issues

Considering the overview of such a legal evolution, by which the individual human being (considered as a person) became the only raw material for building the legal order, it will not escape the reader's attention that the modern conception of things (linked essentially to their corporeality) conceals some deficiencies.

It is especially the rigidity of the dichotomy between persons and things which poses the most difficulties, as evidenced by the argued case of the legal management of the corpse. After death and the consequent extinction of the will of the person, the corpse can, by definition, no longer be considered as a person. It is therefore inevitably placed on the side of *res*, as an outcome that did not seem acceptable from the ethical point of view. Some corrections based on human dignity have been found to be essential to bend the rigidity of the law, but not without generating serious inconsistencies. Consequently, attacks on the body are in Book II of the French Penal Code, which deals with crimes and offences against the person (*crimes et délits contre les personnes*). But the dead are no longer human beings free to exercise any power.

In the same order, one of the greatest difficulties today is the status of animals. Logically, animals should have legal personality since associations are legally entitled to represent them; considering this, it seems inconceivable to exercise a protective mandate for the benefit of 'things'. In this evolutionary perspective, some authors (Regad et al. 2018) have proposed the creation of a non-human physical person status and the creation of a specific legal regime for pets. This orientation comes in the wake of the recent legal reform that led to the French law of 16 February 2015, which defines animals as living beings endowed with sentience. However, they remain subject to the legal regime of property and not of persons.

This consideration leads to more general questions concerning the protection of our environment, even though damage to the environment has inevitable consequences for humankind. There is a major concrete problem with the incapacity to apprehend in law the diversity of beings and elements in nature, as well as nature itself. In such a context, how can we determine on what basis to repair what is called in French legal texts 'pure ecological damage', that is to say the harm which does not affect any property or any legal person? Indeed, several conditions must be met to obtain compensation for such damages, and among them there is the need to prove personal injury.

If biological diversity and its elements, such as animals and plants, do not enjoy the status of legal persons, it is difficult to use the law to seek reparations for the harm or damage caused to them. This was precisely one of the difficulties encountered in the *Erika* case, which ended in September 2012 (Cass. Crim. 25 Sept. 2012, No. 19–82.938). The oil tanker 'Erika' sank off the coast of French Brittany, causing an oil spill that polluted about 400 km of coastline. The Court of Cassation established the civil and criminal liability of the oil company by recognising the ecological harm caused by the spill, which the court defined as an 'attack on non-market environmental assets.' This jurisdictional position has paved the way for an institutionalisation of this recognition: henceforth, article 1386–19–1 of the French Civil Code specifies an action to reparation for ecological damage, but it is only applicable to entities holding legal personality: such as the state, local authorities, associations, the French Agency for Biodiversity.

This is not a coherent development, because in a mature legal system, the first concept of a subject of law is beyond physical and moral persons, who would not necessarily be the only entities apprehended by law, and the door would remain open to other qualifications. Jurisprudence is supposed to develop the conceptual tools necessary to address reality. If the concepts or methods are failing, then we need to adapt, change them or create new ones. Therefore, certain authors (Hermitte 2011: 4) argue for the recognition of a legal personality of nature. This recognition occurred in Ecuador in 2008; and in New Zealand in 2012, in relation to the Whanganui River, due to the Maori community connection with this iconic watercourse (see Chapters 10 and 11 in this volume). But although this approach is an interesting palliative, it does not lead to a modernisation of the subject–object legal categorisation because nature would be protected as a subject of law, without calling into question the ontological dichotomy of legal taxonomy.

Conclusion

Contemporary French law, and civil law systems in general, have almost forgotten all the Roman logic that could very well serve them. It is important to remember that nothing in Roman legal reasoning induced a dichotomy between subject and object. This is confirmed by the conceptualisation that leads us to consider the relation of property in terms of *dominium* rather than *proprietas*, and in the light of the unique consideration of the status of the holder (subject) and not of the object itself. This would make it possible to understand that the status of a thing and a person can coexist for the same entity without any major obstacle other than a philosophical paradigm that can easily be circumvented.

Such an overhaul of the contemporary law according to the original Roman configuration would call into question the very principle of modern law which has become part of our analysis and our mental universe. There are reasons to be hopeful, not least given that legal scholars have developed promising new ideas that could provide the basis for effective solutions. For instance, we can refocus on the relationship with the environment, rethink property as a right that excludes all exclusivity on things and base the qualification on the power of the subject who holds it in a kind of usufruct, in the prolongation of the daring mesological theses of certain authors (Vanuxem 2010).

French civil law has largely forgotten its Roman ancestry by focusing almost exclusively on the category of *res corporales*. However, aspects of Roman terminology endure as an ultimate testimony in French civil law of this distant genealogy. French expressions enshrined in the law, but whose real scope and theoretical stakes were lost in the mists of time, continue to exist. For instance, 'the authority of *res judicata*' (enshrined in article 1350 of the French Civil Code) signifies that all the effects attached to the court decision have legal validity. The expression 'force of res judicata' means it is no longer subject to appeal or that the time limits to act have expired. The expression 'exception of *res judicata*' characterises the refusal (*fin de non-recevoir*, Cornu 1987: 174). In these interpolated clauses, *res* ('thing') means the judgment or the case, according to the direct line of a second meaning highlighted in the legal lexicons, which are linked to the scope of 'question, problem, affair' (Cornu 1987: 174), far from the simple material designation of a good, and this in the line of what the Roman origins of the word expressed. We can hope that future lawmakers will take advantage of these expressions to remember or rediscover the quintessence of *res* and reinvent the concept of 'thing'.

This legal reworking would be one of the major steps to rethink the relationship of humans with their environment to produce a new social representation of partnership with nature. The role of law, as a process of rationalisation of human relations, is also to address integration and partnership with nature which is a shelter and habitat for humanity. To that end, it would be necessary to work on different points:

The question of the porosity of legal categories between things and persons is essential. Nature could be personified without being a subject of will within the current legal meaning. It would be enough to think in good faith and with humility of the interest of nature. Obviously, nature cannot express its will in the modern sense. But humans can nevertheless protect nature and watch over it in the same way as they would protect their own interests.

Along this line, the very concept of property as it is posited and conceptualised in French law is inadequate regarding the appropriation of certain elements composing nature. There are three components of the property right: the *usus* (right of use), the *fructus* (right of enjoying) and the *abusus* (right of disposal). The latter makes it possible to dispose of a good by a material or legal act according to the commonly accepted idea (Cabrillac 2002: 3) and is therefore especially problematic. Legal limitations can be enacted to limit this right of disposal. For example, in French law, landlords have some duties related to the so-called social function of the right of property: the absence of occupation in rented housing may not be allowed in times of crisis or shortage; also requisition of vacant housing may be ordered according to article L 641–1 and following of the French construction and housing code.

However, above all it is the very principle of the existence of *abusus*, applied to certain natural entities that compose our environment, which is incoherent. Indeed, there is a powerful dichotomy between the notion of property considered as the owner's absolute right, while his proper existence depends by extension of this external element. How is it that we can claim to dominate – in the legal sense – that which constitutes the condition of our existence? These external elements will, most of the time, outlive their holder. Whatever legal categories tell us about the predominance of the subject over the object, there are many factual cases which show that the subjects (humans) disappear whereas the object (nature) outlives them. According to this line of reasoning, the owner is pragmatically a holder, a temporary custodian or guardian of a thing, a user and not its owner. The latter term does not really have any meaning concerning nature: this is the very essence of the commons, which are much more the property of anybody before being the common goods to all. Such legal category still remains to be reinvented. *(Parance and de Saint-Victor 2014: 31–32)*

References

Cabrillac, R. (ed.) (2002). *Dictionnaire du vocabulaire juridique*. Paris: Litec.

Carbonnier, J. (1992). *Flexible droit*. Paris: LGDJ.

Cayla, O. and J. L. Halpérin (eds.) (2008). *Dictionnaire des grandes œuvres juridiques*. Paris: Dalloz.

Cornu, G. (1987). *Vocabulaire juridique*. Paris: Presses universitaires de France [10th ed., 2014].

De Visscher, F. (1947). *Le régime romain de la noxalité*. Brussels: Visscher.

Ernout, A. and A. Meillet (1951). *Dictionnaire étymologique de la langue latine*. Paris: Klincksiek [4th ed., 2001, reissued, with additions and corrections by Jacques André].

Gaius (1965). *Institutes*. Julien Reinach (trans.). Paris: collection des universités de France.

Giangrieco Pessi, M. V. (1997). *L'interpretazione prudentium nell'evoluzione dell'actio de pauperie: res mancipi e res nec mancipi, Ricerche dedicate al professor Filippo Gallo*. Naples: Jovene, 1: 285–300.

Giffard, A. (1938). *Précis de droit romain* Paris: Dalloz [3rd ed., 1947].

Girard, P. F. (1929 [2003]). *Manuel élémentaire de droit romain*. Paris: Dalloz.

Girard, P. F. and F. Senn (1967, 1977). *Textes de droit romain*. 7th ed. by a team de Romanistes, 1967, I: *Commentaires*; Paris, 1977, II: *Les lois des Romains*, Naples: Jovene.

Goujard, R. (1975). *Caton l'Ancien. De l'agriculture*. Raoul Goujard (trans.). Paris: Les Belles Lettres.

Guillaumin, J. Y. (2010). *Les arpenteurs romains*. II Hygin – Siculus Flaccus. Paris: Les Belles Lettres.

Halpérin, J. L. (2010). *Propriété et droit subjectif: Deux destins liés?* Conférence faite au Japon aux Université Nanzan et KeioHAL, halshs.archives-ouvertes.fr/hal-00460386/document

Hegel, G. W. F. (1940). *Principes de la philosophie du droit*. André Kaan (trans.), preface by Jean Hippolyte. Paris: Gallimard [orig. pub. Berlin, 1821].

Hermitte, M.-A. (1988). Le corps hors du commerce hors du marché. *Archives de philosophie du droit* 33: 323–46.

Hermitte, M.-A. (2011). La nature, sujet de droit? *Annales: Histoire, Sciences Sociales* 66 (1): 173–212.

Hobbes T. (1921). *Leviathan ou la matière, la forme et la puissance d'un état ecclésiastique et civil.* Traduction française en partie double d'après les textes anglais et latins originaux par Raoul Anthony, I: *De l'homme.* Paris: Marcel Giard.

Kant, E. (1979). *Métaphysique des mœurs: Première partie. Doctrine du droit.* Preface by M. Villey. A. Philonenko (trans.). Paris: Librairie philosophique J. Vrin.

Kaser, M. (1971). *Das römische Privatrech.* I, Munich: Beck.

Krüger, P. (1970). *Code de Justinien, Corpus Iuris Civilis II.* 15th ed. Berlin: Weidmann.

Krüger, P. (1972). *Institutes, Corpus Iuris Civilis III.* 10th ed. Berlin: Weidmann

Laporte, R. (1986). *Une vie: Biographie.* Paris: POL.

Lindsay, W. M. (1965). *Sexti Pompei Festi, De verborum significatu cum Pauli epitome.* Hildesheim: Olms.

Littré, E. (1968). *Dictionnaire de la langue française*, I. Monte Carlo: Editions du Cap.

Mannino, V. (2014). Le 'bien commun': La fausse impasse du droit romain. In B. Parange and J. De Saint Victor (eds.), *Repenser les biens communs.* Paris: CNRS éditions, 35–50.

Meyer C. (2006). *Le système doctrinal des aliments: Contribution à la théorie générale de l'obligation alimentaire légale.* Bern: Peter Lang.

Mommsen, Theodor and Paul Krüger (1973). *Corpus Iuris Civilis I.* 22nd ed. Berlin: Weidmann.

Occam, G. d'. (1970). *Opera philosophica et theologica.* P. Boehner, G. Gal and S. Brown (eds.). New York: St Bonaventure.

Occam, G. (d') (1940, 1956, 1963). *Opera politica.* J. G. Sikes and H. S. Offler (eds.). Manchester: Manchester University Press.

Parance, B. and J. de Saint-Victor (2014). *Repenser les biens communs.* Paris: CNRS.

Paturet, A. (2010). L'individu entre l'homme et la chose: Note sur l'esclave en droit romain. *Droits* 1(51): 3–26.

Paturet, A. (2017). The intriguing fate of the Roman res: From case and trial to modern times in proceedings of the eleventh conference on legal translation. *Comparative Legilinguistics* 30: 67–83.

Piron, S. (2008). *Congé à Villey. L'atelier du Centre de recherches historiques* 1, http://acrh.revues.org/314

Rampelberg, R. M. (2005). *Repères romains pour le droit européen des contrats.* Paris: LGDJ.

Regad, C., C. Riot and S. Schmit (2018). *La personnalité juridique de l'animal.* Paris: LexisNexis.

Scheid, J. (2005). *La religion des Romains.* Paris: Armand Colin.

Sers, O. (2012). *Lucrèce: De rerum natura. De la nature.* Paris: Les Belles Lettres.

Thomas Y. (1978). Le droit entre les mots et les choses: Rhétorique et jurisprudence à Rome. *Archives de philosophie du droit* 23: 93–114.

Thomas, Y. (1980). *Res*, chose et patrimoine (note sur le rapport sujet–objet en droit romain). *Archives de philosophie du droit* 25: 413–26.

Thomas, Y. (1991). *Imago naturae. Note sur l'institutionnalité de la nature à Rome, Théologie et droit dans la science politique de l'Etat moderne.* Rome: éd. EFR no. 147: 201–27.

Thomas, Y. (1998). Le sujet de droit, la personne et la nature, sur la critique contemporaine du sujet de droit. *Le débat* 3(100): 85–107.

Thompson, D. (1993). *The Oxford Dictionary of Current English.* Oxford: Oxford University Press.

Vanuxem, S. (2010). Les choses saisies par la propriété. De la chose-objet aux choses-milieux. *Revue interdisciplinaire d'études juridiques* 64(1): 123–82.

Villey, M. (1964). La genèse du droit subjectif chez Guillaume d'Occam. *Archives de philosophie du droit* 9: 99–127.

9

Environmental Law

Lexical Semantics in the Quest for Conceptual Foundations and Legitimacy

CAROLINE LASKE

Introduction

The environment is a subject that is inhabited by an impressive diversity of points of views, ideas, concepts, philosophies, rules, laws and regulations, to name just a few. As a body of law, developed in a very short period of time, environmental law did not benefit from a more gradual 'organic' evolution. As we can see from the example of the ECOLEX database, a comprehensive global source of information on environmental law, it shows an exponential rise of the number of (all types of) documents it holds from earlier periods in comparison to today: 124 documents in the period between 1789 and 1914 and 321 documents in the period 1915–39, rising to 199,440 documents for the period 1990–2018. Environmental law, together with other sections of emerging law like those relative to employment, social security or equal opportunity, these all arose from primarily political forces mainly during the twentieth century. But while employment or equal opportunity laws find legitimacy in the protection of fundamental rights of people, this is less clear-cut in environmental law. Moreover, some aspects of environmental law are based on scientific research with an ever-changing state of the art.

The rapid rise and success of environmental law comes at a cost: the content and legitimacy of the underlying concepts and principles of environmental protection and governance have been given insufficient attention and time to evolve. Environmental law could not 'expand organically' in view of the rapidity, urgency and political content and context.

Environmental law grew so rapidly and quickly that there was no time, or need, to worry about its jurisprudential underpinnings. It enjoyed the luxury of skipping the stages of debate over fundamentals and incremental growth and acceptance. Debates went directly to the important, but narrower, question about the merits of the suite of policy instruments available to achieve the environmental protection objectives. This 'papering over' has not gone unnoticed … However, as environmental law continues to mature, the largely neglected questions of content and legitimacy become more troubling and need to be addressed if the area is to sustain itself.

(Tarlock 2003–04: 216)

It is the presence or absence of such legal conceptual underpinnings that will condition whether environmental law develops into a fully-fledged and permanent body of law, or whether environmental protection is to be merely a factor in a problem-specific context that will be taken into account in a diversity of established substantive contexts (Tarlock 2003–04: 229).

The approach employed in this chapter is to examine certain terms typically associated with the impact of human activities on the environment, in order to reveal how conceptual meanings have shifted throughout the twentieth century and from one decade to another since the 1960s. This approach is akin to the *Begriffsgeschichte* work undertaken in German-speaking academia, in particular by scholars such as Brunner, Conze, Koselleck and Meier who worked on the encyclopaedia *Geschichtliche Grundbegriffe* (Brunner et al. 2004). This monumental work is a historical study of the concepts and semantic fields that constitute the language of social and political thought and economic structures, and provides insights into the meanings and uses of words and concepts in classical, medieval and modern languages.[1] The aim of the *Geschichtliche Grundbegriffe* project was to test the hypothesis that the main concepts used in German political and social language were transformed during what Kosselleck, one of the principal editors, called the *Sattelzeit* – the period between approximately 1750 to 1850, a century of crisis and transition, during which conceptual change led to transformations in political, social and economic structures (1979: 107–29).

Legal terminology is something of an outsider in the area of specialised language. In law, it is not always possible to draw a clear dividing line between legal conceptions and non-legal conceptions. According to Hohfeld this is because of a failure to differentiate between purely legal relations and the physical and mental facts that create such relations (1913–14: 20). It is reflected in the general ambiguity and looseness of the legal terminology. One of the reasons for this 'looseness' of legal terminology is that although certain terms refer to highly complex legal concepts, the actual language is imported from general language registers and many terms refer to everyday physical things, while actually describing an abstract legal concept. For example, the term 'property' designates the physical object (e.g. land) *and* the legal interests, rights and privileges (e.g. of the ownership of land) appertained to such physical object, and in the latter case the term is used figuratively. This demonstrates perfectly the difference between the notion of

---

[1] There were other similarly important German works: see Ritter et al. (1971–2007); on mainly the history of philosophical concepts, see Reichardt et al. (1985).

concept as a cognitive category (i.e. constituents of thought) on the one hand, and as a linguistic category (i.e. semantic meaning) on the other (Felber 2001: 58–59; Mattila 2012: 27–28).[2] To understand the fundamental nature of legal language, it is important to make that distinction. But it also shows the intrinsic link between the two and the inevitable confusion that can be created when they come together.

Adopted to the context of this chapter, we can observe the evolution of the concepts and semantic fields relating to what we (rather vaguely) call today, environmental protection policy and law. An example of this would be the use of the concept of 'person', which is defined differently in various legal contexts. In most civil and common law systems, it relates to a legal entity, an abstraction or a 'fiction', whereas in legal traditions such as Indigenous law in Canada or New Zealand, it refers to a real entity of land such as, for example, a river. It shows how the understanding of what is the environment and our relationship to it are different depending on the legal context. Revealing such differences can help identify not only steps in the creation of law and in its implementation, but also inform us of the ontological basis underlying specific legal concepts. In the case of the legal personality of the river, both meanings find expression in positive law. This raises the question of whether and how positive law can articulate both concepts, or whether there is a need to reconsider the concept and its ontological foundation. Moreover, in an international or supranational context, legal concepts and terms can be used differently in different languages and studying the semantic content can provide deep-level understanding of such differences, which may be useful, for example, to legal harmonisation projects in European Union law.

In this chapter, we report a very brief study of a few relevant terms, describing what is possible while only scratching the surface of what deserves to be a full research project.[3] The aim is to sketch out an approach and methodology that would contribute to the consolidation of a conceptual foundation for environmental policy and law. Section 9.1 will discuss the basic premise that language is an act of communication, the functioning of which can be better understood, inter alia, through linguistics analysis, which will then be described and explained in Section 9.2, with particular reference to corpus- and concordance-based methodologies. Sections 9.3 and 9.4 each deal with an English-language corpus and an environmental law database, describing brief terminological studies that have been carried out on both collections of texts. The conclusions are summarised in Section 9.5.

9.1 Language

In this quest for conceptual foundations in relation to a body of law with intensifying complexities and unevenness, a linguistic approach has an appropriate

---

[2] Der Begriff ist eine erkenntnistheoretische Kategorie, die Bedeutung eine linguistische (Felber (2001)).
[3] This study was carried out in 2018.

place: linguistics methodologies allow for deep-level understanding of the continuous interaction between the way legal thought creates meaning in language and language creates realities in law. Here, meaning is not approached with the structuralist perspective,[4] but rather from a pragmatic view that stresses the social and communicative functions of the use of language.

If we start from the premise that language is an act of communication, we stress its function, notably the social function of the use of language when people interact with each other. This systemic functional view of language, as first adopted by Michael Halliday in the 1980s,[5] offers an account of language as it is used in actual social situations and is, in this sense, always concerned with the meaning, communicative functionality and rhetorical purposes of language. Therefore, language is an indicator of how meanings are encoded and decoded in a given situation. At the heart of systemic linguistics is the understanding of the communicative properties of written and spoken texts of all types (why a text means what it does and why it is valued as it is), as well as the understanding of the relation between language, on the one hand, and culture, community, social grouping and ideology, on the other (Halliday 1985/94: xxi). For functional linguists, language appears to have developed and is used for three communicative functionalities or meanings, which Halliday has called metafunctions:

1. ideational metafunction encoding experiential meanings, which refer to the use of language to represent experience and construct a view of reality with the various categories language offers to talk about real-world happenings;
2. interpersonal metafunction encoding interpersonal meanings relating to attitudes and relationships which realise tenor of discourse;
3. textual metafunction encoding textual meanings that refer to the use of language to organise the experiential and interpersonal meanings into a coherent, connected and unified entity.

A text, in this sense, is a coherent collection of meanings appropriate to its context. The way the text's meanings are combined gives the text its texture and the text's structure rests on the mandatory structural elements used in the combination of these meanings. Encoding the meaning depends on two surrounding contexts: the *'context of culture'* refers to the general outer cultural environment in which a text occurs. It includes elements such as conventions of

---

[4] Structural linguistics is based on the assumption that language is a coherent system of formal units. Consequently, language is analysed as a system of interrelated structural elements without regard to their historical development. This approach originated from the work of Ferdinand de Saussure (1916/2005).

[5] Also called systemic functional grammar or systemic linguistics. The standard reference works are Halliday (1985/1994); Thompson (1996); Butt et al. (2000); see also Laske (2013: 214–17, 2020: ch. 3).

address, politeness, discourse which shape meanings within a particular culture. It has been described 'as the sum of all the meanings it is possible to mean in that particular culture' (Butt et al. 2000: 3). Within that general context of culture, there is an inner layer, which functional linguists have named the '*context of situation*' and which refers to, as the term indicates, the specific situation in which a text occurs and in which meanings are formed. It includes 'the things going on in the world outside the text that make the text what it is' (Butt et al. 2000: 4). A study of the extralinguistic levels of context of culture and context of situation will show how meanings are encoded and will reveal the (social) function of the use of language.

If language is viewed as an act of communication, the linguistic study aims to understand the communicative properties of texts and their social function. Legal language fulfils several functions, the most important of which is probably to achieve justice by 'producing legal effects by speech acts' (Mattila 2013: 41). Mattila further identifies the transmission of legal messages, strengthening the authority of the law and maintaining order in society, reinforcing the team spirit of the legal profession and, lastly, linguistic policy goals (Mattila 2013: 41–86). Legal language is at the heart of the normative nature of law and of its prescriptive and performative functions, and language is inextricably bound up with the premise that the letter of the law is supreme. These functions are, however, also embodied in non-verbal communication often bound up with historical traditions, such as ceremonials, wigs and robes, the layout of a courtroom.

If we further hypothesise that a central aspect of law lies in its intrinsic and deep-level link to language, in particular to the use of written language, the analysis of the semantic fields of the language and terminology provides an angle beyond the mere content analysis usually practised in the legal sciences. Language offers a reliable indicator of the thinking and contexts in which concepts are established and are shifting in meaning. Legal language, as the linguistic expression of the law and of the legal process, reflects the way (legal) meanings are constructed, encoded and decoded. There is continuous interaction between the way laws create meaning in language and how language creates realities in law (van Hoecke and Warrington 2010: 305). For a better insight into this process, it is necessary to examine language and meaning in their textual context. The use of corpus linguistics methods and concordance software is ideal for such an empirical approach, as it allows for systematic analysis of language in use and thus of authentic evidence. In the case of environmental law, it will improve our understanding of its semantic and conceptual content. In addition, the study of language can also offer other perspectives on legal communication, such as the semiotic approach described in Chapter 5 in this volume.

9.2 Corpus Linguistics

In the process of reflecting on the underlying concepts and principles of environmental protection and governance, corpus linguistics methodologies can be used as cognitive models for a better understanding of the conceptual foundation of the body of law as a whole or of parts of it. Corpus and concordance work as a method of exegesis on the basis of detailed searches of words and phrases in multiple contexts and among a large number of texts, goes back as far as the Middle Ages, when biblical scholars manually indexed the words of the Holy Scriptures. The first computer-generated concordance tools appeared in the 1950s, when it took twenty-four hours to process 60,000 words and researchers used punched-card technology for storage! Modern corpus work, as we know it today, emerged in the 1980s and 1990s, and now employs advanced information technologies.

Corpus-based methodologies consist of the study of naturally occurring language in large bodies of computerised texts using linguistic concordance software, which retrieves alphabetically or otherwise sorted lists of linguistic data from the corpus. This allows for the (legal) language to be examined empirically and in its textual context (so-called KWIC[6] lines), by enabling detailed searches of words,[7] phrases and lexical/grammatical patterns in multiple contexts across a large amount of electronically held texts, providing information on the data that is both quantitative and qualitative, empirical rather than intuitive. Our own intuition of the relative frequency of words, phrases and structures can be little more than vague and general. And while we may be conscious about the frequency of lexis, it is highly unlikely that we have any precise intuitions about the frequency of grammatical categories.

Corpus linguistics methodologies can be purely descriptive and ideologically neutral but can also be used in discourse analysis and coupled with critical approaches. Fairclough saw analysis of text as one aspect of his three-dimensional view of discourse and discourse analysis (Fairclough 1992: 73–100; 1999). Textual/linguistic analysis happens at the micro level (phonology, grammar up to the level of the sentence, vocabulary, semantics, etc.) and is supplemented by meso-level analysis (discursive practice) and the study of intertextuality at macro level. He draws on Halliday's systemic–functional theory of language by breaking down the 'form versus content' distinction and championing textual analysis as providing pragmatic insights on discourse. Critical linguists also drew on systemic linguistics to combine their method of linguistic text analysis with a social theory of the functioning of language in political and ideological processes. Of particular interest to them is the analysis of grammar of a clause or sentence that expresses

---

[6] Key Word in Context.
[7] This includes the possibility of so-called wild-card searches marked by an asterisk (*) at the beginning or end of a word, which allows for all the variations of that particular word to be located.

the ideational meaning, that is, the way it represents reality (Fowler et al. 1979; Kress and Hodge 1979; O'Halloran 2011). Such analysis of texts is best done by undertaking a (diachronic) linguistic and semantic study using corpus linguistics methodologies.

Corpus-based analysis can either be carried out on an existing corpus, such as the British National Corpus (BNC), or using a corpus that had to be purpose-built for a specific research question. The second option was adopted in relation to the ECOLEX database, which does not host a corpus of texts, but just information about texts that can then be accessed through a weblink. Existing corpora, such as the BNC, often come with a number of search tools; some also include concordance tools. The linguistics software used for the purpose-built ECOLEX corpus of this study is the AntConc[8] concordance program, which is fully Unicode compliant, meaning that it can handle data in any language, including all European and Asian languages. Texts selected for uploading to AntConc must be converted to the .txt format. The software then allows us to create word lists and search the text files for words, phrases, patterns, collocates[9] and clusters,[10] as well as advanced proximity searches.[11] Search terms can be displayed in their textual context in a search window, the size of which can be determined. The display in the so-called preset KWIC (Key Word in Context) format is the most common way to show concordance lines and it places the search term in its context as found in the original text. These can then be sorted according to the words to the left and right of the search term and, hence, provide an excellent overview of the type of contexts, textual structure and function in which the search terms occur.

9.3 Analysis in General Language in British English

Before turning to a specifically environmental law database to constitute a corpus, it is of interest to consider how certain terms we traditionally associate with the concerns of the effect of human activities on the environment appear in a general language corpus, like the British National Corpus (BNC).

The BNC[12] is a 100-million-word collection of samples of written (90 per cent) and spoken (10 per cent) language from a wide range of sources, designed to

---

[8] AntConc is a concordance program developed by Laurence Anthony, Director of the Centre of English Language Education at the Waseda University in Japan. There are versions available for Windows, Mac OS X and Linux. The version used for this research was AntConc 3.5.8m (2019), which can be downloaded and which includes links to online guides and video tutorials: www.laurenceanthony.net/software/antconc/

[9] A collocate is a sequence of words or terms that co-occur more often than would be expected by chance, e.g. strong tea.

[10] Clusters are word patterns that group together around the search term.

[11] Proximity searches show two or more separately matching terms occurring within a specified distance, the basic linguistic assumption being that the proximity implies a relationship between the words.

[12] The latest edition is the BNC XML Edition (2007), available at www.natcorp.ox.ac.uk

represent a wide cross section of British English from the later part of the twentieth century. For the present study, only the written part was considered. This includes, for example, extracts from regional and national newspapers, specialist periodicals and journals for all ages and interests, academic books and popular fiction, published and unpublished letters and memoranda, school and university essays, among many other kinds of text. In this way, the BNC provides a fairly representative sample of natural language in use between 1960 and 1993, though it is restricted to British English. The corpus is constructed in such a way that it is possible to subdivide it into three separate time periods: 1960–74, 1975–84 and 1985–93.[13] From the 1960s onwards, the protection of the environment became a more mainstream issue for discussion and legislation, so the subdivision is very useful for the purpose of our study. As we can see from the statistical analysis of the ECOLEX database (see Table 9.1), the production of texts relating to environmental law has increased exponentially in the period 1965–89, and even more so in the time up to 2018. It is safe to assume that this is the period which marked the greatest changes and innovations in the language used. The BNC does not include more recent material and is limited to British English. More comprehensive results would be obtained if similar searches were undertaken on corpora containing other variations of English and text samples from more recent sources. But the brief study using the BNC described here already gives a good indication of tendencies relating to usages of terms and language.

The written corpus contains some 86,072,061 words from 2,978 texts. The relative frequency[14] of specific terms will be calculated in relation to that figure, multiplied by one million. The corpus was searched for six terms: environment, waste, pollution, conservation, ecolog* (wild-card search), biodiversity. The KWIC lines for environment and ecology were also evaluated in greater detail. The number of hits (occurrences), the range (number of documents in which term occurred) and the relative frequency (instances per million words) for each term in every subcorpus and for the total part of the BNC are listed in the Table 9.1 below: The relative frequencies in the three subcorpora are represented in Figure 9.1.

In particular, there was a massive growth in the relative frequency of the terms pollution and conservation, growing to ~8,300 and ~2,700 respectively by 1985 to 1993 on an indexed basis (1960–74 = 100).

---

[13] 1960–74 subcorpus: 1,718,449 words – 46 texts; 1975–84 subcorpus: 4,625,456 words – 155 texts; 1985–93 subcorpus: 79,728,156 words – 2,777 texts.
[14] The relative frequency is the number of occurrences of a term in relation to the total number of words contained in a particular corpus. It is calculated by dividing the number of occurrences by the number of words, multiplying the results by one million in the case of the BNC, or 10,000 in the case of the study on the ECOLEX database (see below).

Table 9.1. *Terminology in the BNC between 1960 and 1993*

	1960–74			1975–84			1985–93			Total		
	Hits	Range	Freq.	Hits	Range	Freq.	Hits	Range	Freq.	Hits	Range	Freq.
Environment	75	18	43,64	604	155	130,58	11,314	1,591	141,91	11,993	1,684	139,34
Waste	95	34	55,28	214	75	46,27	5,714	1,255	71,67	6,023	1,364	69,98
Pollution	1	1	0,58	89	18	19,24	3,836	532	48,11	3,926	551	45,61
Conservation	3	3	1,75	79	12	17,08	3,649	551	45,77	3,731	566	43,35
Ecolog*	10	2	5,82	125	15	27,02	1,509	419	18,93	1,644	436	19,1
Biodiversity	0	0	0	0	0	0	95	35	1,19	95	35	1,19

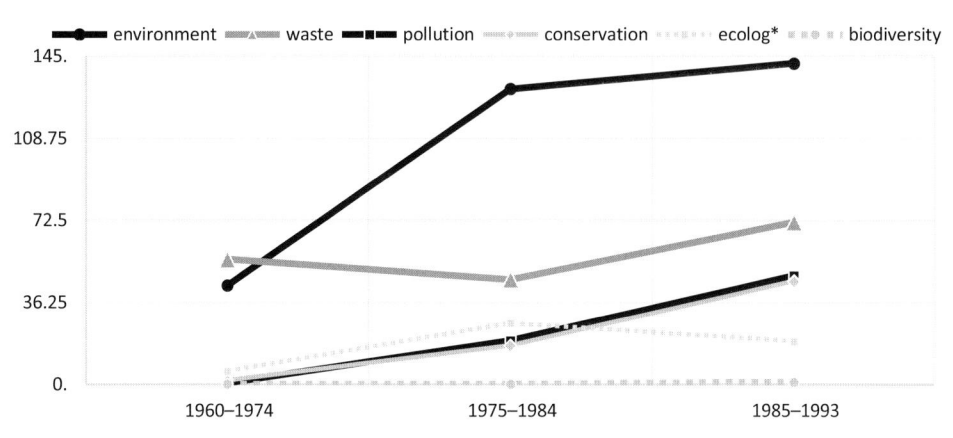

Figure 9.1 Relative frequency of terminology in the BNC

9.3.1 Analysis of the Term 'Environment'

Two terms were singled out for closer evaluation: 'environment', which is probably one of the most generic terms in this context has a multitude of meanings, the semantic fields of which have shifted, as the brief analysis of the BNC below shows; and 'ecology', a more recent term, but similarly to 'environment' it also has a history of semantic shifts. The precise statistical analysis can be found in the notes as well as in Figures 9.2 and 9.3.

Environment features prominently among the six search terms. It not only has the highest frequency but also shows the steepest rise. A rapid glance at the *Oxford English Dictionary* shows that the term has a variety of definitions, of which the effect of human activity on the environment is only one. This is also reflected in the KWIC lines, of which the first one hundred (random order) were examined more closely. During the 1960s and early 1970s, the term 'environment' was used almost exclusively in a general sense, relating to social, economic, political, health factors and conditions, while in only very few cases it refers to the natural/ biological/chemical environment. The concept of environment as the effect of human activity on the environment is absent in the texts of that period.[15] A first shift towards an understanding of environment as the effect of human activity, can be observed between the mid-1970s and mid-1980s where three-quarters of the occurrences of the term relate to a general sense and 6 per cent to natural/scientific

---

[15] 1960–74 subcorpus – 75 KWIC lines for 'environment' (46,64 instances per one million words): 91% – general sense (social, economic, political, health factors and conditions); 9% – scientific sense (natural/ biological/ chemical environment).

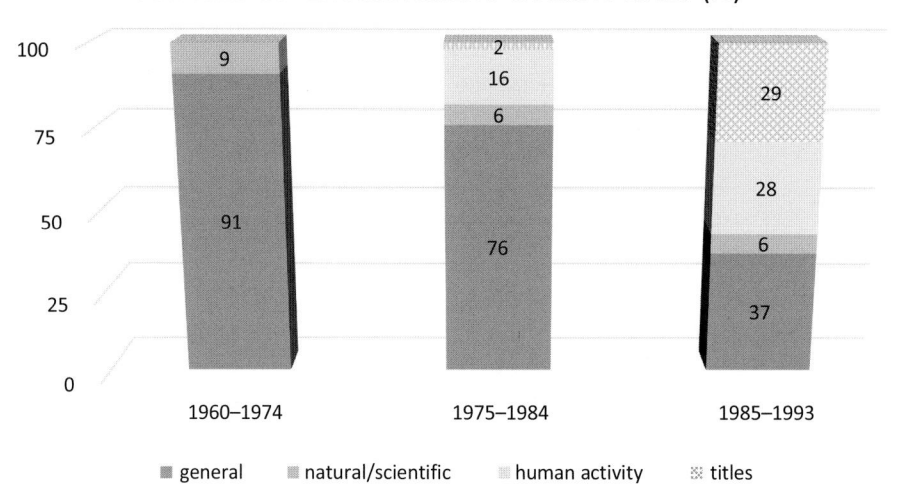

Figure 9.2 Specific meanings and shifts of the term 'environment' in the BNC

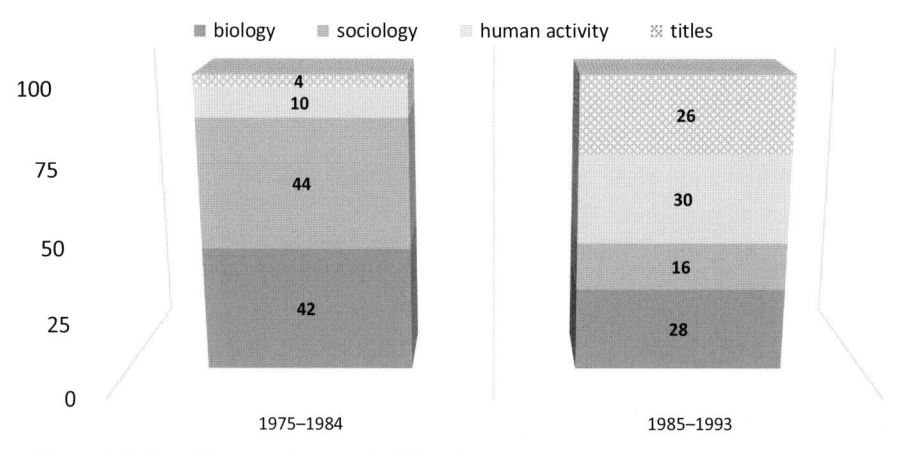

Figure 9.3 Specific meanings and shifts of the term 'ecology' in the BNC

context. However, we find that in 16 per cent of the lines, environment is used in relation to the effect of human activity on the environment and 2 per cent refer to titles, such as government departments or ministers.[16] The substantial change can be found in the late 1980s and early 1990s, when the general context uses have fallen to just over one-third, the scientific context uses remains a very small

---

[16] 1975–84 subcorpus – 604 KWIC lines for 'environment' (130,58 instances per one million words): 76% – general sense, 6% – scientific sense, 16% – effect of human activity on the environment, 2% – titles.

fraction, while the uses in relation to the context of effect of human activity on the environment and to specific titles represents over half of the occurrences of the term environment.[17] This linguistic evidence of general language uses suggests it was during this particular time that the concept of environment took on and consolidated the specific meaning relating to the effect of human activity on the environment, an understanding that is most common today. It is also interesting to note that the general uses show a shift in preoccupation from one period to the other. In the 1960–74 subcorpus KWIC lines, environment would refer almost exclusively to the conditions of social, work and children's education. This gives way in the 1975–84 subcorpus to uses in relation to health and safety in relation to domestic, hospital/patient and road users' situations. The context that is added in the 1985–93 subcorpus are environments in relation to digital technologies, such as specific system or network environments.[18]

From Figure 9.2, we can see how the term environment refers to a series of social, work, educational, natural and scientific environments in the 1960s, and shifts towards a new meaning and to the specific context of the effect of human activity on the environment from 0 to 57 per cent in the period of two decades. Of interest is also the rise in the use of the term in relation to titles of organisations, departments, government ministries, job titles, etc. which points to the fact that there was a steep rise in the creation of such organisations and jobs.

9.3.2 Analysis of the Term 'Ecology'

Ecology[19] is another term that is similarly interesting to consider in its textual context. Both environment and ecology are perceived to today's ears as terms closely related to the effects of human behaviour on the environment. And yet both terms have (a history of) various other meanings. In contrast to 'environment' discussed above, 'ecology' has very low relative frequency in the BNC.[20] Leaving aside the earlier subcorpus in which ecology only occurred twice, we can find the use of the term in the context of the relationship between living organisms and their environment (biology), between people/social groups and their environment (sociology) and between human activities and the environment, as well as in relation to titles. The evolution between 1975 and 1993 is illustrated in Figure 9.3.

---

[17] 1985–93 subcorpus – 11,314 KWIC lines for 'environment' (141,91 instances per one million words): 37% – general sense, 6% – scientific sense, 28% – effect of human activity on the environment, 29% – titles.

[18] e.g. 'Software converted for the Apple–Novell environment will also be portable to the PowerPC'; 'Common Open System Environment'; 'the Windows Open Systems Environment'; 'Open Network Computing environment'.

[19] For the consideration of the KWIC lines, the word ecology was considered rather than the wild-card version of ecolog* as in Table 9.1.

[20] 1960–74 subcorpus: two hits (rel.freq. per 1 million words: 1.16); 1975–84 subcorpus: 48 times (rel.freq.: 10.38); 1985–93 subcorpus: 533 times (rel.freq. 6.69).

Similar to the findings for environment, we can observe a shift during the second half of the 1980s and early 1990s, towards a new meaning and to the specific context of the effect of human activity on the environment. If the category of titles, also relating to the effects of human activity on the environment, is added we can observe a similar situation to the one described: over half of the occurrences of the term ecology relate to the effect of human activity on the environment.[21] It is reasonable to conclude from these observations that the concept of ecology became increasingly associated with the concept of environment relating to the effect of human activity on the environment.

The corpus was also searched for the term 'ecocide', which is a neologism that expresses a very recent concept, which is discussed in Chapter 10 in this volume, and will be examined at greater length below. There were no hits for ecocide in the BNC, neither in the written nor in the spoken part of the corpus. It must be stressed that the term is not restricted to its use in English, but can also be found, for example, in French. It is always of interest to note the possible diversities between the uses of the term and the concept it refers to in different languages.

9.4 Analysis in a Corpus of Environmental Law

The study on an environmental law corpus carried out for this chapter is based on texts brought together in the ECOLEX database,[22] which is an information service on environmental law operated jointly by the Food and Agriculture Organization (FAO), the International Union for the Conservation of Nature (IUCN) and the United Nations Environment Programme (UNEP). Its purpose is to build capacity worldwide by providing the most comprehensive possible global source of information on environmental law. The ECOLEX database includes information on treaties, international soft law and other non-binding policy and technical guidance documents, national legislation, judicial decisions, and law and policy literature. Users have direct access to the abstracts and indexing information about each document, as well as to the full text of most of the information provided. Though access to the full texts is given through links, the database does not host as such a corpus of texts. For the purpose of a corpus-based linguistic study, it was therefore necessary to compile a specific corpus, which will be described below.

Before discussing the study based on the purpose-built corpus, let us look at some of the frequency statistics that can be compiled from ECOLEX. As this

---

[21] 1975–84 subcorpus: 14% of the KWIC lines refer to ecology in the sense of the effect of human activity on the environment (10% for human activity as such, 4% for titles); 1985–93 subcorpus: 56% of the KWIC lines refer to ecology in the sense of the effect of human activity on the environment (30% for human activity as such, 26% for titles).

[22] ECOLEX – Gateway to Environmental Law: www.ecolex.org

Table 9.2. *Number of documents in ECOLEX for specific time periods*

Period	1789–2018	1789–1914	1915–39	1940–64	1965–89	1990–2018
No. of docs	**212,746**	124	312	1,685	11,185	199,440

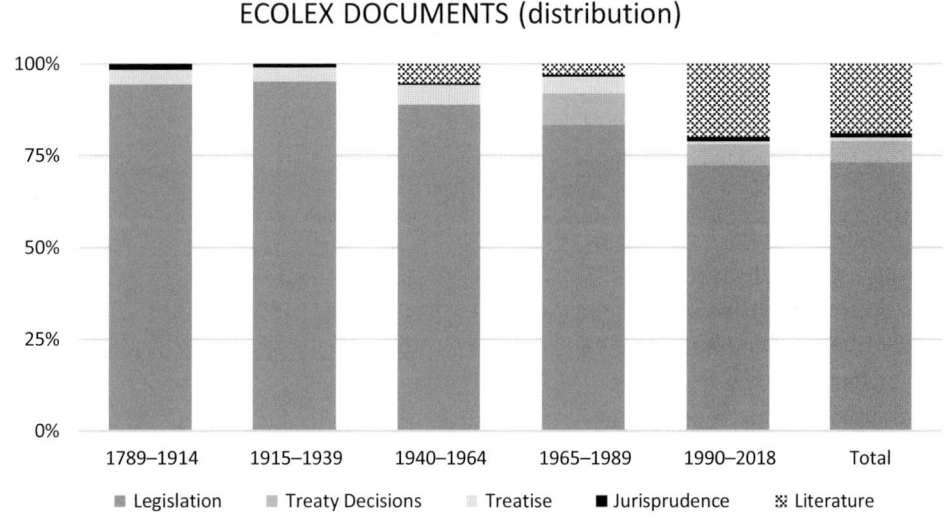

Figure 9.4 Distribution according to different types of documents

database is constantly updated, the information it contains, especially in relation to recent years, fluctuates slightly. At the point of writing (March 2019) and for the period of 1789 to 2018, the database contained just over 212,000 documents of which 73 per cent were pieces of legislation, 5.8 per cent treaty decisions, 1.2 per cent case law/jurisprudence and 1 per cent treaties. It also contains 18.9 per cent of specialist literature, though that represents a great diversity of texts and registers. The number of documents have grown exponentially during the period in question, in particular since the 1960s. If we divide the time span in question into five periods, the first of which includes 125 years[23] while the other four 25 years, we can observe the increase in documents relating to environmental law throughout the last 230 years (Table 9.2).

Yet, the distribution according to the type of documents remains roughly the same (see Figure 9.4). Legislation is the kind of text most used in the area of

---

[23] Dividing this first period into smaller units would have made little sense, as not much happened in terms of environmental law.

environmental policy, though specialised literature adds an important dimension since the 1990s.

ECOLEX was also searched for specific terminological items, as this is likely to reveal the diachronic evolution of the language used in the context of environmental law and policy. As the database does not include the substantive texts, the search was limited to terms appearing in the short titles, long titles, key words and abstracts. Unfortunately, the database does not offer the possibility to ascertain the total number of word tokens, so relative frequency could not be calculated. The search has further excluded the category of 'literature', as some central terms (e.g. environment, ecology) appear in the title of journals rather than in the relevant articles and can thus skew somewhat the results.

List of search terms in alphabetical order:

animal welfare	ecology	land	social justice
biodiversity	ecosystem	negligence	sustainability
climate	environment	nuisance	sustainable development
climate change	fishing	organic	waste
contamination	human rights	pollution	water
ecocide	justice	preservation	

Examining these terms within their textual context reveals the evolution of the language and meanings in relation to newly emerging concepts of environmental law. Some terms have traditionally been associated with environmental issues, such as contamination, environment, fishing, land, negligence, nuisance, pollution, preservation, waste, water. More recently, other terms appeared, such as biodiversity, ecology, ecosystem, organic, and some may express concepts that have been discussed in relation to the environment only during the last few decades: animal welfare, climate (change), ecocide, human rights, (social) justice, sustainability, sustainable development.[24] Unsurprisingly, the more common terms of environmental law are also among those that show the highest frequency. Environment, land, pollution, waste and water occur between 21,000 and 39,000 times. Three notable exceptions are nuisance (1,644 occurrences), negligence (2,638 occurrences) and contamination (4,593 occurrences), all terms that have usually been associated in the common law with early environment case law.[25] It is some indication that the approach of litigating early environmental contamination cases through the common law of nuisance and negligence did not persist on a worldwide level. The figures would no doubt be a little different if carried out on a corpus that only contained texts of common law cases. Similarly, other legal traditions such as Indigenous law in the United States, Canada or New Zealand

---

[24] More recent terminology and terms relating to newer concepts occur less frequently, e.g.: ecocide: 9; social justice: 149; ecology: 1,346; sustainability: 1,959; animal welfare: 4,735; biodiversity: 5,022.

[25] See, e.g. *John Rylands and Jehu Horrocks* v. *Thomas Fletcher* [1868] 3 LR HL 330.

may place different emphasis and/or introduced other concepts, such as 'Mother Earth'. Taking an example given in Chapter 3 in this volume, the cluster for 'water' would be the concept of *Zaagidowin* (love/taking care of), the principle of harmony and healing.

The increase in both the occurrences and diversity of the terms show an important expansion of environmental law language and terminology. The proportions with which the occurrences increase show remarkable similarities. Dividing the time span into the same periods as in Tables 9.1 and 9.2, we can observe very similar proportional increases from one period to the next in the majority of the terms studied. For the first three periods (1789–1914, 1915–39, 1940–64), the occurrences lie between 0 and 1 per cent of the total occurrences, while for the period 1965–89 we are between 3 per cent and 6 per cent. The substantial increase can be observed in the last period (1990–2018) when the percentage lies around 90 per cent and 96 per cent. This brief overview shows the tendency that the environmental law language and terminology is still in full expansion. Long-established preoccupation with issues relating, e.g. to land (increase of 90 per cent in the period 1990–2018), pollution (increase of 94 per cent in the period 1990–2018) or water (increase of 92 per cent in the period 1990–2018) continue to be discussed and are not superseded by newer concepts.

9.4.1 Analysis of a Purpose-Built Environmental Law Corpus

A corpus is usually defined as a systematic collection of naturally[26] occurring texts of both written and spoken language that has been computerised. It offers the empirical basis for carrying out systematic linguistic investigations on authentic evidence. The fact that it is held digitally and searchable electronically offers possibilities that are not otherwise available. Yet, the corpus linguistics methodologies only make sense if a corpus is designed in such a way that it forms a representative basis for making generalisations about a language as a whole or as defined by the underlying premises of the research. The overall corpus design is conditioned by the methods of text sampling and sampling decisions made by the researcher whether conscious or (in part) unconscious. Only a well-defined conception of what the sample is intended to represent will subsequently allow for choices to be evaluated as to the adequacy or representativeness of the corpus. It is less a question of sample *size* and more one of being representative for

---

[26] Natural language, as opposed to artificial or constructed language devised for international communications, computer programming or mathematical purposes, is language that has evolved naturally, is hereditary and in extended use (see definition in *OED*).

the range of text types in the target population (the latter of which has to be defined in turn) and for the range of linguistics distribution in the population (Biber 1993).

For the purpose of this study, and as mentioned above, it was necessary to constitute a purpose-built corpus. The choice was made to concentrate on the texts listed under case law/jurisprudence in the ECOLEX database, which are the complete case reports of the selected environmental law litigation. To the extent that we are dealing with reports of court cases, including at times opinions (e.g. judges, attorneys general), these represent naturally occurring language and a good insight into language usages. Ideally, building a subcorpus for every category of text could have allowed for differences to be highlighted in the usages and evolution of language and terminology. Similarly, it would be of great interest to use more specific legal corpora coming from institutions such as the European Union,[27] the new database on environmental concepts and ontology (LEO) in multilateral documents,[28] or specific issue initiatives, such as Wildlex, the database for wildlife-related law operated by the IUCN.[29] It is hoped that this kind of approach will be adopted in a future study.

The ECOLEX database contains 2,568 case reports from national jurisdictions worldwide as well as from international courts such as the European Court of Human Rights or the European Court of Justice (ECJ). For the period up to 1990, the database contains some 81 cases and 2,487 cases for the period 1990–2018. Some 132 cases were selected for the corpus, 13 of which date from before 1996. For the period between 1996 and 2018, roughly five cases were selected per year. Priority was given to cases that deal with the protection of the environment following adverse effects caused by human activities (e.g. protection of water, animals, land) rather than the discussion of constitutional issues or matters of jurisdiction, legal/administrative procedure, assessment of damages to be paid. The corpus is constituted of 139 files because for six cases that were decided in the ECJ and one case that came from the US Supreme Court, two documents each were downloaded representing two opinions (US) or the judgment and the opinion of the Attorney General (ECJ).

This corpus contains 1,486,541 words or word tokens.[30] On the list of the 200 most frequently occurring word types, environment-related terms can be found

---

[27] See www.eur-lex.europa.eu
[28] See http://sd.iisd.org/news/unep-launches-law-and-environmental-ontology-portal/
[29] See www.wildlex.org
[30] In linguistics, a difference is made between 'word tokens', which represent the total number of words contained in a text regardless of repetition, and 'word types', which express the number of distinct word forms contained in a text; e.g. He was a good shepherd, because his father was a shepherd => 11 word tokens but only 8 word types due to the repetition of three words. To ascertain word types is interesting for calculating the type–token ration which can shed some light on the lexical diversity of a text.

ranked relatively low (relative frequency is calculated per 10,000 words, not 1,000,000 as was the case for the BNC above):

2,213 development (rank 64), rel.freq. 14.89
2,172 environmental (rank 65), rel.freq. 14.61
1,855 water (rank 83), rel.freq. 12.48
1,789 environment (rank 86), rel.freq. 12.03
1,503 waste (rank 100), rel.freq. 10.11
1,476 species (rank 102), rel.freq. 9.93
1,439 protection (rank 106), rel.freq. 9.68
1,322 noise (rank 121), rel.freq. 8.89
944 conservation (rank 186), rel.freq. 6.35

Terms relating to law and the legal/judicial process are more frequent:

5,705 court (rank 25), rel.freq. 38.38
3,460 article (rank 39), rel.freq. 23.28
3,337 law (rank 41), rel.freq. 22.45
3,271 case (rank 42), rel.freq. 22.00
2,406 directive (rank 56), rel.freq. 16.19
1,748 judgment (rank 89), rel.freq. 11.76
1,338 provisions (rank 116), rel.freq. 9.00
1,247 rights (rank 128), rel.freq. 8.39
858 regulations (rank 200), rel.freq. 5.77

In this corpus, we do not find what we had observed with the BNC, which was a multitude of meanings for terms, such as for example, environment or ecology. Instead, we tend to see the search terms in a textual context, the language and terminology of which tend to be semantically restricted to the issues raised by the impact of the human activity on the environment. All terms examined in this study showed that they collocate and cluster with typical environmental protection terminology: e.g. protect/protection, health, effects or impact, water, land, noise, nitrates, agriculture. Also prominent are terms relating to the political, administrative, legal, etc. structures set up as part of the environment protection policy: e.g. department, minister, planning, management, law.

9.4.2 Early Environmental Texts

As with the BNC, it is of interest to examine earlier texts that were written at a time when the protection of the environment due to the threats of human activities was not yet a mainstream concept in our societies in general nor in their legal systems. For this purpose, a small subcorpus was compiled with ten early cases dated between the first case in 1868 and 1975. This corpus contained 126,618 word tokens (7,282 word types). When we search this subcorpus for terms we would use today in a generic way in relation to environmental issues, we find these to produce very few hits. A wild-card search for environment* has one hit for environment (rel.freq. 0.08 per 10,000 words) and the term used in a general sociological sense rather than in a more ecological one. Similarly:

biodiversity, ecosystem, ecology, sustainability: zero hits;
waste, preservation: 1 hit (rel.freq. 0.08);
climate, contamination: 3 hits (rel.freq. 0.24).

These terms, perhaps except for 'waste' and 'contamination', all stand for concepts of environmental protection, as we understand it today. The fact that their use is not prominent in this early corpus reflects how little the discussion centred around conceptual thinking of environmental issues. In contrast, terms that refer to specific environmental law issues occur considerably more, for example:

water* 322 hits (rel.freq. 24.43)
land* 198 hits (rel.freq. 15.64)
fish* 36 hits (rel.freq. 2.84).

In other words, environmental issues as we would call them today in a generic way, were dealt with in relation to specific matters, such as water, land, fishing, rather than ecosystem, climate, biodiversity. The early environmental law cases appear to have dealt with pragmatic issues relating to the environment on a case-by-case basis without necessarily trying to construct a conceptual framework.

9.4.3 Analysis of the Terms 'Environment' and 'Ecology'

In the ECOLEX purpose-built corpus, there are 1,789 occurrences of *environment*, of which 100 KWIC concordance lines, selected at random were examined more closely. If we adopt the same classification of language as for the BNC, we find that in 58 per cent of the lines, environment was used in the sense of the effect of human activity on the environment and 38 per cent refer to titles (see Figure 9.5). Together this comes to 96 per cent. Looking more closely at the contextual language in the 58 lines concerned with human activity, we can observe that in almost every line the word environment is preceded by the definite article 'the' and never linked to a clause that explains or specifies what meaning of environment we are dealing with. It is also interesting to notice that in 78 per cent of these lines, the concept environment is linked to negative notions. We find words such as adverse, destructive or dangerous impact or effect, deterioration, danger, risk in the immediate vicinity of environment. In only 16 per cent of the lines is the term

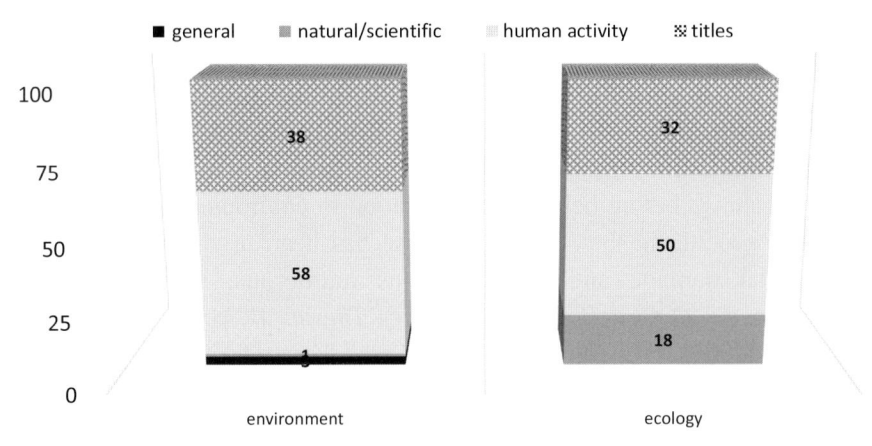

Figure 9.5 KWIC lines for 'environment' and 'ecology' in the ECOLEX Corpus

environment linked to more positive or neutral aspects, such as protection of the environment or clean, green and healthy environment.

The term *ecology* produced only thirty-eight hits in the ECOLEX corpus,[31] but it is comparable to environment to the extent that it has a history of a variety of meanings (see discussion on BNC above). Yet, the one relating to the effect of human activity on the environment has only been used relatively recently, which explains the relative low use of the term in the corpus. From Figure 9.5, we can see that the different meanings for ecology is distributed in proportions similar to those for environment (32 per cent for titles, 50 per cent for human activity). As far as the contextual language is concerned, in 63 per cent of the KWIC lines, ecology is linked to notions that are negative, though less so than was the case for environment. We find words such as concerns, impact, maintain, preserve, respect in the immediate vicinity of ecology. In contrast to the findings for environment, we can observe that ecology tends to be embedded in a different contextual pattern. The term rarely appears as a stand-alone noun preceded by the definite article, signposting a concept that needs no explanations to be understood. Instead, we tend to find ecology together with other nouns and linked by a conjunction, e.g. wealth and ecology, economics and ecology, planned development and ecology. In this, albeit very limited sample, ecology tends to 'behave' less as a generic term, appearing to stand instead for a subcategory in the discussions of the effects of human activity on the environment.

---

[31] The wild-card search ecology* yielded 358 hits and included beside ecology words such as ecological, ecologically, ecologist(s).

9.4.4 'Ecocide'

Before concluding, it is of interest to briefly contrast the findings of studying more established terms with a recent neologism: ecocide, which denotes the concept of criminalising human activities that cause extensive damage to, destruction or loss of ecosystems in a given territory, and which diminishes the health and well-being of species within these ecosystems, including humans. This term is a neologism in the strict sense. Unlike environment or ecology, both of which have had several evolving meanings before being used in relation to environmental protection and governance, ecocide in the strict legal sense has been used mainly to describe environmental damage and destruction as murderous, thus as criminal.[32] According to the *Oxford English Dictionary Thesaurus*, ecocide/ecocidal dates from the late 1960s:

Discarded automobiles, old newspapers and telephone books, tin cans, nonreturnable bottles all add to the growing problems of solid-waste disposal ... Ecocide – the murder of the environment is everybody's business.[33]

The concept of ecocide, albeit without using this specific term, found its way into the Rome Statute of the International Criminal Court, adopted in 1998 and entered into force in 2002. In article 8(2)(b)(iv) relating to war crimes it stipulates that it is to:

Intentionally launch[ing] an attack in the knowledge that such attack will cause incidental loss of life or injury to civilians or damage to civilian objects or widespread, long-term and severe damage to the natural environment which would be clearly excessive in relation to the concrete and direct overall military advantage anticipated.

More recently, this was taken up by Polly Higgins in 2010 when a proposal was presented to the UN Law Commission for ecocide to be recognised as an independent international crime (Higgins 2010; Higgins et al. 2013). The term was defined as: 'the extensive damage to, destruction of or loss of ecosystem(s) of a given territory, whether by human agency or by other causes, to such an extent that peaceful enjoyment by the inhabitants of that territory has been severely diminished'. This proposal was not accepted by the UN, which means that outside of wartime it is not an international crime to cause serious destruction to the environment, to non-human species or to the ecosystem. The criminal law aspect has also been at the heart of concepts such as environmental crime and transnational environmental crime and a new field of study often referred to as green

---

[32] The terms was used fairly widely in the late 1960s and there are multiple usages of the term; see Stoett (2000).
[33] 'Ecocide in Oxford English Dictionary, entry from Third Edition (June 2008), citation from Encycl. Sci. Supplement (1969) Grolier, 159.

criminology. These developments will increasingly provide opportunities and material to study emerging and evolving neologism in the field of environmental law.

When searching the BNC for ecocide, no hits are obtained. The Corpus of Historical American English[34] shows four hits: 1985, 1991 and two in 2005, which represents a relative frequency of 0.01 per one million words. The Corpus of Contemporary American English[35] shows 48 occurrences of the term in its texts dated between 1990 and 2017, which represents a relative frequency of 0.09 per one million words. Searching ECOLEX for ecocide, we find it occurs nine times, all in the category of literature. The first article dates from 1990, one from 1998, 2004 and 2006 respectively, two from 2016 and 2017 respectively and one from 2018. These figures suggest that the term ecocide is not a part of the general environmental law discourse. As mentioned previously, it has not been adopted into any laws, but it does not even appear in the discussions or opinions reported in the case law. Yet, it is being discussed both in academic publications and in the wider press. No doubt a linguistic study a few decades from now will show how that term either gradually became a part of mainstream language or dropped away completely. It will be the linguistic expression of whether the concept of criminalising environmental damage and destruction has become generally accepted outside situations of war.

Conclusion

This brief study describes a pragmatic approach to the examination of concepts by studying language and terminology as the linguistic expression of and reliable indicators for underlying conceptual thinking. Language is essentially an act of communication and reflects the way (legal) meanings are constructed, encoded and decoded. This feeds into a continuous interaction between the way laws create meaning in language and how language creates realities in law. The chapter has sketched out an approach and methodology that can contribute to the consolidation of a conceptual foundation for environmental policy, law and governance. The analysis of language and discourse provides in-depth and empirical knowledge beyond content analysis from the specific angle of observing the shifts in the semantic fields of the language and terminology. As mentioned, this is only a brief examination of a research question that could potentially cover vast amounts of texts and data.

---

[34] COHA, 400 million words, American English, 1810–2009, www.english-corpora.org/coha/
[35] COCA, 560 million words, American English, 1990–2017, www.english-corpora.org/coca/

From searching both the BNC and the ECOLEX database, we can observe that the instances of language relating to the effects of human activities on the environment has risen exponentially since the late 1970s. This coincides with an increasing preoccupation with environmental protection issues, often sparked and encouraged by major environmental policy events or initiatives to codify environmental principles, such as the UN Conference on the Human Environment in Stockholm in 1972 or the Earth Summit in Rio in 1992, just to cite two early examples. In this process of rapid expansion in the discourse, the language and terminology used often evolves by adapting existing terms to new concepts or by creating neologisms.

In this chapter, we have examined diachronically three such terms – environment, ecology, ecocide – by using corpus linguistics and concordance-based methodologies that have allowed us to study the language in its textual context and offers the perfect basis for observations of language in use. We saw that the two first terms have a history of diverse meanings and the linguistic data has shown a clear tendency of how these terms were imported from the general language register and how their semantic fields gradually changed, signposting new conceptual thinking relating to the effect of human activities on the environment. These are excellent examples to illustrate how the change in, what functional linguists call, 'context of situation' conditions the encoding of other/ new meanings in language and terminology. Ecocide, on the other hand, is a neologism that was formed to describe a very new concept, namely the criminalisation of human activities that cause extensive damage to, destruction or loss of ecosystems. In this case, the change in context of situation has meant that new meanings are encoded in a new word. Future linguistic studies will reveal whether and how this term will undergo semantic shifts in meanings.

Concluding on a more general note, the approach and methodology adopted for this study are cognitive models that have allowed us to go beyond the conceptual and doctrinal framework of the law and gain a deep-level understanding of the origins and evolution of legal thinking and the terminology. Studying the language of the law from a diachronic terminological angle in combination with the basic premises of the *Begriffsgeschichte* approach, reveals the etymological, terminological and historical aspects of terms. Such knowl- edge of the emergence and evolution of terminology equips us with a better understanding of how to adapt and use it differently in the present and future. This may be relevant, for example, in the context of new and rapidly emerging bodies of law, extension of legal categories or legal language reforms. Furthermore, a linguistic and terminological approach also contributes to a better comprehension of the sociocultural content of concepts and language. This represents an important contribution to a better understanding of the differences or similarities between legal systems and between concepts/terminology across cultural, legal and linguistic divides. A better grasp of the origins and evolution of specific aspects or elements of the law or a legal system can contribute to a contextual approach for, among others, comparative law, legal translation or legal harmonisation projects.

References

Biber, D. (1993). Representativeness in corpus design. *Literary and Linguistic Computing* 8(4): 243–57.

British National Corpus (BNC) (2007). BNC XML Edition, www.natcorp.ox.ac.uk

Brunner, O., W. Conze and R. Koselleck (eds.) (2004). *Geschichtliche Grundbegriffe. Historisches Lexikon zur Politisch-sozialen Sprache in Deutschland*. Stuttgart: Klett-Cotta, 9 vols.

Butt, D., R. Fahey, S. Feez, S. Spinks and C. Yallop (eds.) (2000). *Using Functional Grammar. An Explorer's Guide*. Sydney: Macquarie University.

Dan Tarlock, A. (2003–04). Is there a there there in environmental law? *Journal of Land Use and Environmental Law* 19(2): 213–54.

Fairclough, N. (1992). *Discourse and Social Change*. Cambridge: Polity.

Fairclough, N. (1999). Linguistic and intertextual analysis within discourse analysis. In A. Jaworski and N. Coupland (eds.), *The Discourse Reader*. London: Routledge, 183–211.

Felber, H. (2001). *Allgemeine Terminologielehre, Wissenslehre und Wissenstechnik. Theoretische Grundlagen und philosophische Betrachtungen*. Wien: Termnet.

Fowler, R., B. Hodge, G. Kress and T. Trew (1979). *Language and Control*. London: Routledge.

Halliday, M. (1985/1994). *An Introduction to Functional Grammar*. London: Edward Arnold.

Higgins, P. (2010). *Eradicating Ecocide*. London: Shepheard Walwyn.

Higgins, P., D. Short and N. South (2013). Protecting the planet: A proposal for a law of ecocide. *Crime Law Social Change* 59: 257.

van Hoecke, M. and M. Warrington (2010). *Legal Cultures, Legal Paradigms and Legal Doctrine: Towards a New Model for Comparative Law*. First published 1998, reprinted in M. Del Mar, W. Twinning and M. Giudice (eds.), *Legal Theory and the Legal Academy*, Library of Essays in Contemporary Legal Theory, vol. III. Aldershot, UK: Ashgate, 291–332.

Hohfeld, W. N. (1913–14). Some fundamental legal conceptions as applied in judicial reasoning. *Yale Law Journal* 23: 16–59.

Koselleck, K. (1979). Begriffsgeschichte und Sozialgeschichte, in: Vergangene Zukunft. *Zur Semantik geschichtlicher Zeiten*. Frankfurt am Main: Suhrkamp.

Kress, G. and B. Hodge (1979). *Language as Ideology*. London: Routledge.

Laske, C. (2013). Translators and legal comparatists as objective mediators. In J. Husa and M. van Hoecke (eds.), *Objectivity in Law and Legal Reasoning*. Oxford: Hart, 213–28.

Laske, C (2020). *Law, Language and Change. A Diachronic Semantic Analysis of* Consideration *in the Common Law*. Leiden: Brill.

Mattila, H. (2012). Legal vocabulary. In P. Tiersma and L. Solan (eds.), *The Oxford Handbook of Language and Law*. Oxford: Oxford University Press, 27–51.

Mattila, H. (2013). *Comparative Legal Linguistics, Language of Law, Latin and Modern Lingua Francas*. Aldershot, UK: Ashgate.

O'Halloran, K. (2011). Critical discourse analysis. In J. Simpson (ed.), *The Routledge Handbook of Applied Linguistics*. London: Routledge, 109–25.

Reichardt, R., E. Schmitt, H. J. Lüsebrink and J. Leonard (1985–). *Handbuch politisch-sozialer Grundbegriffe in Frankreich 1680–1820*. Munich: Oldenbourg Wissenschaftverlag.

Ritter, J., K. Gründer and G. Gabriel (eds.) (1971–2007). *Historisches Wörterbuch der Philosophie*. Basel: Schwabe.

Saussure, F. de (1916/2005). *Cours de linguistique générale*. Paris: Payot & Rivages.

ECOLEX – The Gateway to Environmental Law, www.ecolex.org

Stoett, P. (2000). *Human and Global Security: An Exploration of Terms*. Toronto: University of Toronto Press.

Thompson, G. (1996). *Introducing Functional Grammar*. London: Arnold.

Part III
PERSPECTIVES

10

Rights of Nature, a New Perspective in Law

VALÉRIE CABANES

Introduction

Following the publication of the particularly alarming *Special Report: Global Warming of 1.5 °C* of the Intergovernmental Panel on Climate Change (IPCC) in 2018, and the *Global Assessment Report* of the Intergovernmental Science-Policy Platform on Biodiversity and Ecosystem Services (IPBES) in 2019, no political or economic decision maker can today deny the consequences of climate change and biodiversity loss (Hoegh-Guldberg et al. 2018; Brondizio et al. 2019). The Earth system, our common home, is being destroyed by industrial technologies that disrespect life, leading to mortgaging the living conditions of current and future generations. As stated by Will Steffen's team of researchers:

> The relatively stable, 11,700-year-long Holocene epoch is the only state of the Earth System (ES) that we know for certain can support contemporary human societies. There is increasing evidence that human activities are affecting ES functioning to a degree that threatens the resilience of the ES – its ability to persist in a Holocene-like state in the face of increasing human pressures and shocks.
>
> *(Steffen et al. 2015: 736)*

We have entered a new geological era shaped by human activity. This is the opinion of the Nobel Prize atmospheric chemist Paul J. Crutzen, who named this new era in 2000: the Anthropocene. The new epoch has no agreed start date, but Crutzen proposed, based on atmospheric evidence, to fix it at the time of the invention of the steam engine in 1780 (Crutzen and Stoermer 2000: 17–18). The Anthropocene can be seen as the outcome of a new age, that of capital; a new type of civilisation whose logic of profit guides every step. As a result, the climate has changed, biodiversity has collapsed, pollution has become omnipresent and the very conditions of life on Earth as we know them are threatened. Faced with these scientific facts and the corresponding state of alert, we can no longer remain spectators of our own demise. We need to fix new rules for living together with other species and ecological systems on Earth.

The Earth System is based on a complex set of exchanges that is subject to laws. We are a living species involved in this network of exchanges and should contribute to maintaining its dynamic and balance. Instead, we act as hostile elements, not only with respect to our matrix the Earth, but also among ourselves. We are at war with life. We are biting the hand that feeds us all and yet we close our eyes, eager for distractions, material accumulation and comfort, which give us the illusion of existing. We choose as the foundation of our societies, values and modes of functioning that which are contrary to the principle of interdependence specific to life, with the risk of threatening the essential natural elements such as the air and water. We create laws to protect 'the environment' as if the Earth's ecosystem were external to us, independent, as if the health of our planet did not condition ours. At best, we impose some duties towards it on ourselves, but we do not respect its rights. It is time to recognise the current ecocide, the destruction of our common home. It is vital to recognise the rights of Nature to exist, thrive and flourish.

The ontology grounding such an approach assumes a separation between Nature and culture, between wild spaces and humanised spaces. The anthropologist Philippe Descola explains that this distinction has no place in different cultures, notably Indigenous cultures, which consider that all beings – human, animal or animate – are subjects endowed with life and that all natural areas are inhabited places (Descola 2014: 187). Indigenous peoples do not dissociate their ancestry, existence and fate from all living things and the ecosystems in which they live (see also Chapters 3 and 6 in this volume). Contemporary natural sciences echoes elements of such an understanding, with the idea that humanity is one of the components of a larger system, a tangible reality, we call Nature. From that perspective and with the insight of political science and legal theory, the laws induced by political thought appear as a story that we tell ourselves, a narrative about which we agree, but whose rules are far from immutable (Pfersmann 2004: 55). As we become conscious of our collective biological reality, we should therefore question our failing narratives and ideologies.

10.1 The Crime of Ecocide in Law

Since the rise of multinational companies, corporate law and the rules of global trade have tended to prevail over human rights and disregard ecosystems, thus jeopardising the lives of generations to come. Based on scientific findings, we must have the courage to question our societal choices and the laws that govern us pragmatically. It is necessary to reaffirm the supremacy of human rights over trade law, but also to recognise that our fundamental rights are dependent on our compliance with higher standards defined by biological laws. If the conditions of life on Earth are threatened, how can we hope to ensure humanity's right to water, food, habitat or health?

Yet, no decision maker can be held accountable for destroying the conditions of life on the planet and this should be seen as an international crime. It is urgent to find ways to make industrial activity respect the Earth and its ecosystems, and to question the responsibility of managers and multinationals in the context of the current ecocide. Multinational companies not only benefit from criminal impunity for serious environmental violations but are also allowed to engage in activities which threaten global environmental security, activities supported by financial and political systems.

In the International Criminal Court's founding Rome Statute, damage to the natural environment is only mentioned in article 8, which defines war crimes. The ICC was established in 2002 to put an end to impunity in relation to the most serious crimes of concern to the international community. The Statute stipulates genocide, crimes against humanity and the crime of aggression. The definition of war crimes includes widespread, long-lasting and severe damage to the natural environment. However, there are currently no provisions to protect the environment from such harms during peacetime. In September 2016, Fatou Bensouda, the former ICC Prosecutor, expressed the wish to see the ICC's jurisdiction extended to environmental crimes in peacetime. She founded her opinion on the experience gained by the Prosecutor's Office over the past fourteen years, the experience of other national and international courts and tribunals, and on the legal framework and jurisprudence applicable to the court. In her office policy paper 'Case Selection and Prioritisation', the Prosecutor stated her intention to give particular consideration to prosecuting Rome Statute crimes 'that are committed by means of, or that result in, inter alia, the destruction of the environment, the illegal exploitation of natural resources or the illegal dispossession of land' (Office of the Prosecutor 2016: 14). The ICC Prosecutor thus invites us to take up a major legal challenge stating that the protection of human rights and the protection of the planet are intimately linked.

In fact, the challenge is much broader still if we want the Earth to remain habitable for future generations. In this case, we must also rethink the law in consideration of the long-term consequences of the deterioration of living conditions themselves, which requires us to think beyond humanity alone. Human laws should be integrated into a new remodelled scale of standards, in order to protect first and foremost life on Earth as we know it, which will ensure the transgenerational human right to life. Therefore, the crime of ecocide should be recognised as a distinct crime and be defined in such a way as to truly protect the climate, the remaining biodiversity on Earth, the soils we cultivate, the water we drink, and the air we breathe. Recognising ecocide as an international crime against the safety of the planet has become a moral imperative. This is also the wish expressed by five internationally renowned judges in a legal opinion issued on 18 April 2017, following the testimony heard at the Citizens' Monsanto Tribunal to which they had been invited in October 2016 in The Hague. Among other things, the opinion states:

> In this context, the fundamental value of environmental protection as enabling life on the planet and human wellbeing fully justifies the imposition of criminal sanctions for conduct resulting in serious environmental harm … The Tribunal is of the view that the time is ripe for proposing to set up the new legal concept of Ecocide and to integrate it in a future amended version of the Rome Statute establishing the International Criminal Court.
>
> *(International Monsanto Tribunal 2017: 45, 47)*

Given its severity and global implications, ecocide should be a crime subject to universal jurisdiction. The principle of universal jurisdiction derives from the assumption that certain crimes are so serious that they affect the international community, and consequently states have a duty, if not an obligation, to act in humanity's common best interest and take legal action against perpetrators of international crimes. In this case, state sovereignty cannot be claimed to avoid liability. British barrister Polly Higgins' (1968–2019) first proposal to the International Law Commission in 2010 on the crime of ecocide requests that those in superior positions should be held accountable; it could be a person, company, organisation, partner, or other responsible legal entity but also those who 'assist, support, advise, help' (Higgins 2010: 159). Another particularity of her proposal is that it shifts the focus from the point of view of the estimated risk and its probabilities to the potential consequences of ecocide. An activity with potentially disastrous consequences, even if the risk is considered minimal, should not be allowed. According to this view, strict liability is not only established by malicious intent but also by knowledge of the consequences of the individual or legal entity's action. This new international crime would allow, for the first time, the prosecution of companies and their directors, and most importantly prevent more disasters.

Therefore, the End Ecocide on Earth movement, which has been mobilised on the subject since 2013 in the footsteps of Polly Higgins, reiterates the call for the creation of the crime of ecocide. It only takes a single state to volunteer for any proposed amendment to the Rome Statute to be placed on the agenda of a General Assembly of 122 states parties, through the UN Secretary General. Although the ICC is not a UN body, it is part of the international crisis prevention and management system. Its framework is more favourable to the adoption of binding environmental standards because its member states are of equal status and are, moreover, in the vast majority of cases, victims of predation by multinational companies and the consequences of climate change. Many of them are waiting for a binding legal solution, as demonstrated by their support for the draft UN Treaty, obligating multinationals to respect human rights and the environment. In this perspective, the ICC is a key actor in adopting and implementing a peremptory norm of law, such as the prohibition of ecocide in order to guarantee peace and human security. Therefore in 2015 and 2016, the legal experts of the End Ecocide on Earth movement worked on a proposal of amendments, composed of seventeen articles to be integrated into the Rome Statute. Based on science, the crime of ecocide is precisely defined as are the modalities of its application. The crime of ecocide is characterised by 'severe damage to any part or system of the global commons, or to Earth's ecological system', which threatens the safety of the planet (End Ecocide on Earth 2016: 4). The proposal chooses to consider the protection of Nature, or more precisely of life as we know it, from an ecosystem perspective, by recognising the intrinsic rights of large vital ecosystems and their ecological subsystems. These large vital ecosystems must be recognised as global commons. Today, they are often natural areas over which no state has exclusive rights or legal ownership due to their nature (space, the Earth's atmosphere, etc.) or based on an international agreement (e.g. the 1959 Antarctic Treaty). Such commons include oceans and seas beyond territorial waters, the Arctic and Antarctic, transboundary rivers and migratory species. Their biodiversity must be preserved. The definition also includes the atmosphere, outer space, groundwater, biochemical cycles and gene pools that must be recognised and protected as global commons. It is also imperative to respect the biogeochemical cycles that compose the system of exchange of matter and energy on which all these ecological systems are based. By granting them the right to protection and regeneration, the global commons de facto obtains a legal status, which it had previously lacked, and which has allowed its pollution, overexploitation or degradation.

The safety of the planet is thus recognised as a new higher standard with a scope that goes beyond human security, with the former guaranteeing the latter. Industrial activity must be regulated at least by respecting standards defined according to the limits offered by the planet, those beyond which it becomes inhospitable. Indeed, the crossing of these boundaries would lead us to a 'tipping point' characterised by a process of irreversible mass extinction and catastrophic consequences for humanity (Barnowsky et al. 2012: 52). Encouraging the crossing of planetary boundaries should be recognised as an act of ecocide. To estimate the reality and seriousness of the charges, Barnowsky et al. propose to rely on the concept of 'planetary boundaries' as defined by an international team of twenty-six researchers, led by Johan Rockström of the Stockholm Resilience Centre and Will Steffen of the Australian National University, and recognised by the United

Nations as a relevant framework to determine the objectives of sustainable development. In 2009, the team identified nine processes and systems regulating the stability and resilience of the Earth system which together provide the living conditions on which our societies depend (Rockström et al. 2009: 472–75). Threshold values were defined for each of these processes or systems which must not be exceeded if humanity is to develop safely, that is, avoiding abrupt and unpredictable changes in the global environment. According to these scientists, climate change is linked to the integrity of the biosphere, which has 'fundamental limits'. When the biosphere is damaged, its erosion impacts the climate. The vegetation and soil no longer assume their critical role of direct climate control. In addition, they no longer ensure the functions of carbon storage and recycling. Deforestation results in the permanent local disappearance of clouds and rain. The loss of marine plankton jammed the carbon pump that is the Ocean. Since 2015, the Stockholm Resilience Centre has warned that anthropogenic perturbation levels of four of the Earth systems' processes/features (i.e. climate change, biosphere integrity, biogeochemical flows, land-system change) exceed the proposed planetary boundaries (Steffen et al. 2015). Other boundaries concerning the use of fresh water, ocean acidification, depletion of the ozone layer, atmospheric aerosols and chemical pollution need to be carefully respected. These boundaries are also interrelated. This means that the transgression of one of them may increase the probability of other boundaries being approached or transgressed. These planetary boundaries are part of a scientific approach but, if elevated to standards, they could be integrated into law to better reflect our interdependence with the Earth, and in order for us to live in Harmony with Nature. The ecosystem approach is a central principle in the implementation of the 1992 Convention on Biological Diversity. It offers a strategy for integrated natural resource management based on a holistic approach to managing biodiversity and its components. It involves managing resources at a scale and scope, in order to not only conserve the components of biodiversity, but also protect the essential processes and functions of the ecosystem of which they are part (e.g. nutrient cycling, carbon sequestration, supply of freshwater and food). The ecosystem approach recognises humans, with their cultural diversity, as integral parts of ecosystems. This approach involves managing ecosystems and natural resources in a way that reflects their intrinsic value, as well as the benefits they provide to humans, in a fair and equitable way (Secretariat of the Convention on Biological Diversity 2004).

In 2017, the Stop Ecocide Foundation took up the challenge and started diplomatic lobbying. Vanuatu and the Maldives called for the addition of the crime of 'ecocide' to the Rome Statute at the 18th Meeting of the ICC Assembly of States Parties in 2019, followed by Belgium a year later. In late 2020, at the request of interested parliamentarians from governing parties in Sweden, the Stop Ecocide

Foundation convened an Independent Expert Panel for the Legal Definition of Ecocide. It comprises twelve lawyers from around the world, with a balance of backgrounds and expertise in international, criminal, environmental and climate law. They worked together for six months, charged with preparing a practical and effective definition of the crime of 'ecocide'. The Panel was assisted by independent experts, and a public consultation gathered legal, economic, political, youth, spiritual and Indigenous perspectives from around the globe. The Ecocide definition, presented on 22 June 2021, marks a milestone in the global campaign to prevent future environmental disasters (Stop Ecocide Foundation 2021). The Panel looked at existing precedents in international treaty and customary law, and at the practice of international courts and tribunals, in particular in international criminal law. In the first place, the Panel recommended the amendment of a new preambular paragraph in the Rome Statute: 'Concerned that the environment is daily threatened by severe destruction and deterioration, gravely endangering natural and human systems worldwide'. This sentence provides a normative background for the new crime of ecocide. The formulation 'the environment is daily threatened' is based on the one used by the International Court of Justice in its Advisory Opinion on the Legality of the Threat or Use of Nuclear Weapons, dated 8 July 1996. In that case, the court recognises that 'the environment is under daily threat' and affirms that the 'environment is not an abstraction but represents the living space, the quality of life and the very health of human beings, including generations unborn', and further confirms that 'the general obligation of States' to ensure protection of the environment forms a part of the corpus of international law.

The Panel then provided a definition of ecocide: 'unlawful or wanton acts committed with knowledge that there is a substantial likelihood of severe and either widespread or long-term damage to the environment being caused by those acts'. Allowing the states parties to the Rome Statute to meet current challenges, this definition offers a new and practical legal tool. Each term was chosen thoroughly in the perspective of qualifying an event as a crime:

- 'wanton' means with reckless disregard for damage which would be clearly excessive in relation to the social and economic benefits anticipated;
- 'severe' means damage which involves very serious adverse changes, disruption or harm to any element of the environment, including grave impacts on human life or natural, cultural or economic resources;
- 'widespread' means damage which extends beyond a limited geographic area, crosses state boundaries, or is suffered by an entire ecosystem or species or a large number of human beings;
- 'long-term' means damage which is irreversible, or which cannot be redressed through natural recovery within a reasonable period of time;

- 'environment' is understood as the Earth, its biosphere, cryosphere, lithosphere, hydrosphere and atmosphere, as well as outer space.

The Panel recognised that defining the 'environment' (or 'natural environment'), has proved to be challenging in international law. To date, there is no single agreed definition of these terms. The Panel decided to adopt an Earth-centred approach, considering that criminal law may require greater clarity and specificity. For this purpose, the term used the same definition as the one given by Earth system science, encompassing the Earth and the interactions between its five main spheres which interact in complex ways, but also the outer space. An ecosystemic governance is, therefore, vital to protect the Earth's system as a whole by ensuring that none of its components are overexploited. Unlike the existing four international crimes, ecocide would be the only crime in which human harm is not a prerequisite for prosecution. Moreover, the Earth system would become a subject of law.

10.2 Harmony with Nature and Earth Jurisprudence

In 2009, under the leadership of the Plurinational State of Bolivia, intergovernmental negotiations were initiated at the UN on the principles of Harmony with Nature, which led to the UN General Assembly adopting the first Resolution on Harmony with Nature (A/RES/64/196). On 22 April 2010, the General Assembly held its first Interactive Dialogue on Harmony with Nature to commemorate International Mother Earth Day. The Dialogue session explored ways to promote a holistic approach to sustainable development in Harmony with Nature and facilitated the sharing of national experiences on criteria and indicators to measure the latter. The next such Dialogue session examined scientific findings on the impacts of human activities on the functioning of the Earth system. The General Assembly debated then, the year after, different economic approaches to further a more ethical basis for the relationship between humanity and the Earth. In 2014, key characteristics of a new, non-anthropocentric paradigm were developed in this process, and the Dialogue session identified strategies on how society subsequently would need to function consistent with this paradigm. In its 70th session, the UN General Assembly, adopted a seventh resolution on Harmony with Nature (A/RES/70/208) which, for the first time, initiated a virtual dialogue between, inter alia, experts on Earth jurisprudence worldwide. They were requested to submit a summary to the 71st session of the General Assembly, in order to inspire citizens and societies to reconsider how they interact with the natural world. On 1 August 2016, the first Experts' Summary Report on Harmony with Nature addressing Earth jurisprudence was published. The report, summarising the deliberations and recommendations of

120 experts who participated in the dialogues, recognises 'the intrinsic value of Nature and the need to shift our perceptions, attitudes and behaviors from anthropocentric or human-centered, to non-anthropocentric or Earth-centered' (A/71/266, 2). The report states that:

Currently, under most national laws, all non-human entities are considered as property. While it is not necessary to end the idea of property, the notion that a deed to property conveys with it the right to destroy an ecosystem needs to be changed. Decision-making should be based on a hierarchy of needs defined by the integrity of ecosystems and their ability to thrive. Policies based on this idea would require changes in how we regulate the use of natural resources, and how decisions are made.

The report also specifies that:

This is distinct from current environmental laws, which are ineffective based on the conceptual underpinning: such laws, including an endangered species listing system that cannot keep pace with current extinction rates; after-the-fact litigation that relies on proving individual loss with no obligation to restore ecosystems as systems; and an inability to bring cases on behalf of the injured environment as opposed to on behalf of human beings alone). These laws work by breaking ecosystems into separate parts, which is inconsistent with the fact that they are entwined and interdependent.

(A/71/266, 41–42)

The report explains that:

In the Earth-centred worldview, the planet is not considered to be an inanimate object to be exploited, but as our common home, alive and subject to a plethora of dangers to its health: this process requires a serious reconsideration of our interaction with Nature as well as support for Earth jurisprudence in laws, ethics, institutions, policies, and practices, including a fundamental respect and reverence for the Earth and its natural cycles.

(A/71/266, 2)

There is still a long way to go as our laws do not recognise the elements of nature as individuals. At best, we have started to consider animals as sentient beings or having dignity, but we are far from recognising that Nature has rights.[1] Earth jurisprudence (also known as 'Earth law') refers to an emerging theory of law, which recognises that ecosystems have the right to exist, thrive and evolve – and that Nature should be able to defend its rights in court, just like people can. The term was first used by cultural historian Thomas Berry, who argued that anthropo-centrism was the main cause of the ecological crisis. This implied the urgent need to radically rethink the place of humanity in the world, including a shift towards a

---

[1] The 1976 law in France on the protection of Nature refers to the quality of being sensitive towards animals (*Journal officiel de la République française* 1976). The Swiss Constitution grants dignity to animals and plants but we are far from recognising that Nature has rights (Federal Assembly of the Swiss Confederation 2003, art. 120).

law and governance centred on the Earth. For Berry, the universe is a communion of subjects, not a collection of objects. He advocates humans to see the world from other angles. Western political though, in particular the legacy from the Enlightenment and its conception of law focused on human well-being and respect for dignity, is based on the assumption that the human is the centre and culmination of the evolution of life, a being which can rule the Earth and exploit its resources for its own benefit (Berry 2015: 202). Ultimately, this conception of ourselves as a species is just a story, we tell ourselves. For Berry, our stories are our worldview. They support us and help us structure our world; and express our values and key relationships. In his book *The Great Work*, Berry says that the historic mission of our time is to 'reinvent the human' (Berry 1999: 159). To reinvent ourselves we need to redefine our role within the wider community woven by relationships between species and systems that support life. We must re-examine and change our role in the universe and on our planet. We must recognise the Earth as the primary source of law and consider the regional and local levels as participating bioregions of the life cycle. There are territories whose boundaries are not politically defined; rather, their geographical limits take into account both human communities and ecosystems.

10.3 Rethinking Our Relationship with Nature

In legal terms, the challenge is to find a way to integrate and reconcile the respective rights of all species and natural components, and to find out how to respect them under human laws, considering other laws and temporalities, such as geological and biological laws. In 1972, the year of the first Earth Summit, the lawyer Christopher Stone, anxious to preserve a redwood forest threatened by a project of the Walt Disney Company, wondered 'Should trees have standing?' (as per the title of his book) and proposed to grant rights to the natural environment as a whole by appointing a guardian of the natural object that would also be a guardian for future generations (Stone 1972). Our reframing of the question in the legal domain should also be extended to the meaning of words and concepts that we use.

If we take for example the concept of 'rights': when we think of rights, we usually think of human rights. But when Thomas Berry says, 'The rivers have river rights', he discusses rights in a new context (Berry 1999: 5). Their rights arise from their existence and are structured by the nature of this existence. In *Evening Thoughts*, Berry explains that the natural world's rights originate from the same source as the rights of humans: from the universe that brought them into being (2006: 149). Just as life is differentiated by species, the needs and rights of the different modes of being are differentiated. All rights are also species-specific and limited. Rivers have river rights. Birds have bird rights. Insects have insect rights. Humans have human rights. Difference in rights is qualitative, not quantitative. Therefore, recognising the rights of Nature means recognising the inalienable rights of living systems and species and their specific rights according to the role they play. An inalienable right is a right inherent to an individual by virtue only of what he or she is and therefore by virtue of his or her condition. It must be distinguished from individual liberties. Civil rights are accompanied by duties and linked to the capacity of free will. This is why Berry proposes that the rights of Nature be recognised in national constitutions and courts of law as intangible rights.

With the help of Thomas Berry and based on his reflections, South African lawyer and author of *Wild Law* Cormac Cullinan formulated certain principles to guide the development of this emerging body of law, called 'Earth jurisprudence' (Cullinan 2011b; 2011a: 8–9), as follows:

- The Earth Community and all the beings that constitute it have fundamental 'rights', including the right to exist, to have a habitat or a place to be, and to participate in the evolution of the Earth community.
- The rights of each being are limited by the rights of other beings to the extent necessary to maintain the other beings and the integrity, balance, and health of the ecosystems within which they exist.
- Human acts or laws that infringe these fundamental rights violate the fundamental relationships and principles that constitute the Earth community and are therefore illegitimate and 'unlawful'.

Humans must adapt their legal, political, economic and social systems to be consistent with the fundamental laws or principles that govern how the universe functions. Furthermore, these systems must guide humans to act in accordance with these laws or principles, which means that human governance systems at all times must take account of the interests of the whole Earth community and must:

- determine the lawfulness of human conduct by whether or not it strengthens or weakens the relationships that constitute the Earth community;
- maintain a dynamic balance between the rights of humans and those of other members of the Earth community on the basis of what is best for Earth as a whole;
- promote restorative justice (which focuses on restoring damaged relationships) rather than punishment (retribution); and
- recognise all members of the Earth community as subjects before the law, with the right to the protection of the law and to an effective remedy for human acts that violate their fundamental rights.

Today, recognising Nature as a subject of law is an idea driven by the Earth Law movement together with many organisations around the world; most of these are part of the Global Alliance for the Rights of Nature. This movement was born in the wake of the African Charter on Human and Peoples' Rights (1981) and the World Charter for Nature (1982). It is guided by the thinking and work of Thomas Berry, but also the philosopher Arne Næss, considered the founder of deep ecology and ecosophy, which identifies the ecological crisis as a symptom of the loss of the bond between human and Nature. Arne Næss was one of the first observers to point that our millennium dream to be free of 'natural' constraints is leading us to the abyss. We cannot survive without guaranteeing to other species and living systems their right to exist, and we must learn to look at the biosphere as a living organism worthy of respect that regulates the environment of the Earth. This does not mean that he personifies the Earth by giving it its own will, a criticism levelled at the work of scientist James Lovelock, who named the planet Gaia in reference to the Greek goddess. But Lovelock's Gaia theory has been hailed for allowing us to understand that the biosphere is an entity whose properties are greater than the sum of its parts. This can provide the justification for the readjustment of human laws to take into account the main mechanisms of the biosphere, which is a community of life whose interest takes precedence over individual interests. Lovelock's approach appears in the Amsterdam Declaration on science of the Earth system (2001), which proclaims that 'The Earth System behaves as a comprehensive self-regulating system including physical, chemical, biological and human components'.

In order to rethink our relationship with Nature, Berry, who is also a theologian, suggests we turn to ecological spirituality as exemplified by Hinduism, Buddhism, Confucianism and Taoism, and by Indigenous peoples' cosmologies, which promote respect for all life and consider it to be sacred. According to the sociologist Bruno Latour, we should search in cosmological narratives for the solutions implemented by our ancestors when they had to face great cataclysms (Latour 2017) and apply them to our situation. However, prior to this, we could draw on the experience of Indigenous peoples, when they succeed in preserving their culture in an immemorial territory and interact with the living in a way that preserves or even regenerates it. Through their social organisation, they also show us that values, such as sharing, solidarity and tolerance are necessary for human beings, not only to take care of each other, but also to respect all living beings and live in harmony with them. In this perspective, they favour two complementary levels of governance: community management and the respect of universal rules. This contrasts with the state, which is usually the preferred level of governance. However, the latter is wary of community aspirations and tends to hamper the development of a holistic vision of the world.

For Indigenous peoples, by building a way of thinking that is only concerned with ourselves, we have been uprooted from the Earth and its laws. And it is becoming obvious that we will not survive without also guaranteeing to other species and living systems their right to exist. Ancestral cosmogonies invite us to consider the Earth's ecosystem as a living organism (sometimes called Mother Earth or Pachamama) worthy of respect. This vision inspired the United Nations General Assembly Resolution 66/288 of 27 July 2012, entitled *The Future We Want*, which recognises that: 'planet Earth and its ecosystems are our home and that 'Mother Earth' is a common expression in a number of countries and regions'. State leaders then go on to explain: 'We are convinced that in order to achieve a just balance among the economic, social and environmental needs of present and future generations, it is necessary to promote harmony with Nature.' The resolution also adds: 'We call for holistic and integrated approaches to sustainable development that will guide humanity to live in harmony with Nature and lead to efforts to restore the health and integrity of the Earth's ecosystem.' Moreover, the General Assembly noted that 'some countries recognise the rights of Nature in the context of the promotion of sustainable development' (United Nations General Assembly 2012).

10.4 Upholding the Rights of Nature through Legislation

In Latin America, Ecuador was the first state to recognise the rights of Nature in its Constitution in 2008. Article 71 establishes that:

Nature or Pacha Mama [Mother Earth], where life is reproduced and exists, has the right for that existence to be respected entirely and for its life cycles, structure, functions and evolutionary processes to be maintained and regenerated.

(Constitución de la República del Ecuador 2008)

The precautionary principle is entrenched in order to prevent species extinction, destruction of ecosystems or any permanent alteration of natural cycles. Nature can be represented and defended in court by any individual, community, people or nation and has an inalienable right to restoration. Ecuador has also led the way in the application of these rights. Between 2011 and 2019, thirty-two court cases were brought in the interests of elements of Nature, either by civil society or the state, of which twenty-five were won (Derechos de la Naturaleza 2019). The first case, in 2011, was between the River Rio Vilcabamba and the province of Loja, which was planning the construction of a road disrupting the river's course, thus threatening the flooding of adjacent fields. The river won. In another landmark case, it concerned a 60-metre-high mangrove swamp in the Cayapas-Mataje Reserve won against an intensive shrimp-farming project, based on the swamp's invaluable ecological role for the coasts, its people and marine life. Another case was quite exceptional: the sharks of the Galapagos Islands won against a Chinese boat containing 300 tonnes of fish and 6,223 sharks fished for their fins. This judgment recognised the criminal nature of this fishing, and the captain and crew were jailed.

In 2010, Bolivia enacted a law as an annex to its Constitution, entitled Law on Mother Earth Rights (Gaceta Oficial del estado Plurinacional de Bolivia 2010). The same year, a first proposal in international law emerged during the World People's Conference on Climate Change and the Rights of Mother Earth, held in Cochabamba, Bolivia. The draft Universal Declaration of the Rights of the Earth, which establishes fundamental ethical principles to build a just, sustainable and peaceful global society in the twenty-first century, states that 'the Earth is alive, it is our common home and we must respect it for the good of all and future generations' and that 'to guarantee human rights, it is necessary to recognise and defend the rights of the Mother Earth and all its constituent beings'. Bolivia submitted the declaration to the UN General Assembly for its consideration.

Two years later, at its 2012 quadrennial meeting, the International Union for the Conservation of Nature (IUCN) adopted a resolution (WCC-2012-Res-100-EN) recommending the integration of 'the rights of Nature at all levels and in all areas of intervention' creating a 'strategy of dissemination, communication and defence of Nature's rights'. The resolution also supports the development and promotion of a 'Universal Declaration of the Rights of Nature' as a 'first step towards reconciliation between people and the Earth as the basis of our lives, as well as the foundations of a new civilizing pact' (IUCN 2012).

The necessity to recognise the inherent value of non-human beings to solve the ecological crisis has also been understood by other states and towns passing rights of Nature ordinances. Thanks to the help of US-based organisations like the Community Environmental Legal Defense Fund (CELDF) or the Earth Law Centre, more than thirty cities in the USA, starting in 2006, voted for charters recognising the rights of Nature (CELDF 2019). In 2014, Mexico's State of Guerrero adopted an amendment to its Constitution recognising the Rights of Nature. This was followed by Mexico City in 2017 (formerly Federal District of Mexico), whose new Constitution entered into force on 17 September 2018 (Estado Libre y Soberano de Guerrero 2016; Mexico City 2017). In June 2019, the Congress of State of Colima approved an amendment to its Constitution recognising the Rights of Nature (Blanca Livier 2019). In Brazil, the municipality of Bonito in the State of Pernambuco proceeded with an amendment to its organic law in this direction, followed by the municipality of Paudalho in 2018 (Estados Municípios de Pernambuco 2018; Câmara Municipal de Paudalho 2018).

In Africa, Nature's fundamental rights to be, to habitat, to evolve and regenerate are now formally recognised in Uganda's new National Environmental Act

(Republic of Uganda 2019). The Act grants Nature, its custodians in the form of local/Indigenous communities and their legal allies, the right to sue on its behalf, thereby increasing the legal avenues to hold corporations and other actors responsible for damaging Nature to account.

10.5 The Rights of Nature through Case Law

Courts of justice are often seized to protect rivers from pollution and it is mostly in this context that they create jurisprudence in favour of the Rights of Nature. In 2016, the Colombian Constitutional Court ruled that the Atrato River, which had been polluted by illegal gold mining, thereby sickening communities living on its banks, needed better care. The court decided for this purpose that the river is 'subject to the rights that implicate its protection, conservation, maintenance and in this specific case, restoration' (Republica de Colombia 2016). The suit also calls out the State for its neglectful behaviour and orders that the river be cleaned up. Along its course from the Western Andes Mountain range through Chocó's jungles, down to the Caribbean Sea, it receives water from more than fifteen rivers and three hundred streams and is becoming one of the most contaminated rivers in the country. The ruling also recognised the biocultural rights of riverside communities and their interdependence with the Chocó region (one of the ten biodiversity hotspots in the world and one of the regions most affected by the Colombian armed conflict, even today). The court officially appointed fourteen 'Guardians of the Atrato' belonging to riverside communities, two from each community (one male and one female) alongside the Minister of the Environment. The implementation of this decision in parallel with the ethnic chapter of the Peace Agreement and the Chocó Humanitarian Agreement constitutes the basis for peace building in this region of Colombia. Recognising the rights of Nature as a factor for peacekeeping seems an innovative strategy, in line with the idea that ecocide is a threat to peace and human security.

But sometimes judges lack clarity in their decisions. For example, in March 2017, the High Court of Justice in the State of Uttarakhand (northern India) decided to recognise the Ganges River as well as its tributary, the Yamuna, as a living entity, given the inefficiency of policies to address pollution (ELAW 2017). The court observed that the rivers have been the source of the physical and spiritual sustenance of people from time immemorial, that these 'rivers are breathing, living and sustaining the communities from mountains to sea' and decided to grant them legal personality. But the court defined legal personality in the same way as for humans. It recognised the Ganges and the Yamuna as persons with human rights but also duties. By assigning duties to the rivers, the judge did not apply Berry's recommendations on the specificity and limits of the rights of

Nature. In response, one member of the panel of personalities appointed to act as 'parents' of the Ganges referred the matter to the Indian Supreme Court to block the decision, on the grounds that he – as guarantor of rights, but also assuming duties of the river not to harm anyone – feared being held responsible in case someone drowned in the Ganges.

The High Court of Uttarakhand was more cautious in a second judgment in which it recognised all Himalayan ecosystems on its territory as legal subjects: for instance, the Gangotri and Yamunotri glaciers threatened by climate change; and rivers, streams, lakes, springs, waterfalls, and meadows, valleys, jungles and forests. The court recalled their intrinsic right to exist, maintain and regenerate their own vital ecosystems and not to be polluted (Indian Kanoon Website 2017). In 2018, the court recognised the rights of the animal kingdom, aquatic and avian included. These decisions had a snowball effect at the national and regional levels. On 4 May 2017, the Assembly of Madhya Pradesh State adopted a resolution declaring the Narmada river as a living entity, affirming that the river is the state's lifeline (Ghatwai 2017). While debating the resolution, Chief Minister Shivraj Singh Chouhan announced that a bill to provide a legal framework to the resolution would be brought in the Assembly. He said an officer or an organisation would be given the task of filing complaints on behalf of the river against persons indulging in crimes like illegal mining and the felling of trees.

In Bangladesh, on 30 January 2019, the High Court granted the Turag River the status of a legal person to protect it from encroachment and declared that this status would be applicable to all 450 rivers in the country. The Bangladeshi case had been filed by the Human Rights and Peace for Bangladesh non-governmental organisation in 2016 and concerned the destruction of the Turag through pollution and illegal construction along the river. According to The *Daily Observer* newspaper that followed the case, in 2017 the court ordered an investigation to find out whether there were any illegal structures remaining on the rivers. The court had also asked the authorities to make a complete list of all those implicated in river-filling. The listed individuals and firms became parties to the case. In the orders, the High Court said there would have been no need for it to judge the case if the authorities had properly followed previous court orders to save the four rivers in Dhaka – Buriganga, Shitalakkhya, Turag, and Balu. Consequently, the court justified its decision to grant the rivers legal personality and ordered the National River Protection Commission to serve as their guardian and as the guardian for other rivers (*Daily Observer* 2019). The court seemed to have understood the main goal of the Earth Law movement, which considers that it is no longer sufficient to seek remedy through post facto legal action once damage has already been done or to wait to see whether there are human victims. We need to prevent further degradation of the Earth's ecosystems in order to protect life in the long term in a non-anthropocentric way, which means recognising their intrinsic rights to exist, regenerate, evolve and play their role in the community of life.

This strategy has also been very well advocated by the Colombian Supreme Court in its historical judgment of May 2018 (Republica de Colombia 2018). The judges, seized by twenty-five young plaintiffs denouncing rampant deforestation in the Colombian Amazon forest, acknowledged that the country would face an imminent and serious danger, as deforestation was contributing to the greenhouse effect, transforming ecosystems and altering water resources. The court recognised the obligation of the state to protect not only citizens, but also other living beings, from the effects of climate change. It decided to recognise the plaintiffs' right to life and to a healthy environment, considering them as future generations possessing rights, and it granted legal status to the Colombian Amazon Forest. The rights to protection, preservation, maintenance and restoration were bestowed upon the latter. Though unborn people have no legal rights, the rights of Nature allow us to take into consideration the rights of future generations, human and non-human. The court took the view that those transgenerational rights confer on the present generation the duty to protect future generations.

10.6 Reconciling with Other Legal Traditions

Nature is considered to be property in almost every country's legal system. Considering something as property gives its owner the right to damage or destroy it. People and companies who 'own' natural ecosystems are largely allowed to use them as they wish, even if it means the destruction of the health and well-being of Nature. Indigenous peoples used to define their identity according to the characteristics of the territory to which they belong, but do not consider the territory as their property. They found it difficult to deal with the sacrosanct principle of ownership that Western people imposed on them. Since conquest and colonisation, Indigenous peoples aim to protect their environment through collective land rights, considering their individual rights as finding expression through the collective rights of the group. This can help in building a bridge between their representations of the world and Western law. Collective land rights provide double protection, that of Nature but also that of the customary right of humans to live on their ancestral land which they guard and respect.

The custodians and guardians of Sacred Natural Sites and Territories from four continents – namely Asia, South America, Africa, Australia and the Pacific – and from the countries of Mongolia, the Altai and Buryat republics of Russia, the Kyrgyz Republic, Colombia, Ethiopia, Australia and Papua New Guinea gathered in advance of the IUCN World Conservation Congress, held in Barcelona, Spain in 2008. They made a joint statement requesting legal recognition of sacred sites, territories and landscapes (Custodians of Sacred Natural Sites and Territories 2008). They asked the governments to recognise the full rights of Indigenous peoples to manage their territories in accordance with their traditional ways and customs, and to guarantee the permanence of culture and Nature. They recommended the adoption of appropriate legislation that recognises and endorses local ownership but does not force inappropriate regulation upon custodians. Their presence at the Congress helped secure IUCN Resolution 4.038 for the 'Recognition and conservation of sacred natural sites in protected areas'.

At the IUCN Congress in Hawaii in 2016, the Gaia Foundation promoted what became the most contentious motion, to stop 'environmentally damaging industrial activities and infrastructure development' that impact all protected areas, including sacred natural sites and territories and areas conserved by Indigenous peoples and local communities (Motion 26). It passed by more than 94 per cent of government and 98 per cent of civil society votes.

In Africa, in 2012, the African Custodial Communities made the following statement:

The whole Earth is sacred. Within the body of our Earth there are places which are especially sensitive, because of the special role they play in our ancestral lands. We call these places sacred natural sites. Each sacred natural site plays a different but important role like the organs of our body. All of life is infused with spirit. Sacred natural sites are embedded in territories, which relate to the horizontal, vertical and energetic domains. A territory includes plants, animals, the ancestors' spirit, all life in the land, including humans.

(Chennells et al. 2015)

After many years of advocacy conducted by the Gaia Foundation but also the African Biodiversity Network and partner organisations, the African Commission on Human and Peoples' Rights adopted a new resolution in May 2017 on the recognition and protection of natural sites and sacred territories, as well as on customary governance systems in Africa (African Commission on Human and Peoples' Rights 2017). Liz Hosken, Gaia Foundation's Director, explains that:

Indigenous peoples are facing increasing violation of their ancestral lands in the scramble for Africa's rich natural heritage. The current dominant legal system legitimizes the plundering of the planet. In this landmark resolution, the African Commission opens a space for decolonizing law and affirming plurilegal systems which recognize the Earth as the primary source of law, Earth Jurisprudence, the underpinning of customary governance systems.

(Gaia Foundation 2017)

Decolonising law is also at the roots of the ongoing negotiations between the Maori and the Crown, with great results. In July 2014, a law was passed in New Zealand recognising Te Urewera Park – the ancestral territory of the Tuhoe Maori tribe – as a 'legal entity' with 'all the rights, powers, duties and responsibilities of a corporation' (Department of Conservation of New Zealand 2014). In 2017, the New Zealand parliament signed agreements with other Maori tribes and clans who recognise Whanganui River as a living and legal entity, then recognised Mount Taranaki (New Zealand Government 2017a, 2017b). The agreement on the Whanganui between Ngāti Rangi – the tribe Iwi Maori and Hapu (clans) – and the Crown is particularly interesting. It recognises the Whanganui River as an indivisible whole, from its source to the sea, including physical and metaphysical elements giving life and healing to its environment and its communities. The regulation recognises it as constituting, in its essence, four core values (or *Te Toka Ngā Waiū-o-Te-Ika*): (1) the source of life and inspiration; (2) an interconnected whole; (3) a contribution to the future prosperity of future generations (*mokopuna*); (4) a source of food and power for the Earth and its inhabitants. The latter can benefit physically, spiritually, culturally and economically from the inherent ability of the water to be supportive of life. In return, the Iwi undertake to unite in protecting the river's interests, and to promote, help regenerate and raise its potential. The agreement states that the tribe may designate a person – *Te Punga Tupua* – to interact with ministers regarding matters relating to the implementation of the agreement (New Zealand Government 2017a).

In New Caledonia also, customary land law is challenging the state, in this case the French state. The 2014 Kanak Charter states that the 'lands, resources and the natural environment and related material and immaterial traditional knowledges form the natural heritage of the Kanak people, who is its protector for future generations' (Assemblée du Peuple Kanak 2014, art 80). In April 2016, on this basis and by the political power granted to the Kanak people by the Noumea Accord signed in 1998, the Loyalty Islands Province undertook the drafting process of a new environmental code named the CEPIL (*Journal Officiel de la République française* 1998). The first draft version recognised 'the unitary principle of life' (article 110–3), stating that 'man belongs to the natural environment that surrounds him and sees his identity in the elements of the natural environment which is the founding principle of Kanak society'. To reflect this view of life and of Kanak organisation, elements of Nature may be granted 'a legal status with rights of their own, subject to the laws and regulations in force' (*Journal Officiel de la Nouvelle-Calédonie* 2016). While the Kanak say they are willing to recognise the legal personality and rights of elements of Nature, they do not perceive the Rights of Nature as being opposed to their own rights as human beings. On the contrary, they think that customary land law is the most relevant law to protect the natural elements and to safeguard their clans' interests.

In Australia, after arduous negotiations, the aboriginal Wurundjeri people also managed to translate their customary law into positive law through the adoption of a new law, at the end of 2017 by the State of Victoria (Government of Victoria

2017). The law recognises the Yarra River as Wurundjeri ancestral territory (today in the heart of Melbourne), and as a living and indivisible entity deserving protection. The law also recognises the intrinsic link between the Wurundjeri people and the Yarra River, recognising the former as the guardians of the land and the waterway they call Birrarung.

Switching from customary law to codified law in order to obtain the means to resist industrial projects is an approach being adopted by several Indian nations in the USA too. In September 2015, the Ho-Chunk Nation in Wisconsin voted to enshrine the Rights of Nature in their Constitution after years of severe environmental impacts resulting from frack sand mining,[2] the transportation of oil from the Bakken field in North Dakota, and agro-industry. William Greendeer, who proposed the resolution, explains: 'The Ho-Chunk Nation has always respected the Earth, but we were made to adopt a constitution based on roman law that makes humans more important than everything else; by passing this resolution we are acknowledging how important nature is. We are just one part of Mother Earth, not the centre of it' (De la Terre 2015). Similarly, in 2017, the Ponca Nation of Oklahoma passed legislation recognising the rights of nature in response to its own fight against hydraulic fracturing. In 2019, the Yurok tribe in Oregon adopted a resolution establishing the rights of the Klamath River (Yurok Tribal Council 2019).

Last but not least, at the beginning of 2019, a new step was taken towards the construction of the rights of nature. For the first time, a plant species was recognised as a subject of law, specifically a species of wild rice. This white rice is an all-natural grain that grows wild in the clear, cold waters of northern Minnesota in the United States. It is harvested by hand by an Ojibwe community living on the White Earth Indian Reserve in non-motorised canoes to preserve it. The law of this sovereign nation guarantees its protection on and off reserve, over an area covering nearly 340,000 hectares, as well as the protection of the habitats on which it depends (White Earth Band of Ojibwe 2019: 19–21). According to this law, these rights have been recognised because 'it has become necessary to provide a legal basis to protect wild rice and freshwater resources … for future generations'. Manoomin's rights include: 'The right to clean water and its freshwater habitat, the right to a natural environment free from industrial pollution, the right to a healthy and stable climate, free from the impact of human-induced climate change, the right not to be polluted, patented and contaminated by genetically modified organisms.' It should be noted that the White Earth Band opposed Enbridge Energy's controversial Line 3 oil pipeline in north-central Minnesota. The US$2.6

---

[2] The name 'frac sand' comes from its use in hydraulic fracturing ('fracking'), a method used by oil and natural gas companies to produce natural gas, natural gas liquids and oil from unconventional, low permeability reservoirs such as shale.

billion pipeline is designed to transport oil from the Canada oil sands to the Enbridge terminal in Superior, Wisconsin. Although it would not cross the reserve, it would nonetheless cross the non-tribal waters where tribes have the right to hunt, fish and harvest rice under treaties. In October 2018, Enbridge filed an application for water quality certification for the pipeline with the Minnesota Pollution Control Agency. If the people of White Earth oppose certification, they can go to court – with this new law in hand – because wild rice is specifically mentioned in the 1855 treaty signed with the colonial power. 'Treaties are the supreme law of the country and we Chippewas have constitutionally protected property rights and usufructuary rights to hunt, fish, trap and gather wild rice' explained Frank Bibeau, Executive Director of the 1855 Treaty Authority, to Winona LaDuke, executive director of Honor the Earth in an interview for *Yes!* magazine. 'We understand that water is life for all living things and that the protection of abundant, clean and fresh water is essential to our ecosystems and wild habitats to support us and the Manoomin' (LaDuke 2019).

Laws deriving from the rights of nature prohibit human activities that may affect the capacity and the rights of ecosystems and natural communities to exist and flourish. In this sense, these laws might be in contradiction with property law. They might oppose any owner's right if it interferes in the functioning of ecosystems and natural communities whose existence depends on this property. They do not prevent living from and with nature, but they stop human activities that interfere with the vitality of these ecosystems and jeopardise their existence.

Conclusion

As we cannot expect to live in a healthy environment if we do not protect nature on a global scale, we cannot expect solidarity across our nation if it does not extend to international solidarity. No country can hope to protect its own population from war if it does not live in harmony with other populations. War is fuelled by the idea that there is a division between 'us' and 'them'. And this division occurs when resources are not available, where populations are increasing, sedentary lifestyle is the norm, and where some groups end up being favoured over others. As defended by sociologist and philosopher Edgar Morin:

States can play a decisive role, provided they accept, in their own interest to give up their absolute sovereignty over all major public utility problems especially the problems of life and death which are beyond their isolated competence. Anyway, the fertility of nation-states with absolute power era is over, which means it must not disintegrate, but respect by integrating them into sets and through compliance with the whole of which they belong . . .

A 'dialog' should now complementarize North, South, East, and West. Connectedness [reliance] and the wisdom of living together should replace disjunction.

(Morin 2001: 63)

This duty is not only in the hands of states, but also in the hands of each and every community. We could begin by reorganising ourselves into self-sustaining and self-managed structures to learn to be supportive, while cultivating universal values to respect our common humanity. It is also necessary that everyone agrees to live frugally, and that food resources are preserved and shared. It is a matter of applying to ourselves the systemic functioning of nature, to recognise that each member of the human community is of equal value and that everyone can contribute to maintaining the cohesion of the whole. It is time to experiment with modes of governance at a community level where everyone can be individually recognised for his or her own skills and personality and contribution to the collective wealth of the group, within which the rules to achieve social harmony are aligned with the ones to promote life in harmony with Nature. Those local rules must be aligned with two principles to avoid isolationism: one principle should promote the respect for the cultures concerned and the effectiveness of human rights through the implementation of solidarity in action; the other principle should promote the respect for the diversity of life forms and for universal values, keeping in mind the protection of the habitability of the Earth and the promotion of peace.

We, as human beings, should function as subsystems of a global ecosystem, like the functioning of life. It is from there that a new humanity reconciled with Nature can flourish. By living closer to each other, by associating ourselves instead of falling back on our private sphere, we could build stronger links of solidarity, but also participate more directly in democracy. For this to work, it would be necessary for communities to remain small, like the traditional social organisation of the first peoples, and at the same time adhere to universal values to guarantee peace. We need to rebuild universal and community levels of governance to stop the current ecocide by experimenting with new forms of consideration, consultation and collaboration with all beings, outside of our cultural frames of reference, that is to say new forms of caring and solidarity.

We cannot aspire to peace through war strategies. The way to peace is through a change of consciousness and approach as expressed in our relationship to others and what surrounds us. Denying our kinship with animals, plants and trees is a way to deny the biological reality that we are beings of Nature. This way of thinking has led us to believe in our supremacy in the scale of evolution, in our unlimited rights over the living world. As Casey Camp-Horinek, member of the Ponca Tribal Council, declared once as a call to all peoples: 'It is up to all humans to act because we speak for those who have no voice, for deer, cattle, those who fly … It is time to stand up for our people and defend the Earth' (Biggs 2017).

References

Barnowsky, A. D. et al. (2012). Approaching a state shift in Earth's biosphere. *Nature* 486 (7401): 52.

Berry, T. (1999). *The Great Work: Our Way into the Future*. New York: Harmony Bell Tower.

Berry, T. (2006). *Evening Thoughts: Reflections on Earth as Sacred Community*. San Francisco: Sierra Club Book.

Berry, T. (2015). *The Dream of the Earth*. Berkeley, CA: Counterpoint.

Chennells, Roger et al. (2015). *A Call for Legal Recognition of Sacred Natural Sites and Territories, and Their Customary Governance Systems*. Gaia Foundation, www .gaiafoundation.org/wp-content/uploads/2015/09/CalltoAfricanCommission-1.pdf

Crutzen, P. J. and E. F. Stoermer (2000). Global change newsletter. *The Anthropocene* 41: 17–18.

Cullinan, C. (2010). Earth jurisprudence: From colonization to participation. In Worldwatch Institute (ed.), *State of the World 2010: Transforming Cultures from Consumerism to Sustainability*. New York: Worldwatch Institute/Norton, 143–48.

Cullinan, C. (2011a). A history of wild law in Burdon. In P. Burdon (ed.), *Exploring Wild Law: The Philosophy of Earth Jurisprudence*. Kent Town: Wakefield Press, 12–23.

Cullinan, C. (2011b). *Wild Law*. Claremont: Siber Ink.

Descola, P. (2014). *Beyond Nature and Culture*. Chicago: University of Chicago Press.

Higgins, P. (2010). *Eradicating Ecocide: Laws and Governance to Prevent the Destruction of Our Planet*. London: Shepheard Walwyn.

LaDuke, W. (2019). The White Earth Band of Ojibwe legally recognized the rights of wild rice. Here's why. *Yes! Magazine*. 1 February, www.yesmagazine.org/planet/the-white-earth-band-of-ojibwe-legally-recognized-the-rights-of-wild-rice-heres-why-20190201

Latour, B. (2017). *Facing Gaia: Eight Lectures on the New Climatic Regime*. Chichester, UK: Wiley.

Morin, E. (2001). *Seven Complex Lessons in Education for the Future*. UNESCO.

Pfersmann, O. (2004). Les modes de la fiction: Droit et littérature. In F. Lavocat (ed.), *Usages et théories de la fiction: Le débat contemporain à l'épreuve des textes anciens (XVIe–XVIIIe siècles)*. Rennes: Presses universitaires de Rennes, 51.

Rockström, J. et al. (2009). A safe operating space for humanity. *Nature* 461: 472–75.

Steffen, W. et al. (2015). Planetary boundaries: Guiding human development on a changing planet. *Science* 347(6223): 736.

Stone, C. D. (1972). Should trees have standing? Toward legal rights for natural objects. *South California Law Review* 45: 450–501.

Legislation, Legal Cases and Documents

African Commission on Human and Peoples' Rights (2017). Resolution on the Protection of Sacred Natural Sites and Territories – ACHPR/Res. 372 (LX), www.achpr.org/sessions/resolutions?id=414

Assemblée du Peuple Kanak (2014). Charte du Peuple Kanak sur le Socle Commun des Valeurs et Principes Fondamentaux de la Civilisation Kanak, 26 April 2014, www .senat-coutumier.nc/phocadownload/userupload/nos_publications/charte.pdf

Câmara Municipal de Paudalho (2018). Emenda Ley organica # 3, 5 de janeiro 2018.

Constitución de la República del Ecuador (2008). Publicada en el Registro Oficial No. 449 of 20 octubre de 2008, http://pdba.georgetown.edu/Constitutions/Ecuador/english08 .html

Department of Conservation of New Zealand (2014). Te Urewera Act, Public Act No 51, 27 July 2014, www.legislation.govt.nz/act/public/2014/0051/latest/whole.html

Derechos de la Naturaleza (2019). Casos en Ecuador. Accessed 28 September 2019, www .derechosdelanaturaleza.org.ec/casos-en-ecuador/

ELAW (2017). *Salim* v. *State of Uttarakhand and others*, High Court of Uttarakhand, Writ Petition (PIL) No. 126 of 2014, opinion of 5 December 2016 and 20 March 2017, www.elaw.org/salim-v-state-uttarakhand-writ-petition-pil-no126–2014-december-5–2016-and-march-20-2017

End Ecocide on Earth (2016). Ecocide Amendments proposal, September 2016, http:// cop21.endecocide.org/wp-content/uploads/2016/10/ICC-Amendements-Ecocide-ENG-Sept-2016.pdf

Estado Libre y Soberano de Guerrero (2016). Estado Constitución Política del Estado Libre y Soberano de Guerrero, Fecha de publicación: 05 de enero de 1918, Última reforma incorporada: 8 de noviembre de 2016.

Estados Municípios de Pernambuco (2018). Emenda Lei Organica de 08 de Março 2018, No. 01/2017, Art. 1o–O art. 236 da Lei Organica del Município de Bonito. Diário Oficial do Estado Municípios de Pernambuco ANO IX | No. 2034.

Federal Assembly of the Swiss Confederation (2003). Federal Act on Non-Human Gene Technology, 21 March 2003, status as of 1 January 2018, www.admin.ch/opc/en/ classified-compilation/19996136/index.html

Gaceta Oficial del estado Plurinacional de Bolivia (2010). Ley de los derechos de la tierra madre, 21 diciembre 2010 (071), http://bolivia.infoleyes.com/norma/2689/ley-de-derechos-de-la-madre-tierra-071

Government of Victoria (2017). Yarra River Protection (Wilip gin Birrarung Murron) Act 2017, No. 49.

Indian Kanoon (2017). *Lalit Miglani Versus State of Uttarakhand and others*, High Court of Uttarakhand, Writ Petition (PIL) No. 140 of 2015, 30 March 2017, http:// indiankanoon.org/doc/92201770/

International Monsanto Tribunal (2017). Advisory Opinion, The Hague, 18 April 2017.

Journal Officiel de la Nouvelle-Calédonie (2016). Adoption du Code de l'environnement de la province des îles Loyauté [Adopting the Environmental Code of the Province of the Loyalty Islands], Deliberation No. 2016–13/API 6 April 2016. JONC 9290s, 5941, http://files.harmonywithnatureun.org/uploads/upload704.pdf

Journal officiel de la République française (1976). Act 76–629, 10 July 1976, amendment 28 November 2019. See at www.legifrance.gouv.fr

Journal Officiel de la République française (1998). Accord sur la Nouvelle-Calédonie signed in Nouméa on 5 May 1998. JORF 121, 8039. See at www.legifrance.gouv.fr

Mexico City (2017). Constitución Política de la Ciudad de México 5 de Febrero 2017, No. 1. Gaceta Oficial del Distrito Federal.

New Zealand Government (2017a). Agreement in principle to settle historical claims between Ngati Maru and the Crown, 20 December 2017, www.govt.nz/dmsdocu ment/7262~Ngati-Maru-Agreement-In-Principle-20-December-2017.pdf

New Zealand Government (2017b). Deed of settlement between the Crown and Ngati Rangi, www.govt.nz/treaty-settlement-documents/ngati-rangi/

Office of the Prosecutor (ICC) (2016). Policy paper on case selection and prioritisation, 15 September 2016, www.icc-cpi.int/itemsDocuments/20160915_OTP-Policy_Case-Selection_Eng.pdf

Republica de Colombia (2016). Sentencia T-622/16, diez noviembre de dos mil Dieciséis. Corte Constitucional de Colombia, www.corteconstitucional.gov.co/relatoria/2016/t-622–16.htm

Republica de Colombia (2018). Radicación 11001–22–03–000–2018–00319–01, cinco de abril de dos mil dieciocho. Suprema Corte de Justicia, files.harmonywithnatureun.org/uploads/upload605.pdf

Republic of Uganda (2019). National Environment Act, 24 February 2019, Section 4: The rights of Nature.

Stop Ecocide Foundation (2021). Independent expert Panel for the Legal Definition of Ecocide. *Ecocide Definition. Commentary and Core Text*, 22 June 2021, https://static1.squarespace.com/static/5ca2608ab914493c64ef1f6d/t/60d1e6e604fae2201d03407f/1624368879048/SE+Foundation+Commentary+and+core+text+rev+6.pdf

United Nations General Assembly (2012). The Future We Want (Resolution 66), www.un.org

White Earth Band of Ojibwe (2019). Rights of Manoomin, Resolution 001–19–009, http://whiteearth.com

Yurok Tribal Council (2019). Resolution of the Yurok tribal council establishing the rights of the Klamath river, no. 19–40, 9 May 2019, http//files.harmonywithnatureun.org/uploads/upload833.pdf

Reports and Other Documents

Brondizio, E. S., J. Settele, S. Diaz and H. T. Ngo (2019). Global assessment report on biodiversity and ecosystem services of the Intergovernmental Science-Policy Platform on Biodiversity and Ecosystem Services. IPBES Secretariat, Bonn.

Custodians of Sacred Natural Sites and Territories (2008). A statement of custodians of Sacred Natural Sites and Territories, Barcelona, Spain, 6 October 2008, www.silene.ong/wp-content/uploads/2018/10/Custodians_Statement_Barcelona_2008.pdf

Hoegh-Guldberg, O. et al. (2018). Impacts of 1.5 °C global warming on natural and human systems. In *Global Warming of 1.5 °C, an IPCC Special Report on the Impacts of Global Warming of 1.5°C above Pre-industrial Levels and Related Global Greenhouse Gas Emission Pathways, in the Context of Strengthening the Global Response to the Threat of Climate Change, Sustainable Development, and Efforts to Eradicate Poverty*. Geneva: Intergovernmental Panel on Climate Change, ch. 3.

IUCN (2012). Incorporation of the Rights of Nature as the organizational focal point in IUCN's decision making (WCC-2012-Res-100), http://portals.iucn.org/library/node/44067

NASA Advisory Council, Earth System Sciences Committee (1986). Earth system science overview: A program for global change. National Academies.

Secretariat of the Convention on Biological Diversity (2004). The Ecosystem Approach (CBD Guidelines). Montreal: Secretariat of the Convention on Biological Diversity.

Press Releases and News

Biggs, S. (2017). Ponca Nation of Oklahoma to Recognize the Rights of Nature to Ban Fracking, 1 November 2017. Movement Rights, www.movementrights.org/ponca-nation-of-oklahoma-to-recognize-the-rights-of-nature-to-ban-fracking/

Blanca Livier (2019). Colima hace historia: reconocen los Derechos de la Naturaleza en la Constitución, http//lancalivier.wordpress.com/2019/06/10/colima-hace-historia-reconocen-los-derechos-de-la-naturaleza-en-la-constitucion/

CELDF (2019). Rights of Nature. FAQS. Accessed 28 September 2019, http://eldf.org/rights/rights-of-Nature/rights-Nature-faqs/

De la Terre, J. (2015). Ho-Chunk Nation Gives Rights to Nature. 19 September 2015, http://therightsofnature.org/wp-content/uploads/Ho-Chunk-Nation-R-of-N-pressrelease-09-2015.pdf

Gaia Foundation (2017). Success at international and regional policy level – IUCN and African Commission resolutions, www.gaiafoundation.org/what-we-do/sacred-lands-and-wilderness/regional-international-advocacy/

Ghatwai, M. (2017). Madhya Pradesh Assembly declares Narmada living entity. *Indian Express*, 4 May 2017, http://indianexpress.com/article/india/madhya-pradesh-assemblydeclares-narmada-living-entity-4639713/

Staff Correspondent (2019). River rights commissions appear to be dummy bodies: HC. *Daily Observer*, 1 February 2019, www.observerbd.com/details.php?id=181041

11

Property for Nature

Introduction

While there is some consensus as to the existence of an environmental crisis and the need to protect the integrity of Nature (Bégin 1992), Western jurists disagree about how to resolve this crisis and the theoretical foundation for a sustainable solution. Relying on the theoretical movements of biocentrism and ecocentrism – particularly Thomas Berry and Peter Burdon's *Earth Jurisprudence* (Burdon 2011) and Aldo Leopold's 'Land Ethic' (2012) – this chapter seeks to identify possible solutions that property law could provide with respect to current environmental challenges, by adapting its fundamental concepts to the polymorphism of environmental issues.

Studies have confirmed that common law and civil law are deeply anthropocentric.[1] Under an anthropocentric vision, all that surrounds human beings, namely the natural environment, exists solely for their pleasure and benefit (Bégin 1992: 399). Writers from this line of thought believe that only human beings are worthy – or even capable – of morality (Bégin 1992: 399; Larrère 2010: 406). To put it in Kantian terms, humanity has intrinsic value as it is 'an end in itself'.[2] Some proponents of anthropocentrism have adopted a consequentialist logic, in which Nature is simply considered a 'sum of resources' that merely has instrumental value for human beings (Larrère 2010: 406–07). This is the dominant approach in contemporary Western societies. For example, legislation regarding air or water pollution primarily aims to protect human health and economic growth (Burdon 2015: 5).[3]

In reaction to this anthropocentrism, the philosophical reflection of the 1970s gave rise to the development of diverse branches of moral philosophy, which

---

* This chapter is a modified version of a paper that was published in French 'Vers une reconceptualisation des droits des biens face aux défis environnementaux' (2017) 119 R.d.N. 321.
[1] For the common law, see Burdon (2015: 5–7); Warren (2009: 50). For the civil law, see David (2012: 475).
[2] Larrère (2010: 406–07), translation by author; Kant (1993: 39).
[3] Similarly, parks and green spaces are created first and foremost for human enjoyment: Thiele (1999: 183–84).

sought to create an environmental ethic by integrating Nature within the field of morality (Larrère 2010: 405). The main idea of these philosophical perspectives was that human beings maintained a relationship to Nature and therefore owed duties and obligations towards it (Larrère 2010: 405; see also Bégin 1992: 402). The major schools of thought within environmental ethics, such as biocentrism and ecocentrism, have been adopted by some jurists, mainly from the common law tradition, in an attempt to respond to the environmental crisis (Burdon 2015: 6–9; Stone 1972; Bégin 1992). Similar work has yet to become prevalent in the civil law.

Biocentrism – of which the main proponents are Norwegian philosopher Arne Næss, associated with the deep ecology movement, and American philosopher Paul Taylor – holds that every living entity on Earth has intrinsic value (Larrère 2010: 407; see also Larrère and Larrère 2007: 23; Næss 2005: 18). Biocentrism could help conceptualise the protection of Nature. However, this movement does have limitations, particularly its failure to recognise the value of non-living entities. This could be problematic because protecting nature generally requires consideration of living beings and ecosystems as a whole, and not simply consideration of specific entities in isolation (Larrère 2010: 407–08). Ecocentrism goes a little further, recognising that Nature as a whole has intrinsic value. American philosopher and pioneer of ecology Aldo Leopold was the first to articulate this theory in Western parlance. For Leopold, human morality has historically been extended in concentric circles: from the individual to the family, to the village, to society, and then to humanity. The next step is to extend morality to the biosphere, namely the idea of land ethic (Leopold 1987: 203–04).

These ideas were developed by authors such as Thomas Berry and jurist Peter Burdon (2015: 1). These two authors conceive of the Earth as a community whose members are all interdependent and interconnected (Burdon 2015: 65, 111). Humankind is only a part of a greater whole, which itself bears moral value (Burdon 2015: 10, 47). Thomas Berry argues that law plays a central role in the environmental crisis (Burdon 2015: 1). In his view, '[t]he present legal system is supporting exploitation rather than protecting the natural world from destruction by the relentless industrial economy' (Burdon 2015: 1). Relying on this idea, Peter Burdon contends that a 'paradigm shift' from anthropocentrism to ecocentrism is necessary (2015: 1, 6–7, 49).[4]

---

[4] Burdon relies on the work of philosopher Thomas Kuhn, who argued that a paradigm can only work 'so long as the tools a paradigm supplies continue to prove capable of solving the problems it defines'. Following this logic, property should evolve if, in its current state, it is incapable of effectively responding to the environment crisis that is negatively affecting property and property rights.

Building on the works of authors from the biocentric and ecocentric movements, particularly those of Burdon, this chapter proposes a paradigm shift or, at the very least, a change of perspective in property law, such that it is no longer analysed in purely anthropocentric terms. More specifically, this chapter proposes a reconceptualisation of property law situated somewhere between anthropocentrism, biocentrism and ecocentrism. Property law concepts, particularly ownership, would thus be transformed to account for human beings and their relationship with Nature.

The concept of property is central in our relationship to Nature because it delineates simultaneously what can and cannot be done to things and resources. Given an unprecedented environmental crisis, it is necessary to reflect on the notion of ownership and more generally on property law to determine if these concepts are suitable to address environmental issues. Should Nature itself have rights, and should it be personified so that it would be better protected? Should private property be abandoned in light of these issues, or should we simply modify its narrative? What role should patrimony, a fundamental concept in the civil law, play in the protection of Nature? These are some of the challenges that contemporary property law calls us to address. Moreover, since the environment is a global issue, this reflection must be conducted in both the common law and civil law.[5] While such reflection is well underway in the common law (Burdon 2015: 6–7; Grinlington 2011), little has been written on this topic in the civil law,[6] and even less work has been conducted from a comparative point of view.

Ownership in the common law, if not a vague concept, is at least more flexible than its civil law equivalent. The image of a bundle of rights seems more adaptable to environmental issues than civilian ownership. Title in the common law is often described as relative, which more easily allows other parties to be taken into account (on this point, see especially Debruche 2008). By contrast, the civil law frequently describes ownership as an absolute right over an object. In its most extreme form, no one but the owner has any say with regard to the object of ownership. However, this vision of ownership in the civil law is increasingly falling out of favour. Civilian ownership is not merely an individual right but one that exists within a social context. Today, the absolute nature of ownership is frequently called into question, exceptions to absolutism being so numerous that they arguably have become the rule (Trotabas and Renard 1930: 40).

---

[5] While the two main legal systems throughout the world are the common law and the civil law, there are other types of legal systems (Glenn 2014).

[6] See however the works of François-Guy Trébulle, especially (2007: 659, 674–75). See also Bergel (2001); Zenati-Castaing (1993).

Confronted with different environmental challenges, jurists, particularly property law specialists, are especially well placed to try to respond to the environmental crisis. Since environmental problems are multifaceted, different types of responses can be envisioned. In this chapter, I begin by building on the theory that Nature should be granted personhood and subjective rights, a solution that has notably been suggested by proponents of Earth jurisprudence. I propose a modified version of this theory in which Nature would be the subject of legally protected interests. Next, I offer a reconceptualisation of ownership and its narrative in view of environmental issues, proposing a conception of ownership that is relational, socially limited and functional. Finally, I demonstrate how property law, and more specifically concepts complementary to ownership, such as common patrimony and patrimony by appropriation, can be used to better protect nature as part of a commitment to sustainable development.

11.1 From Subjective Rights for Nature to Nature as a Subject of Legally Protected Interests?

In this section, I begin by examining the theory of the personhood of Nature, which stems primarily from the biocentric and ecocentric movements (Section 11.1.1). Then, I demonstrate that it is clearly possible to recognise Nature as a subject of legally protected interests (Section 11.1.2).

11.1.1 The Theory of Personhood and Subjective Rights for Nature

The theory of the personhood of Nature is widespread, particularly due to the influence of authors from the areas of earth jurisprudence and land ethic. While the theory of personhood and subjective rights has merit in that it allows for better protection of Nature, it nonetheless propagates a way of thinking that furthers a certain anthropocentric vision. While this theory does not place human beings at its centre, its main premises, personhood and subjective rights, are still human-centric. Moreover, this theory can be problematic in the civil law. In this legal tradition, the recognition of legal personhood traditionally implies the recognition of a patrimony,[7] which could cause some difficulty with regard to Nature.

Some authors from the Earth jurisprudence movement, which developed in the United States in the early 2000s, claim that the solution to the current environmental crisis is to give Nature subjective rights. These authors have largely relied on the biocentrism and ecocentrism movements to argue that Nature

---

[7] Under the traditional theory of patrimony by Aubry and Rau, every person has a patrimony, and there is one patrimony per person (1873: 229); Normand (2014a: 17–18).

itself can have moral value and hold subjective rights (Burdon 2011: 6–9; Stone 1972; Bégin 1992).

According to proponents of biocentrism, each living organism considered in isolation is worthy of morality (Næss 2005; Larrère 2010: 407). Each organism, whether a human being, an animal or even a plant, is an equally integral part of the natural order. This school of thought recognises that there are differences between living species but focuses less on these differences and more on the similarities between biological creatures. Therefore, biocentrism brings to the forefront the need to respect each element making up Nature, as human beings are only one living species among others, which, together, form a terrestrial ecosystem (Taylor 2011: 68–69). As indicated by Catherine Larrère, proponents of biocentrism grant each living entity an intrinsic value, and thus a right to protection (2010: 407), which legally translates to subjective rights for these different entities.

Proponents of ecocentrism go a bit further, assigning intrinsic value to the 'biotic community', namely living and non-living entities – of which humankind is only one element – and not only to distinct living entities and resources as suggested by biocentrism (Bégin 1992: 402; Larrère 2010: 408). Ecocentrism thus adopts a more holistic approach, emphasising the 'interdependence between different elements and their common belonging to a greater whole'.[8] The theoretical approach of ecocentrism recognises that Nature as a whole has intrinsic value (Bégin 1992: 402; Larrère 2010: 408). This theory can also serve as a theoretical foundation for granting subjective rights to Nature.

Professor Christopher Stone was the first to legally articulate these theories, by proposing that rights be attributed to the environment and that it have the capacity to take legal action to assert its rights. As early as 1972, the American jurist suggested that natural resources and living entities (like trees) and non-living entities (like mountains) would be better protected if they were granted (subjective) rights and a form of legal capacity or legal personhood (Stone 1972). According to Professor Stone, just because forests cannot talk does not mean that they should not be recognised under the law, and judges would be more sensitive to the protection of Nature if a tree could ask for compensation in its own name (Stone 1972: 17). Nature would be represented by a 'guardian' or representative – already the case for ordinary citizens with legal problems, protected adults without legal capacity, and legal persons (corporations, states, municipalities or universities) (Stone 1972: 17). This would make proving harm to a resource easier as the injury would be more direct, and damages could be directly awarded to the resource itself instead of third parties (Hutchison 2014: 182).

---

[8] Larrère (2010: 408), translation by author.

In *Sierra Club* v. *Morton*, 405 US 727 (1972), the US Supreme Court held that such arguments had merit, through the dissenting opinion of the famous Justice William O. Douglas. In this case, Sierra Club brought a lawsuit to halt the construction of a ski resort at Mineral King valley, in the Sierra Nevada Mountains in California, so as to preserve the beauty and ecology of the region. Sierra Club tried to claim that the project would have a negative effect on the general public. The court rejected this argument, finding that Sierra Club only had the capacity to represent Mineral King valley under section 10 of the American Administrative Procedure Act, 5 USC §§ 701ff., if it could demonstrate that the club itself had suffered injury, which it had not succeeded in doing. Despite this decision, Justice Douglas held in his judgment that natural resources should have legal status and standing to assert their own protection.[9]

The recognition of subjective rights is traditionally linked to legal personhood (meaning one must be a legal person to have subjective rights) (Hermitte 2011: 196–98). Legal personhood must imply legal standing so that people can assert their rights (Parquet 2007: 22). Therefore, the question arises as to how Nature can have rights and assert them before the courts, if it has neither legal personhood or legal standing.[10] The position of the subjective rights theory is as follows: the act of granting subjective rights or legal standing to Nature is a precondition to Nature being able to suffer injury (given that it has become a holder of subjective rights) and to the injury being considered direct (rather than indirect, as is the case when the claim is instituted by a third party). At the same time, this theory allows a representative to assert Nature's rights before the courts.

In his thesis published in France on the legal notion of nuisance, Francis Caballero (1981), influenced by the ideas of Christopher Stone, also considered that legal standing for the elements of Nature was necessary to their protection. Building on this idea, Professor Marie-Angèle Hermitte suggested making Nature a subject of law under French law, as a way of reconciling humankind and nature, human beings being a part of Nature and not the other way around (1988: 254–55). For Hermitte, ecosystems should enjoy the status of a legal subject,[11] and independent guardians should have the role of protecting and exercising their rights (2011: 174).

Over the last ten years, Ecuador and Bolivia have carried out legal and constitutional developments regarding environmental protection unparalleled by other countries (David 2012: 470). In 2008, Ecuador adopted a new constitution making 'Mother Earth' (Pachamama) a subject of law, with different fundamental

---

[9]   *Sierra Club* v. *Morton*, 405 US 727 (1972), 741.
[10] Traditionally in the civil law, only people can be subjects of law: Hermitte (2011: 174).
[11] Moreover, Hermitte emphasises the privileged position of legal subjects (of which physical and legal persons are only examples) while characterising its status as synonymous with legal personhood (2011: fn. 8).

rights. In 2009, Bolivia adopted similar provisions in its Constitution, which was then amended by the Law of the Rights of Mother Earth[12] in December 2010 (David 2012: 470). These two countries thus gave 'Mother Earth' a constitutionally protected right to life and restoration.[13] Moreover, every person has standing to request that governmental authorities enforce these rights.[14] However, the implementation of such protection may be difficult, particularly since the law is unclear regarding the procedures to follow (Whittemore 2011: 666). Furthermore, the text of Ecuador's Constitution is vague, which makes it vulnerable to a restrictive interpretation (Whittemore 2011: 669). Yet, an overly strict application of these provisions could impede important developments in this area (Morris and Ruru 2010: 58).

In the same vein, legal personhood has been granted to a river in New Zealand (Hutchison 2014: 179). On 5 August 2014, the New Zealand government and representatives of the Whanganui Iwi people signed Ruruku Whakatupua, a settlement agreement granting legal personhood to the Whanganui River, the third largest river in the country. Under the agreement, the Whanganui River can sue those who harm it and has two official representatives, one from the Whanganui Iwi and one from the Crown (Davison 2017). On 15 March 2017, the New Zealand Parliament passed the agreement into law (Davison 2017). The personification of Nature is not a novel concept in the Maori culture, which is reflected in their traditional proverb, 'I am the river, and the river is me'[15] (Morris and Ruru 2010: 49). A number of authors have stated that legal personhood is a good model in this context as it articulates a personified conception of the world within existing legal institutions and reconciles Maori and New Zealand legal systems (Morris and Ruru 2010: 50). These authors have also suggested that such an approach forces decision makers to give importance to the preservation of the health and well-being of nature resources, such as rivers (Morris and Ruru 2010: 57).

The idea of personifying Nature and granting it subjective rights can take different forms, varying according to cultural and legal context. Ultimately, the essential task is to find tools appropriate to a given context, tools that would effectively protect Nature. From a civil law perspective, giving Nature subjective rights raises the issue of whether it should have a patrimony, even though Nature is not traditionally recognised as a person. Yet, having a patrimony would mean that

---

[12] Ley de derechos de la madre tierra, 21 December 2010, no. 071.
[13] Constitution of the Republic of Ecuador, 2008, arts. 71–72; Constitution of the Plurinational State of Bolivia, 2009, preamble.
[14] Constitution of Ecuador, 2008, art. 71; Constitution of Bolivia, 2009, arts. 33–34; see also David (2012).
[15] More broadly, for a personified and relational narrative of Nature, its elements and animals in the context of the Anishinaabe Nation, see Borrows (2016: 828); Anker (2017).

Nature would be capable of not just having rights but also obligations.[16] While identifying Nature's obligations is not a straightforward task (Bouchard 1997: 168; Hermitte 1988: 199), some authors have contemplated that such obligations could exist and would be the responsibility of the state (Hermitte 1998: 200; David 2012: 472, 479–80). According to Hermitte, the state would take on this responsibility as 'manager of the nation's biological patrimony'.[17] Even if Nature could be considered to have obligations, the question arises as to how certain rights held by Nature could also belong to individuals and the state. Moreover, things that are traditionally non-commercialised, such as air and water, are generally considered common property[18] and therefore do not belong to any patrimony as they fall outside of the realm of the appropriable. Thus, giving Nature a patrimony would give rise to significant challenges in view of the current state of the law.

We can also consider whether giving Nature or its elements legal personhood would truly represent a clean break from the anthropocentric paradigm. After all, this approach makes Nature more like a person. At the very least, this form of ecocentrism is tainted with anthropocentrism. Furthermore, regardless of the number of rights conferred on Nature, humans would continue to grant themselves rights. Finally, Nature's rights could only be defended and asserted by human beings, using human institutions. Therefore, anthropocentrism seems somewhat inevitable.

11.1.2 Nature as a Subject of Legally Protected Interests?

Despite the traditional link between personhood and the status of legal subject, it is nonetheless possible to consider Nature as new subject of law, without it being a person. Moreover, while legal personhood is typically associated with the subjective rights given to a person as a subject of law, under a less anthropocentric vision, it is possible to suggest that Nature would hold, not subjective rights, but rather legally protected interests.

First, Nature can be envisioned as a subject of law, even if it is not a person.[19] Although the idea that Nature could be considered a legal subject was proposed in French law by Hermitte, she did not go as far as to eliminate all connection between the status of legal subject and legal personhood. While Hermitte uses the

---

[16] On the idea that patrimony, in its proper sense, implies obligations in addition to assets, see Smith (2008: 383). On the traditional conception of patrimony and its connection to legal personhood, see Aubry and Rau (1873: 229).

[17] Hermitte (1998: 300), translation by author.

[18] CCQ, art. 913, with the exception of air or water 'collected and placed in receptables' (para. 2); see also Normand (2014a: 68–69).

[19] For French law, see Hermitte (2011). For Québec law, see Bégin (1992). On the technical nature of the concept of the subject of law, see Demogue (1909: 611). On subjectless rights and subjects without rights, and the existence of subjectless rights in Quebec, see Popovici (2016); Marty and Raynaud (1972: 261).

terminology of 'subject of law' and acknowledges that subjects of law constitute a primary category for personhood, she suggests the procedural personification of Nature and its elements to ensure its protection (2011: 197). Despite Hermitte's terminology, her position remains connected to the idea of giving Nature subjective rights and its personification.

The possibility of recognising a new subject of law, distinct from physical and legal persons, has already been proposed in Quebec civil law in relation to trusts (Cantin Cumyn 2002: 142).[20] For Professor Madeleine Cantin Cumyn, rather than considering a trust to be a patrimony by appropriation with no subject, it is possible to consider the trust to be the holder of the patrimony by appropriation constitutive of the trust (Cantin Cumyn 2002: 142; see also Cantin Cumyn 2010). The trust would not be a legal person but rather a legal subject, with rights and obligations related to its trust patrimony (Cantin Cumyn 2002: 138–39; Cantin Cumyn 2010). While yet to be affirmed by trusts law jurisprudence, the approach of viewing Nature as a new subject of law seems to have sufficient legitimacy from a theoretical point of view as it places on an equal plane legal persons, moral persons, and Nature, a 'non-person' (Cantin Cumyn 2010; Bégin 1992: 7) whose interests deserve strong legal protection. The solution of giving Nature (or even its elements) the status of a legal subject would mean that Nature could be granted subjective rights, without necessarily being conceptualised as a person. This approach has the advantage of being theoretically similar to current legal concepts and therefore relatively easy to implement, even if it remains partially connected to subjective rights, a concept initially developed for (human or legal) persons.

It is no doubt possible to distance ourselves further from the traditional framework of subjective rights and anthropocentric conceptions of law, by recognising Nature as a subject of legally protected interests. This would imply another rupture with traditional legal concepts, as it would involve re-examining the opposition between legal subjects and legal objects (see Chapter 8 in this volume). The notion of legally protected interests was developed in Quebec by Brierley and Macdonald, in the context of trusts.[21] Under this perspective, in which trusts are detached from the notion of real rights, one must think in terms of legally protected interests, beyond the dichotomy of real and personal rights. Indeed, legally protected interests go further than real and personal rights for the very reason that they exist outside the traditional

---

[20] On the conception of subjects of law, see Savigny (1840: 7); Jhering (1888). See also Dijon (1981–82: 86).

[21] See Brierley (1995: 46), who states that 'trusts draw their guiding principles from a different kind of analysis' (translation by author) as the legal relationships that are created through the implementation of a trust can be considered to give rise to powers and duties for the trustee and legally protected interests for the beneficiary and settlor, rather than real or personal rights. See also Macdonald (1994: 802–03). On this point, see also Popovici (2016: 143); Chardeaux (2006: 329, 504).

notion of subjective rights, real and personal rights making up a part of the broader category of subjective rights.

From a theoretical point of view, recognising Nature as a subject of legally protected interests allows us to escape from a purely anthropocentric vision of law. Nature could be granted its own interests, and while these interests would be managed by humans, they should be administered for interests other than those of their managers. From a technical point of view, the legally protected interests of Nature or its elements can be managed by a representative guardian or by an administrator of the property of others (these interests potentially constituting an autonomous patrimony, based on the model of the trust patrimony in the Civil Code of Quebec (CCQ)). Administration of the property of others could serve as a template for managing interests, which can be done in the context of a trust[22] or by property designated for the protection of Nature. Human beings would look after Nature's interests or act as guardian of these protected interests. On the spectrum between anthropocentrism and ecocentrism, this solution is somewhat removed from anthropocentrism.

11.2 Towards a Transformation of Property and Its Narrative?

A number of advocates for the Earth jurisprudence movement have claimed that private property is incompatible with any transition from an anthropocentric paradigm to a ecocentric one (Cullinan 2007) and that Nature should be given subjective rights (Burdon 2015: 102–03). According to certain ecosocialist authors, private property should just simply be abandoned (Lowy 2008: 165–66; Kovel 2011; Tanuro 2012; Durand-Folco 2015: 98–100). A link is established here between the abolition of ownership and rights for Nature.[23] Using the reasoning of Marx or Proudhon, some advocate for the abolition of private property, potentially forming a movement of liberation identical to that of African-American slaves. This movement is less about re-examining mechanisms for distribution of wealth, such as common property, and more about considering ecosystems to have interests independent from those of human beings and therefore to be worthy of independent protection (Burdon 2015: 102–03). However, this philosophical movement would involve a radical change to the design of current Western societies. Moreover, there does not seem to be a logical connection between subjective rights for Nature and the destruction of property. It

---

[22] See Section 11.3, regarding the possibility of creating a trust, a patrimony by appropriation in a technical sense, to protect the elements of Nature.

[23] Traditional societies developed an idea of collective and transgenerational property on their own, not in reaction to the modern notion of property: see notably Chapters 3, 6 and 15 in this volume.

is no doubt possible to adopt a less radical theory to better protect Nature and the environment.

To better contribute to the protection of Nature and to find a sustainable solution to the environmental crisis, a reconceptualisation of property can be envisioned in both the common law and civil law, moving away from an absolutist and purely anthropocentric conception of property rights.[24] In addition to changing the narrative of property, I consider that the idea that property rights are absolute is largely a myth (Section 11.2.1) and propose a transformation of the concept of property (Section 11.2.2).

11.2.1 Recognising Limits to Private Property

The first necessary step towards recognising environmental issues and positive reconciliation between property law and environmental law seems to be the recognition of external limits to private property. Yet, in the civil law, the recognition of limits to property has traditionally conflicted with viewing ownership as an absolute right (Pavageau 2006: 114–15; Zenati-Castaing 1993: 310).

Civilian ownership is commonly defined as having a real right directly in a thing (Normand 2014a: 83; Carbonnier 2000). This right has traditionally been viewed as an absolute right, perhaps even the most absolute of all rights (Pavageau 2006: 114–15). Conceptualised as an absolute right towards the end of the eighteenth century, this conception of ownership was codified in French civil law,[25] in the belief that Roman law recognised the right of ownership as an absolute subjective right. Following the French Revolution in 1789, the right of ownership was elevated to the ranks of fundamental human rights (Sayin et al. 2017: 11; Strickler 2006: 299) and was conceived of as the 'free power that human beings exercise over things' (Pavageau 2006: 114). During codification, this conception of ownership became enshrined in article 544 of the French Civil Code of 1804 (CC), which confirms that '[o]wnership is the right to enjoy and dispose of things in the most absolute manner' (art. 544 CC) thus supporting an absolutist vision of the right of ownership (Pavageau 2006: 115; Goldstein 1990).

The idea that civilian ownership is an absolute right without limits is largely a myth. As one author recently stated, this myth 'was built on an erroneous interpretation of Roman law texts. [Roman law ownership] has been made out to be a limitless power over things, when it simply granted owners full prerogatives

---

[24] On the difference between the modern conception of property rights and *proprietas* in Roman law, see Chapter 8 in this volume.

[25] Liberal ideas, inherited from Enlightenment philosophy which spread at the time throughout continental Europe began to influence the legal sphere. See Sayin et al. (2017: 11); Pavageau (2006: 114).

over their property.'[26] The Roman conception of ownership (*dominium*) referred to full power over things (*plena in re potestas*) (Sayin et al. 2017: 11) even before the emergence of the concept of subjective rights.[27] In fact, article 947 of the Civil Code of Quebec has modified the definition of ownership to characterise it as a free and full right and not as 'the most absolute' of all rights. Moreover, much like its counterpart, article 544 of the French Civil Code, article 947 contemplates that ownership, by its very definition, is subject to 'limits and conditions ... so determined by law'.[28] Therefore, although ownership is defined in French civil law as 'the right to enjoy and dispose of things in the most absolute manner', it is nonetheless limited by competing statutes and the presence of others.

Positive law increasingly challenges the absolutist conception of ownership. In both Quebec and French civil law, there are a growing number of legal and regulatory limits to ownership, such that we might wonder whether the exceptions to a traditional rule regarding the absolute character of ownership has indeed become the principle.[29] Neighbourhood disturbances is a good example of limits to ownership in the civil law. In *St. Lawrence Cement Inc.* v. *Barrette*, 2008 SCC 64, [2008] 3 SCR 392, the Supreme Court of Canada had to adjudicate a class action regarding neighbourhood disturbances related to dust and noise from a cement plant. In this case, the court held that:

Even though it *appears* to be absolute, the right of ownership *has* limits. Article 976 C.C.Q. establishes one such limit in prohibiting owners of land from forcing their neighbours to suffer abnormal or excessive annoyances. This limit relates to the result of the owner's act rather than to the owner's conduct. It can therefore be said that in Quebec civil law, there is, in respect of neighbourhood disturbances, a no-fault liability regime based on art. 976 C.C.Q. which does not require recourse to the concept of abuse of rights or to the general rules of civil liability. With this form of liability, a fair balance is struck between the rights of owners or occupants of neighbouring lands.

(para. 86 [author's italics])

Wallot v. *Québec (Ville de)*, 2011 QCCA 1165, is another interesting example in which limits to ownership related to environmental protection clearly arise. In this case, the City of Quebec adopted a by-law forcing riparian landowners to grow vegetation on their shorelines to protect the supply of potable water. The Quebec

---

[26] Pavageau, 2006: 114, translation by author.

[27] On this point, see the works of Michel Villey, especially (1946).

[28] Under French Civil Code, art. 544: '[o]wnership is the right to enjoy and dispose of things in the most absolute manner, provided they are not used in a way prohibited by statutes or regulations'. While the Civil Code of Lower Canada, art. 406 reproduced verbatim this definition, CCQ, art. 947 states that '[o]wnership is the right to use, enjoy and dispose of property fully and freely, subject to the limits and conditions for doing so determined by law'.

[29] See the new wording at CCQ, art. 947 which no longer uses the phrase 'absolute right'. On the growing number of limits to property, see especially Lafond (2005: 303); Bergel et al. (2010: 139). See also Pichette (1990); Goldstein (1990).

Court of Appeal did not characterise this by-law as expropriation, emphasising its environmental protection objective, which justified imposing positive obligations on owners.[30] By this decision, the Court of Appeal seems to recognise the legitimacy of the state's role, if not as a fiduciary, at least as a guardian of the environment.[31]

In the common law, the idea of limited ownership is recognised without much difficulty. In this tradition, ownership and property are commonly defined as a bundle of rights or as a bundle of rights and obligations (Hamill 2012: 367; Orsi 2014: 372; Cribbet 1986; Arnold 2002; Williams 1998: 356). The fact that property is generally described as relational in the common law implies an automatic recognition of other parties to the relationship, which facilitates consideration of limits in relation to land. Moreover, the common law remains connected to the theory of tenure, which limits the powers that one can have in land (Arnold 2002: 284; Byrne 2005: 682).[32] Furthermore, it is widely accepted in the common law that individuals do not have so much a right of ownership in land as an estate in land (Graziadei 2017: 77–79).

The modern concept of property viewed as a bundle of rights and obligations could be better adapted to an environmental perspective. As explained by Craig Anthony Arnold, the concept of a bundle of rights is one-dimensional. It only deals with legal relationships between individuals and does not consider the relationship between people and the environment (Arnold 2002: 282). This one dimensionality can be seen as contradictory to the principle of interconnectivity between humans and their environment, which has been advocated by Leopold in his land ethic theory (1987). Moreover, some argue that the bundle-of-rights concept aggravates the environmental crisis, by protecting the private and independent use and exploitation of land and natural resources (Arnold 2002: 318). A reconceptualisation of private property and its narrative can thus be contemplated, in the common law and civil law.

11.2.2 *Towards a Transformation of the Concept of Property?*

In both the common law and civil law, one of the most controversial issues stemming from an environmental perspective of property law concerns the reconceptualisation of property rights. Legal innovations and transformations are part of a normal evolution, and they are desirable in a legal tradition that is seeking

---

[30] *Wallot* v. *Québec (Ville de)*, 2011 QCCA 1165, para. 53, citing *Canadian Pacific Railway Co.* v. *Vancouver (City)*, 2006 SCC 5, para. 33.

[31] *Wallot* v. *Québec (Ville de)*, 2011 QCCA 1165, para. 19; Cantin Cumyn (2010: 605).

[32] On the theory of tenure, see especially Moynihan and Kurtz (2005: 4); van Erp (2006: 13–14).

to adapt to social changes. However, these changes are shaped by existing rules and institutions and can take many years to materialise (Doremus 2011: 1094–96).

In the common law, the first reconceptualisation of the concept of ownership occurred during the twentieth century. This led to the development of the bundle-of-rights metaphor (Arnold 2002: 286). This metaphor redefined property as the different legal relationships between individuals, namely a bundle of rights and obligations, and replaced the old definition of property as absolute dominion over things, proposed by Blackstone (1979: 2; Orsi 2014: 372; Arnold 2002: 286). This reconceptualisation of property is attributable to American realists and pragmatists who sought to liberate ownership from its absolutist character. The idea of having absolute power over property has been in decline in American jurisprudence since the end of the nineteenth century, and this decline accelerated after Blackstone's writings were published (Arnold 2002: 286). Since then, the bundle-of-rights metaphor has largely been accepted in the common law world, especially in the United States, though it has been the target of numerous critiques in recent decades (Orsi 2014: 372; Klein and Robinson 2011: 194–95; Penner 1996; 1997: 1; Merrill 1998).

Since the current liberal conception of ownership has contributed to the modern environmental crisis, it may be time to re-examine this narrative. According to New Zealand jurist Burdon, our relationship with Nature must evolve to respond to environmental issues. Since property rights are an essential element of this relationship, they cannot remain unchanged (Burdon 2015: 15–45). Burdon proposes conceiving of our relationship to Nature as a relationship between subjects rather than one between subject (humans) and object (Nature) (2015: 107). Although this position might seem radical as it calls into question the distinction between legal subjects and objects, it nonetheless represents a shift in thinking that not only emphasises limits to property but that also offers a renewed vision of what is appropriable. In this context, limits to property can be seen as part of the very essence of property.

The alternative conceptualisation of property in the common law proposed by Burdon is connected to an ecocentric narrative, which takes into account the fact that we belong to the Earth community, which is more fundamental than membership within any human society. The idea of Earth community 'seeks to transcend the subject/object dichotomy and to place human beings firmly within the web of life' (Burdon 2015: 65). This community has its own normativity, a form of natural law that Burdon, under the influence of Thomas Berry, calls 'great law'. Great law acts as a measure of human law or as a form of natural law (Burdon 2015: 79–80). Burdon defines private property as 'a human institution that comprises a variety of relationships among members of the Earth community, through tangible or intangible items' (2015: 107). For human beings, property 'is characterised by the allocation to individuals or groups of individuals of a degree of control over the use, alienation and exclusivity of scarce resources, as well as a measure of obligation and responsibility to all members of the Earth community in the exercise of the property right'.[33]

This redefinition of property is based on the traditional definition of property in the common law as a bundle of rights or a bundle of rights and obligations, but it also accounts for our membership within an Earth community that is broader than the human community, by imposing on the latter obligations stemming from membership within this community. Thus, property is not only a relationship between human beings but also a relationship between *human and non-human subjects*. Property is no longer an individual right but a social relationship between subjects of law or subjects of legally protected interests, some of which are non-human. This relationship imposes on owners non-reciprocal obligations, as a necessary condition of a mutually beneficial relationship with the Earth community (Burdon 2015: 111). Such a reconception of property is clearly removed from anthropocentric justifications.

It is no doubt possible to transpose this redefinition of property into a civil law context. It is possible to have such a conception of property and ownership in the civil law and common law, even if this analysis is not founded on the traditional conception of civilian ownership. The first step would be to consider that ownership is relational, in both the civil law and common law (Emerich 2008: 339, 355, 376). As indicated by Planiol and the personalists, real rights are not so far removed from personal rights because with real rights, the whole world except the owner has an obligation to not interfere with the owner's right (Planiol and Ripert 1926: 41). Ownership can therefore be seen to impose an obligation on everyone to refrain from interfering with right holders and their property.

The second step would be to recognise limits to property as part of its very essence, as it is a right that exists within a social context. In other words, limits are not extrinsic but *intrinsic* to property. Under the theory of social obligation, property has a social aspect and rights are inseparable from the obligations associated with them (Emerich 2011: 30).[34] As stated by Gregory Alexander, the right to receive and the obligation to give are connected to dependence of individuals on their community (Alexander and Penalver 2009).

While the theory of social obligation is generally associated with the common law, it is nonetheless reflected in the civil law. Civil law scholars including Jhering (1893: 101) and Josserand have also written about the social implications of ownership. As Josserand astutely noted, even in the civil law, positive obligations

---

[33] Burdon, 2015: 107 [author's italics].
[34] On the social function of ownership in the civil law, see generally Duguit, 1912: 150. See also Duguit, 1923: 664.

are increasingly imposed on owners, given that they are members of society.[35] Indeed, the social dimension of ownership must adapt to its context. It is thus possible to conceive of this social aspect of ownership as comprising an ecological dimension.

Furthermore, the social function of property implies a better harmonisation between private and collective property, as property can no longer be considered solely an individual interest but can also be analysed in view of the collective interest. A re-examination of the concepts of private and collective property and their interaction can be useful in finding a solution to the environmental crisis, in both the common law and civil law. This would address the critique of property as necessarily facilitating the private and independent exploitation of land.[36] Caroline Guibet Lafaye proposed a model to reconcile private and collective property regimes (Lafaye 2016: 1249–50). For Guibet Lafaye, we need to stop being prejudiced against collective property, which has been considered undesirable since the end of the eighteenth century (Lafaye 2016: 1232; see also Vanuxem and Lafaye 2015: 9). A reconciliation of the private and collective property regimes would allow individuals to continue being private property owners. However, some goods would be considered 'common', shared among different actors and available to the community (Lafaye 2016: 1250). Ultimately, this re-examination of private and collective property would change the way that we use, share, and preserve the environment and its natural resources (Lafaye 2016: 1249–50). The environment and its natural resources can be held as a form of collective property, placing a common obligation on all members of the community to preserve these resources.[37]

If, from a theoretical point of view, the social function of property can be asserted, this justifies, from a technical point of view, using property to fulfil certain social functions. This is the theory of functional property.[38] In the same

---

[35] Josserand:

> This social function of ownership, which the Civil Code has obscured, has been rediscovered in case law through the concept of abusive exercise of rights. Its social function calls for reexamination of this supposedly absolute and sovereign right. [It makes ownership the centre of an increasing number of positive obligations imposed on the owner]. It makes ownership more flexible and socialises it by attributing to ownership a specific purpose depending on the environment where the right is being exercised and on the object of ownership.
>
> (1927: 41, translation by author)

[36] On the possibility of obligations in the context of property, see especially Lametti (2003); also Moyse (2012). On this critique, see above.

[37] To this end, Professor Gaële Gidrol-Mistral has highlighted the decline of individual property and the emergence of collective property through a form of community property in Québec civil law (Gidrol-Mistral 2016: 140).

[38] See Trébulle (2006), arguing that land ownership must be conceptualised according to function rather than power.

way that property can serve certain technical functions, such as being used as security (Crocq 1995), designated or targeted property can be used as a way to protect Nature and its elements. In particular, this could allow for fiduciary ownership to apply to environmental matters in French law. While designated property has been used for secured transactions in French law, it is entirely possible for property, under a social rather than individual conception, to be used for environmental objectives. This could help justify limitations on the powers that owners have over their property and perhaps even explain positive obligations.[39]

A definition proposed by Burdon affirms that owners have an obligation towards all members of the Earth community in exercising their rights of ownership. That such an obligation is characteristic of property is an interesting idea. As is extending community, not only to other people (such as other owners or neighbours), but also globally to members of the 'Earth community'. Contrary to traditional perspectives, this community could be described as Nature, of which human beings are only a part. Thus, a relational conception of property can go as far as to integrate, not only other human beings, but also Nature and its elements.

Burdon characterises property by looking to the *degree of control one has over the use, disposition and exclusivity of rare resources.* Such a description of property can be refined as it is less of a definition than a characterisation. Ultimately, property can be redefined as *a relationship of exclusivity in relation to things, which includes certain limits in the form of duties and obligations stemming from membership within a community and from the collective interests that characterise this community.*[40] From an environmental point of view, this community should no longer be necessarily comprised of only legal subjects with personhood (traditionally other people) but also non-person, non-human subjects of rights and of legally protected interests, such as Nature or its elements. This perspective is situated at the intersection of ecocentric and biocentric perspectives and recognises that Nature as a whole has value, as do its parts. Not only does this conception of property go beyond anthropocentrism, it can also be harmoniously reconciled with attempts to recognise Nature as a subject of law, or a subject of legally protected interests.

---

[39] For a theoretical foundation for this assertion, see Alexander (2013); Lametti (2010). For an example of practical application of this concept, see *Wallot* v. *Québec (Ville de)*, 2011 QCCA 1165.
[40] On the definition of property as a relationship of exclusivity, see Zenati-Castaing (1993: 308); Emerich (2011: 31). On the possibility of duties and obligations within the concept of property, see Emerich (2011); Alexander (2013).

11.3 The Polymorphism of Patrimony: The Adaptation of Patrimony to Environmental Issues

In this section, I argue that the notion of common patrimony, whether it is the common patrimony of humankind or of the province of Quebec, can be useful, given its symbolic significance, to advance the sustainable development of Nature. Moreover, the concept of patrimony can play an instrumental role in environmental protection, particularly through the concept of a trust patrimony by appropriation. I first discuss the symbolic function of the concept of patrimony (Section 11.3.1) before considering its technical role (Section 11.3.2).

11.3.1 The Symbolic Function of Patrimony

While the image of the common patrimony exists in international law as a common patrimony of humankind (Section 11.3.1.1), it is also a concept in national law, which is demonstrated, for instance, by the common patrimony of Quebec (Section 11.3.1.2).

11.3.1.1 The Common Patrimony of Humankind

On the international scene, the notion of patrimony has undergone a significant transformation in an attempt to address environmental issues. The notion of a common patrimony of humankind was formed around the Roman law concept of *res communes*, which was combined with the doctrine of common property, developed by Thomas Aquinas during the Middle Ages.[41] In the seventeenth century, Diego Suarez applied these notions to international law to make common goods belong to humankind (Rémond-Gouilloud 1989: 149). In the twentieth century, the modern notion of a common patrimony of humankind was affirmed in international environment law.[42]

The common patrimony of humankind was described in the 1990s as the 'new spearhead of planetary ecology'.[43] This notion charged humankind with responsibility for managing natural resources and protecting the environment to ensure its present use, and more importantly, its sustainability for future generations (Flory 1995: 39, 44). One reason why this notion is useful is that the common patrimony of humankind prevents individual or national appropriation of the environment. This notion can also legitimise collective management of the common patrimony, with humans considered to be the managers and guardians of common property (Devost 2012: 58; Flory 1995: 44). Furthermore, the patrimony

---

[41] In so doing, Aquinas sought to ensure the protection of common goods for private and community interests (Rémond-Gouilloud 1989: 149).

[42] Introduced in December 1970, what was meant to govern only the seabed soon grew to encapsulate a lot more: AG Res. 2749 (XXV) 16 December 1970, cited in Salmon (2001: 810–11); see also: Sériaux (1995: 31).

[43] Sériaux (1995: 23, 31) [translation by author].

is reserved solely for peaceful objectives, and resources within this patrimony must be exploited in the interest of humanity as a whole (Flory 1995: 44).

The notion of a common patrimony of humankind has been used in international environment law, in conventions and treaties, and is therefore a source of duties (Rémond-Gouilloud 1989: 151). For example, it is present in the famous Principle 21 of the Declaration of the United Nations Conference on the Human Environment, which indicates that 'States have ... the responsibility to ensure that activities within their jurisdiction or control do not cause damage to the environment of other States or of areas beyond the limits of national jurisdiction'.[44] The notion of the common patrimony of humankind is also found in the United Nations Convention on the Law of the Sea, amended in 1994:

> the area of the seabed and ocean floor and the subsoil thereof, beyond the limits of national jurisdiction, as well as its resources, are the common heritage of mankind, the exploration and exploitation of which shall be carried out for the benefit of mankind as a whole, irrespective of the geographical location of States.[45]

Thus, the common patrimony of humankind has helped advance property law and international environmental law to address environmental issues. It is a concept that promotes ecological responsibility among different states.

The concept of a common patrimony of humankind does, however, have significant limitations. In addition to the practical problems related to large-scale, shared management, considering humankind to be a manager of the environment imposes an anthropocentric approach to the notion of common patrimony as human beings are central and above other living entities. Moreover, the use of the term 'humankind' is not as full and inclusive as one might believe. Presently, the definition of humankind only refers to two-thirds of the states within the United Nations, leaving out states that, while just as sovereign, are perhaps less powerful (Flory 1995: 50). In view of these limitations, it is difficult to argue that the common patrimony of humankind is the ideal solution to protect Nature using property law.

11.3.1.2 The Common Patrimony of Quebec

The notion of common patrimony is recognised by domestic law, particularly in Quebec. The notion of a common patrimony for Quebec was introduced in the Act to affirm the collective nature of resources and to promote better governance of water and associated environments, RLRQ c. C-6.2 (the Water Act), unanimously

---

[44] Declaration of the United Nations Conference on the Human Environment, Stockholm, 16 June 1972, 21st plenary meeting, Ch. 11.
[45] United Nations Convention on the Law of the Sea, Montego Bay, 10 December 1982, in force 16 November 1994, 1833 UNTS 3, preamble.

adopted by the National Assembly of Quebec on 11 June 2009.[46] This legislation was the culmination of research into a solution for water governance and management in Quebec, which began with recommendations in the 1975 Legendre and 2000 Beauchamp Commission reports on water management in Quebec, and included commitments in a provincial water policy, implemented in 2002 (Halley and Gagnon 2009).

The Water Act is part what Professor Madeleine Cantin Cumyn described as a 'new phase of the evolution of Québec law'.[47] This legislation succeeds in advancing Quebec property law by expressly categorising the right to water as a 'common right' in order to respond to related environmental challenges (Cantin Cumyn 2010: 597). In its preamble, the Act states that 'water resources are part of the common heritage of the Québec nation'. The legislation also creates a no-fault cause of action for damages caused to water resources, which can be exclusively exercised by the province of Quebec as a 'custodian of the interests of the nation in water resources' (Water Act, art. 8; Devost 2012: 59). Moreover, CCQ, article 913 sets out the principle that water may not be appropriated and that its use is 'common to all'. Under the Civil Code, water is a common good, and Quebec is responsible for its management.

Despite its advantages, particularly its symbolism, the notion of a common patrimony of Quebec is not without its shortcomings. For one thing, the legislature has not defined, in the Water Act or otherwise, the kind of relationship that is created between the Quebec population and the Province by the concept of a common patrimony of Quebec. It is, however, possible to consider that the Province acts as, if not a fiduciary, at least as a custodian of this patrimony (Cantin Cumyn 2010: 601; Groulx-Julien 2010). Moreover, it is necessary to consider the scope of this concept. With the exception of water, the Quebec legislature has not specified whether there are other natural resources or environmental elements that fall within the common patrimony of Quebec. As indicated by Professor Élise Charpentier, existing Quebec statutes limit public responsibility for the conservation of natural patrimony to certain norms and obligations in particular contexts and does not address environmental issues as a whole. Consequently, the government only takes care of the greatest threats and fails to work towards generally preventing potential environmental threats (Charpentier 2012: 191).[48] Therefore, Quebec's current approach remains anthropocentric, though with some biocentric influence. We are still far from the

---

[46] Quebec, Hansard, National Assembly, vol. 41, no. 44, 11 June 2009.
[47] Cantin Cumyn (2010: 597) [translation by author].
[48] Natural Heritage Conservation Act, c. C-61.01, of Quebec could, however, become an instrument for general planning of environmental protection. See especially Frenette (2005).

ecocentrism movement, which protects Nature as a whole and not only a few of its elements.

11.3.2 The Technical Function of Patrimony

The Civil Code of Quebec has affirmed the objective theory of patrimony by appropriation (Normand and Gosselin 1990: 715), which has German origins (Guinchard 1976: 1), but was revived by French jurist Pierre Lepaulle (1932; Lepaulle 1928: 55; Charbonneau 1982–83: 527; Popovici 2012; Normand 2014b: 600; Zenati-Castaing 2014: 630). Under this conception, in contrast to the traditional theory of Aubry and Rau, patrimony is no longer connected to legal personhood (Terré et al. 2013: 1031). Rather, it forms a detached and impersonal patrimony in which 'the community by appropriation connects the heterogenous elements'.[49] The Quebec legislature has not, however, taken this conception as far as it could go because it has not cut all ties between patrimony and legal personhood, the connection between the two still being the general principle.[50]

As a patrimony by appropriation in the technical sense, the trust patrimony can also serve as a tool to preserve and actively manage certain essential property in the context of environmental protection. Under article 1260 CCQ '[a] trust results from an act whereby a person, the settlor, transfers property from his patrimony to another patrimony constituted by him which he appropriates to a particular purpose and which a trustee undertakes, by his acceptance, to hold and administer'. Furthermore, article 1266 CCQ contemplates different kinds of trusts, which can be constituted for personal purposes or for private or social utility. The social trust 'constituted for a purpose of general interest, such as a cultural, educational, philanthropic, religious or scientific purpose' (art. 1270 CCQ) could thus serve the general interest objective of environmental protection.

It therefore seems possible, in the Quebec civil law, to create a trust, which is a patrimony by appropriation in a technical sense, for environmental ends. Indeed, in the administrative decision *Fiducie du Domaine Saint-Bernard (Re)*, 2006 CanLII 56910 (QC RACJ), it was held that a social utility trust could be created for environmental protection, such as the one implemented for the ecological protection of the Domaine Saint-Bernard. The purpose of this trust was to 'allow the citizens of Mont Tremblant and the general community to enjoy a natural site at a reasonable price'.[51] A social trust, which is a patrimony by appropriation, can be formed for the protection or development

---

[49] Carbonnier 2000: 7 [translation by author].
[50] CCQ, art. 2, para. 1: 'Every person is the holder of a patrimony'. This connection is also found in CCQ, arts. 302 and 911, para. 2
[51] *Fiducie du Domaine Saint-Bernard (Re)*, paras. 5–6 [translation by author].

of a natural element, such as a natural reserve or park.[52] In this case, the resource being protected for environmental reasons (be it a mountain, heritage site or even a park)[53] could be transferred to a trust patrimony, which could potentially entail obligations related to its management, the entire patrimony being managed by one or more trustees. In particular, this would allow the government to unload onto others its exclusive responsibility for certain resources by delegating a more active management role to one or more trustees. The government would still act as a fiduciary, since the settlor can assume this role.[54] The beneficiary in this case would be a relatively broad community of beneficiaries.[55] In this type of trust, the obligations attached to the transferred resources (such as management fees for park use or for the improvement of a contaminated site) would be the patrimonial liabilities.[56] The advantage of this kind of trust is that it would prevent poor (public or private) management of resources.

Conclusion

In conclusion, there are a variety of ways to adapt property law to environmental challenges and for this domain of law, fundamental as it is to our conception of the relationship that exists between people and things, to better respond to the challenges of the current environmental crisis. Nature can be personified in more or less extreme forms according to a given culture, ranging from subjective rights for Nature to a conception of Nature as a subject of legally protected rights. Moreover, the conception of property must be re-examined around a relational, socially limited, and functional conception of property, one that can fulfil its social function without being an exclusively individual right. Finally, the concept of patrimony also has a role to play in environmental protection, either by preserving the domain of the inappropriable using a common patrimony of humankind or common patrimony of domestic law, or through patrimony by appropriation capable of being implemented in a trusts law context.

Environmental issues are diverse, which is why the law has implemented a number of different solutions to address these new challenges. Different concepts and values may be necessary, including the categorisation of certain resources as

---

[52] On the use of trusts as instruments of wildlife preservation or as management or development tools for contaminated soil, see Beaulne and Barette (2015: 101). On the idea that the social utility trust, which is rarely used, can serve as a tool to set aside resources for a sustainable purpose, such as conservation of a natural environment, see Girard (2012: 139). See also Gidrol-Mistral (2016: 138–39). For the common law, see Wood (2013: 143).

[53] In the case of a park, however, its status as a public park would have to be considered in conjunction with the possibility of placing the public good in a public or common trust. On this point, see especially Gidrol-Mistral (2016: 139).

[54] The settlor or the beneficiary may be a trustee but he shall act jointly with a trustee who is neither the settlor nor a beneficiary' (CCQ, art. 1275).

[55] On the possibility of multiple beneficiaries, particularly in the context of social trusts, see CCQ, arts. 1282, para. 2 and 1283. See also *Lachance (Succession de)*, 2008 QCCS 1094.

[56] On the importance of obligations alongside assets when recognising the existence of a patrimony, see Smith (2008: 392–95).

inappropriable through the notion of common things and a more dynamic management of resources using a trust patrimony by appropriation. Alongside traditional public and private interests, the field of common and collective property is now experiencing significant growth.

References

Alexander, G. S. (2013). Ownership and obligations: The human flourishing theory of property. *Hong Kong Law Journal* 43: 451.

Alexander, G. S. and Eduardo M. Penalver (2009). Properties of community. *Theoretical Inquiries in Law* 10: 127.

Anker, K. (2017). Law as … Forest, eco-logic stories and spirits in Indigenous jurisprudence. *Law Text Culture* 21: 191.

Arnold, C. A. (2002). The reconstitution of property: Property as a web of interests. *Harvard Environmental Law Review* 26(2): 281.

Aubry, C. and Frédéric-Charles Rau (1873). *Cours de droit civil français d'après la méthode de Zachariae.* 4th ed. Paris: Marchal & Billard, VI.

Beaulne, J. and André J. Barette (2015). *Droit des fiducies, coll. Collection bleue.* 3rd ed. Montreal: Wilson & Lafleur.

Bégin, L. (1992). La revendication écocentriste d'un droit de la nature. *Laval théologique et philosophique* 48(3): 315–502, 397.

Bergel, J.-L. (2001). Paradoxes du droit immobilier français à la fin du XXe siècle. In *Le droit privé français à la fin du XXe siècle: Études offertes à Pierre Catala.* Paris: Litec.

Bergel, J.-L., Marc Bruschi and Sylvie Cimamonti (2010). *Les biens.* 2nd ed. Coll. Traités/Traité de droit civil. Paris: LGDJ.

Blackstone, W. (1979). *Commentaries on the Laws of England.* Chicago: University of Chicago Press, II.

Borrows, J. (2016). Heroes, tricksters, monsters, and caretakers: Indigenous Law and legal education. *McGill Law Journal* 61(4): 795.

Bouchard, C. (1997). *La personnalité morale démythifiée: Contribution à la définition de la nature juridique des sociétés de personnes québécoises.* Sainte-Foy: Presses de l'Université Laval.

Brierley, J. E. C. (1995). Regards sur le droit des biens dans le nouveau Code civil du Québec. *Revue internationale de droit comparé* 47(1): 33.

Burdon, P. (2011). The jurisprudence of Thomas Berry. *Worldviews* 15: 151.

Burdon, P. (2015). *Earth Jurisprudence: Private Property and the Environment.* New York: Routledge.

Byrne, J. P. (2005). Property and environment: Thoughts on an evolving relationship. *Harvard Journal of Law & Public Policy* 28: 679.

Caballero, F. (1981). *Essai sur la notion juridique de nuisance.* Paris: LGDJ.

Cantin Cumyn, M. (2002). La fiducie, un nouveau sujet de droit? In Jacques Beaulne (ed.), *Mélanges Ernest Caparros.* Montreal: Wilson & Lafleur, 129.

Cantin Cumyn, M. (2010). L'eau, une ressource collective: portée de cette désignation dans la Loi affirmant le caractère collectif des ressources en eau et visant à renforcer leur protection. *Cahiers de droits* 51(3–4): 595–615.

Carbonnier, J. (2000). *Droit civil: Les biens.* 19th ed. Paris: Presses universitaires de France, vol. III.

Charbonneau, P. (1982–83). Les patrimoines d'affectation: vers un nouveau paradigme en droit québécois du patrimoine. *Revue du Notariat* 85(1): 491.

Chardeaux, M.-A. (2006). *Les choses communes*. Paris: LGDJ.

Charpentier, É. (2012). La conservation du patrimoine naturel en droit privé québécois. In Christophe Albiges and Christine Hugon (eds.), *Immeuble et droit privé: Approches transversales*. coll. Axe Droit. Paris: Lamy.

Cribbet, J. E. (1986). Concepts in transition: The search for a new definition of property. *University of Illinois Law Review* 1.

Crocq, P. (1995). *Propriété et garantie*. Coll. Bibliothèque de droit privé, 248. Paris: LGDJ.

Cullinan, C. (2007). Wild law and the challenge of climate change *Soundings* 37: 116.

David, V. (2012). La lente consécration de la nature sujet de droit: Le monde est-il enfin Stone? *Revue juridique de l'environnement* 37(3): 469.

Davison, I. (2017). Whanganui River given legal status of a person under unique Treaty of Waitangi settlement. *New Zealand Herald*, 15 March, www.nzherald.co.nz/nz/news/article.cfm?c_id=1&objectid=11818858

Debruche, A.-F. (2008). Les biens. In Louise Bélanger-Hardy and Aline Grenon (eds.), *Éléments de common law canadienne: Comparaison avec le droit civil québécois*. Toronto: Thomson Carswell, 101.

Demogue, R. (1909). *La notion de sujet de droit: Caractère et consequences*. Paris: Larose & Tenin.

Devost, M. (2012). Le patrimoine commun de la nation québécoise au service de l'indemnisation du préjudice environnemental. *Revue du Barreau* 71: 43.

Dijon, X. (1981–82). Le sujet de droit en son corps: Une mise à l'épreuve du droit subjectif. Thèse, Université catholique de Louvain. Faculté de droit.

Doremus, H. (2011). Climate change and the evolution of property rights. *UC Irvine Law Review* 1: 1091.

Duguit, L. (1912). *Les transformations générales du droit privé depuis le Code de Napoléon*. Paris: Félix Alcan.

Duguit, L. (1923). *Traité de droit constitutionnel*. 2nd ed. Paris: Ancienne Librairie Fontemoing, III.

Durand-Folco, J. (2015). Décroissance, écosocialisme et articulation stratégique. *Nouveaux Cahiers du socialisme* 14: 94.

Emerich, Y. (2008). Regard civiliste sur le droit des biens de la common law: Pour une conception transsystémique de la propriété. *Revue générale de droit* 38(2): 339.

Emerich, Y. (2011). Contribution à une étude des troubles de voisinage et de la nuisance: La notion de devoirs de la propriété. *Cahiers de droit* 52(1): 3.

Erp, S. van (2006). Comparative property law. In Mathias Reimann and Reinhard Zimmermann (eds.), *The Oxford Handbook of Comparative Law*. Oxford: Oxford University Press, 13.

Flory, M. (1995). Le patrimoine commun de l'humanité dans le droit international de l'environnement. In Jean-Yves Chérot et al. (eds.), *Droit et environnement: Propos pluridisciplinaires sur un droit en construction*. Aix-en-Provence: Presses universitaires d'Aix-Marseille, 44.

Frenette, F. (2005). La Loi sur la conservation du patrimoine naturel: Un simple aperçu des mesures de protection édictées et de leur impact sur la pratique notariale. *Revue du Notariat* 107(3): 385

Gidrol-Mistral, G. (2016). L'affectation à un but durable, vers une nouvelle forme d'appropriation des biens communs? Réflexions autour de l'article 1030 du Code civil du Québec. *Revue générale de droit* 46(1): 95.

Girard, J.-F. (2012). La vraie nature de la servitude de conservation: Analyse d'un outil juridique méconnu. In Barreau du Québec (ed.), *Développements récents en droit de l'environnement*. Online document Legal Database CCCLII. Montreal: Yvon Blais.

Glenn, H. P. (2014). *Legal Traditions of the World: Sustainable Diversity in Law*. 5th ed. Oxford: Oxford University Press.

Goldstein, G. (1990). La relativité du droit de propriété: Enjeux et valeurs d'un Code civil moderne. *Revue juridique Thémis* 24: 505.

Graziadei, M. (2017). The structure of property ownership and the common law/civil law divide. In Michele Graziadei and Lionel Smith (eds.), *Comparative Property Law: Global Perspectives*. Cheltenham, UK: Edward Elgar, 77.

Grinlington, D. and Prue Taylor (eds.) (2011). *Property Rights and Sustainability. The Evolution of Property Rights to Meet Ecological Challenges*. Leiden: Brill.

Groulx-Julien, R. (2010). In *Les obligations fiduciaires de l'État pour la protection de l'environnement*. Note de recherche sous la direction de D. Lemieux. Cahiers de la CRCDE 1.

Guibet Lafaye, C. (2016). Récuser le commun pour justifier la propriété privée. *Revista Portuguesa de Filosofia* 72(4): 1231.

Guinchard, S. (1976). *Essai d'une théorie générale de l'affectation des biens en droit privé français*. Paris: LGDJ.

Halley, P. and Christine Gagnon (2009). Le droit nouveau de l'eau au Québec. *Gaïa Presse*, 3 July, www.gaiapresse.ca/2009/07/le-droit-nouveau-de-leau-au-quebec/

Hamill, S. E. (2012). Private rights to public property: The evolution of common property in Canada. *McGill Law Journal* 58(2): 365.

Hermitte, M.-A. (1988). Le concept de diversité biologique et la création d'un statut de la nature In Bernard Edelman and Marie-Angèle Hermitte (eds.), *L'homme, la nature et le droit*. Paris: Christian Bourgois, 254.

Hermitte, M.-A. (2011). La nature, sujet de droit? *Annales. Histoire, Sciences Sociales* 66(1): 173.

Hutchison, A. (2014). The Whanganui River as a legal person. *Alternative Law Journal* 39 (3): 179–82.

Jhering, R. von (1888). *L'esprit du droit romain dans les diverses phases de son développement*. O. De Meulenaere (trans.). 3rd ed. Paris: A. Marescq Aîné, vol. IV.

Jhering, R. von (1893). Des restrictions imposées aux propriétaires fonciers dans l'intérêt des voisins. In *Œuvres choisies*. Octave De Meulenaere (trans.). Paris: A Marescq, II, 101–44.

Josserand, L. (1927). *De l'esprit des droits et de leur relativité: Théorie dite de l'abus des droits*. Paris: Dalloz.

Kant, E. (1993). *Fondements de la métaphysique des mœurs*. Victor Delbos (trans.). Paris: Le Livre de Poche.

Klein, D. B. and John Robinson (2011). Property: A bundle of rights? Prologue to the property symposium. *Econ Journal Watch* 8(3): 193.

Kovel, J. (2011). Cinq thèses sur l'écosocialisme. *Nouveaux Cahiers du socialisme* 6: 66.

Lafond, P.-C. (2005). *Précis de droit des biens*. 2nd ed. Montreal: Thémis.

Lametti, D. (2003). The concept of property: Relations through objects of social wealth. *University of Toronto Law Journal* 53(4): 325.

Lametti, D. (2010). The objects of virtue. In Gregory S. Alexander and Eduardo M. Penalver (eds.), *Property and Community*. Oxford: Oxford University Press, 1–37.

Larrère, C. (2010). Les éthiques environnementales. *Nature Sciences Sociétés* 18: 405–13.

Larrère, R. and Catherine Larrère (2007). Should nature be respected? *Social Science Information* 46(1): 9–34.

Lepaulle, P. (1928). An outsider's viewpoint of the nature of trusts. *Cornell Law Review* 14: 52.

Lepaulle, P. (1932). *Traité théorique et pratique des trusts en droit interne, en droit fiscal et en droit international*. Paris: Rousseau.

Leopold, A. (1987). *Sand County Almanac, and Sketches Here and There*. Oxford: Oxford University Press.

Leopold, A. (2012). The land ethic. *Emergence: Complexity and Organization* 14: 59.

Lowy, M. (2008). Écosocialisme et planification démocratique. *Écologie & Politique* 37 (3): 165.

Lowy, M. (2015). *Ecosocialism: A Radical Alternative to Capitalist Catastrophe*. Chicago: Haymarket.

Macdonald, R. A. (1994). Reconceiving the symbols of property: Universalities, interests and other heresies. *McGill Law Journal* 39(1): 761.

Marty, G. and Pierre Raynaud (1972). *Droit civil: Introduction générale à l'étude du droit*. 2nd ed. Paris: Sirey, vol. I.

Merrill, T. W. (1998). Property and the right to exclude. *Nebraska Law Review* 77(1): 730.

Morris, J. D. K. and Jacinta Ruru (2010). Giving voice to rivers: Legal personality as a vehicle for recognising Indigenous peoples' relationships to water? *Australian Indigenous Law Review* 14(2): 49.

Moynihan, C. J. and Sheldon F. Kurtz (2005). The background. In *Introduction to the Law of Real Property: An Historical Background of the Common Law of Real Property and Its Modern Application*. St Paul, MN: West.

Moyse, P.-E. (2012). L'abus de droit: l'anténorme – Partie II. *McGill Law Journal* 57(4): 1.

Næss, A. (2005). The basics of deep ecology. *The Trumpeter* 21(1): 61.

Normand, S. (2014a). L'affectation en droit des biens au Québec. *Revue juridique Thémis* 48: 599.

Normand, S. (2014b). *Introduction au droit des biens*. 2nd ed. Montreal: Wilson & Lafleur.

Normand, S. and Jacques Gosselin (1990). La fiducie du Code civil: Un sujet d'affronte-ment dans la communauté juridique québécoise. *Cahiers de droit* 31: 681.

Orsi, F. (2014). Réhabiliter la propriété comme bundle of rights: Des origines à Elinor Ostrom, et au-delà ? *Revue internationale de droit économique* 28(3): 371.

Parquet, M. (2007). *Introduction générale au droit*. Coll. Lexifac – Droit. 4th ed. Rosny-sous-Bois: Bréal.

Pavageau, S. (2006). *Le droit de propriété dans les jurisprudences des juridictions suprêmes françaises, européennes et internationales*. Paris: LGDJ.

Pichette, S. (1990). La relativité du droit de propriété. *Revue juridique Thémis* 24: 529.

Penner, J. E. (1996). The 'bundle of rights' picture of property. *UCLA Law Review* 43: 711.

Penner, J. E. (1997). *The Idea of Property in Law*. Oxford: Clarendon Press.

Planiol, M. and Georges Ripert (1926). *Traité pratique de droit civil français: Les biens*. Paris: LGDJ, vol. III.

Popovici, A. (2012). Le patrimoine d'affectation: Nature, culture, rupture. Master's thesis, Université Laval.

Popovici, A. (2016). Êtres et avoirs: Esquisse sur les droits sans sujet en droit privé. Ph.D. thesis, Université Laval.

Rémond-Gouilloud, M. (1989). *Du droit de détruire. Essai sur le droit de l'environnement*. Paris: Presses universitaires de France.

Salmon, J. (ed.) (2001). *Dictionnaire de droit international public*. Brussels: Bruylant.

Savigny, F. K. von (1840). *Traité de droit romain*. Charles Guenoux (trans.). Paris: Firmin Didot Frères, I.

Sayin et al. (2017). Land law and limits on the right to property: Historical, comparative and international analysis. *Law Schools Global League* 5: 1.

Sériaux, A. (1995). La notion de choses communes: Nouvelles considérations juridiques sur le verbe avoir. In Jean-Yves Chérot et al. (eds.), *Droit et environnement: Propos pluridisciplinaires sur un droit en construction*. Aix-en-Provence: Presses universitaires d'Aix-Marseille.

Smith, L. D. (2008). Trust and patrimony. *Revue générale de droit* 38(2): 379.

Stone, C. D. (1972). Should trees have legal standing? *Southern California Law Review* 45: 450.

Strickler, Y. (2006). *Les biens*. Paris: Presses universitaires de France.

Tanuro, D. (2012). *L'impossible capitalisme vert*. Paris: La Découverte.

Taylor, P. W. (2011). *Respect for Nature: A Theory of Environmental Ethics*. Princeton, NJ: Princeton University Press.

Terré, F., Philippe Simler and Yves Lequette (2013). *Droit civil: Les obligations*. 11th ed. Paris: Dalloz.

Thiele, L. P. (1999). *Environmentalism for a New Millennium: The Challenge of Coevolution*. Oxford: Oxford University Press.

Trébulle, F.-G. (2006). Droit communautaire de l'environnement: Vers une consécration de l'analyse fonctionnelle de la propriété ? *Revue de droit immobilier* 6: 436.

Trébulle, F.-G. (2007). La propriété à l'épreuve du patrimoine commun: Le renouveau du domaine universel. In *Études offertes au professeur Philippe Malinvaud*. Paris: LexisNexis/Litec, 659–74.

Trotabas, L. and G. Renard (1930). *La fonction sociale de la propriété privée: Le point de vue technique: le régime administratif de la propriété privée*. Paris: Recueil Sirey.

Vanuxem, S. and C. Guibet Lafaye (eds.) (2015). *Repenser la propriété: Un essai de politique écologique*. Aix-en-Provence: Presses universitaires d'Aix-Marseille.

Villey, M. (1946). L'idée du droit subjectif et les systèmes juridiques romains. *Revue historique de droit français et étranger* 24: 201.

Warren, L. (ed.) (2009). *Wild Law: Is There Any Evidence of Earth Jurisprudence in Existing Law and Practice? An International Research Project*. London: Environmental Law Association/Gaia Foundation.

Whittemore, M. E. (2011). The problem of enforcing nature's rights under Ecuador's Constitution: Why the 2008 environmental amendments have no bite. *Pacific Rim Law & Policy Journal* 20: 659.

Williams, J. C. (1998). The rhetoric of property. *Iowa Law Review* 83: 277.

Wood, M. C. (2013) Ecological Res. In *Nature's Trust: Environmental Law for a New Ecological Age*. Cambridge: Cambridge University Press.

Zenati-Castaing, F. (1993). Pour une rénovation de la théorie de la propriété. *Revue trimestrielle de droit civil* 305.

Zenati-Castaing, F. (2014). L'affectation québécoise, un malentendu porteur d'avenir. Réflexions de synthèse. *Revue juridique Thémis* 48: 623.

Case Law

Canadian Pacific Railway Co. *v.* Vancouver (City) 2006 SCC 5

Fiducie du Domaine Saint-Bernard (Re) 2006 CanLII 56910 (QC RACJ); SOQUIJ AZ-50390964

Lachance (Succession de) 2008 QCCS 1094; JE 2008–846
Sierra Club *v*. Morton, 405 US 727 (1972)
St Lawrence Cement Inc. *v*. Barrette 2008 SCC 64
Wallot *v*. Québec (Ville de) 2011 QCCA 1165

Constitutional Documents

Constitution of the Republic of Ecuador 2008, *Political Database of the Americas*, arts.
    71–72, translation. http://pdba.georgetown.edu/Constitutions/Ecuador/english08
    .html. [Constitution of Ecuador]
Constitution of the Plurinational State of Bolivia 2009, Oxford University Press, preamble,
    www.constituteproject.org/constitution/_Bolivia_2009.pdf [Constitution of Bolivia]
Government of New Zealand (2017a). Te Awa Tupua (Whanganui River Claims
    Settlement) Act 2017, assent 20 March 2017, Government of New Zealand
Government of New Zealand (2017b). Te Awa Tupua (Whanganui River Claims
    Settlement) Act 2017, assent 20 March 2017. Version as 12 April 2022

Legislation

Act to affirm the collective nature of water resources and to promote better governance of
    water and associated environments (the Water Act), RLRQ c. C-6.2, Art. 8 [Water Act]
Administrative Procedure Act, 5 USC §§ 701ff.
Civil Code of Lower Canada
French Civil Code, translated by David W. Gruning, Art. 544, www.legifrance.gouv.fr/
    Traductions/en-English/Legifrance-translations
Natural Heritage Conservation Act, c. C-61.01
Québec, Hansard, National Assembly, vol. 41, no. 44, 11 June 2009

Other

AG Res. 2749 (XXV) 16 December 1970
UN Conference on the Human Environment, Declaration of the United Nations Conference
    on the Human Environment (June 1972), www.un-documents.net/unchedec.htm
UN Convention on the Law of the Sea (adopted 10 December 1982, entered into force
    16 November 1994) 1833 UNTS 3 (UNCLOS)

<h1 style="text-align:center">12</h1>

Reimagining the Common Law

Rights of Nature Tribunals and the Wild Law Judgment Project

NICOLE ROGERS, GRETA BIRD, JO BIRD AND MICHELLE MALONEY

Introduction

In recent years, two exciting and contemporaneous initiatives have highlighted the possibilities in both performance, and performative writing, for opening up extralegal, imaginative spaces for alternative representations of non-human species and Earth itself. These initiatives are the Wild Law Judgment Project and the Rights of Nature and Peoples' tribunals. In this chapter, we explore the performative dimensions of these initiatives and interrogate the extent to which extralegal mimicry of existing legal practices can contribute to radical transformation of the paradigms underlying the common law.

12.1 The Wild Law Judgment Project

In 2014, the Wild Law Judgment Project, a collaborative, cross-institutional endeavour was launched at a workshop in Sydney. The project forms part of a growing number of judgment rewriting projects, of which the most prominent have been the feminist judgment writing projects. These have involved feminist rewritings of judgments from all areas of law, in various jurisdictions (Hunter et al. 2010b; Douglas et al. 2014; Stanchi et al. 2016; Enright, McCandless and O'Donoghue 2017; McDonald et al. 2017). Although the feminist judgment writing projects are the best-known projects, other initiatives have involved rewriting judgments from the perspective of the child (Stalford et al. 2017), rewriting judgments on medical and health issues (Smith et al. 2017) and rewriting judgments of the European Court of Human Rights with a focus on diversity (Brems 2012).

The Wild Law Judgment Project diverged from this growing body of work in that contributors sought to abandon the dominant anthropocentric focus prevalent in all other rewriting projects and experimented instead with judgment writing that focused upon the interests and well-being of other species. At the Sydney workshop, Chief Justice Brian Preston of the New South Wales Land and Environment Court, who contributed a hypothetical judgment to the collection, identified two possible routes for wild law rewriting. The 'more orthodox approach', which has been adopted in the feminist judgment rewriting projects, involves 'accept[ing] the law as it currently exists, but explor[ing] where there is scope for finding, interpreting and applying the law to best meet the justice – including the ecological justice – of the situation' (Preston 2017b: 21). The second approach, which 'falls outside the orthodox technique and logic of judging disputes', is 'to challenge the existing law and mould it to fit the earth's demands' (Preston 2017b: 21). Since our preference was to write wildly, we chose to incorporate both approaches, including the less orthodox, less rigid one; consequently, the collection (Rogers and Maloney 2017) includes existing judgments rewritten within the constraints of existing law, existing judgments rewritten with reference to more desirable but, at this point, non-existent laws, and hypothetical and in some instances futuristic judgments in which there are some quite radical departures from existing laws. The key challenge for contributors was to view judging, and judgments, through a 'wild law' lens.

The extent of this challenge became apparent as participants embarked upon the process of rewriting. Somehow, we had to disregard our own self-interest, our ingrained assumptions and presuppositions as part of the human species, and indeed as part of a particular subset of the human species. Extending the well-established narrative of rights to encompass non-human species provided intriguing possibilities but also created conundrums. Timothy Morton has observed that '[e]xtending rights to everything is absurd since rights language is normative: some beings can have rights to the extent that others do not' (2016: 151). On an even more fundamental level, the challenge of rewriting law wildly required contributors to reflect on whether it is possible to prioritise, or at least recognise and respect Earth and its many communities and life forms through existing intellectual forms and modes of reasoning. This is an important question for us in the Anthropocene as we confront the existential crisis of climate change and the current environmental stresses that threaten the habitability of Earth for all life forms, including humans.

The very concept of judging and the established processes of judgment writing, which require us to deploy accepted forms of legal reasoning in all its measured cadences, can be viewed as part of the intellectual edifice which may have served dominant interests and social groups well during the long-term stability of the Holocene era but is now symptomatic of the 'modes of concealment that [prevent] people from recognizing the realities of their plight' (Ghosh 2016: 11). As Clive Hamilton and Jacques Grinevald have observed, '[t]he Holocene can be no guide to the Anthropocene geologically or intellectually' (2015: 62). Existing legal systems are not only ill-suited to the existential challenges of the Anthropocene, and the radical rethinking required for adaptation to these challenges, but are also singularly ill-equipped to reflect the concerns of and represent the marginal, the ignored and the disregarded. First Nations academic Professor Irene Watson refused to engage in the process of judgment writing in her contributions to both the Australian feminist judgment project and the Wild Law Judgment Project, observing that 'rewriting needs to be done from 'another place', outside the jurisdiction of the Australian common law and the sovereignty of the Australian state' (2014: 53). In the Wild Law Judgment Project she provided, in lieu of a judgment, 'a talking back to colonialism, and a singing up of the decolonial' (Watson 2017: 209; see also Chapter 3 in the present volume). In so doing, she makes it clear that First Nations peoples define and perform law quite differently from those whose interests have always been protected within and served by the colonial political, social and legal order.

Thus, it is important to acknowledge that not all forms of law involve or require judgment writing and that the very process of judgment writing might be antithetical to Earth-centredness and the ongoing challenge of decolonisation. Professor Watson calls First Nations law, 'a natural system of obligations and benefits, flowing from an Aboriginal ontology' (Watson 2015: 1): a 'raw law'. This form of law '[encodes] our obligation to keep our natural worlds living'; 'law is what cares for country' (Watson 2017: 212). Professor Watson's insights and our own misgivings caused us to repeatedly question the assumption at the heart of the Wild Law Judgment Project: namely, that judging and wild law were somehow compatible. In fact, the term 'wild law' itself can be viewed as an oxymoron, as Cormac Cullinan stated in his 2002 seminal text (2002: 8).

Most contributors to the Wild Law Judgment Project were able to reconcile judging and Earth-centredness, and did so with varying degrees of radicalism. As previously stated, the parameters of the project were broader than those of the feminist rewriting projects, in which contributors adopted the more orthodox approach identified by Chief Justice Preston and worked within existing laws and rules to produce plausible and possible outcomes using feminist legal reasoning. Our contributors could, and did, devise new laws with a more Earth-centred focus, and produced judgments based on these. Others sought wild outcomes using existing legal principles or adapted such principles to new challenges.

12.2 Judgment Rewriting as Performance

The above discussion may well lead the reader to wonder whether the process of judgment rewriting is inherently conservative, a way of corralling 'wild' sentiments or other forms of alternative thinking within established, accepted formats and processes and thereby ensuring the ongoing supremacy of these processes. Judgment rewriting is undoubtedly a form of critical scholarship, but a form shaped by particular legal conventions. On the other hand, it can also be viewed as inherently subversive, in that rewriting exposes the bias and arbitrariness underlying the authoritative pronouncements of the judiciary and reveals the performance of judging to be exactly that, a performance that can be undone and reperformed.

In this section, exploring the performative implications of the project, we adopt the second perspective. It is possible to view wild judgment rewriting as a form of performing or playing *within* existing rules, and this view gives rise to the concerns expressed above. Yet it can also be seen as a way of playing *with* the rules themselves, a form of what performance studies theorist Richard Schechner has described as dark play: play which 'subverts order, dissolves frames, breaks its own rules, so that the playing itself is in danger of being destroyed' (1993: 36). When judgment rewriters impersonate judicial insiders in order to articulate outsider perspectives, they are disrupting the playframes of judging itself.

Through judgment rewriting projects, participants are presenting alternative, extralegal and/or pseudo-legal forms of performance to the judicial, authoritative performances that make up the body of common law. It is overly simplistic to point out that legal performances differ from such extralegal performances, that one is real and authoritative, and the other but a game. The inherently disruptive quality in the performances of scholars who are contributing to judgment rewriting projects in ever-increasing numbers lies in the blurring of the boundaries between 'real' judging and judgment rewriting. There are many forms of legal performance and not all of them are exclusively judicial. The Wild Law Judgment Project attempts to answer this specific question: can legal scholars, as both insiders and outsiders, *perform* law differently to achieve wild Earth-centred outcomes?

Focusing on the performative implications of the rewritten judgments may seem peculiar in light of the fact that all rewritings have thus far taken the form of written text. Admittedly, two hypothetical judgments in the collection (Preston 2017a; Cullinan 2017) were originally performed. Nevertheless, the editors of the collection of English feminist judgments have described the very activity of judgment rewriting as 'parodic – and hence subversive – performance' (Hunter et al. 2010a: 8). Margaret Davies has pointed out that the 'judges' in the project 'are dressed up in the law but, having taken it on, it is their law to perform, not a system from which they are simply alienated' (2012: 174–75). She views law as performance and maintains that the performance of law is not confined to 'real' judges (Davies 2012: 175).

As rewriters, we were imitating or mimicking the real process of judging but also, importantly and subversively, departing from the original authoritative text. This process makes apparent the subjectivity of the performance of law. It demystifies and democratises judging. We were reclaiming the activity of judging from the judicial practitioners who have been overwhelmingly drawn from a privileged and unrepresentative subset of human society. And yet, our 'wild' judges are still hobbled by the inescapable, irreducible fact of our inclusion in the *Homo sapiens* species. Conferring standing upon non-human species or ecosystems, as some of our judges chose to do, only permits them representation before human judges and even then, at best, we can only extrapolate from our own human emotions and reactions in representing them. What would non-human judges, members of other species, find if called upon to sit in judgment? Attempting to answer this question involves a somewhat monumental ideological shift, not least because we assume that animals do not judge us. Even in the topsy-turvy world of *Alice in Wonderland*, the judge or King of Hearts is human. Yet as Jacques Derrida wrote in 2002 (Derrida and Wills 2002: 381), reflecting upon the implications of the animal gaze:

As with every bottomless gaze, as with the eyes of the other, the gaze called animal offers to my sight the abyssal limit of the human: the inhuman or the ahuman, the ends of man, that is to say the border crossing from which vantage man dares to announce himself to himself, thereby calling himself by the name he believes he gives himself.

When we attend to the animal gaze, a gaze that may or may not be judgemental, our own very human limitations become apparent.

12.3 Wild Judging in Practice: Systemic Constraints on Judicial Performance

How does the process of rewriting or performing wild judgments intersect with, or imitate the process of 'real' judging? In Chief Justice Preston's judgment in the collection (2017a), he envisaged a time in which a group of green sea turtles could bring legal action in relation to the destruction of their habitat, the Great Barrier Reef. This hypothetical judgment was delivered in a mock trial organised by the Victorian Environmental Defenders Office in 2012, although it is dated 18 February 2032 for the purpose of the project. Its context was climate change, and at issue were the various approvals granted to coal mines in Queensland by the Australian and Queensland governments. The green sea turtles argued that there was a causal relationship between these approvals and various omissions in relation to climate mitigation endeavours, and the damage caused to the Great Barrier Reef by climate change. As a 'real' judge impersonating a future judge, adjudicating a hypothetical claim which can be viewed as improbable in our current legal and political system, Chief Justice Preston granted an injunction to prevent the issue of further coal mine approvals, and to compel both governments to take action to restore the plaintiffs' habitat and enable their adaptation to the damaged areas.

This judgment can be compared with Chief Justice Preston's groundbreaking, recent, 'real' decision in the Rocky Hill coal mine case (*Gloucester Resources Limited* v. *Minister for Planning*), when for the first time in an Australian court a judge refused to approve a proposed coal mine on climate change grounds. The ongoing approval of both new coal mines and extensions to existing coal mines in Australia is a highly contentious political issue and numerous legal challenges have been mounted to such approvals. Three of the rewritten judgments in the *Wild Law Judgment* collection revisited challenges to mining approvals in relation to, respectively, the Isaac Plains and Sonoma projects in the Bowen Basin (Deane and Woolaston 2017), the proposed Wandoan mine in the Surat Basin (Dehm 2017) and the Alpha mine in the Galilee Basin (Galloway 2017). To date, legal challenges have rarely proved successful, and no judge has found against a coal mine on climate change grounds, until Chief Justice Preston handed down his historic judgment in this case in February 2019.

In so doing, the judge was engaged in wild judging even though, by comparison with a case in which non-human species have standing and are presenting legal arguments, the decision is by no means a radical departure from existing legal principles and procedures. Its wildness is most evident in the inclusion in his reasoning of the importance and urgency of climate time (*Gloucester Resources*, para. 699), recently emphasised by the Intergovernmental Panel on Climate Change in its 2018 Special Report (Allen et al. 2018). Of course, a decision to prevent an additional coal mine can be grounded entirely in anthropogenic concerns; humanity will endure much hardship on a 'Hothouse Earth' (Steffen 2018: 8257) once the impacts of runaway climate change are truly felt. However wild law is about resisting the logic of capitalism, contesting the paradigm of endless growth, and prioritising the well-being of all life forms on Earth over the short-term economic benefits associated with an additional commercial endeavour; thus, the decision exemplifies wild judging in practice.

In his overview in the wild judgment collection of what it might mean to write judgments 'wildly', Chief Justice Preston referred to his playful exercise in wishful, extralegal thinking in the green sea turtles judgment and stated that: 'I have to say it was much easier and much more enjoyable giving judgment in a hypothetical case rather than in a real case. There are no disappointed litigants to appeal the judgment, no rebukes from appellate courts and no censure in the media' (2017b: 25). Indeed, by way of contrast to the lack of media attention and minimal public reaction to his hypothetical judgment in 2012, his decision in the Rocky Hill coal mine case created a furore; it was greeted with incredulity and horror by the powerful Australian mining industry and its supporters, and strong enthusiasm by both Australian and international climate activists. Justice François Kunc of the New South Wales Supreme Court, in his role as editor of the prestigious *Australian Law Journal*, has noted that the 'public square ... quickly filled with scathing criticism, not just of the decision but also of the judge' (2019: 253). Media headlines accused him of being, inter alia, an 'activist' judge with 'green links' who had 'tarnishe[d] the rule of law' (Kunc 2019: 253). The New South Wales Bar Association, the Law Society of New South Wales and the Judicial Conference of Australia all released public statements defending the judge and expressing concern about unfounded allegations of judicial bias (Kunc 2019: 253). The reaction to the decision indicated strong resistance in certain quarters to wild judging in practice.

Importantly, Chief Justice Preston had not abandoned the orthodox approach to judging in reaching his decision. He drew upon existing precedents, including the *Urgenda* v. *Netherlands* decision (*Gloucester Resources*, paras. 521–24, 537); upon international law including the 2015 Paris Agreement (*Gloucester Resources*, paras. 439–40, 526–27); and upon the authoritative scientific findings of the Intergovernmental Panel on Climate Change (*Gloucester Resources*, para. 434). His reasoning in rejecting the arguments which had prevailed in previous Australian coal mine case law was cogent and impeccable; these arguments include the so-called drug dealer's defence, according to which coal from the disputed mine would come from 'dirtier' sources if the mine did not go ahead, and the 'drop in the ocean' argument, according to which the coal from the disputed mine would make only an infinitesimal contribution to global greenhouse gas emissions. This, however, did not deter his critics from accusing him of unwarranted judicial activism.

In the next section, we turn to another key case in Australian jurisprudence that also gave rise to such accusations although, as we explain, its implications were far from radical, and its deficiencies inspired wild rewriting.

12.4 Wild Judging and the High Court Performance of Native Title

Mabo (1992) is an Australian case that transcends established legal and other categories. It falls within the ambit of property law, certainly, but it touches on many other categories, including constitutional law, and at its heart is a question, never properly answered, with the potential to disrupt all Australian law and undermine every Australian level of government: was the initial importation of English common law into the colonies and were subsequent British enactments, including the 1901 Constitution Act, ever lawful? This question is arguably unanswerable within the framework of the existing Australian legal system as it generates an aporia: namely, the impossibility of invalidating a system from within the system. In a judgment rewriting exercise enacted outside this framework, however, the aporia is not applicable. Hence it is unsurprising that three authors chose to rewrite *Mabo* (Bird and Bird 2017; Summerhayes 2017) for the purposes of the *Wild Law Judgment Project*, and two of those authors (Bird and Bird 2017) deliberately eschewed the performative embellishments that serve to confer authority upon judges within our existing legal system. The *Mabo* rewritings demonstrate the subversive possibilities in judgment rewriting; as fake judges, the authors are in no danger of being exposed as naked emperors if they explore the lack of legitimacy and the true implications of the fictitious paradox at the heart of the Australian legal system.

In the following section, Greta and Jo Bird reflect upon their rewriting exercise, the manifold performative implications of the *Mabo* decision, its relevance to Earth jurisprudence, and the extent to which a subsequent and very recent decision indicates that the High Court judges continue to adopt a conservative, racist approach in native title decision-making.

12.5 Muckaty, Timber Creek and Sovereignty

In our chapter in the wild judgment rewriting project (Bird and Bird 2017), we reimagined the *Mabo* case. We sought answers to the questions posed in the legal hunt for 'consent' by clan groups to a nuclear waste dump on Muckaty station. We drew on Indigenous knowledges to assert that First Nations peoples have continuing sovereignty over their lands. We questioned the legitimacy of the colonial legal system – one which includes the authority of judges – to unveil the mechanisms of our authority as expert knowers. In doing this we exposed the performance that judges engage in when deciding cases; a performance that feeds into the nation's narrative of identity.

12.5.1 Mabo Case

In *Mabo* the High Court majority found that the legal basis for the British Crown claim to the lands of First Nations people, the *terra nullius* doctrine, was a legal fiction. This left a lacuna in British sovereignty that the judges sidestepped.

We assert that the judges performed a 'smoke and mirrors' judgment. The majority held the title of First Nations people was recognised by the British common law; but only where 'the tide of history' (*Mabo*, 60) had not washed away connection to Country. Further, any recognition of native title was subject to extinguishment. The judges held they must privilege the introduced legal British system. Those bones must not be 'fracture[d]' (*Mabo*, 29). White law was legitimated by the 'act of state' doctrine with a small token tossed to First Nations. Later the government put the *Mabo* case into legislation, called the Native Title Act 1993 (Cth).

12.5.2 Native Title Act

The Native Title Act 1992 (Cth) was the legislative response to the High Court decision in *Mabo*. It was hailed by academic commentators as a progressive law giving recognition to First Nations traditional connection to land.

On examination, 'native title' was a performance by government; one designed to mollify the powerful mining lobby and answer the growing demands for justice for Indigenous people. The Act is a very limited grant of rights. It does not recognise the caring for Country that is at the heart of Indigenous law and sovereignty. It requires proof at white law of the claimants' traditional links to land from time immemorial. Cases such as *Yorta Yorta* (*Members of the Yorta Yorta Aboriginal Community* v. *Victoria*) show the injustice in the test. Colonial laws forbade aspects of cultural expression of the claimant group and their ancestors. Laws forced the taking of children from communities into white families. These genocidal policies and practices were then used as evidence that the Yorta Yorta had broken their traditional links to land. The Yorta Yorta were told by Justice Olney that the 'tide of history had indeed washed away . . . any real' connection to land, a connection that was 'not capable of revival' (*Yorta Yorta*, 461). This finding denied the Yorta Yorta mob recognition by white law of their Country.

Further native title only allows limited rights to hunt and gather and hold ceremonies. There is no recognition of First Nations law. This is because the taking of the land under the doctrine of *terra nullius* and the imposition of British law did not allow for any political or legal power in First Nations peoples; their sovereignty is avoided. The gift of 'native title' in *Mabo*, one that claimed to sweep away the era of racial discrimination in the common law (*Mabo*, 41–42), was deeply flawed. It provided a performance – dressed in judicial robes and sitting on high – to provide political and legal legitimacy. But take away the performance and the myths built on it, and reality was starkly visible.

12.5.3 Muckaty and Sovereignty

As judges in Muckaty we also gave a performance. However, our performance was one that challenged orthodox approaches. Instead of sitting in an imposing court we went on 'Country'. Being on Country, with all your senses connected, is deeply spiritual for First Nations peoples. Generally High Court judges do not go 'on Country' to decide matters of 'native title'.

The judgments contained in law reports impose 'white law'. The judicial wigs and robes hide the reality of whiteness and lay claim to objectivity. The court is like a stage, which creates a sense of awe, where power differentials are inscribed. Reinvention of self occurs, a new costume is assumed, the face of justice appears before citizens, her eyes covered.

And the judges making the decisions have trappings of power, place and authority. Native title rights in these judgments place a mask over First Nations law – no longer is caring for Country the sign of sovereignty. Colonial law turned land into a commodity with market value; damage to land, flora and fauna can be compensated with dollars. And the courts debate the dollars, interpreting the Native Title Act.

The act of performativity we adopted involved unravelling ourselves as judges, indeed unravelling law. The original judgments in *Mabo* demonstrated the impossibility of a judge exposing themselves, the architecture of their power and the law. The judges refused to perform authentically and draw on 'Raw Law' (Watson 2015). Their performance in *Mabo* was based on an 'act of State', a refusal to question the legality of their own authority. And this has served as a precedent.

All judgments that raise questions of sovereignty are cloaked. The judgment in Muckaty did not continue to closure because it risked exposure of the sovereignty question. The curtain had to come down to shield the legal system, to cloak its nudity. The Federal Court judge, Justice North, came on Country, wearing ceremonial feathers in his hat. Gone were his judicial robes. This was his concession to the claimants' law, but the Commonwealth withdrew as a party to proceedings. The matter never reached the High Court.

12.5.4 Raw Law

Contrast this with 'Raw Law'. The common law of Australia was created by First Nations people, eighty thousand years ago. It is birthed from the Country, based on sacred obligations to care for the land, and is not human focused. Professor Irene Watson a member of the Boandik, Meintangk and Tangenekald Nations has described the concept of Raw Law in her book *Aboriginal Peoples, Colonialism and International Law*. There is a lot of performativity in Raw Law, in song and ceremony, in living to care for 'Mother Earth'. But this performance of 'Raw Law' comes from a spiritually truthful space.

In contrast in Western culture, performance can indicate a distance between the real and the fictional, a space where the truth is suspended or disguised, an alternate reality. The majority judges in *Mabo* grappled with the racism embedded in the common law. The dilemma facing them was the centrality of *terra nullius*. This was rejected as a 'legal fiction'; but nothing was put in the space where the doctrine supported the law. Words were twisted, veiled. It is difficult to understand at points what is being said. It is a shifty judgment that aroused differing emotions. In the response of the mining industry, it threatened the backyard. Lawyers trumpeted the case as a 'judicial revolution' (Stephenson and Ratnapala 1993). An aporia opened. But unveiling the judges we see only a small recognition, called 'native title', for some Aboriginal people. The case remains a performance of 'whiteness'.

Whiteness in the Australian context (Bird 2008) has been built upon the spoils of colonisation. Hundreds of years of privilege, of profits from raping the earth, has created the meanings of whiteness. Deconstructing whiteness and its privilege are part of what we were doing in our judgment. We aimed to speak truth to power (Foucault 2001) from Earth's perspective. Colonial power, now in the epoch of late capitalism, is bleeding the lifeblood from the planet. Raw Law is required as antidote.

The basis of the Muckaty litigation was the hunt for a nuclear waste dump. This waste is one of the biggest threats to life on the planet. Political pressure continues to locate a site for a centralised waste dump in Australia – likely it will be on Aboriginal land. The Flinders Ranges, Kimba and Hawker in South Australia have been nominated by the federal government as potential sites. As in the Muckaty case, traditional owners continue to be offered large financial incentives to consent to having a waste dump on their land. Communities are divided. Aboriginal people are denied full services in rural and 'remote communities', so the offer of money is a massive temptation.

In the white courtroom, decades of powerful injustice have been cloaked in the facade, appearance, costume and performance of justice. Part of what makes our reimagining authentic is where the judgment is delivered, away from the stage of the courtroom, and on Country. *Mabo*, decided in the High Court in Canberra, was cloaked in the language of 'native title'; yet is a continuing *terra nullius* in the eyes of many Indigenous people.

12.5.5 *The* Timber Creek *Judgment*

We do not have space to critique in depth the recent judicial performance in the *Timber Creek* case (*Northern Territory* v. *Mr A. Griffiths (deceased) and Lorraine Jones on behalf of the Ngaliwurru and Nungali Peoples*). Suffice to say the case has been described as the most important since *Mabo*. For the first time the High Court was asked to award damages under the Native Title Act for damage to native title interests. The court looked at economic loss and 'spiritual harm'. Once again it fails to deal with the First Nations sovereignty question.

Never before had the High Court sat in Darwin; but in March 2019 it sat there in the *Timber Creek* case and to deliver judgment. The setting was unusual, as the majority of the court's decisions are delivered in Sydney or Melbourne, the centres of colonial commercial and political power.

The court's decision was handed down twenty years after a claim for compensation was lodged in 1999. The claim was started by the Ngaliwurru and Nungali traditional owners through the Northern Land Council under the Native Title Act. The court for the first time examined the compensation provisions in the Native Title Act. The judges had to decide on the value to be attached to 'spiritual harm'. The majority held (*Timber Creek*, para. 3(3)): 'The compensation for loss or diminution of traditional attachment to the land or connection to Country and for loss of rights to gain spiritual sustenance from the land is the amount which society would rightly regard as appropriate for the award for the loss.'

It is difficult to imagine what the terms 'society' and 'rightly' and 'appropriate' mean in this context. The court held that 'the special cultural value to the Claim Group included the spiritual sustenance derived from the land, 'the product of the Dreaming ... considered to be inviolable' (para. 328).

The *Timber Creek* decision, in our opinion, continues *terra nullius* in the law. It is a raced performance. Bridgid Cowling, a senior associate in the native title practice of Arnold Bloch Leibler, has written that the High Court 'has found an elegant way to understand the impact of the extinguishment of [native title] rights and to put a dollar figure on it'. Later in her article she describes the judgment as conservative (2019). We query whether an award of monetary compensation can ever 'understand the impact of the extinguishment of inviolable rights'.

The lead claimants Lorraine Jones and Chris Griffiths spent several years fighting the case in court. 'Mr Griffiths said recognition of spiritual connection was "what our old people wanted". "[T]o prove that our culture is still alive, our law is still in the land, our blood is still running in the country, our tears will fall on the land"' (James 2019). The claimants will continue to care for Country as far as is possible. We ask whether 'white law' can allow this responsibility to be fully realised.

12.5.6 *Spiritual Harm*

While our judgment in Muckaty did not refer directly to spiritual harm, this was embedded in our decision. We went further than the High Court in the *Timber Creek* case and acknowledged the continuing sovereignty of the Muckaty clans. In our judgment, we imagined the hearing took place, not only in the Northern

Territory, but 'on Country'. Away from the benches, the cathedral-like voids, the wigs and the robes of white justice. A place where the judges would have to sit naked in the face of cultural and spiritual law.

This was driven by our desire to perform recognition of First Nations sovereignty – to show the hollowness at the heart of the nation. The building of the nation on the 'act of state' doctrine takes judicial performance to its limits. In our judgment, we reject the native title performance. If judges and lawmakers can embrace the authentic common law of the land – the laws of the First Nations – and care for Country, environmental disaster may be averted.

Nations build cohesion through narratives. In Australia, these narratives of identity are of the 'fair go' and 'mateship' kind. These qualities are exemplified in the ANZAC story, where the blood of the nation's young men was heroically spilled on foreign soil at Gallipoli in 1915. However, the first blood spilt in undeclared wars was on Australian soil. It was the blood of First Nations men and women defending their Country against the British. Until the nation's narrative is revised to tell the truth about history and the laws of First Nations peoples, as requested in the *Uluru Statement from the Heart* (Referendum Council 2017), the judicial system remains a white performance. The strengthening of an Earth jurisprudence and the chance to protect the planet may follow from recognition of First Nations laws.

12.6 The Rights of Nature and Peoples' Tribunals

We turn now to the Rights of Nature and Peoples' tribunals, which also play an important performative role in creating an extralegal space for alternative representations of non-human species. Sitting as quasi-legal bodies before an audience, in quasi-legal forums, the various tribunals are an even more overt exercise in reperforming law than the rewritten judgments. Both internationally, and at a domestic level, tribunals have heard from witnesses and uncovered in a public setting the various elements of the biodiversity crisis confronting our planet. They provide a forum in which tribunal members and the broader audience can bear witness to social and ecological injustice. They also constitute a valuable exercise in civil society organising and advocacy.

The history and practice of Peoples' tribunals are relevant to emerging movements, including the global, climate activist group Extinction Rebellion. Extinction Rebellion is calling for citizens' assemblies to resolve the climate emergency, but such assemblies could well become as mired in procedural delays, as stymied by stumbling blocks created by corporate interest groups, and as compromised by political game-playing as existing parliaments, without rehearsals, practical training and ongoing vigilance on the part of participants. Here the concept of mimetic play becomes important.

Both the judgment rewriting projects and the various tribunals constitute forms of what Davina Cooper calls mimetic play, in which states and state institutions are both imitated and re-envisaged through play (2017: 189). This terminology is not intended to detract from the gravity and importance of both initiatives. These forms of mimetic play have their own rules and structures; they operate as alternative systems (Cooper 2017: 203). Cooper argues that mimetic play can be viewed as part of 'a creative refusal to give up and give way', in 'conditions where institutional formations ... seem radically inaccessible to progressive and radical forces' (2017: 208). It exposes the arbitrary character of existing rules.

In the following section, Michelle Maloney discusses the role of tribunals in offering an important, legitimate and creative space to explore different world views and wild law constructs, drawing specifically upon the International Rights of Nature Tribunal, a recent special hearing of the Permanent Peoples' Tribunal on Fracking, and the Australian Peoples' Tribunal for Community and Nature's Rights.

12.6.1 Earth Laws Tribunals: Rights of Nature and Ecocide

During the past decade, there have been more than a dozen peoples' tribunals focusing on wild law, including Rights of Nature and ecocide. In 2011, the non-government organisation Eradicating Ecocide held a mock trial focusing on allegations against two fictional corporate CEOs, in order to test the validity of model ecocide laws. While this trial was not a traditional peoples' tribunal, as it did not empower people to bring 'real' cases into a public, non-governmental forum, the trial process was a demonstration of what might be possible should an ecocide law be created, and therefore offered an important alternative narrative to existing laws. The trial was not scripted; the jury was vetted and the legal teams included some of the key figures in the United Kingdom legal field. The organisers stated afterwards that the mock ecocide trial 'demonstrated the viability of a law of ecocide' and that 'prosecuting ecocide crime has practical application' (Eradicating Ecocide).

In 2016 and 2017, the Monsanto Tribunal, which defined itself as a 'court of opinion' and which was created at the initiative of civil society to legally investigate certain activities carried out by Monsanto, was held at The Hague (Gerber and Rossler 2016). The Tribunal was held to allow civil society to give a voice to witnesses so that the public could understand the details and impacts of Monsanto's various activities and globally marketed products, such as Agent Orange, glyphosate and other chemicals. The legal opinion drawn up by the Tribunal contains a legal analysis of the questions posed to witnesses, and was based on existing international law and also future legal norms including ecocide (Gerber and Rossler 2016).

A report about the Tribunal prepared by the European Civic Forum claims that the Tribunal had a number of important aspects, including:

The tribunal has raised awareness of the need for a reform of international law, to provide people, who have fallen victim to the practices of multinational corporations, with unfettered access to justice. The conclusions of the tribunal demonstrate that the claims of victims are legitimate . . . The tribunal has established arguments and premises which are now at the disposal of injured parties and their legal representatives to ease the task of taking legal action against Monsanto and other large corporations at national level. This fact could encourage more injured parties to start the process of taking legal action. The expert opinion can also serve as a backdrop for collecting the necessary money for injured parties who do not have extensive resources, so that they can take legal action.

(Gerber and Rossler 2016: 13–14)

Since 2014, peoples' tribunals investigating violations of the Rights of Nature have emerged internationally and in several countries around the world. These tribunals continue the tradition of offering a non-government forum for citizens to raise concerns about injustice, and they also offer a fascinating space to explore the potential operation of emerging and normative Earth laws.

In January 2014, the Global Alliance for the Rights of Nature (the Global Alliance) created the world's first International Tribunal for the Rights of Nature (the International Tribunal) at a summit in Ecuador in 2014. The Global Alliance is made up of around seventy organisations from around the world, including groups from the Global North, the Global South, and First Nations peoples (Maloney 2016). The International Tribunal is comprised of lawyers and ethical leaders from Indigenous and non-Indigenous communities around the world. Its objective is to hear cases regarding alleged violations of the Rights of Nature and to make recommendations about appropriate remedies and restoration (Maloney 2016: 130).

The main source of law for the International Tribunal is the Universal Declaration of the Rights of Mother Earth. The Declaration was created in 2010 by an international group of Earth lawyers and advocates who attended the World People's Congress on Climate Change and the Rights of Mother Earth, held in Cochabamba, Bolivia (Maloney 2015: 42). The lawyers who comprise the founding members of the Global Alliance were part of the group who drafted the Declaration and decided to create a permanent network of people committed to implementing Earth jurisprudence and the Rights of Nature. Despite the fact that the Declaration is not currently recognised in formal international law, it 'represents the agreed values of many thousands of members from civil society' (Maloney 2016: 131).

Cases initially presented to the International Tribunal addressed British Petroleum's pollution of the Gulf of Mexico; hydraulic fracking or hydrofracking in the United States; the Chevron/Texaco case in Ecuador; the failed attempt to protect Yasuni-ITT, Ecuador; the Condor mine case in Mirador, Ecuador; and the Great Barrier Reef case, presented by the Australian Earth Laws Alliance (AELA) (Maloney 2015: 46). In addition, advisory opinions were sought in relation to the dangers of genetically modified organisms and the persecution of Earth defenders by the Ecuadorian government (Maloney 2015: 46–47).

The panel of judges sitting on the International Tribunal included lawyers, First Nations Peoples and ethics experts from around the world. Their statements and judgements reflected an Earth-centred worldview and condemned the violation of the Rights of Nature. Further sessions of the International Tribunal were held in Lima (2014), Paris (2015) and Bonn (2017), in conjunction with the United Nations Framework Convention on Climate Change Conference of the Parties (COP) meetings, and drew attention to environmental destruction around the world. These tribunals also made recommendations for mitigation, restoration and law reform.

As the health of global ecological communities continues to deteriorate, the International Tribunal is an important forum, both for drawing attention to environmental destruction and for reclaiming any notion of justice for state-sanctioned violations of the rights of nature. Written judgments of the International Tribunal, such as the judgment in the Great Barrier Reef case (Cullinan 2017), also provide an important educative tool.

12.6.2 *Permanent Peoples' Tribunal on the Human Rights Impacts of Fracking, Including Rights of Nature*

The Permanent Peoples' Tribunal (Peoples' Tribunal) emerged in the 1970s with a focus on human rights violations and it has heard more than forty cases over forty years, in sessions around the world. In May 2018, the Peoples' Tribunal held its first Tribunal session that also included a focus on the rights of nature. The Peoples' Tribunal framed four questions in its terms of reference: the first three related to the human rights and environmental health impacts of unconventional oil and gas extraction. The final question addressed the rights of nature and asked: 'what is the extent of responsibility and liability of States and non-state actors, both legal and moral, for violations of the rights of nature related to environmental and climate harm caused by these unconventional oil and gas extraction techniques?' (Permanent Peoples' Tribunal 2019).

Oral sessions were conducted entirely online over five days, using zoom web conferencing technology. This enabled people from all around the world to contribute testimonies, at minimal cost (Permanent Peoples' Tribunal 2019: 66).

A team of Earth lawyers from the United Kingdom Earth Law Alliance and the AELA acted as co-counsel for the Rights of Nature submission and oral testimonies. The written submission drew on the provisions of the Universal Declaration of the Rights of Mother Earth and included extensive evidence of the harm caused to nature by unconventional oil and gas extraction. It argued that nature's rights are violated by these industries, including the rights of the climate system as a whole, the rights of rivers, waterways and aquifers, the rights of the sub-surface, and the rights of animals and plants to exist, thrive and evolve. Written and oral evidence was provided by scientists and legal experts, including the Centre for Earth Jurisprudence and the Community Environmental Legal Defence Fund. The Final Report of the Peoples' Tribunal was released in April 2019. The Tribunal stated that:

1. We recognise the full responsibility of State and non-state actors for the commission of systematic violations of human, peoples, ecological, and *nature rights* as they are affirmed and sanctioned in the existing international law.
2. We underline the failure of existing international juridical system and documents to fully address the responsibilities of the same actors with respect to the spectrum of clearly documented violations of peoples and *nature rights* ...
3. We formally recognise and congratulate those countries and sub-state jurisdictions that have banned fracking, and condemn those countries and sub-state jurisdictions that have revoked bans and moratoria on fracking.

(Permanent Peoples' Tribunal 2019: 58, emphasis added)

The inclusion of the rights of nature elements in the 2018 Peoples' Tribunal is a ground-breaking development which represents a broadening out of the world's oldest peoples' tribunal to include wild law and rights of nature.

12.6.3 Australian Peoples' Tribunal for Community and Nature's Rights

As a final example, the AELA has created a permanent Australian Peoples' Tribunal for Community and Nature's Rights (Australian Peoples' Tribunal). Inspired by its participation in the 2014 International Rights of Nature Tribunal in Quito, AELA held a special Rights of Nature Tribunal in Brisbane in October 2014, to bring together further evidence for the Great Barrier Reef case. The findings from this hearing were taken to the 2015 International Tribunal, which was held in Paris to coincide with the COP 21.

In 2016, AELA formally created the Australian Peoples' Tribunal as a permanent space for ecological justice in Australia. Its Charter outlines that the Tribunal may host citizens' inquiries and ecological justice cases. The Tribunal aims to provide an educative and culturally transformative forum in which to present an alternative process for addressing environmental justice in Australia. In hearing citizens' inquiries and ecological justice cases, the Tribunal seeks to: highlight the causes and impacts of violations of the Rights of Nature; highlight the causes and impacts of violations of human rights and community rights to defend their local ecosystems and communities; highlight positive alternatives and community created solutions; explore the development and application of Earth laws; support the human communities who are working to protect the non-human world and their own families and communities; and amplify the voices of non-human beings excluded from our present legal system. First Nations peoples, lawyers and scientists can serve as Tribunal Panel members.

Since its creation, the Australian Peoples' Tribunal has held three public hearings: in October 2016, October 2018 and March 2019. In 2016, ecological justice cases were heard for four ecosystems in Australia: the Mardoowarra/Fitzroy River in Western Australia; the Great Artesian Basin; the forests of Australia; and the Great Barrier Reef. The 2016 Tribunal brought together First Nations Peoples and non-Indigenous citizens to share their concerns about the natural world in a shared, public forum, and to explore in depth, for the first time in Australia, what the Rights of Nature are and how they need to be articulated and protected. The cases were heard from the point of view of the ecosystems themselves, and Earth advocates spoke on behalf of nature and invited expert witnesses from First Nations and local communities, scientific experts and lawyers.

In October 2018, the Australian Peoples' Tribunal held a Citizens' Inquiry into the Impact of Industrial Scale Agriculture on Community and Nature's Rights. The public hearing brought together First Nations representatives, scientists, community members and lawyers to give evidence about the impacts of industrial-scale agriculture (food and fibre production) on various bioregions in Australia. Two bioregions received particular attention: the Brigalow Belt in Central Queensland, and the Darling River ecosystems in New South Wales. The impacts examined included large-scale, devastating vegetation clearing which leads to soil erosion and biodiversity loss, large-scale water extraction, and many other impacts since the colonisation of Australian commenced in 1788. The Tribunal released an initial statement in November 2018 and a final report from the Inquiry is expected in May 2019.

One of the initial recommendations emerging from the 2018 hearing was that a citizens' inquiry should be held to examine the unsustainable extraction of water from the Darling River, a process which is violating the rights of the river to exist and the rights of connected human and natural communities to exist, thrive and evolve. The 2019 Citizens' Inquiry into the Health of the Darling River and Menindee Lakes began in late February and from 19 to 29 March it held two weeks of public hearings in eight towns along the devastated Darling River. Cotton farmers have diverted so much water from the Darling River that a once mighty river system is in its death throes. Towns are surviving on bottled water. Animals are dying. Massive fish kills in January 2019 are symptomatic of an almost complete ecosystem collapse.

At the time of writing the Panel was preparing its final report, which involves a substantial literature review and analysis of more than 100 individual video-recorded testimonies from local people who spoke about the impacts of 'no flow' on nature and human communities. The report is due in June 2019.

The testimonies reveal widespread trauma. At the end of the first week of public hearings, I wrote the following opinion piece:

Tonight the stories and faces of the people affected by the dying Darling/Barka River keep moving through my mind: the man from Menindee who had to stop his friend from shooting all his animals and committing suicide, because they no longer had any water to drink. The woman, a traditional custodian from Wilcannia, who wept as she talked about how the Darling River used to flow clear and deep and all the kids would grow up living, learning and playing around the River . . . The pilot, who for 40 years flew chartered flights around the region, and noticed from the 1990s onwards, the huge, extensive dams being built in the lower parts of Queensland, to hold onto water for cotton and other large scale agriculture, and prevent it from flowing down to the Menindee Lakes and Darling River. The man who described the birdlife, fish, yabbies, mussels and insects that used to flourish in and around the Menindee Lakes, and which survived each dry season to reappear again in the wet, but which are now gone. The woman who simply asked – what will be left for her grand-children?

I keep seeing the looks on peoples' faces when they'd describe how this time, this is different – it's not just drought, they've had bad droughts in the past; they've just never seen the river like this before . . . How it's not just the cotton farms up the river in Queensland, or the fact that so much water is extracted before it even reaches their place – it's also the sheer disbelief that their own State government, their elected officials have let it all happen. Not just let it all happen, but created the 'water crisis' through mismanagement at best, and behind-closed-doors deals and corrupt behaviour at worst. Many people said 'no-one's listening' and 'they don't care about us'.

(Maloney 2019)

A common thread in the literature is that peoples' tribunals offer an important space for people to simply be 'heard' and their concerns validated in a public setting, often for the first time, against a backdrop of state or corporate violation of peoples' rights (Byrnes and Simm 2013: 741–42). This was certainly the case at the 2019 Citizens' Inquiry – people thanked us for visiting their towns, listening to their stories, and caring enough to come and talk to them. A journalist who attended the public hearing in Bourke has written that: '[t]his was a chance for local people to have their stories about the river heard and recorded. To feel the relief of telling at last, and know the succour of having testified against turpitude' (Cameron 2019)

Conclusion

Extralegal and pseudo-legal performances, such as those that take place in Rights of Nature and Peoples' Tribunals, and judgment rewriting exercises, are important partly because they require us to reconsider law as performance. Unlike legal performances, these performances are not anchored in violence and are not recognised by the state.

However, the performative dimensions of the Wild Law Judgment rewriting project and the ongoing Rights of Nature and Peoples' Tribunals offer intriguing possibilities for exploring and reimaging our legal relationships with each other, with non-human species and with Earth itself. Such performances demonstrate possibilities for *doing* (rewriting and enacting) law differently. In exploring such performative possibilities, the rewriting project and the tribunals stimulate new and potent forms of critical Earth-centred thinking in participants, readers and audiences.

The potential for Rights of Nature and Peoples' Tribunals to contribute to a paradigm shift was obvious during various Australian hearings. Expert witness and Tribunal members participated in fascinating discussions about existing environmental laws, and normative legal structures based on an Earth-centred approach and recognising the Rights of Nature. This method of conceptual analysis was extremely valuable because the lawyers, Tribunal members and audience all engaged in an act of creative extrapolation: critiquing existing law in order to pull it apart, lay it bare, reframe it, and begin building something new.

While these powerful, alternative, performative forms of jurisprudence do not offer immediate, increased protection for our Earth community, they can empower lawyers, citizens and activists with new concepts, a new vocabulary, and a transformative vision for how our legal and governance systems could work to protect life on Earth.

References

Allen, M. R. et al. (2018). *Global Warming of 1.5 °C, an IPCC Special Report on the Impacts of Global Warming of 1.5°C above Pre-industrial Levels and Related Global Greenhouse Gas Emission Pathways, in the Context of Strengthening the Global Response to the Threat of Climate Change, Sustainable Development, and Efforts to Eradicate Poverty.* Geneva: Intergovernmental Panel on Climate Change.

Bird, G. (2008). The white subject as liberal subject. *Australian Critical Race and Whiteness Studies e-Journal* 4(2).

Bird, G. and J. Bird (2017). Nuclear waste dump: Sovereignty and the Muckaty mob. In N. Rogers and M. Maloney (eds.), *Law as If Earth Really Mattered: The Wild Law Judgment Project.* New York: Routledge, 237–53.

Brems, E. (ed.) (2012). *Diversity and European Human Rights: Rewriting Judgments of the ECHR.* Cambridge: Cambridge University Press.

Byrnes, A. and G. Simm (2013). Peoples' tribunals, international law and the use of force. *University of New South Wales Law Journal* 36(2): 711–44.

Cameron, A. (2019). The thirsty giants killing our rivers. *Sydney Morning Herald*, 19 April.

Cooper, D. (2017). Transforming markets and states through everyday utopias of play. *Politica and Societa* 2: 187–214.

Cowling, B. (2019). *Timber Creek* decision brings welcome clarity. *The Age*, 22 March.

Cullinan, C. (2002). *Wild Law: Governing People for Earth*. Claremont, S. Afr.: Siber Ink.

Cullinan, C. (2017). *Great Barrier Reef v Australian Federal and State Governments and Others*. In N. Rogers and M. Maloney (eds.), *Law as If Earth Really Mattered: The Wild Law Judgment Project*. New York: Routledge, 39–55.

Davies, M. (2012). The law becomes us: Rediscovering judgment. *Feminist Legal Studies* 20(2): 167–81.

Deane, F. and K. Woolaston (2017). Coal mines and wild law: A judgment for the climate. In N. Rogers and M. Maloney (eds.), *Law as If Earth Really Mattered: The Wild Law Judgment Project*. New York: Routledge, 125–42.

Dehm, J. (2017). Quantifying the environmental impact of coal mines: Lessons from the Wandoan case, *Xstrata Coal Queensland Pty Ltd v Friends of the Earth Brisbane Co-op*. In N. Rogers and M. Maloney (eds.), *Law as If Earth Really Mattered: The Wild Law Judgment Project*. New York: Routledge, 143–60.

Derrida, J. and D. Wills (2002). The animal that therefore I am (more to follow). *Critical Inquiry* 28(2): 369–418.

Douglas, H., F. Bartlett, L. Luker and R. Hunter (eds.) (2014). *Australian Feminist Judgments: Righting and Rewriting Law*. Oxford: Hart.

Enright, M., J. McCandless and A. O'Donoghue (eds.) (2017). *Northern/Irish Feminist Judgments: Judges' Troubles and the Gendered Politics of Identity*. Oxford: Hart.

Eradicating Ecocide Mock Trial, http://eradicatingecocide.com/the-law/mock-trial

Foucault, M. (2001). *Fearless Speech*. Cambridge, MA: MIT Press.

Galloway, K. (2017). *Coast and Country Association of Queensland Inc v Minister for Environment and Heritage Protection*. In N. Rogers and M. Maloney (eds.), *Law as If Earth Really Mattered: The Wild Law Judgment Project*. New York: Routledge, 161–77.

Gerber, E. and M. Rosser (eds.) (2016). *Ecocide: Corporations on Trial. International Monsanto Tribunal, The Hague, 2016*. The Hague: European Civic Forum.

Ghosh, A. (2016). *The Great Derangement: Climate Change and the Unthinkable*. Chicago: University of Chicago Press.

Hamilton, C. and J. Grinevald (2015). Was the Anthropocene anticipated? *Anthropocene Review* 2(1): 59–72.

Hunter, R., C. McGlynn and E. Rackley (2010a). Feminist judgments: An introduction. In R. Hunter, C. McGlynn and E. Rackley (eds.), *Feminist Judgments: From Theory to Practice*. Oxford: Hart, 3–29.

Hunter, R., C. McGlynn and E. Rackley (eds.) (2010b). *Feminist Judgments: From Theory to Practice*. Oxford and Portland, Oregon: Hart.

James, F. (2019). High Court awards Timber Creek Native Title Holders $2.5 million, partly for spiritual harm. *ABC News*, 13 March.

Kunc, F. (ed.) (2019). Current issues. *Australian Law Journal* 93(12): 251–57.

Maloney, M. (2015). Finally being heard: The Great Barrier Reef and the international rights of naturetribunal. *Griffith Journal of Law and Human Dignity* 3(1): 40–58.

Maloney, M. (2016). Building an alternative jurisprudence for the earth: The international rights of nature tribunal. *Vermont Law Review* 41: 129–42.

Maloney, M. (2019). Reflections from the First Days of the Citizens' Inquiry. Australian Earth Laws Alliance website, 23 March 2019, www.earthlaws.org.au/reflections-from-the-first-days-of-the-citizens-inquiry

McDonald, E., R. Powell, M. Stephens and R. Hunter (eds.) (2017). *Feminist Judgments of Aotearoa New Zealand. Te Rino: A Two-Stranded Rope*. Oxford: Hart.

13

Democratic Representation, Environmental Justice and Future People

Introduction

The representations and rights of the environment – the topic of this anthology – should include the question of the representations and rights of future people (overlapping and unborn) with respect to the environment. The latter is one of the key conduits by way of which the present generation affects the future, including generations hundreds or thousands of years from now. This fact foregrounds the importance of environmental governance. Today, however, political decision-making with respect to the future environment is caught in an increasingly perilous paradox. On the one hand, our collective impacts (which, as collective, call for political responses), as well as our knowledge of these impacts – and hence, our responsibilities – reach longer and potentially more harmfully into the future. On the other, the futural time scales that our political decisions take into account tend to get shorter and shorter (Rosa and Scheuerman 2009). It is thus paramount to identify and, if possible, counteract, the drivers of short-termism. In the face of tremendous long-term environmental challenges, recent years witness the birth of new proposals regarding how to reform existing democratic institutions (see, e.g. the proposals collected in Ricoy and Gosseries 2016). Some of these proposals, though by no means all, respond to long-standing complaints that modern democracy, in particular in association with globalising capitalism, inherently favours the present, at the expense of past and future generations. After reviewing, in the next section, the reasons that have been put forward for democracy's short-termism, the argument presented here proceeds in the following steps.

First, I argue that it is preferable to discover and foster pro-futural motivations internal to the democratic heritage. Second, I suggest that taking turns among rulers and the ruled is a normative idea inherent to the concept of democracy. Going back to Aristotle in particular, I present four reasons why 'taking turns' may be relevant to democracy as self-governance. The upshot is that democracy implies the principled consent to others ruling after 'my' turn. I further argue that taking turns is most appropriate as a model of sharing when it comes to indivisible collective goods, such as political institutions – goods that would be destroyed by their division and distribution. The third step of the argument consists in showing why taking turns among rulers and the ruled must be understood to also imply taking turns among generations. To consent to someone else's ruling after my turn is to consent to a generation having its turn with governance after my death.

In conclusion, I stress that many of the drivers of democratic short-termism are related to the dependence of national governments on global markets and the economic movement of capital. Thus, taking democratic turns with generations above all calls for stemming the economic interference in an ecological embedding of democratic institutions.

13.1 Drivers of Democratic Short-Termism

In this first section, I review some of the reasons that have been given for the claim that democracies tend to grant priority to the present generation or generations. For present purposes, I define 'generation' as the totality of all those born in a certain time period whose length is determined by the average time (roughly, thirty years) it takes for children to become parents and parents to become grandparents (see Birnbacher 1988: 23–24). On this definition, 'future people' refers to both non-overlapping individuals (the 'unborn' at that time) and overlapping generations (e.g. from the perspective of an age group roughly 60 years of age and up, children and grandchildren – whether or not individuals in that group have children themselves). Describing the problem of short-termism in terms of the relation between democracy and future generations makes sense because of the central importance of capturing the current environmental crisis – which calls for collective–political, ideally democratically coordinated action – in terms of relations among generations (see Gardiner 2011: 145). Intergenerational politics offers a critical lever in the environmental crisis, not only because of the apparent stark injustices to future people, but also because, initially at least, concern for them promises to bring together, in ways likely unmatched by other facets of the environmental crisis, a broad cross-section of democratic and global publics, from environmental activists and ecologists to policymakers and economists as well as the wider community, whose outlook is often more anthropocentric and humanist.

For present purposes, my definition of democracy is meant to capture both the actual institutional arrangements currently prevailing in many self-proclaimed forms of democratic government of which it has been claimed, with good reason, that they favour present generations, and include the internal link to taking turns (for which I will argue in Section 13.2). Thus, by democracy I mean a set of institutional arrangements and constitutional devices that both give form to the rule of the people (usually by electing representatives) and put restraints (largely liberal rights) upon the actions of the freely elected government. Modern democracies are the result of a historical and variable marriage of the liberalism of individual rights with popular sovereignty, where the latter usually entails majority consent. These institutional arrangements are meant to give expression to the equal liberty and dignity of citizens, who collectively decide their fate, not only by holding regular elections but also by way of a public sphere in which democratic deliberation is fostered through the constitutional right to free speech and free assembly (Habermas 1994, 1996).

It is this democratic institutional set-up that is now increasingly accused of presentism or short-termism; that is, of giving priority to net benefits in the present at the cost of future ones. This allegedly excessive focus on the short term is particularly problematic in policy domains that call for an extended time frame, such as long-term infrastructure, the pension system, nuclear waste management, biopolitical demographic planning, and environmental sustainability, especially action on climate change, loss of biodiversity, pollution, deforestation, ocean acidification. In these areas, successful action tends to impose costs in the short term (e.g. increasing taxes and imposing regulation, divesting from existing energy infrastructure), but the associated benefits typically materialise only in the long run, and in some cases mostly or only for later generations, overlapping and non-overlapping. Given this temporal disjunction, democratic institutions are often tempted to pass the costs on to the next generations, thus failing to adopt the required policies.

In his recent overview, Michael MacKenzie suggests 'four potential sources of short-termism in democratic systems: (1) short-sighted voters; (2) politicians with short-term incentives; (3) special interest groups with short-term objectives; and (4) the fact that future generations cannot be included in decision-making processes today' (2016a, 24; see also Thorseth 2015; Gesang 2015). While the last source depends of course on the definition of 'inclusion' (for future generations could be represented by proxies), I will elaborate and expand on the first three reasons briefly here, beginning with (3) for its importance.

Presentism is often related to the short-term thinking said to be brought on by democracy's relation to free market competition, in particular in so-called post-Fordist and postmodern, increasingly global capitalism since the 1960s, and by the fact that state power is beholden to special economic interests. These interests are often pushed by economic actors that exert a lot of power on states (e.g. by way of the dependence on corporate taxes and investment and the creation of employment) and on politicians (in particular if public financing of electoral campaigns is insufficient). Under competitive conditions, these economic agents often operate with very short and accelerating time frames. As MacKenzie elaborates elsewhere (2016b), the existence of groups with strong short-term preferences and significant political influence may skew decision-making processes in the direction of concessions that distribute the burdens of long-term policies to others and confer short-term benefits on themselves. This line of argument usually focuses on the influence of powerful economic actors with dominant short-term interests in making profits, often under competitive conditions that sideline broader and more long-term goals (Shearman and Smith 2007). Large-scale or well-organised economic agents may influence democratic decision-making processes directly by electoral campaign contributions, funding political advertisements, fielding their own 'insider' candidates, and so on (Mansbridge 2012; Lessig 2011; Nichols and McChesney 2013). Less directly but very powerfully, corporations can affect democratic processes by moving, or threatening to move, to other jurisdictions if regulations that are perceived as adversely affecting their profits are discussed in the legislative arena (e.g. Dryzek 1995; Ekeli 2005; Lindblom 1982; Paehlke 1989). This 'economic dependence' of democratic political systems (Caney 2016; Boston and Lempp 2011) may have become worse during the very time period that environmental crises became so pressing. As Naomi Klein argues specifically with respect to global warming, neoliberalist policies since the 1960s, from deregulation of markets to shrinking of governments, has made concerted action on climate change seem so intractable by weakening the democratic state in the face of increasingly post-national economic actors facing global competition (Klein 2014).

These competitive conditions contribute to the instrumentalisation of rationality and of action, and thus a favouring of narrow interests in the present. While instrumental reasoning, as the focus on the means towards given ends, is important to all action, the so-called Frankfurt School argued that in modernity it comes to progressively eclipse independent rational goal-setting (Horkheimer 1974). In political terms, democratic collective determinations of overall (and typically longer-term) goals are sidelined by the pursuit of all-purpose means, such as money and profits (Schecter 2010). The instrumentalisation of action orientations applies in particular to economic agents, individual and collective, who find themselves in competitive conditions, but also to democratic nation states to the extent they compete with each other for attracting capital investments (Przeworski and Wallerstein 1988; Przeworski 2010).

Economic dependence and instrumental reason may be further enhanced by the growing social acceleration that has gripped all societies in the process of industrialisation, in particular since the Second World War (Scheuerman 2004; Connolly 2002; Rosa 2010). Long-term thinking, we may surmise, has a hard time installing itself in motivational apparatuses of voters and office holders if these are already overstimulated and overstressed (Stiegler 2018). Democracy is particularly vulnerable to acceleration; Rosa and others have argued that technology and economy affect society much faster than democratic (especially deliberative) processes, which merely play catch-up. Information-gathering and deliberation simply take time, as does the verification of legislative proposals against normative standards, existing law and long-standing policies. In response to this desynchronisation, political scientists have noted an increasing displacement of decisions away from elected democratic bodies towards faster but less democratic agencies, from the legislative to the executive branch, to courts, and above all to the private sector, to corporations and to the economic sphere. In turn, it has been argued that overall acceleration is largely caused by global competitive market conditions (Jessop 2009; Connolly 2011). Presentism consists, then, in a favouring of the present rather than the future, but this present is itself fleeting, swiftly giving way to the ever-new future and its latest gadgets.

Presentism has also been related to the frequent change of guards required by the electoral cycles of representative democracy. Simon Caney speaks in this context of 'harmful short-termism', and political scientists King and Crewe argue pointedly: 'politicians lack accountability for the future impacts of their policies, and this leads them not to think policy through, often with disastrous results' (King and Crewe 2014: 356–59, 395).

Another argument that has been put forward for (democratic) short-termism is the intergenerational intensification of the well-known 'tragedy of the commons' (Hardin 1968; for many ways of avoiding it, see Ostrom 1990). Present and future people are said to be caught in a particularly vicious collective action problem that pits individual rationality against collective interests: what is rational from an individual's point of view (an individual consumer, say, or an individual state) is irrational, perhaps even catastrophic, for the collective. In the intergenerational case of such a tragedy, a present generation bent on utility maximisation exploits its asymmetrical power over the future, resulting not in the famous 'tyranny of the majority' (Mill 2003: 76), but in what Gardiner has called the 'tyranny of the contemporary' (2011: 143). While intra-generational collective action problems may be addressed, among other things, by enforcing rules that benefit the collective, in the intergenerational case such enforcement depends on institutions of governance that tend to be weaker the more they have to be shared over time, resulting in a political 'problem of interaction' (Gardiner 2011: 37, 143). Liberal democracies may be particularly vulnerable to such a tragedy of the commons, especially in the case of climate change (Wallimann-Helmer 2015). Supposing we accept this bleak picture – one that assumes largely self-interested agents, perhaps resulting from increasing instrumentalisation of action – part of the conclusion is that we need powerful democratic institutions with sanctioning power to counter the presentist effects. These institutions would have to be more independent of economic power and have global reach (to address a global tragedy of the commons), but they should also survive generational discontinuities and takeovers. Democracies must be able to sustain their sovereignty over time, but they must also understand sovereign power as globally and intergenerationally shared.

Some also argue there is a presentist time preference on the part of the (some add: an increasingly instrumentally oriented or consumerist) populace (MacKenzie 2016a, mentioned above), perhaps justifying the implementation of a positive social discount rate on the part of its representatives. In this context, we could mention a number of psychological, all-too-human factors bearing down on democratic citizens: the difficulty of noticing and properly acting on so-called 'creeping problems', the unidentifiability or invisibility of the future victim, weakness of will, tendency to procrastination, and so on.

Note that only one of the above sources of presentism is germane to democracy, namely, the regular change of guards (I will come back to this). Two of these sources are putatively universal, such as the last one regarding human psychology and the tragedy of the commons (though both are, if not caused then exacerbated by the other, more historically specific factors). The other reasons for presentism – economic dependence, instrumentalisation of action and social acceleration – are concerned with modernity and its capitalist organisation of production and distribution, as well as the path dependence regarding fossil fuels and other infrastructure (Caney 2016). Capitalist markets tend to render democratic self-government short-termist, at least at a certain stage of development.

13.2 Pro-futural Motivations Internal to Democracy

Partly in response to these issues, various proposals have been made to better represent future people in current democratic decision-making processes. Some of the proposals involve specialised institutions meant to specifically promote pro-futural policies, while other proposals seek to increase the future-oriented nature of inherited, existing political institutions. Regarding the former, we could mention regular constitutional conventions in view of updating democratic constitutions (see Thomas Jefferson's famous Letter to James Madison, of 6 September 1789; Jefferson 1904); an ombudsperson for future generations; parliamentary committees dedicated to future generations, such as the Standing Parliamentary Committee for the Future that the Israeli Knesset had (2001–06) (Shohay and Lamay 2006), or the Finnish Committee for the Future within the Finnish Parliament (Caney 2016); a citizens' assembly specifically aimed at safeguarding the perennity of the democratic process (Thompson 2016); a global climate bank (Broome and Foley 2016); and a common heritage fund for future generations (Szabó 2016).

As for proposals that seek to increase the pro-futural consideration of existing democratic institutions, they include explicitly mentioning future people in constitutions (as some already do); reserving a certain proportion (e.g. 5 per cent) of the legislature for elected representatives of the future (Dobson 1996: 132–35; Ekeli 2005: 429–50, 434); making the second chamber that many democracies have a randomly selected one, so as to counterbalance some of the short-term tendencies associated with elected chambers (Mackenzie 2016b); introducing youth quotas in parliament (Bidadanure 2016); demanding 'posterity impact statements' of legislators (Caney 2016); introducing age-differentiated political (e.g. voting) rights; e.g. a system in which parents can exercise votes on behalf of their children (Schmitter 2000: 40–41; van Parijs 1998: 308–14); attaching social and environmental obligations to pension funds so as to render corporate activities more responsible to future generations (Sandberg 2016); setting up an intergenerational endowment requirement, the compliance with which would trigger tax incentives (Cordelli and Reich 2016).

The task I have set myself here is not to assess these different proposals, but to ask why contemporary democrats should be moved to better represent future generations in the first place. Does this motivation come from within the democratic idea, or must democracy be supplemented by other normative sources, cultural, moral or political? In the next section, I will argue that an internal motivation is preferable.

Although I cannot show this here, most work on this issue seeks to reform democracy on the basis of extrinsic (i.e. not necessarily democratic) supplements, such as theories of justice more generally: inadequate treatment of future generations just seems unfair to notions of equality, of rights – notions which need not be related to democracy, but may be so related, of course, at least in a broad way. (Thus, one may feel tempted to challenge the dichotomy extrinsic–intrinsic, though I think it will retain some of its heuristic value.) Discussing some of the reform proposals to better represent the interests of future generations mentioned above, Gonzalez-Ricoy and Gosseries write in their introduction to *Institutions for Future Generations*: 'The institutional proposals included in [this book] are thus assessed on explicit normative grounds belonging to theories of justice and legitimacy' (2016: 4), where these theories need not be explicitly democratic. Further, these theories of justice are usually extended versions that were first meant to apply only to contemporaries, relations among which thus remain the paradigmatic case. What Gosseries writes elsewhere about the method for determining possible rights of members of future generation applies to intergenerational ethics and policies more generally, namely that the 'avenue to examine and decide about what the content of such rights should be' consists 'in starting from our standard theories of justice (utilitarianism, egalitarianism, sufficientarianism, libertarianism) and finding out what they entail in the intergenerational realm' (Gosseries 2008: 447). Extrinsic motivations may thus be doubly extended, or twice removed: both from intergenerational relations, and from democracy.

Let me briefly suggest why pro-futural motivations 'internal' to democracy may be preferable. First, it might be better not to need the external sources, on which there may be widespread disagreement. If future generations are to be treated fairly by any democrat, and pro-futural motivations can be discovered in the concept and history of democracy itself, then it may suffice to be committed to, or participate in, democratic institutions (though of course, here too disagreements as to what this entails must be reckoned with). Second, the internal sources constrain us to care not only for intergenerational ethics in general, but specifically for the democratic institutions and democratic capacities of future people themselves. A broader, not specifically democratic–political conception of intergenerational ethics could serve as a complement for other, non-political claims of future people. (Though, as I will suggest briefly, the turn-taking model can also be seen as embedding democratic societies in environments that generate turn-sharing obligations to future generations on their own.) Third, motivations internal to democracy may lead one more directly to formulate responses internal to democratic institutions, that is, to reforms affecting and protecting these institutions themselves, so as to prevent, for example, outside influence from the economic sector and from self-interested private actors and their psychological tendencies towards short-termism.

One internal argument linking democracy to concern for future people is often said to be the 'all affected' principle in deliberative democracy (Eckersley 2000; Jensen 2015; more generally on discursive ethics and future people, see, Brumlik 2004; Kettner 1992; Ott 2008a, 2008b). According to this principle, a proposed norm, policy or course of action attains normative validity only if all those affected by it could rationally consent to it (Habermas 1990). Many 'green' deliberative democrats or discourse ethicists have argued for the temporal extension of some version of this principle (Dobson 1996; Johnson 2007). The principle can be extended to unborn agents if 'all affected' is interpreted to mean 'all possibly affected' (Heyward 2008) and if the consent requirement is not taken to call for actual, empirically verifiable consent, of which not-yet existing people are of course at present incapable. This is where MacKenzie's fourth point becomes most relevant: 'future generations cannot be included in decision-making processes today' (2016a: 24).

However, one may argue that this virtualisation of consent and fictionalising of discourse robs deliberative democracy of its most distinctive features. It forces it to weaken or abandon the call for actual dialogue, which is replaced, in the manner of

Rawls (1971) or Scanlon (1998), by an inevitably abstract account of moral and political principles the theorist thinks rational agents would consent to, or at least could not reject. While the all-affected principle remains pertinent and important in this context, here I want to propose another, a new and different argument for the claims as to the future-oriented motivations that can be claimed to be internal to democracy. I call it the turn-taking view of democracy.

13.3 Sharing Democratic Institutions by Turns

Given the important role it plays in games and in socialisation processes – from sharing the swing on the playground to board games and language learning (Hayashi 2012) – most of us are familiar with the idea of sharing an object or a game by taking turns with it. In this form of sharing, each participant is assigned a limited temporal duration with a role, the occupation of an office, or a thing. Despite this familiarity, when most people (as well as theorists of distributive justice) approach the task of allocation, they tend to think of sharing an object by division rather than by turns: we cut a cake into parts to be consumed by each individually. Sharing economic benefits of cooperation (income, consumption, and so on) follows this part-sharing model. But in some cases, sharing by turns seems more appropriate than sharing by parts, e.g. when one or more of the following conditions pertaining to item X are met:

1. X cannot very well be shared by division, for dividing it into parts would destroy X as the thing it is (e.g. disassembling a bike renders it unusable, though we can indirectly share it by parts if we have a common metric, like money: then we could rent it out or sell it).
2. X's use(fulness) is typically temporary (e.g. bike-sharing services); for generations, birth and death impose the temporary 'use' of inherited items of sharing that are typically handed on to the future (tradition, language, environment or earth, institutions, and so on).
3. X is 'owned' in common but cannot be appropriated or consumed in toto at a given time (e.g. the earth, or a tradition), and this excess cannot but be passed on to the future.
4. X was received from others earlier in time (together with (3), this means X precedes and exceeds present users; again, one thinks of quasi-holistic items such as tradition, language, and the earth).

As I will indicate, and as Aristotle argued in his *Politics*, these features apply to many political offices generally, not just to democratic institutions. However, I would like to suggest that the link between political institutions and turn-taking is even tighter in the case of democracies. There are a number of reasons why one may take taking turns to be particularly relevant to democracy as defined above. My general point is that it is essential to democracy to ask its members to accept that other members may or will rule after them; accordingly, democrats are committed to letting others have their turn at governing after them. Let me unfold this point more slowly.

I begin with a brief social–ontological account of identity over time, an account which I argue inflects the more political reasons for associating democracy with taking turns. My argumentative strategy here is not to deny that this account would have to apply to all individual and collective political identities, whether democratic or not. Rather, I argue that the various forms of taking turns that I will uncover below in democratic institutions should be understood as expressing the ontology of turn-taking. In other words, part of what makes democratic forms of government unique is the fact that they specifically respect and institutionalise this ontological–temporal condition. And if we can further show (as I will in the subsequent section) that taking turns relates present to future generations, then this institutionalisation of the ontology of turn-sharing is an argument for extending democracies to future people. Indeed, this 'extension' to future generations is then better understood, not so much as undertaken by the theorist, but rather as more fully recognising the ontological inflection of democracies towards turn-taking, an inflection and extension that has, in effect, always already been underway.

The ontological reason I have in mind begins from the fact that to confront democracy with intergenerational concerns is to place democracy in historical time. We should thus reflect on the relation between time and identifying something as this or that (e.g. the identity of an institutional arrangement or individual disposition as democratic, as opposed to dictatorial, monarchical, aristocratic, oligarchic, tyrannical, etc.). Temporally speaking, identity in general is not pregiven as remaining identical to itself, but consists in returning to itself over time from its context, from which it differs. If a self was simply identical to itself over time, then it is hard to see how it could be destroyed, or undergo any sort of change. This means we have to think together both identity over time and its change, and this is what the idea of identity returning, or taking turns with itself as changing, does.

Time 'itself' is nothing without identities existing 'in' time, and it already includes this duplicity of identity and change. Any account of time has to do justice both to what we might call the presentness of the present, and to temporal succession. It cannot be that one moment is first identical to itself, and only then comes to pass away, giving way to another. Rather, every instant ceases to be as soon as it comes to be. And yet, if time were nothing but flow, then no identity could maintain itself in being, as there was no presence, and no difference between one time and another. Now, one way of addressing this duplicity is by thinking time as a taking of turns: each time has its unique and irreplaceable turn, but the 'now' as this singular turn consists only in turning towards or around itself in coming to be from other times, and turning towards another by passing away into yet other times (Derrida 2005). Taking turns, then, is a way of grasping the relation between irreplaceability and replacement, identity and change, or singularity and multiplicity: what is irreplaceable each time is its turn, but such a turn consists only in a granting of presence by past and future. In fact, the English *week* and the French *fois* (as in *une fois*, one time) are derived from the Latin *vicis*, the uses of which range from 'by turns' (*per vices*) and 'in turn' (*vicissim*) to 'succession', 'alternation', 'change', 'reciprocally' and 'in place of' (*in vicem*). Thus, one time takes turns with another time, week by week, one singled-out presence coming to replace a previous one while already being in the process of being replaced by another. Time and identity over time call on us to do justice to the singularity of each time, but this singularity can 'be' only as iterated next time, repeated and to be repeated on the revolutions of the calendar, and generation by generation.

Thus, once we consider an identity over time, we can say that it is not given as the same, but returns to itself from what is other than itself – its past and future other, but also other others in its context. For if identity (the problematically presupposed 'itself' in the previous sentence) is not already given but first of all to be won in this turning movement, then at each turn identity is exposed to, and altered by, that which it is not, or not yet. That is why, at each turn, we cannot (yet) clearly distinguish between future self and the other. If we do not presuppose that the 'itself' remains the same over time, that future self is the same as the past and present self, then the future self is first of all to be reidentified as the self. This reidentification cannot be guaranteed: it is a kind of promise of return that may be broken – and indeed, if by identity we mean the exact same, cannot but be broken. Otherwise, we cannot account for change over time along with identity.

At each turn, identity must make contact with its other in the hope or promise of return, but this alterity induces change in identity. Again, the notion of the turn is meant to help us grasp this duplicity of identity and change: each turn is a unique identity, but only as 'ongoingly' receiving its time by a previous turn and already turning toward the future in a fragile promise of return. Identity takes turns in a context in which it is exposed to change; it takes turns with itself as another (future self), at each turn exposing it to alteration and to others, and thus to alternation. Identities, singular or collective, exist in the mode of taking turns, with themselves (a past self-giving place to a present self-giving place to a future self), but also with others.

Because of this conflictual duplicity in the turning, there cannot be a perfect embodiment of this ontological condition in institutional life, not even a (utopian) ideal that actual governments can approach more-or-less closely, or progressively reach. In this sense, taking turns should be thought of, less as a form of government, and more as a dimension of political experience and institutionalisation that any form of government, democratic or not, has to undergo and negotiate. Nonetheless, institutional arrangements can affirm taking turns to different degrees. For example, a hereditary monarchy will seek to hold onto its rule over time as much as possible, claiming to embody and represent communal political identity over time. Hereditary monarchs typically seek to secure their rule over time, even after their death, by determining successors that preserve their (family) identity. The monarch's acceptance of rule implies no giving way to another. (Of course, this contrast between monarchy and democracy is no absolute opposition; the ontology applies to both and may at times demands complex mixtures.) By contrast, democratic institutions are in principle open to the alternation, to the change of rule while still trying to maintain their identity as democratic. Democracies, on my reading, in principle affirm the turning nature of time, that is, their own constitution, by accepting the alternation, and that means, by the democratic assent to letting others have their turn in governing (Fritsch 2011).

But that is also why democracy is inherently unstable, for in opening itself to the change of rule, its identity as democratic is placed in danger: the next turn-taker may not be democratic. This is a well-known and very contemporary conundrum: can a democracy legitimate its own abdication? To what extent should democracies tolerate non-democrats? Should a constitutional court, in the interest of democratic principles, intervene when an apparently non-democratic (e.g. fundamentalist, or tyrannical or non-egalitarian) party is about to win a general election? There are of course various ways in which institutional arrangements anticipate and negotiate these dilemmas, above all by way of constitutional guarantees that seek to single out and maintain (allegedly) core democratic principles that are then difficult to change even by new democratic majorities. (Elsewhere, I have argued that constitutional guarantees of this sort cannot undo the fundamental duplicity I discussed; see Fritsch 2013.)

I mention these fascinating issues here only to show that the risks stem from the social–ontological constitution of identity and are inherent in any political framework, but especially the democratic. This is because democracy, which is of course only one form of government among others, respects the turn-taking ontological condition more clearly, more expressly. It does that by accepting, in principle, that there may be others after me who I must grant or let have a turn in governing. In affirming my rule (or that of the majority of which I am a part or for which I voted), I affirm that it is temporary, and could change.

In a moment, I will argue that the consent to letting other govern has also – quietly, perhaps, but necessarily – been extended to a generational, rather than just individual, turn-taking. Before elaborating this, let me discuss a bit more this democratic consent as consent to letting others have a turn, by listing some of the ways in which democracies open themselves to turn-taking.

1. The first way stems largely from Aristotle. If democracy is defined (among other things) as rule among the free and equal, but not all can govern at the same time (as there are limited offices, or for pragmatic reasons), then free and equal citizens should take turns in governing. In this way, each one becomes governor and governed in turn, thereby satisfying the freedom and the equality requirement (Aristotle, *Politics*, e.g. 2.2, 1261a; 3.16, 1287a). This basic idea is not specific to democracy only, for the same problem of reconciling freedom and equality obtains among a ruling class in an aristocracy or an oligarchy. Wherever there is no 'natural' hierarchy among human beings in their capacity for rule, as among 'brothers', taking turns recommends itself (*Nicomachean Ethics* 8:11, 1161a25–30; cf. Miller 2013). But this taking of turns is most widespread in democracy because it values freedom and equality above all, and does not tie these to property; thus democracy extends equal political freedom to all citizens, and these are likely to be too numerous to all hold political office at the same time. As Aristotle says, democracy champions freedom and equality, and thus taking turns, the most (*Politics* 6.2, 1317b–1318a).
2. The second reason also stems from Aristotle but this time relates to the application of law to all equally in cases of conflict of interest. In a fascinating and convoluted passage on absolute monarchy (Aristotle, *Politics* 1287a), Aristotle suggests that the need to apply the law already implies the idea of taking turns with law-executing offices. For if the – very human, thus rational but also still 'beastly' and selfish – monarch applied the law to himself, then he would be above the law and thereby violate the very idea of the law as applying to all humans equally. Hence, law and taking turns are closely aligned, not only but especially in democracy, which – as defined above – treats all citizens equally and thus does not take anyone to be above the law. The very idea of constitutionalising (i.e. legally constituting) sovereign political power entails sharing at least some offices (here, law-executing ones) by turns. The fact that humans are finite, temporal beings who do not divinely rotate around themselves in eternity, as Aristotle's unmoved mover does, then, seems to imply turn-taking with others.

Today, many public offices have a substitute officer, for example, a vice president – also from the Latin per vices ('by turns') – not only as substitute in case of illness or other absence, but because the officer may need to excuse herself from a decision for some reason (e.g. conflict of interest), and then hand over her turn to the vice officer.

3. A more modern link between democracy and taking turns lies in protecting minorities. A democracy explains why a minority should consent to majority

rule by suggesting that the minority may become the majority in turn, at the next turn (e.g. the next election). In this sense, the people's right to change the majority through elections is a defining characteristic of democracy. In ruling, every democratic majority consents to possibly shifting majorities and minorities in the future. One way in which this consent is expressed is by committing to fair future elections and to granting pertinent rights to the minority, for otherwise the majority would make itself permanent and become a dictatorship. The minority retains the right and the opportunity to seek to become the majority, and therefore possesses all the rights necessary to compete fairly in elections, including rights to free speech, assembly, association and petition. Perhaps this captures the discomfort many feel in the face of the recent authoritarian turn in democracies, some dimensions of which we can perhaps see as violating the idea of taking turns. For example, if a governing party seeks to shore up its victory by gerrymandering and by stacking up courts, it is acting out of an undemocratic ethos that seeks to forestall the chances of the governed becoming the ruling majority in turn.

4. With this reference to free speech, we have moved to my last link between democracy and turn-taking. It belongs to the democratic ethos, both of citizens and of political–legal organisation, to respect and institutionalise free speech, which entails that democrats must grant the others (e.g. the minority, the official opposition in parliament) a chance, a turn, at speaking. Conversations and dialogue in general, as linguists know well (Hayashi 2012), require taking turns with speech, and so granting free speech in principle to all citizens (or all affected by democratic decisions) calls for the institutionalisation of granting all a turn at being heard. In democratic theory, this insight has above all been elaborated by deliberative or discursive theories that insist on the centrality of pre-voting, pre-aggregative deliberation (Habermas 1996; Gutmann and Thompson 2004; Fontana et al. 2004; Mackenzie and Sorial 2011). That is one of the reasons, we might say, why dialogic search for the truth, for example in universities (ideally independent from the state and from corporations), is so central to democracy, and why democratic education is of paramount significance. Such education should include, in practice and in theory, deliberation on the basis of good reasoning, and listening to others in the context of shared institutions (Morrell 2018), however trite and uncomfortable that sounds in the age of recent trends towards populism, polarisation, internet bubbles, deliberate sensationalist obfuscation, and so on. The so-called authoritarian turn also reminds us, however, that democratic turn-taking carries the risk that democratic alternation results in an anti-democratic turn, which itself can be presented as another democratic turn. By opening itself to the turn-taking nature of time, democracy must risk the turn to the other than democracy, and this precisely to

be what it is (see Derrida 2005). The risk may be reduced by constitutional guarantees that even majorities cannot change easily, but this is unlikely to eliminate the risk altogether (Fritsch 2013).

Despite this risk, if there is an internal link between democracy and turn-taking, then it would be undemocratic to use one's turn to forestall the possibility of an alternation, a turn, in governing. Let us also note that some of the reasons for the link between democracy and turn-taking – reasons 1 and 3 – refer to a feature of democracies that we mentioned as one of the drivers for democratic short-termism, namely the frequent change of guards required by electoral cycles. The changeover, and the commitment to it, belongs to democracy as a defining feature, here expressed as taking turns. To wish to change this potential reason for presentism might thus be to meddle with a core feature of democracy. Despite this connection between short-termism and taking turns, however, I now argue that taking turns is a way to reconceive democracy as not (just) presentist.

13.4 Taking Turns with Future Generations

As indicated, I now want to argue that the democratic, principled assent to the possibility of others having a turn at governing entails a commitment to share one's turn with future generations – those who not only may, but will have a turn with the institutions we are already in the process of leaving to them.

The first premise of this argument, then, is the conclusion to the argument in the preceding section: to say yes to democracy is to say yes to letting others have a turn at governing, others after oneself. The second premise refers to the fact that we are all mortals, and this fact entails that 'others after oneself' includes future generations, in the overlapping and more distant senses defined above, especially the most proximate generation as the next turn-taker. These two premises (affirming democracy is to affirm the next turn-taker, and the next turn-taker will include future generations) yield the conclusion that democrats relate to their political system by already affirming future people as inherently co-occupying and co-owning democratic institutions.

Given what we said about time as taking turns, this result is not surprising. If a present time is present only in receiving its time from the past and is already in the process of turning towards the future, then the past and the future are not cut off from the present, as if by a great abyss. Rather, non-present times are co-implicated in the present. As a result, future generations are already what we might call 'spectrally' present in the here and now. (This co-presence of past and future generations is often defended by various Indigenous views, for instance, the well-known Great Law of Peace (*Gayanashagowa*) of the Iroquois (Haudenosaunee) Confederacy and its reference to seven generations: seven in the future, or, on a different interpretation, three in the past, one in the present, and another three in the future, the latter interpretation not only stressing Indigenous ancestor worship and its relation to profutural care, but also gesturing more towards the idea of taking turns. On the seven-generation principle, see Lyons 1980; Murphy 1997; see also Chapter 6 in the present volume.) There are various ways in which we can understand the spectral presence of future generations in the present.

First, future generations are spectrally present in the political system now, namely, as the next turn-taker already affirmed in the now. This affirmation recognises future generations, first of all as moral–political claimants, that is, most generally as those who have a prima facie claim to have their interests recognised and represented by current decisions. Even if we are thinking of non-overlapping and thus not yet existing generations, some moral–political standing in the present cannot be denied to them. Drawing on the model of taking turns, we should then ask: what is it to let future others have a turn with the democratic institutions with which one is having a turn now? Since a turn-taker owns only her turn, but not the thing with which she takes turns, her first duty to future turn-takers is to pass these institutions on in a well-preserved, well-functioning or even flourishing state (Habib 2013).

Second, this affirmation of future generations as co-owners is expressed and bolstered by the fact that every political system must be concerned about ensuring its survival beyond the currently living, by integrating the newborn (and new immigrant members) into its system. We can approach the significance of this by imagining counterfactually whether it would make sense, for example, to engage in democratic institutions in the absence of any new generations; many of our political projects assume a temporal horizon that does not end with the current generation, but includes the continued existence of political society, and would stop making sense if there were no future citizens. Hence, the importance of education, especially democratic and political.

Third, despite the power asymmetry between present and future (Barry 1989: 189, 246), future generations are spectrally present in that they can in principle overturn decisions made in the past or the present. A generation has to take this into account by considering future generations co-citizens in some way. Generational sovereignty (see Gosseries 2016) cannot – for social–ontological as well as normative reasons – be construed on the model of exclusive property ownership with respect to democratic institutions and territory. Here, the model of turn-taking helps us once more to see that a generation merely owns its turn, not that with which it takes turns. The social–ontological model also helps us to grasp the ontological–temporal status of the institutions in the right way. What is to be avoided is the unpalatable alternative: either each generation is totally sovereign or autonomous in owning (and thus potentially handing on in toto) its institutions (a conception that is very widespread in Enlightenment modernity from Thomas Jefferson and the French Constitution of 1793 to Rawls; see Fritsch 2013), or generations share them equally over time, but then each generation cannot change them, and so is not sovereign.

The turn-taking model avoids this alternative (total or no sovereignty) by viewing institutions as constitutively temporal, that is, as temporally extended quasi-unities (or changing identities) that have been received from the past, and that are already sliding into the hands of the future. What is to be avoided is divorcing citizens from institutions, as if only citizens were generationally replaced, but the institutions stayed the same over time. Institutions are merely quasi-unities that get remade by each generation, and with respect to which no one generation can be exclusive sovereign proprietor. Thus, a generation of citizens is characterised by what we may call auto-heteronomy, that is, an autonomy that co-constitutively depends on inheritance and carrying on by future people. Taking turns expresses this constitutive finitude and temporal humility of power.

Conclusion

Most efforts to reform democratic institutions for future generations are, I submit, extrinsically motivated and exterior to democratic institutions. This permits these efforts to avoid tackling the issue of time despite the motivating worry that democracy is presentist; what would have to be treated by democratic theorists is the relation to the time of generations. By contrast, my internalist, time-focused strategy yields a non-presentist result by grasping the finite generational sharing of democratic institutions, and larger conditions of democratic life, in the turn-taking sense indicated above. This sense is to capture the spectral or virtual presence of future generations in our institutional life, as we find it more often and more expressly in pre-modern or Indigenous societies. The obligations to future people are not just internal to democracy, but also mediated, namely, by way of the (overarching, holistic) context (such as institutions) with which we take turns. It is this sense that the turn-taking model should motivate our reform efforts, such as standing parliamentary committees for the future, second chambers selected by sortition, appointing future representatives or ombudspersons, and so on.

In conclusion, I would like to submit, for further consideration, two points about democracy's relation to the two 'ecos' (ecology and economy) that seem to bound it so problematically, first about democracy and the environment, and second about democracy and the capitalist economy.

Democracy and Environment

The internalist and mediated relation to future people, I would argue, opens the door to better recognising the embedding of democracies in the environment. Of course, democratic societies are themselves territorial and terrestrial, and rely on environmental conditions as the source of life, birth, but also death and generational turnover. Elsewhere, I have argued in detail that sharing by turn-taking (which we have seen should be grasped as internal to democracy) applies in particular to the earth as the global environment (Fritsch 2018). With respect to the earth as history and habitat of human life, the current generation must consider itself a mere turn-taker, not a possessor. Like democracy, earth displays holistic features that recommend a model of sharing, not by division into parts, but by taking turns with a quasi-holistic entity.

Thus, taking turns as a model of collective (and here, intergenerationally collective) sharing applies not only to the institutions of democratic governance, but to other 'items' of intergenerational sharing that have in common a number of features, such as precedence and excess to the turn-takers, indivisibility, temporary use, and the ultimate inappropriability by individuals or single generations. These features are displayed by the earth as the biosphere in which democratic societies are ecologically embedded. Given that future people are affected by the present generation not only through political institutions, but also via the environment as shared context of life, the crucial point is that to take turns with a democratic institutional heritage is to also take turns with the larger environmental context in which it is embedded; similarly, it wouldn't make sense to participate in a bicycle-sharing service without also (if necessary) contributing one's share to what is implied by taking turns with the road and city infrastructure that makes cycling possible.

Above, I suggested taking turns can help us operationalise the view that citizens and inherited institutions are reciprocally co-determining each other over time. This is because, in the case of quasi-holistic objects such as inherited political institutions and the earth, turn-taking does not view its 'object' of sharing as external to the turn-takers: to take turn with these objects is to be in part constituted by them. Similarly, democratically organised generations should not be viewed as external to the earth. Rather, the earth should be understood as co-constitutive of democratic politics – there is no sovereign demos without insertion in an overarching ecological context that precedes and exceeds the turn-takers.

The stakes for this environmental embedding of democracy are quite high, given that the Western heritage has, ever since Plato and Aristotle, conceived of politics as taking place in the city (the polis) defined at least partially by its opposition to nature (Jonas 1986: 2), or the natural world studied by the natural sciences,

sciences that are often conceived as politically neutral or even apolitical. We may thus need a new political constitution that overcomes the oppositions human vs. earth, politics vs. nature, science vs. politics, and so on (see Latour's much-discussed 'parliament of things'; Latour 1991, 2004). Among the oppositions to be rethought, we should count ecology vs economy, so in my second brief concluding note, I turn to the latter.

Democracy and Economy

We saw above that apart from the democratic change of guards (which we have now reinterpreted as turn-taking) and psychological factors, the major drivers of presentism have to do with the influence of a fast-paced, competitive and globalising economy upon democratic decision-making processes. Having reinterpreted democracy as a form of intra- and intergenerational taking turns, what can we say about this?

As the rule of the free and equal, democracy should be understood as entailing the so-called primacy of (democratic) politics: democratic self-governance is to have priority over other institutions of social life, especially the state apparatus, the military and the economy (Ladwig 2009; Rosa 2013: 358). It would not make sense to attribute to citizens the power of self-governance, but then exempt crucial, influential areas of social life from this self-governance. The limit on self-governance would rather be internal to democracy, namely, the demands of freedom and equality themselves, spelled out, for example, by liberal rights enshrined in a constitution that democracies can alter only with great difficulty (e.g. requiring two-thirds majorities, as for US constitutional amendments), or even not at all (e.g. the German Constitution's 'eternity clauses'; Häberle 2005).

In fact, this primacy of democratic politics may also be supported by functional, not just by normative considerations. State institutions are needed for a capitalist economy to function with private capital holders, for instance, to provide infrastructure and guarantee stability and absence of physical violence, provide currencies, enforce contracts. To fulfil this role as 'neutral' or third party, the state has to be perceived as legitimate, at least *grosso modo* and over the long haul. Such legitimacy, however, can arguably only be generated by processes of democratic participation, that is, by all economic actors understanding themselves at least in principle as participants in, or shapers of, this third party (Habermas 1984–85).

Now, if we accept this primacy of democratic politics over the economy, and democratic politics involves a long-term commitment to safeguard democratic institutions for (overlapping and non-overlapping) future people, then a paramount obligation of present democrats is to counteract short-termist and environment-harming tendencies issuing from the economy in particular. Some countervailing evidence linking democracy with intergenerational cooperation and sustainability bolsters this conclusion. In experiments studying people's willingness to sacrifice personal gains so that resources are passed on to future generations, it has been shown that such sharing over time occurs only when defection by free-riders are curbed by majority rule. According to this evidence, if (a big if, perhaps) a majority is willing to sustain a resource for future people, then democratic voting mechanisms help to restrain a minority of non-cooperators, and to align conditional cooperators (those who are willing to sustain the resource only if others do so also; Hauser et al. 2014; Putterman 2014). The failure to cooperate with future generations is driven, according to this research, primarily by a minority of individuals who extract far more than what is sustainable. These results may be particularly important when we have reached a situation in which, as Dipesh Chakrabarty put it recently, the wealthy believe (mistakenly, thinks Chakrabarty) that they can 'buy their way out' of climate disasters, or insulate themselves from their effects, in a way that the majority may not be able to afford (2017: 30). Part of the solution to democracy's short-termism, then, lies not just in addressing intergenerational fairness, but intra-generational equality.

References

Aristotle (1984). 'Nicomachean ethics'; 'Politics'. In Jonathan Barnes et al. (eds.), *The Complete Works of Aristotle: The Revised Oxford Translation*. Princeton, NJ: Princeton University Press, 1729–867; 1986–2129.

Barry, B. (1989). *Theories of Justice: A Treatise on Social Justice*. Berkeley: University of California Press, I.

Bidadanure, J. (2016). Youth quotas, diversity, and long-termism: Can young people act as proxies for future generations? In I. Gonzalez-Ricoy and A. Gosseries (eds.), *Institutions for Future Generations*. Oxford: Oxford University Press, 266.

Birnbacher, D. (1988). *Verantwortung für zukünftige Generationen*. Stuttgart: Reclam.

Boston, J. and F. Lempp (2011). Climate change: Explaining and solving the mismatch between scientific urgency and political inertia. *Accounting, Auditing & Accountability Journal* 24(8): 1000–21.

Broome, J. and D. K. Foley (2016). A world climate bank. In I. Gonzalez-Ricoy and A. Gosseries (eds.), *Institutions for Future Generations*. Oxford: Oxford University Press, 156–69.

Brumlik, M. (2004). *Advokatorische Ethik: Zur Legitimation pädagogischer Eingriffe*. Berlin: Philo.

Caney, S. (2016). Political institutions for the future: A five-fold package. In I. Gonzalez-Ricoy and A. Gosseries (eds.), *Institutions for Future Generations*. Oxford: Oxford University Press, 135–55.

Chakrabarty, D. (2017). The politics of climate change is more than the politics of capitalism. *Theory, Culture & Society* 34(2–3): 25–37.

Connolly, W. (2002). Democracy and time. In *Neuropolitics*. Minneapolis: University of Minnesota Press, 140–75.

Connolly, W. (2011). *Capital Flows, Sovereign Decisions, and World Resonance Machines: A World of Becoming*. Durham, NC: Duke University Press.

Cordelli, C. and R. Reich (2016). Philanthropy and intergenerational justice. In I. Gonzalez-Ricoy and A. Gosseries (eds.), *Institutions for Future Generations*. Oxford: Oxford University Press, 228–44.

Derrida, J. (2005). *Rogues*, Pascale-Anne Brault and Michael Naas (trans.). Stanford: Stanford University Press.

Dobson, A. (1996). Representative democracy and the environment. In William M. Lafferty and James Meadowcroft (eds.), *Democracy and the Environment: Problems and Prospects*. Cheltenham, UK: Edward Elgar, 124–39.

Dryzek, J. (1995). Political and ecological communication. *Environmental Politics* 4(4): 13–30.

Eckersley, R. (2000). Deliberative democracy, ecological representation and risk: Towards a democracy of all affected. In M. Saward (ed.), *Democratic Innovation: Deliberation, Representation and Association*. London: Routledge, 117–32.

Ekeli, K. S. (2005). Giving a voice to posterity: Deliberative democracy and representation of future people. *Journal of Agricultural and Environmental Ethics* 18: 429–50.

Fontana, B., C. J. Nederman and G. Remer (eds.) (2004). *Talking Democracy: Historical Perspectives on Rhetoric and Democracy*. University Park: Pennsylvania State University Press.

Fritsch, M. (2011). Taking turns: Democracy to come and intergenerational justice. *Derrida Today* 4(2): 148–72.

Fritsch, M. (2013). Europe's constitution for the unborn. In A. Czajka and B. Isyar (eds.), *Europe after Derrida*. Edinburgh: Edinburgh University Press, 80–94.

Fritsch, M. (2018). *Taking Turns with the Earth: Phenomenology, Deconstruction, and Intergenerational Justice*. Stanford: Stanford University Press.

Gesang, B. (2015). Is democracy an obstacle to ecological change? In D. Birnbacher and M. Thorseth (eds.), *The Politics of Sustainability. Philosophical Perspectives*, London: Routledge.

Gardiner, Stephen (2011). *A Perfect Moral Storm: The Ethical Tragedy of Climate Change*. Oxford: Oxford University Press.

Gonzalez-Ricoy, I. and A. Gosseries (2016). Designing institutions for future generations: An introduction. In I. Gonzalez-Ricoy and A. Gosseries (eds.), *Institutions for Future Generations*. Oxford: Oxford University Press, 3–23.

Gosseries, A. (2008). On future generations' future rights. *Journal of Political Philosophy* 16(4): 446–74, https://doi.org/10.1111/j.1467-9760.2008.00323.x

Gosseries, A. (2016). Generational sovereignty. In I. Gonzalez-Ricoy and A. Gosseries (eds.), *Institutions for Future Generations*. Oxford: Oxford University Press, 98–116.

Gutmann, A. and D. Thompson (2004). *Why Deliberative Democracy?*. Princeton, NJ: Princeton University Press.

Häberle, P. (2005). A constitutional law for future generations: The 'other' form of the social contract. *Generation Contract Intergenerational Justice Review* 3: 28.

Habermas, J. (1984–85). *The Theory of Communicative Action* (2 vols.). Cambridge: Polity.

Habermas, J. (1990). *Moral Consciousness and Communicative Action*. C. Lenhardt and S. Nicholsen Weber (trans.). Cambridge, MA: MIT Press.

Habermas, J. (1994). Three normative models of democracy. *Constellations* 1(1): 1–10.

Habermas, J. (1996). *Between Facts and Norms: Contributions to a Discourse Theory of Law and Democracy*. W. Rehg. (trans.). Cambridge, MA: MIT Press.

Habib, A. (2013). Sharing the earth: Sustainability and the currency of inter-generational environmental justice. *Environmental Values* 22(6): 751–64.

Hansen, M. H. (2006). *Polis: An Introduction to the Ancient Greek City-State*. Oxford: Oxford University Press.

Hardin, G. (1968). The tragedy of the commons. *Science* 162(3859): 1243–48.

Hauser, O. P., D. G. Rand, A. Peysakhovich and M. A. Nowak (2014). Cooperating with the future. *Nature* 511(7508): 220–23.

Hayashi, Makoto (2012). Turn allocation and turn sharing. In Jack Sidnell and Tanya Stivers (eds.), *The Handbook of Conversation Analysis*. Chichester, UK: Wiley, 167–90.

Heath, J. (2014). Rebooting discourse ethics. *Philosophy & Social Criticism* 40(9): 829–66.

Heyward, C. (2008). Can the all-affected principle include future persons? Green deliberative democracy and the non-identity problem. *Environmental Politics* 17(4): 625–43.

Horkheimer, M. (1974). *Eclipse of Reason*. London: Seabury Press.

Jefferson, Thomas (1904). *The Works of Thomas Jefferson*, Federal ed. New York: Putnam's (1904–5). Vol. 6. Chapter: To James Madison, http://oll.libertyfund.org/title/803/86733/1991883

Jensen, K. K. (2015). Future generations in democracy: Representation or consideration? *Jurisprudence* 6(3): 535–48.

Jessop, B. (2009). The spatiotemporal dynamics of globalizing capital and their impact on state power and democracy. In H. Rosa and W. E. Scheuerman (eds.), *High-Speed Society: Social Acceleration, Power, and Modernity*. University Park: Pennsylvania State University Press, 135–58.

Johnson, G. F. (2007). Discursive democracy in the trans-generational context. *Contemporary Political Theory* 6(1): 67–85.

Jonas, H. (1986). *The Imperative of Responsibility: In Search of Ethics for the Technological Age*. Hans Jonas and David Herr (trans.). Chicago: University of Chicago Press.

Kettner, M. (1992). Diskursethik und Verantwortung für zukünftige Generationen. In P. Fauser et al. (eds.), *Verantwortung* (Friedrich Jahresheft X). Seelze: Friedrich, 124–27.

King, A. and I. Crewe (2014). *The Blunders of Our Governments*. London: Oneworld.

Klein, N. (2014). *This Changes Everything: Capitalism vs. the Climate*. Toronto: Knopf Canada.

Ladwig, B. (2009). *Moderne Politische Theorie*. Schwalbach: Wochenschau.

Latour, B. (1991). *We Have Never Been Modern*. C. Porter (trans.). Cambridge, MA: Harvard University Press.

Latour, B. (2004). *The Politics of Nature. How to Bring the Sciences into Democracy*. C. Porter (trans.). Cambridge, MA: Harvard University Press.

Lessig, L. (2011). *Republic, Lost*. New York: Twelve.

Lindblom, C. E. (1982). The market as prison. *Journal of Politics* 44(2): 324–36.

Lyons, O. (1980). An Iroquois perspective. In C. Vecsey and R. W. Venables (eds.), *American Indian Environments: Ecological Issues in Native American History*. New York: Syracuse University Press, 171–74.

Mackenzie, C. and S. Sorial (2011). The limits of the public sphere: The advocacy of violence. *Critical Horizons* 12(2): 165–88.

MacKenzie, M. K. (2016a). Institutional design and sources of short-termism. In I. Gonzalez-Ricoy and A. Gosseries (eds.), *Institutions for Future Generations*. Oxford: Oxford University Press, 24–48.

MacKenzie, M. K. (2016b). A general-purpose, randomly selected chamber. In I. Gonzalez-Ricoy and A. Gosseries (eds.), *Institutions for Future Generations*. Oxford: Oxford University Press, 282–98.

Mansbridge, J. (2012). On the importance of getting things done. *PS: Political Science and Politics* 45(1): 1–8.

Mill, J. S. (2003 [1859]). *On Liberty*. David Bromwich and George Kateb (eds.). New Haven, CT: Yale University Press.

Miller, F. D. Jr. (2013). The rule of reason. In M. Deslauriers and P. Destrée (eds.), *The Cambridge Companion to Aristotle's Politics*. Cambridge: Cambridge University Press, 38–66.

Morrell, M. E. (2018). Listening and deliberation. In A. Bachtiger, J. Dryzek, J. Mansbridge and M. E. Warren (eds.), *The Oxford Handbook of Deliberative Democracy*. Oxford: Oxford University Press.

Murphy, G. (1997). Constitution of the Iroquois Confederacy, https://sourcebooks.fordham .edu/MOD/iroquois.asp

Nichols, J. and R. W. McChesney (2013). *Dollarocracy: How the Money and Media Election Complex Is Destroying America*. New York: Nation Books.

Ostrom, E. (1990). *Governing the Commons: The Evolution of Institutions for Collective Action*. Cambridge: Cambridge University Press.

van Parijs, P. (1998). The disfranchisement of the elderly, and other attempts to secure intergenerational justice. *Philosophy & Public Affairs* 27(4): 292–333.

Ott, K. (2008a). Diskursethik und die Grundzüge bioethischer Diskurse. In C. Brand, E. M. Engels, A. Ferrari and L. Kovàcs(eds.), *Wie funktioniert Bioethik*. Paderborn: Mentis, 61–95.

Ott, K. (2008b). Ethik und Diskurs. In F. J. Wetz, V. Steenblock and J. Siebert (eds.), *Kolleg Praktische Philosophie*. Stuttgart: Reclam, 111–52.

Paehlke, R. C. (1989). *Environmentalism and the Future of Progressive Politics*. New Haven, CT: Yale University Press.

Pierson, P. (2004). *Politics in Time: History, Institutions, and Social Analysis*. Princeton, NJ: Princeton University Press.

Przeworski, A. (2010). *Democracy and the Limits of Self-Government*. Cambridge: Cambridge University Press.

Przeworski, A. and M. Wallerstein (1988). Structural dependence of the state on capital. *American Political Science Review* 82: 11–29.

Putterman, L. (2014). Behavioural economics: A caring majority secures the future. *Nature* 511: 165–66.

Rawls, J. (1971). *A Theory of Justice*. Cambridge, MA: Harvard University Press.

Rawls, J. (1993). *Political Liberalism*. New York: Columbia University Press.

van Reybrouck, D. (2016). *Against Elections: The Case for Democracy*. London: Bodley Head.

Rosa, H. (2010). *Alienation and Acceleration: Towards a Critical Theory of Late-Modern Temporality*. Ann Arbor: University of Michigan Press.

Rosa, H. (2013). *Weltbeziehungen im Zeitalter der Beschleunigung: Umrisse einer neuen Gesellschaftskritik*. Frankfurt: Suhrkamp.

Rosa, H. and W. E. Scheuerman (eds.) (2009). *High-Speed Society: Social Acceleration, Power, and Modernity*. University Park: Pennsylvania State University Press.

Sandberg, J. (2016). Pension funds, future generations, and fiduciary duty. In I. Gonzalez-Ricoy and A. Gosseries (eds.), *Institutions for Future Generations*. Oxford: Oxford University Press, 197–213.

Scanlon, T. M. (1998). *What We Owe to Each Other*. Cambridge, MA: Harvard University Press.

Schecter, D. (2010). *The Critique of Instrumental Reason from Weber to Habermas*. London: Continuum.

Scheuerman, W. (2004). *Liberal Democracy and the Social Acceleration of Time*. Baltimore: Johns Hopkins University Press.

Schmitter, P. C. (2000). *How to Democratize the European Union . . . And Why Bother?* Lanham, MD: Rowman & Littlefield.

Shearman, D. and J. W. Smith (2007). *The Climate Change Challenge and the Failure of Democracy*. London: Praeger.

Shoham, S. and N. Lamay (2006). Commission for future generations in the Knesset: Lessons learnt. In J. C. Tremmel (ed.), *Handbook of Intergenerational Justice*. Cheltenham, UK: Edward Elgar, 244–81.

Stiegler, B. (2018). *The Neganthropocene*. D. Ross (trans.). London: Open Humanities Press.

Szabó, M. (2016). A common heritage fund for future generations. In I. Gonzalez-Ricoy and A. Gosseries (eds.), *Institutions for Future Generations*. Oxford: Oxford University Press, 385–99.

Thompson, D. F. (2016). Democratic trusteeship: Institutions to protect the future of the democratic process. In I. Gonzalez-Ricoy and A. Gosseries (eds.), *Institutions for Future Generations*. Oxford: Oxford University Press, 184–97.

Thorseth, M. (2015). Limitations to democratic governance of natural resources. In D. Birnbacher and M. Thorseth (eds.), *The Politics of Sustainability. Philosophical Perspectives*. London: Routledge, 17ff.

Wallimann-Helmer, I. (2015). The liberal tragedy of the commons: The deficiency of democracy in a changing climate. In D. Birnbacher and M. Thorseth (eds.), *The Politics of Sustainability: Philosophical Perspectives*. London: Routledge, 20–35.

Zingano, M. (2013). Natural, ethical, and political justice. In M. Deslauriers and P. Destrée (eds.), *The Cambridge Companion to Aristotle's Politics*. Cambridge: Cambridge University Press, 199–222.

14

The Normative and Social Dimensions of the Transition towards a Responsible, Circular Bio-Based Economy

VINCENT BLOK

Introduction

If we take into consideration the Anthropocene and the critics of our current relationship with the environment, as well as the necessary change in approach and mindset they promote, we also need to think of new conceptual foundations for our economic activities. Current developments in new product development based on renewable energy in general and biomass valorisation in particular are promising, and can be seen as the motor behind the transition to the circular bio-based economy (CBE). Although the concept and definition is contested in academic literature (Kirchherr et al. 2017; Birch and Tyfield 2013; Goven and Pavone 2015; Zwier et al. 2015), we adopt a common definition that is provided by the Ellen MacArthur Foundation (2010: 7). They define the CBE as:

an industrial system that is restorative or regenerative by intention and design. It replaces the 'end-of-life' concept with restoration, shifts towards the use of renewable energy, eliminates the use of toxic chemicals, which impair reuse, and aims for the elimination of waste through the superior design of materials, products, systems, and, within this, business models.

Despite this, a transition to the CBE is yet to take place. Recent studies in the CBE indicate that it is a promising way forward, although its actual practices are still marginal (Jonker et al. 2017). This may be explained by the chasm between innovators and early adopters and the majority of producers and consumers. Even where economic actors adopt CBE practices, it is often a side event and not part of the core business of the company. In the sustainability transition literature, it is argued that we are currently between the phase of pre-development, in which only small changes in the system take place that are not (yet) visible, and the phase of take-off, in which these structural changes gain momentum (Bosman and Rotmans 2016).

Normally, the explanation of why the transition to the CBE has not taken off yet is found in the complexity of system transitions. The transition to the CBE is a complex process of co-evolution of economic, technological and institutional developments at multiple levels and at a long-time scale (Grin et al. 2010). From a multilevel perspective, at the micro level new innovation practices emerge, for instance where sustainable entrepreneurs exploit circular bio-based technologies and operate as front runners to promote radical circular bio-based innovations which are adopted by early adopters. This micro level is supported by the meso level of the current regime of institutions and policies, for instance new emerging policies to stimulate the transition to the CBE. In order to enter the next phase of transition to the CBE, therefore, huge investments are made by European policymakers. There are also obstacles at the meso level, for instance the vested interests of the fossil fuel industry that have an interest in delaying the transition. In the end, the meso or regime level of change is influenced by long-term trends at the landscape level, for instance concerns regarding climate change or economic crises (Bosman and Rotmans 2016; Geels 2002; Geels and Schot 2007; Long et al. 2019). It is assumed that the transition to the CBE evolves when developments at these three levels align (Grin et al. 2010; Geels 2002). In a recent study on transitioning to the circular economy in the Netherlands, this dynamic was depicted as shown in Figure 14.1.

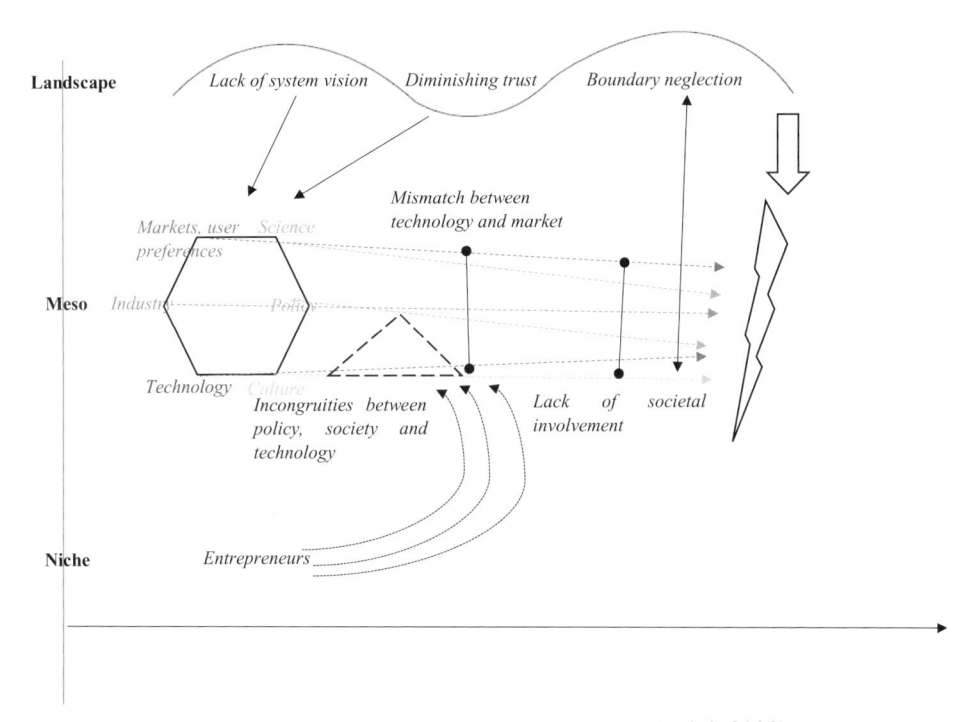

Figure 14.1 Transition to the circular economy (Inigo and Blok 2020)

Why has transitioning to the CBE not yet happened? From a multilevel perspective, the technological challenges and the policy and regulatory drivers and barriers are often highlighted (Bosman and Rotmans 2016). For instance, because residual streams are framed as 'waste', reuse of these materials for food is difficult and requires new rules and regulations (Sira Consulting 2011). What is often missed in the literature, however, are the normative and social dimensions that can be seen as barriers to transitioning to the CBE (Murray et al. 2017; Inigo and Blok 2019). Although we acknowledge the importance of the other barriers to the transition to the CBE, we concentrate on the normative and social dimensions of this transition in this chapter.

In this chapter, we will first argue that current practices in CBE are framed within the market or economic logic and miss the normative dimension of the call for circularity. The transition to the CBE requires a fundamental reflection on the role of economic actors in the social and ecological environment with significant consequences for their business practices. Second, we will argue that the transition to the CBE requires the acknowledgement of the normative and social dimensions of this transition at the meso and macro levels, and the establishment of an environmental and social logic on the micro level of business practices. Third, we will argue that the concept of responsible innovation (RI) can help to articulate the normative and social dimensions of the transition to the CBE, and enables the operationalisation of the environmental and social logic at the micro level. In this respect, RI can be understood as a driver for the transition to the CBE.

14.1 The Normative Dimension of the Transition to the Circular Bio-Based Economy

In current research into the CBE, there is a strong focus on either technical or economic issues. The main question is how we can technologically redesign products in a way that is restorative or regenerative by design, and in an economically viable way. There is a strong focus on economics in new product development, which limits the production of new circular bio-based products to those that are economically viable and for which a business case can be made.

Theoretically, almost everything can be recycled, repaired and reused. In the free market, however, only CBE opportunities are explored and exploited for which a business case can be made. Where a business case cannot be made for a product, this does not lead to the shutdown of its production. Instead, the end-of-life concept of linear economic thinking remains dominant in its continuous production. This explains why the current picture of the circular scenario for 2050 shows only a limited decrease of CO_2 emissions (see Figure 14.2).

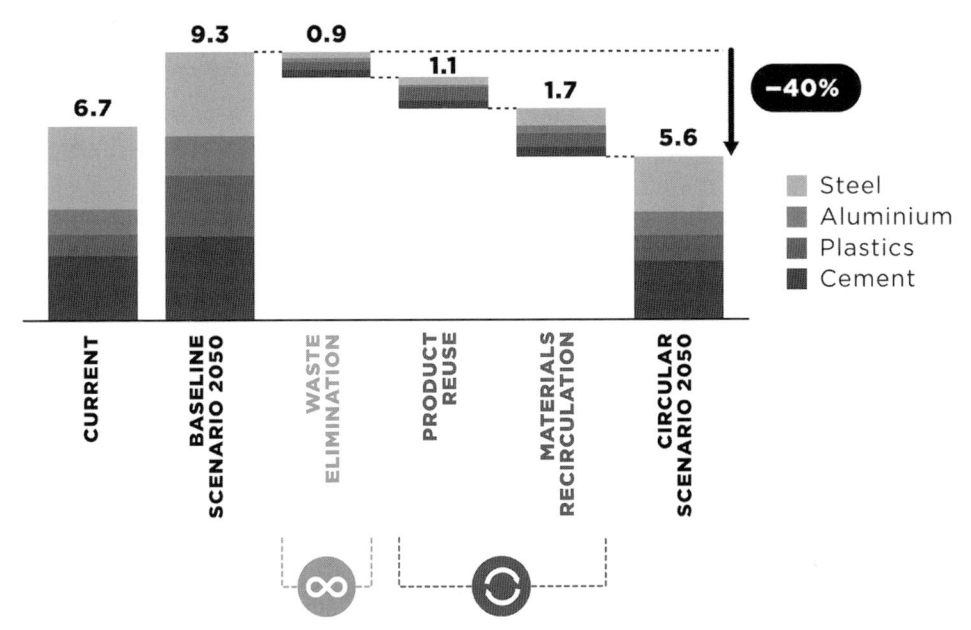

Figure 14.2 Global CO_2 emissions from four key materials production (billion tonnes of CO_2 per year) (Ellen MacArthur Foundation 2019)

This may be explained by the fact that the current conceptualisation of the CBE is not based on the carrying capacity of planet Earth but remains based on economic parameters (Veraart et al. 2019).

The concept of logics has been used to illustrate how values, mindsets and motivations impact what issues are conceived as important and how they are addressed (Stubbs 2017). If an economic or market logic is dominant, actors focus on profits, efficiency and operational effectivity, while if a social logic is dominant, actors focus on the public good and benefits for society (Long and Blok 2019). While the transition to the CBE involves a combination of economic, social and environmental logics, and should therefore lead to radical new circular bio-based products and services, current practices in the CBE are dominated by the market logic. This idea is not only substantiated by the circular scenario for 2050 (Ellen MacArthur Foundation 2019) but also by current practices in the bio-based economy. Currently, the bio-based economy is largely determined by biomass as source of renewable energy and not (yet) by higher value adding bio-products like fine chemicals and biopharmaceuticals. This focus on biofuels does however not automatically lead to the CBE but only to a 'greening of coal-fired power plants', as Bosman and Rotmans (2016: 10) put it, i.e. to CBE practices based on renewable resources. The same can be seen in the circular economy. Although recycling is less environmentally advisable than reduction, reusing and repairing materials, due to energy dissipation and the downgrading of these resources, current practices in the circular economy are largely determined by recycling because of economic reasons, and not (yet) by potentially more sustainable practices (Bilitewski 2012; Stahel 2013; Inigo and Blok 2019). The economic or market logic is appealing to CBE practices as it holds the promise that companies can continue with their business as usual.

We do not object to the idea that technological and economic feasibility is important in the transition to the CBE. Without a feasible business case, the CBE would not get off the ground because front runners in the CBE would go bankrupt before that transition could take place for instance. The question is however whether sustainable development can be achieved within this conceptualisation of the CBE (Beames et al. 2019). In the first instance, we have to acknowledge that sustainable development, which is the main aim of the CBE, is a normative concept; it does not describe the world as it is, but as it should be. The difference can become clear if we compare sustainability with child labour or food safety. The moral question of the acceptability of child labour or the violation of food safety does not concern efficiency or optimisation. The rejection of child labour and obligation to secure food safety is due to a normative standard or principle for what is considered ethical business practice and not to do in business practice. The concept of the CBE is ambiguous, despite its de facto practice as economy-based economy (Veraart and Blok 2019). Under the concept of the CBE the biosphere of planet Earth operates as such a normative standard; it would be an economy based on and relying on the biosphere or the carrying capacity of planet Earth. So although the CBE contains the biosphere as a normative standard for new circular bio-based product development, the restorativity or regenerativity of the natural resources that are required for new product development is not taken as such a normative standard in current business practices, but only as a guideline for optimisation. The problem at hand becomes clear if we once again compare it with the concerns regarding child labour or food safety. If we argued that we should only try to avoid child labour or should only try to guarantee food safety, it would not be acceptable at all.

In fact, in current practice the biosphere of planet Earth is not seen as such a normative standard. On the contrary, the biosphere is seen as a subset of human economy, i.e. as resource for production (Blok 2018a). In this conceptualisation, natural capital is seen as interchangeable with and replaceable by human made capital (labour and technology). But the normative dimension of the CBE raises the questions whether it concerns just a new way of doing business as usual, in which biomass is for instance seen as a source of added value for economic returns, or whether its ambition is to establish a sustainable economy, one that really operates within the carrying capacity of the biosphere of planet Earth and considers the well-being of people (Garver 2013)? While in current management theory business practices are self-evidently depicted as if they lack biophysical foundations (Mead 2014), the massive experience of climate change today shows that natural capital can no longer be seen as interchangeable with human-made capital in business practices. On the contrary, the environmental crisis we face today shows that the economy is a subsystem of the larger biosphere of planet Earth, which sets limits to the growth ambitions of economic actors and functions as a limit in which new product development practices should operate. Climate change shows that the current environmental problems concern an ecosystem failure to provide infinite resources for production and consumption, to provide optimum conditions for sustained production and consumption, and to do justice to intra- and intergenerational equity criteria (Korakandy 2008). As long as environmental problems are seen as market failures, the solution to these failures is found within the economic paradigm, in which the environment is seen as a subset of human economy, i.e. as a resource for production (Blok 2018a).

In the field of ecological economics, it is therefore argued that the transition to the CBE requires a systems transition, namely an economic system that is based on the biosphere and uses the carrying capacity of planet Earth as a normative framework of economic activities (Constanza et al. 2015). Rockström et al. (2009) use planetary boundaries to show to what extent the carrying capacities of planet Earth have been exceeded, and these indicators show absolute boundary conditions within which the CBE has to operate. In other words, what is called for is a new paradigm of the CBE, in which the economic or market logic of the business-as-usual approach is replaced by an environmental logic that guides the further development CBE research and practices. According to such a logic, the economic, societal and ecological spheres are nested systems, in which economics is seen as dependent on society and, in the end, on the biosphere of planet Earth. The biosphere operates as a planetary boundary that affects the space in which economic activities can take place in a normative way. An example can be found in the planetary boundaries provided by Rockström and colleagues. These boundary conditions enable us to reject new product developments that increase climate change, while it allows new products developments that increase chemical pollution (Rockström et al. 2009). Another example can be found in the 'life's principles' provided by the Ellen MacArthur Foundation (2010), which represent overarching patterns of how life on Earth creates conditions conducive to life. One can think of principles like 'adapt to changing conditions', 'be resource efficient' and 'be locally attuned and responsive' (Ellen MacArthur Foundation 2010), that can be used as a measure or standard for circular bio-based business practices (Blok 2016; Muijsenberg and Blok 2019). The CBE constitutes a different economy, namely an economy that operates within the carrying capacity of planet Earth, if circularity is a normative concept that limits and restricts new product development.

To conclude this first section, we have seen that current practices in the CBE are framed within the market or economic logic and miss the normative dimension of the transition to the CBE. Such a transition requires fundamental reflections on the role of economy in ecology with significant consequences for CBE practices. With a few exceptions (Weber and Hemmelskamp 2005; Jacobsson and Bergek 2011; Schlaile et al. 2017), however, the normative dimension of the transition to the CBE is underrepresented in current literature; the lack of attention directed towards this normative dimension can be seen as one of the main barriers to the transition to the CBE.

We are not implying that economic actors should fundamentally reconsider their role in society and adopt a social and environmental logic in their business practices. The normative dimension holds as well for the demand side of the CBE, namely the consumers. Based on a long-term analysis, Verbong and Geels (2007) argued that we cannot expect a smooth transition to a new (circular bio-based) energy system as long as they are not driven by environmental concerns in society. Also, in other fields of the transition to the CBE, like climate smart agriculture, one of the main barriers is the lack of customer demand for climate smart products and services (Long et al. 2019). On the contrary, while consumers may accept recycling, they are less likely to accept the more sustainable opportunities provided by the CBE, like reuse and repair. The transition to the CBE requires that both supply- and demand-side actors adopt a social and environmental logic in their production and consumption processes.

Even if economic actors take responsibility for circular bio-based new product development, transformation to the CBE will not get off the ground if there is no willingness to take care on the side of consumers. The normative dimension of the transition to the CBE holds therefore both for producers and consumers.

One can argue that economic actors are primarily responsible for circular bio-based new product design, as they are primarily polluting to the environment. Accordingly, it can be argued that the expectation that consumers engage in reuse and repair activities actually means that this responsibility is transferred to consumers, and that this transfer is not legitimate. Although we agree that economic actors have a responsibility that cannot be transferred to the consumer, actual engagement in the more sustainable opportunities provided by the CBE like reuse and repair requires the engagement of consumers as well in order to take full advantage of this potential (Schlaile et al. 2017). In this respect, the responsibility of economic actors to redesign their products and services and to engage in new circular bio-based product development corresponds with a willingness to engage in circular bio-based products and services from the side of the consumers. Therefore, we argue that the main barrier to the transition to the CBE is found in a lack of the normative dimension of this transition on both the supply side of circular bio-based products and services, as well as on the demand side.

14.2 The Social Dimension of the Transition to the CBE

Not only is the normative dimension of the transition to the CBE often missing in current conceptualisations: so too is the social dimension. This becomes clear if we reflect on the triple bottom line (planet, people, profit) as the basic idea behind the call for sustainable development. In current conceptualisations of the CBE, the main focus is on the planet (in terms of resource efficiency and waste minimisation) and profit (in terms of economic efficiency and profitability). So while the call for sustainable development involves the economic, environmental and social dimensions, current practices in the CBE seem to cover only the first two dimensions (Kirchherr et al. 2017).

It is especially this social dimension of the transition to the CBE that raises all kinds of questions, for instance ethical issues of intra- and intergenerational equity (Murray et al. 2017). An example is the demand for biofuels that has resulted in the replacement of tropical forests by soy fields (Farigone et al. 2008), which puts pressure on food production in poor countries (Murray et al. 2017). For this reason, Murray et al. (2017) call for the application of social and solidarity principles in order to democratise the CBE beyond economic profitability (Inigo and Blok 2019). The replacement of the market or economic logic by a social logic would lead to a social conceptualisation of the CBE, as is proposed by Murray et al. (2017: 377): the CBE is 'an economic model wherein planning, resourcing, procurement, production and reprocessing are designed and managed, as both process and output, to maximise ecosystem functioning and human well-being'. This conceptualisation enables us to raise questions about ownership of the (public) biomass resources and who may benefit from CBE practices: do stakeholders such as consumers who contributed to restorative and regenerative design by engaging in recycling, reusing and repairing behaviours benefit from the sustainability performance of the economic actor?

Another aspect of the lack of interest in the social dimension of the transition to the CBE is that it leads to the sole focus on the eco-efficiency of new circular bio-based technologies and practices, without taking unknown safety and health risks and unknown impacts and side effects into account. An example is the introduction of precision livestock farming (PLF) in the agricultural sector. PLF can be defined as 'the management of livestock production using the principles and technology of process engineering ... PLF treats livestock production as a set of interlinked processes, which act together in a complex network' (Wathes 2009). By the integration of smart technology and the internet of things – in which computers, sensoring devices, GPS systems but also robots and even animals communicate with one another and function autonomously in an integrated farm management system – farmers can engage in the CBE (Bos and Munnichs 2016). PLF provides concrete strategies to engage in CBE while it at the same time raises social and ethical issues associated with the increased corporatisation and industrialisation of the agricultural sector (e.g. digitalisation of farm animals and mega stalls) (Blok 2018b), in which animals are merely treated as objects of production, and not as living beings.

These circular bio-based technologies have unknown safety and health risks related to the composition of the biowaste that is used as input in bio digesters for instance, and to the residual waste streams that come out of the bio digesters. The health risks of the low frequency sounds produced by wind turbines and heat pumps received less attention in the literature as well but may provoke societal resistance against the adoption of such technologies in local communities. Also, the consequences, impacts and side effects of life science technologies for CBE are unknown. Many circular bio-based technologies have a dark side, for instance if a green technology requires rare earth materials like neodymium that can only be mined at the expense of considerable environmental costs (Zhang et al. 2000), or rely on materials that are hard to recycle (Murray et al. 2017). One of the major targets of synthetic biology for commercial application of synthetic biology is for instance the production of the next-generation biofuels, while the consequences and side effects of synthetic biology are completely unknown and contested.

On the one hand, societal resistance against the transition to the CBE may be fuelled because the high expectations regarding new technology are often not redeemed. On the other hand, we can expect that the more radical circular bio-based technologies are, like life science technologies for CBE, the more it will raise societal questions, requiring more responsibility of actors. In current CBE research and practice, however, the social dimension of the transition to the CBE receives relatively little attention, which may prevent further successful implementation (Winans et al. 2017; Inigo and Blok 2019). The lack of focus on the ethical acceptability and societal desirability of CBE technologies and practices may cause societal resistance and can therefore be seen as one of the key barriers to the transition to the CBE.

The inclusion of the normative and social dimensions of the CBE requires an extension of the economic or market logic with a social and environmental logic in order to safeguard that the CBE does not only focus on ecological efficiency and economic profitability, but starts to acknowledge the limitations of the carrying capacity of planet Earth while contributing to the common good. An example can be found in the conceptual development of biomimetic PLF, which integrates a strong critique of the reification of animals for food production (Blok and Gremmen 2018). Currently there is however little research on how a social and environmental logic can be implemented in CBE research and practice, and exactly how it could be aligned in a constructive manner. Next to normative reflections on the CBE, it would require the involvement of multiple stakeholders involved in or affected by the CBE to address the normative and social dimensions of the CBE collectively, i.e. to prevent the social and ethical risks of circular bio-based technologies and practices, and to better embed these technologies and practices in society.

14.3 RI as Driver of the Transition to the CBE

One way to substantiate the strategy to consider the normative and social dimensions of the transition to the CBE is RI. Responsible Innovation as a concept emerged in the European policy context to prevent failure of promising innovations because ethical and societal questions are not taken into account (Owen et al. 2013). The problem was that innovative developments often start with the promise of positive impact – e.g. genetic modification, nanotechnology and digital technologies like artificial intelligence – but later on turn out to have negative impacts and raise ethical concerns as well. This raised the question how we can steer innovative developments like the CBE in such a way that they meet societal and environmental goals like sustainable development and the common good. The consideration of responsibility issues in new product development requires reflections on how we can explore the potential positive and negative impacts or consequences of innovative developments, and on the question to what extent we can abandon or modify innovations because of ethical and social concerns. These ideas have led to the conceptualisation of RI as 'a transparent, interactive process by which societal actors and innovators become mutually responsive to each other with a view to the (ethical) acceptability, sustainability and societal desirability of the innovation process and its marketable products' (von Schomberg 2012: 9). It provides a systematic framework for the identification, evaluation and management of ethical and social issues within technology development in order to achieve ethically acceptable, societally desirable and sustainable outcomes.

In the literature on RI, two broad traditions can be distinguished. First, there is a normative substantial approach that starts with norms and values as predetermined (substantial) inputs in the innovation process in order to generate responsible outputs, i.e. products and services that serve society (von Schomberg 2012). Second, there is also a procedural approach, which focuses primarily on the innovation process and the way actors anticipate risks, reflect on desirable outcomes and engage stakeholders to this end (Ruggiu 2015). It conceives RI as 'collective commitment of care for the future through responsive stewardship of science and innovation in the present' (Owen et al. 2013). The procedural approach does not proclaim predetermined normative claims regarding the output of the innovation process but focuses primarily on the responsible governance or management of the innovation process itself (Lubberink et al. 2018). According to the procedural view on responsible governance of innovation, RI contains four dimensions: anticipation of possible and unexpected risks (asking what–if questions); reflection on intentions and purposes (asking questions regarding one's own commitments, assumptions and biases); inclusion of and deliberation with societal actors (asking who is involved and how stakeholders are consulted); and responsiveness towards societal concerns and needs (asking questions regarding the alignment of new product development with societal values and concerns) (Owen et al. 2013). While the normative substantial approach of RI can be criticised because unilateral and shared values cannot be identified in case of complex societal problems like the transition to the CBE (stakeholders have in fact different and often opposed value frames), the procedural approach can be criticised because stakeholder inclusion and deliberation cannot replace the ethical considerations that are at stake in new product development (Blok 2019a). Agreement among stakeholders does for instance not necessarily exclude biases regarding intra- and intergenerational equity in new product development. As I have argued elsewhere, the integration of both the substance normative approach and the procedural approach of RI is needed, and requires an action-based conceptualisation of RI (Blok 2019b). For the purposes of this chapter, we consider the contribution which the procedural and the normative substantial approach of RI can provide if it comes to new circular bio-based products in the transition to the CBE.

The procedural approach of RI can help to anticipate possible futures and impacts of the CBE. It helps to identify the negative impacts, unintended consequences and side effects of circular bio-based technologies (e.g. food for fuel), bio digesters (e.g. safety and health risks due to the composition of the biowaste and residual waste streams) and wind turbines or heat pumps (e.g. health risks due to low frequency sounds). It also helps to address these negative impacts in an early stage together with multiple stakeholders, and to anticipate impacts at a more fundamental level, for instance the impacts of the increasing industrialisation and corporatisation of the agricultural sector on social well-being (Blok 2018b).

The procedural approach of RI can help us to reflect on the assumptions and possible biases involved in the transition to the CBE. We can think of reflections on the dominance of the economic and market logic in current CBE practices, which leads to simplistic goals of the CBE, and reflections on the possibilities of adopting a social and environmental logic. And if economic actors already engage in CBE practices that count on consumers' involvement (reuse, repair), RI can help them to engage in second-order reflection on their real intentions and commitments; are we really engaging consumers to serve the common good with our circular bio-based technologies and practices, or are we in fact shifting our 'corporate' responsibility for sustainable development to consumers? Furthermore, we can reflect on the focus on eco-efficiency in circular bio-based technologies and practices, and on the impact, this focus on eco-efficiency has for our understanding of the human condition, which is also associated with enjoyment and wastefulness (Veraart and Blok 2019; Zwier et al. 2015).

The procedural approach of RI can help to include stakeholders in the assessment and redesign of circular bio-based technologies and practices. One can think of citizens who live in the neighbourhood of bio-based factories and facilities. Inclusion may also address the current lack of attention for the role of consumers as systemic barrier to the transition to the CBE (Mignon and Bergek 2016). It may also address the current lack of interest in the role of stakeholder engagement in CBE research and practice (Korhonen et al. 2018; Inigo and Blok 2019). Finally, it enables questions to be asked regarding the diversity of stakeholders involved in the assessment of the ethical acceptability and societal desirability of circular bio-based technologies and practices. These considerations may lead to the inclusion of a more diverse range of stakeholders in order to address ethical issues of intra- and intergenerational equity in the transition to the CBE.

Finally, the procedural approach of RI can help to respond to call for the transition to the CBE and contribute to the common good. One can think of responsiveness at an operational level, for instance the redesign of circular bio-based technologies to address societal concerns and reduce risks, but also of responsiveness at a strategic level of economic actors who decide to adopt the normative dimension of the CBE in their business practices, for instance the adoption of sustainable business models or life's principles in biomimetic design (Muijsenberg and Blok 2019; Muijsenberg et al. 2019).

On the one hand, the four dimensions of the procedural approach of RI may support the transition to the CBE, as they address some of the ethical and social issues that cause societal resistance against the CBE and can be seen as barriers to the transition to the CBE. On the other hand, the procedural approach of RI also requires a normative substantial dimension as we have seen. The contribution of the normative substantial approach of RI is different from the procedural approach, because it mainly helps to reflect on the normative dimension of the CBE, i.e. the core values of the biosphere on which the CBE should be based and the common good the CBE should contribute to.

Because the integration of the normative and social dimensions is often missing in current CBE research and practices, we propose that the concept of RI is a useful strategy to integrate the normative and social dimensions in CBE research and practice. RI can substantiate the social and environmental logic which were claimed to be prerequisites for the transition to the CBE in the previous section. If RI is adopted in CBE research and practice, it can be seen as a driver for the transition to the CBE.

14.4 Philosophical Reflections on RI as Driver of the Transition to the CBE

One can question, however, to what extent RI is able to identify the normative dimension of the CBE as one universal principle that guides circular bio-based practices. Sustainable development is a highly complex or 'wicked' problem (Rittel and Webber 1973). Wicked problems are complex, ill-structured and public problems like lifestyle diseases, poverty in the South and climate change. Several authors have indicated that global warming is such a highly complex problem because it concerns global and interconnected issues like climate change, increasing populations and changing consumption patterns, which cannot be solved in usual ways or by simple solutions (Blok et al. 2016; Brennan 2004; Ehrlich and Ehrlich 2009). Further indications of this wickedness can be found in the dispersion of causes and effects – emissions of greenhouse gases (GHGs) are produced in a particular geographical area but have global effects – in the fragmentation of agency – there is no centralised system of global governance to tackle this global problem, while local agents have the tendency to serve their own (unsustainable) interests (Hardin 1968) – and in institutional inadequacy – local enforceable sanctions to enhance and secure more sustainable behaviour is limited by the current, mainly national institutional context (Gardiner 2006; cf. Jamieson 2007). In such a context, it is difficult, if not impossible, to conceptualise how different human stakeholder groups and institutions, who have a broad variety of perspectives and interests, accept responsibility for the transition to the CBE.

If the key characteristic of wicked problems like global warming is that the distinction between responsible and irresponsible behaviour is difficult because of their complexity, we can critically question whether it is possible for RI to identify a normative principle or value of the biosphere on which the CBE should be based. At the same time, we can argue that planet Earth itself could function as sovereign principle or norm that should guide the transition to the CBE. On the one hand, we can identify the Earth as sovereign principle for our existence, to the extent that human existence emerges, unfolds and expands based on the pre-existence of the Earth, and threatens to go back into the Earth at the end of this era in which humanity is threatened by global warming (Blok 2016). The unique situation of planet Earth that is threatened by global warming unsettles us – we experience our full dependency on the carrying capacity of the Earth for the first time – and calls us to sustain this Earth as supportive ground for human existence. This call is normative, since the Earth as supportive ground operates as norm or regulative idea that guides circular bio-based practices. This normativity of planet Earth can inform the substantial normative approach of RI as driver for the transition to the CBE. At the same time, this norm is 'open' for revision, as opposed to general or universally valid, to the extent that the application of this norm remains always a finite or limited one compared to the wickedness of the problem, remains always questionable, adjustable and improvable. This means that any norm always remains situational – only valid in a limited way and for a specific purpose and time frame – while we have to remain principally critical towards the applicability of such a norm or principle in light of this wickedness of the problem at stake. The critical engagement with the Earth as sovereign principle and acknowledgement of the openness and fallibility of this norm can be established by the procedural approach of RI as driver for the transition to the CBE.

Based on these considerations, we propose the integration of the substantial normative and procedural approach of RI as driver for the transition to the CBE, in which planet Earth itself operates as normative dimension for the CBE. This normative dimension of the CBE acknowledges the ultimate dependency of economic actors on the biosphere and carrying capacity of planet Earth. We develop four preliminary characteristics of a CBE that substantiates the substantial normative and procedural approach of RI, and with this, substantiates the transition to a responsible CBE.

A responsible CBE is characterised by a state of inclusion, namely the inclusion of human existence in the biosphere of planet Earth. This state of inclusion does not only highlight the dependency of circular bio-based producers and consumers on the Earth as supportive ground for their public and private operations, but also their responsibility when it comes to sustaining the Earth as such a supportive ground. The state of inclusion highlights the individual responsibility of circular bio-based producers and consumers as intimately connected with this supportive ground. Circular bio-based producers and consumers are not only held responsible for global warming based on general norms and principles, but also actively take responsibility for the transition to the CBE in actual sustainable action and behaviour (Blok et al. 2016), through which the Earth as *oikos* (home) for human existence and its institutions subsists. At the same time, circular bio-based producers and consumers acknowledge the situational and fundamentally limited character all circular bio-based technologies and practices in light of the wickedness of global challenges like global warming.

A responsible CBE is not only conditioned by the singularity of the circular bio-based producers and consumers, as if the procedural approach of RI as driver for the transition to the CBE is sufficient and does not require the normative dimension of the CBE. This would suggest that an economy that is based on the biosphere as *oikos* of human existence is primarily in the hands of circular bio-based producers and consumers to provide for the needs of human life. But in fact, also the efforts of circular bio-based producers and consumers are always already dependent on the Earth as supportive ground. In this sense, a responsible CBE is always already Earth-bound, i.e. primarily conditioned by grand challenges like global warming that unsettle actors and call them to action to engage in the transition to the CBE, here and now. Circular bio-based producers and consumers are responsive to the normative dimension of planet Earth that operates as a regulative idea or 'open' norm, without being able to derive universally held rules or principles that can be univocally applied.

Because of the situational character of a responsible CBE (characteristic 1) in response to the normative dimension of the CBE (characteristic 2), circular bio-based producers and consumers acknowledge the principal fallibility of our interventions in light of the complexity or wickedness of global warming. This fallibility of the CBE – the possible negative impacts, unintended consequences and side effects of the CBE that we discussed in the previous sections – is not only due to the situational character of circular bio-based production and consumption but may also be due to the instability and volatility of planet Earth itself, as is indicated in the structural possibility of spontaneous environmental events like earthquakes, volcanos and tsunamis.

At the same time, since massive challenges like global warming can be seen as urgent problems, the transition to the CBE can no longer consist in a business-as-usual approach, in which biomass is seen as new a source of added value for economic returns, but calls for a responsible CBE, and establishes an economy that operates within the carrying capacity of the biosphere of planet Earth. It consists in the development of responsible patterns of circular bio-based production and consumption. Responsible circular bio-based production and consumption practices can be seen as enactment of this normative dimension of the CBE, in which the Earth functions as normative principle that enforces circular bio-based practices. Because of the fallibility of any norm or principle, RI for the transition to the CBE does no longer look for perfect solutions to global challenges like climate change, but for satisficing solutions that are, first of all, satisfactory and sufficient to maintain planet Earth as supportive ground for human existence and its institutions and, second, are radically open to future subversions, revisions and improvements (Blok 2018a). Producers and consumers feel responsible for the transition to the CBE and engage in the exploration and exploitation of such satisficing solutions but acknowledge the complexity or wickedness of global warming at the same time.

Conclusion

In this chapter, we argued that current practices in the CBE are framed within the market or economic logic and miss the normative and social dimensions of the CBE. The transition to a responsible CBE requires fundamental reflections on the relationship between the economic sphere and the ecological sphere on which it is based, with significant consequences for CBE practices. We subsequently identified the lack of attention paid to the normative and social dimensions of the CBE as one of the main barriers for the transition to the CBE and called for a social and environmental logic in CBE practices. We then proposed Responsible Innovation as a strategy to address the normative and social dimensions of CBE research and practice and identified RI as potential driver for the transition to a responsible CBE. Finally, we critically reflected on the normative dimension of the biosphere of planet Earth if we deal with highly complex problems like global warming. Based on our reflections, we proposed to integrate both the substantial normative and procedural approach of RI as driver of the transformation to the CBE and developed four preliminary characteristics of a responsible CBE that substantiates the substantial normative and procedural approach of RI, and with this, substantiates the transition to the CBE.

Future research should engage in both conceptual philosophical reflection on the relation between economy and ecology in our conceptualisation of a responsible CBE. More empirical work is needed to address the question how a social and environmental logic can be integrated in CBE research and practices, to what extent the economic and social/environmental logic can align or exclude each other, and how multiple stakeholders involved in CBE practices can successfully address the social issues at stake in current CBE research and practice. Finally, more empirical research is needed on the opportunities and limitations of RI in the CBE and its contribution to the transformation to a responsible CBE.

Acknowledgements

This chapter is partly based on a keynote speech on the normative dimension of the bio economy during the second International Bioeconomy Congress 2017 in Stuttgart (Germany). The chapter benefited a lot from the work I engaged in over the years together with several colleagues, Ph.D. students and post-docs in Wageningen, who enabled me to develop this vision on the normative and social dimensions of the transition to a responsible CBE and the role that RI may play in this transition. I am especially grateful for the conversations with Allistair Beames, Edurne Inigo, Thomas Long, Saskia van den Muijsenberg, Michael Schlaile, Job Timmermans, Roel Veraart and Jochem Zwier.

References

Beames, A., J. Goedhart and A. Kanellopoulos (2019). Biobased economy: Critical foundation for achieving sustainable development goals. In W. Leal Filho et al. (eds.), *Decent Work and Economic Growth*. Dordrecht: Springer, 49–69, https://doi .org/10.1007/978–3-319-71058-7_35-1

Bilitewski, B. (2012). The circular economy and its risks. *Waste Management* 32(1): 1–2.

Birch, K. and D. Tyfield (2013). Theorizing the bioeconomy. Biovalue, biocapital, bioeconomics or . . . What? *Science, Technology and Human Values* 38(3): 299–327.

Blok, V. (2016). Biomimicry and the materiality of ecological technology and innovation: Toward a natural model of nature. *Environmental Philosophy* 13(2): 195–214.

Blok, V. (2018a). Information asymmetries and the paradox of sustainable business models: Towards an integrated theory of sustainable entrepreneurship. In L. Moratis, F. Melissen and S. O. Idowu (eds.), *Sustainable Business Models*. Dordrecht: Springer: 204–25.

Blok, V. (2018b). Technocratic management versus ethical leadership: Redefining responsible professionalism in the agri-food sector in the Anthropocene. *Journal of Agricultural and Environmental Ethics* 31(2–3): 583–91.

Blok, V. (2019a). From participation to interruption: Toward an ethics of stakeholder engagement, participation and partnership in CSR and responsible innovation. In R. von Schomberg and J. Hankins (eds.), *Handbook of Responsible Innovation: A Global Resource*. Cheltenham, UK: Edward Elgar, 243–57.

Blok, V. (2019b). Innovation as ethos: Moving beyond CSR and practical wisdom in innovation ethics. In C. Neesham and S. Segal (eds.), *Handbook of Philosophy of Management*. New York: Springer, 1–14, http://doi.org/10.1007/978–3-319–48352–8_19-1

Blok, V. (2019c). Politics versus economics: Philosophical reflections on the nature of corporate governance. In C. Neesham and S. Segal (eds.), *Handbook of Philosophy of Management*. New York: Springer, 69–87, http://doi.org/10.1007/s40926–019–00118–9

Blok, V. and B. Gremmen (2018). Agricultural technologies as living machines: Toward a biomimetic conceptualization of technology. *Ethics, Policy and Environment* 21(2): 246–63.

Blok, V., B. Gremmen and R. Wesselink (2016). Dealing with the wicked problem of sustainable development: The role of individual virtuous competence. *Business and Professional Ethics Journal* 34(3): 297–327.

Bos, J. and G. Munnichs (2016). *Digitalisering van Dieren. Verkenning precision livestock farming*. Den Haag, Rathenau.

Bosman, R. and J. Rotmans(2016). Transition governance towards a bioeconomy: A comparison of Finland and the Netherlands. *Sustainability* 8: 1017

Brennan, A. (2004). Biodiversity and agricultural landscapes: Can the wicked policy problem be solved? *Pacific Conservation Biology* 10(2): 124–42.

Constanza, R., J. H. Cumberland, H. Daly, R. Goodland, R. B. Norgaard, I. Kubiszewski and C. Franco (2015). *An Introduction to Ecological Economics*. Boca Raton, FL: Taylor & Francis.

Ehrlich, P. R. and A. H. Ehrlich (2009). The population bomb revisited. *Electronic Journal of Sustainable Development* 1(3): 63–71.

Ellen MacArthur Foundation (2010). Iconographics, www.ellenmacarthurfoundation.org/circular-economy/concept/infographic

Ellen MacArthur Foundation (2019). Completing the picture: How the circular economy tackles climate change, www.ellenmacarthurfoundation.org

Farigone, J., J. Hill, D. Tilman, S. Polasky and P. Hawthorne (2008). Land clearing and the biofuel carbon debt. *Science* 319(3): 1235–38.

Gardiner, S. M. (2006). A perfect moral storm: Climate change, intergenerational ethics and the problem of moral corruption. *Environmental Values* 15(3): 397–413.

Garver, G. (2013). The rule of ecological law, the legal complement to degrowth economy. *Sustainability* 5(3): 316–37.

Geels, F. W. (2002). Technological transitions as evolutionary reconfiguration processes: A multi-level perspective and a case-study. *Research Policy* 31: 1257–74.

Geels, F. W. and J. Schot (2007). Typology of sociotechnical transition pathways. *Research Policy* 36(3): 399–417.

Geissdoerfer, M., P. Savaget, N. M. P. Bocken and E. J. Hultink (2017). The circular economy: A new sustainability paradigm? *Journal of Cleaner Production* 143: 757–68.

Goven, J. and V. Pavone (2015). The bioeconomy as political project: A Polanyian analysis. *Science, Technology and Human Values* 40(3): 302–37.

Grin, J., J. Rotmans and J. Schot (2010). *Transitions to Sustainable Development: New Directions in the Study of Long Term Transformative Change*. New York: Routledge.

Harding, G. (1968). The tragedy of the commons. *Science* 162(3859): 1243–48.

Inigo, E. A. and V. Blok (2019). Strengthening the socio-ethical foundations of the circular economy: Lessons from responsible research and innovation. *Journal of Cleaner Production* 233: 280–91.

Inigo, E. A. and V. Blok (2020). System barriers for socio-technical transitions driven by niche and regime-level agents: The case of the circular economy in the Netherlands. Working Paper.

Jacobsson, S. and A. Bergek (2011). Innovation system analyses and sustainability transitions: Contributions and suggestions for research. *Environmental Innovation and Societal Transition* 1: 41–57.

Jamieson, D. (2007). The moral and political challenges of climate change. In S. C. Moser and L. Dilling (eds.), *Creating a Climate for Change*. Cambridge: Cambridge University Press, 475–82.

Jonker, J., H. Stegeman, N. R. Faber and I. Kothman (2017). *Een zwaluw voorspelt veel goeds; resultaten van het landelijk onderzoek 2016–2017 naar business modellen voor de circulaire economie*. Doetinchem: Stichting OCF 2.0.

Kirchherr, J., D. Reike and M. Hekkert (2017). Conceptualizing the circular economy: An analysis of 114 definitions. *Resource Conservation and Recycling* 127: 221–32.

Korakandy, R. (2008). *Fisheries Development in India. The Political Economy of Unsustainable Development*. Delhi: Kalpaz.

Korhonen, J., C. Nuur, A. Feldmann and S. E. Birkie (2018). Circular economy as an essentially contested concept. *Journal of Cleaner Production* 175(544): 544–52.

Long, T. B. and V. Blok (2019). Innovation for grand societal challenges by start-up firms: Overcoming tensions within responsible innovation. Working paper.

Long, T. B., V. Blok and I. Coninx (2019). The diffusion of climate-smart agricultural innovations: Systems level factors that inhibit sustainable entrepreneurial action. *Journal of Cleaner Production* 232: 993–1004.

Lubberink, R., V. Blok, J. van Ophem and O. Omta (2018). Responsible innovation by social entrepreneurs: An exploratory study of values integration in innovations. *Journal of Responsible Innovation* 6(2): 179–210.

Mead, T. (2014). Biologically-inspired innovation in large companies: A path for corporate participation in biophysical systems? *International Journal of Design & Nature and Ecodynamics* 9(3): 216–29.

Mignon, I. and A. Bergek (2016). System- and actor-level challenges for diffusion of renewable electricity technologies: An international comparison. *Journal of Cleaner Production* 128: 105–15.

Muijsenberg, S. van den and V. Blok (2019). Towards a normative framework for conducting business in the bioeconomy: The case of biomimetic enterprises. Working paper.

Muijsenberg, S. van den, I. Boom and V. Blok (2019). Biomimicry as an approach to generate sustainable business models: A typology of biomimetic businesses. Working paper.

Murray, A., K. Skene and K. Haynes (2017). The circular economy: An interdisciplinary exploration of the concept and application in a global context. *Journal of Business Ethics* 140(3): 369–80.

Owen, R., J. Stilgoe, P. Macnaghten, F. Gorman, E. Fisher and D. Guston (2013). A framework for responsible innovation. In R. Owen, J. Bessant and M. Heintz (eds.), *Responsible Innovation*. Chichester, UK: Wiley, 27–50.

Rittel, H. W. J. and M. M. Webber (1973). Dilemmas in a general theory of planning. *Policy Sciences* 4(2): 155–69.

Rockström, J., W. Steffen, K. Noone et al. (2009). A safe operating space for humanity. *Nature* 461: 472–75

Ruggiu, D. (2015). Anchoring European governance: Two versions of responsible research and innovation and EU fundamental rights as 'normative anchor points'. *NanoEthics* 9(3): 217–35.

Schlaile, M., S. Urmetzer, V. Blok et al. (2017). Innovation systems for transformations towards sustainability? Taking the normative dimension seriously. 1–20 *Sustainability*, http://doi.org/10.3390/su9122253

Von Schomberg, Rene (2012). Prospects for technology assessment in a framework of responsible research and innovation. In M. Dusseldorp and R. Beecroft (eds), *Technikfolgen abschätzen lehren: Bildungspotenziale transdisziplinärer Methode*. Wiesbaden: Springer, 39–61.

Sira Consulting (2011). Botsende belangen in de bioeconomy, www.biobasedeconomy.nl/wp-content/uploads/2012/03/Botsende-belangen-in-de-BBE-SIRA-consulting.pdf

Stahel, W. R. (2013). Policy for material efficiency: Sustainable taxation as a departure from the throwaway society. *Philosophical Transaction of the Royal Societal A*, A 371: 20110567.

Stubbs, W. (2017). Sustainable entrepreneurship and B corps. *Business Strategy and the Environment* 26(3): 331–44.

Veraart, R., V. Blok and P. Lemmens (2019). Efficiency versus enjoyment: Looking after the human condition in the transition to the bio-based economy. Working paper.

Verbong, G. and F. Geels (2007). The ongoing energy transition: Lessons from a socio-technical, multi-level analysis of the Dutch electricity system (1960–2004). *Energy Policy* 35: 1025–37.

Wathes, C. M. (2009). Precision livestock farming for animal health, welfare and production. In A. Aland and F. Madec (eds.), *Sustainable Animal Production: The Challenges and Potential Developments for Professional Farming*. Wageningen, Wageningen Academic Publishers, 411–19.

Weber, M. and J. Hemmelskamp (2005). *Towards Environmental Innovation Systems*. Dordrecht: Springer.

Winans, K., A. Kendall and H. Deng (2017). The history and current applications of the circular economy concept. *Renewable and Sustainable Energy Review* 68: 825–33.

Zhang, H., J. Feng, W. Zhu et al. (2000). Chronic toxicity of rare-earth elements on human beings. *Biological Trace Element Research* 73(1): 1–17.

Zwier, J., V. Blok, P. Lemmens and R. J. Geerts (2015). The ideal of a zero-waste humanity: Philosophical reflections on the demand for a bio-based economy. *Journal of Agricultural and Environmental Ethics* 28(2): 353–74.

15

New Perspectives on Guardianship of Nature

Three Traditions of the Global South

DORINE E. VAN NORREN

Introduction: Worldviews and Guardianship of Nature

Guardianship of nature is revered in many Indigenous traditions as a self-evident fact. This contrasts starkly with mainstream Western (economic) thought in which nature is objectified and no longer treated as living or as a sacred force. This chapter looks into three traditions of the Global South: from Asian Buddhism in Gross National Happiness, to African Ubuntu (collective) thought and Latin American *Buen Vivir* (good living) derived from Native American traditions. It looks specifically at South Africa, Bhutan and Ecuador. All three countries actively promote their alternative Indigenous view on international relations and development: South Africa through 'Ubuntu diplomacy'; Bhutan through resolutions within the United Nations on Happiness; Ecuador through stressing harmony with nature (which became a UN network). This chapter is based on van Norren (2017) which takes a critical realist approach (in which interviews are marked A, B, E).

All three traditions have similarities when it comes to care for nature, but also significant differences. *Buen Vivir* law and policies in Ecuador recognise biocentricity most explicitly with rights of nature. Bhutanese Gross National Happiness policies and law contain a concept of guardianship of nature that comes close to *Buen Vivir*. Ubuntu recognises guardianship of nature implicitly in its philosophical outlook on future generations as part of the community, recognised in the constitution, but not in further law or policy in South Africa. The following sections will highlight how Indigenous law and traditional approaches and concepts have been introduced and conciliated with modern positive law in these three countries. This contributes to pinpointing the best practices and limits to such articulation between ancient and modern legal traditions.

15.1 Principles of *Buen Vivir* in South America

The Indigenous concept *Sumak Kawsay*, living well in the Quechua language (*suma* is best and *kawsay* is living), inspired the intellectual movement of *Buen Vivir* in Ecuador (and *Vivir Bien* in Bolivia). It is an Indigenous concept of horizontal coexistence with nature, social justice and multicultural respect as part of a holistic cosmic view of life (Jiménez 2011: 15). It is derived from the Andean Quechua people living mainly in Bolivia, Ecuador and Peru. Philosophies of other Native American peoples of North and South America mirror these beliefs (as was also demonstrated in interviews with different Indigenous groups in Ecuador). Literally, it means living in 'fullness' (plenitude) (van Teijlingen and Hoogenboom 2014: 15). The Indigenous concept of time is cyclical (like nature) and spiral. It thereby defeats Western notions of development, which are linear. It thus breaks through the divide of 'developing' and 'developed' countries (GoE 2009: 17). This 'developmental' distinction, as it is framed in Western philosophy and epistemology, is judgemental; everything simply is, in its various pluralistic forms of being (van Norren 2017).

15.1.1 Environmental Philosophy

Buen Vivir redefines the relationship between human and nature from an anthropocentric world view to a biocentric one. The national plan of Ecuador calls it 'biopluralism' (Guimaraes in Acosta 2008; GoE 2009: 6), which refers both to the centrality of nature and plurality of life as well as to the concept of plurinationality recognising different Indigenous nations. The Indigenous cosmic belief and logic is that the whole is present in each being and each being in the whole and therefore to harm nature is to harm oneself. The right way of living or 'living life to the fullest' therefore requires living in total harmony with the cosmos and the community of life (GoE 2009: 18). The Indigenous understanding of life is 'that the outer world of the stars, planets and everything on the planets was created by the inner human world of images within the heart and the interaction with Great Spirit. Almost all Indigenous peoples know this as a fact of life' (Melchizedek 2008: 266).

An intersubjective relationship with nature means that people communicate with (and pay respect to) plants or animals or even 'inanimate' life like mountains in the same way as they communicate with other humans: 'we communicate with plants. Our parents . . . know when it is the right time to use a particular tree for wood . . . and these dialogues happen spiritually in the forest. So for us, a tree is alive, just like animals' (Akchurin 2015: 21). Reverence for life means recognising the other as equal and mutual exchange (reciprocity):

Complementarity means we are necessary as one for the other and reciprocity means we mutually help each other. Mother Earth gives us life and we have to be grateful for it; how we express that is in taking care of her and feeding her back and making her pretty ... there should be no weeds around the place where the crops will grow.

(E10)

This is reflected in the Indigenous languages, which are dominated by verbs: focused on process rather than object, they avoid turning nature into an object, which human centred – anthropocentric – views of life tend to do (Thomson 2011: 451). This contrasts with noun-based languages such as English.

One has to understand that Pachamama or Mother Earth is not only a physical concept but a spiritual being as well. Mother Earth, including nature has a (right of) existence on her own, to which humans pay their respect and reverence. Even though humans cannot give her rights, as Mother Earth is larger than them, the Indigenous in Ecuador and Bolivia embraced the idea of giving rights to nature so as to incorporate their view of life in the Western legalistic tradition: 'Our discourse has also been incorporated ... such that nature could become a *subject* of legal rights' (Akchurin 2015: 21). A first step was the Universal Declaration of the Rights of Mother Earth adopted in 2010, when Ecuador and Bolivia convened the alternative climate conference in Cochabamba (Peoples Conference on Climate Change and Mother Earth's Rights) (Thomson 2011: 449; Fatheuer 2011: 18; Cullinan 2014).

The legalistic concepts of rights of nature are 'not chiefly Indigenous' (E13, E16, E20, E26): 'To give rights to nature is arrogant; nature gives to you!' (E8). 'The ancestral conception is to ask for permission to use nature' (E16). 'In this system nature is still an object, and you still need the state for the implementation of it, because that is the very idea of rights. Rights are an instrument of the logic of the state. In that you lose the whole concept of *Sumak Kawsay*' (E26). Though 'it is obvious for the Indigenous that nature has rights, she does not need to acquire those from other people, because nature is a person in her own right' (E13; Akchurin 2015); at the same time, it is a solution based on fitting into the dominant system.

15.1.2 Implementation in Law and Policy

The preamble of Ecuador's entirely renewed Constitution of 2008[1] puts *Buen Vivir* at the centre: 'Hereby decide to build: A new form of public coexistence, in diversity and in harmony with nature, to achieve the good way of living, the *sumak kawsay*' (preamble, second paragraph). According to the government of Ecuador 'Good Living posits that humans should use natural resources in a way that allows their natural generation (or regeneration)' (GoE 2009: 6).

[1] Amended in 2011 and 2015.

The new Constitution also accorded rights to nature. The idea of rights of nature in a legal sense, however, finds its roots in the works of Christopher Stone (*Should Trees Have Standing?*) (Stone 1972) and Godofredo Stutzin (Tanasescu 2013: 852–53). The American non-governmental organisation Community Environmental Legal Defense Fund (CELDF) first drafted local ordinances in the United States which inspired the constitutional drafters of Ecuador (Arsel 2012: 155; Cullinan 2014; Akchurin 2015). Indigenous communities in the National Confederation of Indigenous Nationalities of Ecuador (CONAIE) actively supported the inclusion of rights of nature in the Constitution of Ecuador.

There is a modest jurisprudence on the rights of nature giving rights to animals, to forests and ecosystems, yet at the same time not preventing large-scale oil exploration and mining (van Norren 2019). Three constitutional cases mention *Buen Vivir* (Mello 2015: 44–49), but the legal principle of *Sumak Kawsay* or *Buen Vivir* as such has not been worked out (E7).

Buen Vivir was implemented in the National Plans (2009–13; 2013–17), as stipulated by the Constitution: 'Public policies and the provision of public goods and services shall be aimed at enforcing the good way of living and all rights and shall be drawn up based on the principle of solidarity' (art. 85). The constitution, however, also contains provisions promoting development in the traditional sense (e.g. arts. 275–77, 313, 314, 317 and 395–99) (Lalander 2014: 161). The constitution is therefore contradictory with an inherent tension between *Buen Vivir* and development, two concepts which are not necessarily compatible (E1, E17). This is reflected in the haphazard implementation of *Buen Vivir* in practice, whereby the economy is largely supported by large-scale oil exploration and mining, facilitating social bonuses (solidarity), but going at the cost of harmony with nature. These principles were reserved for smaller environmental cases (van Norren 2017). The provisions referring to culture and nature in the constitution both reflect biopluralism (Tables 15.3 and 15.4).

15.1.3 Mother Earth as Chief Principle of Law

The customary right (respect) of Mother Earth is the chief principle of law (Constitution of Ecuador, art. 7.7). This has consequences on how we view human rights, which are then connected to collective rights and rights of nature. Ecuador and Bolivia were the first countries in history to give rights to nature in the Constitution (Fitz-Henry 2012: 268).[2] The Ecuadorian Constitution thus transcends the boundaries between customary and 'ordinary' law.

---

[2] Bolivia adopted it earlier, but ratified later (E21).

Table 15.1. *Ecuadorian Constitution: cultural provisions*

Dimension	Provisions
Buen Vivir *Sumak Kawsay*	Title 6 Development Structure (arts. 275–339) and Title 7 The Good Way of Living System (arts. 340–415) as well as crosscutting through Constitution
Intercultural	• intercultural, *multinational* state (art. 1) • traditional *languages* preservation (art. 2) • 'national unity in *diversity*' (art. 3.3) • natural and cultural *assets* preservation (art. 3.5) • rights to *cultural identity*, creative capacity, cultural manifestation, leisure, scientific and ancestral wisdom (arts. 21–25) • Free, intercultural, inclusive, diverse and participatory *communication* and access; prohibition on violence, discrimination, racism, drug addiction, sexism, religious or political intolerance in media; no confidentiality of information (arts. 16–20) freedom of conscience (art. 20); *free media*: public and private (art. 384) • Protection of *Indigenous 'nations' rights*: ancestral traditions and forms of social organisation; indivisible community territories exempt from tax and use of renewable resources and free prior informed consultation (not consent!) on non-renewable resource exploitation; practices of managing biodiversity; traditional laws; displacement prohibition; traditional knowledge (intellectual protection); holy places; heritage; intercultural bilingual participatory education system with collective administration; teacher protection; right to representation in official bodies; cross-border contact; consultation on relevant legislation; own language media; restricted military activities; garments/symbols/emblems promotion; respect for peoples living in isolation and prohibition of extractive activities in their territory (violation as crime of ethnocide) (arts. 56–57); Afro community and Montubio community protection and right to establish a territory (arts. 58–60) • See also *Duties of citizens* under democracy • *National system for culture*: national identity, diversity and artistic creation promotion; includes languages/oral traditions/ritual, festive productive manifestations; urban monuments/natural and archaeological sites; documents/objects/archives/libraries/museums; artistic/scientific/technological creations; preservation, restitution and restoration of heritage; support artistic teaching to all and art professions; state funding (arts. 377–80) • See also *Education* • See also *Health*

Table 15.2. *Ecuadorian Constitution: nature provisions*

Dimension	Provisions
Nature	➢ 'Non-renewable <u>natural resources</u> of the State's territory belong to its inalienable and *absolute assets*, which are not subject to a statute of limitations' (art.1) 'In the management of these resources, the State shall give priority to responsibility between generations, the conservation of nature' (art. 317) ➢ Right to *healthy environment*: 'Environmental conservation, the protection of ecosystems, biodiversity and the integrity of the country's genetic assets, the prevention of environmental damage, and the recovery of degraded natural spaces are declared matters of public interest' (art. 14) ➢ *Clean technology; alternative energy sources;* primacy of water and food over energy; prohibition on toxic and nuclear waste and genetically modified organisms (art. 15) ➢ *Rights of nature (Pacha Mama)*: integral *respect* for its existence and for the *maintenance and regeneration* of its life cycles, structure, functions and evolutionary processes. All persons, communities, peoples and nations can call upon public authorities to enforce the rights of nature state duty of protection of nature and *ecosystems* (art. 71). Right to *restoration*, duty of state for elimination of harm (art. 72). Prevention of extinction of species and hostile species (art. 73). *Benefit for all*: 'Environmental services shall not be subject to appropriation; their production, delivery, use and development shall be regulated by the State.' ➢ See also *duties of citizens* under democracy ➢ *Economic policy* 'within the biophysical limits of nature and respect for life and cultures' (art. 284(4)) ➢ Prohibition on appropriation of *genetic resources* contained in biological diversity and agricultural biodiversity (art. 322) ➢ *Environmental policies across all sectors*; direct responsibility of all players for restoration of damages; any individual or collective can file legal proceedings with burden of proof on defendant; mechanisms to control pollution; community consultation; decentralised management (arts. 395–99) ➢ *Biodiversity*: state sovereignty over; responsibility between generations; public interest; prohibition on transgenic crops and intellectual property rights (arts. 400–03) ➢ *Natural assets and ecosystem protection:* protected areas with prohibition on extraction of non-renewables; conservation, management, sustainable use, recovery of ecosystems (arts. 404–07) ➢ *Non-renewable resources*: state property and state profit sharing; exploitation in harmony with cycles of nature (art. 408) ➢ *Soil conservation*: combat degradation and desertification; reforestation, revegetation, avoid single crop farming, support farmers (arts. 409–10) ➢ *Water management*: priority on ecosystem preservation and human consumption; conservation in accordance with water cycle (arts. 411–12)

Table 15.2. (*cont.*)

Dimension	Provisions
	➢ *Biosphere*: energy efficiency; clean technology; mitigation of climate change, limiting CO_2, deforestation and air pollution (arts. 413–14) ➢ *Urban ecology*: regulate urban growth, urban fauna, green areas, rational use of water, waste management, priority to non-motorised transportation including bike lanes (art. 415)

15.1.3.1 Collective Rights and 'Free Prior Informed Consent'

Rights of nature are closely intertwined with collective rights and with the principle of free prior informed consent (FPIC). This principle obliges states to consult Indigenous people on matters affecting their territory and is now enshrined in the UN Declaration on the Rights of Indigenous Peoples (2007). Earlier Indigenous customary law was recognised in the ILO Convention 169 (1989), binding signatory states to customary law (Deneulin 2012: 5). As nature is linked to the Indigenous territory, it has a relation to the collective claim to the territory. At the same time nature limits collective rights by its limited resources (E8). The tool to implement the rights of nature is therefore asking free prior and informed consent of its inhabitants who consider themselves 'the defenders of nature, the guardians' (E8; E13). At the same time, it means for example that the right of hunting for Indigenous people can go along with the rights of nature.

15.1.3.2 Human (or Nature?) Rights and Dignity

Buen Vivir reshapes the human rights tradition in that 'the human rights tradition never considered mother nature as her house' (E12). 'In western law you only have a right to a clean environment and can go to court when it personally affects you, but with the right of nature anyone can sue for the restoration of nature' (E15). A new definition of rights emerges from this perspective (Price 2013: 19):

Rights are those obligations owed by Human Society, its members and institutions, to living things, and both human and natural communities. 'Unalienable rights' are those moral, ethical, practical and legal freedoms that human society, its members and institutions are obliged to afford to all living things, upon their birth, and to all interdependent combinations of living things, and to all life-sustaining systems of the earth.

It then follows that the concept of human dignity is much wider than in the Western tradition (Gianolla 2013: 64), adding a wider circle of reciprocity (duties and rights though interpreted in a wider sense when it comes to nature and a relational dimension. It goes beyond civil political rights (prioritised in liberal democracy) and socio-economic rights prioritised in Marxist tradition (Sousa Santos 2008), both of which overlook the dignity of nature and collective rights. The intrinsic value of nature is captured in the concept of rights and notion of inherent dignity. Embracing intercultural human rights may also offer the opportunity for a less instrumental 'rights' approach, focusing more on the human, 'the co-presence narrative, storytelling and human dialogue' (Gianolla 2013: 68). After all, it is an attitude (a mental, practical and interrelational approach) that is promoted, not a mere conceptualisation of other cosmologies into (conventional) rights, which would revert us back to positivism but then in a broader sense. Gianolla rightfully warns for a top-down approach and for co-optation of Indigenous leaders through (liberal) representative democracy with a multicultural facade (Gianolla 2013: 68). Houtart (2012) distinguishes the metaphorical meaning versus the anthropo-morphic[3] position on the rights of nature, the first classic one stressing the need to ensure the reproduction capacity of nature (with moral persons being right holders) and the second Indigenous one as a living Mother Earth (including forces of nature) as a subject of rights. Proponents of rights of nature often do not explicitly distinguish between the two meanings, which leaves the question open whether they are aware of the distinction or consider it important. The Indigenous do consider it very important, as the first one is anthropocentric and the second biocentric in approach. Many authors in general, however, criticise the three traditions of the Global South, as either redundant, romanticised, super-stitious, communist, anti-communist, or as cultural relativism to human rights (van Norren 2017).

15.1.3.3 The Notion of Freedom

Not only does it reconstruct the notion of dignity, but also of freedom: 'the Right of Nature is not only conservation, it sets people free, it constructs justice and freedom and takes care of the seeds of human rights. Firstly, the right of existence of different communities as part of nature ... secondly keeping the vital cycles of nature ... (thirdly the right) of animals' (E8). This means freedom is reciprocity: reciprocity with nature sets humans free; exploitation of earth, and rights centred around humans (modernity) imply a lack of reciprocity. Moreover, rights of nature are 'multidisciplinary' (involving geography and culture), 'multicultural' (involving dialogue with and among Indigenous) 'and combines material aspects (of life), human needs – which are also spiritual – and natural things' (E8). 'Development is not important, what is important is well-being or life. Sustainable life!' (E8) (not sustainable development). 'There are not only legal aspects to rights of nature. It is educational, it is the fascination for natural phenomena, it is mobilising people, and it addresses (conservation) risks' (E8). However,

---

[3] Anthropomorphism is the attribution of human traits, emotions and intentions to non-human entities.

'Conservation is the dissociation of human rights, social rights and nature rights' (E8).

15.1.3.4 Buen Vivir *as an International 'Development' Concept*

Activists are bringing the notions of rights of nature and *Buen Vivir* to the international level by arguing that *Buen Vivir* is the Ecuadorian 'development' concept, which at the same time abolishes the word development in its Western sense, as everything is cyclical and underdevelopment does not exist. Each country or culture has developed certain aspects of life more or less differently from the others. This argument is also brought forward in court: 'In the case for the Inter-American court we argued that *Buen Vivir* is the development concept for us, so it should be recognised as development in the Inter-American Court, and it includes protecting the rights of nature and of water' (E31) (Mirador mining case; van Norren 2017, 2019).

Rights of nature imply that there is a natural limit to the rights of humans, namely whenever the exercise of human rights endangers the existence of other species or the natural world at large (Fitz-Henry 2012: 268, quoting Claude Lévi-Strauss). Since the natural world has been seen as legal property thus far (Fitz-Henry 2012: 265), the right of nature puts limitations to property (as was also demonstrated in the otherwise controversial Esmeraldas small miners case, whereby small miners lost their property; van Norren 2017, 2019). This outlook therefore fundamentally reshapes property law (see also Chapter 11 in this volume). The civil law in Ecuador has however not changed (E7).

15.1.3.5 *Transcending the Separation of Culture and Nature*

Last but not least, *Buen Vivir* starts from the point of departure that culture and nature are intertwined: 'Community and nature … are in permanent dialogue' (E8). This dialogue means (1) being part of nature, (2) interdependence, (3) complementarity and (4) reciprocity (E8). *Buen Vivir* therefore also eliminates the (Western understanding of) boundaries between culture and nature, as nature is part of identity; and collective identity (which comes before individual identity and includes the entirety of life) is the building block for culture.

15.2 The Notion of Gross National Happiness in Bhutan

Gross National Happiness (GNH or 'Happiness') originates in the small Himalayan country of Bhutan. When the king was asked (in 1972) what the gross national product of his country was, he responded that he was more interested in the gross national happiness of his people. Thereafter an explicit government policy was developed which 'measures the quality of a country in more holistic way [than GNP] and believes that the beneficial development of human society takes place when material and spiritual development occurs side by side to complement and reinforce each other' (Ura et al. 2012: 7). Harmony between 'inner skills' and 'outer circumstances'; respect for nature, compassion, and balance 'between spiritual and material aspects of life'; and moderation and interdependence of all things are core principles of GNH (Schroeder 2014: 110, 133, 176; GNH Commission UNDP 2011: 16).

GNH policy consists of four pillars: (a) environmental conservation, (b) sustainable and equitable socio-economic development, (c) preservation and promotion of culture and (d) good governance (NDP Steering Committee 2013). All policies are centred around this and the Buddhist idea of the 'middle path' (harmonious balance). This has further been developed into a protocol for policy formulation; a GNH policy screening tool[4] and a GNH project screening tool (per sector).[5] In 2010, it was complemented with a GNH Index (Ura et al. 2012: 4), using thirty-three indicators which can be further split in 124 variables which are weighed differently. GNH surveys are carried out every five years (2010 and 2015).

The GNH Index has nine domains, of which the first four are not commonly used by most governments (Royal Government of Bhutan 2012: 41): psychological well-being, time use, cultural diversity and resilience, community vitality – complemented by the domains of education, health, good governance, ecological diversity and resilience, and living standards (Ura et al. 2012: 13–39).

Since Buddhism is about individual insight and scientific exploration, rather than believing in God, it is well placed to contribute to new environmental philosophies (Brown 2000: 2).

15.2.1 *Environmental Philosophy*

'Not harming life is the Buddhist concept' (B7) and 'respect for all sentient beings' (B44, B6, B10). Environmental care is closely linked to abstinence from injury to life and non-violence (*Ahimsa* in Sanskrit), and loving–kindness to all living beings (*Metta* in Sanskrit) (Daniels 2011: 45). Buddhism thus has a very specific understanding of nature and its relation to humans (Tashi 2012).

Creation in Buddhism starts from the principle of consciousness which creates the material realm and not the other way round (our body does not create our faculty for thinking; consciousness or the mind creates the body). It is the reverse or exact opposite of the view that our material world creates reality. Creation arises

---

[4] See GNH Commission Policy formulation, www.gnhc.gov.bt/policy-formulation; Schroeder (2014).
[5] GNH Commission Project Tools, www.grossnationalhappiness.com/docs/GNH/PDFs/Project_Tools.pdf

according to Buddhism through the stirring of the (aeonic) wind, and consequent formation of water, then earth, then living beings. These create with their collective karma the wind, in a circular movement of things (Tashi 2012: 93–111). Buddhism does not deny external causes of natural phenomena as described by modern science, but it sees it as limited to direct causes and not addressing the ultimate indirect causes (omitting for example *karma*) (Tashi 2012: 167). It teaches how to achieve ultimate understanding and control over one's life, so one can be master of one's own universe.

Since Buddhism posits that everything is in the mind (the consciousness of all creation; not the human mind), the mind has also created the earth and all its worldly phenomena. Everything is illusionary (vis-à-vis the higher truth) and only real in one's own mind. Everything is interdependently arising (called co-dependent origination). Everything is made of the same elements (Tashi 2012: 105 and 141) (*Sunyatta* in Sanskrit, which can mean both emptiness, intermediate and interconnectedness, Crins 2008: 158). Reality is circular as exemplified by the cycle of reincarnation (Crins 2008: 158).

Jigme Thinley, the former Bhutanese Prime Minister expressed: 'We desperately need an economy that serves and nurtures the well-being of all sentient beings on earth and the human happiness that comes from living life in harmony with the natural world, with our communities, and with our inner selves' (Royal Government of Bhutan 2012: 20).

15.2.2 Implementation in Law and Policy

The Bhutanese state has a clear duty in GNH implementation, including the environment, consistently articulated throughout the Constitution. Cultural provisions protecting Buddhism also ensure environmental protection. The state must strive to promote those conditions that will enable the pursuit of GNH (art. 9.2); and a true and sustainable development of a good and compassionate society rooted in Buddhist ethos and universal human values (art. 9.20). These provisions are not enforceable in court, but 'the promise of happiness ... is its soul', according to the former Chief Justice and co-drafter of the Constitution (Tobgye 2015: 182).

The Constitution defines Buddhism as a spiritual heritage (art. 3), different from state religion. It incorporates 'secular values that are supplementary'. This approach of 'pervasive spirituality' is, according to the drafters, derived from established customs, recognised in Western legal tradition (Edmund Burke) (Tobgye 2015: 108). The Constitution's legitimacy is partly derived from 'divine blessings'; 'the Constitution has become a sacred document ... one copy ... is

Table 15.3. *Constitution of Bhutan: GNH cultural and environmental pillars*

Pillar	Provisions of the Constitution
General *(arts. 1, 9)*	*Kingdom, sovereignty of people* (art. 1) *GNH as principle of state policy*; state creating enabling conditions for GNH (art. 9), including free education, health, etc.
Cultural pillar *(arts. 4, 3)*	The state is 'to preserve, protect and promote the cultural heritage of the country, including … religion' (art. 4.1), recognising it as 'an evolving dynamic force' (art. 4.2) Free cultural participation (art. 9.23) Duty to heritage preservation (art. 8.2) Spiritual heritage of Buddhism: peace, non-violence, compassion and tolerance (art. 3)
Environmental pillar *(arts. 5, 8)*	Whereas every Bhutanese is 'a trustee of the Kingdom's *natural resources*', the state will (a) Protect, conserve and improve the pristine environment and safeguard the biodiversity of the country; (b) Prevent pollution and ecological degradation; (c) Secure ecologically balanced sustainable development while promoting justifiable economic and social development; and (d) Ensure a safe and healthy environment *Mandatory forest cover* of 60% Possibility for enacting protected areas *Fundamental duty*, a Bhutanese citizen shall have the duty to preserve, protect and respect the environment, culture and heritage of the nation (art. 8.2) *Right over mineral resources*, rivers, lakes, forests, vested in the state (art. 1.12)

done in the form of a scripture' (Kinga 2009: 355, 354). Table 15.1 shows the general and cultural provisions as well as the environmental ones.

15.2.3 Buddhism as Chief Principle of Law

GNH clearly advocates that the law, education and government should include the spiritual. Article 9 of the Constitution implies that 'All legislation should directly and indirectly achieve happiness' (B6). Here one should read Happiness in its spiritual Buddhist meaning (not to be interpreted as the Western word happiness or subjective well-being in the Western sense measuring people's life satisfaction). Buddhism is after all about the art of being satisfied regardless of one's situation, and finding the middle road. GNH thus challenges legal theory (constitutionalism) of the separation of religion and state, though one could say Buddhism is also a philosophy.

15.2.3.1 Guardianship of Nature and Culture

'In the Buddhist context human beings are called "milu rimpoche" (human precious one). To the extent that human beings are supposed to be the most highly evolved of all animals, they are supposed to be more mindful and create a more sensitive relationship that binds all phenomena together' (B8). Guardianship of nature can be summarised as follows: 'Buddha's argument (is) … since we are enormously more powerful than other species, we have some responsibility towards them' (Tobgye 2015: 171, quoting Amartya Sen). Buddhism is not anthropocentric (B10, B8), yet not 'biocentric' either. Rather it refers to the sacredness of nature. The Buddhist worldview takes a middle position (Knut Johannessen).[6] 'It is a combination of both anthropocentrism and biocentrism. All life is precious, but the human life is the most precious of all' (B8). From the GNH concept of placing culture at the heart of development follows the idea that culture and nature are not separate, as the care for nature is an elementary aspect of Buddhist culture.

15.2.3.2 Service Instead of 'Duty' and Freedom

Both Hinduism and Buddhism enshrine the concept of *sewa*, service to the community. The constitutional duties of citizens in the Constitution of Bhutan are explicit rather than as implicit correlation of rights (as Western tradition contends). It correlates with this concept of service. 'Freedom must entail duty and responsibility' (Tobgye 2015: 151, quoting the 4th King). Bhutanese responsibilities include (art. 8) preservation of sovereignty, culture, tolerance, nature, respect for the national flag and anthem, as an expression of internal values (e.g. happiness). It includes refraining from torture or killing, providing help (reciprocity), abiding by and aiding the law and Constitution, taxation, non-corruption and last but not least: guardianship of nature. 'A Bhutanese citizen shall have the duty to preserve, protect and respect the environment, culture and heritage of the nation' (art 8.2).

15.2.3.3 Rights of Nature

Bhutanese guardianship of nature comes close to the rights of nature (like in Ecuador). Guardianship of nature is also embodied in article 5 (Constitution) 'every Bhutanese is a trustee of the Kingdom's natural resources'. This implies all citizens can 'seek redress in the court' in the case of 'non-obedience by the state' in

---

[6] Lecture at GNH Conference Paro, 2015.

its duty to protect the natural environment (Tobgye 2015: 125). This seems to imply that personal damage does not need to be established. However, no one has yet invoked this right in court; there is no jurisprudence on guardianship of nature.

GNH does not accord special legal rights to nature or animals; this falls under (strong) biodiversity conservation (B6). The Constitution is unique in containing strong conservation provisions of mandatory forest cover (B6; B7), but it does not give the forest itself rights. This is remarkable since 'in our religion there are also rights for animals and plants ... human rights also extend to the environment' (B7). 'GNH respects the integrity of all life forms' (B8). 'It encompasses all sentient beings' (B10). This expresses itself in a strong vegetarian movement in Bhutan (B7) and conservation laws (B6).

Some parliamentarians suggested 'other living beings' should be included in the provisions of article 8 of the Constitution on prevention of torture. This was, however, rejected out of fear for the legal implications and impact on development policy: namely 'endless ... cases ... for protection of animals and insects' (Tobgye 2015: 177).

15.2.3.4 Intergenerational Justice

The idea of reincarnation and *karma* makes one automatically part of future generations. The Constitution of Bhutan advocates safeguarding natural resources for future generations and ensuring distribution of benefits (art. 9.7). Future generations are also mentioned in the provisions on debt servicing: public debt servicing (which in Bhutan is mainly on hydropower dams) should not go at the cost of the next generation (art. 14.5). Thus, the issue of clean energy, CO_2 reduction, government resource revenues and debt sustainability are all linked. Though in practice many Bhutanese remain concerned about the effects of hydropower dams on ecosystems, biodiversity and on their independence and sovereignty, the constitution attempts to address these various issues. Article 5 regarding protection of nature and article 14.5 on debt sustainability are connected. GNH thus advances constitutional intergenerational justice by looking at the environmental and social impacts of the use of natural resources.

15.2.3.5 Human (Karmic and Co-dependent) Rights and Dignity

Buddhist dignity extends to all living beings. From the human point of view it can be viewed as combining the mind and the heart: 'combining modern reason with Buddhist compassion' (Matsuoka 2005). Contrary to dignity being derived from the individual ability to reason of an independent autonomous being with responsibility for his actions (or in Christian tradition from God), human dignity in Buddhism needs to be viewed from the aspects of:

1. karma (one has more than one life and takes its lessons to the next life);
2. co-dependent origination (everything is simultaneously arising);
3. compassion with Buddhahood in all living beings (all are spirited beings);
4. the path of self-development (awakening and actualising our dignity);
5. being able to contribute to manifesting the world (the mind – the consciousness of all that is – creates reality).

This means:

1. your responsibility for actualising your dignity extends over several lives, not only your current one;
2. all exist in relationship to others, plus the absence of a substantial unchanging self (emptiness) means all can be changed (continuous creativity);
3. a duty to help to emancipate the other and to respect all life; (restoring) the dignity of the other is (enhancing) your dignity;
4. all are able to change and that change will positively benefit others 'everyone is open to possibilities beyond his present individual situation and, although an autonomous being, he nevertheless exists in mutual interdependence with others' (Shiotsu 2001);
5. 'the rationale for the dignity of human beings lies in their practice of compassion as an expression of cosmic subjectivity' ('the individual actively embodies the fundamental power of the Law (of dependent origination) that gives rise to the world in a web of mutually interconnected and interdependent relationships') (Matsuoka 2005).

15.2.3.6 Extra Rights (and Duties) to Community, Leisure and Cultural Participation

GNH has distinct domains in measuring well-being in dimensions that were not measured before. The Bhutanese Constitution formulates extra rights[7] in some of these domains: such as the right to leisure time (art. 9.13),[8] living in strong family and community bond (art. 9.19)[9] and a compassionate society (art. 9.20) and participation in cultural life (art. 9.23)[10] (B9). The right to life has a specific meaning as well. Buddhists argue against all killing including capital punishment,[11] based on the Buddhist principle of *Sokchoepa* (Dzongkhafor no killing, as first negativity of the body). It extends only to persons, not to other beings (art. 7.18; Tobgye 2015: 148 and 164). As we have seen above these are correlated with cultural duties. The separation of culture and nature remains but is less strict

---

[7] Though partly present in the Universal Declaration of Human Rights (UDHR) and the International Covenant on Economic Social Cultural Rights (ICESCR).
[8] Also present in the UDHR (art. 24) and the ICESCR (art. 7).
[9] ICESCR recognises the family as 'the natural and fundamental group unit of society' (art. 10).
[10] ICESCR: 'The right to take part in cultural life' (art. 15.1a).
[11] Abolished by royal decree in 1994, http://bhutanobserver.bt/3042-bo-news-about-buddha_said_it_all.aspx

than in the Western sense. For the (scarce) jurisprudence and implementation issues, see van Norren (2017).

15.3 (South) African Ubuntu Philosophy

Ubuntu offers another organic worldview with deep implications for human–nature relations.

15.3.1 General

Ubuntu means 'I am because we are' and signifies a collective ontology (or way of being in the world), that exists throughout sub-Sahara Africa (see for examples Gade 2012; Broodryk 2002). It is a South African word that is commonly associated with the Zulu/Xhosa saying *umuntu ngumuntu nga-bantu*: a person is a person through other persons. However, it has a deeper meaning when looking at the grammar. The cosmological ordering of the universe is reflected in the structure and grammatical rules of a people's language (Ntibagirirwa 2012: 78, referring to Alexis Kagame (1956)). Mokgoro explains that the translation into Western philosophy is difficult, 'because the African world view is not easily and neatly categorised, any attempt to define Ubuntu is merely a simplification of a more expansive, flexible and philosophically accommodative idea' (1997: 16). As a South African expresses:

> It starts in the communities. I am where I am today because of the other people at home; you should not forget where you come from. They uplifted you and you uplift them, so that you contribute back, you give back to the others . . . You are expected to share with your neighbours . . . if you are raised with those values, the person does not think of what the effect is going to be on his own intake when he gives something . . . Ubuntu is the pulse of everything . . . the pulse of life.
>
> *(A3; van Norren 2017)*

In its deeper meaning *Bu* signifies the general, abstract being in the mind which is not yet manifest. 'In other words, '*bu*' is not another class of beings, but rather an abstracted being which has a mental existence' (Ntibagirirwa 2012: 79). For example, justice (general) versus judge (personal). *Ntu* is the universal force that manifests itself in beings (Mbiti 1990: 11). Bantu language postulates the suffix *ntu* (being) as underlying all other life forms, even space and time (*Hantu*) and the quality/quantity/location all things possess (*Kuntu*) as well as inanimate objects as part of nature (*Kintu*). It is important to note that the human community (*Bantu*) consists of past, present and future generations.

15.3.2 Environmental Philosophy

In the concept of *Ubuntu*, the environment is part of the communitarian concept of life. One way of making this connection is through the concept of *seriti* (Sotho) or *isithunzi* (Nguni) (Boon 2007), which is translated as aura, dignity, personality or shadow. One could say: the clearer the aura, the more dignity the person possesses or the longer the shadow you cast. Those who believe in it refer to *seriti* not only as a personal field, but also as a field which connects all living beings (Cornell 2012: 331). Behrens (2014: 1, 5) deducts from this belief a moral 'considerability' (responsibility) to include all things that are part of the web of life, including inanimate natural objects. One can compare this to the parental earth ethics of Henry Odera Oruka (Haenen 2012: 93). On ecology through the principle of *Ubuntu*, Ramose (1999/2005: ch. 9) remarks that a loss of balance by 'serious disturbance of the ecology' (109) is considered a violation of *Botho*: 'To care for one another ... implies caring for the physical nature as well. Without such care, the interdependence between human beings and physical nature would be undermined' (106). In the traditional African 'animistic' religions, human, community and nature possess a soul (animus) and therefore nature deserves respect; the human is woven into nature, like nature into the cosmos, in relationships that are supposed to be harmonious (Haenen 2012, quoting Gyekye and Oruka). However, 'in urban areas people do not really relate to nature in the same way, it is only in the rural areas; they are still consistent (with Ubuntu) and they pray to the rain gods' (A15).

15.3.3 Implementation in Law and Policy

Despite its omission in the final Constitution, Minister Fransman (2013: 46) refers to a 'Constitution based on the spirit of *Ubuntu*, compromise, consensus, reconciliation and nation building'. South African judges also refer to 'the spirit of *Ubuntu*' underlying the Constitution: a debate has evolved about whether Ubuntu can be a founding principle of law (Cornell 2012a: 326). Justice Mokgoro (1997: 10) claims that the values of *Ubuntu* can provide the South African law with the necessary Indigenous impetus, as the law is under the scrutiny of the Constitution. In her view, Ubuntu is in line with the founding values of democracy established by the new Constitution and the bill of rights. The reference to *Ubuntu* was included in the draft constitution of 1993 to justify the necessity of a national truth and reconciliation commission (see Ramose 2001: s. 17), and thus became part of its (contended) legal history. It can be read into 'the values that underlie an open and democratic society based on human dignity, equality and freedom' or into 'the spirit, purport and objects' of the Bill of Rights (Constitution, s. 39) or as deinstitutionalising customary norms (Keep and Midgley 2007: 34–35). Justice Mokgoro claims that in a hierarchy of legal principles, *Ubuntu* stands higher than 'human dignity', considered to be the mother principle of law (Wewerinkee 2007: 37).

Table 15.4 gives a short summary of constitutional provisions in the dimensions of culture and nature. Cultural provisions do refer to Indigenous language, culture and leadership, though it was probably not envisaged to include the philosophy of language, let alone its environmental implications. Only article 24.2 refers implicitly to *Ubuntu* in that it mentions future generations (part of the concept of Bantu/people). Other provisions embody standard anthropocentric environmental law.

Table 15.4. *Constitution of South Africa: cultural and environmental provisions*

Dimension	Provisions of the Constitution
Culture	➢ *Founding provisions* *Language* protection: art. 6.2 'Recognizing the historically diminished use and status of the Indigenous languages of our people, the state must take practical and positive measures to elevate the status and advance the use of these languages.' *Intercultural protection* by 'A Pan South African Language Board' protecting all official languages; the Khoi, Nama and San languages; sign language; and respect all languages commonly used by communities in South Africa, including German, Greek, Gujarati, Hindi, Portuguese, Tamil, Telegu and Urdu; and Arabic, Hebrew, Sanskrit and other languages used for religious purposes in South Africa. ➢ *Bill of Rights*, Chapter 2, art.: 30. Language and culture: right to use language and to participate in cultural life of choice. 31. Cultural, religious and linguistic communities: right of association/ practice. ➢ Chapter 12: 211–12 *Traditional leaders*: recognition of role, customary law, traditional council.

Nature	➢ Bill of rights: art.:
	 24. *Environment*:
	 Everyone has the right
	
	 1. to an environment that is not harmful to their *health or well-being*; and
	 2. to have the environment protected, for the benefit of *present and future generations*, through reasonable legislative and other measures that
	   a. prevent pollution and ecological degradation;
	   b. promote conservation; and
	   c. secure ecologically sustainable development and use of natural resources while promoting justifiable economic and social development.

In conclusion, one may say that the South African law system is based on a Western Anglo-Saxon and Roman–Dutch system, but efforts are being made by a group of activist judges and legal scholars to reintroduce Indigenous concepts that were omitted from the Constitution for unclear reasons and to use the language of *Ubuntu* to construct a new and more humanely responsive jurisprudence. Critics argue that according to South African jurisprudence, the preamble and epilogue may not be regarded as part of the particular law they refer to, let alone an omitted preamble (anonymous reviewer of van Norren 2014).

The only *Ubuntu* reference in environmental legislation is, according to an expert in environmental law, in the 'environmental management integrated coastal management act' which in the definition section states that 'it must be managed in the interest of the whole community', which according to the drafter is 'wider than only humans'; all other *Ubuntu* provisions were taken out (A16). The Swaziland authorities did adopt environmental legislation on the basis of Ubuntu (A16), e.g. article 4b 'consider the entire environment a whole entity' (Environment Management Act, 2002 Part II – Fundamental Purpose and Principles).[12] The National Environmental Management Act (1998) (NEMA) defines 'environment' as the surroundings within which humans exist. 'The environment', according to NEMA, 'is held in public trust for the people. The beneficial use of environmental resources must serve the public interest and the environment must be protected as the people's common heritage' (s. 2(4)).

Environmental policies are thus not based on a nature–people interdependence understanding of *Ubuntu* (A6; A16). Isolated examples of environmental *Ubuntu* policy exist, such as the former 'program of rural women to uproot invasive plants that were taking a lot of water, carried out under Prof. Kadhar Asmal in the Mandela government. It combined protecting scarce resources of water, with employment for women and restoring the vitality of the earth. It was a very effective and meaningful form of *Ubuntu*' (A14). Jurisprudence based on *Ubuntu* centres around social justice (van Norren 2019).

However, in a Constitutional Court judgment in 2007, Justice Ngcobo pointed out that nature is the basis of life and enables all other human rights: '[t]he importance of the protection of the environment cannot be gainsaid. Its protection is vital to the enjoyment of the other rights contained in the Bill of Rights; indeed, it is vital to life itself. It must therefore be protected for the benefit of the present and future generations.'[13] 'The idea of an environmental right as foundation for basic human existence was confirmed' (Kotzé and Du Plessis 2010). Guardianship

---

[12] www.sea.org.sz/pages.asp?pid=35
[13] *Fuel Retailers Association of Southern Africa* v. *Director General Environmental Management, Department of Agriculture, Conservation and Environment, Mpumalanga Province* 2007 (6) SA 4 (CC), para. 102.

of nature can be furthered by class action.[14] The Constitutional Court held in 2009 that 'the protection of environmental rights will not only depend on the diligence of public officials, but on the existence of a lively civil society willing to litigate in the public interest'.[15]

15.3.4 Mutual Aid as Chief Principle of Law

Like the Buddhist notion of Happiness, *Ubuntu* is rooted in cosmic unity based on natural law, and therefore it goes beyond the framework of positivist legal systems and contributes to their deconstruction. Reformulating the law based on *Ubuntu* would mean upholding the principle 'life is mutual aid'. Truthfulness is considered the foundation of justice, peace and reconciliation. The definition of truthfulness is abstaining from lying. Justice and peace are achieved by helping the other, because it is helping yourself (A13).

An *Ubuntu* moral theory can also be constructed without its metaphysical dimension (Metz 2007), but it unnecessarily diminishes the concept and therefore does not do it justice. In legalism (and analytical positivism), even moral theory has become subservient, as law is defined as a 'logically consistent set of rules constructed in a specialised fashion', which must become 'autonomous and supreme' and must be clearly differentiated 'from other sources of normative ordering' (Trubek, as cited by Bennett 1991: 3). *Ubuntu* goes beyond the rules of the litigation game:

Where law in South Africa is often exclusive (in the sense that it excludes) and adversarial where two parties are opposite *Ubuntu* includes. It links. It shows that I cannot enforce my rights in isolation of other people. And that my enforcement of rights, affect others, and if that effect is inhumane, my enforcement may not be just.

(A2)

15.4.4.1 Relational Rights and Service to the Community

Ubuntu goes beyond Western terminology of social cohesion, social bonds and communitarianism (Cornell and Muvangua 2012: 3–5): it postulates that one does not exist without the other; there is a continuum of being. This suggests an openness 'for a kind of dialogue about what it means to be a human being', that

---

[14] Brandon Abdinor, 'Is South Africa ripe for a climate change class action lawsuit?', *Daily Maverick*, 21 May 2019, www.dailymaverick.co.za/article/2019-05-21-is-south-africa-ripe-for-a-climate-change-class-action-lawsuit/

[15] *Biowatch Trust* v. *Registrar Genetic Resources and Others* (CCT 80/08) [2009] ZACC 14; 2009 (6) SA 232 (CC); 2009 (10) BCLR 1014 (CC) (3 June 2009). www.saflii.org/za/cases/ZACC/2009/14.html. See also GoLegal, 'Environmental law: Sustainable development and planning', www.golegal.co.za/sustainable-development-planning

one is what one is in engagement with others (Cornell and Muvangua 2012: 27, quoting Murungi).

Ubuntu defines who we are by highlighting how an individual is perceived in the eyes of society and how society is perceived in the eyes of an individual. I think it blends well with the promotion of human rights i.e. the denial of one's rights, is denial of societal rights. The reverse is also true.

(A5)

Ubuntu thus asserts a collective ontology and a relational aspect of rights (A8, A13) and thereby offers an alternative legal theory. It adds to human rights an overarching principle of *Ubuntu* which goes beyond human dignity (while encompassing it), including the dignity of the community as a whole. Second, it lays emphasis on duties or rather service to the community. One has the duty to participate in the community and make a difference; duties are therefore more than just correlations of rights (Cornell and Muvangua 2012: 4; A8). Third, it stresses indivisibility of rights, not distinguishing between socio-economic and civil–political rights; both are indispensable for securing our humanity (Cornell and Muvangua 2012: 10): 'In the USA you can be dying of hunger, but still curse the government, that is their definition of freedom ... that is not the way we see it in *Ubuntu*' (A14). *Ubuntu* would have never called such a distinction into being. This comes close to Western notions of interdependence of rights but reasoned from a different vantage point.

15.3.4.2 Community Rights First

One can question the 'fragmentation of the human being' into different rights, undermining the concept of wholeness (Ramose 1999/2005: 138). Different generations of human rights are also ordered in an undesirable hierarchy of rights,[16] according to *Ubuntu* theory, which would accord different priorities. The right to water and food are the most basic for survival; these are the primary claim the individual can put forward towards the community (Ramose 1999/2005: 135). So, socio-economic comes before political rights and collective before individual rights. After all, only the community can assure the actualisation of rights. An *Ubuntu* worldview thus favours a reverse order: first humanity-as-a-whole rights, then solidarity rights, then socio-economic rights, then civil political rights. This ordering originates in the economic development (industrialisation) in the West, according to Ramose (1999/2005: 138).

---

[16] First (civil political), second (socio-economic), third (solidarity rights such as self-determination, peace, development, environment, humanitarian assistance, minorities), fourth (right concerning humanity as a whole; genetic engineering, future generations, etc.). See for example Cornescu (2009).

15.4.4.3 Past, Present and Future Humans (Bantu): One Community of Life

Future generations are automatically part of the '*bantu*' community and enshrined in the South African Constitution (art. 24.2), but the peace of ancestors also needs to be respected. The court extended rights and dignity to those who have deceased in concurrence with the *Bantu* concept. One can extend this collective view on future and past generations to nature, as part of the community. Collective rights are recognised under South African customary law, but not directly in the Constitution.

As the African Charter on Human and Peoples' Rights[17] states: 'Mindful that the ancestral wisdom of Africa teaches that we come into being through our relationships with the whole community of life and that to unfold our full humanity we must respect and live in peace with all beings.' A South African lawyer (A16) remarks:

> There is one community of life, how can human rights cover that? We as a species are a subsection ... the system thinks human beings are separate from the earth and that they have no obligation to other members of the earth community ... (but) there are earth laws ... to guide the human being to play a role as a good citizen of the community ... now law and governance is based on exploitation of the rest of the community. Everything is defined as property ... that means they are slaves, the rivers, the land, the mountain and all other species. It is a dysfunctional relationship that we need to heal ... the human laws need to be modelled such that the system of laws is to live in accordance with nature's law. (Now) everything that causes damage is legal! ... the human right to life is meaningless without water. We need to protect the right of hydrological systems ... before we protect the right to life ... recognise the scientific reality that we are part of the system ... build a new model that makes the old one obsolete ... reasserting the rights of all.

This situation is the result of the separation of positive law from natural law and from any ontological foundation (Carty 2007; David Kennedy 1987; Duncan Kennedy 2001).

15.3.4.4 Relational Dignity Beyond 'Reason'

Cornell points out that 'dignity in *Ubuntu* thinking is not rooted in reason because ... this would deny dignity to too many human beings' (Bennett 2011: 48; Cornell 2012b). Western legal theory places emphasis on rationality, reasonableness, equity, individualism and freedom (Keep and Midgley 2007: 33; Bennett 2011: 48), as well as protection of private property. One could perhaps say it lies in the heart, according to Ubuntu which stresses feeling engagement with the other. Bennett (2011: 53) sums Ubuntu legal culture up as rooted in 'reconciliation, sharing, compassion, civility, responsibility, trust and harmony'. He leaves in the middle whether this constitutes 'embracing a different set of values or simply expressing universal values

---

[17] www.achpr.org/legalinstruments/detail?id=49

differently'. The difficulty in taking a position here is that when one poses that *Ubuntu* upsets conventional legal theory, one is immediately rebuffed as throwing away the baby with the bathwater (the baby being human rights as a concept diminished by cultural relativity); and when one poses that *Ubuntu* reorders universal values in a different way, it is deemed to be unnecessary redundancy. *Ubuntu* shifts the emphasis of conventional legal theory from rational only to being rooted in a natural law that springs from the collectivity of being.

15.3.4.5 *Freedom versus Human 'Bondedness'*

A declaration of human duties might have been more likely from the point of view of *Ubuntu* than one on human rights; proclamation of human 'bondedness' more than human freedom; an emphasis on a socio-economic duty to ensure everyone's 'right to eat' before asserting civil–political rights 'to represent oneself'. One can compare it to a pendulum swing, where both are aware of the full range of the trajectory; they are both at a different moment in the movement of the swing. Traditional African communalism may have benefited from Western notions of individual freedom in the same way that Western individualism may benefit in future from African notions of bondedness. Duties are, however, formulated in the Constitution of South Africa in a general sense: 'Duties and responsibilities of citizenship' (art. 3) are unspecified; the bill of rights recognises 'any duty imposed by the right' (art. 8.2) which 'binds the legislature, executive, judiciary and all organs of the state' (art. 8.1); the state duty to fair administration (33.3b) (resonating in *Batho Pele* (People First) accountability policies); and the bill of rights stipulates provincial and local government responsibilities such as 'developmental duties of municipalities' (art. 153).

15.3.4.6 *Restorative Justice Seeking Harmony*

Ubuntu seeks harmony and rehabilitation with the community (again this could include nature) and does not emphasise punitive justice. *Ubuntu* accords a special meaning to the right to life, stressing every human including criminals are possessing an inherent dignity (laid down in contentious jurisprudence on abolishing capital punishment). *Ubuntu* binding-togetherness could be said to imply that the dignity of all is diminished by taking the life of one. Furthermore, the one who orders and the one who perpetrates the state killing are robbed of their dignity. Capital punishment 'dehumanises the person and objectifies him or her as a tool for crime control' (Justice Mokgoro). 'The value of life is inestimable, and it is a value, which the state must uphold by example', Justice Langa explains, linking it to the new moral way social relations are shaped in the Constitution, undoing the anti-apartheid past (Cornell and Muvangua 2012: 11). The reconciliatory necessity of criminal justice is thus emphasised over the need for punishment or revenge.

15.4 Comparing Guardianship of Nature in Three Worldviews

Similar economic ecological principles appear in all three philosophies, be it in varying degrees. All Native American *Buen Vivir*, Buddhist Happiness and African *Ubuntu* stress unity with nature and unity of being. In terms of economics, sovereignty of people is put over sovereignty of money. Sovereignty of nature ultimately reigns over sovereignty of people. The national policy frameworks of Bhutan and Ecuador mirror these beliefs; in South Africa the environmental *Ubuntu* aspect seems absent, except in the Constitution.

15.4.1 Buen Vivir

In *Buen Vivir*, there is no conceptual starting point at all; rather an ontological approach whereby everything partakes of everything (which is ultimately also recognised by the other two philosophies who start from respectively 'I' in Buddhism and 'We' in *Ubuntu*). Humankind is smaller than nature, and life is biocentric. It is part of the community of life.

Our spiritual belief is harmonious relations; when we cut down a tree, we cut down our brother or sister or grandparents . . . we also kill the spirits, not only the species physically. A little drop is representing the whole of humanity . . . The air we breathe is the same (as other species).

(E38)

It is a feminine culture rooted in Mother Earth (Oviedo 2008). Native Americans see themselves as the keepers of the Earth.[18]

Human life needs the spirit of plants to nourish the soul, not only the food it produces or the water to drink. It needs the air, not only to breathe, but to clear the mind. 'The environment space is not empty. It has many spirits, it is sacred. We believe we become spirits when we die. When the soil is covered in oil and the ecosystem is damaged, we are also damaging human life' (E38). Finally, humans need an emotional-soul connection to nature to nourish their intellect:

When you kill everything to do with the spirits, they also kill intellectual sciences (faculties), if there is no harmony. We know the physical losses, but there are also intellectual losses. When you kill the river, you kill the species of the river and human beings and our feelings and our respect for the spiritual world.

(E38)

15.4.2 Gross National Happiness

This is mirrored in Bhutan: 'All forms of life are valued equally . . . in Bhutan nature as a holistic cosmology is a prime cause and religion a result of this' (Crins

---

[18] Aluna, *There Is No Life without Thought* (2014) [documentary], www.alunathemovie.com

2008: 168). Buddhist teachings on the eightfold path, however, centre on the individual human ('I') and its capacity for reasoning (as well as thinking from the heart), reaching towards enlightenment (last step). On his path to enlightenment the individual expresses detached love (altruism) for others and nature:

According to both Buddhist and pre-Buddhist philosophies, the mountains, rivers, streams, rocks and soils of Bhutan are ... the domain of spirits ... this coupled with the Buddhist tenet that the acts of this life will be rewarded or punished in the next, provides a powerful motivational principle for sustaining Bhutan's natural resource base ... In Bhutanese culture ... the original definition of development was based on the acquisition of knowledge ... the process of communal enrichment was based on a dynamic in which those who possessed superior knowledge imparted that knowledge to others.

(Crins 2008: 155)

15.4.3 Ubuntu

Ubuntu signifies the general inherent quality of everything in the universe (*Bu*). Unity between all beings is articulated through the underlying life force (-ntu) that inspires all beings. This means that there is no hierarchy of things which would distinguish humans as separate from other beings. Therefore, caring for nature is as important as caring for others. The concept of *seriti* also stresses unity with nature and all beings. Sangoma healer Mutwa calls for a more expanded (Mother) mindset (comparable to Oviedo's feminine earth concept): 'we must no longer look at a tree, but must see a living entity in that. I must no longer look at a stone, but I must see the future lying dormant in that stone.'[19]

Ubuntu, therefore, starts from the familial community life which includes future generations ('We'). *Ubuntu* focuses mainly on humanity, human-unity, human bonds within the community (u-Ba-ntu) (the-Human-beings) which possess u-Bu-ntu (general humaneness of humans): 'Man is the centre of this ontology; the Animals, Plants and natural phenomena and objects constitute the environment in which man lives, provide a means of existence and, if need be, man establishes a mystical relationship with them' (Mbiti 1990: 16).

Nowadays, therefore, the initial interpretation seems to come less to the forefront. Interviewees mention the environmental dimension less, if at all. South Africa policies do not articulate specific *Ubuntu* inspired environmental policies; they do stress human civility in public service delivery as well as humanity in social justice and restorative justice. African philosophers such as Ramose, however, maintain *Ubuntu* also refers to the cosmic unity and ecology. It seems that *Ubuntu* has taken a more anthropocentric meaning in practice. Nature is seen

---

[19] Zulu Sangoma (healer) Vusamazulu Credo Mutwa, A Message to the World, Global Oneness Project, www .globalonenessproject.org/search/node/ubuntu

in relation to the next generations that are part of *bantu* (people) (Haenen 2014). On *Ubuntu*, former South African Deputy Minister of Health Nozizwe Madlala-Routledge remarks: 'We have to look after the planet, the earth was given to us and we have got to protect it, we got to, when we pass on, leave it in a condition where those who have come after us continue to exist and enjoy what is given to all of us freely by nature.'[20]

Conclusion: An Alternative to Mainstream Western Views

These three philosophies contrast with mainstream Western views towards nature, which view it primarily as an object. Not only is the Western view anthropocentric: Descartes put the centre of human existence in the human brain – *Cogito, ergo sum* ('I think, therefore I am'). This influenced science and its view of nature. 'It was Descartes who saw animals as 'automatons', a view that has been made definite by our bio-industry' (van Dijk 2015, quoting philosopher Frank Ankersmit). This approach is now progressively being contested in physics, cognitive, neuro and evolutive biology. The Christian philosopher Thomas van Aquino had the opposite view and put forward that everything that animals and humans have in common (survival, sexuality, looking after their young) should be an indicator of mutual duties and rights (van Dijk 2015) (see also Chapter 7 in this volume). So far rights of nature have not been embraced by the West, with some minor exceptions.

Dutch philosopher Ger Groot illustrates the mainstream Western opposition against rights of nature:

> The one who pleads for animal rights is philosophically going off the road. There can be at most a duty that we have to treat animals well. But that duty is often misinterpreted as if animals have rights to a certain treatment, or even to land ... as soon as you want to give a legal meaning to that, one encounters problems ... the law is an artificial construction, and it requires a moral ability and legal consciousness to take part of that. Animals cannot do that. The duty that we have towards animals is therefore something solely between people.
>
> *(van Dijk 2015, my translation)*

This argument is often heard when debating rights of nature (van Norren 2019).

Embracing the concept of rights of nature is a pragmatic way of inserting Indigenous notions of guardianship of nature in the Western law system which is not the same as an Indigenous justice system. The Indigenous consider this an intermediary step that may help us come closer to living in harmony with nature.

The *Ubuntu*, happiness or *Buen Vivir* way of living automatically includes practices and decisions of living in harmony with nature which would then make

---

[20] www.globalonenessproject.org/library/films/ubuntu

rights of nature cases redundant because every human being would have reached the consciousness to respect earth, and would be guided by what the Indigenous North Americans call the precautionary approach (no major actions, unless proven that they will not do harm to nature).

The mainstream West thus has an individualist anthropocentric worldview. The total opposite is the Native American collective biocentric outlook on the world. Buddhism and *Ubuntu* are in between the two opposites. Buddhism has a point of departure which is more understandable for the Western mind (hence Western interest in Eastern spirituality): individual, in between anthropocentrism and biocentrism. *Ubuntu* is closer to the Native American view through its collective outlook embracing ancestors and future generations: in between anthropocentrism and biocentrism. All three views of the Global South lean towards the reverence for nature and ultimately merge in the understanding of the higher unity of being. With the examples entrenched in the law and governance of different countries in South America, Asia and Africa, the Global South can inspire the West with examples of how to embrace the guardianship of nature.

References

Acosta, A. (2008). El Buen Vivir, una oportunidad por construir. *Revista Ecuador* 75.

Akchurin, M. (2015). Constructing the rights of nature: Constitutional reform, mobilization, and environmental protection in Ecuador. *Law and Social Inquiry* 40(4): 937–68.

Arsel, M. (2012). The state, the 'left turn' and nature in Ecuador. *Tijdschrift voor Economische en Sociale Geografie* 103(2): 150–63.

Behrens, K. (2014). An African relational environmentalism and moral considerability. *Environmental Ethics (Special Issue on African Environmental Ethics)* 36(1): 63–82, www.academia.edu/1188836/An_African_Rela6onal_Environmentalism_and_Moral_Considerability

Bennett, T. W. (1991). *A Sourcebook of African Customary Law for Southern Africa.* Wynberg (Cape): Rustica Press.

Bennett, T. W. (2011). Ubuntu: An African equity. *Potchefstroom Electronic Law Journal PER/PELJ* 14(4): 30–61.

Boon, M. (2007). *The African Way: The Power of Interactive Leadership.* Cape Town: Zebra Press.

Broodryk, J. (2002). *Ubuntu. Life Lessons from Africa.* Pretoria: School of Philosophy.

Brown, P. (2000). Buddhism and the ecocrisis: The role of Buddhism in enhancing environmental philosophy and psychology in the west today. *BuddhaZine*, www.buddhanet.net/mag_eco.htm

Carty, A. (2007). *Philosophy of International Law.* Edinburgh: Edinburgh University Press,

Cornell, D. (2012a). A call for a nuanced constitutional jurisprudence: South Africa, Ubuntu, dignity and reconciliation. In N. Muvangua and D. Cornell (eds.), *Ubuntu and the Law: African Ideals and Post-Apartheid Jurisprudence.* New York: Fordham University Press, 324–33, www.newschool.edu/uploadedFiles/TCDS/Democracy_and_Diversity_Ins6tutes/Cornell_Ubuntu,Dignity,Reconcilia6on.pdf

Cornell, D. (2012b). Is there a difference that makes a difference between Ubuntu and dignity? In S. Woolman and D. Bilchitz (eds.), *Is This Seat Taken? Conversations at the Bar, the Bench and the Academy about the South African Constitution.* Pretoria: Pretoria University Law Press, 221–41, www.pulp.up.ac.za/pdf/2012_08/2012_08.pdf.

Cornell, D. and N. Muvangua (eds.) (2012). *Ubuntu and the Law: African Ideals and Post-Apartheid Jurisprudence.* New York: Fordham University Press.

Cornescu, A. V. (2009). *The Generations of Human's Rights, Days of Law: The Conference Proceedings.* Brno: Masaryk University, www.law.muni.cz/sborniky/dny_prava_2009/files/prispevky/tvorba_prava/Cornescu_Adrian_Vasile.pdf

Crins, R. (2008). *Meeting the 'Other', Living in the Present, Gender and Sustainability in Bhutan.* Delft: Eburon.

Cullinan, C. (2014). Governing people as members of the earth community. In Worldwatch Institute (ed.), *State of the World 2014: Governing for Sustainability.* Washington, DC: Island Press, 72–81.

Daniels, P. L. (2011). Buddhism and sustainable consumption. In L. Zsolnai (ed.), *Ethical Principles and Economic Transformation: A Buddhist Approach.* Dordrecht: Springer, 35–61.

Denuelin, S. (2012). Justice and deliberation about the good life: The contribution of Latin American Buen Vivir social movements to the idea of justice. Bath Papers in International Development and Wellbeing 17, Working Paper Series of the Centre for Development Studies. Bath, University of Bath.

Fatheuer, Th. (2011). *Buen Vivir*: A brief introduction to Latin America's new concepts for the good life and the rights of nature. *Heinrich Böll Foundation Publication Series on Ecology* 17: 1–30.

Fitz-Henry, E. (2012). The natural contract: From Lévi-Strauss to the Ecuadorian Constitutional Court. *Oceania* 82: 264–77.

Fransman, M. (2013). Securing democracy, securing business-building a prosperous South Africa for all. *UBUNTU Diplomacy in Action* 3: 46–48.

Gade, C. B. N. (2012). What is Ubuntu? Different interpretations among South Africans of African descent. *South African Journal of Philosophy* 31(3): 484–503.

Gianolla, C. (2013). Human rights and nature: intercultural perspectives and international aspirations. *Journal of Human Rights and the Environment* 4(1): 58–78.

GNH Commission UNDP (2011). *Bhutan National Human Development.* Thimphu: GNH Commission.

Government of Ecuador (GoE) (2009). *National Development Plan, National Plan for Good Living 2009–2013, Building a Plurinational State.* Quito: Republic of Ecuador.

Haenen, H. (2012). *Sage Filosofie, Pleidooi voor Afrikaanse wegen naar zelfstandigheid.* Antwerp: Garant Uitgevers.

Haenen, H. (2014). Afrikaanse filosofie. In J. Borand and E. Petersma (eds.), *De Verbeelding van het Denken, Geïllustreerde Geschiedenis van de Westerse en Oosterse Filosofie.* Amsterdam: Atlas Contact.

Houtart, Fr. (2012). The concept of Sumak Kawsay (Living Well) and how it relates to the common good of humanity. In Birgit Daiber and François Houtart (eds.), *A Post-Capitalist Paradigm: The Common Good of Humanity.* Brussels: Rosa Luxemburg Foundation, 207–33.

Jiménez, R. (2011). Recovering and Valuing Other Ethical Pillars Buen Vivir. Working Paper for the International Workshop Biocivilization for the Sustainability of Life and the Planet (in run-up to Rio+20 Conference, Rio de Janeiro: Forum for a New World Governance (FnWG)), www.world-governance.org/article690.html?lang=en

Keep, H. and R. Midgley (2007). Emerging role of Ubuntu Botho in developing a consensual South Africa in legal culture. In F. Bruinsma and D. Nelken (eds.), *Recht der Werkelijkheid*. Gravenhage: Reed Business, 29–56.

Kennedy, David (1987). *International Legal Structures*. Baden-Baden: Nomos.

Kennedy, Duncan (2001). 'Legal formalism'. In N. J. Smelser and P. B. Baltes (eds.), *Encyclopedia of the Social and Behavioral Sciences*. Elsevier, 13: 8634–38.

Kinga, S. (2009). *Polity, Kingship and Democracy: A Biography of the Bhutanese State*. Thimphu: Ministry of Education.

Kotzé, Louis J. and Anél du Plessis (2010). Some brief observations on fifteen years of environmental rights jurisprudence in South Africa: Environmental rights jurisprudence in South Africa. *Journal of Court Innovation* 3(1): 157–76, https://law.pace.edu/sites/default/files/IJIEA/jciKotze_South%20Africa%203-17_cropped.pdf

Lalander, R. (2014). *Rights of Nature and the Indigenous Peoples in Bolivia and Ecuador: A Straitjacket for Progressive Development*. Stockholm: University Department of Political Science [repr. *Iberoamerican Journal of Development Studies* 3(2)(2015): 148–72].

Matsuoka, M. (2005). The Buddhist concept of the human being: From the viewpoint of the philosophy of the Soka Gakkai. *Journal of Oriental Studies* 15: 50–75.

Mbiti, J. S. (1990). *African Religions and Philosophy*. 2nd ed. Oxford: Heinemann [first pub. 1969].

Melchizedek, D. (2008). *Serpent of Light Beyond 2012*. San Francisco: Weiser.

Mello, M. (2015). *El Buen Vivir y suTutela Jurídica en la Jurisprudencia de la Corte Constitucional Ecuatoriana*. Quito: Centro de Derechos Humanos, Pontificia Universidad Católica del Ecuador, Serie Investigación No. 5.

Metz, T. (2007). Toward an African moral theory. *Journal of Political Philosophy* 15(3): 321–41.

Mokgoro, Y. (1997). Ubuntu and the law in South Africa. In *Seminar Report Constitution and the Law, Organized by Faculty of Law, Potchefstroom University for Christian Higher Education*. Johannesburg: Conrad Adenauer Stiftung Edited Version in 1998, *Potchefstroom Electronic Law Journal PELJ/PER* 1(1): 15–26.

New Development Paradigm (NDP) Steering Committee (2013). *Happiness: Towards a New Development Paradigm. Report of the Kingdom of Bhutan*. New York: Royal Government of Bhutan.

Ntibagirirwa, S. (2012). Philosophical premises for African economic development: Sen's capability approach. Ph.D. diss., Pretoria: University of Pretoria.

Oviedo, Atawallpa. 2008. *Les Marcheurs de l'Arc en Ciel et les Mythes du Développement*. Geneva: Ambre.

Planning Commission (1999). *Bhutan 2020: A Vision for Peace, Prosperity and Happiness* Thimphu: Planning Commission Royal Government of Bhutan.

Price, B. (2013). What are rights, and how can nature 'have' rights? In *Rights of Nature and the Economics of the Biosphere* Rights of Nature Summit Reader, Stillheart Institute, 20–24 October. USA: Global Exchange, www.globalexchange.org

Ramose, M. B. (1999/2005 revision). *African Philosophy through Ubuntu*. Harare: Mond Books.

Ramose, M. B. (2001). An African perspective on justice and race. *Polylog: Forum for Intercultural Philosophy* 3, them.polylog.org/3/frm-en.htm

Royal Government of Bhutan (RGoB) (2012). *The Report of the High-Level Meeting on Wellbeing and Happiness: Defining a New Economic Paradigm*. New York: Permanent Mission of the Kingdom of Bhutan to the United Nations. Thimphu: Office of the Prime Minister.

Schroeder, K. (2014). The politics of gross national happiness: Image and practice in implementation of Bhutan's multidimensional development strategy. Ph.D. diss., University of Guelph (Canada).

Shiotsu, T. (2001). Mahayana Buddhist contributions to the issue of human rights. *Annals of the European Academy of Sciences and Arts* 31(11), www.sgi.org/resources/study-materials/mahayana-buddhist-contribu6ons-to-the-issue-of-human-rights.html

Sousa Santos, B. de. (2008). *Las Paradojas de Nuestro Tiempo y la Plurinacionalidad.* Montecristi, Manabí, Ecuador: Asamblea Constituyente, http://constituyente .asambleanacional.gov.ec/documentos/expositores/boaventura_sousa_santos.pdf

Stone, Christopher D. (1972) Should trees have standing? Towards legal rights for natural objects. *Southern California Law Review* 45: 450–501.

Tanasescu, M. (2013). The rights of nature in Ecuador: The making of an idea. *International Journal of Environmental Studies* 70(6): 846–61.

Tashi, K. J. (2012). *View of GNH and Environment: Way to the Golden Age.* Thimphu: Kuensel Corporation.

Thomson, B. (2011). Pachakuti: Indigenous perspectives, *Buen Vivir, Sumaq Kawsay* and Degrowth. *Development* 54(4): 448–54.

Tobgye, L. S. (2015). *The Constitution of Bhutan: Principles and Philosophies* [pub. unknown], www.kuensonline.com

Ura, K., S. Alkire, T. Zangmo and K. Wangdi (2012). *A Short Guide to Gross National Happiness Index.* Thimphu: Center of Bhutan Studies.

van Dijk, M. (2015). Mensenrechten voor het dier. *Trouw* 5 juni (De Verdieping religie&-filosofie), 8.

van Norren, D. E. (2014). The nexus between Ubuntu and global public goods: Its relevance for the post-2015 development agenda. *Development Studies Research* 1(1): 255–66.

van Norren, D. E. (2017). Development as service: A happiness, Ubuntu and Buen Vivir interdisciplinary view of the Sustainable Development Goals. Ph.D. diss., Tilburg University, Tilburg, the Netherlands, http://pure.uvt.nl/portal/files/198559816/Van_Norren_Development_18_12_2017.pdf

van Norren, D. E. (2019). The right to happiness in three traditions of the global south: Buddhist happiness, African Ubuntu and Indigenous American Buen Vivir. *Revue Juridique du Bonheur/ Legal Review of Happiness* 1(1): 89–109. France: Observatoire International du Bonheur (OIB), www.oib-france.com/wp-content/uploads/8.-The-right-of-Happiness-in-3-tradi6ons-of-the-global-south_D.Van-Norren.pdf

van Teijlingen, K. and B. Hoogenboom (2014). Development discourses at the mining frontier: BuenVivir and the contested mine of El Mirador in Ecuador. Engov Working Paper No. 15, www.engov.eu

Wewerinkee, M. (2007). Human through others: Towards a critical participatory debate. Master's thesis, Radboud University Nijmegen, www.sosci.ru.nl/maw/cidin/bamaci/scriptibestanden/641.pdf

Index